The New France

A COMPLETE GUIDE TO CONTEMPORARY FRENCH WINE

The New France

Andrew Jefford

PHOTOGRAPHS BY JASON LOWE

MITCHELL BEAZLEY

Dedication

To my parents, Peter and Celia Jefford, in
gratitude for their unfailing love and support –
and for taking me to France in the first place

www.andrewjefford.com

New France
by Andrew Jefford

First published in Great Britain in 2002
by Mitchell Beazley, an imprint of Octopus Publishing
Group Ltd, 2-4 Heron Quays, London E14 4JP

First published in paperback 2006

A CIP catalogue record for this book is available
from the British Library.

ISBN-13: 978 1 84533 000 2
ISBN-10: 1 84533 000 5

Photographs by Jason Lowe

Commissioning Editors: Rebecca Spry, Hilary Lumsden
Executive Art Editor: Yasia Williams
Design: Grade Design Consultants
Managing Editor: Gill Pitts
Senior Editor: Lara Maiklem
Index: Laura Hicks
Production: Alix McCulloch

Typeset in Gill Sans and Monotype Spectrum

Printed and bound in China

Contents

No word matters more to the New France's best cooperatives (like the Cave
◄ *de Rasteau) than sélection: only great grapes make great wine.*

Introduction

Elemental Alchemy France, historically, has turned its earth and air into wine of greater beauty and profundity than any other nation on earth. Today's fine wine, though, comes from many lands. Why, at the beginning of the twenty-first century, buy French?

To write this book has been a privilege. France first marked me almost forty years ago as a little English boy on a family holiday, perplexed by difference, yet overjoyed to discover it existed. I was sent to buy five ice creams (*cinq glaces*), and the teasing vendor, seizing on my uncertain British accent, told me with great relish that he was happy to sell me one hundred (*cent glaces*). I still recall my panic as I tried to work out some way of averting this creamy catastrophe, but there was none. "*Cinq glaces, s'il vous plaît*" had exhausted my French. I had no idea how to say "No, that wasn't what I said, I said just five, please don't give me a hundred, I only want five, honest, I promise I only said five." How could I tell my parents and brothers that I had bought them twenty ice creams each? How would I carry them? How would we find the money to pay for them all? Perhaps we would have to head back across the Channel that very night, our holiday cut short by damp and sticky armfuls of melted ice cream. The man noticed my consternation and stopped, smilingly, at five, but by the time I had finished licking ten minutes later, filled with relief and reflection, the hook was in me: otherness existed, and I wanted to understand it.

I grew to love much about France: its low railway platforms and majestically high, heavy trains; the smell of Gauloises on a sunny street corner; esplanades of plane trees; pointing road signs; chewing gum ingratiatingly called Hollywood; the oven-warm paradise of the *boulangerie* and the little plastic dishes where the baker's wife would toss your change. Then, of course, came cafés, restaurants, wine. Everyone drank wine, all the time. It was the Frenchman's tea. It seemed to make everyone happy, and turned no one into a hooligan or a roaring thug, which was what I had seen beer do in Britain. It was France's trump card.

Not only that, but wine was how you could take France back home with you. Wine was France for those who could not be in France; drinking wine grafted a bright French moment into a glum domestic elsewhere. I read books about it, experimented with it; for years, I never bought the same bottle twice. Sometimes, of course, it was better than at other times, but even when it was poor, I still contrived to enjoy it. When it was good, by contrast, it was an experience like no other. It often took a glass or two to comprehend, just as it takes fifty pages before you learn the rudiments, inflections, and discourse of a great novel; then it would seize and delight you, stimulating not just the nose and the mouth but the mind, too, triggering an avalanche of allusions to the natural world, satisfying you with an earthy, deep-rooted profundity which no other alcohol seemed to begin to match. It would surge in this way still more strongly with food; the bottle and the meal completed, it would leave a profound digestive calm. A spiritual calm, too, as if the wine had lifted the meal from out of the

rattle of daily repetition, glazing it with a sudden, Zen-like benediction. You were not, of course, entirely sober at the end of the process, but the wine's alcohol seemed to have refined and polished your spirit, rather than sent it sprawling as rawer alcohols did.

That was thirty years ago. Since then, a world of good wine has grown up around France. My purpose in this book is not to convince you that France still produces the greatest of all wines, though I happen to believe this; it is to demonstrate the ways in which France has changed and progressed.

When I have talked to others about the writing of this book, my interlocutors have assumed that "The New France" means principally Languedoc and Vin de Pays, the cliché for which is "France's New World". I have pointed out that the book covers all of France, and that "new" doesn't simply refer to what didn't exist before, but also to the present, changed state of that which has long existed. Despite its over-use, though, "France's New World" remains an interesting phrase, even if a few moments are needed to chew it down to its gristle.

New World competition has been very good for France, as all the most intelligent French wine-growers readily acknowledge. (The unintelligent ones use it as an excuse for the hooliganism which I once believed had nothing to do with wine.) A spell in South Africa, Chile, or Australia is now an essential part of the education of many young French wine-growers. What they tend to learn, I have been happy to discover, are the best lessons of New World winemaking. Rethink every action; do nothing for precedent's sake alone; understand as much as possible; and practice your vocation with absolute commitment. What has not been brought back to France so far is the worst lesson of New World winemaking: that it can be a brand-driven industry like any other. That vineyards are just a home for venture capital; that winemaking is no more than applied chemistry; that the purpose of wine production is shareholder value; and that marketing strategies are more important than scent and flavour in selling wine.

Which brings me to ethics. My research for this book took me to every region of France in search of good wine. I found it, as I hope you can comprehend in the pages that follow, and discover for yourself by buying some of the wines I describe. But more than that, I also began to see and to understand more clearly exactly what "good" might mean in relation to the growing of vines and the making of wine.

It means first of all the possession of a certain attitude to the physical world: that of loving and tender curiosity. Wine lends a sensual print to geography and geology (*see* Terroir, pages 16-21). No other agricultural crop can do this. The good wine-grower, thus, has three primary aims: to understand his or her land; to respect that land by cultivating it sustainably; and to allow its unique qualities to

"I respect not his labours, his farm where everything has its price, who would carry the landscape, who would carry his God, to market, if he could get anything for him... on whose farm nothing grows free, whose fields bear no crops, whose meadows no flowers, whose trees no fruits, but dollars; who loves not the beauty of his fruits, whose fruits are not ripe for him till they are turned to dollars. Give me the poverty that enjoys true wealth."

HENRY DAVID THOREAU, *WALDEN* **(1854)**

◄ *Vines mimic families, in that rootedness is all; the duty of care for both knows few limits.*

characterize the wine it surrenders so generously to us. I would argue that it is only in this way that truly great or profound wine can be created, though you are welcome to disagree. In this respect, France leads the wine world, as it has done since the system of *appellations d'origine contrôlée* (much derided today, but a creation of infinite preciousness) was first established in the 1930s.

Given this, good winemaking means ensuring that the sensual print of place emerges with maximum limpidity in a wine. In this respect, France leads the wine world, too, since almost every one of the great young winemakers I met in the course of researching this book is engaged in a quest for vineyard endeavour and for solicitous winery inaction.

Return to the vineyards

There is a growing realisation not just in France but around the wine world that while the final decades of the twentieth century may have been years of great progress in the winery, they were also years of catastrophe in vineyards. These were the years when the sellers of chemical and mechanical shortcuts made themselves fortunes; they were consequently years of soil poisoning, of soil compacting, of a war of attrition against vineyard biodiversity, of the sensual totalitarianism of over-productive grape variety clones, and of repeated physical abuse enacted against vine plants and their fruits. It is no good being Stradivari in the winery if you are Stalin in the vineyard. Great wine can only be made from great grapes. Great grapes must be picked carefully and sorted fastidiously; they grow on healthy, hard-pruned, and clonally diverse vines whose roots spread deeply through living, breathing, microbially pullulating soils. To create these conditions (frequently but not invariably by using organic or biodynamic viticulture) takes hard work. *Labour* (ploughing) is something many older French vignerons thought had gone forever; their sons and daughters have returned to it. Domains whose workforce had been cut back to a single worker or two have more than doubled their number of hands as they have discovered the benefits of painstaking

User guide

The following abbreviations and conversion rates are some of the most common used in this book:

abv alcohol by volume
AOC appellations d'origine contrôlée
CIVB Comité Interprofessionel des Vins de Bordeaux
INAO Institut Nationale des Appellations d'Origine
plc plafond limite de classement
SGN Sélection des Grains Nobles
VDN Vins Doux Naturels
VDQS Vins Delimités de Qualité Supérieure

cm centimetre (1cm = 0.3937 inches)
g gram (1g = 0.0353 oz)
ha hectare (1 ha = 2.47 acres)
hl hectolitre (1 hl = 100 litres)
l litre (one litre = 2.11 US pints)
kg kilogram (1 kg = 2.205lb)
km kilometre (1 km = 0.621 miles)
m metre (1m = 3.28 feet)

Please note that all producers in the "People" sections should be contacted before attempting to visit them.

viticulture in improving wine quality. What is the most important piece of winery equipment? For France's avant-garde, is it no longer the press, the vat, or the barrique, but the *table de tri*, the sorting table. After that, many growers believe, the less you interfere, the better.

In winery terms, France is a giant experimental laboratory of inaction at present – willed inaction, understood inaction, observed inaction – and it is this, together with dramatically reduced yields and healthier vineyards, which has spawned a new generation of wines of shattering articulacy and strange beauty. It often requires daring: doing nothing is sometimes the winemaker's equivalent of exhibition acrobatics, of pulling out of the dive at the last possible moment, of skimming the tree line with a shaking fir cone to spare. I will not enumerate the tenets of non-interventionist winemaking since they are much described in what follows, but no oenology school will ever recommend them.

Nor would many company accountants sanction them, which brings me to the final element of truly good wine. The number of those growing, making, and selling their own wine in France is increasing. Doing all three is what matters; it is this which is precious. The pernicious consequences of separating these activities is the main challenge facing Champagne today (*see page 22*). Small, family domains across France's vineyard areas are thriving, while it is cooperatives and négociants who have found life hard over the last decade. This complexity and fragmentation is France's strength, not (as is sometimes claimed) France's weakness. Families mean children; children mean succession and continuity; succession and continuity mean sustainability and sane stewardship of the land. Families mean aesthetic freedom, too; since the economic unit is a small one, it need find only a small market. Families mean a healthy and vibrant countryside, which can only deepen what is already a rich cultural relationship with the land. And yes, family domains mean a hugely diverse offering of French wine to the world. This may, for the time being, be perceived as a disadvantage, since fashion and the economic power of capitalism have succeeded in gulling individual human beings (who may not have given much thought to the matter) into putting a high value on hollow mass-marketed products which leave them both physically and spiritually unsatisfied. When it comes to good wine, however, human beings are more swiftly ready to step off the treadmill of monotony than they are for soft drinks, electronic equipment, or hamburgers. France is perfectly placed to welcome them when they do. Complexity is not a problem; it is a badge of virtue. The worthwhile is never easy; only the worthwhile endures.

France does have a weakness, of course, and a very great one, which is that it has failed to communicate the beauty and worth of its complex and fragmented wine culture. Notions of "prestige" and "image" are accorded far too much respect in France; other, more pragmatic cultures simply laugh and go elsewhere when confronted with the absurd pretentiousness, pomposity, and waffle of much French wine promotion. An understanding of something as complex as France's AOC system is no one's birthright, and a huge effort of accessible, friendly communication will be needed in the years ahead if France is to continue to thrive when its rivals can sell themselves with facile brand-marketing alone.

This matters. French wine culture is as great an achievement as French literature or French cinema; the bottles of Vincent Dauvissat, the Brunier brothers, or Olivier Zind-Humbrecht enrich lives differently but no less profoundly than do the novels of Zola, the films of Renoir, or the scripts and poems of Prévert. I hope this book will reveal just how vivid and vibrant French wine culture is at the beginning of the twenty-first century. Above all, though, I hope it will help you to love French wine.

▲ *The wine harvest is never quite as clean and carefree as the imagery suggests, even in bright, airy Corsica.*

Personal thanks

Many people have helped me enormously in the preparation of the book, and I compiled a list of their names in order to thank them on this page. Shortly before completing the book, however, my laptop computer was stolen, and this list of names was lost with it. I have tried to recreate it, but if any of you who have helped me find yourselves unaccountably omitted, please accept my sincere apologies for your anonymity.

A particular thank you to Rebecca Spry for commissioning me to write this book; to Hilary Lumsden and Gill Pitts for editing it with such commitment and courtesy; to Jane Aspden for her forbearance when the book doubled in length and demanded an extra six months to complete; to Jason Lowe for seeing what he saw; and to Catherine Manac'h of Sopexa for having arranged the majority of my research visits. Thanks, too, to Yasia Williams and Peter Dawson for finding space for so many words and still creating such an elegant book. And thank you to the following:

Eric Aracil, John Arnold, Sara Basra, Dr Neil Beckett, Christine Béhy-Molines, Mike and Liz Berry MW, Patricia de Bona, Adam Brett-Smith, Ken Brook, Stephen Brook, Stephen Browett ("Come on you Eagles"), Françoise Brugière, Alison Buchanan, Jim Budd, Thierry Cabanne, Lars Carlberg, Lorraine Carrigan, Nathalie Chassard, Jean Clavel, Sabine Cleizergues, David Cobbold, Claire Contamine, Daniel Craker, Clémence de Crécy, Jean-Luc Dairien, Matthew Dickinson, André Dominé, Emmanuel Drion, Robert Drouhin, James Dunstan, Paula Eyers, Jacques Fanet, Debbie Feickert, Simon Field MW, Harry Gill, Sue Glasgow, Jean-Michel Guiraud, Peter and Christine Hall, Lindsay Hamilton, Adrian Heaven, Rosamund Hitchcock, Maryse Jeannin, Matthew Jukes, Jonathan Kinns, John Livingstone-Learmonth, Wink Lorch, Daniel Lorson, Patrick McGrath, Antony Marrian, Ginny Martin, Fay Maschler, Anne Masson, Jean-Christophe Mau, Patrick Matthews, Matthew McCulloch, Thierry Mellenotte, Chris Mitchell, Fiona Morrison MW, Eric Narioo, Christine Ontivero, Françoise Peretti, Sue Pike, Michel Pons, Rupert Ponsonby, Tuukka Puolakka, Florence Raffard, Christophe Reboul-Salze, Dominique Renard, Jancis Robinson MW, Anthony Rose, Sophie Roussey, Johana Salanson, Michael and Monica Schuster, Christian Seeley, Tina Sellenet, Michel Smith, Bernard Sonnet, Kit Stevens, Peter Stone, Matthew Stubbs MW, Charles and Philippa Sydney, Charles Taylor, Jacques Thienpont, Gaylene Thompson, Dominique Vrigneau, Frank Ward, Michael Warlow, Jessica Worsley, and Philippe Verdier. Remaining errors are my responsibility.

French Wine Law

The Beautiful Bulwark Often considered gratuitously bureaucratic, the common property rights enshrined by French wine law exist to combat fraud, sustain individual endeavour, and frame research into terroir.

Vines have been grown in France's vineyards, and wines made in its cellars, for over 2,000 years, or at least 300 successive working generations. For most of this time, and to a greater extent than in present-day Australia, Chile, or California, wine production was subject to no rules whatsoever. Anything could be grown anywhere, and made anyhow. Under such circumstances, some wines proved more successful than others. Occasionally this gave rise to a little local legislation (Philip the Bold expelling Gamay from the Côte d'Or in 1395, for example); mostly it just raised the price.

When we consider French wine law, then, it is worth remembering that it is recent. French wine itself developed in conditions of absolute freedom. And developed, moreover, to a remarkably sophisticated extent. When the brokers of the Médoc classified its best properties into five tiers in 1855, there was no wine law stipulating grape variety, yield – or, indeed, the boundaries of the Médoc itself. Most of Burgundy's lacework of appellations reflect a pool of local knowledge accumulated over the previous 500 years. The Romans knew that Côte Rôtie was a great vineyard site long before the French, as a nation, even existed.

Why, then, was law necessary?

Engines, in a word. Steam engines; diesel engines: boats and trains. Throughout most of those 2,000 years, wine was, overwhelmingly, a local product. The rise of modern transport systems meant that one place on earth could produce wine for another. Wine began to travel. A few of the very finest wines had, certainly, travelled before the industrial revolution; after it, all wines travelled, often swiftly. If wine was made in one place and sold a short while later in another, the surety that it was what it claimed to be began to be open to question. Fraud became a profitable possibility. And a reality, especially after the chaos engendered by the epidemics of oidium and phylloxera in the latter half of the nineteenth century.

The first attempts by the French to protect the names of their best wines failed. The law of August 1st, 1905 gave protected status to certain wine-growing areas (including Bordeaux), but failed to specify anything other than general geographical boundaries. Quality remained wildly variable; fraud continued; prosecutions were difficult.

The law of May 6th, 1919 gave growers (rather than administrators) the possibility of claiming an appellation, subject to a judges' decision. Those fraudulently using such an appellation could be challenged in court. This was the moment that an important principle of French wine law was born: place names belong to a community of producers.

It was with the law of July 27th, 1927 that production methods were first specified as being a part of the authenticity of an

appellation, though it was left to a judge's discretion to define those appellations and methods. The notion of an *appellation d'origine* as a collective property right was strengthened. Nonetheless this law failed too, since the multitude of claims for appellations led to confusion and chaos in the market. There were also abusive claims for appellations during these years of overproduction and surplus, since an appellation exempted a region from obligatory distillation and overproduction penalties.

The French state tried again on July 30th, 1935, when *appellations d'origine* became *contrôlée* (AOC), and a dedicated supervisory body was instituted to oversee these. It was called the Institut Nationale des Appellations d'Origine, or INAO. The motive political force for this law came from a former agriculture minister called Joseph Capus, by then one of France's senators; he became the first president of INAO.

Let me just pause for a moment before I describe exactly how French wine law works – to sing its praises. French wine law is much criticized outside France at the beginning of the twenty-first century, for reasons I will also describe. Despite these (often valid) criticisms, I believe it is a great law, one very close to the spirit and ideals of the French Revolution. French wine law is splendidly resistant, furthermore, to the depredations of capitalism and the abusive perversions of the free market. It is a major reason why French wine has achieved the level of refinement, beauty, and complexity that are its hallmarks.

The fundamental greatness, indeed, of the AOC system is only now becoming fully apparent. The roots of this lie in the notion that an AOC is a collective property right, belonging in some cases to tens of thousands of individual wine-growers. It is a single name, often one that enjoys worldwide celebrity, which small-scale, economically vulnerable individuals jointly own. You, reader, may be a French wine-grower with only a few acres of vines. Nonetheless, provided you follow certain rules (which in most cases are no more than the codification of the wisdom of several hundred years of agricultural research), your wine can be recognized and understood as offering a certain sensory experience in every country of the world. Until you reach the very highest branches of the French wine tree, indeed, the appellation name will be more important than your own name. And when your own name finally becomes world-famous in its own right, you will still struggle as far as possible to absent yourself from your wine. Instead you will try to express, above all, the characteristics of the land you tend for a short while but will leave to others after you. Mechanisms of this sort to protect that which is held in common against that which is privately owned are increasingly rare in a world in which even genes can be patented and turned to private profit. They are precious.

"The charming landscape which I saw this morning is indubitably made up of some twenty or thirty farms. Miller owns this field, Locke that, and Manning the woodland beyond. But none of them owns the landscape. There is a property in the horizon which no man has but he whose eye can integrate all the parts, that is, the poet. This is the best part of these men's farms, yet to this their warranty-deeds give no title."

RALPH WALDO EMERSON, *NATURE* **(1836)**

AOC gives each of these Maury grapes a birth certificate – and a passport to
◀ the world's markets.

This is particularly true in a wine world dominated by the homogenizing fetish of the "brand". Branded wines are everything that appellation wines are not. Brands are privately owned, and are geared to generate maximum profit by crushing rivals; appellation wines coexist happily, merely asserting their difference. Brands offer consistency and reliability, something that no vintage appellation wine (which reflects nature's gifts in a particular year) will ever do. The flavour of a brand is engineered for maximum consumer appeal; the flavour of appellation wines is derived, as limpidly as possible, from the realities of site and season. The success of brands is measured economically; the success of appellations is measured at a community level. Appellations, therefore, are most emphatically not brands — though their often powerful consumer appeal makes them an ideal tool with which to combat the influence of brands.

How French wine law works

All French wines fall into one of four categories: Vins de Table (table wines), Vins de Pays (country wines), Vins Delimités de Qualité Supérieure (VDQS wines or "delimited wines of superior quality") and Vins d'Appellation d'Origine Contrôlée (AOC or appellation wines).

Most readers of this book will rarely if ever encounter French Vins de Table (which are in almost all cases rough wines of lowly quality and rock-bottom price). French Vins de Table cannot be labelled with either grape variety or regional names, nor with vintage dates. The only case in which table wines are likely to be of good quality occurs on those very rare occasions when producers of appellation wines fall foul of rules and regulations in areas that have no Vins de Pays alternative to AOC (such as Bordeaux, Burgundy, or Alsace). They are also being used for the production of sweet wines in areas with no ancestral sweet wine tradition.

The VDQS category was created in the 1950s as a kind of waiting room or proving ground for aspirant AOCs: the twelve terroirs of the Coteaux du Languedoc, for example, began as VDQS wines in 1963 before communally forming this AOC in 1985. INAO considered abolishing this category altogether in 1990 when most of the former Mediterranean VDQS regions became AOC; in the end, though, it decided to persist with VDQS as an incentive for those zonal Vin de Pays regions that wished to become AOCs. Since 1990, for example, the Côtes de Millau has graduated from Vin de Pays to VDQS (in 1994) and the Coteaux du Quercy did so in 1999; Vin de Pays de St-Sardos and Vin de Pays de la Meuse have applied to do so. But it is a small category.

Vins de Pays and Vins d'AOC are far more important than VDQS. I will describe AOC wines first, since in many ways the definition and destiny of Vins de Pays has been crafted as a deliberate contrast to AOC.

The basis of France's AOC system is the notion of "terroir", described in full on pages 14 to 19. The point of the system, with its rules and regulations, is to ensure that this sense of "placeness" emerges with maximum clarity in the wines of each appellation. When modifications are made to the rules, or when decisions are made regarding those techniques which might or might not be allowed in an appellation, the primary consideration of INAO is always respect for the terroir itself.

Logically, therefore, the first and most important regulatory aspect of an appellation is its geographical boundaries. Geology plays an important part in deciding where these should fall, but by no means an exclusive one; slopes, aspects and climate factors are also taken into account, and so too (less logically) are some political boundaries. Demarcations on the ground are not as simple and straightforward as they might appear from the coloured splodges on a wine book map; they are usually defined parcel by parcel, after much thought and study. If you visit vineyard regions, you will sometimes find the boundaries starkly apparent – as in Champagne, where halfway down a gentle slope, and for no apparent reason, some of the world's most valuable vineyards cede their place to muddy tracts of sugar beet. On other occasions distinctions are much less easy to spot, particularly when the AOC system within a region takes hierarchical form, as in Burgundy. If you take a walk around the upper sections of the grand amphitheatre of Chablis' Grand Cru vineyards, you will see vineyards stretching continuously away over the top of the slope and onto the plateaux beyond. At some point towards the top of the hill, Chablis Grand Cru becomes mere Petit Chablis, a quality category three notches below, though it is not obvious to the casual walker exactly where this happens. Naturally, too, such a demarcation is a compromise, since the reality of terroir is at all times gradual: towards the boundary line, you are likely to find weak Grand Cru Chablis and exceptionally good Petit Chablis.

Grape varieties are specified, in some cases with maximum and minimum proportions within a blend. These varieties are generally the traditional ones, used for many years within a region, on the basis that (to use Emile Peynaud's words) "tradition is an experiment which has worked." The system is not as immutable and frozen as critics sometimes make it out to be. Changes to the varietal composition of an AOC are sometimes made to massage down the importance of less interesting varieties (like young or flat-land

AOC: The Gospel according to Joly

Perhaps the most radical, all-embracing and poetic notion of AOC is that of Nicolas Joly, biodynamic evangelist and proprietor of the ancient vineyard of Coulée de Serrant (a single-property AOC within Savennières; see page 55). Joly believes that all the life forms found in a certain area – birds, flowers, bushes, insects, even the manure of local breeds of cattle – contribute towards the identity of an AOC. "To reinforce the special life of a place is to accentuate diversity and diminish uniformity," he writes in Wine from Sky to Earth *(Acres USA, 1999).*

As a biodynamicist, moreover, Joly looks up as well as down towards "the atmospheric and solar world" which also constitutes and defines an environment. Naturally such a complex spectrum of factors is entirely beyond the scope of the legislator. The moral duty of each wine-grower, according to Joly, would be to foster and cherish those natural, localizing factors. Wine-growers should reject the abomination of artificial chemical inputs and of electrical and atmospheric pollution, all of which come from a wider, man-made environment and deform, erode, and destroy "the special life of a place". They should seek out and salvage, as far as possible, the nourishment of the local. The result will not necessarily be better wine, but it will be "truer" and "more authentic" wine.

Carignan in the Languedoc) and to increase the use of promising though non-traditional varieties (like Syrah in the Languedoc). Vine density is stipulated: the higher the better, since high planting densities mean low yields per vine. Vine-training systems and pruning regimes are also specified.

Yields themselves – in other words the amount of wine that you can make per hectare of vineyard land – are limited, though there have been many complaints in the past that these limits are overly lax. They certainly vary a great deal: Châteauneuf-du-Pape restricts itself to thirty-five hectolitres per hectare (hl/ha); Alsace permits itself eighty hl/ha. These yield figures have in the past, in any case, been treacherous. They represented what is called a *rendement de base* (base yield), which could be increased after a good year, giving a higher *rendement annuel*. Thus in the Côtes du Rhône, for example, the base yield of fifty hl/ha could be extended in a good year to an annual yield of sixty hl/ha. Nor was that all. Individual growers could also ask for a further excess of up to twenty per cent (called a *plafond limite de classement* or plc), provided certain conditions were met, such as that all of his or her wines were greeted with approval by the tasting panel. Thus our Côtes du Rhône grower could now claim a yield of seventy-two hl/ha – making the "base yield" figure look slightly comical. To be fair, there were valid reasons for this: great vintages are often relatively generous vintages. The fine 2000 vintage in Bordeaux produced much higher yields than the weak 1997 vintage; the excellent 1999 Burgundy vintage produced higher yields than the difficult and inconsistent 1998 vintage. Nature is unfair at all times. The system was abused, however, as INAO realized; so in 1993 the *rendement annuel* and the plc were capped by a single *rendement butoir* (literally "yield stopper"), which could never be exceeded, and which is usually about twenty per cent above the base yield (in Côtes du Rhône, for example, it is sixty hl/ha).

Bordeaux is trialling another system called the *rendement moyen decennal* (rmd). The idea here is that the *rendement de base* cannot be exceeded, though it can be aggregated out over a ten-year period. In poor years, therefore, there is a strong incentive for growers to reduce yields to the maximum (thereby improving quality), since it will mean that they are banking excess yields for good years (when their wine should be better in quality and is likely to sell for a higher price).

For a few appellations (such as Beaujolais, Champagne, Monbazillac, Bandol, and Coteaux du Layon) hand-harvesting is stipulated, and machine-harvesting is banned; in general, however, this decision is left to the grower. Minimum ripeness and alcoholic strength are specified, as is the extent to which wines can be either chaptalized (adding sugar or grape concentrate to the must to increase alcoholic strength) or acidified. The general rule is that you cannot do both, and that northern regions are permitted to chaptalize but not to acidify, while southern regions can acidify but not chaptalize. (The best producers go to great lengths to avoid doing either.) There are also AOC stipulations in some regions governing certain winemaking techniques, such as removing the stems from bunches before vinification, using whole berries for pressing or vinification, and pressing the harvest in certain ways in order to separate parts of it for different purposes. There are also minimum ageing regulations before the wines can be sold for many AOCs.

The end result of all this is an intricate and complex system with a heavy bureaucratic weight. Criticisms of it are examined overleaf. The AOC ideal, however, is that all of France's best pieces of vineyard land are sold under a regional badge that acts as a property right held in common. If you purchase an AOC wine, you are purchasing the true scent and taste of a place, defended and controlled by the AOC rules and regulations.

Beside this strict, pure, and almost ascetic ideal, the principles underlying Vins de Pays ("country wines") are relatively free and easy – though not uncomplicated. The basic fact to grasp is that, while there is only one type of AOC, there are in fact three types of Vins de Pays: regional, departmental, and zonal.

Regional Vins de Pays come from one of four very large areas into which most of wine-growing France has been divided: Vin de Pays du Jardin de la France (the Loire); Vin de Pays des Comtés Rhodaniens (most of the Rhône Valley, Beaujolais, Jura, and Savoie); Vin de Pays du Comté Tolosan (Southwest France excluding Bordeaux); and Vins de Pays d'Oc (Languedoc).

Departmental Vins de Pays come, as their name suggests, from a single wine-producing *département* (a *département* is the very approximate equivalent of a British county or an American state). Among the most common departmental Vins de Pays are Vins de Pays de l'Hérault and Vins de Pays de l'Aude, both from the Languedoc.

Before we look at the third type of Vins de Pays, let us just pause to consider the first two categories. These mark a genuine and radical departure from the AOC system, since terroir need play no role in their flavours. They are not quite geographically meaningless, since climate plays some role in their flavours: Vins de Pays du Jardin de la France will always produce cool-climate wines, for example, while Vins de Pays de l'Hérault will always produce Mediterranean-style wines. Nonetheless they allow considerable freedom to the winemaker, and the grape variety or varieties chosen, in the creation of flavour. When the phrase "France's New World" is used of Vins de Pays, it is these two categories that it generally refers to.

By contrast the third category of Vins de Pays, zonal Vins de Pays, introduces the notion of terroir, albeit at a rudimentary level. These are wines that come from a hundred or so small zones scattered preponderantly over the southern half of France. Many are resoundingly obscure or even unused; a few (such as Vins de Pays des Côtes de Gascogne) have achieved international celebrity.

Overall, it is the regional and departmental categories which have been most successful. This is unsurprising, but a shame nonetheless, since the heart and soul of the "country wine" ideal is found among some of the delicious obscurities of the zonal Vins de Pays. It may be that some of these zones in future set off on the long hike towards winning an AOC for themselves. On the other hand, they may just fade away. It's a tough wine market.

What about rules and regulations? There are fewer of them than for AOC wines, but they exist nonetheless. The grape varieties used must be selected from a recommended list, and are generally local varieties for zonal Vins de Pays and include "international" varieties of French origin (like Chardonnay, Sauvignon Blanc, Cabernet Sauvignon, and Merlot) for departmental or regional Vins de Pays. Yields must never exceed ninety hl/ha, and some zonal Vins de Pays have a lower limit. There are various technical parameters (such as minimum and maximum levels of alcohol, and maximum levels of sulphur and volatile acidity); all Vins de Pays, too, are tasted before sale.

Most Vins de Pays are straightforward varietal wines sold under the regional or departmental names; a small minority are zonal Vins de Pays which bear the stamp of terroir. In theory, however, many of those with vineyards in France's AOC areas could use the Vins de Pays legislation to make "alternative" wines from international varieties if they wished. It is remarkable how few do this. Why not? The truth is that varietal Vins de Pays from France are facing sales difficulties at present. In a world awash with Chardonnay, Cabernet, and Sauvignon Blanc, they have no particular competitive edge. For all the failings of the AOC system, it still creates wines whose scents, flavours, and identities can be duplicated nowhere else.

Wine Law Flak

France's wine law is widely criticized outside the country, by international journalists, merchants, and wine-producing rivals. Interestingly, most French wine-growers I have talked to are broadly content with the system, and happy to work within it. Here are the ten most widely voiced criticisms, together with some counter-arguments culled from my conversations with officials and French wine-growers.

French wine law stifles creativity

The usual sources of this frequently voiced criticism are international journalists and winemakers from New World countries who cannot understand, say, why those with AOC vineyards in France are not allowed to plant any grape variety they chose. Why should there, for example, be no Chardonnay on the best sites in the Médoc? Wouldn't it be great to taste Merlot grown in Côte Rôtie?

In the main, those growing wines on the greatest Grand Cru vineyards in France have absolutely no desire to experiment with other varieties. They seem satisfied that experiment by their ancestors over the course of the centuries has delivered the best solution for these sites and soils, and cannot imagine (probably correctly) that alternative wines would bring them a better livelihood.

These criticisms, though, are sometimes made by wine-growers working in less sought-after AOC areas, or in AOC areas where the regulations are still in some flux. There is a celebrated producer in Faugères, for example, who would like to use pure Syrah but is constrained (at least officially) to blend in some Mourvèdre and Grenache to his wine. A Bandol vineyard cannot (officially) be planted with Mourvèdre alone, though this is perhaps the greatest spot on earth for Mourvèdre.

I put it to Jacques Fanet of INAO that a producer in Faugères, which has a superb terroir of schist, might very well want to compete on an equal footing with the best varietal Shiraz from Australia or Syrah from California. "Yes," he replied, "but if that's what they want to do, they can always produce Vins de Pays." This would indeed be an option in Faugères. The fact is, though, the French wine producers still seem to prefer what they perceive as the cachet of AOC to the ignominy of Vins de Pays – in areas where both exist.

The true error of French wine law in this respect is that some of the key parts of France, such as Bordeaux, Burgundy, and Alsace, have no Vins de Pays alternative to AOC. If producers in these areas did want to take a creative, unconventional route (as many in Alsace do, and as many in Bordeaux should), then their only alternative is the highly restrictive Vin de Table legislation, which forbids them to mention either vintage or grape variety.

French wine law is protectionist

This criticism is made by rival producers from other countries, on the basis that wine-growing in France receives support both as part of the European Union's Common Agricultural Policy and from the French Government. French wine production provides employment for around half a million people, including many of the country's most economically vulnerable citizens in threatened rural communities; thirty per cent of all of those involved in French agriculture work with wine. Given these figures, the attempt to maintain a healthy wine economy is understandably an important part of French social policy.

France's wine culture, moreover, of which the appellation system is the coded abstract, is not only a national treasure but also a precious human achievement. Free-market capitalism often has a corrosive effect on cultural wealth of this sort, since it privileges economic success over the broader human value systems on which cultures are founded. This is recognized by governments of all political hues in France, as is the need to protect such cultural achievements.

French wine law fails to guarantee quality

Appellations, remember, are *d'origine contrôlée* (of controlled origin) and not *de qualité garantie* (of guaranteed quality). The primary duty of French wine law is to protect the uniqueness of a wine's place of origin; achieving the best quality in every bottle is the duty of each wine producer. Nonetheless, as Michel Pons of ONIVINS points out, "we have learnt that we aren't the only fish in the pond, and that we need to improve quality in order to be competitive." Since all French wines are tasted before sale, the evident quality lapses which sometime occur are humiliating, and INAO is working hard to improve the standards of *agrément* (quality testing) at present.

Yields are too high

"This is a permanent problem," says Jacques Fanet, "and it's never easy to control." Yields have been reduced across French appellations since the high water mark represented by the 1988, 1989, and 1990 vintages, but they need to come down further, particularly in regions like Alsace and Champagne. Both INAO and ONIVINS recognizes this.

French wine law is too complicated

For ordinary consumers, this is undoubtedly true. Yet those complications are the faithful reflection of cultural depth, of human achievement over hundreds of years. The plays of Shakespeare or the music of Bach could also be said to be too complicated – yet people still derive enjoyment from them without necessarily understanding every nuance of a soliloquy or a fugue. To simplify would be to betray and to impoverish. A little understanding is all that is necessary to open up long avenues of exploration and enjoyment. A far greater problem than the complications themselves is the catastrophic ineptitude with which French wine is explained and promoted.

French wine law is inconsistent

This criticism is often made when innovative producers are penalized for unorthodox practices in viticulture or vinification (the barrel-fermentation and wood-ageing of Alsace wines, for example), while the slackness and sloppiness of those who care little for quality goes unpunished. Sometimes, too, advances in technology catch French wine law off-guard. Is it right, let's say, to outlaw the use of plastic sheeting to protect vineyards from excess harvest rain in Bordeaux while permitting the use of reverse osmosis and vacuum evaporation machines to "concentrate" musts which have been rain-spoiled?

Many of these criticisms are valid. All legal systems (and the bureaucracies that enforce them) tend to be unresponsive or even antagonistic to innovation. In the long run, though, such systems must adapt if they are not to wither, and French wine law is no exception. If it is to survive and prosper, it will need to accommodate innovation – provided, of course, that the sanctity of terroir is respected. It is on this basis, indeed, that the use of plastic sheeting in vineyards has been outlawed, since in preventing fallen rain from reaching the vine roots, those sheets are thought to modify terroir. Concentration of dilute musts in the winery, the argument runs, merely concentrate terroir. A theological distinction? You decide.

French wine law is consumer-unfriendly

This serious criticism is true at present, and is a problem France urgently needs to resolve if it wishes to compete with the hugely successful branded wines of the New World. A case in point is the much-publicized refusal of INAO to allow AOC wines to state the grape variety (or varieties) from which they are made on the front label. This is seen as marketing stupidity of the first order, since most consumers in all of France's major export markets now choose and buy their wines on the basis of varietal labelling. I have been told by Jacques Fanet of INAO that this ruling is not enforced for AOC wines sold outside France, which seems a sensible compromise.

The boundaries of many AOCs have been too laxly drawn

This criticism applies particularly to the dramatic expansion in vineyard area of popular and highly saleable AOCs such as Chablis and Côte Rôtie. This debate, of course, is crucial whenever any geographical boundaries are defined anywhere in the world; controversy often ensues, as Australia discovered in setting boundaries to Coonawarra. Defining the boundaries of Champagne led to riots in the streets.

Whether the criticism is valid or not has to be examined on a case-by-case basis. Côte Rôtie is at present one of France's most admired AOCs, so the expansion of the AOC area must be regarded as a success. Chablis is commercially successful, though not all Chablis is high in quality or even particularly marked by terroir. The cause of this, however, is more often bad viticulture and careless winemaking than the source of the fruit, as those growers who produce exemplary Petit Chablis prove. Sometimes, too, the redefinition process sees AOCs contracting, as in St-Joseph, whose appellation boundaries have actually been reduced by a third in recent years.

Those who break the rules don't get caught

Wherever rules exist, they are broken. Unnamed experts, quoted in *La Revue du Vin de France 449*, estimate that up to six per cent of French wine might be subject to fraud of various sorts, and that only a small fraction of this (0.01 per cent) is brought to light and punished. Among the most common instances of rule breaking are excessive or illegal chaptalization by growers and the selling of ordinary table wine under grandiose AOC names by merchant fraudsters. The victims, overwhelmingly, are gullible French consumers, since such scams are usually local, and in any case almost all of France's worst wines are sold to undiscerning and bargain-hungry French shoppers.

Most French wines don't taste of terroir anyway

Terroir, I have heard Australian winemakers allege, is just an excuse for bad winemaking. What they mean is that when French wines don't taste of fresh, ripe fruit but instead of dry cardboard this is baptized "terroir" and used as a marketing gimmick to sell wine which by rights should be condemned. There are certainly cases when this criticism is fair.

Few, though, would dispute that the greatest wines of most of France's AOCs do indeed have a strong regional stamp to them, even if they don't always live up to the more fanciful descriptions found in some wine reference books. Competent wine tasters can routinely distinguish between red wines from Margaux and red wines from Pauillac, even though the two are grown only a few miles from each other and using exactly the same blend of grape varieties. Terroir exists, in other words, and it should be the aim of every French wine-grower to draw out that character as vividly as possible at all times. Most try; some succeed.

SAFERs: Helping Hand or Red Menace?

A subject guaranteed to raise the blood pressure of French wine-growers in 2002 is that of SAFER – the acronym stands for Société d'Aménagement Foncier et d'Etablissement Rural. In one short trip to Burgundy as I was preparing this book, I heard two or three growers complaining about SAFER in the strongest possible terms. "Ça me fait chier" (it really pisses me off) said one celebrated Côte d'Or producer who had recently bought land in the Mâconnais. "If I was looking to expand any further, I'd go abroad." Another claimed that the system penalized and frustrated good growers, and held overall quality standards in check. The celebrated Burgundian négociant Robert Drouhin resigned his post at the BIVB in protest over the issue.

So what are SAFERs? They are governmental bodies, reporting to the Ministry of Agriculture, charged with preventing rural depopulation and amalgamation of agricultural enterprises. "The state," summarized Jean-Luc Dairien of ONIVINS, "would in general rather see ten domains of one hectare than one domain of ten hectares. That has been absolutely consistent government policy in France, no matter who was in power, for the last forty years." It is, of course, a check on the free market. "If you let the free market alone decide things," says Dairien, "then money will always win."

SAFERs work by supervising agricultural transactions. If a property passes from one generation of a family to another, the SAFER is content. If an agricultural property is sold, by contrast, the SAFER takes an interest in the potential purchaser. And, crucially, it has the right to pre-empt the transaction if it considers the purchase will not serve the national interest as defined above. It would do this by purchasing the property itself (at "the going rate" – which may well be a lower price than that already decreed), then selling it on, in whole or in part, to other purchasers it approves of. In Provence, for example, a property developer might wish to buy a hillside planted with 110-year-old olive trees, tear them out, and build a luxury hotel. The SAFER would insist (to the probable fury of both vendor and developer) on buying the olive grove itself – at the going rate for an olive grove, and not as building land. It would then sell it, perhaps divided into three parcels, to a trio of young and impecunious would-be olive farmers with a cooperative project for producing top-quality organic olive oil. The vendor's only option, should he or she consider this unwarranted interference, is not to sell.

An example such as the one above shows that the system has some merits. There are, however,

three main problems with the application of SAFER principles in the viticultural context.

The first problem is that holdings are often already too small anyway, and further division and parcellation serves no useful purpose.

The second is the assumption which many feel SAFERs make that any large-scale, moneyed purchaser is necessarily "the enemy". In many wine-growing areas, indeed, the opposite is likely to be true. Were a top Bordeaux producer to decide that Entraygues is a superb terroir and perfect for major investment, and were he to purchase the largest estate in Entraygues in order to prove this, Entraygues as a whole (and its entire community of wine-growers) could only benefit.

Thirdly and perhaps most seriously, SAFERs do not seem to consider raw ability when they select beneficiaries for their schemes. "While the general goal is understandable," says Robert Drouhin, "I strongly disagree on the criteria to select the potential candidates. It is based only on social criteria: a small producer, a young producer, the one with the lowest revenue and so on. No quality criterion is taken into consideration." The risks of this are evident. The potential of a fine piece of vineyard land might be squandered, thus damaging France's cultural patrimony.

Terroir

The Print of Place Consistency, varietal character, depth of fruit, oak integration: these are qualities of absolute irrelevance to French AOC wine. Instead, its aim and its reason for being is to lend a sensual print to rock, stone, slope, and sky.

In the December 1999 issue of the British wine magazine *Decanter*, readers happened upon an article called "The Soul of Wine". It was written not by a journalist, but by the Californian winemaker, intellectual jester, and former philosophy student Randall Grahm. In it, Grahm describes how, while tasting a bunch of wines including some of his own Santa Cruz creations, he came across one wine, a non-Californian, which stood out. "It was not simply that it had *more* of one particular quality than the California wines but the wine seemed to possess a very different order of qualities, as if it might have come from another planet (and I know how *that* feels). It was ontologically different, of a different order of being." Grahm said that the other wines were "winningly exuberant" and "eager to please". The wine that stopped him in his tracks "was indeed very pleasing but *it wasn't there to please.*" It had, he said, "a sort of stony resoluteness at its very core — the impression one sometimes gets in shaking the hand of a particularly wilful or rugged individual... one could be shaking the hand of a mountain."

I will return to this article later, and tell you just what wine it was that stopped the extra-planetary Californian in his salivary tracks. Let's just consider, though, Grahm's perceptive phrase "shaking the hand of a mountain". Was there ever a better analogy for the pleasure procured by drinking what the French would call a *grand vin de terroir*?

If you are taking the time to read this book, then you enjoy wines. Not wine, but wines: diverse, multifarious, copiously plural, endlessly different. As most wine drinkers do.

That, after all, is what distinguishes wine from other food and drink products: its pullulating variety. We may have the chance to sample, say, six types of cabbage, a dozen varieties of apple or twenty species of fish in the course of a year. If we worked hard with our recipe books, we might produce one hundred different dishes over the next twelve months. Cheese enthusiasts could perhaps collate several hundred slabs of gently decomposing milk as the four seasons turn. Give most of us a phone and a credit card, though, and we could fill our houses with 10,000 wines in a matter of days.

What makes wines different from one another? A number of things, which I would suggest can be grouped into three categories: false differences, shallow differences, and deep differences.

Labels, bottles, marketing stratagems, and advertising campaigns create false differences. These are the make-up, the silicon implants, the hair dye, and the toupees of the wine world. It is for this reason that the only trustworthy wine tastings are those that are conducted "blind", that is without sight of bottles or labels. Better than tastings in assessment terms, of course, and by a very long margin, are drinking sessions, with the wines served in

plain decanters. No wine can be properly assessed until it lies quietly in the stomach: that is its purpose and destiny.

Winemaking creates shallow differences: pre-fermentation maceration, for example, or barrel fermentation, tank fermentation, percentages of malolactic fermentation, lees contact, racking, micro-oxygenation... the list of possibilities is a long one. When winemaking interventions actually involve changing the chemical composition of a wine, as is the case when one adds acid to the must or adjusts a wine's tannin content, then these shallow differences can take on a dramatic or lurid allure. Such wines are denatured; we move from agriculture towards industry. (Denatured wine is what the Loire Valley biodynamic wine-grower Nicolas Joly calls "false wine"; natural wine is what he calls "true wine". You can, of course, have good "false wine" and bad "true wine", depending on the skills with which the denaturing operations are carried out – or the lack of skill with which natural wines are grown, harvested, and vinified.)

Thus, finally, to the deep differences between wines. These derive from the place on earth in which wine comes into being. The sum of these environmental influences is what is meant by terroir, a French word which we could translate as "placeness".

A vine cannot move. It is rooted to its spot on earth. It makes its grapes from water and minerals absorbed through the roots as they rummage some ten or fifteen metres (thirty or forty-five feet) down into the soil and subsoil, and from the light which fills the sky above it. (The sky, indeed, may be more important than the soil. According to soil scientist Claude Bourgignon, eighty-eight per cent of vegetable matter is derived, via photosynthesis, from carbon dioxide in the air. Terroir lies above as well as below.)

If you prefer poetry to science, you might enjoy the French writer Colette's version of this process. "Alone in the vegetable kingdom, the vine makes the true taste of the earth intelligible. What a faithful translation it is! The vine feels, expresses through its bunches the secrets of the soil. Flint, via the vine, makes us understand that it is living, fusible, nourishing. Poor chalk weeps, in wine, its golden tears."

"Everywhere," to use Nicolas Joly's simple phrase, "the earth has a different face." No vineyard is ever quite the same as any other. Soils grow thinner or thicker, stonier or loamier, more acid or more alkaline; hillsides rise and fall; watercourses approach and retreat. The sky, too, changes incessantly, both from day to day and from place to place. Not merely the shadowplay of local topographic features, meaning that it is dark in Pernand's Caradeux long before the sun has set on Corton-Charlemagne across the valley; but also the presence of the shadowless sea on all sides of the Médoc, or the protection of the Vosges which makes wine-growing in Alsace

"Seule, dans le règne végétal, la vigne nous rend intelligible ce qu'est la véritable saveur de la terre. Quelle fidélité dans la traduction! Elle ressent, exprime par la grappe les secrets du sol. Le silex, par elle, nous fait connaître qu'il est vivant, fusible, nourricier. La craie ingrate pleure, en vin, des larmes d'or."

COLETTE, "VINS" IN PRISONS ET PARADIS **(1932)**

Healthy soil is a world apart, packed with life. Wine provides the sensual link
◀ *which enables us to taste that otherwise inarticulate world.*

▲ *Terroir is sky and sea as much as soil – if, like Latour or Margaux, your vines are beached in the Médoc.*

possible. The land – or its absence – affects the sky. The sun shines in Colmar as much as it does because it stands in the lee of granite mountains which claw water out of the sky. The Médoc, by contrast, is almost part of the sea: infinitely open, ready for a dozen meteorological mood-changes a day. Add to this torrent of chance and complexity the grand lottery of a season's weather, during which no minute replicates any other, and you will begin to understand why each vine's experience of life is unique.

The vine is a scholar among plants. It records everything. In the middle of a windless January night, it outfaces the cold stars. The flowers that will create the following summer's fruit already lie in its tightly clenched buds at that moment of ice and silence. Something is happening; something is noted. The vine grips its stones in an equinoctial gale as the sodden, ash-grey clouds race across the sky on a dark March afternoon. This is different from an unseasonably warm, bright March afternoon; the vine will inscribe both on its fruit. It is there, recording, for the dewy hour before dawn on a limpid June day, and in the fierce heat of a white August noon. The grapevine, *seule dans la règne végétal* as Colette puts it, has the ability to lend those annual records a sensual print. It does this by making grapes, which become wine.

When the hurly-burly of vinification is over, and provided the chemical composition of the grape juice has not been altered, then a drinker can smell and taste everything that has happened to the vine in the course of its season, and the precise place in which it finds itself on the earth's surface. This is the chief source of joy and astonishment to thoughtful wine drinkers. This is how, in drinking a wine, you can shake the hand of a mountain. This is terroir.

Analogies sometimes help. Imagine one of your favourite pieces of music. It matters little what it is – John Lennon's "Imagine", let's say. The song is the wine, there to be enjoyed; John Lennon was (or is) the terroir, the creator; and whoever is performing the song is the winemaker. Lennon's words and music can never be altered, just as a terroir can only be itself. But if the performer is a hobbled busker who drank beer for breakfast you will probably not enjoy the performance much, no matter how deep your love for the song; even the greatest terroirs can be battered into silence by inept viticulture (in particular over-high yields), crass winemaking interventions, or a fundamental dereliction of care. To claim, in other words, that the deep differences between wines are a function of terroir is not to denigrate or deny the vital role of the winemaker. Winemakers stand at the gate that brings wines into life (hence the "midwife" analogy of which so many French wine-growers are fond); they can open the gate wide or slam it shut. What is accepted by all of France's greatest winemakers without exception is that only the sympathetic and courageous restraint of non-interventionist winemaking can help terroir towards maximum articulacy within wine. "*Il faut avoir le courage de ne rien faire,*" as Dominique Lafon's father, René Lafon, used to say: a winemaker must have the courage to do nothing. If you want terroir to speak in your wine, you must let that wine be what nature intends. "To sincerely pursue terroir," Randall Grahm confirms, "one must, as a winemaker, learn to subordinate one's ego, to put one's stylistic signature at the corner of the wine-painting rather than squarely in the middle... (I might remark parenthetically how difficult this discipline is for New World winemakers. If we were not already in hormonal overdrive to 'make a statement', our Mephistophelean marketers continually coo in our ears about the need for 'stylistic differentiation'.)"

We also need to state the obvious, which is that not all terroirs are born equal. France, because of its long wine-growing history, offers starker examples of this than any other wine-producing country in the world. In Burgundy, you can walk just a hundred paces from

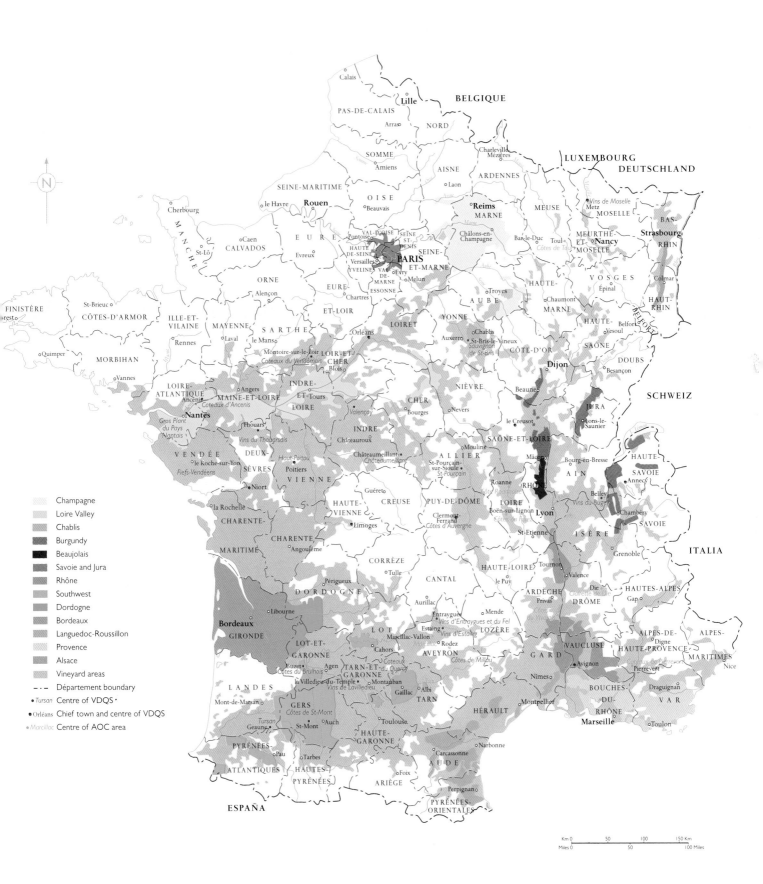

Olivier Jullien

Olivier Jullien's story illustrates two fascinating aspects of terroir.

The first is the struggle for understanding – in Languedoc. "In 1989," he recalls, "no one liked my wine. 'OK,' I thought, 'I'll make a wine that you'll all like and I'll sell it to you more cheaply than the wine that you find disgusting.'" Thus was born, in 1990, Jullien's Etats d'Ame (which means "Moods"), a "sociable" wine in which, he says, he makes "efforts to please". It's built on fruit. Mas Jullien, by contrast, is a wine made with "an absence of effort" (another way of describing non-interventionism). It's the pure expression of his white stonefields and, he says, is "beyond seduction". It can, in other words, be difficult; it needs time. It is always more expensive than Etats d'Ame: Jullien's decision, against market logic. The creator rates nature, thus, more highly than his own craft.

The second aspect, though, is that terroir itself sometimes needs to be crafted. Since Jullien has both limestone and schist vineyards, he used to make two "top" red wines: Les Cailloutis from the former, and Les Despierre using the latter. "It bothered me. I wasn't getting the equilibrium I wanted, the digestibility." Now he just makes one red wine using both soil types: Mas Jullien. "I feel much more at ease with it now. It works." Nurture now helps to interpret nature.

▶

some of the most expensive and prized vineyard land in the world to land of viticultural uselessness. This is not the dead hand of bureaucracy persecuting less fortunate landowners, as critics of the AOC system sometimes allege. "*Le législateur en 1936,*" as Henri Jayer says, "*n'a fait que confirmer les trouvailles empiriques de nos ancêtres. N'oublions pas que la classification, avant l'officialisation des classements, se faisait à la tasse, par des personnes qui avaient bon goût.*" ("The legislators back in 1936 only confirmed the empirical observations of our ancestors. Don't forget that classifications, before it was sanctified by officialdom, was done in the glass, by people who knew how to taste.") The work of uncovering terroir, of peeling back the skin of the land to discover what lies beneath, is well-advanced in regions like Burgundy, but in other parts of France (and in the rest of the world) centuries of exciting discoveries lie ahead of us. The Grands Crus of Languedoc, of Southwest France, and of Provence have still to be unearthed. There are many surprises ahead in Bordeaux, too, while Alsace's complex terroirs are at an early stage of differentiation. We can, though, be certain that there are no terroirs in Muscadet to equal those of Corton or Montrachet. Life is unfair; so is land.

Why, though, should we privilege the print of terroir over all other traces and prints in wine? Wine also contains alcohol, which statistically is what most drinkers enjoy most about it. Particularly when young, wine is full of fruit flavours, too. The British wine commentator Oz Clarke has throughout his career championed

This young vine may live to see one hundred harvests, its roots rummaging ever deeper into rock and soil, mining beauty. ▶

fruit flavours in wine, memorably appearing on television with his slogan "Fruit, fruit, fruit" emblazoned on his T-shirt. It is fruit above all, Clarke claims, which ordinary drinkers enjoy in wine, not the more abstruse and sometimes even disagreeable flavours of terroir. (Australian critics, as mentioned on page 15, sometimes go further than Clarke, alleging that the concept of terroir is no more than "an excuse for bad winemaking," as one of them once said to me.) Statistically speaking, once again, Clarke is right, not least because it costs much less to create fruity wines (for which high yields are possible) than it does to create wines in which terroir comes to the fore (where high yields are impossible). Compare the following two tasting notes for white wines from the same producer, in the same vintage. The first wine is a "fragrant effort exhibiting scents of tropical fruits and orange rind, crisp acidity, and a lively, medium-bodied, citrusy finish." The second wine is a "restrained, well-delineated white... [which] represents the essence of granite liqueur. There is no real fruit character, just glycerin, alcohol, and liquid stones." The first wine costs around £15 or $24 a bottle; the second wine around £290 or $440 a bottle. We are comparing Chapoutier's 1999 Crozes-Hermitage Blanc Les Meysonniers and the same producer's 1999 Hermitage Blanc L'Ermite; the tasting notes are those of Robert Parker (the fruity wine, by the way, scores 84; the unfruity one 93-95).

There is nothing wrong with preferring the taste of fruit to that of terroir in a wine; unlike terroir, taste is genuinely democratic, and every taster has a moral duty to decide for themselves what brings them most joy and well-being. If you love fruit more than stones, rejoice in your good fortune. It will save you much money — and you barely need bother with French wine at all. To discover, though, why people are prepared to pay more to taste stones and shake the hand of mountains than they are to drink fruit, let's go back to Randall Grahm.

Grahm's article addressed the difficult question of whether or not wine has a soul. He had, he said, "been brooding about this subject for a long while," and he had concluded that terroir, "the sense of belongingness, of coming from somewhere, is very much connected to the idea of soulfulness in a wine." The discovery of terroir in wine, he continued, constitutes "a meditation for the winemaker as well as for the wine drinker." And what is soul? It is "the part of ourselves that is abiding, never changing, the part somehow hidden beneath the surface, representing our truest self, the part beyond public ascription." It was this that he encountered in the wine that took him aback so, which was an Alsace Riesling from the Muenchberg vineyard, made by André Ostertag.

I have been lucky enough to drink wine for thirty years now. There is no doubt in my mind that the most profound satisfaction that wine can bring is based on the scents and tastes of stones, earth, and minerals in wine. Alcohol is available elsewhere; so is fruit. It is only via wine that a drinker can shake hands with a mountain. I also agree with Grahm that it is in meeting these scents and flavours that we encounter what we might justly describe as the soul of wine: its essence, its eternal truth, which is precisely its articulate empathy with the natural world. To drink a great *vin de terroir* is to lose yourself in nature, to be awed by natural beauty as affectingly as when you stand on a wind-buffeted hilltop, wake up to a snow-hushed world, or watch a rising moon scatter silver over an ink-black sea. Experiences of this order bring a pleasure and a well-being, I would argue, of infinitely greater profundity than that procured by the rude slug of alcohol and caffeine in a vodka and Red Bull, or by the empty and desolating blandness of a watery industrial lager or an oak-smeared Chardonnay. This is wine's final, joyful sobriety.

▼ Merlot vines planted at Bon Pasteur in Pomerol, the family property of the most influential French winemaker of the 1990s: Michel Rolland.

Champagne

The Turning Point Champagne is on the verge of profound change. There is a growing realization in the region that its viticulture has become slovenly and the subtleties of its terroir have been neglected. The era of great growers and great vineyards is just beginning.

It was midwinter, in leafless Sussex. I was with an old friend who had suffered. His life had, over the previous four months, undergone dislocating reverses that eroded everything for which he had worked with ceaseless energy over the previous twenty-five years. His circumstances, never more than modest, had begun to flirt with squalor. In his mid-fifties now, this usually good-humoured stoic seemed defeated. We talked amid the metaphorical ruins for an hour or two. He barely smiled.

"I think," I said, as midday passed, "we should drink some champagne." He looked at me, pulling on his hand-rolled cigarette. He loved good wine, but he had particular reasons for loving good champagne above all good wines. I had, in my car, a bottle of Mumm de Cramant. It was a cold day, and the champagne had acquired a light chill. We lodged the bottle in his fridge's freezer compartment for a few final chilling minutes while I cleaned the glasses, breaking one in the process.

I poured. The wine gleamed greenly, topped with enticing snow. It was our first drink of the day. The Cramant smelled fresh: sweet apples. It tasted green – yet round, vivid, surging. We carried on talking; we ate some *saucisson*, *chorizo*, bread, avocado. The champagne grew finer and finer. We were hypnotized by its seeming contradictions: its crispness, its edginess, its sappiness... and yet its roundness and fullness, too. Would any other wine have served us as well? Perhaps; yet this champagne memory will abide while all the others – the dull receptions, the tedious parties, the routine markers for the stations of the year – have long faded. My friend's spirits were raised; we laughed and smiled; his eyes gleamed again. As we stepped outside later to confront his mud-slide of difficulties, I remembered that quotation attributed to Lily Bollinger which I never trusted; it always seemed too pat and polished to be true. Just now, though, the phrase "... I drink it when I'm sad..." came tumbling, as if new-minted, from the twig-covered place in the mind where it was lying hidden.

I detain you with this story only because it illustrates an essential truth of champagne: that this is, more than most, a wine of general appeal rather than particular excellence. My friend and I drank Mumm de Cramant, but it could have been any other good champagne; the point was that it was good champagne. No other wine carries the same weight of symbolical significance; no other wine was in quite the same position to lift the spirits, almost outrageously, at such a moment. Its taste, of course, makes it suitable for drinking at any time; meals are never obligatory, as they would be for a fine bottle of Hermitage or Madiran. It is an occasion as much as a wine. And what, in any case, does "quality" mean for champagne?

Does it have its customary significance in the wine world, meaning that our wine showed outstanding concentration, power, and individuality? Or does it mean that it merely incarnates an ideal of snowy finesse with rapturously neutral fidelity? Probably, in truth, the latter more than the former. We weren't seizing on the particular, unique felicities of Mumm de Cramant; indeed it didn't have that many. We were simply lancing our gloom on the rapier point of champagne acidity; buoying our damp hopes on its absurd foam; nourishing our serotonin on its yeastmeal.

All of which is exactly why the Champagne region finds itself in something of a conundrum at the threshold of the twenty-first century. Its wine is one of the most successful processed agricultural products in human history. It is prized worldwide, and intimately associated with luxury and wealth. The average price of a bottle of branded, non-vintage champagne is, to be frank, several times more than a wine of its sometimes modest concentration (made from France's highest-yielding AOC vines) should cost. It is able to command those exorbitant prices because it has built an impregnable image over the last 150 years, and because (thanks to its climate and soils) at present it has no rival on earth for piercing and disarming finesse. Champagne is France's only region of strong brands; Champagne is France's only region of monolithic, consumer-friendly simplicity. We are prepared to pay that much for champagne not because it is worth it, but because there is no functional alternative and that is what the experience of drinking it costs.

The New France, by contrast, is building itself on the cultivation of every quality that has to date eluded Champagne. Almost without exception, the New France's greatest wine producers are engaged in a battle to allow the nuances of terroir, in all their variety, to speak with maximum articulacy. Almost without exception, France's greatest wine producers are fastidious viticulturalists and fanatical fruit-sorters, checking over every bunch which goes into their vats. These brilliant and passionate wine-growers are almost always working with half the yields of their fathers — or less. In terms of vinification, theirs is a course of increasingly watchful and solicitous inaction. These hundreds of French growers are, naturally, profoundly "unbranded"; indeed their work (in which no vintage or *cuvée* is ever the same as another, sold under names which tend to change from moment to moment, from generation to generation, and whose only absolute guarantee is fidelity to a place of origin) is subversive of everything that brands stand for. Naturally, Champagne doesn't want to be left behind as France mounts its counter-attack to the gradual, worldwide industrialization, abusive commercialization, and brand-driven

"In the 1980s we used to say that the cellarmaster was everything in Champagne. In the 1990s we realized that grapes were everything. The cellarmaster can add five or ten per cent — or destroy your reputation. But the base of everything is, truly, the grapes."

JEAN-MARIE BARILLERE, CEO, CHAMPAGNE MUMM

◀ *The 2001 vintage in Champagne made everyone pause to think. It's time for a more stringent vineyard policy.*

▲ *No vineyard area is colder or drearier in winter than Champagne. Vines on the Montagne de Reims slumber through the gloomy months.*

homogenization of wine; Champagne wants to be part of the French avant-garde, too. Yet the structure of Champagne production is such that the region finds this very difficult. Champagne also realizes that its gleaming success to date has been built on ignoring or rejecting all these tendencies. Champagne, if you like, was "France's New World" – eighty years ago. It is now beginning to realize the limits of that approach.

Let's look at these issues in turn, beginning with terroir. In its recent publicity, the Comité Interprofessionel du Vin de Champagne (CIVC) has stressed "the diversity of Champagne wines for a multitude of different occasions" – yet the region has at present no conceptual framework to hang such diversity on. In terms of appellations, Champagne is France's most primitive and backward region, since it has but a single AOC: Champagne. Is the whole region a mono-terroir? Certainly not, as we'll discover in "Adventure of the Land"; Champagne contains many different terroirs. Yet present wine law does not permit their identification, and consumers are left in the dark about them. All that we are allowed to know is whether or not a wine is made from grapes grown in villages that are classified as Premier Cru or Grand Cru. These terms refer to Champagne's internal grading system, originally used to fix the price of grapes: Grand Cru villages (of which there are seventeen) are classified at "one hundred per cent", and Premier Cru villages (of which there are forty-one) at "ninety to ninety-nine per cent". The Grand Cru system in Alsace, we might note in passing, has been widely criticized for its laxity by comparison with the Burgundy model; yet Champagne's is far worse. At least in Alsace it is a large parcel on a single slope or hillside that is classified; in Champagne it is an entire village. "I'm sorry," says vigneron Didier Gimmonet, "but wine from the *tailles* grown on clay under the hill at Cramant is not and will never be Grand Cru." "Classing a whole village," as fellow vigneron Pierre Larmandier points out, "is fairly meaningless, but you have to remember history. In the old days, a négociant would come to a press house in the village and buy. What he was buying, though, was already a village blend, made up of wine from all over the place. The problem is that the system hasn't changed since then." Champagne urgently needs a more terroir-sensitive AOC system, and the CIVC's ten-year-old *zonage* project under researcher Laurent Panigaï, looking at the entire region on the basis of fifty-square-metre (538-square-feet) parcels, could provide a basis for this when complete. Yet there is liable to be substantial resistance to change, since

defining Grands and Premiers Crus in Champagne more satisfactorily would mean defining them more stringently. That in turn would mean many growers losing their right to these illustrious names – and thus losing income. No change that involves an overall loss of income will ever take place.

The march of "reason"

The situation in the vineyards themselves, too, is often unsatisfactory, with yields ballooning out of control, the vineyards being poorly maintained, and with little of the fruit-sorting fastidiousness found in other regions of France evident here. (Philippe Secondé of Champagne Barnaut owns a sorting table, but says he knows of only two others apart from his.) These problems are examined more minutely in the Flak section on page 31, as are some of the reasons why the problems are difficult to solve. The question of vineyard quality is, however, one that the Champagne authorities are taking seriously – by promoting a "Viticulture Raisonnée" scheme throughout the entire region. This "reasoned wine-growing" involves, among other things, encouraging growers to consider *enherbement* and the use of cover crops and mulches, better choice of rootstocks, and a more thoughtful use of sprays and synthetic vineyard treatments. It has, of course, nothing whatsoever to do with organic grape-growing or biodynamic production, which is difficult in Champagne and in which very few growers as yet show much interest. It is hard to say how closely growers are likely to follow the scheme, and there are at present no sanctions involved for those who choose to ignore it – though in the long run the plan is to make awarding the AOC itself conditional on following the Viticulture Raisonnée rules. If a sizeable majority of growers apply the CIVC's recommendations, however, then there is no doubt that the quality of Champagne's grapes will begin to rise. "Viticulture," confirms Pierre Larmandier, "is getting better in the region. I'm president of the growers in our village, and there's a lot of progress among the younger members. They're not about to switch to organics, but they do at least realize that if we put toxins into our soils then we will be the first to suffer." Despite this, Larmandier – one of the few in Champagne to use *enherbement* at present – still gets accused of having "dirty" vineyards by those for whom a "clean" vineyard means one whose soil is drenched in herbicide.

The question of yields, alas, is even harder to solve – because, as with the revision of terroir, it directly affects each grower's income. Since Champagne's climate is an uncertain one, few growers are prepared to take the risk of pruning and green-harvesting for low yields, and there are at present no financial incentives for them to do so. Quite the opposite, indeed: *see* "Flak". The question of yields is one that the Viticulture Raisonnée "*guide pratique*" dances around nimbly, stressing only that there should be a "balance" between "economic viability" and "quality potential". This, of course, can justify almost anything.

The move towards a less interventionist style of champagne production, one that would let the nuances of terroir emerge more limpidly in the wines, is beginning to get underway. Few would go as far yet as Anselme Selosse, who told me "our ideal schema of vinification is the following. No *débourbage*, no chaptalization, no acidification, no added yeasts, no yeast nutrient, no sulphur, no fining, no filtration." Yet Selosse has become Champagne's most celebrated individual grower, and his influence is spreading swiftly among those of the younger generation who are able to overcome their jealousy of his success. ("You're a lousy vigneron and you know it," one fellow grower told him. "You just know how to communicate more effectively than we do.") Others have found that, despite champagne's singularity as a wine style, they can learn much from producers in other regions, as Francis Egly has from Dominique Laurent in Burgundy and Michel Tardieu in the Rhône, or Pierre Larmandier has from Pierre Morey at Leflaive and from Marc Kreydenweiss in Alsace.

Most growers, of course, don't make wine and never will; eighty per cent of champagne is made not by growers but by cooperatives and large merchant houses. One might assume that whoever's name is on the bottle has actually made the wine – yet even this is far from being the case. Many champagne names are pure fiction, and even well-known companies often buy wine *sur lattes*, in an undisgorged state, to bolster their own stocks, making basic champagne a traded commodity. Given all of this, it is perhaps just as well that the winemaking practices of Champagne's cooperatives and large houses are, for the time being, highly interventionist and formulaic, with swift pressing, extensive use of chaptalization, and other adjustments (including on occasion the addition of acidity – though theoretically acidification is forbidden whenever chaptalization takes place), cultured yeast strains, enzymes, nitrogenous yeast nutrients, rapid temperature-controlled fermentations in stainless steel, repeated racking to avoid the problems of reduction that come with the extensive use of stainless steel, and eventual fining and filtration of the wines before the second fermentation. The way raw materials are generally treated in Champagne leads Philippe Aubry to describe himself and his fellow vignerons as *betteraviers de luxe* (luxury sugar beet growers). Such techniques are perfect for turning often indifferent raw materials into a satisfactory, fault-free, and consistent branded product, which is what most non-vintage champagne is. The vinification ideals of the region remain, above all, those of "zero faults". These techniques, though, obscure and obliterate the nuances of terroir rather than accentuating them. If Champagne is serious about wanting to be a *vin de terroir*, then there must be a return towards the artisanal methods now followed by most of France's greatest wine producers.

Oh yeah?

Or must there? Why should Champagne change? Don't things work pretty well as they are in this prosperous region? Shouldn't other French regions, in fact, try to emulate Champagne?

"*Terroir? On est contre.*" The speaker is Régis Camus, successor to the brilliant Daniel Thibault as cellarmaster at Charles Heidsieck. "We're against terroir; we're very much in favour of blends. We try to make our blends a reflection of the entire Champagne region. That's as far as we want terroir to go." Even a grower like Didier Gimmonet, who might be expected to champion terroir, says he is "anti-mono-parcel,

and anti-mono-terroir. The more different *cuvées* you make, the less complex your different *cuvées* will become." Gimmonet self-sacrificingly follows his own theories in that he blends up to twenty per cent Premier Cru wine from Cuis into his Grand Cru from Cramant and Chouilly because he feels the blend is better – even though he thereby deprives his wine of the right to call itself "Grand Cru", and sell at Grand Cru prices. "It is very difficult," summarizes Hervé Gestin of Duval-Leroy, "to find a terroir in Champagne that is one hundred per cent complete."

Similarly, the questions of yield and ripeness in Champagne are less straightforward than they at first appear. Champagne's greatest vintages have usually been high-yielding years. The glorious 1982 vintage, for example, had an average yield of ninety-four hl/ha, which is well over twice the permitted yield in Châteauneuf-du-Pape. Even the quality-obsessed Anselme Selosse is looking for an

▲ *Vine wood ash nourishes soil – and a brazier helps keep pruning fingers warm in French wine's far north.*

average yield of around fifty-five hl/ha – or three times that of a Leroy Grand Cru in Burgundy, a Rayas, or a Gauby old-vine Grenache in Roussillon. "If you reduce yields too much in Champagne," says Jean-Marie Barillère of Mumm, "you get little burgundies." "Harvest a Chardonnay at 12.8 per cent potential alcohol in Champagne," says Didier Gimmonet, "and you're already halfway to Meursault or Chassagne. The wines are too varietal, too personalized to make good champagne." Leading grower Gimmonet is also doubtful about lees ageing and *batonnage* for champagne (since he feels they make the wine too weighty) and questions the ideal of intense concentration of flavour for champagne (since he believes it undermines elegance and finesse). His ideal is not a classic *vin de terroir* as it might be defined by Mark Angeli in the Loire or by Olivier Zind-Humbrecht in Alsace. "You want something *hautement expressif*," he says, "but not more than that."

We're back, in other words, to the fundamental question with which this chapter opened: is great champagne that which conforms most winningly to the Platonic or generic ideal of "champagne", or is it a sparkling wine of depth and rigour, bearing the clear stamp of terroir, and expressing a complex and usually challenging individuality? This question has no conclusive answer at present – though at least, with the arrival of great growers' champagnes like those of Egly-Ouriet, Selosse, or Larmandier-Bernier, we are in a position to begin to make comparisons. The fact that Moët et Chandon has released its "Triologie des Grands Crus", that Mumm has released a Grand Cru, and that a cooperative like CVC has done the same with the Nicolas Feuillatte Grand Cru wines shows that the large concerns do not want to be left behind. They, too, want to produce new, more distinctive champagnes whose appeal is based on an expression of terroir rather than the blending skill of a *chef de cave* and the packaging pretensions of the marketing department. (Even though Charles Heidsieck is a house which has officially declared itself against the value of specific terroirs in Champagne, its own Mise en Cave approach to Brut non-vintage wines shows that it, too, realizes the limitations of the old, monotonous approach to brands and is looking for an alternative.) I consider this fundamental question a heartening and exciting one, at any rate, since it is precisely this that will make the coming decades in Champagne such a fascinating period for those who love this Arctic fox among wine styles.

Pierre Larmandier

Pierre Larmandier, who says he comes from a family of "gentle madmen", is tall, quiet, apparently diffident, yet with a keenly polished sense of irony. He inherited a third of his attractive twelve-ha (thirty-acre) domain from his father (the Cramant parcels); the other two-thirds, based in Vertus, came from his mother. He thinks; he travels; he's worked (this is still unusual for a Champagne grower) in Alsace and Burgundy. "What surprised me in Alsace and Burgundy was that top growers had as elevated a reputation as the big merchant houses. That's far from being the case in Champagne. The big houses are at the summit, and the wine-growers are miles below." Why? "The big houses have suffocated the vineyard. They haven't allowed the individualities of terroir to develop as they have in other regions. That is our main problem in Champagne. We have a superb terroir – but we only make good wines from it." Larmandier's pure, vinous, almost salty Né d'une Terre de Vertus and Cramant Vieilles Vignes cuvées constitute a magnificent challenge to that orthodoxy.

Francis Egly

"My father Michel," says Francis Egly, "and my grandfather Charles were great vignerons. They always worked the vines, they rejected gadoux [see page 31], they used to defoliate; we haven't changed our methods for years. We green-harvest, sometimes half the crop; no one knows how to do that in Champagne. You have to fight nature; it's not a gift. The difference between me and my father and grandfather was that I have had the chance to meet people. Wine-growing is also a matter of meeting people." With his friend the French wine critic Michel Bettane, Egly has refined his philosophy of picking at full ripeness and giving all his wines up to four years' age before sale; with his friend Dominique Laurent he is slowly exploring the possibilities of wood fermentation and of working the lees (and of producing a superb still Coteaux Champenois, too). What Larmandier-Bernier achieves with Chardonnay, so Egly-Ouriet manages for Pinot Noir: wines of riveting purity and concentration.

Anselme Selosse

Anselme Selosse is to Champagne what Jean-Michel Deiss is to Alsace or Claude Papin to the Loire Valley: a profound and original thinker whose vocation happens to be that of vigneron. He's known for having pioneered biodynamics in Champagne and for his complex and rigorously non-interventionist oak-matured champagnes made from fully ripe grapes. In truth, though, few growers understand the region's geology with even half the sophistication of Selosse; few think as profoundly about terroir; and few see their work in the same universal context (Selosse practises what José Bové and the Confédération Paysanne, of which he is a member, preach). He also smokes Lucky Strikes and, like Jean-Luc Thunevin of Valandraud in Bordeaux, has remarried his wife.

He shares Deiss's linguistic fastidiousness. He's not, he'll tell you, an exploitant but a cultivateur; he's not a manipulant but an éleveur. How much land does he own? "No one owns a terroir. I can work with its fruit, and pass that work on to my children, but I don't consider myself a proprietor." In viticultural terms, his chief aim is to optimize the activity of micro-organisms in the soil, since he is convinced they are the catalyst of terroir. Biodynamics is a "tool" to help achieve this, though Selosse has misgivings about the dogmatic aspect of biodynamics. When I met him he had just sacked his biodynamic counsellor and taken on Claude Bourgignon instead. "I'm more for Goethe than for Steiner. Steiner didn't like wine; he called it 'a dangerous element for man'." Even a matter as straightforward as raising his prices proceeds on a philosophical basis here. "I don't want to capitulate to the law of offer and demand. I apply a coefficient based on my cost price. Everything is calculated on a healthy, true, and transparent basis."

What makes Selosse stand out so starkly is the fact that his methods are studiously artisanal in a region where the scientific, industrial approach is now the norm. "Winemakers in Champagne generally like fermentation to take 144 hours. They've got it all calculated. To achieve that, you have to use selected yeasts and feed them. I use wild yeasts, with no starter. Fermentation begins spontaneously. I even want apiculate yeasts – those that begin fermentation and die quickly at about four per cent or five per cent abv. Oenologists don't want them because they say they give 'off' flavours. I want them, because they are part of the terroir." Selosse is very careful to keep and use his bourbes (settlings), which most discard because of residues from sprays; much of the perfume of a wine, he says, comes from essential oils in the grape skins. Fermentation always takes place in barrels, and the wine stays there until it is bottled for the second fermentation.

Selosse's barrel supplies are wide-ranging. "I don't like mono. I don't have a single container, a single forest, a single tonnelier, a single age of wood. If I work in mono, I can only achieve average quality. I prefer to roll the dice – since then occasionally the sublime arrives."

The Adventure of the Land

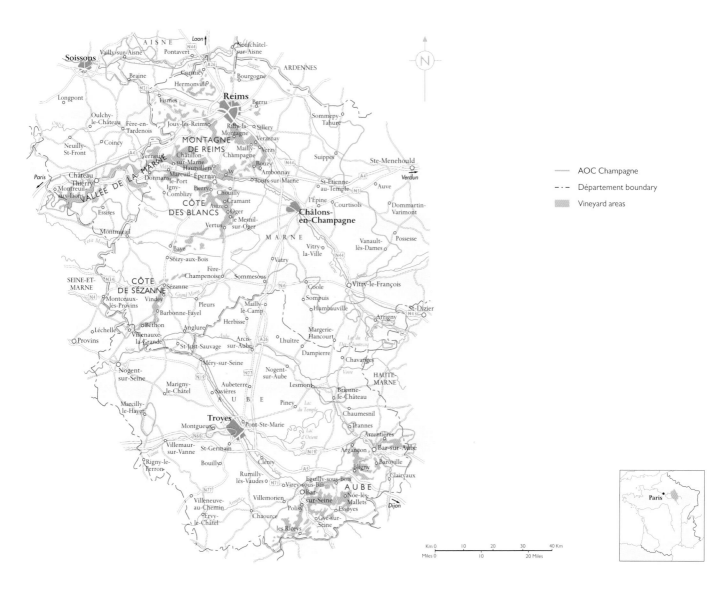

AOC Champagne

– – – Département boundary

Vineyard areas

I ought to begin this section with one word: mystery. French wine law tells us that there are such important differences of terroir between Coteaux du Tricastin and Côtes du Vivarais, between Côtes de la Malepère and Cabardès, and between Saussignac and Haut-Montravel that separate AOCs are needed – but that, in the whole of Champagne, there are no differences of terroir of this order. It is, of course, false.

The reason for this falsehood is that the vast majority of champagne has long been sold by large houses under brand names. In order to service these brands (and the Brut non-vintage alone often accounts for well over half a champagne house's production) and keep their flavour substantially consistent from year to year, vast blending operations are required. Wine from the entire region will find its way into most large producers' non-vintage blend. Such blends obliterate the nuances of terroir. Champagne has the primitive appellation system it has because the all-powerful merchant houses have never needed the concept of terroir to sell

their wines; they sell on "image", house style, and distributive strength instead. Terroir (other than Champagne's regional generality) is an embarrassment to them, because they know that their work snuffs out its expression; hence the dogma that "complete" or "great" champagne must be a blended product. This dogma may, with time, prove to be perfectly true; as we have seen earlier in this chapter there are even some growers who believe this to be true. But until we have several hundred great *champagnes de terroir*, skilfully produced from the finest vineyards across the entire region, we simply cannot tell whether it is these, or the blends, that will prove to be the greatest champagnes of all. Until then, open minds are in order.

There are moral reasons for attempting to recover the nuances of terroir in Champagne, too, since this would enable those in whose hands the all-important land lies to assume both the responsibility and credit they deserve. The key moment in the professional life of champagne grower Philippe Aubry came in 1989 when he took a business trip to Italy. He offered his champagne to a Bolognese restaurateur. The Bolognese tasted it, and told Philippe Aubry that it "wasn't intelligent." Aubry was nonplussed, and asked him what he meant. "It's too rich," the Italian replied. "Rich champagnes should be called Krug. You're just a seller of little champagne; you should produce something light and easy." "It made me mad," recalls Aubry, "but it also made me think. I decided at that moment to become a real vigneron, and not just to be 'a seller of little champagne'."

So what is the reality of terroir in Champagne? What every student of wine quickly learns about the region is that Champagne's grapes grow in chalk. Yet as Daniel Lorson of the CIVC points out, this image of the "classic" terroir of Champagne – an east-facing slope of thin, poor soil over deep chalk – covers no more than a third of the region. The whole of the Côte des Bars, some twenty per cent of Champagne, is on Kimmeridgean marl and not on chalk at all. There are sizeable tracts of clay and of sand in the less well-known parts of Champagne; slopes and aspects, too, vary enormously in this strikingly morsellated vineyard area. Any champagne blender will quickly confirm that the vineyards of Cramant, Avize, and Le Mesnil, apparently so similar, produce very different raw, still wines. None of this is yet apparent to the drinkers of the world.

Let's sketch out what we can nonetheless. Champagne covers 34,000 ha (84,000 acres) of which 31,000 ha (76,600 acres) are planted in three *départements*: Aisne (2,800 ha/6,900 acres), Marne (21,600 ha/ 53,350 acres), and Aube (6,600 ha/16,300 acres). It is France's most northerly major vineyard area (and the closest to Paris), and it is made up of hundreds of scattered fragments: propitious little parcels where a bit of a slope, a bit of shelter, a bit of chalk, and the luck of happy drainage makes vines viable. Otherwise it's wheat and sugar beet – which are far less profitable than champagne grapes.

The region is usually divided up into five broad subregions: the Vallée de la Marne, the Montagne de Reims, the Côte des Blancs, the Côte de Sézanne, and the Côte des Bars (also known as the Aube). Even this is a simplification: west of Reims, the Massif de St-Thierry and the Vallée de l'Ardre have their own identities; as does the Vallée du Surmelin stretching southeast from the Vallée de la Marne. There are a string of "lost" producing villages north of the Côte de Sézanne and south of the Côte des Blancs with no identity at all; while one of the most famous vineyards of the Aube region, Montgueux, is sited well away from the rest, just southwest of Troyes. Montgueux is known as the "Montrachet of the Côte des Bars" for its fascinating and distinctive Chardonnays – but who in London, New York, or Tokyo has ever tasted champagne made from them?

Three grape varieties are used to make champagne: Pinot Meunier (the most widely planted), Pinot Noir, and Chardonnay (the least widely planted, with about twenty-eight per cent of the total). Since Champagne is overwhelmingly a white wine made with red grapes, there are strict rules on pressing: just 2,550 litres of juice from every 4,000kg of grapes, with the last 500 litres (the *taille*) being of second quality. All non-vintage champagne must be aged for twelve months, and all vintage champagne for three years; reputable houses and growers always exceed these minima. The initial codes at the bottom of champagne labels tell you whether the wine has been produced by a négociant (NM), a cooperative (CM or RC), or a grower (RM). The ND and MA initials signify that the brand name does not relate in any way to the producer of the champagne (there are many wholly meaningless, fantasy brand names used in the champagne world which make life harder for true grower-producers).

If Champagne was to acquire different terroir-based internal AOCs, there would presumably be five of these, at least initially. (Any of the small vineyard areas that didn't fall into one of these five categories would, under this theoretical scheme, continue to enjoy the overall Champagne AOC, as would blends.) The first of these terroir-based zones would be the **Vallée de la Marne**, running from west of Château-Thierry to Epernay itself. (There would, of course, be some tricky decisions to be made about where exactly the Vallée

▲ *A windmill on the Montagne, captured in this sunny mural, proves the value of its modest dominance over the dusty plain.*

ends on both sides of the river, with the Montagne de Reims taking over the relay on the north side, and the Côte des Blancs beginning on the south side.) The chalk at this point dips under the more recent clay and sand deposits of the Paris basin, though the subsoils are often chalky enough. The attraction of these vineyards, well over half of which are planted with Pinot Meunier, is more topographical than geological: there are some fine south-facing slopes here, which of course is why most of the vineyards are on the northern bank of the river.

The second of Champagne's putative terroir-based AOCs would be the **Montagne de Reims**: a large horseshoe of vineyards perhaps running from Ay in the south, facing Epernay, round to Jouy-lès-Reims and Ville-Dommange in the north, facing Reims. These vineyards are, in the main, classic chalk slopes though with a variety of orientations (northeast, west, southeast, and southwest). Above

▲ *The River Marne is Champagne's mournful artery, its name recalling a brace of gruesome battles more readily than seething wine.*

the chalk, at heights whose relative coolness means that viticulture is not possible, there are mixed younger strata including deposits of the lignite that has traditionally been used to nourish the vines, chalk being an austere and impoverished soil medium. Internal differences within this area include more sand, marl, and clay in the zone known as the Petite Montagne, the Reims-facing sector; and intermittent outcrops of clay and of gravel in a number of places. Pinot Noir is the main grape variety cultivated here, though there are also substantial plantings of Pinot Meunier and Chardonnay is on the increase, too.

The **Côte des Blancs** would run from Chouilly on the outskirts of Epernay south to Vertus. The geological profile here is very similar to that of classic Montagne de Reims vineyards (low and mid-slope chalk, topped with younger mixed strata where woodlands take over from vineyards), though once again sand and clay breaks the monotony on a regular basis. The big difference between this sector and the Montagne, though, is that the majority of the vineyards face east or southeast. Just like, in other words, Burgundy's Côte d'Or — which may account for the fact that Chardonnay finds itself so comfortable here, with ninety-six per cent of plantings.

The **Côte de Sézanne** would be the smallest of the five putative internal AOCs of Champagne. It is, if you like, a southerly continuation of the Côte des Blancs, in the same way that the Côte Chalonnaise continues the Côte d'Or in Burgundy, though the slopes are less majestic, less extensive, more morsellated, and there is lots of sand interrupting the chalk, too. Plantings in the Côte de Sézanne are seventy per cent Chardonnay with most of the balance coming from Pinot Noir.

Finally would come the eccentric **Côte des Bars**. Eccentric, not because its champagnes are inadequate; they aren't, and in such an AOC regime this subregion seems likely to produce more interesting *champagnes de terroir* than the Côte de Sézanne and perhaps than the Vallée de la Marne. Eccentric, though, in that it really belongs to another geographical region altogether, the "secret" region of the Kimmeridgean chain which links it with Sancerre and Pouilly-Fumé, via Chablis. It lies no less than 160 km (one hundred miles) from Reims and Epernay. There is no chalk at all down here, close to Troyes and to Chablis itself; instead there is the typical limy marl you'll find in both Sancerre and Chablis. The vineyards along the Ource and around Les Riceys even look rather like they do in Chablis: scattered, well-sited plots nestling around a little river valley.

This is the most northerly part of the Kimmeridgean chain, and yet paradoxically it is planted chiefly with Pinot Noir. Why? Partly it is due to its sparkling wine vocation (almost all this Pinot will end up as white wine), but partly it is historical accident, too, in that when the Gamay that was planted here was chased away in the 1950s, its "noble" red counterpart replaced it. The truth, though, is that the Côte des Bars would also be a great site for Chardonnay and for Blanc de Blancs. If and when it gets its own AOC, then this development seems inevitable.

For the record, there are also two still-wine AOCs in Champagne: **Coteaux Champenois** (for still red, white, and rosé wine produced throughout the whole area) and **Rosé des Riceys** (for Pinot Noir-based rosé produced in the Aube commune of Les Riceys). These wines quench curiosity more effectively than furnish pleasure for the majority of non-local drinkers, who find their acidity levels a challenge without bubbles, yeast flavours, and dosage. Nonetheless, once you have become accustomed to their challenging balance, these can be wines of considerable finesse and nuance.

Champagne Flak

Feeding the birds

Champagne has one major structural problem, which stands, pylon-high, above all others. It is this: the region's 15,000 growers neither make nor sell its wine.

It is universally accepted that great wine can only be made from great grapes. Champagne is no exception. I asked grower Pascal Agrapart what he would do if he wanted to sell grapes. "Simple – make a telephone call." All he would have to do is say which village they came from, and they would be bought over the phone, sight unseen and regardless of yield. At harvest, they would be taken to a local pressing centre, and the juice would eventually find its way to the purchaser from there. Grower Philippe Aubry confirmed that there is no supplementary payment for grapes whose must contains at least ten per cent potential alcohol rather than the legal minimum of 8.5 per cent (some were even lower than this in 2001). When large houses have their own pressing centres, fruit-checking can take place: Mumm's cellarmaster Dominique Demarville says the company's seven pressing centres look after up to forty-five per cent of its supplies and there, "*on surveille tout*" (we check everything). The rest, though, is a commodity purchase – from some seventy-three further pressing centres in the case of Mumm. Checking individual purchases on this scale, says Demarville, is impossible. The only large house I have come across which claims to check every grape purchase it makes is Roederer.

Yelds in Champagne have been steadily creeping up since the early 1980s – due to over-fertilization, improved disease treatments, the planting of young vines following the winter frosts of 1985, and global warming (many growers I spoke to told me that the region is warmer and wetter than it used to be). Average bunch weights have increased from 85g in 1980 to over 150g in 2001. "We think that 11,000kg per ha," says Didier Gimmonet, "is a small harvest; my father's generation used to think that was an abundant year." Gimmonet says that the average over the last decade has been between 13,000 and 14,000kg per ha (equating to about 80 hl/ha), and he admits that sometimes they are higher – equating to 150 hl/ha or even more, as in the notorious 2001 harvest. In such circumstances, most growers simply leave the excess fruit on the vines for the birds to eat, though a fastidious grower like Gimmonet who presses and vinifies for himself will press more lightly and extract less (and finer) juice. At the time this book goes to print, Champagne has the biggest problem of excess yields in France. Philippe Aubry told me that 10,000 ha (24,700 acres) in Champagne are not fully picked each year.

Rewarding mediocrity

Another chronic problem, as grower Anselme Selosse points out, is that growers in Champagne actually prefer to pick their grapes under-ripe rather than ripe. Once again, this is chiefly done for financial reasons (even if the excuses are "to avoid rot" or "to maintain acidity") – in the knowledge that disposing of the resulting thin, dilute wines will not be the growers' problem. "If one takes the maximum yields and then adds another two per cent abv by chaptalizing," says Selosse, "that is the way to financially maximize your harvest since you are increasing the final volume at minimum cost. That sugar you can legally add will benefit from the Champagne AOC. If you pick fully ripe grapes and can't chaptalize, then financially you've made a loss." There is a financial incentive to

produce lower quality, in other words: an extraordinary state of affairs for what is the most valuable vineyard land in the world. Given the fact that wine quality is directly linked to grape quality, it is an irrefutable truth that the quality of wine produced by the Champagne region at present could be better than it is. Until more growers become involved in making and selling their wine, or until the large houses which at present sell seventy per cent of champagne begin to be more exigent about every one of their purchases (which, with 14,500 growers owning an average of 1.6 ha/6.3 acres divided among fifteen tiny parcels, is a nightmarish challenge), Champagne will continue to be a region of unfulfilled potential.

Vineyards: young and full of rubbish

Champagne's vineyards, even the most prestigious, are often in a surprisingly dilapidated condition, and are still visibly full of the notorious and persistent Paris city rubbish or *gadoux*. The idea that domestic rubbish from France's capital city (and later from Reims) could be ground up and spread over the nation's most expensive agricultural land is barely credible today – yet that was exactly what happened between the early 1960s and 1998. On my desk in front of me I have a crushed plastic cosmetics bottle, polystyrene fragments, a green plastic rawlplug, a green plastic disc, broken glass, shredded blue plastic, and a white plastic tag saying "Renault 992" on it, collected in a matter of seconds from a prestigious Grand Cru vineyard in Le Mesnil on the Côte des Blancs. City rubbish was distributed as "fertilizer" over the vast majority of Champagne vineyards during these decades – though not all: a few fastidious growing families like the Egly family in Ambonnay and the Champs family of Vilmart in Rilly always refused to allow *gadoux* on their vines; the Larmandiers abandoned *gadoux* from 1978. "The problem," says Pierre Larmandier, "was that the rubbish changed. To start with it was potato and apple peelings, which was fine. But then all sorts of other things started turning up...." A key question is whether the rubbish contained persistent and toxic heavy metals; so far, analyses have not revealed cause for concern. This might change in the future according to Anselme Selosse who, like Francis Egly, works with the soil analyst Claude Bourgignon (*see* page 87). "We're lucky enough in Champagne," says Selosse, "to have intensely alkaline soils. But because they aren't worked any more, they are in the process of slowly acidifying. And the more they do that, the more of those heavy metals they will liberate."

Another vineyard problem for Champagne is that the average age of vines here is one of the youngest in France – in part because of the 1985 frosts, but in part once again because growers don't have to sell the wine and are thus not financially motivated to grow for quality. "Champagne has a young vineyard," says Dominique Demarville of Mumm. "The average is around twenty-five years; it should be nearer forty." Quantity, though, pays, and younger vines produce more amply and more reliably than older vines.

There is no doubt that the Champagne authorities have grasped the implications of the fact that vineyards in this region are far from exemplary – and the Viticulture Raisonnée project is a welcome response to this. Yet it will take many years to change the working philosophy of 14,500 small growers – and without financial incentives from those buying the grapes, change will come more slowly than it should.

Champagne: People

Agrapart
51190 Avize, Tel: 03 26 57 51 38, Fax: 03 26 57 05 06

Brothers Pascal and Fabrice Agrapart have a 9.5-ha domain planted with 90% Chardonnay (including 4.5 ha in Avize, one ha in Oger, and one ha in Cramant and Oiry); there is also a little Pinot at Avenay. Some 70% of the vines are over 40 years old, and the vines are worked (in part by a white Boulonnaise horse called Venus) rather than herbicide used in order to encourage healthy, deep-rooted vineyards: the aim here. The brothers have been tempted by biodynamics – but the fact that they have no fewer than 53 parcels makes this difficult. Natural yeasts, restrained *dosages* of around 6 g/l, and the use of old wood to bring managed oxidation to reserve wines are two hallmarks of this impressive and improving range. The gentle oxidation brings beautiful mayflower complexities to the Brut Blanc de Blancs; the Brut Réserve is a more generous, ripe and sturdily constructed champagne. The 1996 vintage is a pure expression of chalklands; the 1995 more exuberant and biscuity. Best of all is the 1995 Avizoise (based on the finest mid-slope parcels and 55-year-old vines) with its fine butter and nut scents and lively, dancing, seething style.

Arnould
51360 Verzenay, Tel: 03 26 49 40 06, Fax: 03 26 49 44 61

Michel Arnould's 12-ha domain is based at Verzenay, whose vinous, tautly riveted style is evident throughout the range. These are pushy Pinot Noir-based champagnes which reward storage. The rosé offers best value for money.

Aubry
51390 Jouy-lès-Reims, Tel: 03 26 49 20 07, Fax: 03 26 49 75 27

This old family domain (the same 16 ha have been owned since 1790, though wool and rye were once produced as well as wine) includes 11 ha of Premiers Crus, though its primary claim to fame is the fact that Philippe Aubry is fast becoming the Robert Plageoles of Champagne. He works with his brother Pierre and brother-in-law Noël Poret and, ever since the traumatic meeting with a Bolognese mentioned on page 28, has been trying to give expression to Champagne's indigenous varieties such as Arbanne and Petit Meslier, as well as Pinot Gris (whose local name was Fromenteau) and Pinot Blanc. Champagne's customary three grapes are grown as well, and from 1998 Aubry's Nombre d'Or *cuvée* includes all of these except Pinot Blanc, though when Aubry can get hold of low-yielding Alsace plant material this will be included too. This *cuvée* is subtitled Campanae Veteres Vites – "Champagne's Old Grape Varieties" in Latin. The 1996 Nombre d'Or was based on Fromenteau (40%), Pinot Meunier (30%), Arbanne (20%), and Petit Meslier (10%) and was primitive and savage in flavour, though it smelt appealingly of waffles; the 1997 (40% Fromenteau, 40% Petit Meslier, and 20% Arbanne) was more accessible though still with a bite of rustic acidity. Aside from this "archeological" *cuvée* there is more historical interest with Aubry's Sablé *cuvées*: authentic crémants at half normal pressure in rosé and Blanc de Blancs guise. The Ivoire et Ebène *cuvée* blends Chardonnay with Pinot Meunier (which in Aubry's Petite Montagne terroir gives better results than Pinot Noir), while best of all are probably the subtle and aromatic Aubry de Humbert vintage wines based on Chardonnay from Jouy, Pinot Meunier from Pargny, and Pinot Noir from Ville-Dommange.

Paul Bara
51150 Bouzy, Tel: 03 26 57 00 50, Fax: 03 26 57 81 24

The champagnes of Paul Bara and his daughter Chantal are essential references for anyone who wants to enjoy and understand the ripe, dry richness of Bouzy, where their 11-ha domain is situated and about which Bara has written a book. Value is very good here, especially for the profound and dark rosé.

Barnaut
51150 Bouzy, Tel: 03 26 57 01 54, Fax: 03 26 57 09 97

This 15-ha domain, run by the affable Philippe Secondé, includes a mouth-watering 12.5 ha in Bouzy with the balance at Brasles in the Marne Valley. Avoiding heaviness, says Secondé, is his "obsession"; he sorts the fruit before pressing (unusual in Champagne), separates the juice into five fractions, uses selected yeasts, and prepares his blends on the basis of blind tasting only. Among the stars of an impressive range is the bready Grande Réserve, the vinous, pungent Extra Brut Sélection, the round-edged Blanc de Noirs, and the strawberry-laden Rosé Authentique (based on a *saignée* of Bouzy Rouge). Vintages here tend to contain as much as 50% Chardonnay, "so as not to have something that gets too heavy in time"; the 1995 is surprisingly graceful and floral, with a hop note in the finish. The Cuvée Edmond is where most of the Marne fruit fetches up, but this is a carefully crafted wine of vinosity and depth, and its packaging makes it look like a *prestige cuvée* rather than a range-opener.

Beaumont des Crayères
51318 Epernay, Tel: 03 26 55 29 40, Fax: 03 26 54 26 30

This small co-operative, based in Mardeuil, does not have the best-sited vineyards, but its multitude of growers (over 200, with an average holding of just 38 ares) grow for quality and not quantity. The result is an attractively priced range, with the vintage-dated Fleur de Prestige and Grande Prestige offering best value of all.

Billecart-Salmon ✪
51160 Mareuil-sur-Ay, Tel: 03 26 52 60 22, Fax: 03 26 52 64 88

This medium-sized house in Mareuil-sur-Ay has a good and largely well-deserved reputation, though its sweet-edged Brut non-reserve can disappoint on occasion, as do the equivalent wines of nearly all of its rivals except those who can supervise their own viticulture (Billecart's own vineyard holding is small). The Blanc de Blancs has also been inconsistent in the past. The range is extensive; the better wines include both the plump Brut rosé and the rumblingly deep vintage rosé Cuvée Elisabeth Salmon, as well as the consistently pure vintage Cuvée Nicolas-François Billecart. Look in general for a clean, limpidly expressive style allied to rounded, soft fruit which is less drivingly vinous than some.

H Blin
51700 Vincelles, Tel: 03 26 58 20 04, Fax: 03 26 58 29 67

Another of Champagne's small cooperatives whose many members grow a gardenful of vines each. As you'd expect from the Marne Valley location, Pinot Meunier is much in evidence here giving champagnes of jolly fruit that quickly turn biscuity.

Boizel
51200 Epernay, Tel: 03 26 55 21 51, Fax: 03 26 54 31 83

French direct mail-order specialist now part of the group (presided over by Bruno Paillard, but not including his own company) which also brings together Alexandre Bonnet, Chanoine, Philipponnat, and de Venoge. The Boizel range is generally good, ranging from its crisp, mineral-salty Brut through a relatively light and fragrant Blanc de Blancs to what is generally a much more deeply structured vintage (like the resonant 1996). The oak-fermented Cuvée Sous Bois from 1990 is of gluey style; the oak integration may improve with subsequent versions.

Star rating system used on producer spreads ✪ Very good wine ✪✪ Excellent wine ✪✪✪ Great wine

Bollinger ✿✿
51160 Ay, Tel: 03 26 53 33 66, Fax: 03 26 54 85 59

This Ay-based négociant has the considerable advantage over many other houses of owning 150 ha of its own vines (providing two-thirds of its supplies) and therefore being able to rely on a core of first-class raw materials on which to build its wines, especially the reserves (stored painstakingly in magnums under cork) and the top cuvées. Bollinger's "Charter of Ethics and Quality" was also designed to underline its commitment to best practices at a time when other so-called Grande Marque houses were transparently unable to do so; this charter is now alluded to on the back labels. Special Cuvée is the name of the Brut non-vintage, a pure and forthright wine of reliable depth and some complexity (half the component wines are oak-fermented). The vintage Grande Année, the RD (Récemment Dégorgé) series, and the rare Vieilles Vignes Françaises, based on three small parcels of ungrafted Pinot Noir vines at Ay and Bouzy, are all among the Champagne region's summits. The style in these wines is deep, dark, sober, serious. Not necessarily austere: there is too much Pinot-built power and push for that, and indeed in youth the wines can be off-puttingly massive, jangling, and unresolved. They are, though, concentrated at all times, making few concessions to the timid drinker, and age magnificently towards an articulate and finely detailed maturity. They are also laudably subversive of the concept of the brand, in that everything in the range (and not simply the RD, which is the same as the Grande Année but given extra years on yeast) remains undisgorged until around three months before dispatch. Needless to say, this leads to "lack of consistency" – something that makes brand builders' knees knock. Bollinger's champagnes, in other words, do not always taste exactly the same as their putative brand "prototype" because the taste of a champagne depends on when it was disgorged. I welcome this, since there does not seem to me to be a standardized and predictable "moment of perfection" to disgorge a particular champagne, and in any case the strategy of serial disgorgement reflects the living, changing nature of wine, a product of agriculture rather than industry. When you taste a great Bollinger, such as the RD 1985 as tasted in 2002, you will find such a wealth of allusions to the natural world and such craft and nuance in its layered flavours that to carp about apparent differences with previous releases seems misguided.

Bonnet
51100 Reims, Tel: 03 26 84 44 15, Fax: 03 26 84 44 19

Fine value champagne from the Aube, full of rounded Pinot exuberance. Now part of the BCC group (see Paillard).

Brice
51150 Bouzy, Tel: 03 26 52 06 60, Fax: 03 26 57 05 07

Small Ay-based négociant specializing in the purchase and sales of single-village Grand Cru wines designed to underline differences of terroir between villages rather than stamp each wine with a "Brice" house style (though blended wines are also available). This approach is timely and topical – though not as new as it might seem, since Jean-Paul Brice took the same philosophy when he was one of the creators of Barancourt. Of four recent releases, the Ay and the Bouzy were more successful than the Verzenay and an over-dosed Cramant.

Le Brun de Neuville
51260 Bethon, Tel: 03 26 80 48 43, Fax: 03 26 80 43 28

The wines of this 145-grower cooperative offer a relatively inexpensive taste of the full-on Chardonnay style of the Côte de Sézanne. Don't expect great subtlety, but there is much to enjoy in the custard-cream softness.

Pierre Callot
51190 Avize, Tel: 03 26 57 51 57, Fax: 03 26 57 99 15

Thierry Callot's small 5-ha domain in Avize includes the fine vineyard Clos Jacquin, used for an intense and ambitious Blanc de Blancs of textured and creamy style (and beautiful packaging).

Cattier
51500 Chigny-les-Roses, Tel: 03 26 03 42 11, Fax: 03 26 03 43 13

This small house based in Chigny-les-Roses owns the Premier Cru Clos du Moulin (though the old Larmat Atlas lists no such vineyard); it is bottled as a three-vintage blend, and is composed of 50% each of Chardonnay and Pinot Noir. The wine is well-aged and exuberant in style, though it seems slightly over-dosed and less concentrated and lingering than, for example, the Moët Grands Crus.

Charlemagne
51190 Le Mesnil-sur-Oger, Tel: 03 26 57 52 98, Fax: 03 26 57 97 81

This is a great name for any wine-grower, and the forebears of Guy and Philippe Charlemagne have used it for many years now. This 15-ha domain has some beautifully sited Côte des Blancs vineyards, and the style, for both the Grand Cru and "lesser" wines, combines elegance with the confident force that only comes from fully ripe fruit.

J Charpentier
51700 Villers-sous-Châtillon, Tel: 03 26 58 05 78, Fax: 03 26 58 35 59

Jacky Charpentier's 12-ha domain in the Marne Valley provides carefully crafted, consistently pleasure-giving Pinot Meunier-based champagnes.

Chartogne-Taillet
51220 Merfy, Tel: 03 26 03 10 17, Fax: 03 26 03 19 15

This old-established 11-ha domain near Château-Thierry is a good source of soft, toasty, mellow champagnes.

Cuvée Orpale see Union Champagne

CVC see Nicolas Feuillatte

Delamotte
51190 Le Mesnil-sur-Oger, Tel: 03 26 57 51 65, Fax: 03 26 57 79 29

Delamotte is the alter ego, if you like, of Salon, that rare bird of the Côte des Blancs. The company does have 11 ha of its own vines (in Le Mesnil, Oger, and Avize) and makes a number of its own purchases, but it also inherits all of the Salon wine not required by Salon – which, in years when Salon doesn't declare, means the entire harvest. Like Salon, it is owned by Laurent-Perrier; indeed it was at Delamotte that the great Bernard de Nonancourt began his career after his distinguished war years (at that time, Delamotte was a larger house than Laurent-Perrier). The fresh, smoky non-vintage Brut is 50% Chardonnay from Mesnil, Avize, and Oger, plus 30% Grand Cru Pinot Noir from Ambonnay and Bouzy; it lies on its lees for three years. The non-vintage Blanc de Blancs is, in 2002, 30% 1996 with 70% 1997, giving a wine of powdery, sweet-blossom purity but also palate-slicing acid levels; the 1995 vintage Blanc de Blancs has had six years' ageing, by contrast, and this (plus the riper vintage) gives a fuller, more statuesque style. In theory, Delamotte undergoes malolactic fermentation whereas Salon does not, which implies that the eventual destiny of all raw materials is decided swiftly after alcoholic fermentation.

Delbeck
51053 Reims, Tel: 03 26 77 58 00, Fax: 03 26 77 58 01

Delbeck has been of late a much-traded Champagne name, but one of its present owners, Pierre Martin, is (like Jean-Paul Brice) a former Barancourt man, and the same terroir-based approach is chosen for the top wines. Of the available Grands Crus, the Cramant is short, sherbetty, and disappointing, whereas the Ay and Bouzy are deeper, richer, and more carefully crafted (as at Brice).

De Sousa
51190 Avize, Tel: 03 26 57 53 29, Fax: 03 26 52 30 64

Erick De Sousa has 7 ha in Avize, Oger, and Cramant; the vines have an average age of 38 years. "The more natural it is, the better it is," believes De Sousa, and in pursuit of this ideal he has switched to biodynamic cultivation, uses natural yeasts, has lowered his dosages, and has given up filtration. There are also excellent, explanatory back labels. The Blanc de Blancs Cuvée des

Caudalies, barrel-fermented and made from vines of over 50 years, is unquestionably De Sousa's best wine with its mineral notes, almost orange-like fruit and the long finish to which its name alludes (a *caudalie* is a French "unit of persistence" for wine).

Paul Déthune
51150 Ambonnay, Tel: 03 26 57 01 88, Fax: 03 26 57 09 31
Pierre Déthune's Ambonnay domain is, at 7 ha, not a large one, but the wines (oak-fermented in large casks) have depth, ripeness, roundness, and vinosity, and the prices are no less attractive by comparison with large-company equivalents.

Deutz
51160 Ay, Tel: 03 26 56 94 00, Fax: 03 26 56 94 10
This Roederer-owned house based in Ay produces crisp, classic, firm champagnes based chiefly on purchased fruit (just 42 ha are owned). Both the Blanc de Blancs and the rosé (especially the "prestige" version William Deutz Rosé) are memorable and complex. Amour de Deutz is a new super-selection Blanc de Blancs.

Doquet-Jeanmarie
51130 Vertus, Tel: 03 26 52 16 50, Fax: 03 26 59 36 71
Well-sited 15-ha domain on the Côte des Blancs (based at Vertus) whose concentrated style is one reason for a visit. The other is a fine range of older vintages sold under the Coeur de Terroir label. The rosé is good, too.

Drappier
10200 Urville, Tel: 03 25 27 40 15, Fax: 03 25 27 41 19
Aube-based Drappier's champagnes are fruity, lively, and exuberant, and offer excellent value for money. The vigorous Grand Sendrée *cuvées* are based on fruit from a single vineyard in the Aube (but one planted with both Chardonnay and Pinot Noir).

Duval-Leroy
51130 Vertus, Tel: 03 26 52 10 75, Fax: 03 26 52 37 10
This house is run by the pessimistic Carol Duval, who is convinced that France is being slowly turned into "a kolkhoz". For the time being, at any rate, Duval and her sons still own their 150 ha, providing a quarter of the company's needs and ensuring its present reputation, which is above average. The talent of Chef de Cave Hervé Jestin helps, too. The style is graceful and elegant, marked by the prettiness of the Côte des Blancs; the triteness of the Fleur de Champagne labels doesn't do the wines justice. The 1990 Femme de Champagne (a "prestige" *cuvée* based on almost 90% Chardonnay) is brioche-scented, voluptuous, sumptuous, and mouthfilling. An organic champagne is imminent.

Egly-Ouriet ○○
51150 Ambonnay, Tel: 03 26 57 00 70, Fax: 03 26 57 06 52
This is a very serious and well-run domain with 9 ha of Grand Cru vineyard divided between Ambonnay (7.2ha), Verzenay (1.5ha), and a morsel of Bouzy; the average age of the vines is 35 years. Francis Egly works with soil analyst Claude Bourguignon on "common sense" principles: ploughing, soil aeration, manuring, the fewest treatments possible. He combats the general problem of yields in Champagne by green-harvesting up to half the crop – which enabled him to have wines of 9.8% in the miserable vintage of 2001 when many winegrowers were harvesting fruit at a mere 7.8%. His normal finished alcohol level is between 12.5% and 13%. "Maturity is great in champagne; *sur-maturité* I'm not so sure. But in any case, our biggest problem in the region is under-maturity." Slow pressing, natural yeast, fermentation in barriques and enamelled tanks (not stainless steel, which Egly dislikes) without racking, and bottling for the second fermentation without fining or filtration are Egly's current methods. All the wines receive between three and four years' ageing before release. The Brut Tradition, with its minimal *dosage* of between 5 and 6 g/l, is a wonderful expression of Pinot Noir: old-gold colours; scents of warm fruits; deep, powerful, resonant flavours. The Blanc de Noirs Vieilles Vignes, generally bottled with no *dosage* at all, is even deeper with an almost shockingly chalky charge.

There is also a tiny quantity of red Coteaux Champenois Grande Côte without the tannic mass of a Côte d'Or red, but sweet-fruited and oak-cosseted nonetheless.

Nicolas Feuillatte
51210 Montmirail, Tel: 03 26 59 55 50, Fax: 03 26 59 55 82
These wines, produced and marketed by CVC, a group of 85 cooperatives, have traditionally had rather a soft and slushy style. Recent releases of the Grand Cru series (the 1995 Chardonnay vintages from Chouilly, Cramant, and Le Mesnil-sur-Oger and a Pinot Noir from Verzy) have, however, brought some refinement and finesse into the picture.

Fleury
10250 Courteron, Tel: 03 25 38 20 28, Fax: 03 25 38 24 65
The wines of this biodynamic producer based at Courteron in the Côtes des Bars are light, gentle, graceful, and well-constructed.

Gardet
51500 Chigny-les Roses, Tel: 03 26 03 42 03, Fax: 03 26 03 43 95
Boisterous and satisfying champagnes from Chigny-les-Roses.

Gatinois
51160 Ay, Tel: 03 26 55 14 26, Fax: 03 26 52 75 99
Pierre Cheval-Gatinois' 7.2-ha domain occupies fine slopes in Ay, and is planted exclusively with Pinot Noir (Bollinger is a customer). The Gatinois champagnes are firm and well-constructed, meriting a spell in the cold and the dark. Unsuprisingly, the trenchantly fruity rosé is a particularly good buy here.

Pierre Gimmonet ○
51530 Cuis, Tel: 03 26 59 78 70, Fax: 03 26 59 79 84
With no fewer than 25 ha to his name, all in the Côte des Blancs and exclusively planted in Chardonnay, Didier Gimmonet has one of the most enviable domains in the region. There are 14 ha in the Premier Cru Cuis, and 12 ha in the Grands Crus Cramant and Chouilly. No less notable is the fact that in a region afflicted with generally young vine stocks, Gimmonet has 70% of his vines over 30 years old, of which some 40% are over 40 years old (the oldest of all, planted in the *lieux-dits* of Le Fond du Bateau and Buisson in Cramant, were planted in 1913). "Cramant," says Gimmonet, is "very expressive and round"; Chouilly is similar in style but slightly less concentrated; Cuis is much more "neutral, acid, fresh, aerial": this north-facing village is the coolest in the Côte des Blancs. In defence of his belief in blending, Gimmonet says that Cramant can be grand, but that it ages more swiftly on its own than when it is aged with wine from Cuis. He says that yields of 50 hl/ha are "utopian" and "unrealistic", admitting that his own are higher – a 10-year average of 80 hl/ha, "which is low for the Côte des Blancs". He presses more lightly than most. In vinification terms, he says he is moving away from the prevailing philosophy of zero faults towards something more expressive; stainless steel, selected yeasts, fining, and filtration are still used, though. These are sappy, crunchy, refreshing champagnes of acupuncturally tonic qualities; the best is the non-dosed, vintage Cuvée Oenophile with its lingering, salty purity.

Michel Gonet
51190 Avize, Tel: 03 26 57 50 56, Fax: 03 26 57 91 98
The heart of this enterprising and old-established grower's 40-ha estate is in the Côte des Blancs, but Michel Gonet also has vineyards in the Côte de Sézanne and the Aube (and even produces sparkling wine in Bordeaux's Graves de Vayres). The best wines are the fragrant and rich Grands Crus Blanc de Blancs. Gonet is also the owner of the Marquis de Sade label, which doubtless has a specialized following.

Gosset
51160 Ay, Tel: 03 26 56 99 53, Fax: 03 26 51 55 88
In the ownership of the wealthy Cointreau family, this négociant should be surging in quality. The Brut Excellence is fair, while the "upper crust" non-vintage Grande Réserve has better concentration and an appealingly frank, vigorous

style but still not, perhaps, the intensity and refinement of the great. The best wines are the resonant Grand Rosé and the intense, Chardonnay-dominated vintage wines and "prestige" Celebris, all of which share the Gosset hallmark of forthright exuberance.

Gratien
51201 Epernay, Tel: 03 26 54 38 20, Fax: 03 26 54 53 44

This smallish house produces champagnes which are rather taut and unyielding in their youth (the malolactic is blocked), but which age superbly towards a pure and articulate old age. Its low profile may change now that it has been sold by former owner Alain Seydoux to the German sparkling wine specialists Henkell; let's hope, at any rate, that the company doesn't abandon its commitment to fermentation in oak-casks, surely responsible for many of its latent or overt complexities.

Charles Heidsieck ✪
51200 Epernay, Tel: 03 26 59 50 50, Fax: 03 26 52 19 65

When Daniel Thibault died, tragically early, in 2002, Champagne lost one of the greatest Chefs de Caves of the twentieth century. Few had been able to stamp personality so strongly onto a range; few had created so many great champagnes from what at times were modest raw materials; few had innovated as daringly and successfully. Thibault's successor Régis Camus has quite a challenge on his hands, even though he has worked with Thibault for 8 years. The single word that most aptly sums up the Charles Heidsieck style is "cream": these are soft, caressing champagnes of ample grain and texture; their flavours are accessible, soothing, nourishing. Reserves stored on their lees, as you might guess, are a key element for achieving this: the Mise en Cave series, which has replaced the non-vintage Brut Réserve at this house, contains up to 40% reserves, some of 10-year antiquity. These wines, which are released in batches of three different "mises", are labelled with the date at which they trundle down into the cellars for their second fermentation. They are based, in other words, on 60% of wine from the previous vintage from that shown on the label. It does mark a break with Champagne tradition and a move away from branded ideals since difference, rather than consistency, is the point; the back labels and neck labels, too, are radically informative. This house also produces two of the most reliably great of all "prestige" champagnes: the lengthily aged, sumptuously creamy, almost fig-fruited vintage Blanc de Millénaire and the deeper, more Pinot-rich Champagne Charlie, packed with tangerine and peach and with a lassoo-round style (though with an off-puttingly vulgar label).

Henriot
51066 Reims, Tel: 03 26 89 53 00, Fax: 03 26 89 53 10

The changes brought about by Joseph Henriot when he repurchased his family domain have not been quite as stark as those achieved at Bouchard Père et Fils in Burgundy and William Fèvre in Chablis, but the time lag between undertaking change and seeing it materialize is a longer one in Champagne. Henriot's style at its best (which means the vintage wines, the Blanc de Blancs, and the Cuvée des Enchantaleurs) is based on exuberant, lemon-cream scents in which fine Chardonnay purchases show well, backed by deep, round, forthright, extrovert flavours.

M Hostomme
51530 Chouilly, Tel: 03 26 55 40 79, Fax: 03 26 55 08 55

The soft, bready qualities of Chouilly come to the fore in these accessible and friendly Blanc de Blancs wines produced from a mixture of domain and purchased fruit.

Jacquesson ✪
51530 Dizy, Tel: 03 26 55 68 11, Fax: 03 26 51 06 25

This old, small house is run with great passion and enthusiasm by brothers Jean-Hervé and Laurent Chiquet. It owns just 26 ha, yet the small scale means that this is around two-thirds of what the company needs. Everything is done with great attention to detail, including traditional pressing methods and

fermentation and storage of reserves in oak. The style throughout the range is one of intricacy and finesse, built on relatively complex blends; the wines age well. Perfection is the modestly titled Brut non-vintage, a wine with more concentration than most of its rivals (though some way short of its name); the company begins to approach perfection with the best of its Signature vintage range (like the complete and stately 1990 or the arrestingly intense 1988) and with its Dégorgement Tardif series of late releases. The labels are as elegant and refined as the wines (which is surprisingly rare in Champagne).

Krug ✪✪✪
51100 Reims, Tel: 03 26 84 44 20, Fax: 03 26 84 44 49

Of all the wine world's luxury brands, Krug is perhaps the most glittering. No expense is spared in its production, though the techniques used are in fact remarkably artisanal, including fermentation in small, old wooden casks and, Henri Krug once told me, "no idea" whether the malolactic fermentation takes place or not. (It is not provoked, but happens anyway.) Time is of the essence: the overall ageing cycle is the best part of a decade here, with all wines being aged for at least six years sur pointes (upended, after the "ordinary" ageing period that follows the second fermentation is concluded). No expense is spared, either, in the pricing of its five wines, the cheapest of which, Grande Cuvée, costs as much as many rival houses' top cuvées. This is the only Krug champagne I have been able to taste on a regular basis: it is a wine of magnificent complexity and layered richness, nourishing and diverting, as detailed and textured as a Gobelin tapestry. It contains wines from a decade's worth of vintages and from at least 20 different crus (not all of them Grand or even Premier, one might note); Krug makes no secret, too, of its need and love for Pinot Meunier. (The Krug 1928 vintage, regarded by the family as the greatest ever, contained 20% Meunier, and there is 18% in the finely honed 1988.) There is also a relatively understated rosé of pale tawny hue, and a series of vintage wines of magnificent stylistic oscillation, fully respecting the potential of each year. The Collection vintage wines have spent more years in the Krug cellars in Reims; disgorgement took place at the same time as for "ordinary" vintage wines. Finally, a champagne de terroir: the pure Chardonnay Clos du Mesnil, vinified from wines in a genuine 1.9 ha walled vineyard within the village of Le Mesnil, purchased by Krug in 1971, and released as a vintage wine beginning with 1979. In great years (like 1988) it is magnificent and multidimensioned, but many feel that regular comparison with the Grande Cuvée would mostly be to its disadvantage, despite the price differential, thereby advancing the case for the superiority of blends over single-site champagnes.

Lanson
51100 Reims, Tel: 03 26 78 50 50, Fax: 03 26 78 53 88

Lanson is today the flag-carrier for the enormous own-label specialist Marne et Champagne. Many commentators noted the worrying implications behind the fact that Moët et Chandon gobbled up Lanson's magnificent vineyards when it traded the company briefly in 1991; the predicted plunge in quality for Lanson, though, hasn't yet happened. As with all large houses it is the small production, top-of-the-range cuvées (like the vintage Gold Label, the Blanc de Blancs, and the Noble Cuvée, magnificently intense and complex in the 1988 vintage) that provide most interest; the mature vintages of these, of course, were made under the administration of previous owners. Black Label, the last big-selling (6.5 million bottles a year) Brut non-vintage to be made with blocked malolactic fermentation, is a vigorous palate-cleanser rather than silken-robed séductrice; give it some age if you want complexity.

Larmandier-Bernier ✪✪
51130 Vertus, Tel: 03 26 52 13 24, Fax: 03 26 52 21 00

Pierre Larmandier's gentle, questioning approach, combined with his 11-ha holdings in Vertus, Cramant, Chouilly, Oger, and Avize, produce finer and finer wines with every vintage. The emphasis is very much on fastidious viticulture and an ever lighter touch in the cellar; he prefers foudres to smaller casks because they are perfect for the kind of controlled oxidation that builds complexity into great champagne. The Brut Tradition strikes a clear house note with fine mineral-salt depths; these are amplified and filled out with lemony freshness and biscuity depths in the Blanc de Blancs. Larmandier produces two of the greatest *champagnes de terroir* with his Né d'une Terre de Vertus and the Vieilles Vignes de Cramant: both are intensely mineral, as if they had had a dry residue of Ste-Yorre or Vichy water mixed into them, and reward long ageing, after which the Vertus sings with vinous purity while the Cramant turns on the ivy-leaf charm. The Spécial Club is "a Grand Blanc more in the spirit of *assemblage*": the 1996 vintage, for example, is rather lacier, more sweet-scented, and more accessible than the Vieilles Vignes de Cramant in the same vintage. Larmandier also produces a red Coteaux Champenois based on Pinot grown in Vertus which is sharp but perfumed and strangely compelling. Few growers' ranges in Champagne are as consistently outstanding as that of Larmandier-Bernier.

Laurent-Perrier
51150 Tours-sur-Marne, Tel: 03 26 58 91 22, Fax: 03 26 58 77 29

This house, slowly built by Bernard de Nonancourt from modest beginnings after World War Two, has won an enviable reputation for its consistent wines, blended with great intelligence by one of the Champagne region's most outstanding Chefs de Caves, Alain Terrier. The Brut non-vintage (which sells 7 million bottles a year) is simple, and like most big-name brands offers less good value than most leading growers' champagnes – though this is perhaps unsurprising, given the fact that the domain holdings are only 90 ha or so. The non-vintage Brut rosé, by contrast, is the model of this style which all others try to emulate: soft, crowd-pleasing, teasing, charming, though a few thrills short of exquisite. The more expensive champagnes are good, and none more so than the Grand Siècle series, in principle a three-vintage blend (La Cuvée) but since the mid-1980s also available as a vintage wine. Grand Siècle La Cuvée is the ballerina among "prestige" *cuvées*: full of energy, poise, and enchantment, and given such slow and unhurried ageing that the aromas are always ready to lead your nose a dance. (Rival "prestige" *cuvées* are often released too early, when still mute.)

Leclapart
51380 Trépail, Tel: 03 26 57 07 01, Fax: 03 26 57 07 01

Biodynamic grower with vineyards at Trépail on the Montagne de Reims. There are three *cuvées*, all Blanc de Blancs: l'Amateur (steel-vinified), l'Artiste (wood-fermented), and the old-vines l'Apôtre. Bitter notes can be a problem here, but l'Apôtre has fine concentration and depth; there is also a good Coteaux Champenois l'Eden, full of rounded curranty fruit.

Leclerc Briant
51204 Epernay, Tel: 03 26 54 45 33, Fax: 03 26 54 49 59

This small house in Epernay is a triple pioneer: of *champagne de terroir*, with three non-vintage single parcel wines; of sparkling red champagne (the powerfully fruited rosé Cuvée Rubis de Noirs); and of biodynamics, which is the cultivation method used for the three single-parcel wines. (The rest of the 30-ha domain is in conversion at present.) The three named parcels are all in the Premier Cru village of Les Cumières: Les Chèvres Pierreuses is a 60/40 Pinot Noir-Chardonnay blend made from a south-facing mid-slope 2.8-ha site, giving the roundest, fullest wine of the three; Les Crayères is just over one ha, and blends 90% Pinot Noir with Pinot Meunier, its pure chalk soils giving a wine of lunging incision; Le Clos des Champions is the smallest at just under half a hectare of softly sloping limy clay, sited close to the village, its 70% Pinot Noir and 30% Chardonnay giving a wine of striking purity and depth.

Lenoble
51480 Damery, Tel: 03 26 58 42 60, Fax: 03 26 58 65 57

Small Damery-based négociant (which should in truth be called Graser, the founder's name, or Malassagne, the name of his present-day descendants who run the company; "Lenoble" was an early marketing decision). Its 18 ha are well placed, with Grand Cru Chouilly for Chardonnay, Premier Cru Bisseuil for

Pinot Noir, and Pinot Meunier near the Damery base, supplying 50% of requirements; the rest is bought near Damery. Ten to 15% of cask-fermented wine (new wood for the first fermentation; old for the reserves) is used in all the *cuvées* "to spice the food," as Anne Malassagne puts it. These are excellent champagnes, the quality of the raw materials shining through in the undosed Extra Brut (the same blend as the Grand Cru Blanc de Blancs).

Lilbert Fils ✪
51530 Cramant, Tel: 03 26 57 50 16, Fax: 03 26 58 93 86

This tiny 4-ha Cramant domain is the source of some very fine and long-lived Blanc de Blancs made by Georges Lilbert and his son Bertrand. The style is less soft, creamy, and flowery than the Blanc de Blancs of most large houses might leave the drinker expecting: Cramant here has a taut, steely, rigorous quality, even in riper vintages like 1995.

Mailly Grand Cru
51500 Mailly-Champagne, Tel: 03 26 49 41 10, Fax: 03 26 49 42 27

The Grand Cru village of Mailly is the furthest west on the northern side of the Montagne de Reims, adjacent to Verzenay and Verzy; this small village cooperative only has vineyards here, making its wines a fine and rare opportunity to taste the terroir. The vintage La Terre *cuvée* sums up the mélange of flowers and nuts, the citrus-style fruits, and the finishing minerality of this Pinot-dominated location which produces wines of less power and resonance than Ay or Bouzy.

Henri Mandois
51530 Pierry, Tel: 03 26 54 03 18, Fax: 03 26 51 53 66

Small, consistent house whose range is based on a widely scattered 35-ha domain. The 1996 Victor Mandois *cuvée* is beautifully constructed and will age even better than the 1995 and 1993 did, and both the Cuvée de Réserve and the rosé Premier Cru offer fine value.

Margaine
51380 Villers-Marmery, Tel: 03 26 97 92 13, Fax: 03 26 97 97 45

The vintage Blanc de Blancs from this grower based in the little-known village of Villers-Marmery at the far eastern end of the Montagne de Reims is refined, incisive, and vinous, built on understated lemon fruit, and acquiring tantalizing walnut-butter notes with time; 1996 is a great success here.

Marne et Champagne *see* Lanson

Marquis de Sade *see* Michel Gonet

Le Mesnil
51390 Le Mesnil-sur-Oger, Tel: 03 26 57 53 23

This cooperative offers a relatively inexpensive taste of one of the Côte des Blancs' very greatest *crus*, though quality could presumably be much higher if all the vineyards were tended as carefully as those of the 18 Salon growers. Look out for the Réserve Sélection.

Moët et Chandon
51200 Epernay, Tel: 03 26 51 20 00, Fax: 03 26 54 84 23

Moët is the elephant of Champagne, its 25 million bottles sold annually being more than twice the number sold by its nearest competitor, Veuve Clicquot (the two are in the same ownership in any case, both being part of the LVMH group). Scale, naturally, obliges Moët's winemaking team of Dominique Foulon and Richard Geoffroy to be masters of *assemblage*; the company's Brut Impérial is a true brand, and consistency is part of its appeal. As a champagne, it is pleasant and easygoing, ageing relatively swiftly towards a toasty old age. The Brut Premier Cru is barely more interesting. Without an overall improvement in the region's viticulture, and particularly lower yields, riper fruit, and more effective fruit sorting, it is hard to see much changing. Moët does, though, have a fine 550-ha vineyard portfolio of its own, and its more expensive champagnes are everything they should be thanks to this estate (which includes the old Lanson vineyards and recently appropriated Pommery vineyards). The Brut Impérial vintage is a model of its style, ageing with grace and articulacy; the vintage Dom Pérignon is very powdery and pure, though it is often released well before it has reached expressive plenitude. In contrast to the often teasing and pretentious hints given as to Dom Pérignon's vineyard origins (which include the Premier Cru Hautvillers, as well as the Grands Crus Ay, Bouzy, Cramant, and Verzenay), Moët began to tear up the sacred texts of *assemblage* when in 2001 it released a series of three "Grand Cru" wines: Pinot Meunier from Sillery (Les Champs de Romont), Chardonnay from Chouilly (Les Vignes de Saran), and Pinot Noir from Ay (Les Sarments d'Ay). The aim, I was told by Chef de Cave Georges Blanck, was "not to make a garage wine; it's just the origin of the grapes which is the focus." No markedly lower yields, then, and no use of wood; and the blending philosophy still permeates them, too, in the sense that they are multi-vintage blends. They are good champagnes and will improve with storage time; yet whether they truly reflect terroir or are rather top-quality varietal champagnes is an intriguing question. The powdery refinement of Les Vignes de Saran and the bready, fruited roundness of Les Sarments d'Ay are both "typical" of their origins in that these are the classic grape varieties from those sites; Les Champs de Romont, however, is arguably more of a varietal Pinot Meunier (vigorous and orchard-like) than an expression of terroir (the little-seen Grand Cru of Sillery, until now known chiefly through the wines of Francis Secondé). The real significance is that it is Moët that has made this break with Champagne theology. Can we expect a response from Laurent-Perrier, from Taittinger, from Veuve Clicquot? I hope so.

Pierre Moncuit ✪
51190 Le Mesnil-sur-Oger, Tel: 03 26 57 52 65, Fax: 03 26 57 97 89
Nicole and Yves Moncuit's 20-ha domain in Le Mesnil-sur-Oger is the source of some superb Blanc de Blancs Grand Cru champagne, all single-vintage (though only wines from what are considered great vintages actually carry dates on them). The 1995 vintage is profoundly ripe, persistent, concentrated, and mineral, needing only time to calm it and refine its component parts. There is a Vieilles Vignes *cuvée* named after Nicole.

Jean Moutardier
51210 Le Breuil, Tel: 03 26 59 21 09, Fax: 03 26 59 21 25
Terroir enthusiasts who want to lay taste-buds on Meunier-dominated champagne from the Surmelin Valley should try these soft, supple yet impressively intense champagnes.

Moutard Père et Fils
10110 Buxeuil, Tel: 03 25 38 50 73, Fax: 03 25 38 57 72
Together with Aubry, this 20-ha domain at Buxeuil in the Côte des Bars is one of the few to research Champagne's antique varieties; there is a pure-Arbanne *cuvée* here (this domain spells the variety "Arbane"). Curiosity aside, the dark, fruit-infused rosé is a better buy.

Mumm
51100 Reims, Tel: 03 26 49 59 69, Fax: 03 26 40 46 13
The purchase by Hicks, Muse, Tate, and Furst of Mumm from Seagram in 1997 looked, from the outside, like a catastrophe in the making; happily, the American financiers proved to be consolidators rather than asset-strippers. They not only put a fine team in charge but also gave them the resources needed to drag this historic house out of the marshes into which Seagram had allowed it to sink. The Americans duly took their profit and departed in 2001, and new owners Allied Domecq have had the sense to leave the team – and in particular the intelligent CEO Jean-Marie Barillère and the talented young Chef de Caves Dominique Demarville – in place. Because of champagne's ageing requirements, improvements take some time to filter through, but already the low-pressure Grand Cru Blanc de Blancs Mumm de Cramant is as fine, fragrant, creamy, and seethingly gentle as it's ever been in the last two decades, while the basic, jolly Mumm Cordon Rouge has much more of a spring in its step than a few years ago (it has replaced Moët as Formula One's spraying champagne). Look out, in the coming years, for improved Cordon Rouge vintage wines – and also for the new "Grand Cru" cuvée, a vintage blend

of wines from the five Grands Crus most associated with Mumm: chiefly Cramant and Verzenay, with supplements from Bouzy, Ay, and Avize. This welcome nod to terroir began with the modestly concentrated 1995 vintage, but watch for better releases subsequently.

Bruno Paillard
51100 Reims, Tel: 03 26 36 20 22, Fax: 03 26 36 57 72
The founding of a Champagne house in modern times is an extraordinary financial challenge; 20 years on, former broker Bruno Paillard's eponymous house is not only still in existence, but apparently thriving. Paillard himself is sole owner, as he is of de Nauroy; he is also a major shareholder (around 43%) in the complicated, publically quoted BCC group which unites Boizel, Alexandre Bonnet, Chanoine, Abel Lepitre, Philipponat, and de Venoge. Paillard's own champagnes are taut, tight, slender, and pure, with low *dosages* and impressively informative back labels which tell you much about the composition of the blend and the date of disgorgement. The Brut non-vintage, which contains a high 33% of Chardonnay, is incisive and scalpel-like, needing a little time to find aromatic articulacy; there is a fine, refreshingly fruit-scattered rosé; while the Chardonnay Réserve Privée, founded on Paillard's own 3 ha in Oger, takes the surgeon-like incision to new depths, though around the cut you will find sap, leaf, and grapefruit. There are up to three wines carrying a vintage date: a Blanc de Blancs, a classic vintage (the 1995 is vigorous and thrusting, with a slightly broader, more vinous style than the Paillard norm), and the prestige NPU (only Grand Cru components from seven villages; only oak-fermented wines).

Palmer
51100 Reims, Tel: 03 26 07 35 07, Fax: 03 26 07 45 24
This classy and small Reims-based cooperative bases its wines on a core of Montagne-grown Pinot Noir. Best buy is the non-vintage Amazone which enjoys plenty of age and goes to market in an oval-shaped bottle.

Pannier
02403 Château-Thierry, Tel: 03 23 69 51 30, Fax: 03 23 69 51 31
Another of the region's "A-team" of fighting cooperatives, the Château-Thierry-based Pannier produces tasty and consistent champagne, even if the modest vineyard sources fail to ignite the two "prestige" wines Egérie and Louis Eugène. The basic Brut Sélection is as near to a cert as this difficult climate can provide.

Joseph Perrier
51000 Châlons-en-Champagne, Tel: 03 26 68 29 51, Fax: 03 26 70 57 16
The wines of this smallish house based in Châlons-en-Champagne are worth a look for lovers of the apple-roundness that Pinot Meunier and Pinot Noir can bring to a blend: the Cuvée Royale is a typically gentle, easygoing Brut non-vintage. It's with the vintage Cuvée Josephine that real concentration and refinement break through, like sunbeams piercing mist.

Perrier-Jouët
51201 Epernay, Tel: 03 26 53 38 00, Fax: 03 26 54 54 55
Perrier-Jouët has, like its sister house Mumm, undergone two changes of ownership in recent years, but finds itself in a happier situation at the start of the noughties with Allied Domecq than at the start of the nineties. While Mumm's style is built on Pinot Noir from the Montagne de Reims, Perrier-Jouët has a backbone of Chardonnay from the Côte des Blancs (especially Cramant) and Meunier from the Marne. It's hard to make much of a case for its trivial basic Brut non-vintage (called Grand Brut), but the non-vintage Blason de France is a wine with some pleasantly biscuity depths. The vintage wine is light but pure-flavoured, and the Blason de France rosé often shows pretty fruit characteristics. The "prestige" *cuvée* here is the lavishly bottled Belle Epoque, complete with its enamelled anemones designed by Gallé, which appears in vintage, vintage rosé, and vintage Blanc de Blancs guises. The latter is a palpable *champagne de terroir*, coming exclusively from Cramant; the other two are graceful blends built on Chardonnay from Cramant complemented by lighter Pinots. In youth, this is a champagne which can underwhelm, given its extravagant packaging; with age, it sweetens fragrantly.

Philipponnat

51160 Mareuil-sur-Ay, Tel: 03 26 56 93 00, Fax: 03 26 56 93 18

Philipponnat has, for many years, been a kind of Jekyll and Hyde among Champagne houses. Bottles from its 5.5-ha vineyard Clos des Goisses, spectacularly sited above the Marne canal at Mareuil, provided one of champagne's greatest sensorial insights into the region's terroir, yet the rest of the range was barely worth pulling the cork on. When Bruno Paillard acquired the company via BCC in 1997, he said he found the basic stocks in such a poor state that two years' work was needed in order to get the Brut non-vintage back into shape. The range is now much deeper and more concentrated. The Clos des Goisses itself, meanwhile, continues to be magnificently ripe and full-flavoured, amply rewarding a decade or two's cellar patience with wave after wave of hazels, bread, and resonant orchard fruit. (Part of this vineyard lies on one of Champagne's most impressive and steepest south-facing slopes, with the rest on plateau land above it, hence the ripeness even in difficult years. The vineyard is planted with both Chardonnay and Pinot Noir.)

Piper-Heidsieck

51100 Reims, Tel: 03 26 84 43 00, Fax: 03 26 84 43 49

Owned (like Charles Heidsieck) by Rémy Cointreau, Piper-Heidsieck passed several years in the remedial hands of the late Daniel Thibault, who altered it from a non-malolactic to a malolactic style. Nonetheless, compared to creamy and luxuriant brother Charles, young Piper is all about "impertinence, freshness, vivacity, fun, and cinema," to quote Thibault's successor Régis Camus. It is cleanly made, but as an "inexpensive" marque, Piper is one of those champagnes in which the region's viticultural problems are often evident with a lack of concentration and a difficult rawness of style. As usual, the vintage Brut is much better.

Pol Roger

51206 Epernay, Tel: 03 26 59 58 00, Fax: 03 26 55 25 70

The family-owned house has, in part thanks to the enthusiastic endorsement of Winston Churchill, for long been regarded with great generosity and indulgence on the British market; in size terms, it is just a little larger than Bollinger, but much smaller than regional giants such as Moët, Laurent-Perrier, or Lanson. Stylistically, its range is much lighter and more delicate than Bollinger, for example, and the Brut non-vintage has often tasted disappointing over the last decade, particularly when purchased in France. The Blanc de Blancs, by contrast, is all that it should be, full of early-flowering grace and vanilla charm, while the vintage wines have a fine track record for slow, steady ageing. The "prestige" cuvée, named after the company's most famous customer, was only launched in the mid-1980s and requires age before it begins to show the surging intensity and grandeur of dimension of some of its rivals; when first released it can be underwhelming.

Pommery

51053 Reims, Tel: 03 26 61 62 06, Fax: 03 26 61 62 99

Alas, poor Pommery: the perfect illustration of how little a brand is worth and how fragile its existence becomes once it is severed from the family and vineyard roots that created it in the first place. As this book goes to print Pommery is about to be traded by LVMH in the same way that Lanson was traded a decade ago, with 400 ha of vineyards amputated from the rest of the body and shared between Moët and Veuve Clicquot; the purchaser is the commercially successful but qualitatively disappointing Vranken Monopole group (which also owns Heidsieck Monopole). The stocks in Pommery's cellars vary from the callow Brut non-vintage (called Brut Royal) to the serious and carefully crafted Louise cuvées. Pommery's graceful, charming, sketch-book style, of course, blinks a little when dragged into the limelight and compared with obvious regional thunderers such as Bollinger; yet the non-vintage Apanage, the Summertime Blanc de Blancs, and the Wintertime Blanc de Noirs have all managed, in recent years, to combine depth with that grace and charm, and the vintage wine (a Grand Cru here) is quietly and consistently excellent, beautifully blended (in his trademark yellow scarf) by the dapper Prince Alain de Polignac. Let's hope all of this remains sacrosanct under Vranken's administration.

Roederer ✪

51053 Reims, Tel: 03 26 40 42 11, Fax: 03 26 47 66 51

The strength of the much-admired and still family-owned company of Roederer is customarily said to reside in its 200-ha vineyard estate, though in fact it is not the size of this which counts so much as the fact that 115 ha are Grand Cru land and 70 ha Premier Cru; that Roederer's viticultural practices (including green-harvesting) are genuinely and unusually stringent; and that it supplies two-thirds of the company's needs. The rest of the company's supplies are contracted, and all purchases inspected; even so, Jean-Claude Rouzaud says that with hindsight he wishes he had refused to expand sales earlier in his career so that the company could now be self-sufficient in grapes. "I am very discouraged by what I see in Champagne today. Quality is not an issue for too many people." Brut Premier is a reliable and always well-aged (3.5 years) Brut non-vintage built on a core of Pinot Noir. It contains up to 20% of Roederer's famous wood-aged reserves, and malolactic fermentation is prevented for most of the blend (though the exact proportion varies). High-tech filtration techniques (at 0.65 microns) ensure that Roederer's non-malolactic proportions are stable. The style is bell-round, nonetheless, with the reserves being used to tickle in extra ripeness in years when nature has not delivered. The rest of the range is exclusively vintage-dated, thus stylistically diverse, though always dignified, concentrated, firm, and slow to unfold; the aromatic, creamy Blanc de Blancs perhaps offers most appealing value, though nothing in the range is sold at prices competitive with those of the great champagne growers. Cristal is, with Moët's Dom Pérignon, one of the world's two most celebrated "prestige" cuvées, and is a carefully crafted and beautifully packaged champagne of considerable finesse and penetrating intensity. The 1995 seems to combine the incision and minerality of great Côtes des Blancs sites with the booming, rounded fruit of the Montagne de Reims; its faintly oxidative complexities (honey, beeswax) and biscuity notes indicate finely judged cellarwork, too. Few wines truly deserve the epithet "iconic", but should a latter-day Andrei Rublov chose to work with grapes rather than paints, Cristal might be the kind of thing he'd create.

Ruinart ✪

51053 Reims, Tel: 03 26 77 51 51, Fax: 03 26 82 88 43

Ruinart has contrived to make a virtue out of its low profile, even though this quiet, studious pupil in the noisy LVMH class does, in fact, produce over 2 million bottles a year, making it bigger than either Pol Roger or Bollinger. Ruinart is Chardonnay, stylistically speaking; even the Dom Ruinart Rosé here is Blanc de Blancs with a splash of red wine, as its cream-and-custard scents reveal. In fact the Brut non-vintage (called "R" de Ruinart) contains just 40% Chardonnay, but they stamp the wine firmly nonetheless; this is a much better Brut non-vintage than most. The Dom Ruinart Blanc de Blancs is a most beautiful wine, complex and enchanting, faint notes of controlled oxidation added dazzling mayflower complexities to its graceful, mineral style. The blend includes relatively large amounts of Chardonnay from the Montagne de Reims, lending the wine a sappiness not always evident in the cream of the Côte des Blancs.

de Saint-Gall see Union Champage

Salon ✪

51190 Le Mesnil-sur-Oger, Tel: 03 26 61 82 36, Fax: 03 26 61 80 24

This, the "personal Champagne house" of founder Eugène Aimé Salon, a rabbit-skin millionaire of the early twentieth century, is a living historical monument. The company has only ever made just one wine, a vintage Blanc de Blancs produced in great years only from 21 original parcels in Le Mesnil; the wine is given between 8 and 10 years' ageing before release. Salon itself (part of Laurent-Perrier) owns just 3 ha; the rest of the wine comes from 15 ha owned by 18 growers, all of whom sell all their wine to Salon (which in undeclared years becomes Delamotte or Laurent-Perrier). Most of the decision as to whether to declare a Salon, according to director Didier Depond, is taken at harvest, and the rest after fermentation. Officially, Salon does not undergo malolactic, whereas Delamotte does. (According to Bruno Paillard, the only way that malolactic can effectively be prevented in champagne is by microfiltration, heavy sulphur use, or permanent temperature control until the point at which the wine is served. Neither of the former techniques takes place at Salon, and the latter is not possible to control.) What is sought, says Depond, is an "equilibrium between sugar and acidity." This can sometimes lead to some surprise omissions, as with 1989 ("there was a lack of acidity") and 2000 ("too much rot: it was not a great year"). On the mathematical basis of declarations, Salon has, perhaps surprisingly, judged the decade of the 1990s superior to the 1980s; it was the first since the 1940s with five declarations (1990, 1995, 1996, 1997, and 1999). Wood is not used, and there is no late harvesting: "freshness" is the prime aim. The 1990 (a year which the house considers to be one of the two greatest of the twentieth century, with 1928) is still young, massive as Chardonnay in Champagne rarely is, and soberly forceful, a paste of minerals: it needs a further decade.

Francis Secondé
51500 Sillery, Tel: 03 26 49 16 67, Fax: 03 26 49 11 55

Pure, lingering, intense, and citric wines from Sillery, based on Pinot Noir and Chardonnay and thus providing an interesting contrast to Moët's Champs de Romont. Give them time.

Selosse ✪✪
51190 Avize, Tel: 03 26 57 53 56, Fax: 03 26 57 78 22

The "madman of Avize" may turn out to be the "prophet of Avize" – by which I mean that it is hard to think of a single individual in Champagne today whose work (though by no means uniformly admired) is more influential than that of Anselme Selosse. Fastidious viticulture (which happens to be biodynamic); ripeness levels previously thought unattainable in the region; radically non-interventionist methods; the use of a wide variety of wood containers and long ageing (the 1995s are to go on sale in 2004) are some of the lodestars of the *méthode* Selosse. The veneer of eccentricity (he decided to bottle his 1997s in magnums alone) conceals a sharp and scholarly intelligence, and if the future of Champagne truly is going to be one in which terroir plays more of a role then the region as a whole will have to pay more attention to Selosse and less to its accountants and brand managers. "We need a hundred Selosses," as Daniel Lorson of the CIVC puts it. "I choose my recipients," Selosse says in explaining the 1997 decision, "not in terms of commerce but in terms of wine. You need time for the wine to leave its fruit behind and to assume its terroir. I don't want to make a beautiful Chardonnay; I want to make a beautiful Avize." He even has a still "solera" of pure Avize wines from which he removes 22% each year for blending purposes to provide the "*vécu du vigne*", the "lived experience" of the vine, catalyzed by time. The range here is extensive, and the names chosen with extreme care: Brut Initiale is the "good humoured" introduction wine; Version Originale is the Extra Brut; Exquise is the "*cuvée gourmande*"; Substance has matter; Contraste is a Blanc de Noirs; there is a Masculin Rosé with "skeleton and muscle" in which Selosse's Chardonnay meets Francis Egly's Pinot Noir. Perhaps the greatest wines of all, though, are the vintages – like the magnificent 1990, large yet fine-boned, its 14.2% of finished alcohol barely perceptible amid the mineral finesse of its Avize origins and the slow, honeyed descent of time's intricacies.

Taittinger
51100 Reims, Tel: 03 25 85 45 35, Fax: 03 26 85 17 46

This house is owned by the Taittinger family, whose other interests include Baccarat crystal and the haunting, connoisseur's perfumes of Annick Goutal. For a company of its size (5 million bottles per year) the 270 ha of vineyard holdings is relatively small, which may explain why the basic *cuvées* (Brut Réserve and Brut Prestige Rosé) are relatively simple, short champagnes. The vintage wines are much better and admirably faithful to the style of each year, coming into full articulacy in the medium term. The top-of-the-range Comtes de Champagne is one of the region's greatest Blanc de Blancs, built on wines from the Côte des Blancs given a little tickle of oak; it needs age, and rewards it with banks of scent.

Union Champagne
51190 Avize, Tel: 03 26 57 94 22, Fax: 03 26 57 57 98

This massive, Avize-based entity is an ensemble of 10 cooperatives and 1,200 growers, and the key supplier for many well-known big name Brut non-vintage blends. Among the better known of its own labels are Pierre Vaudon and de Saint-Gall; the fragrantly lush vintage Cuvée Orpale wines (only the best years, only Grand Cru fruit) also begin life here. All offer good value, though few provocative challenges or sublimities.

Pierre Vaudon *see* Union Champagne

de Venoge
51200 Epernay, Tel: 03 26 53 34 34, Fax: 03 26 53 34 35

Interesting house which is now part of the Bruno Paillard controlled BCC group. It has no vineyards of its own, but the purchases include about 30% from the Côte de Sézanne, which director Aymeric de Clouet says help bring complexity to blends when young. Age, by contrast, is something the house means to specialize in: look out for releases of the forthcoming Cuvée Vingt Ans (champagnes which, like vintage Madeira, will go to market on their twentieth birthday, beginning with the 1983 in 2003) and a wine which de Clouet says will be called "LBV" (for Late Bottled Vintage – though the Portuguese authorities are unlikely to be happy about this). This latter wine is based, if you like, on pure reserves: wines held over for a year (two-thirds oak-aged Chardonnay and one-third steel-aged Pinot Meunier) before being bottled for the second fermentation. Among the present releases are the impressively complex non-vintage Cordon Bleu and beautifully labelled, mouthfilling Blanc de Noirs. The 1995 vintage is sappy and firm, needing a few calming years in the cellar, while the 1993 Grand Vin des Princes is a much creamier, softer affair, continuing the tradition of showy lushness which this wine has established.

Veuve Clicquot
51054 Reims, Tel: 03 26 89 54 40, Fax: 03 26 40 60 17

In size, Veuve Clicquot is Moët's nearest competitor; the two are siblings within the LVMH group. In general, Clicquot produces the more characterful champagnes: rounded, deeper, fuller, more pungent, and – as far as the non-vintage is concerned – more age-worthy. The vintage wines are chunky and full and their rosé counterparts exuberantly fruity. La Grande Dame is the name of Veuve Clicquot's "prestige" *cuvée*, built on eight Grand Cru villages in which Veuve Clicquot herself originally owned vineyards: it is firm, vinous, and sinewy.

Vilmart
51500 Rilly-la-Montagne, Tel: 03 26 03 40 01, Fax: 03 26 03 46 57

Few cellars in France are as impeccably clean and well-ordered as this one, and the fact that the now-retired René Champs is an artist working in stained glass, examples of which glow throughout, makes the experience of tasting here a quasi-ecclesiastical one. Only the plainsong is missing. The family business is now in the hands of the likeable Laurent Champs, the fifth generation; there are 11 ha of vines, all Premier Cru and sited at Rilly and Villers, with a minimum age of 28 years. The philosophy, Champs says, is "to make wines, not bubbles." In general, the non-vintage wines are vinified in impeccably maintained *foudres* and the vintage wines in barriques (of which a quarter are new or second-use). The plainsong analogy fits the wines, too: they are very pure and fine drawn, with occasional austerities that the combination of blocked malolactic fermentation plus oak seems to intensify. The Grande Réserve (70% Pinot Noir, 30% Chardonnay) is vinous and crisply defined; the Grand Cellier (70% Chardonnay, 30% Pinot Noir) is more piercingly intense. The vintage Grand Cellier d'Or ups the intensity still further, though the acid levels (as in 1997) can seem almost Saar-like. The vintage Coeur de Cuvée is built on the heart of the pressings of an 80% Chardonnay, 20% Pinot blend from vines of over 50 years given barrel-fermentation and bottled for its second fermentation unfiltered. The 1996 vintage is still very young, its scything acidity fighting somewhat with the wood notes, yet the 1991 suggests that the scrap is not necessarily happily resolved in time. Is a blocked malo really the best strategy for wood-fermented champagne?

The Loire Valley

River of Difference Few regions of France can match the Loire for singularity. Challenging grape varieties; edgy balance; a spectrum of sweetness, minerality, or the print of lees in place of fruit – this northern ribbon of vineyards flutters to its own breeze.

It is hard, in the Loire Valley, to imagine wilderness. In the idle heart of a summer day in Saumur, when time slows to the pace of a sleeper's breath, to figure wolves, torrents, and impenetrable forest on every side requires a determined imagination. The Loire is where French is spoken with more pouting perfection than elsewhere. The bridges that cross the river do so with leggy grace; the château libraries salt centuries away in the cow-scented dust of leather bookbindings; the gardeners outdo each other with feats of absurd vegetative symmetry. The river seems so vastly placid that it can seldom be bothered to gather its watery flab into a single channel. If this was ever a place of sores and fear, of banditry and of disorientation, it was a long time ago.

Yet stone rarely looms as large in French life as it does here. If we know the Loire at all, we know it for its castles, the perfect source material for every illustrator of fairy tales and Sadean fantasies. To gaze on these is to understand the French Revolution. Yet such exercises in monumental patisserie were possible in part because of plentiful local supplies of malleable limestone – the celebrated local *tuffeau*. The same rock is responsible for the pale glow of plainer homes which falls, at summer dusk, down the village streets. The Loire is barely less famous for its mushrooms and cheeses than for its châteaux: both grow and ripen in the moist darkness of the thousands of caves that lie beneath the vines. I have seen Angevin mushroom growers come whistling out of the gloom of their underground farms by bicycle, so long are their subterranean tracks and avenues, so extensive their dark and dripping fields. It is here, too, even at the beginning of the twenty-first century, that men and women of ease and income choose caves in which to make their homes or offices. You might not be able to afford a château, but your *maison* in the Loire can still be *troglodyte*, your roof a vineyard, its tiles bunches of grapes.

Thus the Loire continues to live out its long and refined stone age. Wine, needless to say, fits happily into this schema. Grapes love to feed on stone; the poorer and purer, the better. Moreover we are in the northern half of the country, the half of France where viticulture is only viable where a hillside points its flank at the sun, where a stream cuts a south-facing bank, where a sheltered terrace lies in the lee of the wind. The adventure of the land is unusually adventitious here, a game of hide and seek. Growers pounce on the warmth of angled stone.

Today's Loire rises on a lonely mountain in the Massif Central, France's high southern heart. Its journey is one long, slow decline northwards and then west, culminating in a muddy dissolution in the Atlantic, within sight of the stacked containers and sea-lizard

tanker ships of St-Nazaire. The water that drains into the Loire from forest and field leaves one-fifth of France behind it. This is France's Nile; this is France's Ganges.

It links at least three different wine regions which, were it not for the common thread of the river, might be thought to share little. The wines of the Nantes region, based on the Melon grape variety, offer a fresh, limpid neutrality. The Central Loire – France's garden, as it's called, linking Anjou, Saumur, and Touraine – is a generous, dappled landscape where Chenin Blanc and Cabernet Franc produce a spectrum of wines both white and red, both stone-dry and syrup-sweet. The Upper Loire, finally, forms part of the Kimmeridgean limestone chain, extending through Chablis to Champagne's Aube sector. Sauvignon Blanc finds its most pungent French expression here in a series of sparely drawn, sometimes smoky wines of taut ripeness.

Many differences, thus – yet also a strong sense of unity despite the 600 or so miles that separate the first of the Loire's wine-growers from the last. To some extent, it is a unity borne of adversity. This is France's third largest wine region; there are 16,000 ha in the Nantes region; 30,000 ha in Anjou, Saumur, and Touraine; and 4,300 ha in the Upper Loire (which the French call the *vins du Centre*, meaning the wines of Central France). As a northerly wine region, it is vulnerable to the petulance of the weather (as in 1998, 1999, 2000, and 2001). Most of the Loire's wines are white, nervy, and relatively acidic in a world which increasingly favours big, rich red wines. Many of them sell at those modest prices where competition from new wine-producing countries is greatest. Sales of the most important wine of the Nantes region, Muscadet, fell during the year 2000 in Britain by no less than sixteen per cent. And the Loire can ill afford these losses, since it is already a region which relies more heavily than most on the home market (only twenty-two per cent of its production is exported, compared with a national average of twenty-seven per cent). The consolation for the Loire is that it is Paris's own vineyard, providing quick, lively wines for a nervy, high-spirited city – and Paris isn't about to become unfaithful.

The quest for golden Chenin

What, though, of the New Loire? In some ways, developments in the Loire over the last ten years have shadowed those of its northern neighbours, Alsace and Burgundy. Two chief concerns have emerged. The first of these is a far greater respect for the environment than that shown by the retiring herbicidal generation. The stewardship of vineyards is a longer-term venture than that

"To keep free wine-growers who work on a family scale, we have to cultivate the understanding of terroir. We must inform; we must educate. Every day, every day, every day. Marketing? We will always lose. Those who drink our wines, our clients, have to take over the educational relay from us if free winemakers like us are to continue to exist. Otherwise we will all finish like Heineken or Kronenbourg."

CLAUDE PAPIN

◀ *When a river grows this grand, it provides few sun-trap slopes; the Loire's vineyards often cluster around tributaries.*

undertaken by any planter of forests, and it has not taken long to
realize that the lazy use of chemicals in vineyards to replace hard
physical work was poisoning the most precious asset of all for any
wine-growing family: its land. The further north you go, the less
easy organic and biodynamic viticulture becomes, but this has
not dissuaded the region's greatest wine producers, like Guy
Bossard, Noël Pinguet, or Mark Angeli, from following this path.
Biodynamics is profiled below.

The second great leap forward concerns the practices of
viticulture, and particularly harvesting. In contrast to Alsace, the
appellation system in the Loire provides an adequate, even over-
complicated template for the expression of terroir; that is not a
battle which has needed fighting here. The Loire, though, has
Chenin Blanc. If any white grape can be said to throw up
difficulties equivalent to those posed by Pinot Noir, it is Chenin
Blanc. The great few are among the finest white wines on earth,
rivalled only for longevity, and for the beauty of its cellar
metamorphoses, by Riesling (Chardonnay isn't even in the
running). The dismal masses are harsh and raw. The very fact that
the Loire produces as much biting, Chenin-based sparkling wine as
it does is an admission of failure.

The Loire also has Cabernet Franc and Cabernet Sauvignon. The
Central Loire is, with Burgundy, France's most northerly red wine-
producing region. Beaune, for the record, is a little further north
than Chinon, but only by a few minutes' daylight in midsummer.
Cabernet Franc is the grape that makes Cheval Blanc one of the
most voluptuous red wines in Bordeaux; Cabernet Sauvignon is the
Hamlet of the Médoc. Ripening Cabernet fully this far north is, to
put it mildly, a challenge.

Ungrateful, harsh Chenin Blanc; difficult, raw Cabernets: the
lesson has been learned. The second great development of the New
Loire is the cult of the *trie*: of successive harvest passages through the
vines to pick, at each moment, only the ripest fruit. This time-
consuming practice has completely altered the horizon of possibilities
for Loire wines, as the new generation of ripe, flavour-saturated dry
white wines and deeper, more structured red wines proves.

Biodynamics: the upward gaze

Rudolf Steiner (1861-1925) was the founder of the movement known
as anthroposophy, often described as "spiritual science". Steiner's
teachings (profoundly influenced by Goethe, whose scientific works
Steiner edited in his youth) cover a wide variety of applications, most
notably education, medicine, and therapeutic practices. In 1924, the
year before his death, he gave a series of lectures on agriculture.
Working from these, followers of Steiner such as Maria Thun have
established a practical system of cultivation called biodynamics.
During the 1980s and 1990s, a number of leading French wine-
growers – most notably Nicolas Joly in Savennières – began to
cultivate their vineyards on these principles.

Biodynamics is, at the practical level, a specialized branch of
organic viticulture. There is, for example, a rejection of synthetic
chemical inputs such as insecticides, herbicides, and artificial
fertilizers; plant and mineral teas are used in their place. These are
made according to homeopathic principles; in other words they are
based on successive dilutions, combined with prescribed stirring
techniques, until only the minutest traces of the original substance
remains. The solution is then understood to be "dynamised".
Biodynamics also makes extensive use of composts and preparations

which are made (by specialist suppliers) according to the often visionary and poetic instructions outlined by Steiner in his lectures. These composts are stored in glass jars packed inside peat-lined wooden cases, which in turn need to be kept well away from other sources of contamination (such as electrical currents).

A further key element of biodynamic practice is the use of the seasonal calender established by Maria Thun. Steiner's vision of vegetation was that of a "middle world" sandwiched between the earth, or the forces of minerality in which plants bury their roots; and an upper, ethereal world of exposure to the cosmos. The sun, of course, is the key element of this upper world, but not, for Steiner, the only one. The stars, the planets of the solar system, and the moon have a considerable influence also; astral forces match solar ones, biodynamicists assert. Maria Thun's calender is based on the movement of the moon through the twelve houses of the zodiac; the association of each of these with one of the four elements furnishes the basis for treatments in field or vineyard. Earth houses, for example, rule root formation; water houses rule leaves; air houses rule flowers; and fire houses rule the formation of fruits and seeds. If you need to treat the leaves of your vines against incipient mildew, then you would do so on a day when the moon was passing through a water sign such as Pisces.

Like all organic wine-growers, biodynamic practitioners use sulphur (to combat powdery mildew, as an anti-oxidant, and for general winemaking hygiene) and Bordeaux mixture (copper sulphate and lime, used to combat downy mildew). Sulphur is not viewed as problematic: this element makes up 0.5 per cent of the earth's crust, and occurs naturally as a by-product of fermentation. Biodynamicists do, however, lament the need to use Bordeaux mixture, and limit it as far as possible: Nicolas Joly uses ten kg of Bordeaux mixture per hectare per year, equivalent to 2.5 kg of copper per hectare per year. He would rather not do this, admitting that copper "inhibits life in the soil". Growers like Raimond Villeneuve of Château de Roquefort in Provence are experimenting with alternatives to copper, which the EU is due to outlaw over the coming decade in any case.

Critics say that some wine producers use (or claim to use) biodynamic techniques for marketing reasons alone. I have never seen these allegations substantiated. There is no doubt, however, that some among France's fine wine community are offended by what they see as the woolliness of biodynamics, and its lack of scientific rigour. This anti-biodynamic position is particularly evident in Bordeaux and Champagne, two areas of deep conservatism and great wealth, where the ruthlessly pursued business aspects of fine wine production tend to eclipse other considerations. The director of Château Latour, Frédéric Engerer, described biodynamics to me in 1999 as "a giant intellectual swindle"; two days later Jean-Guillaume Prats of Cos d'Estournel dismissed it as "a cult". By contrast, the regions where biodynamics has its most enthusiastic following – Burgundy, Alsace, and the Loire Valley – are regions where the very best vineyard sites are in the hands of small grower-producers. Interestingly, they are also regions where minute differences in terroir are most palpable, and where great vineyard sites tend to be held in common. The remarks of Engerer and Prats contrast most strikingly with those made to me by growers like Dominique Lafon in Burgundy, like Olivier Zind-Humbrecht MW in Alsace, or like Noël Pinguet of Huët in the Loire, all of whom have switched to biodynamics for overwhelmingly pragmatic reasons. They began by converting a part of their domains for comparative tests; they found that biodynamics, quite simply, produced better fruit and better wine.

▲ *No sight is, paradoxically, more gratifying to a sweet-wine maker than a tubful of well-rotted grapes.*

Yet perhaps the most compelling aspect of biodynamics, and certainly one that Steiner would wish to underline were he still alive today, is its moral dimension. Steiner believed that spiritual processes were as real, and as important, as material processes, and that it was the duty and the privilege of human beings to rise above material goals in order to achieve spiritual understanding of the higher human self. Science – the study of the material world – needed to be completed and balanced by "spiritual science" to avoid disequilibrium and catastrophe.

This moral dimension is most clearly in evidence in the work of Nicolas Joly (a former merchant banker and Columbia MBA) at Coulée de Serrant, and is one of the reasons why he is a singular wine-grower. The *fiche technique* (technical specification sheet) produced by Joly begins with his credo: "*Avant d'être bon, un vin doit être vrai*" ("Before being good, a wine should be true"). This is a moral statement, and moreover a revolutionary one in its context, since it reverses the unspoken assumption that in the assessment of wine quality is paramount. No, Joly is saying, quality is not primordial: the truth of wine (which he defines as "the ability to make manifest the subtleties of the place from which it comes") is actually more important. An unpleasing true wine is morally better than a pleasing false wine. Some practitioners of biodynamics would follow Joly in this radicalism; others would not. It is philosophically problematic, since such a truth relies on subjective analysis (by tasting) for verification. Joly's theoretical point is clear, however, and it makes one of the most challenging contributions to wine aesthetics of the beginning of the twenty-first century.

Didier Dagueneau

My first meeting with Didier Dagueneau was in an underground cavern in St-Emilion. Vinexpo was happening; this was Château Belair; and "les gens du métier", a greenish collection of France's avant-garde, were showing their wines. Maybe it was chance or maybe it was somebody's mischievous sense of humour, but Didier Dagueneau's tasting table had been positioned under an opening in the cave, and the sunlight was cascading down onto

France's most physically messianic winemaker in a bacchic parody of the Annunciation. Jason Lowe was with me; he took this photograph at that moment. Dagueneau glared at the tasters; he poured samples with studiedly curt swiftness; all questions were met with monosyllabic replies. He would rather, one felt, have been racing huskies in Finland (as he did for three months the following winter). So we tasted. His wines smelled not of Sauvignon

Blanc, nor of gooseberries or asparagus or of micturating felines, but... of spring. Sipping the Buisson Renard was like standing beneath a waterfall: the flavours were clean, limpid, eerily palpable, a soft shock. The Silex was not the parody flintlock of popular myth; it was pure, sappy, soaring, rich, finishing with just a hint of stone after rain. I had not been expecting this calm and majestic retreat from the varietal. I learned something new.

Claude Papin

You need to concentrate when you talk to Claude Papin. Words not only tumble swiftly from the lips of the President of the Technical Institute of the Vine and of Wine, but so, too, do concepts like that of the "climatic space", questions about the effect of hydric stress on grape polyphenols, and observations about the electrical charge of the clay-humus complex. None of this, though, is showy; none of this is merely for effect. Papin's knowledge is grounded in reverence for simple observation, like that of his father-in-law -- who pruned vines for sixty years. "We don't know any more than they did. We are just better at explaining things." He is a poet of the Chenin Blanc, that "super-rustic" variety "perfectly adapted to our half-maritime, half-continental region" -- once a red variety, he claims, and one that needs botrytis to perform at its best, whether for sweet or dry wines. His work on his pierre bise (spilite) soils has given us some of the greatest vins de terroir of the New Loire; he is also wryly sceptical about the poses of the organic and biodynamic movements, even though some of his greatest wine-growing friends (like Deiss and Zind-Humbrecht) are biodynamicists. Above all, though, he makes wines of shattering singularity. No one, thus, sums up his region better than this modest questioner.

Guy Bossard

"There are more than 13,000 ha cultivated in Muscadet," says Guy Bossard, "and to say that the only difference between them is that they are either sur lie or not isn't, in my opinion, adequate. Our present subregions are based on geographical and human factors, not terroir. Muscadet is a region with problems, and our only hope is to isolate the best terroirs, identify them, and bring them to consumers' attention." No one can accuse Bossard of not practising what he preaches: terroir-differentiation is exactly what he has done with his own three old vine cuvées, abandoning his previous "prestige" cuvée in the process. This tireless biodynamic producer says that his cellar work is behind him now. "My future work is all in the vineyard: making old massal selections for vinestocks, looking after the health of the oldest vines, and above all trying to improve the quality of the roots. That work will never end."

The Adventure of the Land

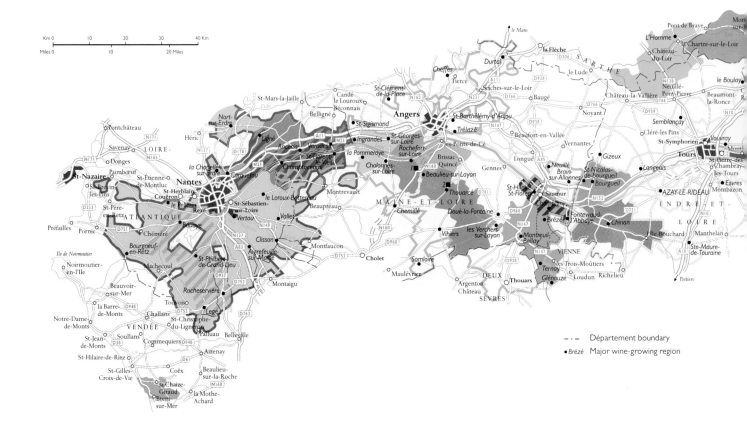

Km 0   10   20   30   40 Km
Miles 0   10   20 Miles

- - - Département boundary
• Brézé Major wine-growing region

You could call the Loire's first wines Mountain Beaujolais. The **Côtes du Forez** and the **Côtes Roannaises** are both high-sited (the vineyards at Forez are some of France's highest, at between 400 and 600 metres/1,312 and 1,968 feet) and granite-soiled, with Gamay the only permitted grape variety. Production is small, and their proximity to Lyons makes them a paler, sharper, Canteloube-like echo to the vineyards of the northern Rhône and of Beaujolais itself.

The Loire is raced for the first 322 km (200 miles) of its course by a rival river, the Allier; the two join near Nevers, and the Loire claims the victory of nomenclature. Allier, nonetheless, is a name of huge significance in the wine world – for its oak trees, which many consider the very best of all for barrel-making. Its two vineyard areas, both VDQS, are the **Côtes d'Auvergne** and **St-Pourçain**. The former is a third Gamay-based appellation, though the fact that the soils are relatively limy gives the Côtes d'Auvergne wines an even greater tenuousness; many are a pale metallic pink, with a vinaigrette-like sharpness. St-Pourçain, by contrast, is aesthetically a kind of lost Burgundian appellation, cast adrift on the crystalline mineral sea of Central France. Aligoté, Chardonnay, and the tart white variety Sacy, together with Pinot Noir and Gamay account for its blade-edged whites and palely incising reds and rosés.

A fifth and final vineyard area, the VDQS of **Châteaumeillant**, is found further west still, on the very northern edge of the Massif Central. The soils, once again, are granitic, meshed with schist and sandstone; Gamay is joined by Pinot Noir and Pinot Gris. The VDQS is best known for its pale, dry, faded, piercing rosé of the type known here (and in Morocco) as *vin gris*.

Downstream of the junction of the Loire and the Allier, the now unified river breaks through the chalky scarps of the Kimmeridgian chain. Reuilly, Quincy, Menetou-Salon, Sancerre, and Pouilly: these are the vineyards of the west-east escarpment at the edge of the Paris basin, not of the river itself. The river is an interruption, but the fact that it is flowing northwards at this point means that it has little to offer wine-growers (the great south-facing slopes are provided when rivers flow east-west, as we'll discover in Anjou). There are, it is true, some river-clinging vineyards here for the **Coteaux du Giennois** AOC and, further down, the VDQS of the **Orléanais**, but these wines have none of the wealth, power, and pungent splendour of those from the escarpment vineyards. Those of the Giennois are light pink-reds based on Gamay and Pinot Noir, while there are some reed-slender Sauvignon Blanc whites. (Some of the villages in the AOC may add **Cosne-sur-Loire** to the name). The Orléanais, traditionally Paris's vineyard until the railway opened up the Languedoc, makes a speciality of rosé from the Pinot Meunier grape called Gris Meunier; there is also a little tart red from Cabernets Sauvignon and Franc as well as Pinot Noir, and white from Chardonnay and Pinot Gris, all grown on river sands.

The five escarpment AOCs are known for one wine style above all: pungent, fist-like, stone-juice whites based on the Sauvignon Blanc

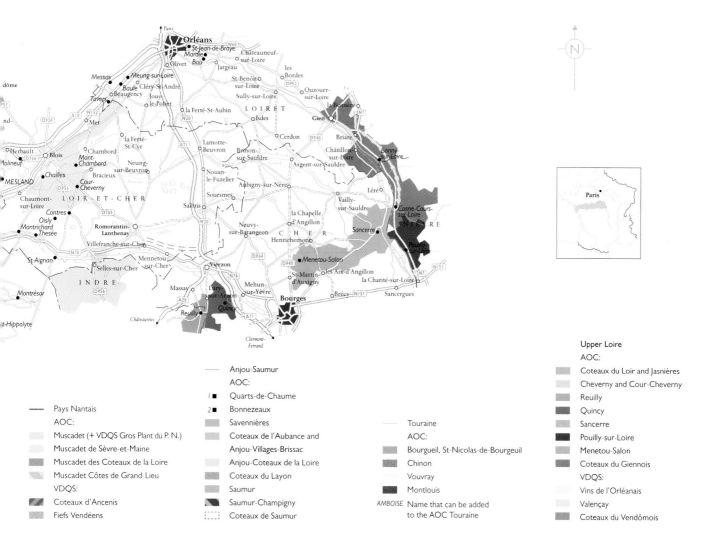

grape variety. Indeed this is the only wine style you will find under the names Pouilly-Fumé and Quincy. Where Chasselas is grown in the vineyards of Pouilly the AOC becomes **Pouilly-sur-Loire**, and the Sancerre, Reuilly, and Menetou-Salon AOCs also embrace red and rosé wines based on Pinot Noir.

The two grandest of the AOCs are Sancerre, west of the river, and Pouilly-Fumé to its east. **Sancerre** is a hill town poised on a big fault block of Cretaceous limestone. Behind the town and away from the river, the strata of Kimmeridgian limestone have weathered and sorted in different ways to produce three main soil types. The first is known locally as *terres blanches* (white earth), a marl which contains exactly the same comma-shaped fossil as is found in Chablis and the Aube, *Exogyra virgula*. The second type, locally called *caillottes* (little stones), is a rubbly limestone formed by the weathering of other, harder Kimmeridgian strata. There are also sizeable deposits of flint, called *silex* in French. (Flint is formed from silica either precipitated and recrystallised from seawater or from the remains of dead sea creatures, and contrasts strongly with the calcareous materials in which it is found.)

Pouilly, across the river, is flatter and more geologically various than Sancerre, with river deposits and Portlandian limestone joining the Kimmeridgian limestone. There is also more flint (red here, rather than the grey of Sancerre) as well as sand and gravel, with the sandier vineyards being used for the Chasselas of AOC Pouilly-sur-Loire. The main topographic feature of Pouilly is the hill (or *butte*) of

St-Andelain, whose flints and gravels mingle with the surrounding Kimmeridgian limestone to provide a superb wine-growing environment; Les Loges, overlooking a particularly idle stretch of the river, mixes its limestone with conglomerates and sandy clays. The two AOCs are not a sharp contrast to one another; the main differences between wines derive, as ever, from the skill or ineptitude of the grower, and then from the different terroirs (marl, limestone rubble, sand, gravel, and flint) within each AOC. In general, flint soils do seem to produce the smokiest wines in both Sancerre and Pouilly-Fumé – though it should also be said that Sauvignon Blanc is less articulate a transmitter of terroir characteristics than Chardonnay, Riesling, or Chenin Blanc.

Menetou-Salon tends to be regarded as the poor man's Pouilly-Fumé or Sancerre, and with good reason. The limestones here begin to mix with an underlay of iron-bearing sandstones, and the results of this geological change appear to be wines which share some of the limpid freshness of the major AOCs but integrate it with a simpler, more affable, less austerely mineral style of Sauvignon Blanc fruit. By the time **Quincy** and **Reuilly** are reached, gravels and sands washed down from the Massif Central cover the rapidly sinking limestones, but good producers in both appellations can still craft Sauvignon Blanc of recognizably ripe, pungent style. There is, though, more juiciness to the wines here than you will find in, say, either Touraine or Sancerre; in Reuilly, too, you can find a delicate spicy muskiness filling out the livid green.

▲ *The Loire, a parliament of cool rivers, helps attract the botrytis which (Claude Papin believes) propels Chenin towards greatness.*

The river has, as it leaves Orléans behind it, turned definitively west; all is now set for its languid lunge towards the sea. This central part of the Loire opens up like a luxurious fan, studded with orchards, wheat fields and many-turreted châteaux. The vineyards spread out both to the north and to the south here, many of them taking advantage of the slopes carved out by tributaries such as the Cher, the Vienne, and the tiny, masculine Loir.

Let's deal with the satellites first. **Haut-Poitou** is a VDQS island sited near Poitiers producing unexceptional varietals on limestone soils; a slender, clean though rather anodyne Sauvignon Blanc is the most successful of these. **Vins de Thouarsais** is a nearby VDQS of similarly slender style, though Chenin Blanc is more important here (it abuts the southernmost reaches of Anjou); this area is also known as **Coteaux du Thouet et de l'Argenton**. **Valençay** is a new AOC lying between Reuilly and Touraine, where a wide variety of soils (sand, chalk, flint, and clay) produce a range of tart reds and rosés, plus a little white, sold on the historical shirt-tails of local grandee Talleyrand. To the north of the river, the **Coteaux du Vendômois** is another VDQS producing a slender, bracing *vin gris*.

The exceptions to this picture of general inconsequentiality are found with the AOC of **Jasnières** and the larger neighbouring AOC of **Coteaux du Loir**. Jasnières is the *cru* of these slopes, and its AOC is for white wines based on the Chenin Blanc grape alone, grown on flint, clay, and limestone soils into which the tinkling Loir has carved its course. The geology, however, is less important here than topography and latitude: these are, for the late-ripening Chenin Blanc, almost Arctic conditions, and its cultivation is only possible thanks to south-facing slopes and tough-minded growers. Great

Jasnières is France's riposte to Germany's classical Saar Rieslings. These are, in other words, piano-wire wines out on the far edge of ripeness. Their apple and grapefruit flavours can have a shocking, jangling intensity; the juices seem drawn from a cold stone well rather than from vines on a sun-warm hillside. Yet with late harvesting even these wines can begin to hint at honey and apricot. Coteaux du Loir offers growers a little more flexibility: as well as Chenin-based whites, red and rosé wines can be made here from Pineau d'Aunis, Cabernet Franc, Gamay, Malbec, and Grolleau. Of these, the pale Pineau d'Aunis, with its perry tannins and redcurrant flavours, is most memorable.

The preamble to the giant sprawl of Touraine's vineyards comes with the small AOC of **Cheverny** and the tiny fifty-ha (124-acre) AOC of **Cour-Cheverny**. The latter is an exercise in viticultural rescue: it is for the near-extinct variety Romorantin alone, whose wines combine a rounded apple acidity with some honey and nougat. Cheverny itself, meanwhile, is for red, white, and rosé wines based on seven different varieties. Once again, full ripeness is hard to achieve.

This, the central portion of the Loire, is divided between two historical provinces of Celtic tribal origin: Anjou (its capital Angers) and Touraine (its capital Tours). The **Touraine** AOC is a catch-all covering over 5,000 ha (12,350 acres) of vineyard land and 150 communes sited above, below, and around Tours itself; varietal names can be used here. Three sectors of Touraine, too, have the right to add their own name to that of Touraine itself: **Touraine-Mesland**, **Touraine-Amboise**, and **Touraine-Azay le Rideau**. The latter two zones have some potential, yet none of the three has suceeded in developing much of an identity for itself other than locally, and Touraine remains known chiefly for its Sauvignon and Gamay – and for its sparkling wines.

The two great white wine vineyard areas of Touraine are **Vouvray** and **Montlouis**. Vouvray is sited on the right bank of the Loire, and Montlouis on the left, sandwiched between the Cher and the Loire itself. The rivers have, over the centuries, cut fine, sunny sites into the preponderantly chalky soils. *Tuffeau* or *tuf* are the terms used locally to describe the pale white-yellow rock, a distinctive soft limestone from the Turonian age (about 90 million years ago) in which calcium carbonate is mingled with iron and magnesium oxides. (This is nothing to do with the purer, travertine "tufa" or the volcanic "tuff" which are erroneous though often-used English-language equivalents.) The exposed slopes, frequently covered with clay and gravel topsoils, allow the vines to bask in sunlight, with Vouvray in particular having some superb vineyards overlooking the river. The flat, lazy lagoons, ponds, and braids of the river, separated by vast and lonely gravel banks discovered by summer's low waters, in turn reflect light back up into the vines. This is more or less the point at which the continental climate that typifies Sancerre and Pouilly-Fumé modulates towards the maritime, Atlantic climate of the Nantes region. In theory the result should be a gentle, sunny summer declining with slow grace towards a luminous, clear-skied autumn, perfect for bringing the late-ripening Chenin Blanc (locally called the Pineau) to perfection. Sometimes it is; botrytis develops; great sweet or semi-sweet wines can be made. At other times the region is hit by intemperate rains and early chills, and the harvests then tend to be used to make sparkling wines or dry still wines.

Touraine's other main claim to fame is its possession of three of the Loire Valley's four main red wine appellations. Geologically speaking, what happens here is a kind of mini-Médoc; during a past Ice Age, the Loire took a large bite out of the right bank of its present course, depositing terraced layers of gravels, clays, and sands as the waters tumbled about. Much of this right bank gravel now nourishes the Cabernet Franc vines of **Bourgueil** and **St-Nicolas-de-Bourgueil**, though these two red wine AOCs also include vineyards on the *tuffeau* of the higher slopes, too. Naturally, wines from the two soil environments are said to be different: gravel wines are fragrant and easy-drinking; chalk wines are denser and slower to mature. Blends of the two make the best wines of all. The division between Bourgueil and St-Nicolas is political rather than being justified in terms of terroir.

Chinon, by contrast, whose vineyards cover the south of the Loire at this point, as well as both banks of the tributary River Vienne, is different. The Cabernet Franc vines here grow in chalk and sand; there is just a little gravel along the banks of the Vienne. Much, of course, depends on the grower, but in general the Bourgueils are marginally deeper than Chinon, which tends at best to be fresh, vivid, and juicy. There is a little white wine production in Chinon (from Chenin Blanc) but none in Bourgueil.

The point at which the Vienne joins the Loire marks the boundary between Touraine and Anjou. North of the river, the catch-all and widely scattered AOC of **Anjou** itself commences, while on the south side of the Loire lies Saumur. Both of these appellations are for red and white wines, and Saumur has a sparkling Mousseux, too. At the heart of Saumur is the red wine only AOC of **Saumur-Champigny**, while a tiny thirty-ha (seventy-four acre) enclave within Champigny is classified AOC **Coteaux de Saumur**, an appellation for sweet and semi-sweet white wines from Chenin Blanc.

Large areas like these resist easy generalization. Anjou is particularly dangerous, since its widely scattered vineyards begin on a continuation of Bourgueil's gravel terraces, include some chalk sites, grow elsewhere on schist, slate, and volcanic spilite, and end deep in

▲ *The "Garden of France" is as famous for its tender vegetables (grown here at Langeais) as for its succulent wines.*

the granite loams of the Muscadet region. In an attempt to give these 3,000 ha (7,400 acres) of vineyard encompassing at least six terroirs a little more sense, sub-appellations have been created for **Anjou-Coteaux de la Loire** (a small fifty-ha/124-acre zone of dry and sweet Chenin Blanc on schist and limestone soils next to Savennières), **Anjou-Gamay** (a varietal option) and the red wine only AOCs of **Anjou-Villages** and **Anjou-Villages-Brissac**. If growers in the great terroirs of Savennières or Coteaux du Layon want to make red wine, remember, Anjou-Gamay and Anjou-Villages are the names they will use. The pink wine AOCs of **Cabernet d'Anjou** and **Rosé d'Anjou** also play an important commercial role.

As far as the adventure of the land is concerned, we have begun a new chapter. The biggest general change to the Loire's soils since Sancerre occurs at this point. Saumur is, geologically, a continuation of Touraine. As anyone who has ever visited this beautiful white town will know, limestone predominates; the finesse and pungency of the best Saumur wines are typical of France's chalk vineyards. Indeed Saumur's vineyards are some of the most difficult in France from the point of view of the vine disease chlorosis, caused by too much lime in the soil.

In Anjou, by contrast, an older geological song returns: the Celtic notes of the Massif Armoricain. We've left the basin, and the vines between here and the Atlantic dig their roots into some of France's oldest rocks. The differences are perhaps most clearly tasted in the red wines. The very best reds of the Anjou-Villages and Anjou-Villages-Brissac AOC, which grow in clay soils on top of weathered schist, have a tannic substance and a depth of meaty fruit quite unfamiliar in Chinon, Bourgueil, and Saumur-Champigny.

For contemporary international tastes, they are often more appealing than the nervous and chilly reds of Touraine.

The truth is, too, that many of the Loire's greatest dry and sweet white wines are found in Anjou, growing on schist. Chenin Blanc on limestone (as in Vouvray and Montlouis) can be superb; Chenin Blanc on schist can be even better. For dry white wines, there is no contest at all: AOC **Savennières** (together with its AOC *crus* **Savennières Roche-aux-Moines**, nineteen ha/forty-seven acres, and the single-property **Savennières Coulée-de-Serrant**, 6.85 ha/ 16.9 acres) is the only place in the Loire Valley where dry Chenin can genuinely rival Montrachet and Corton-Charlemagne. This 100-ha (247-acre) AOC offers perfectly positioned, south-facing slate, schist, and sandstone slopes on the Loire's north bank just south of Angers (Savennières has some plateau land, but the two *crus* are both on sunny, exposed slopes). The result is white wine of great aromatic allusiveness combined with extraordinary substance, chewiness, and mineral density – when it is carefully vinified from fully ripe grapes grown on low-yielding vines. It's an airy site – thus botrytis is uncommon. Unfortunately the AOC's indifferent reputation has been based on too many wines carelessly vinified from higher yields and unripe Chenin, which tends to give dry, bitter flavours that are as unpleasant as the fully ripe flavours are sublime.

Once again, we cross the river – this time to find the AOCs of **Coteaux de l'Aubance** and **Coteaux du Layon**. The 200-ha (494-acre) Coteaux de l'Aubance has the same soils as Savennières, but not quite the same good fortune with its slopes and aspects. Nonetheless good sweet Chenin-based whites of gentle, supple style can be made here, and this AOC occupies exactly the same zone as the potentially impressive Anjou-Villages-Brissac reds (see above).

Coteaux du Layon, by contrast, is a much larger AOC (over 1,500 ha/3,700 acres), and it contains within it the sweet wine *crus* of AOC **Bonnezeaux** (100 ha/247 acres) and **Quarts de Chaume** (thirty-three ha/81.5 acres). It's a confusing appellation, since the hamlet of Chaume itself can also attach its name to the general AOC (for **Coteaux du Layon-Chaume**) as can six different villages (giving you, potentially, **Coteaux du Layon-Beaulieu-sur-Layon**, **Coteaux du Layon-Faye d'Anjou**, **Coteaux du Layon-Rablay-sur-Layon**, **Coteaux du Layon-Rochefort-sur-Loire**, **Coteaux du Layon-St-Aubin-de-Luigné**, and **Coteaux du Layon-St-Lambert-du-Lattray**). There are proposals afoot to reform this chaos into a three-tier structure of Crus, Premier Crus, and Grand Crus.

This is a special place. The Layon is another tributary of the Loire, but an altogether smaller and more meandering one than bigger siblings like the Cher or the Vienne. It bumbles, idles, and prevaricates its way through a variety of soils and rocks, creating many hill slopes of varied orientation as it does so: schists, sandstones, and older limestones and marls are all found here. What's the result? A Chenin Blanc-based spectrum of often superb sipping whites of hugely varying sweetness. Some are based on regular botrytis (like Quarts de Chaume, a shallow-soiled, well-protected hillside cove); others more commonly on *passerillage* (like the long, schistous, high-sited Bonnezeaux or the hilltop Coteaux du Layon-Chaume). The best age superbly. Also worth noting are the red wines produced by the Coteaux du Layon's leading growers, many of them on the volcanic intrusions of a rock called spilite which are found in this area; they are sold as Anjou-Villages and Anjou-Gamay.

After Anjou, the smell of the sea reaches the air; the Loire wallows towards the Atlantic through an increasingly flat and fertile landscape. The bedrock here is granite, but the action of the river itself and its manifold past courses are no less important; deep loams and clays of granitic origin are much more common than glittering stone vineyards of pebbles and sands. The winds have dumped fine materials here over time; and the original granites, gneisses, micas, schists, and gabbros have been ground and weathered to a tilth, to which centuries of vegetation and cultivation have added much organic matter. Rich soils combined with a northerly maritime climate and two grape varieties (the Melon and the Gros Plant) of limited quality potential mean that the speciality of the Nantes region is simple white wine, not fine white wine. At its best, of course, these crisp, refreshing whites with their faint flavours of bread and lemon can be superb partners for oysters and fish. Thus, over a lunch table, the simple wine acquires grandeur, and the act of drinking it becomes an epiphany. You will never, though, find any great complexity of concentration of flavour in these wines; they are best drunk as soon as purchased, by the mouthful, without the magnifying glass of scrutiny. Muscadet is, if you like, white Beaujolais. Thus the river ends on a similar note to that with which it began.

There are four appellations with "Muscadet" in their formulae: **Muscadet** on its own, plus **Muscadet de Sèvre-et-Maine**, **Muscadet des Coteaux de la Loire**, and **Muscadet de Côtes de Grand-Lieu**.

▲ *Botrytis installs itself in three stages, all seen here: speckled grapes, full rot and "roasted" or confit berries.*

The biggest is Muscadet de Sèvre-et-Maine; indeed at over 10,000 ha (24,700 acres) this is one of the largest AOCs in France. Muscadet *tout court* covers almost 2,000 ha (4,940 acres), and the other two AOCs occupy about 300 ha each (740 acres). Any one of these AOCs may add the words *sur lie* to its appellation formula provided the wines have been bottled directly off the fine lees (one racking to remove the wine from its gross lees is permitted) before November 30th of the year after harvest in the cellar in which the wine was originally vinified. The purpose of this lees contact is to help fill out Muscadet's naturally spare, adolescent profile with a little yeasty flesh and fat, and to maximize freshness. It works, sometimes. Hard against the Atlantic, finally, come the coastal VDQS zones of **Gros Plant du Pays Nantais** and, further south, **Fiefs Vendéens**. The "big plant" of the former is not the Melon but the Folle Blanche, normally a distilling grape; it makes an even shriller wine than Muscadet. Fiefs Vendéens, by contrast, is an ambitous zone of both red, rosé, and white wine production using no fewer than eleven varieties; the style, nonetheless, cannot be anything but slender. **Coteaux d'Ancenis**, for the record, is a VDQS occupying the same area as Muscadet des Coteaux de la Loire and used for whites made from Chenin Blanc and Pinot Gris, as well as red and rosé wines mostly based on Gamay.

Loire Valley Flak

Name chaos

The appellation situation is unsatisfactory in most regions of France, and the Loire is no exception. As any cartographer will tell you, trying to map the appellations of the Loire with simple clarity is a task which rapidly skids towards failure; there are simply too many AOCs of wildly varying size here, and a frustratingly large number of them actually overlap with each other or share identical borders. It's hard to see a simplifying revision of all the Loire's AOCs as anything but a good idea, though none is planned (apart from some talk of hierarchizing the confusions of Coteaux du Layon). At the same time, Sancerre and Pouilly-Fumé, beyond question the most commercially successful of the Loire AOCs, both deserve to have their leading *lieux-dits* systematically classified into an official Premier Cru system. At present, names like Monts Damnés, Chêne Marchand, or Les Loges are used almost as brands, a practice so evidently untrustworthy that some of those owning plots in these fine parcels actually refuse to pass on this information. A carefully defined Sancerre Premier Cru Les Monts Damnés or Pouilly-Fumé Les Loges would be much more useful to consumers than the existence of Anjou-Coteaux de la Loire, Vins de Thouarsais, or Cour-Cheverny.

Picking holes in progress

I have mentioned that one of the great advances recorded by the New Loire is the readiness among the best growers to pick much later than they once did, which in the Loire's often difficult climate means picking by *tries*, in stages, leaving the healthiest fruit until last. There is, though, an even stronger tendency pushing the majority of growers in the opposite direction, which is the desire (and, to be fair, sometimes the necessity) to switch from hand harvesting to machine harvesting. Machines are robotic thugs which knock every grape off a vine; machines are incapable of understanding the concept of the *trie*. In Sancerre, I have been told that less than ten per cent of growers still pick their fruit by hand, yet this is no easier a climate than any other in the Loire in which to grow perfect grapes. Young Fabien Mollet, one of the few growers who does pick by hand, described the clouds of white fungus spores that accompanied the advance of the machines through neighbouring vineyards during the 2001 harvest, merrily gathering up rotten grapes: *"moi, j'ai trié à mort,"* he said. "Sorting to death" was the only way to produce great Sancerre in 2001. If a Premier Cru system is established in the Central vineyards, the requirement that all Premier Cru wines should be hand harvested will be essential.

Dry dreams

There is an assumption in "France's garden" that the greatest destiny any Chenin Blanc grape can aspire to is dissolution within a grand Moelleux. Why? Because such wines are rare; because they will endure a hundred years; because they can taste sublime when mature. True; all true. Yet great dry Chenin can be no less profound a wine – as Coulée de Serrant, the Trie Spéciale of Baumard, and Papin's Clos de Coulaine all prove. In drinking terms, too, a dry wine is ten times as useful as a sweet one. Internationally, the ancient "bush vine" Chenins of South Africa are beginning to create a climate of appreciation around the world for these welcome alternatives to Chardonnay. It is time for the Loire to make its dry Chenin Blancs with the same reverence as it makes Moelleux.

Sparkling temptation

There are some great sparkling wines produced under the Crémant de Loire and various Mousseux and Pétillant appellations of the Loire – but not many. These appellations are all too often used as dustbins for the region's inadequate, under-ripe fruit; unsurprisingly the finished wines taste raw, tart, and charmless. Until sparkling wine becomes a positive rather than a negative choice for most Loire producers, their chief appeal will remain the ill-starred one of low price.

Loire: People

Philippe Alliet ✪
37500 Cravant-les-Coteaux, Tel: 02 47 93 17 62, Fax: 02 47 93 17 62

Philippe Alliet is, like many of the New France's best winemakers, an inveterate traveller to other wine regions (including Italy's Piedmont), and if the Bordeaux influence can be said to have shaped any Chinon domain then it is probably this one: Alliet visits Bordeaux several times a year. It runs much more deeply than merely stocking a few second-hand barriques from Château Margaux in the cellar: Alliet's challenge is to achieve the kind of levels of density and ripeness that the greatest wines of Bordeaux have, at the same time as imbuing them with the distinctively pungent, sappy shock of inky freshness that the local terroirs deliver. By dint of reducing yields down to a maximum of 40 hl/ha, sorting the grapes after harvesting, working slowly and unhurriedly, and bottling without fining or filtration, he has begun to achieve this during the 1990s. Comparisons between the Coteau de Noiré, a new-barrique-aged wine grown on limestone, and the Vieilles Vignes Cuvée, grown on gravel and aged in one-year barriques, generally favour the latter, perhaps testifying to the worth of 50 years' root-searching; these are deep, resonant wines of uncommon ripeness for this latitude. Remember, though, that the vines on the Coteau de Noiré were only planted in 1996; in the long run, Alliet is convinced that they will surpass the gravels (which lie on flat land). The domain now occupies nearly 12 ha.

Thierry Amirault
37140 St-Nicolas de Bourgueil, Tel: 02 47 97 75 25, Fax: 02 47 97 97 97

The best wine from Thierry Amirault's 25-ha St-Nicolas-de-Bourgueil estate is the deep, mineral-charged Le Clos des Quarterons, based on old-vine (30 year) Cabernet Franc.

Yannick Amirault
37140 Bourgueil, Tel: 02 47 97 78 07, Fax: 02 47 97 94 78

Those who want to compare Loire Cabernet Franc grown on gravel with that grown on limestone should hunt down Yannick Amirault's two finest old-vines cuvées, both from St-Nicolas-de-Bourgueil: the juicy, succulent Les Graviers and the darker, more brooding Les Malgagnes. Other wines from this assiduously run 16-ha red-wine domain include an old-vines cuvée of Bourgueil, La Petite Cave, as well as the slightly silkier and more sumptuous Le Grand Clos and Les Quartiers. The young-vine cuvées La Coudraie (from Bourgueil) and La Source (from St-Nicolas) are both deliciously graceful and pretty.

Mark Angeli *see de la Sansonnière*

Aubuisières
37210 Vouvray, Tel: 02 47 52 61 55, Fax: 02 47 52 67 81

Vouvray-based Bernard Fouquet's 23-ha domain has been hit hard by recent difficult vintages, but his winemaking is as sure, as clean, and as limpid as ever, as wines like the crystalline 2001 Les Girardières Demi-Sec prove. There is also a lively Cuvée du Silex and an elegant barrel-fermented Vouvray, too, grown on limy clay soils: Le Marigny.

Bablut
49320 Brissac-Quincé, Tel: 02 41 91 22 59, Fax: 02 41 91 24 77

This large estate in Coteaux de l'Aubance run by Christophe Daviau is one of a growing number in the Loire to switch to biodynamic methods. Sweet wines are a particular speciality here (Daviau has studied and worked in both Bordeaux and Australia, so his perspectives are broad): the Vin Noble and the Grandpierre were both remarkable successes in the often difficult 1999 vintage.

Balland-Chapuis
45420 Bonny-sur-Loire, Tel: 02 38 31 55 12, Fax: 02 48 54 07 97

This 40-ha domain, part of the Guy Saget empire, is the biggest producer of the willowy wines of Coteaux du Giennois. Its best wines, though, are the salty Sancerre Vallon and the more structured and vinous Chêne Marchand. It also owns the 42-ha Sancerre Domaine de la Perrière, whose 1.5-ha flint-grown Mégalithe is splendidly earthy and mineral.

Baudry
37500 Cravant-les-Coteaux, Tel: 02 47 93 15 79, Fax: 02 47 98 44 44

Former lab technician Bernard Baudry now has an enviable 29-ha domain in Chinon (including a tiny parcel of Chenin for one of the rare white Chinons). In addition to the reliable "domain" wine, Bernard and his son Matthieu produce two top cuvées, once again playing on the terroir differences between deep gravels (for the Grézeaux, one of the AOC's most age-worthy gravel wines) and the oaked, limestone-grown La Croix Boissée. Les Granges is juicier and simpler. Clos Guillot is a new wine made from ungrafted vines.

Baumard ✪✪
49190 Rochefort-sur-Loire, Tel: 02 41 78 70 03, Fax: 02 41 78 83 03

This estate (the family has been here since 1634, though winemaking is only in its third generation; before that the forbears were nurserymen) is run by Florent and Isabelle Baumard, and has a mouth-watering spread of vineyards on both sides of the river, including 15 ha in Savennières and 25 ha in Rochefort (for Coteaux du Layon and Quarts de Chaume). The wines are exemplary. There are four different Savennières: lightest and soonest ready is Les Sables, while Clos St-Yves is deeper, though still fresh and balanced; the profound Clos du Papillon is richer and more fiery. In great years there is also a Trie Spéciale, which can be (as in 1997 and 1989) the apotheosis of Chenin Blanc, and unquestionably a wine to rival Corton-Charlemagne and Montrachet: dense, glycerous, and flavour-saturated, packed with honey, nuts, and flowers. The Coteaux du Layon Carte d'Or tends to be vivid and apricot-rich, while the Quarts de Chaume in ripe years is perfumed, sweet, and succulent, weighty with lime-blossom honey. In lighter years it can be more vivid, its plunging yet ripe acidity lending the honey a dancing quality. The domain also produces two red wines in Savennières: Anjou Rouge Clos de la Folie and La Giraudière. Florent Baumard is proud, too, of his small parcel of old Verdelho vines used for the sweet table wine cuvée Vert de l'Or – though Chenin Blanc has nothing to fear from this Madeiran interloper.

Bellivière
72340 Lhomme, Tel: 02 43 44 59 97, Fax: 02 43 79 18 33

Nine hectares spread over no fewer than six communes in Jasnières and Coteaux du Loir are cultivated with extreme care by thoughtful, quiet Eric Nicolas. Vine densities have been increased to 9,300 plants per ha, and yields reduced to around 20 hl/ha; indeed a small experimental parcel has been planted "en foule" (higgledy-piggledy, as in times past) at a density equivalent to 40,000 vines per hectare. The aim is to leave one bunch per vine on this propitious site and wait for noble rot to develop, autumn weather permitting. All the Bellivière wines are given descriptive and sometimes gnomic names: L'Effraie is the young vines cuvée of Coteaux du Loir, and Vieilles Vignes Eparses that based on older vines (50 to 70 years old); occasionally a Cuvée Philosophale is made from nobly rotten grapes when conditions permit. Les Rosiers is the "basic" blend of Jasnières, with Discours de Tuf and Elixir de Tuf

---

being made from botrytized grapes. Nicolas is also a great believer in the red variety Pineau d'Aunis; his red wine is called Le Rouge-Gorge (the robin). The white Jasnières and Coteaux du Loir have the shocking, invigorating characteristics of their appellations; the Nicolas touch is palpable in their cleanness, purity, and length.

Jacky Blot *see* La Taille aux Loups

Guy Bossard *see* Domaine de l'Ecu

Henri Bourgeois ✪
18300 Sancerre, Tel: 02 48 78 53 20, Fax: 02 48 78 53 20

Large but high-quality Sancerre-based négociant whose own 65-ha domain provides around half the company's needs. It's run with deafening energy by the unforgettable Jean-Marie Bourgeois, one of whose favourite subjects is "French hypocrisy" (and whose latest venture, perhaps tellingly, is a vineyard in New Zealand's Marlborough region). Bourgeois has taken tentative steps towards a more radical non-interventionist approach with his Sancerre Jadis (an unfiltered, floral wine made from Sauvignon Rose planted on the Côte de Chavignol) and the Sancerre d'Antan (an old-vines, flint-planted *cuvée* which combines exotic fruits like pineapple and passion fruit with rich, smoky depths). Etienne Henri is the conventionally vinified and handled top *cuvée*, produced from old vines on flint in the best years only. Le MD de Bourgeois (from Monts Damnés) and La Bourgeoise are both excellent "standard" *cuvées*.

Bouvet-Ladubay
49400 Saumur, Tel: 02 41 83 83 83, Fax: 02 41 50 24 32

The Loire Valley is the most important sparkling wine region in France after Champagne, and the two leading producers in the region – Bouvet-Ladubay and Langlois-Château – are both owned by Champagne houses (Taittinger and Bollinger respectively). Is this a good thing? It certainly means that the understanding of how great sparkling wine is created is there; the suspicion must be, though, that the final supreme effort of will needed to make Loire Valley sparkling wine truly rival or even eclipse Champagne is missing. Perhaps I'm being unfair: Bouvet is still run with great vigour by the latest generation of its custodial family, Patrick Monmousseau, who retains a quarter of the shares. Bouvet is based in Saumur; its two finest sparkling wines are the vintage Saphir, a wine of real depth and structure though a slightly cloying finish; and the "prestige" *cuvée* Trésor, a Chenin-Chardonnay blend which is in part barrel-fermented and aged, and which ages for three years before release. This is the Loire Valley's most allusive, complex, and multi-layered sparkling wine, though it, too, can have a bothersome *dosage*. There is also a Trésor Rosé made from Cabernet Franc, and a demi-sec christened Grand Vin de Dessert. Bouvet-Ladubay also produces some exciting still wines on a micro-négociant or "garage" basis: the Extrême *cuvées* of Anjou Cabernet Franc and Cabernet Sauvignon, and the Les Nonpareils versions of varietal Merlot and Cot (sold as Vin de Pays du Jardin de la France). If you want to taste Loire red wines taken out towards the climatic limits of depth, extract, and power, try these.

Brédif *see* de Ladoucette

Champalou
37210 Vouvray, Tel: 02 47 52 64 49, Fax: 02 47 52 67 99

Didier and Catherine Champalou's 20-ha estate produces model Vouvray: vivid, clean, sappy wines in which a range of orchard fruits dangle and tinkle. The Cuvée des Fondraux is based on fruit grown on clay-flint soils aged in old casks; it often seems fresher and lighter than its residual sugar analysis would suggest.

Chéreau Carré
44690 St-Fiacre-sur-Maine, Tel: 02 40 54 81 15, Fax: 02 40 54 81 70

Leading Muscadet négociant working, for the best wines, with a variety of different named domains from its own 120-ha estate. Look out for those of the Château du Coing de St-Fiacre (there is even an unusually successful Cuvée Fûts de Chêne here) and the Grande Cuvée St-Hilaire.

Clos de Coulaine *see* Pierre Bise

Clos de la Coulée de Serrant *see* Joly

Closel
49170 Savennières, Tel: 02 41 72 81 00, Fax: 02 41 72 86 00

This 16-ha domain owned by the de Jessey family has been typical of Savennières: the quality of the terroir has provided occasionally brilliant bottles as if in reminder of how much better the standard could be here with a more painstaking approach. Since 1998, there are signs that this is happening: the barrel-fermented Clos du Papillon has become denser and more articulate, while Les Coulées and Les Vaults are well-balanced and cleanly defined.

Clos Naudin ✪✪
37210 Vouvray, Tel: 02 47 52 71 46, Fax: 02 47 52 73 81

This 12-ha Vouvray estate is immaculately run by Philippe Foreau, who brings a cook's questing intuition to his work in the vineyard and the cellar. Foreau is also a great philosopher and evangelist for Chenin Blanc, and when one tastes wines like the Clos Naudin Demi-Sec, Moelleux Réserve, or the occasional Goutte d'Or super-selections one can believe, with their creator, that this is one of the world's very greatest white grape varieties. All age superbly, for as long as any one human life is ever likely to require; they are always ripe (including the Secs and the fine sparkling wines), clean, graceful, and acrobatically balanced, packed with the enchanting orchard hints and allusions so typical of this fecund and sunny little riverbank world. Foreau's main soil type is a flint-studded clay called *perruches*; yields are kept down to 30 hl/ha or so; there is no chaptalization or use of added yeast, and fermentation is in large old wood for the sweeter wines and steel for the dry and sparkling wines. A reference domain, in sum.

Clos Rougeard ✪
49400 Chacé, Tel: 02 41 52 92 65, Fax: 02 41 52 98 34

The Foucault family's pace-setting 10-ha Saumur-Champigny domain produces three red *cuvées* and one white (this last, from centenarian vines, in minuscule quantities only). The reds include the richly fruited Poyeux and the fine-grained Le Bourg. All are produced with very low yields, wild yeasts, long and soft macerations, oak-ageing (with a proportion of new oak), and are bottled without filtration; they age as well as any.

Cotat ✪
18300 Sancerre, Tel: 02 48 54 04 22, Fax: 02 48 78 01 41

Small 9-ha domain producing Sancerre Chavignol La Grande Côte and Sancerre Les Monts Damnés by fastidiously non-interventionist methods which, because of the presence of residual sugars after particularly sunny years, have cost the Cotats the appellation on occasion. These are the Sancerres to get hold of if you wish to see what age can bring; indeed in youth their quiet unshowiness can often leave drinkers nonplussed.

Couly-Dutheil
37500 Chinon, Tel: 02 47 97 20 20, Fax: 02 47 97 20 25

Large 65-ha Chinon producer whose basic *cuvées* are light and disappointing. The Clos de l'Echo, however, and its new-oak counterpart Crescendo, offer a fine trumpet blast of fresh, meaty fruit.

Cray
37400 Lussault-sur-Loire, Tel: 02 47 57 17 74, Fax: 02 47 57 11 97

This is the largest estate in Montlouis, and since September 1993 the vines have been leased by owner Michel Antier to Briton Paul Boutinot. "It could be a jewel," says Boutinot. "The soil is superb. I think it's easily the best in Montlouis, and one of the best in the Loire." It isn't yet, because the vineyard needs improving, and the 1998, 1999, 2000, and 2001 vintages have all been largely declassified by Boutinot (a fanatical and thoughtful taster) and his winemaker Pierre Laroche (whom he hired on the basis of his tasting ability). The energetic, complex, and vinous 1997 Clos du Cray Montlouis Signature hints at what's to come.

Crochet

18300 Bué, Tel: 02 48 54 08 10, Fax: 02 48 54 27 66

Lucien Crochet and his son Gilles have a well-sited 35-ha Sancerre estate of their own, and also produce a range of wines on a négociant basis. The domain wines are, unsurprisingly, the best: clean, frank, and fresh. The domain includes a 5-ha parcel in the prized Bué *cru* of Chêne Marchand, and this serves as the basis for the lingering, sappy Le Chêne *cuvée*, the best in the range. Reds have improved recently, especially the subtle and graceful La Croix du Roy.

Didier Dagueneau ✪✪

58150 St-Andelain, Tel: 03 86 39 15 62, Fax: 03 86 39 07 61

There are less than 12 ha at this celebrated Pouilly-Fumé domain, and they get cut up six ways (sometimes more). En Chailloux is, so to speak, the basic and largest volume *cuvée*, and is typical of Dagueneau's pure, limpid yet generous style; the slightly crunchier, limier Buisson Renard comes from a parcel called Buisson Menard, I believe, but the wine was renamed once it had been misnamed by the celebrated French critic Michel Bettane. Pur Sang and Silex are both barrel-fermented, from old-vine stock; the former is almost creamy, the latter more mineral, though the siliceous notes are at all times nuanced rather than overt here. You are in a green glade, not a grey stonefield, with Dagueneau, even if the ground underfoot is rock hard. Finally (though anecdotally, since quantities are so small) comes Astéroïde, made from ungrafted vines, and the Clos du Calvaire. All the wines merit the experiment of age. Dagueneau's methods include massive plant densities (up to 14,000 per ha), low yields and, naturally, hand-harvesting by *tries*.

Deletang et Fils

37270 St-Martin-le-Beau, Tel: 02 47 50 67 25, Fax: 02 47 50 26 46

Well-run 20-ha domain specializing in late harvest wines (there were six different versions in 1997) in Montlouis. The vineyards cover 20 ha at present. Les Petits Boulay (grown on limestone with a greater admixture of clay than usual, giving intensely fruited wines) and Les Batisses (limestone with flint, giving smokier flavours) make an instructive comparison. These are Montlouis wines of great purity and classicism, always clean, with fine ageing potential – when they acquire honey and marzipan notes.

Pierre-Jacques Druet

37140 Benais, Tel: 02 47 97 37 34, Fax: 02 47 97 46 40

Low yields and an unusual vinification system (the must is briefly heated to 62°C to avoid, Druet says, the extraction of clumsy tannins) make the Bourgueils produced at this 22-ha domain some of the most delicious and toothsome in the AOC. Blackberry fruit notes in the Grand Mont reveal the warmth of this fine site, and the unfiltered Vaumoreau (produced from low-yielding, 90-year-old vines) hints at chocolate behind the svelte fruit.

L'Ecu ✪

44430 Le Landereau, Tel: 02 40 06 40 91, Fax: 02 40 06 46 79

Guy Bossard's 20-ha domain has been organically run since 1975, and biodynamic since 1986. The skilled Bossard is at present taking Muscadet as far as it can go (given a grape variety as shyly articulate as the Melon de Bourgogne) towards the expression of terroir in his three top *cuvées*: Expression de Gneiss (from 4 ha), Expression d'Orthogneiss (from 2 ha), and Expression de Granit (from 3-ha). In 1999, the Gneiss was the most scented (moist stones and spring flowers) with vivid, full, pebble-hard mineral flavours; the Orthogneiss was plumper and more fully fruity; while the Granit was slender, long, and lemony, with a mineral-salt finish. The Cuvée Guy Bossard, also grown on granite, has a slightly fuller, smokier style, and Bossard's sparkling wine is a revelation, too, made from a fascinating blend of Melon with Folle Blanche, Chardonnay, and Cabernet.

Fesles *see* Germain

Foreau *see* Clos Naudin

Gaudrelle

37210 Vouvray, Tel: 02 47 52 67 50, Fax: 02 47 52 67 98

Alexandre Monmousseau's 15-ha Vouvray domain produces wines of delicious classicism, particularly the teasingly off-dry Sec-Tendre château wine. When vintages allow, this is a good source of sweeter wines, and recently Monmousseau has been putting great efforts into producing his Sec wines, with extensive fruit sorting to eliminate all traces of rot and unripeness, followed by barrique-fermentation.

Bernard Germain

49380 Thouaré, Tel: 02 41 68 94 00, Fax: 02 41 68 94 01

This ambitious and dynamic Bordelais, in charge of the group that owns Yon-Figeac among 11 other châteaux, acquired the Loire châteaux Guimonière, Roulerie, Varennes, and Fesles from the retired *pâtissier* Gaston Le Nôtre in 1996. The aim was to produce great sweet wines by the "*méthode Germain*" (fastidious vineyard work plus careful use of new oak), though vintages since 1996 haven't been helpful. Germain and his team (which includes winemaker Gilles Bigot, who already worked for Le Nôtre) have nonetheless succeeded in producing some excellent wines from each property, especially the Les Aunis parcel at La Roulerie (for sweet butter-and-marzipan wines) and the unctuous Bonnezeaux from Fesles. The wines that the "*méthode Germain*" produces by renting 1 ha from Savennières proprietor Pierre Soulez at Chamboureau are also markedly better than Soulez's own versions.

Thierry Germain *see* Roches Neuves

Gigou

72340 La Chatre-sur-Loire, Tel: 02 43 44 48 72, Fax: 02 43 44 42 15

The greying, pony-tailed Jasnières grower Joël Gigou has recently been joined by his 22-year-old son Ludovic. "He's self-taught, just like I was. I'm wayward (*marginale*) but he will be even more so." Look out Jasnières. Gigou's distinction was not only to produce classic, stony, austere dry Jasnières and Coteaux du Layon by traditional methods at a time when most of the handful of producers couldn't be bothered, but he's also pioneered wines based on botrytized grapes in this very cool, northerly climate. Don't expect these to have anything like the sweetness of a Coteaux du Layon or a Vouvray Moelleux: they are, instead, hauntingly off-dry, and sipping them is as invigorating as eating the first apples of summer's end.

La Guimonière *see* Germain

Huët ✪✪

37210 Vouvray, Tel: 02 47 52 78 87, Fax: 02 41 47 66 74

This historic Vouvray domain has been run for over a decade along biodynamic lines by the son-in-law of war hero Gaston Huët, Noël Pinguet. The three vineyard sites are Clos de Bourg, Haut Lieu, and Le Mont, and as well as producing Sec, Demi-Sec, and Moelleux versions, there are also distinctions among the latter according to *trie*. The Demi-Sec and Moelleux wines are exemplary and often brilliant, with fine acid balances and classic flavours of buttered walnuts and autumn leaves. Some of the Sec wines, by contrast, can provide difficult drinking for all but the most committed Chenin Blanc aficionados. In 2000, Pinguet bought the Domaine de Vodanis in Vouvray, a 5-ha estate being converted to biodynamics at present. Anyone who wants to hear the pragmatic, down-to-earth arguments for biodynamics after a visit to the inspirational but sometimes anti-gravitational Nicolas Joly should make their way to this domain. "We began trials," Pinguet told me, "and the results were satisfactory, so we carried on. What counts is the result. We don't pollute the environment; we pick healthy grapes and the wine is good. Why should we deprive ourselves of that just because we don't understand it in its entirety?"

Hureau

49400 Dampierre-sur-Loire, Tel: 03 41 67 60 40, Fax: 03 41 50 43 35

Philippe Vatan's Grande Cuvée and Cuvée Lisigathe show a different route forward for Saumur-Champigny than that carved out, for example, by the ambitiously extracted wines of Thierry Germain. The Hureau wines are lush, spicy, ripe, and full – but soft-textured.

Charles Joguet
37220 Sazilly, Tel: 02 47 58 55 53, Fax: 02 47 58 52 22
Celebrated though often rather light wines from this important 38-ha domain in Chinon, run by Alain Delaunay and his cellarmaster Michel Pinard. The Clos du Chêne Vert (on limestone soils) and the Clos de la Dioterie (on sand and gravel over limestone) are by some way the two most serious *cuvées*, exhibiting true roastiness and depth in good vintages.

Joly ✿✿✿
49170 Savennières, Tel: 02 41 72 22 32, Fax: 02 41 72 28 68
This superb 13-ha estate was purchased by the Joly family in the 1960s. In 1977, Nicolas Joly quit his expatriate banking job with Morgan Guaranty and returned to look after the family vineyards. There are three parcels of vines. The largest parcel, the Clos de la Coulée de Serrant, is one of only two non-Burgundian AOCs in France that are in single ownership (the other is Château Grillet in the Rhône Valley). The vineyard, which occupies a superbly sited south-facing hillside of slate and schist above the River Loire, was planted by Cistercian monks as long ago as 1130. Adjacent to the Coulée de Serrant (whose name actually refers to the moist depression between the two hillsides) is the larger Roche aux Moines vineyard, a *cru* of Savennières rather than an AOC in its own right, which Joly shares with other growers (he has 3 ha). Finally, he also has 3 ha of "ordinary" Savennières.

When he took over in 1977, Joly began as a conventional wine-grower, but was dissatisfied with the results. "The colour of the soil had begun to change, there weren't any insects left in the vine parcels, there were no more shadowy partridges flitting about the thickets... I had the impression that I was helping to destroy a harmonious universe." In 1979, he found a second-hand copy of Rudolf Steiner's agriculture lectures in a bookshop in Paris; the chance discovery launched him on a long journey. Not only did he convert his estate from conventional to biodynamic cultivation between 1980 to 1984, but he has subsequently become the evangelist-in-chief for this movement among French wine-growers. He writes and argues copiously and often pugnaciously for biodynamics, and pays exhortatory visits to those on the verge of conversion.

The '"Joly problem", if one might so phrase it, is that the biodynamic project is for him a moral imperative, and it is thus one that eclipses all other considerations. He much prefers talking about biodynamics to talking about winemaking; he would rather show visitors his herds of rare local cows (which he keeps for their manure alone) than conduct a vertical tasting. Some of his ideas (including a deep conviction of the ill effects of household electrical pollution, and the notion that barrels are the ideal recipients for new wine since their shape duplicates that of an egg, which is the source of life) encourage the view that he is a crank. When he announces that "sulphur is a form of light," he is liable to leave even open-minded listeners nonplussed. His winemaking techniques, too, have come in for much criticism, though many of them are now becoming standard practice among France's new generation of radical non-interventionists. He leaves the must on its lees; relies solely on wild yeasts for fermentation, and never cold-stabilizes or fines his wines, giving them only a very light filtration. He ferments and ages his wines in old wood alone, using 600-litre casks; any residual sugar left at the end of fermentation is accepted. All of this is uncontroversial; Olivier Zind-Humbrecht MW does exactly the same. Altogether more startling, however, is Joly's assertion that he racks his wines as often as possible. "Wines produced by biodynamic agriculture are more likely to suffer from reduction than from oxidation. Indeed wines made from healthy grapes are more likely to be improved by oxidation than to suffer from it." Joly urges drinkers to decant his wines a full 24 hours before serving them and to serve them at a cool room temperature, and in any case never below 12°C. He claims they will improve in half-empty bottles over a three-day period.

How good are his wines? My own view, based on a series of tastings and purchases, is that something happened in the mid-1990s to improve Joly's winemaking enormously; perhaps this was the production of a fine though only gently sweet Moelleux in 1995 itself. Vintages of Coulée de Serrant since the mid-1990s are far riper and more allusive than the sometimes disappointing, under-ripe, hit-and-miss wines which preceded them (though in good vintages like 1990, the vineyard could shine through in what is a magisterial wine of prodigious aromatic power). The 1997, 1998, and 1999 vintages of Coulée de Serrant are all superb – and very different from one another, too. The 1999, for example, despite being in earliest infancy smells of baked almond pastry, while on the palate it shows the astonishing chewy depth and inner fire that Chenin Blanc only ever seems to acquire in Savennières, together with the palpable tannin that is another feature of this white AOC when it is vinified from truly ripe fruit. The 1998 is scented with honey and nougat, and is intensely mineral, not so much characterized by fruits as by walnuts and walnut shells; it is rich yet vivid with surging acidity too, giving it a powerful and hypnotic balance. Coulée de Serrant from the superb 1997 vintage smells of nuts and pollen and warm hay; in the mouth it is voluptuous, the minerals in this vintage acquiring a melting quality, interleaved with warm ferns. Joly's other wines are Becherelle and the Cuvée du Château from Savennières itself, as well as the Clos de la Bergerie from Roche aux Moines. None has the grandeur or ability to endure in time which Coulée de Serrant has, but each lights intriguing new facets of this, one of France's most provoking yet rewarding AOCs.

de Ladoucette
58150 Pouilly-sur-Loire, Tel: 03 86 39 18 33, Fax: 03 86 39 18 33
This, at some 65 ha, is the largest property in Pouilly-Fumé, and it is also the most spectacular; the many-turreted château building itself is enough to make AXA's Pichon-Longueville look like a modest country cottage. Owner Baron Patrick de Ladoucette also buys in grapes and must, and produces Sancerre under the Comte Lafon label (yes, there is a distant family link with Burgundy) and owns the reliable Marc Brédif in Vouvray. The wines (and particularly the top-of-the-range Baron de L) are ambitious, structured, serious, produced with more than a glance towards Burgundian practices – which in a way (and paradoxically) makes them more Graves-like than most Sauvignon Blancs hereabouts. Whether they also succeed in capturing the mouth-watering pungency of this grape variety and this place on earth seems to me less certain.

Lafon *see* de Ladoucette

Langlois-Château
49400 Ste-Hilaire-Ste-Florent, Tel: 02 41 40 21 40, Fax: 02 41 40 21 49
Together with Bouvet-Ladubay, the Bollinger-owned Langlois-Château is one of the better Loire sparkling wine producers; the vintage Crémant de Loire is given plenty of age before being released on to the market, and replaces the taut neutrality, so characteristic of most wines of this appellation, with some yeasty complexities and sinewy fruit.

J-YA Lebreton
49320 St-Jean-des-Mauvrets, Tel: 02 41 91 92 07, Fax: 02 41 54 62 63
This large 52-ha domain is one of the best producers of red Anjou-Villages, often a difficult and shocking wine but here one of substance and depth. Look out for the pure Cabernet Sauvignon La Croix du Mission.

V Lebreton *see* Domaine de Montgilet

Henri Marionnet
41230 Soings, Tel: 02 54 98 70 73, Fax: 02 54 98 75 66
This large (60-ha) Touraine domain is unusual in that it is mostly planted with red varieties; Marionnet is the region's great Gamay and carbonic maceration expert. With his Premier Vendange (made with no sulphur and no chaptalization) and Vinifera (ungrafted Gamay) *cuvées*, he is the only grower to begin to approach Claude Papin's achievements with Gamay grown on spilite. These are both sweet-fruited wines of wonderfully crisp definition. Another curiosity here is the Provignage, an odd but haunting, nougat-like wine made from ancient (pre-phylloxera) Romorantin, sold as a Vin de Pays.

Alphonse Mellot ✪
18300 Sancerre, Tel: 02 48 54 07 41, Fax: 02 48 54 07 62

With their precise and elegant flavours, their avant-garde labels and their heavy bottles, Alphonse Mellot's wines are among the most showy in Sancerre. This domain is one of the few in the AOC still to pick by hand alone, and the two top *cuvées*, the Génération XIX and the Edmond, are both based on fruit from vines of 60 years or more, made with fastidious attention to detail.

Mollet-Maudry
18300 St-Satur, Tel: 02 48 54 02 26, Fax: 02 48 54 02 26

This 17-ha domain has vineyards in both Sancerre and Pouilly-Fumé, and is run by Jean-Paul Mollet and his fiercely ambitious son Florian. "I want to be the best. Being average doesn't interest me," Florian told me, echoing Didier Dagueneau. Low yields and hand harvesting result in a range of good though not yet great wines, especially the unfiltered l'Antique *cuvées* in both AOCs.

de Montgilet
49610 Juigné-sur-Loire, Tel: 02 41 91 90 48, Fax: 02 41 54 64 25

This 37-ha domain run by Victor and Vincent Lebreton is the source of some of the richest and most unctuous of all Coteaux de l'Aubance whites (Les Trois Schistes is, as the name suggest, the *cuvée* most firmly ballasted with mineral depths, though Les Tertereaux is more sweetly ambitious). The two Cabernets come darkly and sometimes violently together in the red Anjou-Villages from Montgilet, and there is also a fine-value dry white Anjou, too.

Eric Nicolas *see* Bellivière

Ogereau
49750 St-Lambert-du-Lattay, Tel: 02 41 78 30 53, Fax: 02 41 78 43 55

Few Loire domains can manage the consistency of Vincent Ogereau's 24 ha of Anjou-Villages and Coteaux du Layon-St-Lambert. The pure Cabernet Sauvignon Anjou-Villages Côte de la Houssaye is one of the reference reds of the New Anjou, and Ogereau's basic Anjou-Villages is not far behind.

Claude Papin *see* Pierre Bise

Papin-Chevalier *see* Pierre Bise

Henry Pellé
18220 Morogues, Tel: 02 48 64 42 48, Fax: 02 48 64 36 88

The wines at this, Menetou-Salon's leading estate, are now made by Henry Pellé's daughter-in-law in tandem with cellarmaster Julien Zernott. Pure and clean, thanks to fastidious viticulture and stainless steel winemaking, all of the range offers good value, with the southeast-facing Clos des Blanchais particularly crisp and fragrant.

La Perrière *see* Balland-Chapuis

La Perruche *see* La Varière

Pierre Bise ✪✪✪
49750 Beaulieu-sur-Layon, Tel: 02 41 78 31 44, Fax: 02 41 78 41 24

If the Loire Valley can offer a theoretician and polemicist of terroir to match Alsace's Jean-Michel Deiss, then it has to be Claude Papin. The two, indeed, are friends. Once Papin begins to explain to you his search for "aromatic polyphony", or how important "the personality of a wine is linked to the slowness of the evolution of its polyphenols", then you know you are dealing with a mind of considerable sophistication. This, of course, would be worth nothing if his wines were disappointing, but the fact is that Papin has produced some of the greatest modern-day Chenin Blanc and Gamay not just in the Loire, but in France.

"The Chenin," says Papin, "is made by botrytization. If there isn't any, it always makes hard wine. Even my dry wines are made with around 50% botrytization. This translates in the wine as honeyed notes." I remember tasting Papin's Savennières Clos de Coulaine directly after trying a Joël Gigou Jasnières, and the contrast was so overwhelming that it was hard to believe the two wines were made from the same grape in the same

region. The Savennières was herb-scented (even Chartreuse-like) with rich substance and depth, tasting of smoke and dissolved minerals, a total contrast to the quicksilver freshness of Gigou's wine. Papin's remarks, one might note, also go some way to explaining why most sparkling Loire wine (made from barely ripe Chenin) makes such ungrateful drinking. Another of Papin's beliefs about Chenin is that "it was once a red grape" – and he is one of the French avant-garde actively macerating white grape skins to the extent of extracting tannins from them which, he says, helps give the wines longevity. Tasting his white Anjou Haut de la Garde and finding it has palpable tannic depth supporting its clean, honeyed wealth of flavour is surprising at first – but it works. Papin's Coteaux du Layon wines from Rochefort (sandstone) and Beaulieu (schist) offer an instructive contrast, the Rochefort Les Rayelles all lime-flower fragrance and dancing acidity, the Beaulieu L'Anclaie rather deeper and more fiery. There is also a Beaulieu les Rouannières grown on volcanic spilite (for which the local name is *pierre bise*) which seems to add delicious earthy marzipan dimensions, and provide both unctuous glycerol and ample, ripe acidity. There are further fascinating contrasts between the chiefly *passerillé* Coteaux du Layon Chaume, apparently a wine of massive sweetness, and the Quarts de Chaume, an even richer wine yet whose botrytized component often makes it tastes less sweet. Instead it is packed with fresh, dense peach fruits and apricot fruits which in youth mask the mineral notes that will emerge with time.

Unusually among Loire growers, Papin is as skilled with his red wines as he is with his whites. He makes a red wine from sandy soils in his Savennières vineyards, sold as Anjou-Villages, though it doesn't have the plunging grandeur of the white wine; indeed it is the most disappointing wine in this otherwise superb range. By contrast the red Anjou-Villages (made from the two Cabernets grown on schist) and Anjou Gamay he produces from his *pierre bise* vineyards are magnificently meaty, chewy wines of much greater substance than most Chinons or even Bourgueils. Indeed his 1996 Gamay "sur spilite", made from late-harvest fruit ("I picked when the skins began to shrivel") at a low yield of 35 hl/ha, was the most astonishing Gamay I have ever tasted: improbably dark, prune scented, its profound depth and extract balanced by challenging acidity. Despite having been filtered, the wine throws a glorious sediment. Even in the difficult 2000 vintage, this implausibly majestic wine was almost as good. Papin is surely the greatest winemaker in "France's garden", and the good news is that he and his sons René and Christophe now have 54 ha to work with.

Vincent Pinard ✪
18300 Bué, Tel: 02 48 54 33 89, Fax: 02 48 54 13 96

One of the most skilled of present-day Sancerre producers, Vincent Pinard's two finest *cuvées* are the aptly named Nuance, with its passion fruit notes, and the coolly smoky old-vine Harmonie, packed with dense and succulent fruit.

de la Ragotière
44330 Vallet, Tel: 02 40 33 60 56, Fax: 02 40 33 61 89

This historic and expansive (68-ha) Muscadet property has taken on a recent turn of speed in the hands of the Couillaud brothers, who have given the wines an appealingly rich, firm style. The Clos Petit Château is a step up in intensity from the "basic" *cuvée*, but best by some measure is the Premier Cru Vieilles Vignes *cuvée*, full of pungent purity. Varietal Vins de Pays are also produced under the Auguste Couillaud label, including an over-hopeful Viognier which proves that granite soils alone can't make up for a shy sun. Château La Morinière is in the same ownership.

Renou
49380 Thouarcé, Tel: 02 41 54 11 33, Fax: 02 41 54 11 34

The domain of the current president of France's wine-growing community consists of just 8-ha of Bonnezeaux, though this will rise by 2 ha when the domain is fully planted. René Renou is one of those behind the renaissance of the *tri* as a fundamental viticultural technique in the Loire Valley; his own top *cuvée* is the elegant, creamy, and sumptuous Cuvée Zenith.

Richou
49610 Mozé-sur-Louet, Tel: 02 41 78 72 13, Fax: 02 41 78 76 05

Highly consistent 38-ha family domain based in Coteaux de l'Aubance: Les Trois Demoiselles is almost always one of the appellation's best wines. Look out, too, for Anjou Blanc of unusually rich structure and depth from this property as well as juicy Gamay and darkly brisk Anjou-Villages.

Château de la Roche aux Moines *see* Joly

Roches Neuves
49200 Varrains, Tel: 03 41 52 94 02, Fax: 03 41 52 49 30

Thierry Germain, the son of Bernard Germain, preceded his father to the Loire from Bordeaux, and with his Terres Chaudes and La Marginale *cuvées* has pushed the boundaries of red winemaking and oak use in Saumur to the limit. These are ambitious and exciting wines of explosive flavour.

La Roulerie *see* Germain

Saint-Just
49260 St-Just-sur-Dive, Tel: 02 41 51 62 01, Fax: 02 41 67 94 51

The top *cuvées* from Yves Lambert's 40-ha Saumur domain (La Coulée de St-Cyr, Les Terres Rouges, and Montée des Roches) are all among the ripest and fullest wines of this heterogenous AOC.

Jacques Sallé *see* Silice de Quincy

de la Sansonnière ✪✪
49380 Thouracé, Tel: 02 41 54 80 80, Fax: 02 41 54 80 80

Mark Angeli, his cap perpetually perched on his head, is one of the most committed of the Loire's keen team of biodynamicists; indeed for Angeli biodynamics is just part of an ongoing and occasionally apocalyptic struggle against the idiot distractions, deviations, and "zombifications" of the modern world. There are just 8 ha here, but the standard is impeccable: Anjou La Lune is a dry wine of magnificent internal architecture of flavour; Anjou Les Fouchardes is a more glycerous and tangy wine of soft balance; while the sweet Bonnezeaux Coteau du Houet has arresting purity and focus, packed with the scents of mint, limeflower, and verbena. There is a wonderfully grown-up Rosé d'Anjou, too: yellow-orange and decadently sippable. It's Angeli's intention only to produce sweet wines in future in great vintages of plentiful botrytis – despite the fact that it was to make sweet wines that this Provençal stonemason first set his chisel to one side in Anjou.

Sauvion
44330 Vallet, Tel: 02 40 36 22 55, Fax: 02 40 36 34 62

Muscadet négociant whose "Haute Culture" Cardinale Richard and "Tradition" Baron du Cléray *cuvées* both manage more multidimensionality than most of their peers.

Silice de Quincy ✪
18120 Quincy, Tel: 02 54 04 04 48

Former journalist Jacques Sallé's 7-ha biodynamic domain is one of the outstanding sources of Quincy: a fine, mouthfilling expression of Quincy's terroir and with memorable vintage differentiation, too. Moss, wells, and stones are typical notes, with vivid lime fruit; in warmer years (like 1997) the wine acquires touches of honey, and more glycerous textures. Silicette is the second wine. Sallé says he was shocked when he first began as a wine-grower to discover how many chemical products were routinely used in conventionally farmed vineyards, and it was this (as well as a chance meeting with Mark Angeli and Nicolas Joly) which pushed him towards biodynamics. It has, he says, been hard – because "biodynamics costs about five times the price of normal viticulture" and it is difficult in lesser-known areas like Quincy to obtain the kind of prices that make biodynamics viable. Nonetheless it has been worth it "to see life coming back into the vineyard; biodynamics wakes everything up. This has been very important to me because many of my vines are very old; one vineyard is almost 100 years old. Biodynamics has given those old vines a second life."

Suronde
49190 Rochefort-sur-Loire, Tel: 02 41 78 66 37, Fax: 02 41 78 68 90

Francis Poirel has just 7.5 ha in his meticulously run, organic domain, but with 6 of them in Quarts de Chaume and the other 1.5 in Coteaux du Layon-Chaume, they could hardly be better positioned. The wines are dense, succulent, and concentrated.

La Taille aux Loups ✪
37270 Montlouis-sur-Loire, Tel: 02 47 45 11 11, Fax: 02 47 45 11 14

Former wine merchant Jacky Blot turned winemaker due to frustration at the incompetent winemaking of many small Loire growers; he's now built his Montlouis and Vouvray domain to 14 ha. He's self-taught, and prefers to work alone: "If you hire consultants, everything tastes the same." He claims never to have chaptalized a single wine, and that his average yield over the last ten years has been no more than 35 hl/ha. Hard work in the vines includes severe fruit sorting; everything is fermented in wood (10% of which is new each year). Why? "In order to have slower fermentations and more complex flavours. Stainless steel simplifies and schematizes wine. It also means you often have to use artificial yeasts, and I only use wild yeasts."
Everything Blot does, he says, is aimed at making great sweet wines, but he modifies each harvest in order to best match what nature has given him (in 1994, for example, he made only Pétillant). "Stylistically", he says, "my obsession is cleanliness and precision." This is a fine range, peaking with the Cuvée Remus (which uses the oldest Montlouis vines, deftly barrel-fermented with up to 50% new oak to give an unusual dry succulence), the chewy Clos de Venise from Vouvray, some fresh-flavoured Demi-Sec wines, and Moelleux wines with ample botrytis characters and fine sustaining acidity.

Vacheron
18300 Sancerre, Tel: 02 48 54 09 93, Fax: 02 48 54 01 74

This impeccably run, 37-ha family domain is a consistently good source of both white and red Sancerre of pure and limpid style; the oak-aged Romains, from flint vineyards, is perfectly judged (the oak is used, Jean-Louis Vacheron says, "to confirm the amplitude of the wine itself"), while the red Belle Dame has the true warm breath of ripe Pinot blowing though it. This is one of the largest Sancerre domains to continue with 100% hand harvesting.

Varennes *see* Germain

La Varière
49320 Brissac, Tel: 04 41 91 22 64, Fax: 04 41 91 23 44

Jacques and Anne Beaujeau's superb 95-ha estate includes parcels in Quarts de Chaume, Bonnezeaux, Coteaux de l'Aubance, Coteaux du Layon-Faye d'Anjou, and Anjou-Villages-Brissac; they also own the 43 ha Domaine de la Perruche in Saumur. Late harvesting is very important here for the dry as well as sweet wines, and both the reds and the dry whites have a depth of extract (balanced by new or young oak) unusual in Brissac. The top red *cuvée*, La Grande Chevalerie, pushes Cabernet Sauvignon to its exciting Anjou limits. Recent vintages of the sweet wines have been disappointing, though the 1997 Bonnezeaux was excellent. The dry white Saumur from Perruche is dense, chewy, and honeyed, while the red Saumur-Champigny Le Clos du Chaumont is dark and packed with black cherry fruit.

Villeneuve ✪
49400 Souzay-Champigny, Tel: 02 41 51 14 04, Fax: 02 41 50 58 24

"All my work," says Jean-Pierre Chevallier, "is designed to create concentration." This outstanding 31-ha Saumur domain is a reference source for both white and red wines, with even the "'ordinary' *cuvées* offering arresting ripeness and depth, and the old vine *cuvées* Les Cormiers (a fine-honed, stone-polished white) and Le Grand Clos (a dark, chewy, powerful red from great years only) are better still.

Alsace

Frontier Zone This narrow strip of vineyard land gazing across at Germany's Baden marks a border in more senses than one. Few other French growers can match the environmental respect shown by Alsace's vanguard, and few, too, are investigating terroir as searchingly.

A geranium is a tough, tenacious little fistful of colour: street decoration to pin to summer. It's a paradox: the bright, scentless flower attached to the pungent leaf. It's a statement of civic aesthetics: yes, living here, as we do, is a joy.

I doubt that anyone has ever worked out the ratio of geranium blooms per head of population for a given area. Were they to do so, this statistic of jubilant futility might well reveal that Alsace is the most geranium-rich spot in Europe. Clustered around the village fountains, crowding the sills, dangling in the air in spongy baskets: June in Alsace is speckled by a million geranium petals. The heads detonate pinkly in the stillness of early morning; they nod redly as the afternoon breeze steals through the timbered alleys. They add to the sense that this place is a gigantic stage set, a contrivance, a morsel of the sixteenth century tumbled by accident into the twenty-first.

To be an Alsacien is to be different from most of your French compatriots. To begin with, you are likely to speak at least three languages: French, German, and the local dialect (which is closer to German than French). Your grandfather spoke no French at all; your two uncles fought (quite involuntarily) on opposing sides in the Second World War. You may well be a fervent believer in the ideal of the new Europe. Historically, your homeland has changed nationality with confusing regularity in the last five hundred years; enough is

enough. You view politicians, especially those who crash the cymbals of nationalism, with a cautious and cynical eye. You are proud, though, of your village and your street: to have emerged as prettily unscathed as it has through so much turbulent history is remarkable. (Other villages – Bennwihr, Sigolsheim – weren't so lucky.) Your doorstep is kept swept; your wrought-iron sign freshly painted. It's your mother who tends the geraniums on the fountain. And then...

Then there are the vines. With those, you have the same sense of good fortune constantly threatened by external forces. Many times, wine-growing has flourished in Alsace; many times, too, it has been destroyed by war (most comprehensively during the Thirty Years' War, the French Revolution, and the two twentieth century World Wars). When Alsace has been part of Germany, its wines have been those of the warm south: cheap, simple, plentiful, varietal, reliable. When Alsace has been part of France, by contrast, its wines have been those of the scented north, entirely unable to compete with the factory vineyards of a different, more southerly south, thus sent lurching from bulk status back to a quality vocation. And after each upheaval, decades elapse before the region is allowed back into the fold. The AOCs of Arbois and Bandol had been in place for twenty years or more before Alsace finally made it to AOC status in 1962. Alsace has had to fight hard for French viticultural acceptance. Even

now, some question its good faith – in part because, at eighty hl/ha (more than twice those of Châteauneuf-du-Pape), its official yields remain the highest in France, and in part because of its varietal legacy, seemingly at odds with the ideal of terroir.

If we want to understand just why it is that Alsace's leading wine-growers are the most avant-garde in their thinking among any in the New France, we would do well to bear all this in mind. They husband a precious, beautiful, sunny but repeatedly violated strip of land. They have been mistrusted outsiders to all but themselves for centuries; they have much to prove. The irony is that, as they do so, they are slowly dismantling the old certainties that made Alsace, for many consumers, such a safe bet.

Unpeeling the land

It seems astonishing nowadays, but it was only with the arrival of the Grand Cru system that terroir officially came into being within Alsace. The decree establishing the Alsace Grand Cru AOC dates from November 1975, though it took eight years for the first delimitations to emerge, and the process of defining the fifty Grand Cru sites was only completed in the 1990s. Prior to that, Alsace was just... Alsace, a uni-terroir. It wasn't even equivalent to Champagne, since there was no internal *echelle des crus* by which the price of grapes was fixed.

This was, in the context of French wine law, an astonishing anomaly. Geologically, as we will discover in The Adventure of the Land, Alsace is perhaps the most complex wine region in France, even more complex than Burgundy (which has managed to accumulate over 500 potential AOCs). None of this complexity and difference was reflected in the appellation system; Alsace growers, thus, had no way of drawing attention to the realities of terroir that they could smell and taste in their own finest *cuvées*.

Putting an end to the monolithic status of Alsace and beginning to pick out its nuances of site was long overdue, yet the way in which this was done proved hugely controversial, to the extent that Alsace's long-term reputation was damaged. Historically, cooperatives have been very important in Alsace: the average landholding here is one-tenth of a hectare (a quarter of an acre), and eighty-seven per cent of Alsace's vineyard land belongs to domains of less than two hectares (under five acres). Political pressure from cooperatives meant that the Grand Cru system met broad social criteria rather than strict viticultural criteria. "I am a socialist," Mark Kreydenweiss told me. "But in viticulture one cannot be a true socialist. All terroirs aren't born equal." The fact is that the Grands Crus of Alsace, as presently defined, are by no means all grand. There are too many of them; their boundaries are

> "What is a terroir? It is a matrix by which the possible can be uttered. History robbed us of our memory; it robbed us of our terroirs. We no longer knew what Ribeauvillé meant, or what Bergheim might say. We have to find out what is possible once more."
>
> **JEAN-MICHEL DEISS**

Autumn draws on in Bergheim, and the struggle for sweetness grows more unequal as the clouds gather.

often drawn too generously; the maximum yield of sixty-six hl/ha (including plc) is at least twice the size it should be. The names are confusing (there are three Altenbergs; and distinguishing Moenchberg from Muenchberg or Pfersigberg from Pfingstberg requires considerable linguistic talent even for Parisians, let alone those who live in Manchester or Minnesota). Moreover the initial varietal specifications (Muscat, Riesling, Pinot Gris, and Gewurztraminer were allowed, while all other varieties were forbidden) failed to respect local knowledge and historical precedent for these sites. Calling these vineyard areas "Grands Crus", with its Burgundian overtones, was a gross error. (Though not an isolated one: St-Emilion is no less culpable.) The market, of course, treated this *folie de grandeur* with disdain. Consumers are prepared to pay lavishly for a wine that comes from the eleven ha (twenty-seven acres) of Musigny or the eight ha (twenty acres) of Richebourg, because many historical bottles exist which prove the distinction of the sites; no one is prepared to make a similar gesture for a wine from the unproven fifty-three ha (131 acres) of Marckrain or the nineteen ha (twenty-two acres) of Praelatenberg. Ideally, *crus* should have been created which were neither Premier nor Grand, and some decades should have been allowed to elapse before these *crus* were hierarchized based on the prices their wines achieved and their performance over the years in blind tastings.

The Grand Cru system did have one great advantage, though: it made all the growers of Alsace begin to research terroir. The issue was on the table. "Better poorly defined Grands Crus," says André Ostertag, "than no Grands Crus at all. The Grand Cru movement has been a great *révélateur de terroir* in Alsace." It is more orderly than the chaotic usage of *lieux-dit* names, clos names and often meaningless "Réserve" bottlings and special *cuvées* (all of which continue in any case, though with less resonance than before). The large producers like Hugel and Trimbach who spurned the Grand Cru system claim to have done so because its quality controls were inadequate. "We are opposed," Hubert Trimbach told me with typical forthrightness. "There is not enough discipline. Yields are too high; quality is questionable; prices are ridiculous and criminal. Over fifty per cent of the Grand Cru juice comes from co-ops. This is a political time bomb. No, no, and no." His criticisms may be valid; yet it is also true that these large producers refuse the Grand Cru system because they wish to protect their brand names. Branding is selfish: it works to the benefit of the brand-holder alone, and uses the concept of terroir expediently. For Trimbach and Hugel to enter the Grand Cru system (as I believe they should) would mean surrendering some of their branded exclusivity, and sharing the glory of the land. They do not seem ready to make this gesture.

In any case, the real interest lies elsewhere – with those producers who, like Jean-Michel Deiss, are rethinking the very meaning of terroir; or who, like Olivier Zind-Humbrecht MW, are taking non-interventionist viticulture and winemaking to its absolute limits, and in so doing are expressing terroir in their wines with almost shocking forcefulness. In 2001, too, the Grand Cru regulations changed for the better. More of this below.

The varietal conundrum

Over eighty per cent of AOC Alsace wines are sold as varietal wines. Just how far back into Alsace's history this varietal thinking stretches is a matter of some controversy, but it was reinforced at the beginning of the twentieth century when many of Alsace's vineyards (under German administration) were planted with hybrids. The use of the names of "noble" pure-vinifera varieties served as proof, by the mid-century accession to AOC, that the bad old past of hybrid production

▲ *Varieties first – or soils? The debate in Alsace is lively. The region's best wines, never more profound than at present, underscore its importance.*

had been left behind. They also proved comprehensible and welcoming to non-French consumers. They were popular, and remain so. Over eighty per cent of Alsace's wine is still varietal, with blends (Edelzwicker or Gentil) accounting for under five per cent; the rest is sparkling wine (Crémant d'Alsace).

In a region officially regarded as a uni-terroir, moreover, they marked difference. Nine varietal names were permitted or allowed: Pinot or Pinot Blanc (which could include any member of the Pinot family – Blanc, Gris, or Noir – plus Auxerrois), Tokay-Pinot Gris, Pinot Noir, Riesling, Gewurztraminer, Muscat, Sylvaner, Chasselas (minute amounts only), and, unofficially, Auxerrois itself. Why so many? In part, because of the hugely diverse terroirs of the region. A fractured and heterogenous land demanded varietal plurality. Or, to put it in Jean-Michel Deiss's language, before the arrival of *crus*, varietal diversity was the only way in which Alsace's terroir could speak.

It was a primitive language, he maintains. "We had 150 varieties in the Rhine Valley in 1840. Now there are officially seven. Do you realise that eighty per cent of all the Riesling in Alsace is clone 49? All of that genetic generosity has been lost. How can I spell my name with one letter? How can my terroir express itself in one syllable? How can I make music with one note? All I can do is exclaim – no more than that. The absolute necessity here, the absolute first priority, is to re-find complex varietal plantings in order to give utterance once again to the complexities of our terroir." Deiss's solution is a return to what he claims is the oldest tradition of all in Alsace – "*la vieille tradition de complantation*". "Complantation" means (heresy of heresies) planting a range of different grape varieties on a single site. He likes to show visitors a fifty-year-old parcel in Engelgarten where all the varieties can indeed be found muddled, even within a single row. The resulting wine is a varietal blend, sold under the site's name alone. Deiss returns to his favourite linguistic analogies. "To write a phrase, I need consonants, vowels, commas, full stops, verbs, subjects, complements. I need contradiction. Syntax is a way to organize contradictions so that you understand the message. Terroir is a space that takes contradictions and organizes them in a logical manner so that you recognize them. Cheval Blanc is not the same as Domaine de Chevalier. Pétrus isn't Merlot." Deiss's Grand Cru Altenberg de Bergheim, thus, is based on a mixture of

▲ *Dark clouds over Turckheim. Olivier Zind-Humbrecht, a winemaker of genius, coaxes scent and succulence from these low hills.*

Riesling, Pinot Gris, and Gewurztraminer, though it includes other varieties, too. He stresses, though, that the precise proportions of the varieties don't matter much. "When you listen to Mozart, you don't ask what percentage of violin there is, or what percentage of oboe. It doesn't matter. What matters is that they all play harmoniously together. If I can distinguish the varieties, then it's no longer wine. Wine is music; wine is harmony."

Needless to say, not everyone shares Deiss's views. Laurence Faller of Domaine Weinbach, for example, is quite happy with varietal wines. "We're very lucky in Alsace. We have great grape varieties and great terroirs. We're the only French region to be able to play on these twin assets, and we should make the most of them." "Complantation may well be right for Jean-Michel," says Frédéric Blanck, "but not for everyone, and not everywhere. We feel that our granite terroir of Schlossberg is best conveyed by growing Riesling on it. On other terroirs, though, like Rosacker, varieties do come to resemble each other in their perfumes, at least, so he has a point there." Hubert Trimbach once again is most forceful of all. "Mixing Riesling with Pinot Gris, Gewurztraminer, or Muscat doesn't help terroir to emerge. The terroir comes out best, *with no question at all*, with Riesling. And Deiss knows it better than anybody. Riesling has the facility to express minerality better than any other grape. *Ça, c'est clair.*"

So is complantation allowed? Now it is. The Grand Cru regulations were altered on January 24th, 2001 to permit Grand Cru wines to be produced from varieties other than the original four, and from blends if wished. More importantly still, though, the growers themselves can now adapt their own Grand Cru regulations if they so desire – to lower the yield, alter the official harvest date, change planting densities, or even agree to produce only sweet or dry wines. This system of *gestion locale* gives producers the chance to begin to rectify some of the failings of the Grand Cru system as originally conceived. Rangen has already upped its planting density to 6,000 vines per hectare rather than 4,500, and raised its minimum potential alcohol from eleven per cent to twelve per cent; Altenberg de Bergheim has cut its maximum yield to fifty hl/ha. Putting the impetus for change in the hands of the growers themselves is a laudable and wise move: other French regions should take note.

Less is more

For organic and biodynamic wine production, Alsace leads France. The region now has thirty domains officially working organically or biodynamically, with more in conversion and following these methods unofficially. The producers' organization Vignes Vivantes has established collective compost piles (the recipe is fifty per cent cow manure, thirty-three per cent horse manure, seven per cent sheep manure, seven per cent pomace, and three per cent vine prunings). France's first biodynamic domain was in Alsace (that of Eugène Meyer); as in Burgundy, the region's greatest domains (most notably that of Zind-Humbrecht) are preponderantly biodynamic.

The importance of this, though, is not its literal and mundane reality; it is the thinking and the rationale that underlies the decision to reject conventional, chemical agriculture. For Olivier Zind-Humbrecht as for Anne-Claude Leflaive or Dominique Lafon, the decision was initially empirical. "My scientific training," says Zind-Humbrecht "told me that experiment is the key to knowledge." Experiments began in 1997 – but the results were so dramatically superior to those on conventional plots that the whole domain was quickly converted. For Jean-Michel Deiss, biodynamics provided "the ignition key" to fire up vines so that they can plunge beneath the soil, rummage deep into rock and thus express terroir most memorably. But the ethical aspects are important for Deiss, too: "You can make 1,000 hectolitres of wine from ten hectares with one man, using herbicide, fertilizer, all the technology that is poisoning the planet. Or you can make 1,000 hectolitres of wine from twenty-five hectares with seventeen men – using biodynamics and physical effort. Whether you like my wine or not I don't know and to some extent I don't care. This is not taste; this is ethics."

The same philosophy infuses the winemaking work of many of the region's greatest growers: the ideal (as at Zind-Humbrecht) is maximum ripeness, maximum purity, maximum concentration – and minimum intervention. The use of natural yeasts, unhurried fermentations, malolactic or not at the wine's pleasure, minimum racking, no fining, no filtering, with the result that every wine emerges at a different spot on the spectra of alcohol, sweetness, perfume, and substance. Commercially this can create problems, as we'll discover in the "Flak" section; ethically, however, the strategy is impeccable, for only like this can full voice be given to site, vintage, and varieties. The result is a delicious democratic babble, rather than the eerie and hollow conformity achieved by industrial methods.

Jean-Michel Deiss

Sometimes ideas, in Alsace, can be as luscious as late-harvest Gewurztraminer. If any French wine-grower deserves to be called the Roland Barthes of botrytis or the Jacques Derrida of the demi-muid, it is Jean-Michel Deiss. This accolade (or insult) would be granted him not only for the deconstructive and subversive originality of his thought, but also for the rich metaphorical drapes with which he is able to clothe it. So intoxicated does a lecture from Deiss leave you that the tasting afterwards is almost sobering. He can shift into professorial mode with such elective ease that the idea that he is also able to prune a vine, operate a press, and fork marc seems improbable. (Or perhaps not: he is also a keen biker.) The introduction to this chapter contains samples of his beguiling rhetoric and capacity for memorable abstraction; here are a few more, on his favourite subject: the vine's revelation of terroir. "What is my technology? It is a technology of depth. I try to do everything from January 1st to December 31st to make the vine descend. Vines aren't made to live in the liquid solution found in the soil. The vine is a superior, evolved plant, created to make soil where there isn't yet any. The Romans understood this, and planted vines near Marseille where they wanted to create soil. To plant vines where you grow wheat is the ultimate idiocy; wheat consumes soil whereas vines create it."

"How do you force a vine to go downwards? By deep planting, first of all. If I plant a vine at four cm, I'm saying to it 'Be beautiful, enjoy yourself, and shut up, baby.' Whereas if I plant at sixty cm, I'm saying 'You're going to suffer in order to exceed your own expectations. You'll suffer in order to say something that will surprise you, to produce something that will be there after you're gone.' Secondly, I use high planting densities, up to 10,000 plants a hectare for new plantings. Thirdly, I work the earth, to put oxygen into it. Fourthly, I use biodynamics, as a starter, until the vine takes over and begins to create its own new soil."

"What is a man? A man is the network of all his genes; that's his 'possible'. Beyond that, though, a man is all he's learned. Every day he lived, he learned. He suffered; he became enthusiastic; he fell in love; he became disappointed. When I meet someone, what do I want? I want what he has lived (his vécu), his humanity; I don't want his genetic material. Why, when I taste a wine, do you want me to taste its genotype and not its vécu? A vin de terroir is how a vine communicates everything that it has learned beyond its genotype. And this apprenticeship is the cultivation of depth. Every day the vine descends, it learns something new, and that's what is manifested in the grapes."

Deiss says he has proved this by organizing grape tastings for his fellow growers. "When we tasted the Sylvaner, the Pinot Blanc, the Pinot Gris, the Riesling that grow in Schoenenbourg, we discovered that they all had the same taste. The character of the place is stronger than the taste of the varietal. That's what we learned together."

Olivier Zind-Humbrecht MW

To say that Olivier Zind-Humbrecht stands head and shoulders above most of France's makers of white wine is to do no more than state the obvious: he's 1m 95cm (6'4") tall. Within that lofty frame, more unusually, is a brilliant mind. Anyone who has ever considered taking the British Master of Wine examination will know that it is a fierce intellectual as well as sensorial challenge. Olivier Zind-Humbrecht was the first Frenchman to pass both parts of it – as a young man in 1988, having written his answers in a foreign language.

More impressive than either his height or his exam achievements, though, are his wines: voluptuous with fruit, yet dignified with stone essences which lie saturated within that rich fruit like oil in an olive. They are arrestingly articulate – and gloriously variable, too. When I tasted twenty of the complete range of thirty-two Zind-Humbrecht 1998 wines in London in March 2000, I remember being astounded not only by their individual felicities but by their virtuoso differences, such a striking contrast to the patterned uniformity generally found within a domain range. And it's here that the most striking aspect of this forty-eight-year-old's greatness is revealed. A winemaker of his abilities could have done almost anything, so skilled is his controlling hand. Yet he stood back. He unpicked the knots of modern oenology and let the threads lie as they would – in trusting absolutely the raw materials delivered him by his father Léonard. Despite having a magician's touch, he let nature's spells take precedence over human dexterity. To a basketball player's height and a masterly mind, then, we need to add vision and courage – to discern this way forward, and be prepared to pursue it in the face of criticism and the cynicism of others (about biodynamics and rigorously non-interventionist winemaking, for example). Head and shoulders? And then some.

The Adventure of the Land

I have mentioned, by way of caution, that Alsace's earthly adventure is one of astrophysical complexity. Considered at the largest scale, however, it is simple enough; indeed it echoes another of the adventures we will discover a little later. Geologically speaking, Alsace and Burgundy are twins.

Both lie on the western side of a formation known to geologists as a graben; both are part of the rift system that links the Mediterranean with the North Sea. A graben is a large trough formed when two parallel faults give way, leaving the collapsed central section, like the bottom of a bathtub, lower than the sections to each side. Rivers take advantage of such troughs, though they have not had a principal hand in their formation. So it is with the Saône in Burgundy; so it is with the Rhine in Alsace. It is not the river that has sculpted the slopes on which the vines bask, but the shearing of faults. (The vineyards of the northern Rhône or of Anjou, by contrast, are most definitely the work of the river.) On the other side of the Saône graben lie the vineyards of the Jura; on the other side of the Rhine graben lie the vineyards of Germany's Baden.

If you look at a relief map of the area, the perky Vosges mountains can be seen forming an abrupt western boundary to the Rhine Valley from just south of Colmar to just north of Strasbourg. Wine exists in Alsace thanks to the Vosges. They mother the vineyards by shielding the region from the prevailing westerlies: Strasbourg and Colmar to the east are much hotter, sunnier and drier than exposed Nancy and Epinal to the west. Mountains? Well, they're 1,200 metres (3,900 feet) or so high: lushly forested rather than craggy. (This is great hiking country.) The higher the crest, the better the shielding effect.

You can divide the slopes into three wine-growing zones, top to bottom: the Vosges, the sub-Vosges hills, and the alluvial fans.

Uppermost come some of the genuine Vosges slopes (vines peter out at about 400 metres/1,300 feet). These are preponderantly granite – as the Vosges themselves are.

Most of the vineyards, however, are sited below the Vosges proper, on the undulating sub-Vosges hills. A huge variety of soil types is found here, thanks to the fact that these hills are slashed and hatched by step-faults and cross-faults into a harlequin design of different geological origins: limestone, sands, clays, loess, conglomerates, mica, scree, gypsum, tufa, ash, even schist.... Geology is rarely simple, but these hills are the most geologically complex in viticultural France.

The alluvial fans at the base, finally, provide the growing environments dismissed as "wheatlands" by Francis Burn, Jean-Michel Deiss, and others; those who drew up the AOC boundaries, perhaps under local pressure, disagreed. Wines from these sites are generally disappointing, though Zind-Humbrecht's Herrenweg shows what might be achieved.

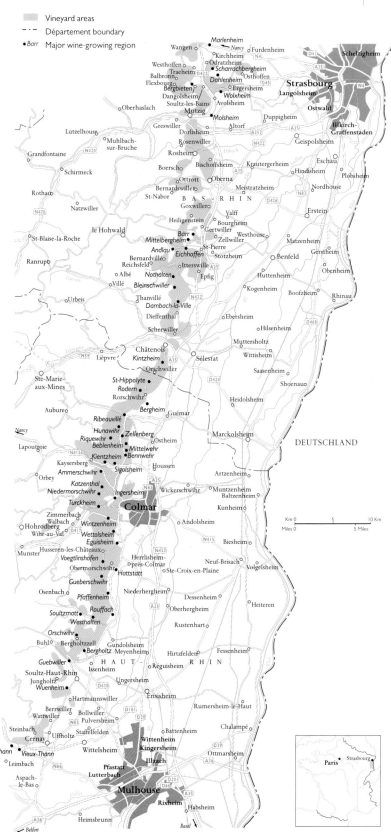

▲ *Harvesting grapes by the trailerload means lower quality: top growers will always use small, stacking boxes.*

Terroir, as we already know, only steps officially into the AOC system at the Grand Cru level. The overall AOC **Alsace** covers around 14,500 ha (35,800 acres), making it just a bit bigger than all of the Muscadet AOCs together, but less than half the size of the Côtes du Rhône. **Riesling** is the most widely grown varietal, followed by **Pinot Blanc** (including **Auxerrois**, and sometimes sold as **Klevner** or **Clevner**), **Gewurztraminer**, **Sylvaner** (in decline), **Pinot Gris** (also, unhappily, called **Tokay**), **Pinot Noir**, **Muscat** (both d'Alexandrie and Ottonel), **Chasselas** (which theoretically can be sold as **Gutedel**), and **Klevener de Heiligenstein** (a local speciality of this Bas-Rhin village: Klevener is said to be a Traminer variant). Sparkling **Crémant d'Alsace** suffers, as so many of such wines do in France, from being produced from second-rate raw materials rather than the cream of the crop (though this AOC is notable for being the only one to permit Chardonnay in Alsace). **Vendange Tardive** (late harvest) and **Sélection des Grains Nobles** (botrytis-affected) wines can be produced within the context of both Alsace and Alsace Grand Cru – but from Riesling, Muscat, Pinot Gris, and Gewurztraminer only. These designations are awarded on the basis of the original sugar level in the juice, rather than the final sugar level in the wine – which is why some Vendange Tardive wines sometimes taste almost dry. The most ambitious producers, by contrast, routinely exceed or even double the basic required sugar levels (the rules in any case were tightened in September 2001) – and many "ordinary" Alsace wines, too, now taste sweet, further muddying the conceptual distinctions underlying the creation of these wines.

And so to **Alsace Grand Cru**: fifty named sites from gentle Steinklotz above Marlenheim in the north to dramatic Rangen soaring over Thann in the south, making a total of around four per cent of the entire vineyard area. Sizes vary from the tiny 3.2-ha (7.9-acre) Kanzlerberg (west of the larger Altenberg de Bergheim) to the grandiose eighty-ha (198-acre) Schlossberg, above Riquewihr. I do not name all these sites; the curious will find them in reference books. Instead, let's explore the temper of the land and some of the great historical terroirs of the region, whether sanctified by Grand Cru or inexplicably excluded. The *département* of Bas-Rhin lies to the north of the *département* of Haut-Rhin (since the river is flowing north at this point). We'll tackle each separately.

Bas-Rhin

There are few great vineyards in Bas-Rhin: the Vosges are markedly lower in this northern sector, offering less shelter from the westerlies and less steep vineyard slopes, too. Wissenbourg, on the border with Germany's Pfalz, begins the region; there are even German-owned vineyards here. Real wine-growing interest, however, only begins some eighty or ninety km (fifty or fifty-six miles) south, almost exactly the point when the Vosges summit line begins to crest 700 metres (2,300 feet) or so (it has rarely been over 500 metres/1,640 feet thus far). The four villages of Barr, Mittelbergheim, Andlau, and Eichhoffen drop the flag on the action. **Zotzenberg** is the most northerly Grand Cru of interest – though more for what it might surrender in the future than for what it has achieved in the past. This southeast-facing calcareous marl vineyard enjoyed historic fame for its Sylvaner which, under *gestion locale*, should begin to make a welcome reappearance. Little **Kastelberg** is a granite vineyard (this is the Vosges rock basement, rather than the kaleidoscopic sub-Vosges hills), perfect for taut, sinewy Riesling; nearby **Wiebelsberg** is similar though slightly larger and sandier, giving slightly slacker wines. **Moenchberg**, gazing down on Eichhoffen, is a scree, clay, and

▲ *Horses harnessed to ploughs are plodding back to the vineyards; quadrupeds don't crush soils as tractors do.*

conglomerate slope where Gewurztraminer shares the honours with Riesling. Treacherously, there is a **Muenchberg** just a little further south near Nothalten, described by André Ostertag as "a sandstone amphitheatre"; this terroir can give Riesling a fine mineral backbone. At Andlau, **Clos Rebgarten** is a small, unclassified sandy site from which Kreydenweiss produces a hauntingly pure and scented Muscat Ottonel.

Haut-Rhin

St-Hippolyte and Rodern, the first two villages in the *département*, both have a local reputation for Pinot Noir – though the appeal of these dawn-pale reds (and of Alsace Pinot Noir in general) tends to elude non-locals. South, then, to Bergheim and Ribeauvillé, two villages of unquestioned grandeur; and with **Altenberg de Bergheim** we come to the first of the Grands Crus which, even viewed from Burgundy, might justify the name. "Bergheim is a closed valley, protected, warm, exposed. Bergheim's wines? Malabar: muscular, powerful. The deep valley of Ribeauvillé is cool, airy, freshened by winds from the Vosges. The difference between Deiss" – yes, it is Jean-Michel Deiss speaking once more – "and Trimbach is the difference between a closed, hot valley and an open, cool, fresh, airy valley." We are among limestone marls here, sometimes growing heavier and clayey (as in Ribeauvillé's **Osterberg** and Bergheim's tiny **Kanzlerberg**) and sometimes rather sandier (as in **Geisberg** and **Kirchberg de Ribeauvillé**). Deiss describes Geisberg as having *une vibration acide*; unsurprisingly, it is the source of a portion of the raw materials for Trimbach's Cuvée Frédéric Emile Riesling (though most of this blend comes from Osterberg).

There then follows perhaps the prettiest stretch of one of France's most exquisite vineyard regions, and the source of many of Alsace's greatest wines, too: Hunawihr, Riquewihr, Beblenheim, Mittelwihr (a rebuilt replica following destruction in World War Two), Bennwihr,

Sigolsheim (another replica), and Kientzheim. Hunawihr has **Rosacker**, and within it the one hectare (2.47 acres) of **Clos Ste-Hune**: dolomitic limestone with a little sandy scree, producing some of Alsace's most enduring and intense Riesling. **Clos Windsbuhl** is also found in Hunawihr, a shelly clay-limestone site from which Zind-Humbrecht produces magnificently thick-textured and luscious (though rarely botrytized) Pinot Gris. Riquewihr's pale-soiled **Schoenenbourg**, Mittelwihr's hot **Mandelberg**, but above all Kientzheim's **Furstentum** and the mighty **Schlossberg** are the other great sites of this stretch, while the lower-lying **Clos des Capucins** of Weinbach is also found at Kientzheim. Riesling from Schlossberg should be congenitally different from Rosacker, Schoenenbourg, and Furstentum: Schlossberg has granitic, acid soils; the other three are limy and alkaline. **Wineck-Schlossberg**, **Sommerberg**, and the hot **Brand** continue the granite theme down to Turckheim and the break in the hill-line caused by the little River Fecht flowing down from Munster; the 1.4 ha (3.5 acres) of Zind-Humbrecht's **Clos Jebsal** is another hot site next to Brand, though this has alkaline marls and gypsum rather than acidic granites and micas.

There are more worthy sites across the Fecht and south to Wintzenheim, Wettolsheim, and Eguisheim. The warm, stony-marl flank of **Hengst** is Wintzenheim's official Grand Cru, but **Clos Hauserer** (underneath Hengst) and **Rotenberg** are other worthy sites: the limestone is returning (it's red in Rotenberg), though there are still granite boulders and screes from time to time, too. These disappear the further south one goes: **Steingrubler** retains some granite, whereas dry Eichberg and sunny Pfersigberg have none. In this warm sector, Gewurztraminer comes into its own, and Gueberschwihr's **Goldert**, and the five-ha (12.4-acre) **Clos St-Imer** within it, make uniformly powerful wines (fine Pinot Gris from the Clos St-Imer, too). Goldert, with its limy soils, is also one of Alsace's greatest sites for Muscat. Pfaffenheim and its **Steinert** may prove the place to hunt for Grand Cru Pinot Blanc in the future under *gestion locale*, since there is a grand pedigree for this variety here; while Rouffach's **Vorbourg** is best known because its southern sector (south-facing and steep rather than east-facing and gently sloping like the rest) is constituted by the sixteen-ha (39.5-acre) **Clos St-Landelin** of Muré. The **Zinnkoepflé** between Westhalten and Soultzmatt echoes Clos St-Landelin, though it is hotter and dryer still, producing fierce Gewurztraminer. Schlumberger's Rieslings and Gewurztraminers are the great performers in rubbly **Saering** and **Kitterlé**. After these sites, there is only one more outstanding Alsace terroir, some thirteen km (eight miles) further south: the volcanic, acid-soiled **Rangen**, whose steep nineteen ha (forty-seven acres) constitute the majority of the vineyards of Thann. This is a furnace in high summer, and the black soils a repertoire of minerals including iron, fluorine, manganese, and magnesium. This inaccessible and demanding site, positioned at between 300 and 400 metres (984-1,312 feet), is perhaps the very greatest in the entire region. It had largely been abandoned by the 1960s; its renaissance is due to the pioneering work of Léonard Humbrecht, father of Olivier, who bought three of

the remaining 4.5 ha (11.1 acres) in 1977 and was called "crazy" at the time. The Grand Cru includes Zind-Humbrecht's **Clos St-Urbain** and Schoffit's **Clos St-Theobald**. Terroir notes not infrequently dominate varietal character in Rangen, giving earthy, pumice-like, salty or even iodine characters in place of lush fruits, though acidity levels remain surprisingly tenacious here.

Finally, for the sake of inclusiveness, three further vineyard areas of northeastern France should be mentioned. The VDQS of **Côtes de Toul** lies just west of Nancy: it produces mostly slight red and rosé wines based on Pinot Noir and Gamay. Around Metz, the VDQS of **Vins de Moselle** is used for tenuous, often sharp whites (these are more impressive a little further north, in Luxembourg). Producers making Vins de Pays from the *département* of **Meuse** have also applied for VDQS status. A taste of any wine from these areas underlines the vital role played by the Vosges mountains in creating the wines of Alsace: the difference in structure and depth is huge.

Alsace Flak

Cru blues

A *cru* system in Alsace was long overdue, in that until 1983 wines from what is perhaps France's most complex terroir were gagged and bound, unable to articulate anything other than their basic varietal character and their producer's vinificatory skill. Yet the Grand Cru system as instituted was lax to the point of meaninglessness, misnamed, and in its early years a divisive failure. In 2002, the "Grands Crus" are looking a little less blue thanks to the *gestion locale* initiative described on page 61, yet there are still too many of them, and they are still too large to be taken seriously as genuine Grands Crus. Let's hope that *gestion locale* leads the way to further reform, including the difficult but essential step of downgrading sites and locations which fail to prove their worth. With the possibility of complantation and the use of previously excommunicated varieties like Sylvaner, the truly great sites should begin to emerge over the next two decades.

Sweet nightmares

I have mentioned the ethical desirability of the radically non-interventionist stance adopted by the Alsace vanguard, yet in one respect it has made consumers (including this one) swear and curse. Why? Sugar, in a word. The amount of residual sugar left in a wine radically alters its gastronomic profile. A Pinot Gris with three g/l of residual sugar might be perfect to partner grilled sea bass; a Pinot Gris with twenty-three g/l of residual sugar will murder the fish anew. You will find both wines on restaurant lists and shop shelves, and you will not be able to tell from the label which is which.

This came about, according to Olivier Zind-Humbrecht, for the best of reasons. "The average ripeness of the grapes in Alsace has increased dramatically. Today's best vineyards are harvested at levels that our grandfathers would only dream to have once every twenty years. In a non-interventionist attitude, the winemaker must give time to the wine to finish its fermentation. If all that has been done and the wines still have residual sweetness, then I would call it natural and harmonious." Other producers, like Frédéric Blanck and Laurence Faller, point out that it is not the grams of sugar that count so much as the balance in the wine. "The only problem with residual sugar," says Blanck, "is when it's out of

balance with acidity. Ten g/l sugar with 8.5 g/l acidity is no problem." Blanck offered me his 1999 Patergarten Pinot Gris to try (twelve g/l sugar) – and, sure enough, it tasted merely succulently dry rather than sweet, thanks to its seven g/l acidity.

Needless to say, Hubert Trimbach is vigorously opposed to the burgeoning sugar levels in Alsace wines. "It's done to please American wine writers. That's all it is. Honestly. More fatness, more richness, more voluptuousness: that's how you get high ratings from Parker. We have been taken in a direction that is not the classical direction of Alsace. Crisp acids, freshness, a clear aspect, no compromise with malolactic or leaving the wine a long time in vats with the sediment to give fatness: that is how you get the clean, dry, refined, precise classicism of Alsace. These rich, thick, heavy wines are aberrant, crazy. The rest of the world can beat us on the rich style, but they cannot beat us on the dry, crisp style."

Ideologically, in fact, no one need to belong to one camp or the other (and both have their merits); all that matters is that those buying the bottles need to know what is inside them. In this respect, the decision by the Comité Interprofessionel des Vins d'Alsace to introduce a sweetness scale of one to nine for back labels is welcome, and I look forward to its introduction from the 2001 harvest onwards.

Vines in wheatfields

As is the case throughout this book, this chapter concerns an elite. Ordinary Alsace wines, the kind you will find filling the shelves in any French supermarket, the kind that supply the own-label ranges of foreign supermarkets, have changed very little over the last decade. They are often thin, over-chaptalized, and produced from exaggerated yields. When I last visited Alsace, a litre of Sylvaner was worth less than a litre of petrol. "The big problem for Alsace," says Francis Burn, "is all the wheatlands. In the Middle Ages, vines were only found on the hillsides. But nowadays wine is more profitable than wheat. There are too many vines in wheatfields in Alsace." This is exactly the same problem that dogs German wine-growing, and ruins its reputation abroad. Things could, of course, be worse; Alsace has no Liebfraumilch and, scandalously, Champagne's yields are even higher. Will Alsace show its northern neighbour the way?

Alsace: People

Barmès-Buecher ✪
68920 Wettolsheim, Tel: 03 89 80 62 92, Fax: 03 89 79 30 80

François Barmès-Buecher is, like so many of Alsace's leading growers, a passionate advocate both of biodynamics and of the limpidity of aroma and of flavour he says it allows. Auxerrois, Pinot Blanc, and Sylvaner are all taken very seriously at this 15-ha domain, with the Sylvaner Vieilles Vignes from Rosenberg among the region's best. The two greatest Rieslings here are the peaches and cream version from the "lime valley", Leimenthal, and the more massive and mineral version from Hengst; look out, too, for four Gewurztraminers from different sites, the richest being that from Pfersigberg. Barmès-Buecher's personal passion is Pinot Noir; his Vieilles Vignes *cuvée*, produced from tiny yields and given extensive lees "feeding", is a benchmark bottle for the region.

Léon Bayer
68420 Eguysheim, Tel: 03 89 21 62 30, Fax: 03 89 23 93 63

Négociant house with a 20-ha domain producing, as Trimbach does, food-friendly dry styles of the classic varietals sold under Réserve and brand names but not Grand Cru names (despite owning land in both Eichberg and Pfersigberg). The wines are consistent, nervy, and pure.

Blanck ✪
68240 Kayserberg, Tel: 03 89 78 23 56, Fax: 03 89 47 16 45

Why is it that Alsace growers are so articulate? Anyone who has ever met Philippe Blanck, in charge of the commercial side of this 36-ha domain based in Kientzheim, will not forget the torrent of information, passion, and opinion that tumbles from his lips. His cousin, winemaker Frédéric Blanck, is barely less voluble – and the wines, too, constitute a crowd of different voices. The five Grands Crus (Schlossberg, Furstentum, Mambourg, Sommerberg, and Wineck-Schlossberg) account for more than a third of plantings, and the Blancks also differentiate another four *lieux-dits* (Patergarten, Altenbourg, Grafreben, and Rosenbourg). Great efforts go into drawing out nuances of terroir; the contrast between the knife-edged purity of granitic Schlossberg and the softer, more comely fruits surrendered by the calcareous pebbles and sand of Furstentum just across the valley is particularly instructive, and never delineated more clearly than here. (Altenburg and Grafreben, by the way, lie adjacent to and beneath Furstentum, while Patergarten is on the alluvium and gravels of the Weisbach river valley down below.) The overall style is one of elegance and purity; after a sometimes steely, inarticulate youth, the wines age well. Frédéric Blanck is not a winemaker who overvalues high sugar levels; his favourite vintages, he says, are those like 2000 ("incredible, unpredictable, indomitable") where you can pick early. He's honest, too. "We were too pretentious in 1997. We all picked too late, and everything got too sweet and flabby."

Bott-Geyl
68980 Beblenheim, Tel: 03 89 47 90 04, Fax: 03 89 47 97 33

Jean-Christophe Bott is another up-and-coming star of the new generation in Alsace, working hard to produce expressive, richly flavoured wines from the fine range of sites held by the 13-ha domain. Late harvesting and the refusal to force fermentation means that these wines often have residual sugar levels, which "work for white wine in the way that tannin does for red – provided that it isn't just make-up, and there is extract and acidity to support it beneath," claims Bott. Star wines include pithy Riesling from Mandelberg and elegant,

impeccably defined Gewurztraminer from Furstentum. There is also the Cuvée Apolline for those who would like to see what Burgundy's great white grape can do on its own when barrel-fermented in Alsace.

Albert Boxler
68230 Niedermorschwihr, Tel: 03 89 27 11 32, Fax: 03 89 27 70 14

Jean-Marc Boxler's 10-ha is worth noting for its taut and concentrated wines from Brand and Sommerberg.

Burn ✪✪
68420 Gueberschwihr, Tel: 03 89 49 28 56

"It takes about 20 years," Francis Burn told me, "to move from being a good wine producer to being a great one. Why? Because at first you can't charge more for higher quality. My father was less free economically than we are. We can pick very late, sort the fruit, do everything we feel is necessary for quality. He didn't have that luxury." Ernest Burn still managed to build a fine small (9.5-ha) domain in Gueberschwihr based on the Clos St-Imer, a 5-ha parcel within the heart of Goldert, where the Burns have erected a little stone chapel of their own. "We can both pray and shelter from the sunshine there," says Francis – and, he might have added, admire the wild yellow tulips that fill the vineyard in spring. Goldert is indeed a hot site; its dry limy clays are ideal for Gewurztraminer and Muscat, and these two varieties provide some of the most outstanding bottles of this fine domain. The Muscats are weighty, almost smoky, with mineral grapefruit notes infusing the purer, sweet grape flavours; the Gewurztraminers are an attar of roses, smelling like a warm and windless summer evening. Riesling from the Clos St-Imer is dancing and vigorous, packed with fruit; while Pinot Gris is, even by the lush standards of this variety, extravagant and honeyed, a syrup of quince.

Clos St-Landelin *see* Muré

Marcel Deiss ✪✪
68750 Bergheim, Tel: 03 89 73 63 37, Fax: 03 89 73 32 67

Jean-Michel Deiss is such an compelling talker that he runs the risk of eclipsing his own wines. This would be a shame, since the range that he and his wife Clarisse produce is one of the most stimulating in the region. There are 20 ha, quite widely scattered (120 different parcels on the chaotic mass of tiny fault blocks that lie between St-Hyppolyte and Sigolsheim), giving this arch-terroiriste a wide palette of raw materials to work with. In particular, Deiss has vineyards on the two basic, contrastive Alsace soil types: acid, crystalline soils (as in Schoenenbourg, where these are mixed with marl) and alkaline, limy materials (as in Altenberg de Bergheim). Riesling from the former Grand Cru site is purer, harder, full of sinewy fruit, more enduring in time; Riesling from the latter Grand Cru site is richer and more billowing, floral as well as fruited.

Other pleasures of the Deiss range include Rieslings from five other locations (look out for the smokily luscious Grasberg and the pure, elegant, serene Engelgarten), and Gewurztraminer and Pinot Gris coaxed into more mineral expressions than usual. Deiss uses oak for some of his Pinot Noir and Pinot Gris wines; there is Chardonnay in the Pinot Blanc, too. Above all, though, this is the domain to patronize if you want to judge the success or otherwise of complantation (varietal blends). The Gentil de Burg is a delightful, provocative wine full of teasing scents and spiced, vanillic fruit (it blends Riesling with Gewurztraminer). At the top of the tree is Deiss's Grand Vin de l'Altenberg, which includes "all the traditional varieties" according to its maker (not

---

Star rating system used on producer spreads   ✪ Very good wine   ✪✪ Excellent wine   ✪✪✪ Great wine

forgetting 1% Chasselas) and spends time in barrel. Whether or not it has, as Deiss claims, "plus d'humanité" (more humanity) than other Alsace wines I am not sure; what is certain, though, is that it is deep, concentrated, plump, long, and complete. As with the Gentil de Burg, it teases, fascinates and provokes by its nuances (orange, tangerine, honeysuckle, bacon fat) tricked out in the glass over half an hour, rather than telling its story in open-hearted purity as a single varietal might.

Dirler-Cadé
68500 Bergholtz, Tel: 03 89 76 91 00, Fax: 03 89 76 85 97

This 12-ha domain based in Bergholtz is another name for the notebook of those who prefer their Alsace wines (Gewurztraminer included) clean and dryly pungent rather than plump and sweet.

Dopff & Irion *see* Cave de Pfaffenheim

Frick
68250 Pfaffenheim, Tel: 03 89 49 62 99, Fax: 03 89 49 73 78

This 12-ha domain based in Pfaffenheim was one of the pioneers of both organic and biodynamic production in Alsace: look out in particular for a cool, intensely mineral Steinert Riesling and a limpid, textured Vorbourg Gewurztraminer. Low sulphur use means that some of the wines are best decanted before service.

Hugel
Hugel et Fils, 68340 Riquewihr, Tel: 03 89 47 92 15, Fax: 03 89 49 00 01

This much-loved négociant company is actually one of the region's biggest landholders, with over 120 ha to its name. It was a pioneer, in both a legislative and practical sense, of Vendange Tardive and Sélection des Grains Nobles wines; like Beyer and Trimbach, it has decided to have nothing to do with the Grand Cru system, despite being initially enthusiastic in principle. Varietals occupy the first tier of quality, "Tradition" the second, and "Jubilée" the third (and finest). Wines of particular excellence appear under the Hommage à Jean Hugel banner, and the Vendange Tardive and Sélection des Grains Nobles *cuvées* are only made in great vintages. The style is dry, though more softly so than in the case of Trimbach.

Josmeyer
68920 Wintzenheim, Tel: 03 89 27 91 90, Fax: 03 89 27 91 99

Jean Meyer's 25-ha domain (which includes holdings in Hengst and Brand) is complemented by purchases from a further 12 ha. The aim is to produce delicate, carefully crafted, and above all food-friendly wines that reflect their terroir; surprise helpings of residual sugar are rare here. Some of the base-level wines can be over-quiet, almost dull; the better *cuvées*, by contrast, are polished and racy. The Riesling Les Pierrets, for example, combines minerality with succulence; while the Riesling from Brand is incisive, deep, and stony. The Gewurztraminer Les Folastries makes an unusually food-friendly bottle of this varietal: creamy, vinous, dry-spiced, while the Hengst Gewurztraminer ages better than many thanks not only to its fiery minerals but also sustained supporting acidity. From 2001 the family domain is being run biodynamically.

Kientzler ☉
68150 Ribeauvillé, Tel: 03 89 73 67 10, Fax: 03 89 73 35 81

André Kientzler is yet another great wine producer working among the manifold faults of Bergheim and Ribeauvillé. His perfectionist approach means that every wine here is noteworthy, including the superb Chasselas and Auxerrois wines. Muscat from Kirchberg can rival the best from Burn's Clos St-Imer. Greatest of all, though, are the profound, deep-flavoured and cellar-seeking Rieslings from the Grands Crus of Geisberg and Osterberg.

Kreydenweiss
67140 Andlau, Tel: 03 88 08 95 83, Fax: 03 88 08 41 16

Marc Kreydenweiss was the great pioneer of biodynamic viticulture in Alsace from his 12-ha estate in Andlau; he also advises the Bürklin-Wolf estate in Pfalz, and has bought his own estate in Costières de Nîmes, at present in conversion to biodynamics. "Finesse and length" are his stated aims; compared with many of the fashionably baroque wines of the New Alsace, Kreydenweiss's wines are almost austere and edgy, like Gothic cathedrals. (Unusually, he favours early harvesting for Riesling in some sites.) For example, the Clos du Val d'Eléon, a 70% Riesling, 30% Pinot Gris blend produced in grey schist (the same terroir, Kreydenweiss says, as Coulée de Serrant) is super-stony, almost raw, interesting rather than pleasurable. The best, though, are characterized by great purity and limpidity of flavour, like his silvery, nervy Pinot Gris wines from Moenchberg and Lerchenberg and the subtle, almost delicate Gewurztraminer from Kritt.

Seppi Landmann ☉
68570 Soultzmatt, Tel: 03 89 47 09 33, Fax: 03 89 47 06 99

The forceful Seppi Landmann may have only 8.5 ha to his name, but he makes a better range of wines with them than most growers with twice as much. Like all Alsace's best growers, he is constantly pushing at the boundaries of nomenclature and style – with the Sylvaner Z, for example, coming from the Grand Cru of Zinnkoepflé, though he is not yet allowed to say as much; or with the Sylvaner Hors La Loi, a magnificently dense exercise in late harvest brinkmanship. Both Gewurztraminer and Riesling from Zinnkoepflé are balanced and long-lasting, while the Crémant here is a finely crafted sparkling wine rather than just a way to use up second-rate grapes.

Albert Mann
68920 Wettolsheim, Tel: 03 89 80 62 00, Fax: 03 89 80 34 23

"We're looking after the land for our children," says Maurice Barthelmé, explaining why he and his brother Jacky have chosen to take the domain into organic production and, for certain, parcels, biodynamic, too. They produce a generously flavoured, often luscious range from their 20 ha, peaking with exuberant Gewurztraminer from Furstentum and Pinot Gris from Pfersigberg.

Muré
68250 Westhalten, Tel: 03 89 47 64 20, Fax: 03 89 47 09 39

There are two strands here: the first, René Muré, is a négociant producing a sound range of varietals from the Côte de Rouffach (Sylvaner, Riesling, and Crémant are all above average). The second strand is the large, 15-ha Clos St-Landelin, evidently the finest portion of the Grand Cru Vorbourg, constituted by a series of terraced, south-facing, limy slopes, of which Muré is the sole proprietor. Riesling produced here is deep, intense, and unusually richly fruited, while Gewurztraminer in this hot site is chewy and sappy, full of earthy power rather than boudoir scent.

Ostertag ☉
67680 Epfig, Tel: 03 88 85 51 34, Fax: 03 88 85 58 95

The impish André Ostertag is a key grower among the band who are rethinking the fundamental principles of wine production in Alsace. His 12-ha domain is best known for its barrique-fermented wines (which the appellation authorities do not like, hence the cadastral designations and enigmatic song names they have appeared under). It is primarily members of the Pinot family (Blanc, Gris, and Noir) that Ostertag treats in this way, reasoning that their Burgundian origins mean that this is the most suitable and sympathetic system of *élevage*. His own years of study in Burgundy, indeed, and work with Dominique Lafon, were seminal; he has spoken of "*la bouche Lafon* – ample, dry, and mineral" as being one of his winemaking ideals, "a palate very far from that of the habitual Alsace wine". He has also experimented with oak for his Heissenberg Riesling, though the rest of the Ostertag range is unoaked, classical and fresh.

Ostertag's poetic streak comes out in his division of all of his wines into three categories: *vins de fruit* (fruit wines or basic varietals); *vins de pierre* (stone wines, from named Grands Crus and *lieux-dits*); and *vins de temps* (time wines: late harvest and Sélection des Grains Nobles wines which seek cellar solace.) He practices biodynamics "as a tool", yet goes out of his way to conceal the fact, distrusting its cultish overtones. "I detest Nicolas Joly," he told me. "He's the sort who gives a bad name to biodynamics. He's an intellectual, a guru. But the whole point about biodynamics is that it should serve the terroir; the terroir is what comes first." Among the pleasures of the Ostertag range are his Vieilles Vignes Sylvaner, based on 30- to 60-year-old vines: the earthiness, sap, and pepper of the variety emerge with great precision. Riesling from Fronholz is delicate, crystalline, and bell-like; Riesling from Muenchberg, by contrast, is more assertively mineral, though its fruit qualities are still limpid; the Heissenberg Rieslings tend to be plumper and spicier. This is one of the most distinctive Pinot Gris ranges in Alsace: fundamentally dry, but spicy, smoky, occasionally vanillic, sometimes salty. The Zellberg can rival the Muenchberg in certain vintages. Gewurztraminer is the one varietal in which Ostertag allows residual sugar, since he found that fully ripe versions emerged over-hot with alcohol if he pushed them to dryness.

Cave de Pfaffenheim
68250 Pfaffenheim, Tel: 03 89 78 08 08, Fax: 03 89 49 71 65

In a region lucky enough to have half a dozen or more great cooperatives, that of Pfaffenheim is one of the best. The wines of Dopff & Irion are beginning to flourish under its ownership, and its own Grand Cru selections (particularly the Gewurztraminer from Steinert and the Pinot Gris from Zinnkoepflé) bear comparison with many of the wines of private domains in these sites.

Cave de Ribeauvillé
68150 Ribeauvillé, Tel: 03 89 73 61 80, Fax: 03 89 73 31 21

If the Cave de Pfaffenheim is an elephant, then Ribeauvillé is more of a squirrel – there are just 40 members, but they have some very well-sited parcels, including fine Riesling from both Altenberg de Bergheim and Osterberg.

Rolly-Gassmann
68590 Rorschwihr, Tel: 03 89 73 63 28, Fax: 03 89 73 33 06

No Grands Crus here, but a range of soft and succulent wines produced from 31 ha around Rorschwihr in which many nuances of terroir can be discerned, in particular from the Moenchreben de Rorschwihr and the Pflaenzerreben de Rorschwihr. This fine domain is a good source of Sylvaner, Muscat, and varietal Auxerrois (which can suggest strawberries and white chocolate with age). The new generation is taking the domain towards biodynamics.

Schlumberger ✪
68501 Guebwiller, Tel: 03 89 74 27 00, Fax: 03 89 74 85 75

The 140 ha of superbly positioned vineyard owned by Schlumberger makes it Alsace's largest domain. Apart from Gewurztraminer, for which Schlumberger seems to have a deep affinity, the basic *cuvées* are rather dull. The Grands Crus, by contrast, are covetable: this is the reference domain for Saering, Spiegel, Kessler, and Kitterlé planted with Riesling and Gewurztraminer. (Less so for the Pinot Gris *cuvées*, which can be mawkish.) Vendange Tardive and Sélection des Grains Nobles are taken very seriously here.

Schoffit ✪
68000 Colmar, Tel: 0389 24 41 14, Fax: 03 89 41 40 52

This fine 16-ha domain is based in Colmar, even though its greatest wines have, since 1986, come from much further south – from the Clos St-Théobald in Rangen. If you're curious to try Alsace Chasselas at its best, then Schoffit's Vieilles Vignes (they're 70 years old) is the version to seek out. Like Zind-Humbrecht and Blanck, Bernard Schoffit proves that the best growers are still able to make excellent wine from flatland sites – with his wines from Harth,

sited around Colmar (especially an overachieving Pinot Blanc). But it's indubitably the Clos St-Théobald that produces the greatest Schoffit wines of all, especially the intricately constructed Rieslings.

Bruno Sorg
68420 Eguisheim, Tel: 03 89 41 80 85, Fax: 03 89 41 22 64

The Eichberg Gewurztraminer can be superb, but it's the haunting Muscat and the concentrated Riesling Vieilles Vignes *cuvée* from this 10-ha domain for which François Sorg is most often singled out.

André Tempé et Fils
68770 Ammerschwihr, Tel: 03 89 47 18 29, Fax: 03 89 78 15 63

Former INAO worker Marc Tempé is going from strength to strength at his small 7.5-ha biodynamic domain based in Zellenberg, with parcels in Mambourg, Schoenenbourg, and other local sites. "*La vendange, c'est mon dada,*" he told me ("the harvest is my hobby-horse"): absolute ripeness, which combined with low yields and very gentle pressing gives rich, concentrated, highly aromatic musts. No chaptalization, no acid adjustments, no selected yeasts, and fermentation in wood (90% of the 1999 harvest was still fermenting when I called in June 2000): this natural approach gives wines of splendid focus and definition. Tempé's touch is particularly sure for Gewurztraminer: his wines are saturated in spice and rose essences, yet finish clean and pure.

Trimbach ✪✪
68150 Ribeauvillé, Tel: 03 89 73 60 30, Fax: 03 89 73 89 04

If the textured, scent-saturated, often extravagantly powerful wines of Zind-Humbrecht occupy the south pole of Alsace excellence, Trimbach stands waving its flag in the far north. "Restraint" is the watchword. A short, severe written lecture on "The Trimbach Style", produced by the family itself, puts it thus: "The Trimbach Style produces harmonious wines that are concentrated, not heavy; fruity, not sweet; bracing rather than fat; polite rather than voluptuous. Trimbach wines are reserved, steely, elegant, even aristocratic; never obvious or flashy." You have been warned. The Trimbachs (Bernard and Hubert run the company, which has been in family hands since 1626; Bernard's son Pierre is winemaker) own 27 ha of their own vineyards, which supplies about a quarter of the company's needs. This ownership includes the 1.25 ha of Riesling in the Grand Cru of Rosacker that makes the great Clos Ste-Hune, the Alsace Riesling by which all others are judged; as well as 0.65 ha of Geisberg and 4 ha of Osterberg which are blended for its slightly less expensive sibling, the Cuvée Frédéric Emile. (Needless to say, the Grand Cru names are not used by this scourge of the system's laxities.) Fermentations are cool and slow; the wines are removed from their lees as soon as possible; malolactic is avoided; they are filtered, fined, and bottled early "so as to preserve the freshness of the fruit." The Trimbachs then store all their wines for a year in bottle, and the greatest wines for five years or so before release.

The entire range tastes much as you would expect, given this singular, vigorously pursued and proudly championed aesthetic. The basic wines are clean, pure, and classic, though some (like the Pinot Blanc) can seem over-austere, lacking the fun factor. The higher qualities (there is a hierarchy of Réserve, Réserve Personelle, and named *cuvées*) are impeccable: pure, usually though not uniformly concentrated, elegant, classical. The pinnacle, in other words, of French varietal wine production and thus (ironically) a model of the New World approach in France. Terroir may be important – but the fact is that terroir is hidden, not proclaimed and explored, behind the series of brand names and identities. For those weary of the copious residual sugar found in so many contemporary Alsace wines, Trimbach's are a refuge – indeed even the Vendange Tardive wines (like the Frédéric Emile Vendange Tardive 1990, with a mere 15 g/l of residual sugar) are barely off-dry. I will give the last words to the articulate and provocative Hubert Trimbach, with his laughing eyes, ginger eyebrows, and white hair. "We are Protestants. Our wines have the Protestant style – vigour, firmness, a beautiful acidity, lovely freshness. Purity and cleanness, that's Trimbach. No wood: I hate wood! Purity and cleanness, always. Parker has taken us in the wrong direction. He has a sweet tooth. The Americans have corrupted the taste of wine drinkers. These wines are long in cask, they do the malolactic, they sit on their sediments, they get so fat that only Americans can drink them. Zind-Humbrecht is made by Parker. Everything I say you take with a little grain of salt, *n'est-ce pas?*"

Weinbach ○○
68240 Kayserberg, Tel: 03 89 47 13 21, Fax: 03 89 47 38 18

Or, to give the domain its full name, Madame Théo Faller et ses filles. This superb 26-ha domain is known for three things: the splendid walled Clos des Capucins, at the heart of which lies the family house and cellars; the good looks and charm of Madame Colette Faller and her daughters Catherine (sales) and Laurence (the winemaker); and a range of wines which, under the magnetic Laurence, seem to have acquired more finesse and breed without sacrificing their approachability and comeliness. The 5-ha Clos itself is flat, on sandy silt, but there are also mouthwatering parcels in the unclassified Altenbourg (3 ha) as well as the contrastive Grands Crus of Schlossberg (10 ha), Furstentum (1 ha) and Mambourg (50 ares). Names, here, are confusing: in addition to the Grand Cru and *lieu-dit* single-vineyard varietals there are also Réserve and Réserve Personelle wines (from the Clos); Cuvée Theo (from better parts of the Clos); Cuvée Sainte Catherine (from the lower parts of Schlossberg and sometimes the best parts of the Clos, often harvested around Sainte Catherine's day on November 25th) and Cuvée Laurence wines (richer wines from even later harvested grapes). There are also some astonishingly showy Vendange Tardive and Sélection des Grains Nobles wines. A huge range, thus, but one of impressive consistency, never better to my mind than in the various Rieslings from the magnificent Schlossberg, by turns suggesting orchard fruits, mineral salts, honey, and (with time) butter and nuts. The perfumed, oily Gewurztraminers from Altenbourg, too, suggest that this site should be a Grand Cru.

Zind-Humbrecht ○○○
68239 Turckheim, Tel: 03 89 27 02 05, Fax: 03 89 27 22 58

If I had to pick one French domain out of all those mentioned in this book as being emblematic of The New France as a whole, it would be this one. Why? Firstly, because France's new generation are above all engaged in a quest to peel back the land, to discover the truths and the beauties of terroir, and no domain in France has done this more effectively over the last four decades than Zind-Humbrecht. The work was begun by Léonard Humbrecht who married Geneviève Zind in 1959, before Alsace had been awarded its mono-terroir AOC; during the 1960s and 1970s, where convenience was the watchword of most Alsace wine-growers, Léonard Humbrecht was buying and salvaging great, difficult vineyards, and in particular the now legendary (but then abandoned) Rangen of Thann. The winemaking arrival of their prodigiously talented son Olivier in the late 1980s has enabled Léonard to continue his vineyard research at the 40-ha domain with renewed zeal, while Olivier's wines offer a dazzling lesson in site differentiation.

The second great theme of The New France is that of environmental respect. This is a consummately professional domain; Olivier Zind-Humbrecht MW has a brilliant mind, and one forged on scientific pragmatism. The fact that biodynamics was adopted as swiftly as it was here is both a comprehensive endorsement of its empirical benefits and proof of the environmental commitment of the Zind-Humbrechts. (It was no easy choice: permanent staff had to be upped from 15 to 26.) Yields here are often a third or less than the regional average, and the ideal is always to harvest perfectly ripe, perfectly balanced grapes (never, of course, requiring chaptalization or added acid).

The third great development of the last decade in France is the courageous pursuit of the non-interventionist ideal in the cellar. Few could use the battery of modern winemaking techniques to greater effect than the skilled Olivier Zind-Humbrecht; instead he has chosen to follow the non-interventionist route as far as it leads. It takes courage to press grapes so gently that 48 hours are required to extract all the juice; to allow wines 14 months to ferment; to let them rest for ten months on their lees with no added sulphur dioxide; to permit them to make their own decision as to whether or not they undergo malolactic fermentation in a region where the malo has traditionally been avoided. It takes courage to bottle wines containing residual sugar without fining or filtration. It takes courage to present a range to market in which residual sugar levels vary widely. It has involved Olivier Zind-Humbrecht himself in a change of heart on more than one occasion. "I wouldn't have considered it 15 years ago," he told me, when we discussed his 1998 wines finishing their fermentations in January 2000. "But only idiots don't change their minds." It's also risky. "We can afford to be non-interventionist only if the grapes are of irreproachable quality and maturity; otherwise the results might be catastrophic." Anyone who has ever had the chance to taste through the complete offerings of a vintage chez Zind-Humbrecht will know that this experience is akin to stepping into an immaculately tended garden or walking around a quiet gallery full of masterly paintings. Here is the earth's wealth given sensory expression; here is a glittering spectrum of cultured nuance and difference. We are as far as it is possible to be from the drab monotony of industrially produced, branded wine, or from the surly harshness of wines made in unthinking and ignorant agricultural traditions.

And in practice? The first characteristic that immediately alerts you to the quality of Zind-Humbrecht wines is their density. These are white wines of matter and substance; they lie like essences or pulp on the tongue. Their scents aren't always pleasing, particularly shortly after bottling; as with all low-sulphur practice, reduction can be a problem, and no one should ever hesistate to decant these wines if necessary. Mostly, of course, they smell magnificent, yet each wears a different personality, and scent is meshed to flavour here with rare intimacy. The grape essence of the Herrenweg Muscat (a bargain, based on 50-year-old vines), for example, contrasts with the floral power of the Goldert Muscat. Zind-Humbrecht's Pinot Blanc seems beautifully typical of this varietal; surprisingly, it contains Auxerrois from Herrenweg and Chardonnay from Clos Windsbuhl as well as Pinot Blanc from Rotenberg. Riesling, for Olivier Zind-Humbrecht, is "the most elegant white wine in the world", and there are up to ten to chose from. Among them the limestone Clos Hauserer (beneath Hengst in Wintzenheim) is lively and darting; the sheltered Clos Windsbuhl (in Hunawihr) is stony, intense and driving; the young-vines Heimbourg (in Turckheim) is softer and creamier; the granitic Brand is powerful, brash, almost uncivilized, packed with walnuts and cinders (most of the vines here are over 40 years old); while the volcanic Clos St-Urbain is complex and calmly composed, a synthesis of flowers, orchard fruits, and butter with a finishing mineral flourish. Zind-Humbrecht's Pinot Gris wines often contain residual sugar, even the "ordinary" Vieilles Vignes *cuvée* (from 50-year-old-plus vines in Herrenweg), yet their density and extract provides the necessary weight to anchor this sweetness. Clos Jebsal (a south-facing, gypsum-rich vineyard above Turckheim) is the flagship vineyard for this varietal, and Zind-Humbrecht often produces boundary-pushing, essence-like, fruit-dripping late harvest and Sélection des Grains Nobles wines here, characterized by super-succulent summer fruits. Heimbourg and Rotenberg are slightly fresher and smokier, while the Clos St-Urbain turns on the mineral power of this extraordinary vineyard. Gewurztraminer, finally, is rarely as explosively exotic as here, with the "ordinary" Turckheim version being one the region's absolute benchmarks. Above that, almost everything is special: fine village examples from Wintzenheim and Geuberschwihr which easily outpower many other producers' Grand Cru wines, as well as the masterful, often fully dry Herrenweg de Turckheim. The doughty, spice-bomb Hengst; the almost painfully intense and structured Heimbourg (from 50-year-old vines); the succulent, candied citrus Goldert; and the honeyed, fiery, steamroller-like Clos Windsbuhl are all crowned by tiny quantities of the multi-faceted, salty, mineral Clos St-Urbain, a sublime wine but one which proves Jean-Michel Deiss's thesis that in great sites in Alsace, the voice of the vineyard is far louder than that of the varietal.

Chablis

Keeping Faith Chablis is made with the world's favourite grape variety — and yet no wine in the world tastes like Chablis. That happy chance is easy and profitable to exploit. In the New France, thus, Chablis' main challenge is to do itself justice.

If there is to be sunshine like this, you'd want it for a Sunday. The warmth carries no moisture. There's a powdered perfection in the air. The squat, white building stones of this small, self-sufficient town seem to be minutely settling, one on another, cladding the air with the dust of marine bones as they do so.

There is, in the rue du Maréchal de Lattre de Tassigny, a market. It's hard to avoid its languid magnetism; the gentle current of people outside your hotel will guide you there anyway. You pass the rue des Juifs: dark, crumbling, and poor. The river glints greenly at its end, and just round the corner is the *ancien lavoir*, a small cloister where the women of the town once bent over their washing. Today it's sombre and still, decorated with a little innocent graffiti ("*SL aime V*" inside a crude heart). You carry on down the rue Porte Noël past the pharmacy, whose window is full of pink balloons. "*Charbon de Belloc*," reads the handwritten poster, "*digère l'air qui vous ballonne*" ("Belloc carbon digests the air that makes you swell up like a balloon.") One balloon displays a painted face, smiling with the unconditional happiness of the deflatulated. Across the street, a large black Newfoundland dog pads responsibly up the street with a basket of Sunday goods held between her teeth. Her owner, a slim man with graying, messy hair, walks a little way behind her. If she strays away from the kerb, he says something to her, quietly, and she slips back on course.

The market begins at the crossroads. The baker opposite (Didier Martin — *votre artisan boulanger*) has put a table outside his shop, covered with the more original turns in his repertoire: huge, crusty country loaves looking like giant burnt snails. The first two stalls face each other across the street: a bored blonde selling nightclothes to no one, her surly man reading a newspaper in the sunlight behind the stall; and facing it a busy vegetable stall on which pumpkin-yellow *girolles* gleam. "*Produits de terroir*," says a crude handwritten notice on a sheet of exercise-book paper. There are strings of bright red peppers hanging from the stall's framework: "*Piments de l'Espelette*," explains a brochure: "*l'épice du pays Basque*." There are white peaches and dark, bloomy figs from Provence; trays of haricots verts as fine as quills; radishes in two military lines in another box, and parsley stuffed into a third. Three colours of garlic (white, violet, and pink) beckon the eye. At the stall where a stout woman sells hot black pudding, the queue is a dozen souls long. Every table on the shaded café terrace is taken; as the day's heat rises, the drinkers sit quietly, reading papers, watching movement, smoking unhurriedly. And, from chill-beaded café glasses, they sip a near-silver white wine. An old lady passes me in a side street: white hair, thick glasses. "*Fait chaud, hein?*" she says, as if she needed confirmation from someone else before she'd believe it. "*Fait chaud*," she mutters again as she walks on by, uncontradicted.

Chablis is a fortunate spot. Its name slides, slippery as a mango stone, off the tongue; its reputation long ago travelled as far as wine itself. If imitation is flattery, this should be a wine with the ego of a pampered rock star: before the protection of French appellation names became widespread in new wine-producing countries, every one of them made a "Chablis". A few still do.

There isn't much of it: just over 4,000 ha (9,880 acres) for its four appellations, making it barely bigger than Coteaux d'Aix en Provence. That's but a drop to satisfy a world of demand. Above all, though, the reason why Chablis is so prized is its taste. It is quite unlike any other wine on earth (though it comes closest, for reasons we will discover in a moment, to old Champagne and to the Sauvignons of the Upper Loire). There are many New World Chardonnays that can manage a passable imitation of Meursault; almost none even attempts to understudy Chablis. It smells of smoke and stone and winter air; it tastes as quick and fresh as a chill, pebbly stream tumbling off a dark, rain-draped mountain. Do you doubt the influence of soil on wine flavour? If you do, buy yourself a bottle of Chablis from any of the starred producers below. Buy five other Chardonnays, muddle the bottles up together, and taste all six blind with a few friends. If the bottle of Chablis isn't constitutionally different from the other five Chardonnays, then dismiss this book as fraudulent.

"Can I tell you a story?" said Vincent Dauvissat to me, when I asked him about Chablis' stony, mineral flavours. "About ten years ago, several geologists came to Chablis to try to understand terroir, the links between the soil and the wine. The day they came, though, it was pouring with rain and they couldn't get into the vineyards, so they decided to tour round the cellars and taste various wines instead. I opened a very old bottle for them at the end, and they were very struck by its scent. Now I've also got a lovely old block of stone full of *Exogyra virgula* [the comma-shaped fossil that characterizes the Kimmeridgian marly limestone on which classic Chablis grows] and they exclaimed how beautiful it was, and said they wanted to take it away with them. I said no, no, it's too beautiful, I want to keep it, but I will give you a bit of it. So I went and got a hammer and knocked a bit off. And at the point at which it broke, it gave off truly the same smell that we'd just found in the bottle of old wine, that same note of smoke and stone. They were astounded."

I have a piece of *Exogyra*-rich stone in front of me as I write; I picked it up from Les Clos one ferociously hot afternoon in September 2000. A close look reveals the foliated fossil shells packed densely together like pasta, glued with a hard grey-white marl which resembles dried potter's clay. The visual composition, though, is by no means the most extraordinary characteristic of this 160-g pebble. The fact is that

"In the 1970s we took an aspirin every day just in case we got a headache. In the 1980s we took an aspirin only when we had a headache. And in the 1990s we began to ask ourselves 'Why do we get headaches?'"

MICHEL LAROCHE

◄ A bud is a promise. Inside this one, inflorescences already marked by their singular environment await a season's fulfilment.

▲ *Little in this view betrays the uniqueness of Chablis. One sip reveals all. Wine's landscapes are decoded by scent and taste, not sight.*

this stone smells. One sniff catches its aroma. What is it like? Imagine a box of classroom chalk lightly sprinkled with water and placed in an airtight container for a day or two. This smell is that which would greet you as you opened that box.

It's not, of course, only the pungency of fossiliferous pebbles that makes Chablis stand out from other Chardonnays. Acidity is another element: good Chablis is sour. Not the sort of raw sourness you'll find in unripe fruits, but ripe sourness, full sourness, rich sourness, milky sourness. There are other Chardonnays in the world that are lashed as tightly to the mast of acidity (most notably those of Tasmania and New Zealand's Marlborough), but those acidities have a very different quality. They are usually profoundly citric, riven with lemon and lime, and in Marlborough often leafy, too; Chablis' acidity is vinous, structural, sinewy, crackling through the wine with a sort of mute electrical force.

Fruit flavours, indeed, are likely to be restrained, and there is certainly nothing of the billowing sumptuous fruit of most warm-climate Chardonnay in Chablis, or even of some white burgundies grown further south in the Côte d'Or. You need to poke around in a Chablis to find its exquisite little wicker basket of orchard fruits; it is often hidden beneath a pile of white stones. With time (and good Chablis, like good Riesling, needs time) there will be other things, too: flowers, moss, fresh bread, cut white mushroom, forest floor, a little honey. These, though, are contingent; nothing in surfeit. The only rival Chardonnay that might confuse you (though this would be cheating) would be an old Blanc de Blancs Champagne from a ripe vintage which you had let stand in the glass until it had exhaled all its gas.

This wine, then, is a treasure of the natural world, like a perfect harbour on an inhospitable coast, or a lode of diamonds stowed beneath a grim mountain. The pressures on Chablis wine-growers are accordingly rather different from those faced by growers in Corbières or Quincy. There is no case to prove or challenge to meet in order to gain acclaim and acceptance. The pressure, rather, is to keep faith with the promise of the soils and the trust of the market. To make, in other words, the very best Chablis that can be made. Not to take short cuts; not to give way to indiscipline on yields and concentration; not to exploit the easy sales that the name ensures.

Chablis' record in this respect is a patchy one. The vineyard area has expanded greatly in the last three decades of the twentieth century: it was 500 ha (1,235 acres) in the 1950s and had grown to 1,000 ha (2,470 acres) by 1970; now it is four times that size. There was a great deal of shockingly mediocre Chablis sold cheaply during that

time, and even Premier Cru and Grand Cru Chablis too often disappointed. The evidence for this decline is glaring, and should be painfully obvious to the producers themselves. If all Chablis was as great as it could be, why is its average price so much lower than that of Puligny-Montrachet? Why is the average price of Premier Cru Montée de Tonnerre so much lower than Meursault-Genevrières, and the average price of Grand Cru Le Clos so much lower than Corton-Charlemagne or Bâtard-Montrachet? Walk these vineyards, taste their best wines, and you will know that the terroir is in no way inferior to the most exquisite sites of the Côte d'Or. The problem has been bad faith, easy sales, shortcuts, and laziness. Until recently, for example, forty per cent of Grand Cru Chablis was harvested mechanically. At a time, in other words, when the physical handling and sorting of fruit, bunch by bunch and even (in 2001 at Pape Clément) grape by grape, is considered more and more important in France's greatest vineyards, almost half of the cream of Chablis' fruit was being knocked off the vines by batons and taken back to the winery by the trailerload. Other Chablis vices include a mania for the flavour-stripping "cleanliness" that puts low temperatures, stainless steel vessels, fining agents, and filter pads together to devastating effect. The result is then baptized, quite erroneously, as "terroir".

Change, happily, is underway; there is a palpable sense in this small region that it is time to leave behind its commodity-wine past and become, as it deserves to be, a more consistently pure, fine, and expressive wine, watermarked with the knife-grinder's smile that its astonishing terroir surrenders. The most tangible sign of this is the formation of the Union des Grands Crus de Chablis, created in March 2000, with the all-important Charter of Quality being signed by 18 producers (including Billaud-Simon, La Chablisienne, Drouhin, Laroche, and Fèvre) on January 24th, 2001.

The quotation from Michel Laroche with which this chapter opens describes the evolution in thinking in Chablis, as the shortcuts, prophylactics, and palliatives of the past have gradually given way towards a clearer understanding of what quality is and how it can be achieved. The Union, originally Laroche's idea, is intended to be a method not only of giving back to the Grand Cru wines some of their lost grandeur, but also a way of showing an example to the region as a whole. The Union now includes 18 producers, accounting for two-thirds of the 100 ha (247 acres) currently in production. The Quality Charter lists, among its stipulations, future plantings at 8,000 plants per hectare; a vineyard inspection in July by other Union members to verify that crop levels are not too high; no machine harvesting; no bottling any earlier than fifteen months after harvest; and blind tasting by other Union members before the Union's seal of approval is issued.

Vincent Dauvissat

Few political quotations are as well known as Charles de Gaulle's reported remark about the ungovernability of a nation that produces as many cheeses as France does. Wine-growers are no more compliant.

"When I heard about it," said Vincent Dauvissat, referring to the creation of the Union des Grands Crus, "I thought it was as if the Chablisiens weren't conscious that they had a great terroir, as if they were afraid of something. I saw financial calculation behind it. It was if they wanted to drag the price of Chablis up with this Union. Our work shouldn't be at this level, with salesmanship of this sort; our work should be in the vineyards. Every wine-grower in Chablis already makes a very good living. One shouldn't speculate on something noble – which is what wine is."

Those who know Vincent Dauvissat will instantly recognize this pure-spirited objection (a fellow producer describes him as a doux-reveur,

a "sweet-dreamer"), even if they may regret – as I do – the fact that Dauvissat is not a member of the Union, making it by his presence a stronger one.

Let's, though, look at it another way. Do winemakers make wines in their own image? If so, who would you rather have make your Chablis for you than a pure-spirited vigneron? Chablis, after all, should be the purest of wines, limpid and uncluttered, acquiring with time only those notes that naturally well up from the moist stones into which the roots spread and percolate. That more or less sums up the Dauvissat style, which might be described as that of intense and finely detailed purity. "The fundamental theme," he told me, "is that we are lucky enough to have some truly great terroirs here, and we have to preserve them. I was brought up in surroundings where people were close to their soils, where they loved what they were doing, and where they were able to transmit that love for their vine, for each plant, for wine itself. I try to pass that on. No more."

Jean-Marie Raveneau

Shyness, you might say, goes with the territory. There are one or two ebullient extroverts in Chablis (like Gilles Collet, perhaps, with his flamboyant aviator's moustache), but most growers round here are hard to draw out, live very much in the stony, wind-sung loneliness of their vineyards or in the darkness of their own cellars, and keep their thoughts to themselves. To this profile, one must add in the case of Jean-Marie Raveneau an almost palpable intensity. Just find the key, one feels, and all the secrets will tumble out, hurly-burly.

Principles and methods are very similar here to those chez Dauvissat: much hard work in the

vineyards, then classic vinification and slow, unhurried élevage in old wooden feuillettes. Like Dauvissat, too, Raveneau has chosen to remain outside the Union des Grands Crus, though his reasons are perhaps a little more pragmatic than Vincent Dauvissat's.

"In principle," he says, "I'm in agreement. I just think it all happened too quickly; they put the cart before the horse. They should have begun with the Charter of Quality, worked slowly towards achieving it, then once that was done set about forming the Union. Until the quality standards really do improve, then my answer to the Union is 'no'."

Didier Séguier

Bordelais Didier Séguier, placed in charge of Chablis' finest estate (which bears the name of former proprietor William Fèvre) by owner Joseph Henriot, is one of the few outsiders to be making wine in Chablis. Séguier was born in Cognac, but grew up in Blaye; despite this Chardonnay-free background, he seems to have developed a profound affinity for the region and its wines. The William Fèvre estate owns no less than fifteen per cent of all the Grand Cru land; if only those

with the other eighty-five per cent would model their fruit-handling techniques on William Fèvre principles. All the fruit is picked by hand into small trays holding no more than thirteen kg; they are then sorted on a table de tri before going off for pressing. It is this, combined with lower yields and a much more cautious use of new oak than before, that has helped bring about the remarkable results that were achieved here in 1999 and 2000.

The Adventure of the Land

Chablis does not belong in Burgundy. Ask any geographer: the two are doubly different. Different on the basis of water; different on the basis of stone.

France contains four great river basins: the Seine, the Loire, the Rhône, and the Garonne/Dordogne. Burgundy forms part of the Rhône basin; Chablis (and Champagne) forms part of the Seine basin. You have to cross the Plateau de Langres and the Morvan to get from one to the other. Not much of an upland, admittedly, but water only spills over its sinewy shoulder by dint of the locks on the Canal de Bourgogne. The fact that Chablis is part of the Seine basin is why the Yonne was once (mind-bogglingly) the largest viticultural *département* in France. Before phylloxera, the vineyards covered not 4,000 ha (9,880 acres) but 40,000 ha (98,800 acres).

Geologically, too, we are somewhere other than Burgundy. We are, in fact, in the region to which the geologist James Wilson gives the name "The Kimmeridgian Chain" in his fine book *Terroir*. The stone maps are, for once, unusually clear. Reuilly, Quincy, Menetou-Salon, Sancerre, Pouilly-sur-Loire, Irancy, Chablis, Tonnerre, les Riceys, Bar-sur-Seine, Bar-sur-Aube: all lie within easy reach of each other on a long white baguette of Upper Jurassic limestone. This is a two-tone composition: lower down lies a soft, chalky fossil-bearing marl called Kimmeridgian, which is capped by hard limestone called Portlandian. It comprises the rim of the Paris basin (which dips below the English Channel and rises again in Britain's southern counties – hence the Dorset nomenclature). By contrast, almost all of Burgundy (apart from a few peaks of the Hautes Côtes) is on Middle Jurassic. Geologically,

thus, Chablis has more in common with the Upper Loire and the southern sector of Champagne than it does with Meursault or Mâcon.

But then there is the little matter of grape variety. Sauvignon Blanc does grow in the Yonne, but in a few vineyards only. Overwhelmingly (since phylloxera; not before) this is Chardonnay country, with a little pale Pinot Noir grown too. Grape varieties are sometimes thought secondary to considerations of terroir in France, but in truth it is grape variety above all that has given Chablis its Burgundian profile. This is today the northern outreach of the greatest stretch of Chardonnay country in the world.

Chablis occupies a splodge surrounding the town of Chablis; the vineyards lie each side of its river – the prettily named and habitually indolent Serein (which means "serene"). Charter a microlight to overfly the splodge, and you'll see a pastoral and evolved landscape in which at least fourteen side valleys cut down to the Serein. This means a multiplicity of slopes and aspects – thus subdivision. Chablis' other appellations are subsumed within it.

The coolest, often highest patches of vineyard are **Petit Chablis**; this usually (though not uniformly) coincides with the point at which the Kimmeridgian marl gives way to the harder Portlandian limestone that overlies it. Take a walk up the Grand Cru slopes that superintend the town of Chablis, and almost all of the long stretch of vineyards that lie above them, as the slope rounds off into a plateau, are Petit Chablis. Aside from a small morsel of land above the Valmur-Vaudésir border, there is no transition zone of Premier Cru or "ordinary" Chablis between the two.

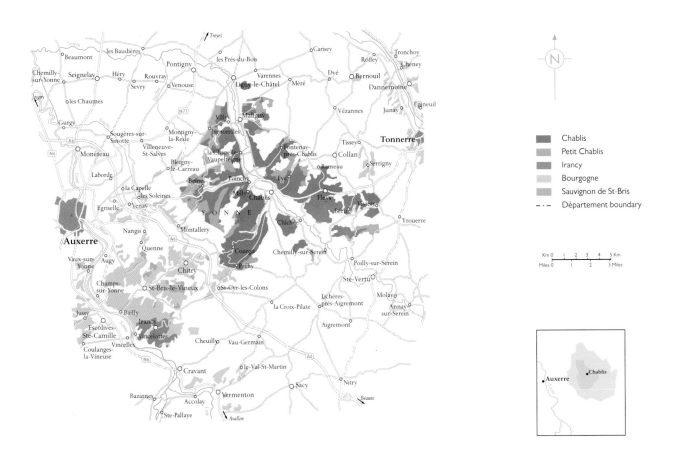

■	Chablis
■	Petit Chablis
■	Irancy
■	Bourgogne
■	Sauvignon de St-Bris
– – –	Département boundary

Favourable mid-slope sites that face southeast or southwest are classified as **Chablis Premier Cru**, which leaves the vast majority of slopes (facing in all directions and at various heights, but preponderantly on Kimmeridgian marl) as plain Chablis. There has been considerable controversy surrounding the 1967 and 1976 extensions (both finally ratified in 1986) to the boundaries of both Chablis and Chablis Premier Cru. Why? The reason is that the original 1938 AOC decree was unusual in that it specified the precise geological strata from which Chablis should in principle come (Kimmeridgian marl), and many of the 1967 and 1976 extensions made to the 1938 boundaries have been on Portlandian, or on other sorts of marl or on clay. Topographical features, in other words (the right slope in the right place), are now regarded as being of equal importance to geological origin. Maybe this is why not all Chablis and not all Chablis Premier Cru is as good as it should be; personally I suspect it has more to do with shabby viticulture, over-high yields, and slapdash winemaking.

What is irrefutable is that there is a chaos of Premier Cru names (forty all told, covering 747 ha/1,845 acres). As in the rest of Burgundy, using these names is optional; you can simply call your wine Premier Cru and leave it at that. In any case, only seventeen or so names are in common use, and some of these (like Beugnons or Butteaux) are rarely seen. Others (like Forêts) are spelled in different ways. The great Premiers Crus are those that lie each side of the Grands Crus (Fourchaume to the north, and Montée de Tonnerre and Mont de Milieu to the south), plus the three that face the Grands Crus across the Serein Valley (Montmains, Vaillons, and Côte de Léchet). Fôrets is in effect the southern end of Montmains.

It is a great relief to reach **Chablis Grand Cru**, since this is simple to understand. Well, almost. Chablis Grand Cru is a single, contiguous 106-ha (262-acre) stretch of hillside sited exactly opposite the town itself and an easy walk from it. The slope is intriguingly shaped, and divided into seven Grand Cru parcels (though the appellation here is Chablis Grand Cru and not the parcel name alone). Blanchot (12.7 ha/31.4 acres) lies at the southeastern end of this choice morsel of land, occupying the steep drop to the Fyé Valley, which separates it from Montée de Tonnerre. Les Clos, at twenty-six ha (64.2 acres), is the biggest and hottest parcel, glowering down at the town itself; Valmur (13.2 ha/32.6 acres) occupies a cooler side valley to the north of Les Clos. Grenouilles (the smallest at 9.4 ha/23.2 acres) is also the lowest: a gentle mound of frog-hopping height close to the river. That mound creates a little curling valley behind it which reminds me of the shape of *Exogyra virgula* itself; the slopes that look down on this valley are those of hot, quick-ripening Vaudésir (14.7 ha/36.3 acres). Finally, at the northeastern end of the Grand Cru zone are Les Preuses (11.4 ha/28.2 acres) and Bougros (12.6 ha/31.1 acres); the two form a sloping plateau which, at the southern end of Bougros, suddenly drops down steeply to the D91 road. La Moutonne is a name of monastic origin used by one producer (Long Depaquit) for a 2.35-ha (5.8-acre) parcel at the western end of Vaudésir; it also includes a snippet of Preuses. William Fèvre, meanwhile, produces two Bougros wines, one from the higher plateau land (simply called Bougros) and one from the steep slope at the southern end of this parcel (called Bougros Côte Bouguerots).

Stylistically speaking, Les Clos makes the biggest, chewiest, most slowly evolving yet most long-lasting wines. Vaudésir, every bit as warm a site, tends to be more seductive, ripe, and voluptuous. Les Preuses is full of floral finesse, while Valmur is often the most austere and nervy of the seven: the Chablis classicist's choice. Grenouilles is softer and lighter. Blanchots is as accessible as Grenouilles, though it tends to have a little more mineral depth, while Bougros is the most controversial in that some tasters consider it doesn't fully justify its Grand Cru status. Perhaps it depends on where in the *cru* a grower's

vines are sited: one taste of Fèvre's Côte Bouguerots, with its fine, sappy intensity and clattering mineral finish, is proof positive of grandeur.

The two links to either side of Chablis in the Kimmeridgian Chain provide perfect material for wine quiz enthusiasts, as well as some of the least readily loveable of all France's still wines: a little portfolio of the curious, acidic, and obscure. These are, in effect, the last remnants of the great pre-phylloxera vineyards of the Yonne, struggling to make their way in a world full of naturally richer wines. To the southwest of Chablis lies the new AOC of **Sauvignon de St-Bris**. St-Bris le Vineux is the full name of its home village, and "vinous" sums up the style of this Sauvignon: it is fuller and more sinewy than its leafy neighbours further down the chain in Quincy or Menetou-Salon. **Irancy**, just to the south of St-Bris, now has its own AOC for tenuous Pinot-based reds. The village itself occupies an arrestingly sunken site surrounded by the vineyards that rise up over its roofs, making the buildings appear as if they are about to disappear forever down some geological plughole.

Other villages in the surrounding area can attach their names to that of the basic Bourgogne AOC, in the main for both red and white wines: **Bourgogne St-Bris** (not, obviously, for Sauvignon-based white but for Chardonnay and Pinot Noir), **Bourgogne Coulanges la Vineuse**, **Bourgogne Jussy**, **Bourgogne Chitry**, **Bourgogne Aligoté Côtes de Chitry** and **Bourgogne Côte d'Auxerre**, all in the Auxerre area (known as the Auxerrois). **Bourgogne Joigny Côte St-Jacques** lies northwest of Auxerre, around Joigny (this area is called the Jovinien); **Bourgogne Vézelay** lies to the southeast, around the much-visited town of the same name (the, Vezelien). Northeast of Chablis lies **Bourgogne Epineuil** and **Bourgogne Tonnerre** (the Tonnerrois). Finally, further northeast once more lies the magnificently obscure wine-growing district of the Châtillonais, based around Châtillon-sur-Seine (very different, note, from the Rhône's Châtillon-en-Diois). This is just a few kilometres from les Riceys, and is thus in effect another still-wine producing sector of Champagne's Aube – yet administratively it finds itself in the *département* of the Côte d'Or rather than the Aube, so its still wines (which tend to be based on Pinot Blanc rather than Chardonnay for white) are sold as **Bourgogne**. Every bottle referred to in this paragraph is still – yet in truth if this area does have a vocation, Chablis aside, it is for the production of some of the best of all sparkling **Crémant de Bourgogne**. The naturally high levels of acidity found here, often so challenging in still wines, come into their own for sparkling-wine production.

▼ *Chardonnay loves to dig its roots deep into these pebbles of Kimmeridgian lime – and rabbits love new shoots.*

▲ *The Grand Cru view from Bougros towards Preuses and Vaudésir, each vine lounging expectantly on its sun-ramp.*

Chablis Flak

New oak smoke

No discussion of Chablis at any time over the last twenty years has neglected to comment on, usually ruefully, the amount of new oak in which some producers have fermented and raised their wines. William Fèvre, in particular, picked late and used lavish new oak; the La Chablisienne cooperative, too, liked the ample, internationally appealing style that new oak brought. The arrival of new oak in Chablis coincided with hot vintages such as 1989 and 1990, and this intensified the impression tasters received that the old days of slender, rapier-like Chablis were gone forever. Another problem is that reviewing magazines tend to taste Premier and Grand Cru Chablis at around the two to three year mark, often an awkward, adolescent phase, which is when its oak is likely to be most obtrusive.

In fact "the oak crisis" was much exaggerated. It is true that the use of new oak, even for Grand Cru Chablis, needs to be cautious, but the vast majority of Chablis producers (for reasons of economy, if nothing else) were always parsimonious with new oak anyway. Today, new oak is disappearing as a "problem" in Chablis; both La Chablisienne and William Fèvre (under the talented Didier Séguier, the winemaker appointed by new owner Joseph Henriot) use new oak with great discretion. Laroche only ever uses a maximum of twenty-five per cent new oak for Les Clos and Blanchots alone; Drouhin uses fifteen per cent for Les Clos and Vaudésirs. Dauvissat himself varies the amount he uses according to the vintage, but it is usually around the twenty per cent mark; Jean-Paul Droin says much the same thing; the average age of Raveneau's barrels is between seven and eight years. The majority of wood in Chablis, thus, is old wood, though the size of container varies from the traditional Chablis *feuillette* of 132-litres to large *foudres*. And, make no mistake, Chablis works exquisitely well with judicious amounts of both new and old oak, as the greatest wines of Raveneau and Vincent Dauvissat and present-day Fèvre bottlings confirm. This is not a question of vanillins; the subtle oxidation of cask ageing also speckles the wine with complexity. (Some producers, of course, like Louis Michel and Jean Durup, reject oak entirely: *see* below.) The new oak issue is becoming a non-issue in Chablis.

The march of the machine

Oak may now be a non-issue, but machine harvesting is a hot issue in Chablis; it was the requirement to abandon machine harvesting that proved the most difficult hurdle to stride as the Union des Grands Crus charter was fought over. (Since its formation, one domain has withdrawn because of this stipulation.) The quality of harvesting machines, claim their users, is improving all the time. It is much cheaper to harvest mechanically than by hand; in principle (though not always in practice: those who hire machines have to book their slots in advance) machine harvesting permits more flexibility about the harvest date, avoiding rainy days and sweltering afternoons. Above all, though, it has been the sheer difficulty of finding pickers that has led to more and more producers using machines to harvest their grapes; these difficulties have been aggravated by recent strictures in French employment law, which have succeeded, ludicrously, in dissuading both the unemployed and the retired from helping with harvesting. Yet great wine, especially great white wine, cannot be made with bruised, shocked, or damaged grapes, and even the most sophisticated mechanical harvesting is a necessarily violent process. The great present-day Grand Cru wines of Fèvre, for example, are hand-picked in trays that contain no more than 13kg of grapes, so that none are crushed or bruised; they are then sorted further by hand at the winery. The machine that can do this has yet to be invented; those who wish to make the greatest Chablis need skilled human hands to pick their grapes. Indeed machine harvesting, along with extensive use of stainless steel, selected yeasts, refrigeration for fermentation and tartrate precipitation, reductive winemaking, routine fining, and secure filtration is part of the "technological" mentality that has invaded the Chablis mindset more extensively than in any other fine wine region in France. If Chablis is ever to be as great as its terroir suggests it should be, it needs to step back from this, to recover the simple reverence for raw materials and methods of the past.

The chaos of Premiers Crus

In some regions, INAO seems extraordinarily parsimonious with its AOCs; in Greater Burgundy, by contrast, almost anything goes. The nomenclature of Chablis' Premiers Crus is chaotic, confusing, and arbitrary, and to judge by the quality of some of the Premier Cru Chablis available on the market, the delimitations of Premier Cru land have been disappointingly lax. The lesson should be clear. If Chablis wants its Premiers Crus to be taken as seriously as those of Meursault, Puligny, or Chassagne, and to rise above the joke status that those of Rully or Montagny command, then it needs to refine, simplify and tighten its Premier Cru system.

Chablis: People

Billaud-Simon ✪
89800 Chablis, Tel: 03 86 42 10 33, Fax: 03 86 42 48 77

This 18-ha domain, assiduously run by Samuel Billaud and his uncle Bernard, produces a worthwhile range of wines including Vieilles Vignes *cuvées*, 9 ha in four Premiers Crus and small holdings of 1 ha or less in four Grands Crus (Les Clos, Blanchots, Vaudésirs, and Les Preuses). Hand-picking and oak fermentation is used for the Vieilles Vignes (40 years+) and the Grands Crus; the rest of the wines are machine harvested and steel-fermented. The overall style is pure, fresh and limpid.

Pascal Bouchard
89800 Chablis, Tel: 03 86 42 18 64, Fax: 03 86 42 48 11

Medium-sized, 32-ha domain with small Grand Cru holdings (1.7 ha of Les Clos and 1.6 ha of Vaudésir, plus a little land in Blanchots) but with an attractive range of Premier Cru wines including 8 ha of Fourchaume and 5 ha of Mont de Milieu. There is also now a range of négociant wines. Low yields give wines with better intensity than the norm, ageing well. The Grands Crus are oak-fermented; the rest of the range generally not.

Jean-Marc Brocard
89800 Préhy, Tel: 03 86 41 49 00, Fax: 03 86 41 49 09

Jean-Marc Brocard is a great businessman and a good wine producer. He began back in the 1970s with a single hectare; as I write he has 80; there will probably be more by the time this book is published. In addition to his own domain, he also buys fruit from both Chablis and the wider Yonne in general to sell on a négociant basis. He is an astute marketeer: the "Chardonnay collection" (the rounded Jurassique, the mineral Portlandian, the delicate Oxfordien, and the perfumed, deep Kimmeridgien) is an attractive idea for the geologically romantic, as is his division of Sauvignon de St-Bris into "Rive gauche" and "Rive droite", and his location-based Chablis AOC *cuvées*. Winemaker Clotilde Davenne oversees a range of clean, consistent Premiers Crus (with an especially good Montée de Tonnerre) and satisfactory Grands Crus (including a pleasant Bougros).

La Chablisienne
89800 Chablis, Tel: 03 86 42 89 89, Fax: 03 86 42 89 90

Well-run and market-orientated cooperative whose wines, palpably authentic and impressively reliable, provide the first taste of Chablis for many consumers around the world. With around 300 members and one-third of the AOC production, it dominates its region – and not just at the lower levels. Some 7 ha of the total 9 ha of Grand Cru Grenouilles is made by the cooperative, part of this being the "estate" of the Château de Grenouilles. There are thus two Grenouilles *cuvées* here; the Château version is made from old (50 year) vines in the top part of the vineyard. La Chablisienne also has 1.5 ha of Blanchot and 3.3 ha of Preuses, as well as morsels in all the other Grands Crus save Valmur. The style in general is easygoing, full, and expansive, with the blandishments of generous oaking and ample creamy lees making up for a lack of the drill-bit intensity that only low yields can bring.

Anita et Jean-Pierre Colinot
89290 Irancy, Tel: 03 86 42 33 25, Fax: 03 86 42 33 25

This small, 9-ha estate run by the chatty Jean-Pierre Colinot and his wife Anita is one of the best sources of cherry-fresh Irancy. Côtes du Moutier and the "César" version of the Les Mazelots *cuvée* both show this new appellation in its best (though always flickering) light.

Jean Collet et Fils
89800 Chablis, Tel: 03 86 42 11 93, Fax: 03 86 42 47 43

This 34-ha domain run by the characterful Gilles Collet has a substantial 9.6 ha holding in Premier Cru Vaillons, as well as 5.7 ha in Montmains and a worthwhile 2 ha of Montée de Tonnerre; there is also half a hectare in Valmur. Good vintages bring wines of fine intensity and sinew here, though in less generous years they can be thin. Look out for a fine Petit Chablis.

René et Vincent Dauvissat ✪✪
89800 Chablis, Tel: 03 86 42 11 58, Fax: 03 86 42 85 32

This outstanding 11-ha domain's wines are also sold under the Dauvissat-Camus label (wines labelled Jean et Sébastien Dauvissat, by contrast, issue from a different domain altogether). Vincent Dauvissat, often accompanied by his Newfoundland dog Isis – we spotted them both in the introduction to this chapter – is the consummate craftsman-vigneron, all his efforts going into impeccable viticulture and careful, unhurried vinification. There is no marketing, by contrast; the wines sell themselves, generally to long-standing clients whose outlook Dauvissat finds congenial. Sold (and it is rare to be able to say this of great white burgundy) almost too cheaply; Dauvissat's 1999 Grand Cru Les Clos cost less than a quarter of the price of Etienne Sauzet's 1999 Grand Cru Bâtard-Montrachet, a ludicrous disparity. Some 90% of the domain's holdings are in Premier and Grand Cru sites: 1.7 ha of Les Clos, 1 ha of Les Preuses, 4.5 ha of La Forest (sic), 1.4 ha of Vaillons plus a morsel of Séchet. The vines average 40 years old and are all hand-picked. Dauvissat, like Raveneau, is not fond of ostentatious late harvesting: "Over-ripe Chardonnay isn't very interesting," he says. They are part steel-fermented and part wood-fermented (including a small proportion of new oak). All of the wines then rest in old wood until they have naturally stabilized; "...long *élevage*," continues Dauvissat, "helps tone down the Chardonnay-ness of the wine, and emphasize its minerality." Despite what seem like high yields (Dauvissat says his 1999 average was 70 hl/ha; perhaps he is just more honest than his *confrères*), they have superb concentration and length. Among the Premiers Crus, the Forest is honeyed, full of white flowers, humus, and straw; while the Preuses (Dauvissat's parcel is next to La Moutonne) is creamy and elegant, ageing with great grace toward an old age which can suggest mint and lemon verbena. The Les Clos is big, statuesque, almost oily, profoundly mineral.

Jean-Paul Droin
89800 Chablis, Tel: 03 86 42 16 78, Fax: 03 86 42 42 09

This 20-ha domain has a magnificent spread of vineyards, including land in seven Premiers Crus and five Grands Crus. This is a domain where machine harvesting is widely used, and Droin is also a winemaker who has enjoyed experimenting with age, type, and size of oak container (Russian and American oak have both been tried and discarded) and with more lees contact and *batonnage* than many Chablis winemakers use. The result is a range with both highs and lows, the former being more common after richer, lower-yielding vintages (the 1999s seem rather dilute while the 1996s are over-slender).

Joseph Drouhin ✪
21200 Beaune, Tel: 03 80 24 68 88, Fax: 03 80 22 43 14

In contrast to most of the Côte d'Or's large négociants (including Jadot), Drouhin actually owns a sizeable (45-ha) domain in Chablis. This includes over a hectare of Les Clos and Vaudésir among the Grands Crus, and Vaillons, Montmains and Séchers (sic) among the Premiers. The grapes are hand-picked

---

Star rating system used on producer spreads   ✪ Very good wine   ✪✪ Excellent wine   ✪✪✪ Great wine

and pressed at the Moulin de Vaudon in Chichée, then transported to Beaune for fermentation and *élevage* (which for the Grands Crus takes place in oak, most of it old). As with Verget, though in a slightly more restrained register, one can say that the Drouhin style emphatically suits Chablis: these are wines of finesse and grace that, with more concentration, could be outstanding.

Durup
89800 Maligny, Tel: 03 86 47 44 49, Fax: 03 86 47 55 49

Jean Durup's enormous 170-ha domain has no Grand Cru land, but Premier Cru holdings include 17 ha of Fourchaume (13 of these in the sub-*cru* known as l'Homme Mort, the "dead man") and 15 ha in Vau de Vey (sic). Durup himself is a Paris-based tax consultant; the domain is run by his son Jean-Paul, and sells its wines under a variety of different names. Jean Durup has been the leader in the expansionist tendency within Chablis; he harvests by machine, and is opposed to the use of oak (steel, concrete, and fibreglass are all used here). The best of the wines are clean and correct, sometimes acquiring an appealing nuttiness with age; less successful examples are neutral, empty, and inarticulate.

L'Eglantière *see* Durup

William Fèvre ✪✪✪
89800 Chablis, Tel 03 86 98 98 98, Fax: 03 86 98 98 99

The story of Bouchard Père et Fils since its takeover by Joseph Henriot has been a happy one; what has happened chez William Fèvre is more heartening still. As it should be, this is the greatest domain in the region. Its 40 ha (average vine age 40 years) include 12 ha of Premiers Crus and 16.3 ha of Grands Crus; this is the only domain, indeed, to own land in six of the seven Grands Crus (only the Blanchot is from purchased fruit). If there is a single domain in Chablis whose wines should be able to express every nuance of these unique soils and sites, Fèvre is its name. Should; now does. Much of the credit for this must go to Bordelais Didier Séguier: he seems to be one of those uncommon winemakers whose intrinsic lightness of touch is in spherical harmony with the Chablis idiom. No doubt, too, Henriot's own wealth permits the decisions (yield, equipment, labour, time) that enable these wines to be what they have been since 1998: consistently outstanding. The most obvious change in practice from the old regime at Fèvre has been far greater restraint in the use of new wood: barrels are now used here for six vintages, with on average only 5% new wood each year; most of the wines, including some of the Grands Crus like Grenouilles and Bougros, now have a stainless steel-raised component; and Séguier has also experimented since 2000 with a return to the use of large wood *foudres*. He was pleased with the results: "*Foudres* are very good at preserving freshness and minerality." Other changes include minimum rackings and a longer *élevage*, which in turn permits lighter filtration. The *bâtonnages*, says Séguier, are "*très, très léger* – just to give body but not enough to denature the flavours." The ordinary Chablis is now an appellation model: clean, green fruits, full of stone whispers. Among the Premiers Crus, Les Lys (hilltop Vaillons, looking straight out across the Serein Valley towards the Grands Crus) is a masterpiece of fruit purity, while the Montée de Tonnerre almost seems to have a mineral smokiness to it. The Fourchaume Vignoble de Vaulorent is the richest and most resonant – though a typical example of the muddy chaos of Chablis' Premier Cru nomenclature. This vineyard actually lies next to the Grand Cru Preuses and across the Fontenay Valley from the main expanse of Fourchaume; a different terroir altogether, in other words. Fèvre's Grand Cru holdings are particularly strong in Bougros (where the company owns almost 50% of the *cru*), Les Preuses (22%) and Les Clos (16%); one of the two Fèvre holdings in Vaudésir is next to the La Moutonne parcel of Long-Depaquit, and the Valmur parcels are in two of the warmest parts of this cru (one next to Les Clos). And the wines? Fèvre's Côte Bouguerots bottling of Les Bougros (from the steepest parts of the *cru*) is multifaceted, elegant, and long, certainly the greatest wine from this site; the Valmur is arrestingly pure, while the Vaudésir contrives to be both piercingly intense and charming at the same time. Fèvre's is one of the showiest of all Preuses: leafy, mineral yet creamy too; the Les Clos, finally, is definitive: textured, mineral-dredged, cellar-seeking.

Goisot
89530 St-Bris-le-Vineux, Tel: 03 86 53 35 15, Fax: 03 86 53 62 03

The non-Chablis vineyards of the Yonne are a tough call in which to produce great white and red wine, but Ghislaine and Jean-Hugues Goisot's 24-ha estate succeeds in producing excellent Bourgogne Côtes d'Auxerre (red and white) and sappy Sauvignon de St-Bris. The top *cuvées* are called Corps de Garde.

Grossot
89800 Fleys, Tel: 03 86 42 44 64, Fax: 03 86 42 13 31

This 18-ha domain has some very well-sited AOC Chablis parcels (used for the *cuvée* La Part des Anges) as well as almost 5 ha of Premier Cru vineyard, the largest parcels being in Vaucoupin and Fourneaux. Look out for the uncommon (and gratifyingly mineral) Côte de Troèmes. Corinne and Jean-Pierre Grossot are unafraid of oak, and the wines in general are fresh and fragrant. Corinne's maiden name was Perchaud; Domaine Perchaud is another label.

Jadot
21203 Beaune, Tel; 03 80 22 10 57, Fax: 03 80 22 56 03

Jadot owns no vineyards in Chablis, but the purchases are astute (they include Valmur, Preuses, and Grenouilles) and all receive the sympathetic, almost psychoanalytical Lardière touch. Buy with confidence.

Laroche ✪
89800 Chablis, Tel: 03 86 42 89 28, Fax: 03 86 42 89 29

This large domain has put on a turn of speed in recent years under the restless and ambitious Michel Laroche, the instigator of the Union des Grands Crus. Most of the 100 ha is in the Chablis AOC; there are 30 ha of Premier Cru land (10 ha in Vaudevey) and 6 ha of Grands Crus (4.5 ha of Blanchots with just over 1 ha of Les Clos and a morsel of Bouguerots). Laroche has adopted a policy of later picking since 1997; other obsessions are gentle pressing ("about what you do with your two fingers"), slow fermentations using part-wild yeasts, and discreet use of oak for fermentation of the bigger wines (15-25% for the Premiers Crus; 80% for Blanchots; 100% for Les Clos, of which just 15% is new wood). The Laroche Chablis St-Martin comes from 10 villages and 60 ha of vines of between 25 and 30 years old, all steel-fermented: it's a good argument for the extension of the AOC to non-Kimmeridgian soils, since its purity, classicism, and mineral limpidity belie the fact that some of it is grown on deeper clay. The leading Premier Cru wines are Vieilles Vignes *cuvées* from both Fourchaumes and Vaillons; in youth, at any rate, the latter is more charming, riper, and seemingly richer, though it may be that the terse rigidities of the Fourchaumes ease with age. Unsurprisingly, Laroche is the domain for benchmark leafy, fresh Blanchots. The Réserve de l'Obédience is a Blanchots taken from two plots of 50-year-old vines given 100% barrel-fermentation with up to 33% new wood: look out for toothsome, nutty succulence stealing into the cool fruit after a year or two in bottle. Les Clos and the Réserve de l'Obédience are bottled unfiltered.

Long-Depaquit
89800 Chablis, Tel: 03 86 42 11 13, Fax: 03 86 42 81 89

Substantial 62-ha estate owned by the Bichot family with holdings in five of the Grands Crus; the company also owns the 2.35-ha *monopole* of La Moutonne (see "Adventure of the Land" above). The style is cool, steely, and pure, requiring time to show at its best.

des Malandes
89800 Chablis, Tel: 03 86 42 41 37, Fax: 03 86 42 41 97

Lyne and Bernard Marchive's 25-ha estate is a good source for the Grand Cru Vaudésir, of which they have almost a hectare: it is complex, intense, and long, despite the fact that no wood is used. Among the Premier Cru holdings are over a hectare each of Fourchaume, Montmains, and Côte de Léchet, plus 3.5 ha of Vau de Vey.

de Maligny *see* Durup

Louis Michel
89800 Chablis, Tel: 03 86 42 88 55, Fax: 03 86 42 88 56

This 22-ha domain has a fine spread of Premier Cru sites (including 4 ha in Montée de Tonnerre and 6.5 ha in Montmain, with a further 2 ha in both Vaillons and Forêts) and much smaller Grand Cru holdings. The style is modern, austere, targetting both oxygen and wood as enemies. Harvesting is by machine; fermentation and *élevage* are in stainless steel; bottling for the Premiers and Grands Crus comes after a year with both fining and filtration. It is nonetheless a scrupulously run domain, and many admire a perceived concentration and purity in the wines and claim they have the ability to age towards full articulacy. When young, certainly, many are neutral and unyielding: try decanting before serving. Domaine de la Tour Vaubourg is an alternative label.

Alice et Olivier de Moor
89800 Courgis, Tel: 03 86 41 47 94

Chablis needs more young, talented, and iconoclastic outsiders – like this pair of winemakers from Dijon whose small 6-ha estate is divided between Chablis and St-Bris. There are no Premiers or Grands Crus here, but the Chablis La Rosette and Bel Air are both from promising sites and are intense and floral, with more texture and depth than many Premier and Grand Cru wines (thanks to careful lees contact and the refusal to fine or filter). The Sauvignon de St-Bris is an old-vines *cuvée* with unusually vivid fruit, while there is also a fine old-vines Aligoté with far more sensual personality than most.

Moreau
89800 Beine, Tel: 03 86 42 87 20, Fax: 03 86 42 45 59

The négociant company of this name (J Moreau & Fils) is now owned by Boisset, and produces undistinguished wines. Domaine Moreau, however, comprises the Moreau family vineyard holdings, no longer sold to the négociant arm. This is a recent arrangement – but with no less than 7.2 ha of what is often thought to be the greatest of the Grands Crus, Les Clos, to work with, as well as 2 ha of Valmur and one of Vaudésir, this domain run by Louis and Fabien Moreau looks like one to follow.

Sylvain Mosnier
89800 Beine, Tel: 03 86 42 43 96, Fax: 03 86 42 42 88

This 15-ha domain is noteworthy not so much for its Cru holdings (though there are 1.6 ha of Premiers Crus Côte de Léchet and Beauroy) but for its old-vine Chablis (55 years+), exuberant and deep-fruited.

Perchaud *see* Grossot

Pinson ✪
89800 Chablis, Tel: 03 86 42 10 26, Fax: 03 86 42 49 94

Laurent and Christophe Pinson's 12 ha domain includes an attractive 2.5 ha holding in Les Clos; once aged, the Pinson version has the true breadth of flavour that this site promises. The rest of the range (which includes Montmains, Forêt, and Mont de Milieu) is concentrated, long, and intense, thanks in part to an average vine age of 30 years, as well as low yields, hand picking, and some use of oak (new and old) for *élevage*. The AOC Chablis comes from a site close to Mont de Milieu, and offers excellent value for money.

Denis Pommier
89800 Chablis, Tel: 03 86 42 83 04, Fax: 03 86 42 17 80

Small but ambitious 8-ha domain run by Denis and Isabelle Pommier with three small Premier Cru holdings (including an especially good Côte de Léchet, half of which is barrique-fermented).

Denis Race
89800 Chablis, Tel: 03 86 42 45 87, Fax: 03 86 42 81 23

A substantial 14-ha estate with major holdings in Montmain, including a 60-year-old Vieilles Vignes parcel. The philosophy here rejects oak.

Raveneau ✪✪
89800 Chablis, Tel: 03 86 42 17 46, Fax: 03 86 42 45 55

There are just 7.5 ha here, alas, to satisfy a world thirsty for the sharp stone redeemed by woodland honey that make mature bottles of this domain's Chablis a benchmark for the entire region. The methods here have none of the technophilia that marks so many Chablis estates: genuinely low yields (just 35 hl/ha in 1996); a damp cellar in which the wines rest in old *feuillettes* for a year; bottling without fining and with a light filtration only. Jean-Marie Raveneau says that the changing climatic conditions at the end of the 20th century (fewer frost problems; warmer summers) means that picking here is now earlier than it used to be. On average, he told me, over the last 15 years the picking date here has advanced by one day per vintage. Thanks to low yields, of course, chaptalization is barely necessary: the sugars are high but the all-important structural acidity remains fresh. All of the holdings are either in Premier Cru sites (almost 6 ha, including nearly 3 ha in Montée de Tonnerre) or Grand Cru sites (just over half a hectare each in Les Clos, Blanchot, and Valmur). Raveneau's Montée de Tonnerre can rival the Blanchot for mineral exuberance; this is a domain, too, where the shy magnificence of Valmur, its nervous, half-hidden fruits and flowers, its blue sky purity crossed by mineral vapour trails, reaches full articulacy. The Les Clos is, as you might expect, dense and shelly, a stone carpet whose dust time will brush aside.

Servin
89800 Chablis, Tel: 03 86 18 90 00, Fax: 03 86 18 90 01

Old-established 32-ha domain whose wines have great elegance, purity, and length. The holdings are well spread, with useful parcels in three Premiers Crus and four Grands Crus (including almost a hectare in Les Clos, Blanchots, and Preuses). The Grands Crus are hand-harvested and part oak-fermented (Les Clos entirely so); look out for the Preuses here which comes from older vines (between 40 and 50 years).

Simmonet
89800 Chablis, Tel: 03 86 98 99 00, Fax: 03 86 98 99 01

Négociant Simmonet-Fèbvre is Chablis' sparkling wine specialist, but there is also a small domain that produces good Chablis including an invigorating Les Preuses (whose vines are tended for the Simmonets by Vincent Dauvissat).

La Tour Vaubourg *see* Louis Michel

Laurent Tribut
89800 Chablis, Tel: 03 86 42 46 22, Fax: 03 86 42 48 23

Small 5-ha domain run by Vincent Dauvissat's brother-in-law along much the same lines (careful viticulture; fermentation in enamelled tanks; slow *élevage* in older wooden casks until the wine is naturally stable and can be bottled without fining and with a light filtration only). There are small Premier Cru holdings in Beauroy, Côte de Léchet, and (40-year-old vines) Montmains; the wines are finely balanced and pure, ageing well.

Vauroux
89800 Chablis, Tel: 03 86 42 10 37, Fax: 03 86 42 49 13

Most of this well-run 30-ha domain lies in AOC Chablis, but there are also small holdings in Montmains, Montée de Tonnerre, and Bougros. The quality is high throughout the range, with plenty of fresh, crunchy fruit.

Verget ✪✪
71960 Sologny, Tel: 03 85 51 66 00, Fax: 03 85 51 66 09

It is my belief that it is from Chablis' raw materials that Jean-Marie Guffens has created some of his greatest wines. The pared back, super-pure, limpid Verget style (he treats Chardonnay as if it was Riesling's first cousin) is intrinsically in harmony with Chablis' spirit of place and its terroirs. Not, though, that Guffens himself is popular in Chablis: his criticisms of the failings of Chablis' own local talent (gross yields, mechanical harvesting, school-book winemaking) are typically immoderate and amusingly undiplomatic. Guffens buys grapes – but the deal begins with pruning and continues right through to harvesting. The Vaillons and Fourchaumes (there are "normal" and Vieilles Vignes *cuvées* of both) have ravishing depth: how, one wonders, can wine-fruit taste so challengingly green yet feel so glycerous? Guffens uses new oak, yet give the wines time and all is digested.

Burgundy

Terroir's Dreamland Of all of France's wine regions, Burgundy is the only one where minute geological nuance, sensually etched into human consciousness by centuries of winemaking and tasting, is given the force of the law. Justly?

My room, this November evening, is in the Hôtel des Remparts in Beaune; indeed two of the walls seem to be made of *remparts*. I'm facing brightly lit blocks of limestone, none of the same dimensions as any other. When was this stone lifted from the earth? And when did the seas which created these blocks, from its million-year midden of bones and shells, retreat?

Beaune is quiet tonight. The summer's tourists have all gone home to their northern cities and their hurried, profitable lives; this is the time when the wine merchants tour, paying the visits that they hope might eventually result in a dozen cases of wine to sell from a favoured or famous grower. They scuttle from hotel to restaurant clutching mobile phones, to wire them wirelessly to their roots. As they eat their solitary meals, they look with observant envy at the easy articulation of French provincial life, basking in its second-hand warmth. Solitary diners have their part to play in the ritual, too.

Night has closed in on a dull, wet day. The vineyards are dark chess squares lurking in the moist gloom; the cars shuttling up and down the RN74 mark an ant trail of light at their base. The headlights illuminate only moist tarmac; the drivers' eyes soak up only the glare of the oncoming vehicles. Each vine, now, is lost in its own loneliness, rooted in the stony ramp that leads up towards the silent hilltop forests. Each vine basks in photosynthetic rest, its long summer work

finished. A fox steps, with light-footed unseen grace, up the dark rows of vines. The starlings that swarmed in a single undulating wave over the vineyards at dusk, stripping the vines of their secondary fruit, roost in a dark tree. They digest, in their sleep, a Grand Cru meal.

An hour ago I tasted the 1999 Montrachet of the Domaine des Comtes Lafon. Under the earth, of course: burgundy cellars are uniformly subterranean. Perhaps the blocks of limestone that surround me now were lifted in the excavation of such a place. Dominique Lafon, as usual, has been generous with his time and his wine; he has talked with us for two hours, answering our questions and telling us his impressions of the 2000 vintage, which took place a month or two ago. Those, though, are not the wines we are tasting; many have barely finished their first fermentation; they're rough; they're troubled. We're tasting the vintage before last, 1999, born a year ago and now beginning to approach the end of its period in cask. The Montrachet smells very sweet at this moment, its bread and its fruit sheathed in the puppy velvet of youth, like an almond robed in pink sugar. To taste, though, it's altogether more intense and mouthfilling: a pure green fruit slides across the tongue with the weight of a freight train. After we swallow (no one spits this, the final wine), the ghost of its fruit seems to turn and pulse, aromatically, filling the mouth with a perfumed wineyness. We've just tasted the

spicy Meursault-Goutte d'Or, the floral, honeysuckled Meursault-Genevrières, the glycerous Meursault-Perrières, the graceful and intricate Meursault-Charmes; none, though, has quite the push, the shove, and the thrust of the Montrachet.

"When you're up in the vineyard," I asked Dominique, "what's the difference between Meursault and Montrachet? Do the vines have another look? Is there less fruit, smaller grapes, quicker ripeness? What makes this wine just that little bit better than all the rest, year after year?" "Nothing's different," he says, and pauses. "Nothing's different. Okay, the vines are a bit older, but they don't really look any different. They look the same; they behave the same." He shrugs, smiling at the fact that we all know what he's going to say next, and yet it would be dishonest not to say it. "It's the soil. That's it. It's what's under your feet."

And, he might have added, above your head. The next afternoon, I visit the hill of Corton with Jean-Charles le Bault de la Morinière of Domaine Bonneau du Martray. We're in the westernmost part of this open carousel of hillside, looking over to the pretty village of Pernand-Vergelesses. The vines have lost most of their leaves now, exhausted after the long summer. I poke the white marl, curious to unearth its secrets; it returns my gaze inarticulately, a mere sticky mud. I look across the valley to the hillside opposite. This slope is echoed there; as

here, those vines bathe in what seems an equal light. The wine grown here is worth £80 a bottle in the UK; the wine over there would sell for £15. It's the obscure Caradeux. Yet even the marl looks the same. Again the same question: why?

We retreat into the cellar to taste and talk. Two hours later, we leave, our mouths perfumed by Corton-Charlemagne, thrilled by what vigorous, soaring, sappy white wine can do and can be. As we drive down the little road, I check my watch: 4.35 pm, November 9th. Corton-Charlemagne is impossible to ignore: it gleams above us, bright with sunlight. The sun is shining from the west up the valley with the clean glow of a lamp illuminating a tomb; it hits this part of the hillside full on, fierce as a floodlight, cutting the vineyards below into shadow like a belt. That superb hill I gazed at across the valley two hours before, Caradeux, has long slipped into cool shadow. What's true for 4.30 on a November evening finds its echo at 9.30 on a summer one; the sun quits Corton-Charlemagne last.

"Burgundy vineyards," points out Le Bault de la Morinière, "face east and south. The great exception is here: we face west. It's extraordinary, because in June, if you are here at seven am, you are in the sunshine. If you come back at nine pm at night, you are still in the sunshine. That's fourteen hours of sun exposure. Not heating sun, because it's not due south, but good light, cool light. And I think it has

"The term terroir refers as much to climate as to the nature of soils and sub-soils. That's why we use the term "*climat*" in Burgundy... These parcels... always correspond to natural entitities that are made palpable by the character of the wines that come into life there. The age of the vines and the "paw mark" of the wine-grower have their own importance, but it's always the character of the wine itself that dominates."

HENRI JAYER, QUOTED IN *ODE AUX GRANDS VINS DE BOURGOGNE*, J RIGAUX (1997)

◀ *Long shadows tell tales in Burgundy. Up here in the Hautes Côtes, every minute of sunshine counts in the race for ripeness.*

something to do with the special structure of Corton-Charlemagne, which I feel is a little apart from other white burgundies. The structure and the balance. It is an unusual wine. The pH is always extremely low; we have high levels of total acidity, all natural of course, as well as good alcoholic potential. No interest, one year after the bottling. Needs ten years, fifteen years sometimes, sometimes twenty years. The mature vintage today is 1976."

All vineyards, of course, are many-dimensioned grid references: a sounding in earth, with its mineral nourishment, its biological life, its structural possibilities; a sounding in air, based on the fall of a piece of land among neighbouring mounds and vales, and positioned in a certain way in relation to a moving fireball some 150 million kilometres distant. The vines are a kind of soft, green instrument for measuring these phenomena – subject, of course, to the further mutations of a particular season, and a guiding human hand of varying sensitivity. Wines are the data we take from the instrument. We read the data by sniffing, and by sipping.

Of no region on earth is this more true than Burgundy. Charlemagne gave his vines to the monks of St-Androche de Saulieu in 775; they kept them for 1,000 years, cultivating them for the glory of God and the furtherance of their order, until the French Revolution dispossessed them. Every vintage gave new voice to beauty and to difference. Gradually, the whole of this fifty-km (thirty-one-mile) stretch of vineyard, the Côte d'Or (golden slope), began to reveal exactly what it was capable of. Caradeux could not do what Corton-Charlemagne could do, no matter how hard the monks and their vine-tenders tried. A terroir can only be itself; a terroir cannot surpass itself.

In this sense, very little is new in this ancient area. Burgundy unquestionably has France's most complicated AOC system, but this expensive puzzle is history's gift to us: it is a piece of geographical scholarship reflecting 1,300 years of human endeavour. Our understanding of the soils and sites of the Médoc are recent by comparison, and in many other parts of France, like the Languedoc or the villages of the southern Rhône, we are still peeling back the skin of the land to discover what lies beneath. The Adventure of the Land provides a brief guide to what one might expect from the different villages and vineyards of Burgundy (see below).

In another sense, of course, much has changed, and there is a New Burgundy just as there is a New France.

You could call this Articulate Burgundy. Many of the struggles of the last century in this region were concerned with authenticity: establishing definitively that red burgundy was not a thick, soupy, or hearty red wine bolstered by Alicante Bouschet from the Languedoc, or Carignan from Algeria, but a red wine of light body, seductive perfume, and aerial grace. The new challenge for the twenty-first century is to make such a wine speak with maximum articulacy.

Not easy. Red burgundy is the most difficult wine in the world to make well. What's true now must have been still more true in the ninth or thirteenth centuries; there will certainly have been many vintages in history here when the drinkers of Burgundy, sitting in their smocks, their clogs, their rags, were grateful for little more than its alcohol. This is a northern wine-growing region where full ripeness is often a gamble against the closing of the year, where hail can strike at any time, and where spring frosts are waiting around the corner like a madman with a knobkerrie. Pinot Noir, moreover, the grape of red burgundy, is multi-cloned, thin-skinned, rot-prone, and virus-susceptible; and its vinification consists of a tightrope walk between various forms of failure, such as over- or under-extraction, hardness, hollowness, slenderness, tartness, or (when yields are too high and the wines have been heavily chaptalized) a dull and skulking emptiness. Chardonnay-based white burgundy is easier to produce and to vinify, yet careless vineyard and winery work can easily send it, too, into a chilly and untender taciturnity. The great struggle is now against these forms of failure, and the weapons are fastidious work both in vineyard and cellar.

Flat vineyards and Chardonnay grapes by the tubful will limit the articulacy of this wine. The story is different on the golden slope beyond. ▶

This rotation crop provides holiday nourishment for a resting vineyard before the vines return for another vintage century.

The search for articulacy

It is perhaps no accident that Burgundy is the region where biodynamic viticulture (*see* page 24-43) has had more influence than any other. The scale of viticulture here is relatively small; average holdings, over a dozen or so sites, stretch to twenty ha (fifty acres) at most. (Château Lafite in Bordeaux, by contrast, occupies ninety-four ha/232 acres.) The top domains can, thus, afford the investment in hard vineyard labour that biodynamics requires (a bare minimum of double the number of vineyard hours required by conventional cultivation). And the quest for purity that biodynamics implies was always going to be of maximum appeal in an area as structurally committed to the notion of terroir as is Burgundy. The fact that domains of the importance of Leroy, Leflaive, and Lafon practice biodynamics provides a powerful tractor to drag lesser domains towards more environmentally respectful systems of viticulture than were common in the past.

In the cellar, too, there has been evolution. Not so much in what wine producers are actually doing to their grapes, but in the care with which they are doing those things. There was, it's true, a fashion for cold-macerating the fruit before fermentation in the early 1990s, based on the consulting advice of Guy Accad — yet this was no more than basing a system (some would say fetish) on what was already an old-established practice. Henri Jayer, now retired but widely regarded as being Burgundy's first and finest modern winemaker, was using a week's "cold soak" — to leach perfume out of the grape skins without

extracting fierce and unbalanced tannins — as long ago as the 1970s. In still earlier times, before producers had the wherewithal to heat or cool cellars and vats, Nature herself would often have imposed a cold soak: autumn tends to close in swiftly in this northern French vineyard region with its continental climate. "I noticed," says Jayer, "that in seasons where the harvest weather was very cool and when fermentations took a long while to get going, the wines were much fruitier than usual. And their colour was prettier. Applying this technique in warmer years by using temperature control gave very fruity, balanced, and complex wines."

Pinot Noir, as I mentioned above, is a thin-skinned red grape, which in turn makes it prone to rot (*Botrytis cinerea* or "grey rot", as it is called when it affects healthy red grapes). Vineyard work, careful harvesting, and sorting out of unhealthy from healthy grapes before fermentation are all regarded as an essential part of serious winemaking in Burgundy, and a vintage like 1983 (in which many wines were clearly made from rot-affected grapes) seems unlikely to be repeated.

Wines are more often destemmed than in the past (the Domaine de la Romanée-Conti is a celebrated exception), and excessive chaptalization of musts is rarer than in the 1970s and 1980s, too. Growers are more ready to risk all for ripeness than in the past. It also reflects an understanding that low yields are essential if burgundy is to reflect its terroir. Wild yeasts as opposed to cultured yeasts are favoured by almost all serious domains; extraction levels for red wines, by contrast, vary widely among producers and among villages, too. Many feel that the early 1990s was a period marked by excessive extraction, and that this constituted a denaturing of the very quality that should be red burgundy's hallmark: its perfumed grace. Others, by contrast,

Jean-Marie Guffens

To be a Belgian in Burgundy is bad enough, but to be a motormouth who talks about fellow winemakers in the same tender terms which boxers use to needle their opponents has turned Jean-Marie Guffens into a celebrated pariah. Everyone has a favourite Guffens quotation; I remember asking him how he marketed his wines. "Marketing," he said loudly to me across a table at London's River Café, where we were no doubt surrounded by marketeers, "is the art of selling rubbish to idiots."

Yet he is also a demanding viticulturalist, a consummate winemaker, and an astute analyst of burgundian reality. Back in 1990 when he and Jean Rijckaert founded Verget, no one else had thought of the cherry-picking, micro-négociant role that is now so important throughout Burgundy, and increasingly in the Rhône and Languedoc too. While the clean, almost monkishly pure Verget style may not appeal to those brought up on traditional, cheesy white burgundy, there is no

doubt that he has managed to imbue his wines with a greater sense of terroir than many traditional négociants, and he has been a quality trailblazer in both Chablis and the Mâconnais. Indeed with his own Guffens-Heynen domain in the Mâconnais, he is working at the absolute vanguard of quality for the AOC. Before Guffens, no one knew that Mâcon Pierreclos or even Pouilly-Fuissé could rival Corton-Charlemagne or Bâtard-Montrachet. Now they do.

welcomed the added depth and structure that increased extraction brought, pointing out that Burgundy's fatal flaw had always been a tendency to thinness, tartness, and hollowness. The later 1990s have seen a more thoughtful approach to extraction from most producers, with fewer wines either harshly inky, or lean and skinny.

The question of red burgundy's eventual balance and wealth of flavour once bottled, of course, is only partly answered by discussing extraction. No less important are the questions of racking, fining, and filtering. How long, in other words, do you keep burgundy in cask before bottling, and to what extent do you claw flavour out of the wine by fining and filtration in order to sleep secure in the knowledge that your bottled wine is lifelessly stable?

The truth, as anyone who ever visits Burgundy to taste wines from barrel will confirm, is that all red burgundy would ideally be sold directly from the cask. Burgundy, especially red burgundy, hates being bottled. This is a wine of such delicacy, whose qualities of excellence are so intimately associated with butterfly-wing nuance, that any fining and filtering tends to have a damaging effect. Choosing the best

moment to bottle is another intuitive skill, as is gauging how much new oak during *élevage* would help enrich a particular wine without drying and dominating it. All credit to American journalists and importers such as Robert Parker, James Suckling, Peter Vezan, and Kermit Lynch for pressuring producers to abandon "secure" fining and filtration practices which left their wines sterile and hollow. Among the wines of those who have abandoned fining and filtration (they include almost all of Burgundy's top domains) there is little sign of the "bacterial time-bombs" which wine writers Hugh Johnson and James Halliday alleged would result. Many producers now sell an unfiltered version of their wine to the USA alone; purchasers and importers from other markets are culpably remiss in not applying similar pressure for their own allocations.

The New Burgundy, then, means wines of increased articulacy, fullness, and concentration thanks to greatly increased vineyard work, lowered yields, ever more sensitive winemaking and the abandonment of crass filtration practices. Just as important as all these elements, though, is what we might call the family franc – or euro.

The major generational change dividing those running family domains today and their parents concerns not winemaking or viticulture, but the philosophy of the vineyard environment. The "advances" of science – artificial fertilizers, pesticides, herbicides, insecticides, and fungicides – appeared beneficial to the post-war generation. Today it is hard to find a single great grower in France who is not either eliminating their use (organic or biodynamic viticulture) or reducing it (la lutte raisonnée). Anne-Claude Leflaive-Jacques is no exception.

She arrived at Domaine Leflaive in 1990 and co-ran it until 1994, when her cousin Olivier Leflaive left to work exclusively on his négociant business; since then she has been in sole charge. Its twenty-two ha (fifty-four acres) are eye-rubbingly well-sited: there are two ha (five acres) in both Chevalier- and Bâtard-Montrachet, as well as a morsel of Montrachet itself, sold by the single bottle. Premier Cru holdings include almost five ha (twelve acres) of Clavoillon. Precious vines, in other words, whose average age varies from twenty-three years in Clavoillon to fifty years for Montrachet.

Her approach to biodynamics was cautious, beginning in 1990. Leflaive's British agent, Adam Brett-Smith of Corney & Barrow, recalls six years of blind tastings in which wine from the biodynamic parcels consistently emerged as superior to that from conventional parcels. By 1997, the entire domain was converted; since then Leflaive has been a passionate advocate of biodynamics. Fining and filtering have been abandoned, too. Leflaive, described by Brett-Smith as "a lady of some steel: very clear-thinking, with strong convictions", has now launched into a new campaign: to keep Burgundy's vineyards free of genetically modified organisms, which she describes as "incompatible with the idea of controlled appellations of origin."

▶

Anne-Claude Leflaive

Bourgignon by name…

In point of fact, he grew up in Paris, the son of a 6th arrondissement doctor. Claude Bourgignon, though, responded to the pull of the natural world even in that most urban of environments: he started a Parisian ornithology club, and undertook a census of the city's birds of prey. This was the first stage on the long journey (via the gorillas of Zaire, the birds of Turkey, and the tigers of the Himalayas) which led to Bourgignon becoming the most influential soil scientist in viticultural France today, working from his base just north of Dijon. Nowhere is his influence more important than in Burgundy itself, where his client list includes Domaine de la Romanée-Conti, Leflaive, Lafon, Lafarge, and Trapet. All of these estates, you will note, are working either organically or biodynamically; Bourgignon's soil studies, both in France and in the Third World, have convinced him

that the chemical crutches of conventional agriculture have had a catastrophic effect on microbial life in the soil. Bourgignon advises these estates on ways in which they can improve the activities of the millions of tiny creatures which live in healthy soil (they include fungae and algae as well as bacteria); he gauges their numbers and their vital biochemical workrate. "Bacterial fermentation," he says, "is at the beginning of all life." The agrochemicals, pesticides, and herbicides used in conventional farming kill off this life in the soil; Bourgignon is famous for having pointed out that there is less microbiological life in some of Burgundy's vineyards than in the Sahara Desert. Composts, inter-row cultivation, and traditional ploughing techniques (DRC now prefers a horse to a tractor) are three means of revitalizing the soil.

Bourgignon himself is not a biodynamicist, but as a soil scientist he confirms that biodynamic parcels do contain more microbial life in deep soils than organic parcels (levels in topsoils are similar); he is also impressed by the intense levels of activity in the horn preparations used by biodynamic practitioners. Moreover, as Bourgignon describes in his magnificent book Le sol, la terre et les champs, eighty-eight per cent of all plant matter (including, of course, vines and grapes) is formed by carbon and oxygen photosynthesized from the atmosphere. (In dry weight this rises to ninety-two to ninety-eight per cent, with only two to five per cent of the dry weight of plants coming from the soil.) Conventional agriculture regards soil as the source of all growth; only biodynamics gives equal importance to what lies above the ground as well as what lies below.

"When you have a wine in the mouth, nothing should shock. It should be like a caress." Etienne Grivot's journey towards this gentle, sensual ideal began with restless experiment in the 1980s, including work with the consultant Guy Accad in the practice of pre-fermentation maceration or "cold soaking". Accad, he says, helped him put the density into his wines which he had felt was missing. He still cold soaks, though less lengthily than in the past: "My obsession is to preserve the freshness." He is "contre les vins excessifs": he speaks of managing his extractions as if the grapes were held within a silk scarf; his late harvesting is intuitive rather than dogmatic. Like so many great burgundian growers, he now uses only natural yeasts, avoids fining and filtration, and bottles by gravity alone. "I feel very serene with my winemaking now. I still analyze, but more calmly." Grivot's compellingly articulate wines are emblematic of the New Burgundy: it is almost as if his own serenity can be perceived in the exquisite shapeliness of his Richebourg, the sumptuous grace of his Vosne Beaumonts, the fruited purity of his Clos Vougeot, or the glowing wealth of his Echézeaux. Like many of his generation, he acknowledges the debt owed to the New World (he worked for six months in California). "The improvement in the quality of French wine is directly related to the challenge posed by New World wines. That's clear." Like others of his age, too (he was born in 1959), he sees himself as a wine-grower first and a Burgundian second. "We are part of a wine civilization. I think it's wonderful that great wine-growers can form a big family, wherever we are."

Who makes burgundy?

In the past, it was merchants, or négociants as they are called, who made and sold burgundy to the world. They didn't actually own the vineyards — those belonged (at least from the French Revolution onwards) to the growers. The situation in Burgundy thirty years ago was not dissimilar to that of Champagne today: thousands of growers, yet for consumers outside the region only a dozen or so widely recognized names.

There was, though, one big difference. Champagne has one AOC; Burgundy has over 500. Most négociants didn't make a very good job of expressing the subtle and sometimes fugitive differences between the different vineyards; indeed they didn't always make good wines at all. There was every incentive for growers to take their own estates in hand, looking after their own vinification and sales, and during the second half of the twentieth century more and more of them did this. Négociants, meanwhile, either disappeared or merged.

The result wasn't an instant leap into articulacy and fidelity to terroir for burgundy, though, because very often these first-generation grower-winemakers lacked the necessary cellar skills to produce great wines. In the early decades of the twenty-first century, by contrast, it is their sons and daughters, or even grandsons and granddaughters, who are in charge. The new generation has brought a surge in winemaking skills, and it is now incontrovertible that the very greatest red and white burgundies of all are produced by individual growers such as Jean-François Coche, Etienne Grivot, Dominique Lafon, Emmanuel Rouget, or Vincent Dauvissat, to name but five.

This is true to such an extent, indeed, that a reverse trend is now under way. Skilled growers sometimes find that a family split or the end of a *métayage* agreement means that they have fewer vineyards than they would like. The solution under such circumstances is to become small-scale négociants themselves. Among those who have taken this route (from a variety of different departure points) are Olivier Leflaive, Jean-Marie Guffens, Dominique Laurent, Nicolas Potel, Gérard Boudot of Sauzet, and Jean-Nicolas Méo of Méo-Camuzet. These new-wave micro-négociants produce finely crafted wines that rival those of the best growers. Another alternative for Burgundy's best is to make for other parts of France in which to produce wine with the same attention to detail but in larger quantities, as Dominique Lafon is now doing in the Mâconnais, Jacques Seysses is doing in Var, or Jean-Marie Guffens himself does in Lubéron. At the same time, the surviving large négociants have also, in some cases, raised their game to compete with the best growers, too. Top vineyard wines from Jadot, from Drouhin, or from the astonishingly revitalized Bouchard Père et Fils under Joseph Henriot's stewardship prove the point. Others (Boisset, Jaboulet-Vercherre, Patriarche), alas, don't.

The Adventure of the Land

Chablis, the Côte d'Or, the Côte Chalonnaise, the Mâconnais, and Beaujolais: these five regions constitute Greater Burgundy. Chablis and Beaujolais have, in this book, separate, short chapters of their own. Beaujolais certainly merits separate treatment, since its grape variety and soils stand in complete contrast to those of Greater Burgundy. Chablis, apparently, doesn't: limestone-rooted Chardonnay is wholly typical of Greater Burgundy. There is, nonetheless, something different about the taste of Chablis, something that links it more closely to the wines of the Kimmeridgean geological chain that runs from Sancerre and Pouilly-Fumé through Chablis to the Aube district of Champagne – hence the separate chapter.

Here we track the length of the **Côte d'Or**, which lies between Dijon and Chagny; the **Côte Chalonnaise**, between Chagny and St-Boil, to the southwest of Chalon-sur-Saône; and the **Mâconnais**: the swathe of comfortable vineyard land to the west of Tournus and of Mâcon itself.

The Côte d'Or

Enjoy a crossword puzzle? Work out differential equations on the train home from work? If you have any sort of appetite for complication, Burgundy is the right place in the wine world for you. There are, potentially, over 500 different appellations in this fifty-km (thirty-mile) stretch of vines. Why? I'll try to explain as simply as I can.

It's customary to describe Burgundy's AOCs as a pyramid. At the bottom are the general regional appellations: Bourgogne Grand Ordinaire (for wine made chiefly from Gamay rather than Pinot Noir), Bourgogne Rouge (Pinot Noir), Bourgogne Blanc (Chardonnay), and Bourgogne Aligoté (from the Aligoté grape).

Next step up are subregional AOCs: Bourgogne-Hautes Côtes de Nuits and Bourgogne-Hautes Côtes de Beaune for vineyards up in the hills. The Côte d'Or is also divided into two sections: the Côte de Nuits (between Dijon and Nuits-St-Georges) and the Côte de Beaune (between Beaune and Chagny). Wines not classified in any other way from the former area can be called Côtes de Nuits-Villages and from the southern area Côte de Beaune-Villages. (For the record, there is also a weak little Côte de Beaune AOC.)

Climb a little higher and you come to the twenty-five villages (or communes) of the Côte d'Or: each has its own AOC. Famous examples include Gevrey-Chambertin, Nuits-St-Georges and Meursault. Easy!

Most villages – take a deep breath – have a number of Premiers Crus, and these vineyard names are permitted to attach themselves to that of the village in the AOC formula: Appellation Nuits-St-Georges Premier Cru Les Cailles Contrôlée, for example, or Appellation Meursault Premier Cru Les Genevrières Contrôlée. This marks a giant leap forward in complication, since there are over 450 Premiers Crus in Burgundy (Beaune alone has forty-four). To add to the headache, there are also named vineyards (*lieux-dits*) without Premier Cru status which turn up on the labels of village wines sometimes. Some Premiers Crus, horribly enough, are also *lieux-dits* (in other words part of the vineyard is Premier Cru, but part only classified as village wine). Premiers Crus can also belong to more than one village (or be attached to one village if the wine is white and another if the wine is red, as with the white Santenots of Meursault and the red Santenots of Volnay). Wines from a blend of Premiers Crus can be sold as "Premier Cru" without any vineyard name whatsoever. The same vineyard names occur in different villages (both Beaune and Santenay have a Clos des Mouches, for example), and the spellings of the Premier Cru names are notoriously variable.

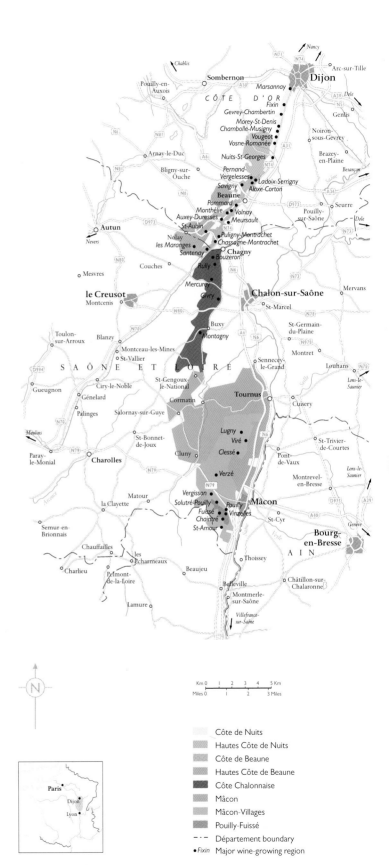

Côte de Nuits

Hautes Côte de Nuits

Côte de Beaune

Hautes Côte de Beaune

Côte Chalonnaise

Mâcon

Mâcon-Villages

Pouilly-Fuissé

– – – Département boundary

•Fixin Major wine-growing region

To resuscitate you after that onslaught of complication, I should point out that Burgundy's Premiers Crus offer the francophone drinker some of the jolliest names in the wine world. Fixin has a Premier Cru Herring Tail (Queue de Hareng), Chambolle-Musigny a Lovers (Les Amoureuses), Vosne-Romanée a Bad Companions (Les Malconsorts), Meursault a Drop of Gold (La Goutte d'Or), Blagny an Under the Donkey's Back (Sous Le Dos d'Ane – don't ask), St-Aubin an On The Path of the Nail (Sur Le Sentier du Clou) and Chassagne-Montrachet a Dog's Teeth (Les Dents de Chien). The practice known nowadays as mooning is commemorated in an old *lieux-dit* vineyard in Dijon called Montreculs.

Finally, at the very top of the pyramid, come the Grands Crus. There are thirty of these in the Côte d'Or, and they appear in an appellation formula that makes no reference to the village from which they come: Appellation Chambertin Contrôlée, for example, or Appellation La Grande Rue Contrôlée. The label should state, too, that this is a Grand Cru vineyard. Price, however, will already have alerted you to this fact.

What reality does this torrent of names reflect?

In its overall geological structure, as mentioned on page 64, Burgundy resembles Alsace. At first glance, in other words, it seems to be a vineyard region sunbathing on the fortunate slopes of a river valley. The river here is the Saône; as with the Rhine in Alsace, the river itself seems to have meandered, over a few million years, some distance away from the vineyards. In fact, to be more geologically accurate, faulting has torn the two walls of the valley apart and provided a route for the far-away river, with its burden of silt, to idle along. This giant trough is called a graben. Way across on the other side of the Saône graben lie the vineyards of the Jura, Burgundy's curious and stunted twin. (Alsace has just such a twin, too, on the other side of the Rhine graben: the vineyards of Germany's Baden.)

The long, north-south slope on which Burgundy's vineyards find themselves is interrupted by further small faults and tilts. Little streams and rivers have come breaking through this slope from the hills beyond, forming the small side valleys called combes. The "slope of gold" is broken into a thousand pieces.

The base rocks are limestones and marls (a limy clay) of various sorts. Indeed at Comblanchien, the transition zone between the Côte de Nuits and the Côte de Beaune, stone suddenly becomes more important than vines. One layer of Burgundy's limestone was formed in a balmy sea which nourished oysters – who deposited themselves, multi-millennially, on the sea bottom. Their corpses were compressed into the beautiful *dalles nacrées* (pearly slabs) quarried at Comblanchien. This stone, not recrystallized as marble would be, nonetheless resembles it in taking a glowing polish. It's dyed a soft dawn pink by iron oxides precipitated into the limy mixture at an earlier stage in its geological life.

Faults, tilts, and combes, all going to work on a variety of limestones and marls, with slope wash, scree, and pebbles intermingled and interfingered: yes, the Côte d'Or is geologically complex. You don't, though, find the wild, symphonic, Sorcerer's Apprentice geological complexity of Alsace here. Instead you have something more akin to Bach's Goldberg Variations: exquisite, brilliant, and with minute geological nuance. Thousands of wine-growers over hundreds of years have tasted differences in their wines from different parcels. They have noted them, and talked about them to each other: these are now logged in the appellation system, providing growers with challenge and inspiration. "The legislators back in 1936," to requote Henri Jayer, "only confirmed the empirical observations of our ancestors. Don't forget that classification, before it was sanctified by officialdom, was done in the glass, by people who knew how to taste."

The Côte de Nuits

The Côte d'Or begins in the suburbs of Dijon at Chenôve. In practice, however, it is at **Marsannay** – the only village in Burgundy that is allowed to produce red, white, and rosé wine – that wine-growing first gets the better of suburban building. The Côte de Nuits slope pattern is established here, though the hills are less expansive than further south, and the potential of the soils, too, is reduced by admixtures of alluvial river deposits. Marsannay's wines (most of its 225 ha/556 acres are given over to red and rosé) are light, clear, fresh, and delicate. The wines of the next village, **Fixin**, are overwhelmingly red and relatively chunky: the slope is warming. After Fixin comes the unclassified village of Brochon, the wine from whose flat, shaley vineyards is sold as AOC Bourgogne; wine from nearby hill sites is bottled as Gevrey-Chambertin. The Côte de Nuits quickly gets into its stride here.

Just south of the next village of **Gevrey-Chambertin** lies the first of the Côte d'Or's major combes or slope interruptions, Combe Lavaux. To the north of the combe, looking down from a prominent knoll above the village, is a roulette wheel of Premier Cru land swinging round in orientation from the east to the south; in the middle lies the outstanding Clos St-Jacques, one of those Premier Crus which locals consider a Grand Cru in all but name. South of Gevrey, meanwhile, is the first of the Côte d'Or's quietly majestic Grand Cru hill slopes: Chambertin. And more. The next major slope-break is the Combe Ambin at Chambolle-Musigny. The stately Chambertin slope extends steadily southwards, taking in (in Grand Cru terms) Clos de la Roche, Clos St-Denis, Clos des Lambrays, Clos de Tart, and Bonnes Mares, before the village of Chambolle is reached. Chambertin itself is subdivided and (inevitably) hierarchized, with Chambertin and Chambertin-Clos de Bèze at the head, and Chapelle-, Griottes-, Latricières-, Mazis-, and Charmes-Chambertin (or its alternative name Mazoyères-Chambertin) all standing in a beatific second place.

Look up from the famous N74 road here and you will see, in vineyard terms, the classical Burgundian sandwich. The best vineyards, in other words, are mid-slope: this is where the sun is warmest, the drainage is best, and often (for erosional reasons) the soil is stoniest and thinnest, with the limestone bedrock closest to the surface. Up at the top of the hill, underneath the woods, the sites are a little cooler and the limestone less yielding; down at the bottom of the hill, the soils are

▲ *Mid-slope vineyards, like talented children, enjoy all the advantages: sun, stone, and snugly dry roots. Their wines endure when others have faded.*

richer and moister, and the bedrock more deeply buried. Chambertin and some of its associated vineyards are an exception, in that the Grand Cru land here stretches right to the top of the hill, just underneath the woods that customarily cap the Côte d'Or (as they do the Vosges in Alsace, too). The Grands Crus of **Morey St-Denis** are more typical: there are Premier Cru and Village vineyards both above and below. The style of Gevrey is expressive, full-flavoured, almost meaty; Morey is more elegant and pure-fruited.

With **Chambolle-Musigny** and its combe (down which mighty waters have sporadically rushed in the past), the vineyard pack gets a shuffle. The waters have brought much lime-rich stone to Chambolle itself; this, combined with the cool air that drifts through the combe, is a reason for the elegance and refinement of the red wines at this point on the Côte. The combe's depositional fan lowers the quality of the vineyards around the village itself, but travelling south again Le Musigny, Clos de Vougeot, Grands Echézeaux, and Echézeaux re-establish the mid-slope avenue of Grands Crus. Indeed after a perplexing little break where the Premiers Crus of Les Suchots, Les Beaux Monts, and aux Brûlées interrupt the avenue, it resumes with the grandest of all Grands Crus: Richebourg, La Romanée, Romanée-Conti, Romanée St-Vivant, La Grande Rue, and La Tâche. To those who come expecting drama, this gentle slope surprises. Great red burgundy should be perfumed, light, and aerial, vividly fruited in youth then sweetly animal with age, seemingly delicate yet indefinably powerful, robust, and mouth-seizing too. Wines bearing these names should incarnate this ideal. Sometimes they do.

In terms of village wines, Chambolle is graceful, fragrant, and seductive, qualities it shares with its Grands Crus of Bonnes Mares and the ethereal Musigny; **Vougeot** and **Vosne-Romanée** are darker and more masterful. Clos Vougeot's fifty ha (124 acres), it is obligatory to point out, run down to the road, where there are deep soils over marl: this is land of village quality, classified as a Grand Cru. Why? The magnificent walls of this Clos were raised and mortared five centuries ago, while the vineyard's origins go back to 1110; even the bureaucrats of INAO didn't have the heart to subdivide what the monks of Cîteaux had considered unitary. There are eighty owners today, and the wines of those with the best, upper part of the vineyard bear little resemblance to carelessly vinified young-vine Clos de Vougeot from the lower slopes.

Why is the earth so particularly favoured just up behind the village of Vosne-Romanée? In some ways, it is precisely because the formula is so simple there: a metre of topsoil and pebbles made from a nourishing blend of limestones and marls, seasoned with a little lightening sand, and lying over unfaulted, gently sloping bedrock of classic, centre-slope crinoidal limestone. The vines' roots love this pure, clay-moistened cake of dead sea-creatures; the vines themselves relish their sheltered, sunny spot. Yet it's also true that history plays a role there, too: these plots were already celebrated in the twelfth century by cowled vignerons, and squabbled over later by aristocrats and royal mistresses; no owner has ever considered them anything less than Burgundy's best, and cultivated them accordingly. Were they planted with Gamay or Merlot and cropped at one hundred hl/ha for France's answer to Jacob's Creek, our reverence would be less choral.

After Vosne-Romanée, the Côte de Nuits loses the geological plot, in that the River Meuzin comes bustling through the slope, with the small town of **Nuits-St-Georges** sitting on its depositional fan; south of Nuits the classic formula briefly resumes before the cap rock of hard Comblanchien stone cascades from the hilltop and the quarrymen get to work. (The jagged topography would make viticulture difficult here.) The sandwich formula works well, though, for Nuits' Premiers Crus, especially those south of the town; the sharp scarp back acts as a suntrap. These are bugle-burgundies: blasts of fierce, proud red fruit.

Vineyard areas
Département boundary

▲ *Tomorrow and tomorrow and tomorrow: choosing the perfect moment to harvest is never an easy decision.*

The Côte de Beaune

Odd, really: the Côte de Nuits lies to the north of the Côte de Beaune, yet it is in the latter that you find Burgundy's greatest white wines, while reds are the speciality of the former. Why? Grower Henri Jayer and writer Jacky Rigaud describe the revelatory process of trial and error. Pinot Noir has been grown the length of the Côte d'Or for ten centuries; the use of Chardonnay for white wine is much more recent. Initially Chardonnay was grown here and there along the whole stretch of vineyards, but it was found to do better in the southern part. The climate differences are minimal over thirty kilometres (18.6 miles) (and in any case according to Jayer the Côte de Nuits is actually cooler and dryer than the Côte de Beaune). What seemed to make the difference was that there was much more marl in the Côte de Beaune than the Côte de Nuits, where the limestones were purer.

What's certain, by contrast, is that the Côte de Beaune is twice as large as the Côte de Nuits, and that despite its white wine celebrity most of its production is in fact red. In landscape and geology terms, the Côte de Beaune almost resembles the southern Rhône, while the Côte de Nuits resembles Côte Rôtie and Hermitage. The thread of hillside, in other words, that is so characteristic of the Côte de Nuits becomes broken, dislocated, and disjointed in the Côte de Beaune. The vineyards fan out spreadingly; they gaze more to the south, and less fiercely at the east. The soils, too, are less uniform, as we'll see.

It all begins excitingly with the commanding hill of Corton, the Côte de Beaune's answer to Chambertin up on the Côte de Nuits. Corton is a high, elongated, wood-topped stump, dropping down on its southeastern side to the villages of **Aloxe-Corton** and **Ladoix-Serrigny**, and sculpted at the back by fugitive watercourses, at the intersection of which sits the tranquil village of **Pernand-Vergelesses**. The entire hillside is Burgundy's biggest Grand Cru (148 ha/365 acres).

Until the mid-nineteenth century, it produced only red wine. It was then discovered (slowly, of course) that white wine from the cream-coloured, marly upper slopes of the west-facing Pernand side (known as En Charlemagne) could be mouth-shiveringly good; this, now, is where the white Corton-Charlemagne grows, with the rest of the hillside (redder soils, more iron) producing red Corton. Confusingly, Corton can carry up to twenty other names hyphenated to it, depending on exactly where on the hillside the wine originates. Since white Grands Crus command a higher price than red, Chardonnay is gradually spreading along the top of the hill on the Corton side also.

There's a sea of vines hereabouts, and the Pernand combe is not the only one to interrupt the slope here. The little River Rhoin flows out past **Savigny-lès-Beaune**, too, providing a junction of slopes with widely varying aspects and soil types. A mass of low-lying vineyard behind **Chorey-lès-Beaune** provides plentiful quantities of light village wine. The best Premiers Crus of both Pernand and Savigny are pungent and raspberryish.

Then comes **Beaune** itself, the Côte d'Or's capital city. Typically, the main slope here is nibbled by a number of small combes, and the slope falls away from the woods at the top relatively abruptly, without the space for the mid-slope grandeur that gave rise, further north, to Échézeaux, Musigny, or Bonnes Mares. No Grands Crus, thus, but a mass of Premiers Crus, some of which are on steep, stony soils and some of which are on flatter, richer soils (indeed some vineyards, like Grèves, have both). Deep wines, light wines, even thin or sharp wines: Beaune has them all, but the most typical are soft, comely, and supple.

Pommard is odd in that its best vineyards are not found up on the slopes above the village, and sited to each side of its combe, but rather in the low, flat, and gentle land that flanks the village itself. Even more oddly, those Premiers Crus produce relatively deep-coloured, tannic

▲ *Great wine is created as much by what you leave out as what you include. These discarded bunches mean less, but better.*

reds with decided black-plum fruit and even, on occasion, a sprinkling of chocolate. Why? The reason seems to be that a seam of iron-rich ferruginous oolite is brought, by mild faulting, to the surface more or less in the middle of this near-flat Premier Cru land, where it is washed and tumbled about by the rain and frost. One of the vineyard names, Rugiens, refers to the reddish colours of the soils here. Underneath the surface, too, there is plenty of almost clay-like sticky marl, giving what one might almost describe as a mini-Pétrus effect; Pommard is Burgundy's Pomerol. The next village, **Volnay**, is in principle similar, save that the red, iron-rich soils are more widely scattered and interspersed with pebbly limestones and brown marls. The Premiers Crus (of generally high quality here) climb back up onto the hillside proper, where the soils are lighter and thinner, and the wines of this village seem at best to strike a voluptuously happy medium between the rippling flesh of Pommard and the grace and charm of Beaune.

What next? Chaotic complications. The Côte de Beaune forks into what we could call a high road to the hills, and a low road south. Let's deal with the high road first.

Monthélie sits next door to Volnay, though its orientation swings more toward the south; two combes flank the village. The main slope then disappears altogether as a side valley opens up past **Auxey-Duresses** to **St-Romain**, the latter village being more properly regarded as part of the Hautes Côtes, despite having its own AOC since 1967. Further south, **Blagny**, the unclassified village of Gamay, and **St-Aubin** all form part, too, of this "highland" thread of villages producing cool, light reds and correct though rarely fleshy whites. Lower down, however, more exciting things are happening.

In vineyard terms, the reddish, northern side of **Meursault** is intermingled with Volnay: the Santenots Premier Cru is regarded as belonging to Volnay if it's red, and Meursault if it's white. Land-wise,

things change to the south, or white, side of Meursault. What occurs here is that the seam of Comblanchien stone (in slightly modified geological form) reappears at this point. It, too, has been quarried, though it is so no longer. Up above the old quarries is good village land; the fine white Premiers Crus of Meursault are found below, on a pure limestone, marl, and old quarry rubble. This is a sheltered situation; you can taste the butter and fat of the sun's warmth in the wines here, though there is mineral finesse behind. Perrières is commonly regarded as the finest vineyard of all, and indubitably Grand Cru-worthy; Lavalle's nineteenth century vineyard ranking placed it just below Montrachet. The name itself is an old word for a quarry ("stoneyard").

South of Meursault (and underneath the little hamlet of Blagny, whose wine only appears under this name if it is red), the spread of fine white Premier Cru vineyards continue into **Puligny-Montrachet**. This strip of land ends with the Grand Cru Montrachet flourish: white wine considered by many to be the greatest found on our planet. Geologically (and there is nothing much else to account for the difference in quality between Meursault and Montrachet), some subtle changes have taken place. The basic formula of strata of hard limestone locked into place by sticky marl is the same, though their constitution is different: the limestone known as Pierre de Chassagne replaces Comblanchien, and the *Ostrea acuminata* marls of further north are now succeeded by beds of *Pholadomya bellona* and *Digonella divionensis* marls. Small faults break this Grand Cru up into its three fundamental divisions: stony Chevalier-Montrachet high on the hillside; Le Montrachet itself on a gentle mid-slope; and the three Bâtard-Montrachets on almost flat, moister land. Montrachet, like Corton-Charlemagne, needs many years to evolve; at its peak it is every bit as articulate, yet more fulsomely so: exuberant wild mushroom and nut characters in place of the nervy quality and mineral flavours of Corton. The great, almost flat sweep of superb Premier Cru land that began at Meursault continues southwards through both Puligny-Montrachet and **Chassagne-Montrachet**, sited on the other side of the combe that opens up beneath St-Aubin and Gamay. White wines dominate and convince; red wines now merely complement the whites.

The slope continues into the next village, **Santenay**, then turns right at **Dezize-** and **Sampigny-lès-Maranges**. The Côte d'Or ends here in considerable geological confusion; indeed not only is the southerly orientation of the Maranges vineyards completely different to the rest of the Côte d'Or, but its soils are different, too, with magnesium-rich dolomite and shale taking the place of classic limestone. Santenay, the final shout of the classic Côte, has some juicy, raspberryish reds to offer. Finally, the vineyards of the Couchois region, lying southwest of Maranges and due west of the the northernmost vineyards of the Côte Chalonnaise, received the **Bourgogne Côtes du Couchois** AOC in early 2001 for Pinot-based red wines.

The Hautes Côtes

Behind and above the main slope of the Côte d'Or lies what are known as the "high slopes" or Hautes Côtes. These are divided into **Hautes Côtes de Nuits** and **Hautes Côtes de Beaune**. The soils are no longer as limy; the sites are fractured and widespread; the climate is notably cooler. This is a viticulture of opportunism, grabbing a good slope here or there in order to try to get a vineyard full of grapes ripe. It is blackcurrants (for crème de cassis) that are the real glory of the Hautes Côtes, while Aligoté can be tautly good here, too. Alas, most of the Pinot-based red and Chardonnay-based white from this sector that reaches the market is thin and ungrateful. Were it not for the magical names "Nuits" and "Beaune" on the label, it would be very hard for this wine to find any but a local market.

The Côte Chalonnaise

The slope continues – on the other side of the River Dheune. It is already fissured in the Côte d'Or; along the Côte Chalonnaise, the slope is frankly discontinuous. This thread of hill vineyards wends circuitously through five villages: Bouzeron, Rully, and Mercurey in the north of the region, then Givry and Montagny further south. A patchwork of sites, broken up by multiple faults, and a patchwork of soils, too: limestone, sandy clay, marl. You'd expect a bit of everything here, and that's exactly what you get. It's more exposed, and therefore cooler, than in the Côte d'Or; quality aspirations are modest but sometimes memorably achieved. But treat "Premier Cru" with a raised eyebrow here; they are defined far more laxly than in the Côte d'Or.

The first and smallest village, **Bouzeron**, has an AOC for Aligoté only, for reasons more historical than geological: there is no reason why Chardonnay shouldn't prosper on its limy soils. If you like the citric glint of Aligoté, though, or if you're fond of a good Kir, Bouzeron is worthwhile. **Rully**, to the south, is classified for red and white wines, and has a ludicrous twenty-three Premiers Crus. The cool, elegant whites are more successful than the tenuous reds. The next village, **Mercurey**, pumps out red wine that, at best, can be a pungent, juicy, rough-hewn, honest, grafter's burgundy; its tally of thirty Premiers Crus, though, is again wildly over-flattering. There is a little white. In **Givry**, on the doorstep of Chalon-sur-Saône, the balance is the same: mostly red. Here the structure is a little lighter, the perfumes a little more intriguing, with another great fistful of so-called Premiers Crus (twenty-two). The Premier Cru nonsense finally gets out of hand in the last, white-only village, **Montagny**, where there are no fewer than fifty-three. (At least it's an improvement on the situation prior to 1991, when any white wine was regarded as Premier Cru providing it got up to 11.5 per cent abv.) Marl and sandstone soils make for Chardonnays with a little more weight and substance than elsewhere in the Côte Chalonnaise; the best can compete with many Côte d'Or village whites.

The Mâconnais

The Mâcon region is soldered, at its southern end, with Beaujolais: the limestone of St-Véran meshes, in the space of a few kilometres, with the granite of St-Amour. Two different soils, and two different wines, yet they share at least one thing in common: accessibility. There's an artless generosity and charm about these straightforward white wines – recognizably Chardonnays (with their soft and creamy lemon), yet at the same time still very much burgundy, too, with a vinous structure and depth that lifts them above the level of the simple varietal. Like Beaujolais, they are sympathetic food wines in the classic French tradition – yet they are fun to drink too, their deliciousness never quite shading into the serious and sometimes ponderous grandeur of the Côte d'Or or the Médoc. They can offer some of France's best white wine value.

Most of the Mâconnais is rumpled pastureland on which vines perch wherever a promising hill shows up. They share this sweet and comely landscape with Charolais cattle (at home here), goats, and orchards; the region's 9,000 or so wine-growers are on average mixed farmers with less than a hectare each – hence the importance of cooperatives. Limestones predominate, but there are also clays, sandstones, and alluvial soils, too. The Mâconnais, though, is a big fellow: it produces as much wine as the Côte d'Or and the Côte Chalonnaise combined.

The AOC system here is pyramid-like, as in the Côte d'Or. At the bottom is **Mâcon** and **Mâcon-Supérieure**: passable whites and often dismal reds. **Mâcon Rouge** is one of the few French AOCs of which I can say that I have never had a good one – though some must exist. Almost all are Gamay, and Gamay hates the limestone it finds in Mâcon. The idea is that this crystal-loving variety should be planted on the Mâconnais' patches of sand and granite, though the results suggest that this happens either infrequently or unsuccessfully. When Pinot Noir is grown down here, which is altogether a better idea, it gets called Bourgogne Rouge.

Mâcon-Villages (or Mâcon Blanc-Villages, since all must be white) is where quality begins. There are forty-three of these villages, and each has the chance to hyphenate its own name to that of Mâcon if it wishes: Mâcon-Lugny, for example, or Mâcon-Igé. You may even see Mâcon-Chardonnay – since Chardonnay is a village here (which may or may not have given its name to the grape variety). Two villages, Viré and Clessé, managed to win an AOC of their own in 1999 (**Viré-Clessé**), though the regulations are no more stringent than for any other village.

The geology becomes most interesting in the far south of the Mâconnais where typical Burgundian limestone collides with Beaujolais granite. This geological hiatus sees a number of different marls and limestones packed together like playing cards, with the most famous feature of the local landscape being the cliff-rocks of Vergisson and Solutré. They rear up out of the landscape like calcareous waves; in prehistoric times, thousands of wild horses, deer, and anything else four-legged and edible were sent tumbling over these precipices by tribes of marshalling hunters. Their bones lie two metres (six feet) deep beneath the rock. The three Pouilly appellations, **Pouilly-Fuissé**, **Pouilly-Loché**, and **Pouilly-Vinzelles**, form a limestone bowl; surrounding it is the **St-Véran** AOC, which unites the wine production of half-a-dozen villages to the north and south of Pouilly. These wines, the best of the Mâconnais, have a substance and a fire to them missing among the generally softer whites of the Villages area.

Chance proximity? Not necessarily: hand-harvesting into small boxes helps create the quality that marks Jadot out from many other négociants.

Burgundy Flak

Varietal controversy

Most of those who have passed their professional lives tasting and drinking wine believe that this region is where the greatest Pinot Noir and Chardonnay wines of our age are grown. Chardonnay, we might note in passing, is now the world's most popular grape variety. But what is the one nugget of information a white burgundy producer is not allowed to inform the drinker of via the label? That the wine is made from Chardonnay. No bottle of AOC Bourgogne Rouge, similarly, can proclaim itself "Pinot Noir". The appellation authorities are resolute, no grape varieties for the front labels of appellation wines except in regions where varietal labelling is "traditional" (like Alsace).

In many French regions, of course, if you want to label wine varietally, you at least have the option of making a Vin de Pays; not in Burgundy, though. It's AOC or nothing. Small wonder that many flout the law and label Bourgogne Blanc as Chardonnay and Bourgogne Rouge as Pinot Noir. Why not? The official argument is that these are not wines that taste of varieties; they are wines that taste of their place of origin – Burgundy. Indeed so. Yet a little varietal labelling would at least allow consumers to make up their own minds. This law sacrifices accessibility on the altar of dogma. Changing it would not endanger the expression of terroir; it would be a simple communicative gesture, and a retreat from arrogance.

The madness of Burgundy's appellations

As we discovered above, the Côte d'Or contains more than 500 appellations for fifty km (thirty-one miles) of vineyards. Is this mad?

In theory, no. In theory, Burgundy's appellation system is as near perfection as you can find in the wine world: it reflects every nuance of soil, aspect, and exposure, these distinctions not having been decreed by myopic administrators in a dusty Paris bureau, but proved by hundreds of years of back-straining viticulture. The quotation from Henri Jayer on page 83 is no mere rhetoric: the man worked all his life in this open-air laboratory; these were his findings; tens of thousands of others have confirmed and confirm them. The AOC boundaries give that sweated peasant research the force of law. Indeed, complex as they are, it could be argued that they don't go far enough. "What we call Echézeaux," points out Henri Jayer, "is in fact an assembly of eleven different *lieux-dits* situated in different ways on a hillside." Jean-Charles de la Morinière of Bonneau du Martray cultivates sixteen different parcels and makes sixteen different wines for his one Corton-Charlemagne.

In practice, however, whose interests does such a system serve? Do they help the world's drinkers, or are they rather a way for the majority of producers to glorify inadequate wines with the theology of terroir? An appellation system pursued to this degree of precision is like religion in another way, too: everyone necessarily falls short of the perfection it prescribes. Time and time again, I have embarked on a burgundy tasting looking for minute differences between sites – and found only the stark differences between growers' winemaking abilities. Why not, then, confine one's search to the different wines of one, talented grower? This I have done, too. Differences between adjacent vineyards certainly emerge – in one vintage; another vintage can reverse them. I don't doubt that the best growers understand these things and can testify to their reality, by dint of tasting all of their own wines repeatedly and thoughtfully over a twenty- or thirty-year cycle. No ordinary consumer will ever have the chance to do this. My suggestion is that you accept, as I have done, Burgundy's appellation system as one of a number of possible ways of tracking chaos and anarchy. It has great abstract beauty, but chaos and anarchy is the reality to which you will constantly, as you drink burgundy, return. The consuming truth of burgundian wine quality, sadly, is that it is eighty per cent due to producer and vintage, and at best twenty per cent due to vineyard of origin.

Inadequate red burgundy is the world's worst "fine" wine

Much red burgundy remains, even today, of insultingly low quality: raw, thin, and inarticulate. It was, admittedly, worse in the past; but this is still a wine region that relies more than most on a wine dream in order to sell an often unlovely reality. It is hard to blame the region's producers entirely for this: they are working with one of the world's most challenging red grape varieties in a small, much-morselled area towards the northern limit for successful red wine production. Those responsible for appellation tasting committees, however, ought to place their loyalties to the world's drinkers above those to their fellow producers. It is alarmingly easy to prove that the worst producers' Grand Cru wines are of inferior quality to the best growers' village or even regional wines. One reason for this is that Burgundy's wines (including, amazingly enough, the Grands Crus) do not have to be tasted prior to receiving their AOC; a producer's whole production is approved on the basis of one or two "representative" samples. To reject the region's disgracefully poor Grand Cru and Premier Cru wines – as the tasting panels should be doing – may have divisive social implications within the communities in which they take place. Burgundy's reputation, however, will never wholly emerge from the shadowlands in which it has spent much of the last fifty years so long as the terrible disappointments that leap out of expensive bottles of burgundy persist. It remains to be seen if the "Project Burgundy" scheme agreed in summer 2001, one of whose aims is "downstream monitoring", will improve matters.

Names, names, names

Burgundian nomenclature is the most confusing in France. This is partly the fault of its baroque appellation system, but it is also a side effect of a region whose wines are made by a huge number of producers each of whom owns a few small parcels of vines. Family domain names, furthermore, may last less than a lifetime, and change with the marriages and alliances of succeeding or even existing generations; since burgundy is made in small villages which form part of a rural community, many of these names are held in common. To say that you have bought a bottle of burgundy made by Boillot, Gagnard, or Morey is a profoundly ambiguous statement. Bordeaux, with its château system (the name stays the same no matter who owns the property and, more questionably, no matter what the property's boundaries) and with its infinitely simpler AOC system, is far easier for the world's drinkers to understand. This is one reason for Bordeaux's greater international popularity; it also explains why burgundy fans tend to be the nerds of the wine world, delighting in trivial arcana. Should Burgundy attempt to simplify its jungle of names? Since it has no difficult selling the comparatively small pool of wine it produces, there appears to be no pressing need. When time and history have bestowed a terroir-based system of the sophistication of Burgundy's appellations, too, it is sad and perhaps philistine to retreat from it. But if Burgundy wants to be understood a major effort of interpretive simplification is needed. Incomprehensibility is France's biggest problem in the world wine market, and no region is more incomprehensible than Burgundy.

Burgundy: People

François d'Allaines
71150 Demigny, Tel: 03 85 49 90 16, Fax: 03 85 49 90 19

A new wave négociant (founded in 1996), d'Allaines' wines were until recently made by the talented Hautes Côtes winemaker Jean-Yves Devevey. The speciality is Burgundy's lesser village wines, including a rich, blossomy Mâcon La Roche Vineuse and a deep, citrussy white St-Romain.

Bertrand Ambroise ✪
21700 Premeaux-Prissey, Tel: 03 80 62 30 19, Fax: 03 80 62 38 69

This Nuits-St-Georges producer crafts almost atypically exuberant, powerful, chewy red burgundies including a spendidly dark and brooding Premier Cru Les Vaucrains that can almost match the quality of his Corton Le Rognet, and sometimes exceeds that of his Clos Vougeot. Look out, too, for Ambroise's Corton-Charlemagne (one of the richest of all), and a pure, nutty Chassagne-Montrachet Premier Cru La Maltroie. The white Ladoix Premier Cru Les Gréchons offers great value for money, as does the sturdy Bourgogne Rouge.

Guy Amiot
21190 Chassagne-Montrachet, Tel: 03 80 21 38 62, Fax: 03 80 21 90 80

A delicious portfolio of Chassagne Premiers Crus led by a tight, intense, and slowly evolving Caillerets; Amiot also has a plot of Montrachet, giving a profound, mineral-charged wine needing 10 years or more to unfold.

Pierre Amiot
21220 Morey-St-Denis, Tel: 03 80 34 34 28, Fax: 03 80 58 51 17

This Morey-based producer's wines have greatly improved since he has worked with the broker Patrick Lesec; Amiot's sons Jean-Louis and Didier have now taken over from their father, and quality continues to rise. Look out for the deep Gevrey-Chambertin Les Combottes, a Premier Cru enclosed, significantly, by Grand Cru land.

Amiot-Servelle
21220 Chambolle-Musigny, Tel: 03 80 62 80 39, Fax: 03 80 62 84 16

The graceful, silky wines of this Chambolle-based domain are made by Pierre Amiot's son Christian; they include the warmly fruited but little seen Chambolle Premier Cru Derrière La Grange.

Marquis d'Angerville
21190 Volnay, Tel: 03 80 21 61 75, Fax: 03 80 21 65 07

Aristocratic Volnay estate run along conservative lines. The Premiers Crus Taillepieds and *monopole* Clos des Ducs, with their round and resonant fruit, typify the sythesis of grace and power that is Volnay. This was the first domain in Burgundy to bottle its own wines, forced into this leap forward by négociants angry at the then Marquis d'Angerville's campaigning for labelling transparency.

Domaine de l'Arlot
21700 Nuits-StGeorges, Tel: 03 80 61 01 92, Fax: 03 80 61 04 22

Former accountant Jean-Pierre De Smet, who trained with Jacques Seysses of Domaine Dujac, created and runs this estate on behalf of its owners, AXA Millésimes. The style of the wines is, unsurprisingly, Dujac-like: in other words you'll find great purity of fruit here and graceful elegance, rather than muscle and power. They model Pinot Noir, burgundy-style, to perfection.

Comte Armand ✪
21630 Pommard, Tel: 03 80 24 70 50, Fax: 03 80 22 72 37

One of the beacons of Pommard, especially for the 5-ha Clos des Epeneaux whose wines can be amongst the chewiest in the Côte d'Or. The recent celebrity of this biodynamic estate was built on the winemaking of French-Canadian Pascal Marchand. Marchand has now been head-hunted by Boisset to run the Domaine de la Vougeraie, and his place taken by young Benjamin Leroux. The show-stopper here is the dense, regal, often powerfully tannic and liquorice-like Clos des Epeneaux; Leroux is aiming to refine the tannins.

Domaine Robert Arnoux ✪
21670 Vosne Romanée, Tel: 03 80 61 09 85, Fax: 03 80 61 36 02

This estate illustrates the truth that it is not always those who have been born to wine who make the best wine; sometimes a perspective from outside brings fresh insights and fresh rigour. Trained pharmacist Pascal Lachaux has, since his arrival in 1993, brought down yields, improved the care with which the fruit is vinified, increased the proportion of oak used and abandoned fining and filtration. The result is a superb range of wines from Nuits and Vosne-Romanée: deep and fleshy yet soft-edged, and packed with perfumed fruit.

Domaine d'Auvenay ✪✪
21190 Saint-Romain, Tel: 03 80 21 23 27, Fax: 03 80 21 23 27

This is the personal domain of Lalou Bize-Leroy (see Domaine Leroy), based in St-Romain but with village and Premier Cru vineyards in Auxey-Duresses, Meursault, and Puligny, and with the Grands Crus Criots-Bâtard-Montrachet, Chevalier-Montrachet, Mazis-Chambertin, and Bonnes Mares. Rare and expensive, yet what are often the lowest yields in the Côte d'Or combined with rigorously non-interventionist winemaking produce wines of extraordinary concentration and aromatic power.

Daniel Barraud
71960 Vergisson, Tel: 03 85 35 84 25, Fax: 03 85 35 86 98

Daniel Barraud is one of those who shows just what the Mâconnais might achieve with higher expectations on the part of producers and consumers alike. Low yields, late harvests, and the exclusive use of small casks (rather than big steel vats) produce a superb range of wines from single-vineyard sites in Vergisson, St-Véran, and Pouilly-Fuissé. Most of the wines stay on their lees for 15 months, and are bottled unfined and unfiltered. Barraud's Pouilly-Fuissé En Bulands Vieilles Vignes (from 70-year-old vines) is startlingly lush and exotic.

Ghislaine Barthod-Noëllat
21220 Chambolle-Musigny, Tel: 03 80 62 80 16, Fax: 03 80 62 82 42

This small, well-run Chambolle domain produces relatively full-bodied, vigorous, sometimes peppery wines from low-yielding vines. Perfume is one of this village's hallmarks; Barthod's wines ballasts this with earth and spice. The basic Bourgogne is often a good buy here. It's a shame Ghislaine Barthod has no Grands Crus to work with, but the Premiers Crus are well differentiated.

Domaine des Beaumont
21220 Morey-St-Denis, Tel: 03 80 51 87 89, Fax: 03 80 51 87 89

Former motorbike-racer Thierry Beaumont's vivid and exuberant Gevrey-Chambertin and Morey-St-Denis wines were previously sold to merchants; they offer fine value. The Beaumont style mirrors the exuberant fruit and freshness of his friend and fellow bike-enthusiast Vincent Géantet. Look out for the little-seen, superbly positioned Gevrey Premier Cru Les Cherbaudes.

Jean-Claude Belland
21590 Santenay, Tel: 03 80 20 61 90, Fax: 03 80 20 65 60

A Santenay domain, but one with fine holdings in Chambertin and Corton thanks to Jean-Claude's mother, born a Latour. The wines are unshowy, but dense and carefully made, rewarding cellaring.

Bertagna
21640 Vougeot, Tel: 03 80 62 86 04, Fax: 03 80 62 82 58

This Vougeot estate is run by a German-English couple, Eva Reh and Mark Siddle. The holdings are attractive (Chambertin and Clos St-Denis as well as Clos Vougeot) and fastidious viticulture is bringing quality levels up swiftly.

Star rating system used on producer spreads   ✪ Very good wine   ✪✪ Excellent wine   ✪✪✪ Great wine

Vincent Bitouzet-Prieur
21190 Volnay, Tel: 03 85 51 00 83, Fax 03 85 51 71 20

A fine spread of red Volnay and white Meursault wines from this carefully run domain. Both are classical: the Volnays (especially a fine Caillerets) lively with warm red fruits; the whites lush, nutty, and buttery.

Simon Bize
21420 Savigny-lès-Beaune, Tel: 03 80 21 50 57, Fax: 03 80 21 58 17

Consistent, elegant, and refined red wines from a number of different sites in Savigny-lès-Beaune is Patrick Bize's speciality, bottled without fining or filtration (particularly important for the delicate wines produced by east-facing scree slopes here). These light, lithe, digestible burgundies are ideal drunk cool.

Jean-Yves Bizot
21100 Vosne-Romanée, Tel: 03 80 61 24 66, Fax: 03 80 61 24 66

Henri Jayer's young neighbour has learned much from the old master; his Echézeaux and Vosne-Romanée wines are made and bottled, quite literally, barrel by barrel, with minimum use of sulphur dioxide and no fining or filtration. They are characterized by grace, depth, and fragrance, though those placed in new barrels sometimes need some time to digest their oak.

Blain-Gagnard
21190 Chassagne-Montrachet, Tel: 03 80 21 34 07, Fax: 03 80 21 90 07

Part of Jacques Gagnard's vines are tended by his son-in-law Jean-Marc Blain and sold under the Blain-Gagnard name: small quantities from starry vineyards, though in the past only intermittently successful (the 1990 Bâtard-Montrachet I purchased had oxidized and foundered by 2000). This domain took over Jacques Gagnard's parcel of Montrachet in 2000.

Daniel Bocquenet
21700 Nuits-St-Georges, Tel: 03 80 61 24 48, Fax: 03 80 62 15 98

The mischievous Monsieur Bocquenet, hidden away in one of the most obscure cellars I have ever visited, is becoming well-known for his gloriously juicy, deep Echézeaux, as well as some good Nuits-St-Georges.

Jean Boillot
21190 Volnay, Tel: 03 80 21 61 90, Fax: 03 80 21 29 84

Prepare to be confused. This domain is run by Henri Boillot, the brother of Jean-Marc Boillot (and, by the way, the brother-in-law of Gérard Boudot of Sauzet); he has also recently created a micro-négociant business for white wines only called Maison Henri Boillot. Standards are high, with the white wines in particular being vivid and intricately defined.

Jean-Marc Boillot
21630 Pommard, Tel: 03 80 22 71 29, Fax: 03 80 24 98 07

Many of this Pommard-based estate's wines are smooth, articulate, and juicily accessible early in life, though the Pommard Rugiens can be extraordinarily dense, dark and almost raisiny (the vines are over 80 years old). This estate also has a superb range of white wines (it was the destination for those parcels Domaine Sauzet had to relinquish in the early 1990s), including generously endowed Bâtard-Montrachet and Puligny-Montrachet Premier Cru Les Combettes. Boillot believes that the best vintages for white burgundy are those of larger rather than smaller crops; he is an enthusiastic lees-stirrer in such clean, generous years. Like his brother Henri, Jean-Marc Boillot (formerly the winemaker for Olivier Leflaive Frères) also has a négociant's licence.

Domaine du Bois Guillaume *see* Jean-Yves Devevey

Jean-Claude Boisset *see* Domaine de la Vougeraie

Domaine de la Bongran
71260 Clessé, Tel: 03 85 36 94 03, Fax: 03 85 36 99 25

Jean Thévenet's superb Mâcon-Viré and Mâcon-Clessé wines are the result of low yields and late harvesting – which, when combined with natural, unhurried, wild-yeast fermentations can often give wines with some residual sugar (the same vineyard and cellar improvements in Alsace have given similar results).

They make tasting and drinking Thévenet's wines an exciting, exotic experience – but they also give him problems with the AOC authorities, who have effectively excluded him from the new Viré-Clessé AOC (the regulations outlaw wines containing residual sugar). He now sells as Mâcon-Villages. Thévenet was elected President of the Sapros association in 2001: this brings together producers of unchaptalized, botrytized wines from different regions of France.

Bonneau du Martray ✪✪
21420 Pernand-Vergelesses, Tel: 03 80 21 50 64, Fax: 03 80 21 57 19

Inheriting a domain like this, as former architect Jean-Charles Le Bault de la Morinière did from his father Jean in 1994, must be both a huge stroke of good fortune and a grave responsibility: the 11 ha are all found within the Grand Cru of Corton. Most are planted with Chardonnay, producing nuanced, finely detailed Corton-Charlemagne that unfolds in time at a glacial pace; there is also a little red Corton (from a parcel of Pinot entirely surrounded by Chardonnay). Le Bault de la Morinière's aim, he says, is "precise wines". In mysterious support of this almost ascetic ideal, this former architect quotes Ingres: "*le dessin est la probité de l'art*" (drawing is the truth of art). There are other aesthetic maxims, too. "All architecture students learn the maxim of Mies van der Rohe, that God is in the details... Well, the same is true of winemaking, which like architecture is a similar combination of technology and aesthetics, and of thinking now about things that will matter in years ahead." In addition to precision, he also wants great intensity. "It would be nice if the wine could last 10 minutes. One sip. It's not a dream. It could exist." The main reason for the notable improvement in the wines of this domain (both white and red) under Le Bault de la Morinière is reduced yields, giving the 1999 Corton-Charlemagne, in particular, a dramatic, eye-watering intensity unusual in that generally high-yielding year. Oak is used with extreme caution. "How can we find enough wood to present the wine well but gentle enough to disappear?" His solution is a maximum of one-third new wood for 12 months, with the Charlemagne then spending a further six months in stainless steel ("the wine carries on nourishing itself on the finest part of the lees"). A similar practice is followed at Leflaive. The wine's fermentation is also begun in steel, "to observe the tempo of the vintage." Once bottled, he insists, it needs about 20 years.

Bouchard Père et Fils ✪
21200 Beaune, Tel: 03 80 24 80 24, Fax: 03 80 24 97 56

Bouchard Père et Fils (a different company altogether to the Boisset-owned Bouchard Aîné) has, since its purchase by Joseph Henriot in 1995, propelled itself back into the front rank of Burgundy négociants. Indeed Bouchard, together with Jadot and Drouhin, proves that large négociant companies can compete, appellation by appellation, with all but the most single-minded growers. (In one way, of course, this is a grower: its 30 ha of Grands Crus and 74 ha of Premiers Crus make it the largest landowner in the Côte d'Or, though wines from its own vineyards are not distinguished on labels.) Star wines among Bouchard's reds include its velvety Beaune Grèves Vignes de l'Enfant Jésus and pretty Clos de la Mousse, both with better depth and texture than many Beaune wines; and its Volnay Taillepieds and Volnay Caillerets Ancienne Cuvée Carnot, both much deeper and more resonant than in the past. The superbly sited Grand Cru *monopole* of La Romanée should be one of Burgundy's greatest red wines; beginning with the 1995 vintage, it has been. The whites are finely balanced, with brilliantly judged oak influence; stars include an outstanding Montrachet and Chevalier-Montrachet, but the Meursault Genevrières is barely off the pace, and wines like the Beaune Clos St-Landry and St-Aubin Les Murgers des Dents de Chiens offer excellent value. The Rully les Thivaux has the fresh elegance of the Côte Chalonnaise at its best. Bouchard is now what it always should have been: a name to trust.

Michel Bouzereau et Fils
21190 Meursault, Tel: 03 80 21 20 74, Fax: 03 80 21 66 41

Carefully crafted, remarkably intense white Bourgogne Blanc, plus a range of Meursault including the *lieux-dits* Grands Charrons (soft), Limozin (rich), and Tessons (mineral). Michel Bouzereau's son Jean-Baptiste is refining the style.

Louis Carillon ⊙
21190 Puligny-Montrachet, Tel: 03 80 21 30 34, Fax: 03 80 21 90 02

This old-established Puligny producer, run at present by Jacques and Philippe Carillon, makes a range of initially unshowy whites that slowly unfold over time into finely detailed articulacy and creamy sumptuousness. The Bienvenues-Bâtard-Montrachet is outstanding, though produced in pitifully small quantities.

Carré-Courbin
21190 Volnay, Tel: 03 80 24 67 62, Fax: 03 80 24 66 93

Small but very promising Beaune domain run by Philippe and Maëlle Carré-Courbin: the holdings are in Volnay (including an old-vine parcel in Taillepieds) and Pommard. Their 1999s were packed with bright and perfumed fruit.

Château de Chambolle-Musigny *see* Frédéric Mugnier

Champy Père et Cie
21200 Beaune, Tel: 03 80 25 09 99, Fax: 03 80 25 09 95

Burgundy's oldest négociant house (founded in 1720) is now owned by the Meurgey broking family, and produces a worthwhile range of elegant, poised, and softly spoken reds and whites.

Chandon de Briailles
21420 Savigny-lès-Beaune, Tel: 03 80 21 52 31, Fax: 03 80 21 59 15

Conservatively styled and beautifully labelled wines from the 13-ha domain of the Comte and Comtesse de Nicolay. Old oak is favoured in order to underline the purity and finesse of these silky, stealthy, sometimes slightly skinny red wines and pure, racy whites.

Chanson Père et Fils
21206 Beaune, Tel: 03 80 25 97 97, Fax: 03 80 24 17 42

Burgundy négociant now owned by the Bollinger group. These are delicate, soft yet sustained wines of great grace and charm; the 1999s were particularly successful, and further improvements can be expected.

Philippe Charlopin
21220 Gevrey-Chambertin, Tel: 03 80 51 81 18, Fax: 03 80 51 81 18

Fine Gevrey grower whose 13-ha domain includes a superb Clos St-Denis. The dense and resonant Gevrey Vieilles Vignes is hard to get hold of, but offers superb value for money.

Baron de la Charrière *see* Vincent Girardin

Chartron et Trébuchet
21190 Puligny-Montrachet, Tel: 03 80 21 32 85, Fax: 03 80 21 36 35

Jean Charton and Louis Trébuchet's partnership offers burgundy lovers a wide spread of preponderantly white wines from some superb sites, including the Clos du Cailleret and the Clos de la Pucelle in Puligny; the finest vineyard holding is the Chevalier-Montrachet Clos des Chevaliers. Quality varies from fair for some of the lesser wines to outstanding for the best Premiers Crus (such as the Clos de la Pucelle) and Grands Crus.

Jean Chauvenet
21700 Nuits-St-Georges, Tel: 03 80 61 00 72, Fax: 03 80 61 12 87

Jean Chauvenet's son-in-law Christophe Drag has added depth and amplified differences between this estate's fine spread of Nuits-St-Georges Premiers Crus, partly through near-total conversion to organic cultivation, and partly through longer maceration. The results are accessible, warm, and dependable.

Robert Chevillon ⊙
21700 Nuits-St-Georges, Tel: 03 80 62 34 88, Fax: 03 80 61 13 31

If the style of Nuits-St-Georges (bright, bold, fiery fruit) appeals, then this is the first name to remember. Robert Chevillon and his sons Bertrand and Denis have around 13 ha, exclusively in Nuits-St-Georges, including parcels in all of the finest Premiers Crus. Moreover their holdings in Les St-Georges,

Les Cailles and Les Vaucrains are planted with very old vines (75 years), giving multi-dimensional, dense red burgundies of unusual power and richness.

Bruno Clair
21160 Marsannay-la-Côte, Tel: 03 80 52 28 95, Fax: 03 80 52 18 14

Marsannay-based estate (though among the 20 ha of vineyards are holdings up and down the whole of the Côte d'Or) run by Bruno Clair with winemaker Philippe Brun. Among the best wines in 1999 were a sweet-fruited Vosne-Romanée Les Champs Perdrix, a liquorice-charged Gevrey-Chambertin Premier Cru Clos St-Jacques, and an explosively deep Chambertin-Clos de Bèze. The Corton-Charlemagne was a fine bottle, too, flower-scented and honey-charged.

Coche-Bizouard
21190 Meursault, Tel: 03 80 2128 41, Fax: 03 80 21 22 38

Alain Coche is a cousin of the celebrated Jean-François Coche and a maker of fine white wine in his own right, though with less fortunately positioned vineyard parcels. Late harvesting and late bottling create complex, structured, slowly evolving Meursaults.

Coche-Dury ⊙⊙
21190 Meursault, Tel: 03 80 71 24 12, Fax: 03 80 21 67 65

Jean-François Coche is one of Burgundy's legendary makers of white wine, producing the Meursaults by which all others are measured, as well as a superb Puligny-Montrachet Premier Cru Les Enseignières and a Corton-Charlemagne of definitive finesse. All are crafted with great care, layering dense fruit with sumptuous yet seamlessly integrated oak over a long, 18-month *élevage*. They are bottled unfiltered, and age superbly: in a tasting of fine white burgundies in 2000, Coche-Dury's 1988 Bourgogne was still showing well, while the golden-flavoured 1990 Corton-Charlemagne was just getting into its stride. Coche suffered the very contemporary misfortune of having a helicopter crash into his Corton-Charlemagne vines in July 1998 (it was spraying a neighbour's parcel) damaging 10 rows of 40-year-old vines, but fortunately not polluting the soil with chemicals or aviation fuel.

Marc Colin et Fils
21190 St-Aubin, Tel: 03 80 21 30 43, Fax: 03 80 21 90 04

The sons of Marc Colin, Pierre-Yves and Joseph, have now taken over from their father, working the Puligny and Chassagne plots from their cellar in the side-valley village of Gamay. Despite extensive *bâtonnage* (Pierre-Yves has Californian experience), these are generally fine, nervy wines requiring time in bottle to unfold. A great source of St-Aubin too.

Michel Colin-Déléger
21190 Meursault, Tel: 03 80 21 32 72, Fax: 03 80 21 32 72

Michel Colin and his son Bruno make a fine range of wine from nearly 20 ha of vineyards in and around Chassagne-Montrachet, including both Bâtard- and Chevalier-Montrachet and the Puligny Premiers Crus La Truffière and Les Demoiselles. All the wines begin their vinification in stainless steel tanks, before being transferred to barrels to finish fermentation and to age; bottlings are early. The best are complex, ripe, and characterful, achieving articulacy relatively swiftly.

Jean-Jacques Confuron
21700 Premeaux-Prissey, Tel: 03 80 62 31 08, Fax: 03 80 61 34 21

The JJ Confuron domain is run by Alain Meunier and his wife Sophie Confuron; Meunier has also recently begun a micro-négociant business called Féry-Meunier. The domain wines are red burgundies of elegant, expressive fruit, hedonistic rather than intellectual, with fine drinking balance. The top parcels include Romanée-St Vivant, a fine Vosne-Romanée Les Beaux Monts, and one of the most reliably exciting Clos Vougeots, from plots sited behind the château itself. The Féry-Meunier wines are based on purchased fruit, albeit much of it owned by Meunier's friend Jean Féry and grown by Alain Meunier.

Confuron-Coteditot
21700 Vosne-Romanée, Tel: 03 80 61 03 39, Fax: 03 80 61 17 85

A fine spread of vineyards and the sensitive, expressive winemaking of Yves

Confuron make the richly fruited wines of this domain worth seeking out, especially the graceful Vosne-Romanée Premier Cru Suchots and a voluminous Charmes-Chambertin.

Cordier Père et Fils ✪
71960 Fuissé, Tel: 03 85 35 62 89, Fax: 03 85 35 64 01

This, one of the finest domains in the Mâconnais, is now run by Christophe Cordier, who has taken over from his father Roger. Christophe has a curious mind, and he experiments with as wide a variety of techniques as anyone in Burgundy, including *microbullage*, extensive *bâtonnage*, and late harvesting. The result is a spectacular and stimulating range from low-yielding vines which shows just how articulate Pouilly-Fuissé, Pouilly-Loché, and St-Véran can be; even the simple Mâcon Blanc here is a wine of many dimensions.

Coste-Caumartin
21630 Pommard, Tel: 03 80 22 45 04, Fax: 03 80 22 65 22

Vigorous, firm, juicy reds from Pommard are the best buy from this estate run by enthusiastic Jérôme Sordet.

de Courcel
21630 Pommard, Tel: 03 80 22 10 64, Fax: 03 80 24 98 73

The owner of this Pomerol domain, Gilles de Courcel, works for Calvet in Bordeaux; it is run in his absence by Yves Confuron (see Confuron-Coteditot) – and well run, too, taking the raw power of Pommard and giving it sweet and approachable accessibility.

Pierre Damoy
21220 Gevrey-Chambertin, Tel: 03 80 34 30 47, Fax: 03 80 58 54 79

A fortunate estate with superb Côtes de Nuits holdings, including one-third of Clos de Bèze. The present Pierre has reduced yields and raised quality, with the Chambertin in particular providing pungent, deep and resonant wines.

Vincent Dancer
21190 Chassagne-Montrachet, Tel: 03 80 21 94 48, Fax: 03 80 21 94 48

Young grower producing clean, incisive Meursault, Beaune, and Pommard, as well as a dense old-vine Bourgogne Rouge.

Darviot-Perrin
21190 Monthélie, Tel: 03 80 21 27 45

Cleanly delineated, precise, elegant and classic wines from this Monthélie-based grower with some good sites in Volnay, Meursault, and Chassagne, including the Chassagne Premier Cru Blanchots-Dessus, adjacent to Montrachet.

Marius Delarche
21420 Pernand Vergelesses Tel: 03 80 21 57 70, Fax: 03 80 21 58 96

The wines that Philippe Delarche produces in conjuction with American importers Peter Vezan and David Hinkle (labelled Réserve, and bottled by hand without fining or filtering) are deeply and vividly flavoured, packed with intense fruit. Delarche is based in the pretty village of Pernan Vergelesses, with his vineyards lying on both sides of the valley beneath the village, including parcels of Corton and Corton-Charlemagne.

Denogent *see* Robert-Denogent

Bruno Desaunay-Bissey
21640 Flagey Echézeaux, Tel: 03 80 62 80 06, Fax: 03 80 82 87 38

This little-known Flagey domain has some exciting vineyard holdings, including an excellent parcel of Grands Echézeaux (some of which is sold to Dominique Laurent to cosset). The succulent, flavour-saturated Vosne-Romanée Premier Cru Les Beaumonts is very nearly as good.

Domaine des Deux Roches
71960 Davayé, Tel: 03 85 35 86 51, Fax: 03 85 35 86 12

Fine, subtle St-Véran from this domain provides excellent value for money.

Jean-Yves Devevey
71150 Demigny, Tel: 03 85 49 91 11, Fax: 03 85 49 91 59

Skilled winemaker Devevey produces some of the best (and thus ripest) wines from the generally disappointing Hautes Côtes, and also now has a parcel of Beaune Pertuisots to work with.

Joseph Drouhin
21200 Beaune, Tel: 03 80 24 68 88, Fax: 03 80 22 43 14

Together with Jadot and Bouchard Père et Fils, Drouhin is part of the great triumvirate of present-day Burgundy négociants. Quality is high throughout the range, with the Drouhin style one of great finesse and purity; vulgar extract and lavish oak are both frowned upon here. The flagship wine, both for its comely, rounded red and delicately nutty white, is the beautifully labelled Beaune Clos des Mouches, a Premier Cru site of which Drouhin owns nearly 14 ha. The Drouhin style is perfectly matched with the nervy finesse of Corton-Charlemagne, while the emperor of these white wines is the extraordinarily concentrated Montrachet Marquis de Laguiche (Laguiche is the biggest owner of Montrachet, and Drouhin has made and marketed the wines since the 1940s). Amongst the white Premiers Crus, the Puligny-Montrachet Les Folatières is particularly dense, rich, and spicy. The reds are no less consistent, yet at the same time splendidly true to their origins, as a comparison of the graceful, cherry-packed 1999 village Chambolle-Musigny with the plummy 1999 Pommard proves. Among the stars are a Musigny of great presence, depth, and grace, and an entrancing Griotte-Chambertin, suggesting both the cherries of the name and something altogether deeper and meatier. Patriarch Robert Drouhin has now been joined by his daughter Véronique (who also looks after Domaine Drouhin in Oregon) and sons Philippe and Frédérique; Laurence Jobard is the winemaker.

Claude Dugat ✪
21420 Gevrey-Chambertin, Tel: 03 80 34 36 18, Fax: 03 80 58 50 64

Claude Dugat proves both that there is no formula for the making of great burgundy, and that avant-garde techniques are not necessary either; attention to detail is all that is required. These are wines of what one might call complex simplicity: they reward scrutiny with a wealth of notes and allusions; they match any gauge for quality one might choose; yet at the same time they make delicious, fresh-fruited drinking from the moment they are bottled. All of Dugat's vineyards are in and around Gevrey, peaking with a Griotte-Chambertin of heady, enchanting scent and powerful, perfumed flavour.

Bernard Dugat-Py ✪
21220 Gevrey-Chambertin, Tel: 03 80 51 82 46, Fax: 03 80 51 86 41

Another Gevrey domain, run by Claude's cousin Bernard with, if anything, even more fastidiousness. This all-too-small 7-ha estate is lucky enough to have extensive old-vine resources, resulting in a series of Vielles Vignes *cuvées* that truly deserve the name. Overall, the style is deep, dark, and full of meaty spice: the apogee of Gevrey.

Domaine Dujac ✪
21220 Morey-St-Denis, Tel: 03 80 34 01 00, Fax: 03 80 34 01 09

Given land prices in Burgundy today, the creation of a fine domain without benefit of inheritance seems almost impossible. Almost. Jacques Seysses managed, beginning in the mid-1960s, and today this Morey-based domain has an enviable 12 ha, including parcels in five Grands Crus. Seysses doesn't use press wine, keeps the fermentation and *cuvaison* relatively cool, and racks as often as necessary in order to get rid of savoury flavours – yet he does (like his friend Aubert de Villaine at DRC) use all the stems, and he also uses new, lightly toasted wood lavishly. The result is often wine of relatively pale colour and soft texture, yet great depth, fruit, and refinement, and with memorable drinking balance. Seysses' widely travelled son Jeremy is becoming increasingly involved.

Vincent Dureuil-Janthial
71150 Rully, Tel: 03 85 87 02 37, Fax: 03 85 87 00 24

This enthusiastic, Rully-based grower working with old vines and late harvesting has produced (especially the Cuvée Unique bottlings for the USA) some exotically dense, dark, succulent reds and rich, multi-layered and sometimes lavishly oaked white wines: a wake-up call for the often rather dull winemaking of the Côte Chalonnaise, and a perfect contrast to Rully's other star, Jacqueson.

Maurice Ecard et Fils
21420 Savigny-lès-Beaune, Tel: 03 80 21 50 61, Fax: 03 80 26 11 05

This Savigny-lès-Beaune producer produces a fine range from the commune's different Premier Cru sites, with more ripeness and tannic depth than most of his peers. These are graceful, satisfying lunchtime-style red burgundies.

René Engel
21700 Vosne-Romanée, Tel: 03 80 61 10 54, Fax: 03 80 62 39 73

The Vougeot, Echézeaux, and Vosne-Romanée wines of this domain have been usually among the best of their peers, thanks to the energetic efforts of the late Philippe Engel. They have flesh and depth, and offer grateful, lush drinking.

Arnaud Ente
21190 Meursault, Tel 03 80 21 66 12, Fax: 03 80 21 66 12

A bottle of Vega Sicilia positioned among the empties outside Arnaud Ente's cellar indicates that this quiet young Meursault grower has both catholic taste and high ambitions. The range of wines is not huge, but it includes a stunning Meursault Vieilles Vignes made from a parcel over 100 years old in En l'Ormeau as well as a large-scale Puligny-Montrachet Premier Cru Les Réferts. "Elegance and purity" are what Ente says he is looking for.

Faiveley
21701 Nuits-St-Georges, Tel: 03 80 61 04 55, Fax: 03 80 62 33 37

Larger holdings (117.5 ha) than Bouchard Père et Fils, Jadot, or Drouhin make this négociant's position an enviable one, and there are outstanding wines within the portfolio at all quality levels. Inexpensive wines to seek out include the sappy white Givry Blanc Champ Lalot, the richer, leesier Mercurey Blanc Clos Rochette, and the chewy, cherryish Mercurey Rouge Premier Cru Clos du Roy; the stars of the range include the various Chambertin Grands Crus. All the reds spend 18 months in oak, and the majority of Grand and Premier Cru wines are hand-bottled unfiltered, directly from the cask. Faiveley is based in Nuits, and it always seems to me that the Nuits style itself marks the whole range: these are forceful, energetic, vivid burgundies of exuberance and pungency rather than finesse and subtlety.

Féry-Meunier *see* Jean-Jacques Confuron

Jean-Philippe Fichet
21190 Meursault, Tel: 03 80 21 28 51, Fax: 03 80 21 28 11

This young Meursault-based producer believes in vinifying all his parcels separately, giving a range of *lieu-dit* bottlings: the Gruyaches (a small vineyard beneath Les Charmes planted in old vines) is particularly deep and resonant.

Follin Arbelet
21420 Aloxe-Corton, Tel: 03 80 26 46 73, Fax: 03 80 26 43 32

Fine holdings, whose fruit formerly went into Louis Latour bottlings, include Corton-Charlemagne, Corton (a red produced from the En Charlemagne white wine sector of the hillside) and Corton-Bressandes. The style is pungent, vivid, lively, and incisive: piquant sloe rather than creamy plum.

Fontaine-Gagnard
21190 Chassagne-Montrachet, Tel: 03 80 21 35 50, Fax: 03 80 21 90 78

One of the two heirs to the Gagnard-Delagrange holdings, these wines are made by Richard Fontaine, a former aeronautical engineer. They are more richly oaked than the Blain-Gagnard wines; despite this, I have found them slightly understated, given the notoriety of their vineyards.

Château de Fuissé
71960 Fuissé, Tel: 03 85 35 61 44, Fax: 03 85 35 67 34

This 30-ha domain has been owned by the Vincent family since 1852; Jean-Jacques Vincent is the present encumbent, aided by his daughter Bénédicte. The range includes three single-vineyard Pouilly-Fuissé wines: Les Brûlées, Le Clos, and Les Combettes, in addition to Château Fuissé and (the top wine)

Château Fuissé Vieilles Vignes. These are firm, tight-knit, oak-spiced wines which need time to soften and unfold.

Jean-Noël Gagnard
21190 Chassagne-Montrachet, Tel: 03 80 21 31 68, Fax: 03 80 21 33 07

Jean-Noël Gagnard's daughter Caroline Lestimé took over in the mid-1990s, and since then the domain has gone from strength to strength, with ever-increasing levels of concentration in a fine range of Chassagne Premiers Crus: the tautly fruited Masures, the sheer and sinewy Chenevottes, the lush Chaumées, the firm Morgeots, and the mineral Caillerets. There is, too, wonderful bready substance to the Bâtard-Montrachet. Red wines, however, seem to be less well-understood; even in a generous vintage like 1999 they tasted rather light and tenuous, despite the use of 25% new oak and the abandonment of filtration.

Gagnard-Delagrange
21190 Chassagne-Montrachet, Tel: 03 80 21 31 40, Fax: 03 80 21 91 59

A gradually diminishing domain, as the veteran Jacques Gagnard hands his vineyards over to his daughters (whose wines, through their marriages, are labelled as Blain-Gagnard and Fontaine-Gagnard). Gagnard's own wines continue to reflect his philosophy of low yields, scrupulously clean fruit, and low sulphur levels. Sinewy and vigorous, they last well.

Geantet Pansiot
21220 Gevrey-Chambertin, Tel: 03 80 34 32 37, Fax: 03 80 34 16 23

Jolly, juicy red wines from this Gevrey-based domain run by biker Vincent Geantet peak with a soft-tannined, deep-fruited Charmes-Chambertin. Geantet picks and bottles early in order to capture maximum fruit freshness.

Génot-Boulanger
21190 Meursault, Tel: 03 80 21 49 20, Fax: 03 80 21 49 21

The wines of this intriguing, Meursault-based domain were sold to négociants until the early 1990s. Since then, the Delaby-Génot family has invested a considerable amount in the 27-ha estate, which is run by François Delaby. The prize parcel is in the middle of Corton-Charlemagne producing a wine of unusual depth and dimensions for this Grand Cru, but there are also fine sites in Chassagne-Montrachet (Chenevottes) and Meursault (Clos du Cromin). Reds include a Clos Vougeot and a Corton. The domain also produces good red and white Mercurey.

Emilian Gillet *see* Domaine de la Bongran

Vincent Girardin
21190 Chassagne-Montrachet, Tel: 03 80 21 96 06, Fax: 03 80 21 96 23

Vincent Girardin, like Gérard Boudot of Domaine Sauzet, combines running a domain with a flourishing micro-négociant business; some of the wines are also sold under the Baron de la Charrière label. The domain itself is based in Santenay, and Girardin's own Santenay red wines are models of digestible, silky purity, while the whites (rare in this AOC) are fresh and lemony. For the négociant business, Girardin buys fruit (never juice or wine) from old-vine parcels up and down the Côte de Beaune (which, thanks to its size, is where most of Burgundy's bargains are to be found). There is no fining and filtering. The consistency of these wines is astonishing, given the burgundy region's historical unreliability, with even the most modest AOCs (like the Maranges Clos des Loyères Vieilles Vignes) amply meriting a punt. Among Girardin's many star red wines are three powerful yet luscious Premiers Crus from Volnay (Champans, Clos des Chênes, and Santenots), and another superb, dense and tight-knit old-vine trio from Pommard (Les Chanlins Vieilles Vignes, Clos des Lambots Vieilles Vignes, and a Premier Cru Les Rugiens Vieilles Vignes; there is also a gutsy Premier Cru Les Epenots). High spots among the whites come with more Vieilles Vignes parcels in the Chassagne-Montrachet Premiers Crus (especially Morgeots) and a multi-dimensioned Corton-Charlemagne.

Henri Gouges ✪
21700 Nuits-St-Georges, Tel: 03 80 61 04 40, Fax: 03 80 61 32 84

This 14.5-ha domain, tightly focused in the southern side of Nuits-St-Georges, has a splendid history; it has been domain bottling since the 1920s, and the original Henri Gouges helped draw up Burgundy's appellation system in the 1930s. It is run today by Pierre and Christian Gouges, and low yields and lengthy, extractive vinifications give wines for long ageing. Little oak is used, so the focus remains firmly on the roar of fruit so typical of Nuits. Another speciality of the domain are the two white Nuits (Clos des Porrets and Les Perrières) produced from mutant white Pinot Noir grapes.

Jean Grivot ✪
21700 Vosne-Romanée, Tel: 03 80 61 05 95, Fax: 03 80 61 32 99

This 15-ha Vosne-Romanée estate is run by the sensitive and reflective Etienne Grivot (see page 88) with great skill and articulacy. The bottles of non-burgundian wines at the entrance to the cellar (Kistler, Niepoort ports, Château Latour) testify to broader horizons than many burgundians enjoy. Aesthetically, Grivot is looking for structure subsumed within a caressing harmony: his analogy is: "the square within the circle. No part of the square must ever stick outside the circle." His 15 ha of vineyards give him no fewer than 20 AOCs, including five Vosne Premiers Crus, three Nuits Premiers Crus, and three Grands Crus; the average age of the vines is over 30 years. This age, combined with Grivot's thoughtful winemaking, produces a range of fresh, sweet, cleanly defined, and resonant red burgundies with outstanding purity of fruit, subtlety, and expressivity. The tannins are sumptuous, and the oak perfectly judged, giving great harmony; I was reminded, as I tasted the 1996 Vosne-Romanée Beaumonts, of a Monteverdi mass echoing around the high arches and vaults of a cathedral. Great burgundy can do this.

Robert Groffier et Fils
21220 Morey-St-Denis, Tel: 03 80 34 31 53, Fax: 03 80 34 31 53

This estate is based in Morey-St-Denis, though it also has good holdings in Chambolle-Musigny and Gevrey-Chambertin (including Chambertin itself); Robert is now joined in the vineyards by his son Serge. These are dense, ripe, hedonistic red burgundies, with the Côte de Nuits stamp of power to them.

Anne-Françoise Gros
21630 Pommard, Tel: 03 80 22 61 85, Fax: 03 80 24 03 16

This well-endowed Vosne-Romanée estate produces lush, full wines which peak with a flamboyant Echézeaux and a pure, deep, tight-sewn Richebourg of enormous depth and substance, requiring long ageing.

Guffens-Heynen ✪✪
71960 Sologny, Tel: 03 85 51 66 00, Fax: 03 85 51 66 09

Jean-Marie Guffens, more *sui generis* than any other individual in Burgundy today, is best known as an uncompromising, hyper-energetic and ruthlessly plain-speaking micro-négociant whose company Verget (co-founded with Jean Rijckaert, though the two have since parted company) has been hugely successful in creating vivid, concentrated, piercingly pure white burgundies. This Mâcon domain is personally owned by Jean-Marie Guffens and his wife Maine (see Verget), and run in a different, more artisanal way to the Verget operation: on an intuitive basis, with all decisions made by taste and not technical analysis, and characterized by the late harvesting so typical of the work of all the Mâconnais' greatest growers. The cellar is under their home; there is no chaptalization, acidification, fining, or filtration; a 17th-century press is used. The wines (Mâcon-Pierreclos and Pouilly-Fuissé, sold under different *cuvée* and parcel names) are rich, challenging, and dense, sometimes luscious, always long and pure, expanding the boundaries of the appellation possibilities.

Pierrette et Marc Guillemot-Michel
21420 Savigny-lès-Beaune, Tel: 03 80 21 50 40, Fax: 03 80 21 59 98

Biodynamic estate producing clean, rich, and mouthfilling Mâcon-Village Quintaine based on late-harvest, low-yielding vines. Pierrette Guillemot is Jean-Thévenet's cousin and god-daughter (see Domaine de la Bon Gran) and, like Thévenet, she is keen to exploit the potential of the region for late-harvest wines; both maintain these are an ancient local tradition. The Guillemot-Michel late-harvest wines have been christened "Sélection des Grains Cendrés" – selection of "ashy" grapes, based on their degenerate and bearded appearance.

Antonin et Dominique Guyon
21420 Savigny-lès-Beaune, Tel: 03 80 67 13 24, Fax: 03 80 66 85 87

A large, 50-ha estate with some fine vineyard holdings up and down the entire length of the Côte d'Or, but with a spotty past reputation for quality. Recent improvements, however, suggest that this may become a name to watch.

Hudelot-Noëllat
21640 Chambolle-Musigny, Tel: 03 80 62 85 17, Fax: 03 80 62 83 13

This Vougeot-based domain owns, amongst its 10 ha, small parcels in some fine sites (including Romanée-St-Vivant and Richebourg). Alain Hudelot abandoned fining and filtering back in 1990, earlier than many of his peers, and his winemaking has followed a long, steady march towards intensity and expressivity.

Henri et Paul Jacqueson
71150 Rully, Tel: 03 85 87 18 82, Fax: 03 85 87 14 92

Rully's star, producing fine, flinty, mineral-filled wines much appreciated in France's best restaurants: fine value.

Jadot ✪
21200 Beaune, Tel: 03 80 22 10 57, Fax: 03 80 22 56 03

Burgundy's large négociants have been the favoured punchbag for disappointed tasters, drinkers, and writers for many decades. One négociant, though, has passed those years in a permanent state of public absolution: Louis Jadot. The reason? Its wines are often among the very best examples of their appellations. The American proprietors (Patricia Colagiuri, Sue Mueller, and Brenda Helies, the three Kopf sisters who own Kobrand, Jadot's US agent) give manager Pierre-Henri Gagey a free hand, and he has built Jadot to its present-day pinnacle of success, coincidentally expanding its holdings considerably in the process. His secret weapon (if you can describe such an articulate and eye-catching individual as secret) is winemaker Jacques Lardière, an astonishing source of information, philosophy and wine-scented poetic enigma. The company has 70 ha in the Côte d'Or spread among 38 appellations, including 50 ha in Premier and Grand Cru sites, though this is just a small portion of the total production. Tasting your way through the entire range is an exhausting business – as is superintending the vinification of these wines, since all are fermented and aged separately. It's a huge and immensely complicated portfolio, even by burgundian standards – which makes it all the more remarkable that standards are so high.

Lardière is in many ways an unusual winemaker: he likes very hot fermentations and long *cuvaisons*; the wines receive less new oak after good vintages than after less good. The whites do not always undergo malolactic fermentation; rackings and fining are kept to a minimum, and the wines are bottled unfiltered. It is hard to pick stars from such a large portfolio, but the Beaune wines offer excellent value for money, particularly the Clos des Ursules exclusivity (part of Premier Cru Vignes Franches); Jadot's Bonnes Mares and Musigny combine perfumed finesse with unusual richness of structure. Among the whites, there is a superb Montrachet here, but the Chevalier-Montrachet les Demoiselles can be almost as good. It is not often in Burgundy that one can buy with confidence across a range; from Jadot, you can.

Patrick Javillier
21190 Meursault, Tel: 03 80 21 27 87, Fax: 03 80 21 29 39

This thoughtful, analytical, and intelligent Meursault-based grower produces a superb range not merely of different vineyard wines but also of different Bourgogne Blanc *cuvées*; moreover many of these are subject to alternative bottling dates, the later bottlings being christened Mise Spéciale. Javillier's Cuvée Oligocène shows just how good Bourgogne Blanc can be when no expense or effort is spared in making it, though in price it compares with many lesser growers' village wines. From the fine Meursault range the stars are an exotic Les Narvaux and the dense, focused, and explosively long Cuvée Tête de Murger. This is composed of one-third Casse-Tête (which Javillier feels has attack but no finish) and two-thirds Les Murgers (which he feels are long but can lack opening impact and excitement): a typical example of the questing Javillier approach.

Georges Jayer ✪
21640 Flagey-Echézeaux, Tel: 03 80 62 84 56, Fax: 03 80 62 86 61

Wines grown and made by Emmanuel Rouget, but bottled under this label, reflecting the vineyards' ownership. The situation is the same with Lucien Jayer wines.

Henri Jayer *see* Georges Jayer, Méo-Camuzet, Emmanuel Rouget

Jayer-Gilles
21700 Magny-les-Villers, Tel: 03 80 62 91 79, Fax: 03 80 62 99 77

Dense, tight-packed, oaky wines from Echézeaux, Nuits-St-Georges and the Hautes Côtes. Gilles Jayer has now taken over from his father Robert. The estate was prosecuted in 1998 by the French government on the basis that some of its 1996 wines had been over-chaptalized, though this was never a fault that was evident in the bottles themselves, all of which have remarkable aromatic thrust.

François Jobard
21190 Meursault, Tel: 03 80 21 21 26, Fax: 03 80 21 26 44

Quiet and craftsmanlike, François Jobard makes some of the most long-lived of all Meursaults, insisting unfashionably that the practice of *bâtonnage* serves only to age white wines prematurely. His own wines (including a quivering Genevrières and a deep and stony Charmes) are challenging to drink young, but rewardingly resonant after a decade in the cool dark.

Rémi Jobard
21190 Meursault, Tel: 03 80 21 20 23, Fax: 03 80 21 67 69

The young Rémi has taken over from his father Charles; he is the nephew of François Jobard (and of Jean-Pierre Jobard, François' brother, who is winemaker for Louis Latour). Like François, he is not a *bâtonnage* enthusiast, though long lees contact is practised; his mother bottles the wines by hand. Rémi Jobard's commitment to low yields and quality shine out in these concentrated and finely structured Meursaults.

Joblot
71640 Givry, Tel: 03 85 44 30 77, Fax: 03 85 44 36 72

Jean-Marc Joblot is, like Jean-Michel Deiss in Alsace or Claude Papin in the Loire, one of those wine-growers who you feel could easily hold down a professorship at the Sorbonne, so articulate are they in describing their work, so profound and broad-horizoned is their knowledge of their vineyard environment, and so gloriously metaphysical are some of their speculations. Joblot's lavishly oaked wines, meanwhile, take Givry out to its limits of amplitude and power.

Michel Lafarge ✪
21190 Volnay, Tel: 03 80 21 61 61, Fax: 03 80 21 67 83

Michel Lafarge and his son Frédéric run one of the most admired domains in Burgundy – admired for its un-Burgundian trait of consistent quality, year after year and for every AOC (the Bourgogne and Bourgogne Passe-Tout-Grains are superb here). Small crops provide great depth; late harvesting when the weather permits gives ripe, vivid, succulent fruit. The estate began conversion to biodynamics in 1996. Its finest wines include the Premier Cru *monopole* Clos du Château des Ducs, as well as parcels in Caillerets and the Clos des Chênes.

Comtes Lafon ✪✪✪
21190 Meursault, Tel: 03 80 21 22 17, Fax: 03 80 21 61 64

Dominique Lafon has, since he took over from his father in 1987, been lifting the quality of this domain's wines steadily higher and higher; it has also undergone considerable expansion, as vineyards that were formerly *en métayage* have returned to the family fold. Does this mean that everything has changed since his father's time? Not really. Dominique Lafon once told me (as he has others) that the best single piece of advice he had ever received as a winemaker came from his father: "*Il faut avoir le courage de ne rien faire*" – you have to have the courage to do nothing. To let, in other words, nature's gifts emerge untrammelled in the wines you are making. In order to do this, Lafon has slowly converted all of the domain vineyards to organic, and then to biodynamic cultivation, this decision being taken for the most pragmatic of reasons: it has given the wines more energy, density, and purity. "The differences between vineyards are more marked; the earth is healthier, and the vines are looking better." Lafon's latest venture is a purchase in the Mâconnais: 10 ha at Milly, sold as Herétiers du Comtes Lafon. It makes for a lot of driving at harvest time, but Lafon feels that he understands the soils and grapes more intuitively than he would in another region. Because the Milly estate has been over-fertilized in the past, Lafon says, it will take a few years before he can achieve the low yields and high quality he is sure the site can provide.

The 13-ha Meursault estate is superbly sited, and includes Charmes, Clos de la Barre, Désirée (on SO4 rootstock, thus slightly higher yielding and less intense than the others), Genevrières (whose floral finesse and refinement make it my personal favourite), Goutte d'Or, Perrierès (a white wine of massive substance), and a third of a hectare of Montrachet. The Lafon Montrachet has become, since it returned to Lafon hands in 1991, a beacon of dramatic, multi-layered intensity – one of those transcendent wines that seems to detonate in the mouth. Lafon added Champs Gain in Puligny-Montrachet in the mid-1990s. There is less red wine available, but Lafon's touch with it is no less sure: the Volnay Champans, Santenots, and Santenots de Milieu are all vividly fruited, with superb balance between fruit, tannins, and extracts, and even the Monthélie is fragrant and ravishing.

Domaine des Lambrays ✪
21220 Morey-St-Denis, Tel: 03 80 51 84 33, Fax: 03 80 51 81 97

This ambitious, German-owned estate's flagship wine, the Grand Cru Clos des Lambrays (of which it owns almost the totality) produced its best vintage ever with the fleshy, sumptuous 1999. Winemaker Thierry Brouin has been able to cut yields, declassify wines where necessary, and use a higher proportion of new oak since the change of ownership in 1995.

Hubert et Olivier Lamy
21190 St-Aubin, Tel: 03 80 21 32 55, Fax: 03 80 21 38 32

This is one of two domain names to remember if you want to understand the subtle flavours (and appreciate the value) of St-Aubin in a variety of Premier Cru and *lieu-dit* sites: the other is Marc Colin. Cultivation here is more serious than that practiced by many growers in more prestigious vineyard sites; 20% new oak is used; and there is little or no fining and filtering. The pretty Premier Cru Clos de la Chatenière and the dense, weighty Premier Cru Les Murgers des Dents de Chien can both be outstanding.

Louis Latour
21204 Beaune, Tel: 03 80 24 81 00, Fax: 03 80 22 36 21

Despite its 45 ha of fine holdings, this large négociant produces soupy, low-definition, hollow red wines, something that most commentators attribute to the company's seemingly perverse desire to persist with its technique of heating all its reds to 70°C after fermentation. The company is also oddly out of step with the entire region in downplaying the role of terroir in the creation of wine flavour – though this has endeared it to some New World viticultural commentators. Its white wines are better than its reds (they do not undergo the same hot ignominy), and the 9 ha it owns in Corton-Charlemagne often results in a wine of structure, flesh, and length (richer though less intense and nervy than the Bonneau du Martray version). Look out for the fine value Montagny Premier Cru La Grande Roche, full of sappy warmth.

Latour-Guiraud
21190 Meursault, Tel: 03 80 21 21 43, Fax: 03 80 21 64 26

In renaissance during the 1990s, this Meursault-based estate produces an excellent range of Premiers Crus (topped by the Genevrières Cuvée des Pierres) and *lieux-dits*.

Dominique Laurent ✪✪
21700 Nuits-St-Georges, Tel: 03 80 61 31 62, Fax: 03 80 61 49 95

The work of this rotund, former pastrychef is innovative and influential in terms of the redefinition of what the négociant's role might be; indeed in some ways what he does is closer to the work of the Bordeaux garagistes (see page 169) than to traditional Burgundy négociants. Laurent owns no vines. A small portion of his raw material is purchased as fruit, but most of the wine he sells is bought already vinified: he describes himself as an *éleveur*, a "raiser" or "schooler" of wines. "My work is a mixture of innovation and highly traditional approaches. I try to recreate the Golden Age of Burgundy, the period between the two world wars. What I'm looking for is *vieux Pinot fin*: old clones, old vines. They have a quicker ripening cycle, thicker skins, and a higher proportion of skins to juice than modern, younger plants. I work with small oak casks, leaving the wines in freedom as far as possible and as long as possible, and always on their lees. It's very rewarding but it's also very difficult, since they can easily acquire odd or reductive flavours. I use about one-twentieth the level of sulphur that most producers use – just a homeopathic dose, really. I never pump anything; all the wines are bottled by hand, without sulphur, without filtration." Some of the wines receive 200% new oak. Laurent's range (almost all red) is evidently diverse, with rich oak showing in some of them, but also plenty of ripe, creamy fruit and soft tannins. Many are multi-parcel blends marketed under numbered *cuvées*, but even the most modest are treated with fanatical care. Laurent's Passe-Tout-Grains, for example, is a fake in that it contains no Gamay; in fact it's pure Pinot from a parcel on the wrong side of the road in Pommard which Laurent feels isn't quite good enough to go into his Bourgogne Rouge Cuvée No. 1. (It's also sold as Bourgogne La Taupe.) Even that spends two years in wood, and is bottled by hand. Some of the Laurent wines (like the 1996 Nuits-St-Georges Premier Cru Richemone) attain a gob-smacking exoticism quite unparalleled in Burgundy before his arrival: cherry liqueur, crème de cassis, chocolate and havana are all wrapped up in extraordinarily concentrated and showy flavours. This is burgundy that pushes at the boundaries, that provides altogether new quality perspectives that should make all of the region's red winemakers think about their work again. Not all the wines, though, are successful; some have an odd medicinal quality as well as unpredictable and sometimes surprising acidity levels (though Laurent never adds acid), and they can be over-bulky and unbalanced in textural terms. Greater control over viticulture and vinification might give Laurent's wines more consistency, and in any case there is a measure of acknowledged risk in Laurent's approach. Laurent, finally, is a skilled marketeer of his own wines, playing on their rarity and exclusivity in various ways, including specially packaged mixed cases called Séries Rares. It is all the more surprising, therefore, that the labels are so uninspiring.

Lécheneaut
21700 Nuits-St-Georges, Tel: 03 80 61 05 96, Fax: 03 80 61 28 31

Brothers Philippe and Vincent Lécheneaut from Nuits-St-Georges produce powerful, sinewy wines from Les Cailles and Les Damodes, as well as one of the deepest and most resonant interpretations of Clos de la Roche.

Leflaive ✪✪
21190 Puligny-Montrachet, Tel: 03 80 21 30 13, Fax: 03 80 21 39 57

This celebrated domain has improved enormously under the direction of Anne-Claude Leflaive, daughter of patriarch Vincent, who initially took over in collaboration with her cousin Olivier. He left in 1994 to concentrate on his own négociant business, and Anne-Claude now works with Pierre Morey as winemaker. The estate is one of those that gradually converted to biodynamic viticulture during the 1990s; as at Lafon, the appeal was chiefly pragmatic (comparison of wines produced from biodynamic and non-biodynamic fruit showed the former possessed more substance and definition). The breakthrough vintage was 1995 (those of the early 1990s were uncertain and sometimes disappointing), and since then the wines have deserved their reputation and their prices. The 21-ha domain includes a legendary and unobtainable Montrachet (only 25 cases of the 1995), as well as intense though expensive village wines from Puligny and some racy, floral, thoroughbred Puligny Premiers Crus including Pucelles and Combettes.

Olivier Leflaive
21190 Puligny-Montrachet, Tel: 03 80 21 37 65, Fax: 03 80 21 33 94

This new wave négociant business in Puligny now sells over 60 different AOCs, 90% of which are white. All purchases are of either grapes or must; Olivier Leflaive's aim, helped by winemaker Franc Grux, is to vinify wines of elegance and finesse – and the wager is largely won. St-Aubin En Remilly often offers best value; the Corton-Charlemagne is pure, fine-lined, and reverberative.

Leroy ✪✪✪
21190 Auxey-Duresses, Tel: 03 80 21 21 10, Fax: 03 80 21 63 81

Lalou Bize-Leroy was once the joint-manager of Domaine de la Romanée-Conti, and remains a part-owner. Her management activities there ceased in 1993, and since then Domaine Leroy has been DRC's main rival in terms of price, rarity – and quality. The 22-ha spread of vineyards, built up with major investment at the end of the 1980s (one third of Leroy is Japanese-owned), is mouthwatering; it includes nine Grands Crus. Lalou Bize, however, was one of the first of burgundy's great winemakers to adopt biodynamic cultivation methods, and the ferociously low-yielding rigour with which these are applied in some ways marks the wines more distinctively than the vineyards themselves (the 1995 average was 15 hl/ha). Prodigious concentration and rich extraction, in sum, which since the wines are bottled without fining or filtration should be amply palpable in bottle. Among the supernovas in a very starry collection are a muscular, forceful Richebourg and an exquisitely perfumed Romanée-St-Vivant; the masterly grace of Musigny. Leroy's Clos de Vougeot, too, provides the peak that others struggle to attain. (See also Domaine d'Auvenay and Maison Leroy.)

Maison Leroy ✪
21190 Auxey-Duresses, Tel: 03 80 21 21 10, Fax: 03 80 21 63 81

This is the négociant arm of Lalou Bize-Leroy's Domaine Leroy. Its wines are purchased, blended, and bottled but not necessarily grown or vinified by Leroy. Do not, therefore, expect the same levels of concentration, though the Leroy name still guarantees character and typicity.

Hubert Lignier
21220 Gevrey-Chambertin, Tel: 03 80 34 37 79, Fax: 03 80 51 80 97

A typical example of the quality of wines that, formerly, disappeared into the anonymity of big négociant *cuvées*, this Morey-based estate run by Hubert Lignier and until his death in 2004 his son Roman produces pure-fruited and perfumed red wines. Look out for the dense, long-lasting Morey-St-Denis Premier Cru Vieilles Vignes, a blend of the oldest-vine parcels the domain holds.

François Lumpp
71640 Givry, Tel: 03 85 44 45 57, Fax: 03 85 44 46 66

Solid, well-rounded Givry, both red and white.

Michel Magnien et Fils
21220 Morey-St-Denis, Tel: 03 80 51 82 98, Fax: 03 80 58 51 76

This Morey-based domain has made great leaps forward under the direction of the widely travelled Fred Magnien, Michel's son, who aims above all for natural wines or, as he puts it, "alert wines", achieved by (among other stratagems) putting sheep manure on the vines, never chaptalizing and using little new wood. Best value is offered by the little-seen Morey Premier Cru Les Chaffots.

Méo-Camuzet ✪
21700 Vosne-Romanée, Tel: 03 80 61 11 05, Fax: 03 80 61 11 05

The 15 fine hectares of this domain includes the vineyards (Vosne-Romanée Aux Brûlées and Nuits-St-Georges Aux Mergers) that the young Henri Jayer was offered en métayage by the then mayor of Vosne and regional député, Etienne Camuzet, at the very start of his career. Other vines went to other growers, and the family share of the fruit to large merchants. When these arrangements came to an end, Jean-Nicolas Méo, heir of the Camuzets, took over, basing his methods of those of Henri Jayer, which accounts for the sumptuous style of the wines. Méo's business and economics training, and work in California, is perhaps one reason why these seem to me to be some of the most urbane and internationally articulate of all fine burgundies; they also perhaps explain Méo's decision to become a micro-négociant.

Olivier Merlin
71960 La Roche, Tel: 03 85 36 62 09, Fax: 03 85 36 66 45

Clean, bright, sometimes austere Mâcon wines purchased from growers in Pouilly-Fuissé and Viré-Clessé on a négociant basis, as well as from Merlin's own Domaine du Vieux Sorlin.

Lucien Le Moine
21200 Beaune, Tel: 06 07 56 76 07, Fax: 03 80 24 99 98

New micro-éleveur operation established in a Beaune backstreet by Lebanese winemaker Mounir Sawma (who works for Picard) and his fiancée Rotem Brakin. Tiny production so far (just 31 barrels in 1999), but the wines (chiefly white, including a barrel of Montrachet) are succulent and showy.

Mommessin ✪
21220 Morey-St-Dennis, Tel: 03 80 34 30 91, Fax: 03 80 24 60 01

Beaujolais and Mâconnais négociant (now owned by Boisset) whose Côte d'Or jewel is the 7.5-ha monopole Grand Cru Clos de Tart. Since 1998, this Grand Cru in Morey has become, under the stewardship of the writer and cartographer Sylvain Pitiot, a reference point for perfumed vivacity, intensity and elegance – hence the rising star. Prices have followed suit.

Château de Monthélie see Eric de Suremain

Hubert de Montille
21190 Volnay, Tel: 03 80 21 62 67, Fax: 03 80 21 67 14

Volnay-based estate owned by lawyer Hubert de Montille and his son Etienne. Light extraction, minimum chaptalisation and little new oak mean that these are rather reserved, austere red burgundies in their youth, though those that know them after 15 years' ageing say that the wait is worth it.

Bernard Morey
21190 Chassagne-Montrachet, Tel: 03 80 21 32 13, Fax: 03 80 21 39 72

Morey, along with Colin and Gagnard, is one of the most confusing names in Burgundy since it forms a vital component of the identity of so many domains, as well as a village. This Chassagne-based Morey is both a domain-owner and a micro-négociant (Domaine for the former, Maison for the latter) whose wines are characterized by intense and well-rounded fruit flavours. Like many white winemakers in Burgundy, Morey has reduced the amount of lees-stirring he gives his wines in recent vintages, so as not to tire the wines, reduce their longevity and obscure their fruit flavours. The result is best seen in Morey's fine range of Chassagne Premiers Crus (including an outstanding Les Caillerets), as well as one of the finest Bâtard-Montrachets produced. The red wines are no less consistent; look out for Morey's supple, svelte Beaune Grèves.

Jean-Marc Morey
21190 Chassagne-Montrachet, Tel: 03 80 21 32 62, Fax: 03 80 21 90 60

Another Chassagne-based Morey whose wines (including, too, a fine Caillerets) occupy a mid-point between the exuberant fruit of his brother Bernard and the restraint and purity of the Marc Morey wines made by Bernard Mollard.

Marc Morey
21190 Chassagne-Montrachet, Tel: 03 80 21 33 52, Fax: 03 80 21 90 20

The Marc Morey wines are made by son-in-law Bernard Mollard, and include a fine spread from Chassagne as well as some Bâtard. The style is taut, austere, and tight-sewn, with low yields providing impressive concentration.

Pierre Morey
21190 Mersault, Tel: 03 80 21 21 03, Fax: 03 80 21 66 38

In addition to working with Anne-Claude Leflaive, this Meursault grower has a small domain of his own and also runs his own micro-négociant business, Morey Blanc. The style throughout is pure, fine-drawn, and elegant, with the domain wines showing great depth and concentration.

Albert Morot
21200 Beaune, Tel: 03 80 22 35 39, Fax: 03 80 22 47 50

Beaune's portfolio of Premiers Crus offers some of the best value red burgundy of all, as the Morot wines prove: concentrated, crunchy, pungent fruit. Both the Bressandes and the Teurons can be outstanding.

Denis Mortet ✪
21220 Gevrey-Chambertin, Tel: 03 80 34 10 05, Fax: 03 80 58 51 32

Denis Mortet, the nephew of Charles Rousseau, raised the reputation of this estate throughout the 1990s with fastidious attention to vineyard detail (in 1999 he green-harvested twice in some vineyards) and a commitment to minimal handling: no racking, no filtering. Oak, too, has been lavishly used; yet Mortet's devotion to and understanding of his different terroirs was profound. The results were dark, hedonistic Gevreys and one of the biggest of all Clos de Vougeots. The premature death of this talented perfectionist is a sad loss for Burgundy.

Georges Mugneret
21700 Vosne-Romanée, Tel: 03 80 61 00 97, Fax: 03 80 61 24 54

Vosne-Romanée domain, run in tandem with Mugneret-Gibourg, whose Ruchottes-Chambertin and Clos Vougeot are both outstanding. Georges Mugneret's daughters Marie-Christine Teillaud and Marie-Andrée Nauleau continue to refine the winemaking, adding depth and richness.

Mugneret-Gibourg see Georges Mugneret

Frédéric Mugnier
21220 Chambolle-Musigny, Tel: 03 80 62 85 39, Fax: 03 80 62 87 36

The intensity and grace of the Château de Chambolle-Musigny's wines, made by Frédéric Mugnier, memorably combine prettiness and profundity. Mugnier's father, a Parisian lawyer, used to lease the vines to Faiveley; Mugnier has been gradually recuperating them to make his graceful yet sustained wines (from yields of no more than 30 hl/ha, and with little oak influence). The return of the Clos de la Maréchale from the 2004 vintage lifts the domain further.

Philippe Naddef
21160 Couchey, Tel: 03 80 51 45 99, Fax: 03 80 58 83 62

Small domain based up in Couchey specialising in old-vine parcels and producing lushly flavoured red wines using considerable lees contact (Dominique Laurent, unsurprisingly, is a purchaser here).

Michel Niellon ✪
21190 Meursault, Tel: 03 80 21 30 95, Fax: 03 80 21 91 93

For long one of white burgundy's great names, Chassagne-based Michel Niellon now works with his two sons-in-law in maintaining his wine's reputation for intense and luscious multi-dimensionality. Getting the two bottles together would be an expensive nightmare, but if you want to taste the vineyard differences between the nervy, mineral-dredged Chevalier-Montrachet (high slope) and the plumper, ripe-fruited, butternut Bâtard-Montrachet (low slope), Niellon's would be fascinating bottles to chose. The Premier Crus are impressively varied, too.

Annick Parent
21190 Monthélie, Tel: 03 80 21 21 98, Fax: 03 80 21 21 98

Child physiotherapist Annick Parent now makes the wines of her father Jean Parent (formerly sold to négociants) from vineyards in Monthélie, Volnay, and Pommard. The 1999s had fine balance and deep, spicy, mouthfilling flavours.

François Parent
21200 Beaune, Tel: 03 80 22 61 85, Fax: 03 80 24 03 16

François Parent is the husband of Anne-Françoise Gros (see Domaine Anne-Françoise Gros) and the wines of the two domains are made together in the same cellar in Beaune, though the labels are very different (Parent's feature a truffle). These well-made wines often exceed their appellation expectations.

Jean Parent *see* Annick Parent

Domaine des Perdrix
21700 Premeux-Prissey, Tel: 03 80 61 26 53

A Nuits-based domain owned by the director of Antonin Rodet, Bertrand Devillard, producing impressive, expressive Echézeaux and a typically satisfying Nuits-St-Georges Aux Perdrix.

Paul Pernot
21190 Puligny-Montrachet, Tel: 03 80 21 32 35, Fax: 03 80 21 94 51

Fine 19-ha Puligny domain, though the fact that 80% of production goes to Drouhin means that the name is not as well-known as it might be. The best barrels are kept back for the domain bottlings, meaning that this is an excellent if hard-to-find source of top white burgundy, including a revelatory Bienvenues-Bâtard-Montrachet.

Perrot-Minot ✪
21220 Morey-St-Denis, Tel: 03 80 34 32 51, Fax: 03 80 34 13 57

Former courtier Christophe Perrot-Minot's domain has some fine sites, planted with old vines, including deeply flavoured Charmes-Chambertin and the much rarer Mazoyères-Chambertin. Methods here are non-interventionist, with no racking, fining, or filtering, and the very minimum of sulphur injected into the lees. The results show new, articulate Burgundy at its best: fruits, flowers, and spices soar in the wine's perfumes, with textured and deep flavours.

Jean Pillot
21190 Chassagne-Montrachet, Tel: 03 80 21 33 35, Fax: 03 80 21 92 57

This 10-ha Chassagne-based estate is now run by Jean Pillot's son Jean-Marc: the wines combine breadth of fruit with generous oak. Look out for the Premier Cru Chenevottes, from 60-year-old vines.

Ponsot
21220 Morey-St-Denis, Tel: 03 80 34 32 46, Fax: 03 80 58 51 70

This Morey-St-Denis domain can, at best, produce wines of great purity and depth; bottlings have, however, been inconsistent and unsatisfactory on occasion, perhaps because of Ponsot's refusal to use sulphur. Those who have kept the wines for a long period speak highly of their mature qualities.

Nicolas Potel
21700 Nuits-St-Georges, Tel: 03 80 62 15 45, Fax: 03 80 62 15 46

The son of former Pousse d'Or manager Gérard Potel, Nicolas Potel has established himself as a micro-négociant from his Nuits base working with a range of wines from up and down the Côte d'Or, but with (as one might expect) a particularly wide range from Volnay (14 wines in 1999). Those of more modest origin can taste unusually classy thanks to generous new oak, while fruit sings out of the top wines. Better 2000s than most.

Domaine de la Pousse d'Or
21190 Volnay, Tel: 03 80 21 47 38, Fax: 03 80 21 40 27

This Volnay domain was much admired when run by Gérard Potel, who died in 1997 on the day its Australian owners signed the deeds for its sale. The new owner, Patrick Landanger, has had a shaky start, but the 1999s bode well for the future. Top parcels include the *monopole* Clos de la Bousse d'Or, and the "60 Ouvrées" parcel within Caillerets.

Jacques Prieur ✪
21190 Meursault, Tel: 03 80 21 23 85, Fax: 03 80 21 29 19

Wonderfully well-endowed Meursault domain, whose white wine holdings include parcels of Corton-Charlemagne, Chevalier-Montrachet, and Montrachet itself. The days of unexciting winemaking are now over, thanks to the arrival of the Antonin Rodet team and the new generation of the Prieur family, Martin Prieur. The white wine style is now lavish and ample, with finely judged new oak influence. Red wine holdings include Chambertin, Clos Vougeot, Corton-Bressandes, Echézeaux, and Musigny, but the voluptuous Volnay Clos des Santenots can match all these, and the red Meursault Clos de Mazeray is an intriguing, cherryish curiosity.

Prieuré-Roch ✪
21700 Nuits-St-Georges, Tel: 03 80 62 00 00, Fax: 03 80 62 00 01

This 4-ha domain belongs to Henri Roch, co-manager (with Aubert de Villaine) of the Domaine de la Romanée-Conti; it includes parcels of Clos de Vougeot, Clos de Bèze, and an ex-DRC *lieux-dit* in Vosne called Clos Goillotte, a short distance only from La Tâche and La Grande Rue. The winemaking is similar in style to that at DRC, giving meaty wines of slow evolution and stately grandeur.

Château de Puligny-Montrachet
21190 Puligny-Montrachet, Tel: 03 80 21 39 14, Fax: 03 80 21 39 07

Owned by Crédit Foncier, this 20-ha estate has a wide sweep of holdings, and under winemaker Jacques Montagnon has made great strides forward towards consistency and articulacy. The Meursault and Puligny Premiers Crus (especially Meursault Perrières and Puligny Les Folatières) are perfect examples of their vineyard styles, while the St-Aubin En Remilly is a generous, fine-value bottle.

Ramonet
21190 Meursault, Tel: 03 80 21 30 88, Fax: 03 80 21 35 65

A much revered Chassagne-based domain, whose 18 ha include a splendid spread of Premiers Crus and a little Montrachet. The best of these wines are intense and pure, with fine mineral breed; consistency, though, is irregular.

Reine Pedauque
21420 Aloxe-Corton, Tel: 03 80 25 00 00, Fax: 03 80 26 42 00

Improving négociant house whose own 40-ha domain produced some excellent 1999 wines, including a pungent Beaune Clos du Roi.

Jean Rijckaert
71570 Leynes, Tel: 03 85 35 15 09, Fax: 03 85 35 15 09

Jean-Marie Guffens' former partner has now established his own micro-négociant business, specializing in Burgundy's less celebrated white wines from both the Mâconnais and the Côte d'Or (including a concentrated Maranges En Borgy), as well as from the Jura region.

Daniel Rion
21700 Premeaux, Tel: 03 80 62 31 28, Fax: 03 80 61 13 41

Pungent yet accessible red wines from Nuits, Vosne, and Chambolle, produced, now, by two brothers (Christophe and Olivier Rion) and sister Pascale, based on a long tradition of near-organic viticulture and ceaseless cellar experimentation. (Patrice Rion left in 2001 to concentrate on his own domain and micro-négociant business.) In addition to the fine spread of reds, you'll also find one of Burgundy's leading Pinot Blanc whites (Nuits-St-Georges Les Terres Blanches).

Michèle et Patrice Rion
21700 Nuits-St-Georges, Tel: 03 80 62 32 63, Fax: 03 80 62 49 63

Small 2.5-ha domain run by the inventive Patrice Rion and his wife Michèle, with holdings in Chambolle-Musigny les Cras and the Nuits Premier Cru Les Argillières. One to watch, as is the new micro-négociant business Patrice Rion.

Antonin Rodet
71640 Mercurey, Tel: 03 85 98 12 12, Fax: 03 85 45 25 49

This fine, Mercurey-based négociant house, run with great acumen by Bertrand Devillard, was sold in 1997 by its former owner, Champagne house Laurent-

Perrier, to the Worms conglomerate; Nadine Gublin is its thoughtful winemaker. The finest wines from the stable are from Domaine Jacques Prieur (of which it owns 50%), but this is also an excellent source of expressive, subtly differentiated négociant wines, especially those sold under the Cave Privée label (all purchased as grape juice and vinified by Rodet). Look out, too, for some of the best of the Côte Chalonnaise via the Château de Chamirey, Château de Rully, and Domaine du Château de Mercey wines, all of which are either owned or run by Rodet.

Robert-Denogent
71960 Fuissé, Tel: 03 85 35 65 39, Fax: 03 85 35 66 69

A first rate source of top quality Pouilly-Fuissé (including four superb Vieilles Vignes *cuvées*) and Mâcon-Solutré, based on low yields, late harvesting and oak fermentation by the fastidious Jean-Jacques Robert.

Rémi Rollin et Fils
21420 Savigny-lès-Beaune, Tel: 03 80 21 57 31/50 35, Fax: 03 80 26 10 38

Elegance and finesse characterize this domain, whose whites (both Aligoté and Corton-Charlemagne) are more successful than its light reds.

Domaine de la Romanée-Conti ✪✪✪
21700 Vosne-Romanée, Tel: 03 80 62 48 80, Fax: 03 80 61 05 72

This is, by common consent, Burgundy's most fortunate domain, and its wines are among the world's most expensive; in 2001, the 1998 Romanée-Conti was launched in Britain at £540... per bottle. Few of us will ever own or even taste such wines. The domain's holdings are not extensive – just over 26 ha in all. They are, though, of platinum quality. All the parcels are Grand Cru: they include the 1.81-ha La Romanée-Conti, Burgundy's finest vineyard, in its entirety, as well as the whole of La Tâche (6 ha). Its other parcels are in Richebourg (3.5 ha), Grands Echézeaux (3.5 ha), Echézeaux (4.7 ha), Romanée-St-Vivant (5.3 ha) and Montrachet (0.7 ha). A morsel of Bâtard and some village Vosne are sold on in bulk. Despite the glittering quality of its holdings, the estate is run quietly, with becoming humility, by Aubert de Villaine and his co-manager Henri-Frédéric Roch on behalf of the owning families. Gérard Marlot is vineyard manager, and Bernard Noblet *chef de cave*. The prices achieved mean that no expense need be spared in the single-minded pursuit of quality.

The vineyards are cultivated organically (and 5 ha of La Tâche and Grands Echézeaux biodynamically), and are all old – 61 years in the case of Montrachet, 52 years for Romanée-Conti, while the youngest vines are those of Echézeaux at 31 years. Around 50 different clones have been estate-selected for future replanting needs. The consultative work of the influential soil specialist Claude Bourguignon has been key here. The estate makes its own compost by mixing all the prunings with the residues from winemaking and about 25% manure; this mixture (which de Villaine describes as "an injection of microbial life, a sort of forest system") is applied to the soil every three years. A horse is now used for ploughing, as at Coulée de Serrant in the Loire and Magdelaine in St-Emilion. Yields are very low: an average of just 22 hl/ha for the red wines in 1998, and a 10-year average of no more than 24 hl/ha. Harvesting includes crop-sorting both in the vineyard and then back again at the cellar. Most unusually, all stems go into the vats; DRC is one of the few producers to maintain this most traditional of practices. The fermentation takes place at just under 30°C, with a *cuvaison* of up to a month. The wines are then run into lightly toasted new casks from François Frères, where they remain for a full 16 to 20 months, with a single racking. They are bottled without fining or filtration. De Villaine says that the aim is to make wine by "pre-oenology" methods, just as he is trying to return the vineyards to their "pre-phylloxera" vine density and health.

Those who know these wines well find generosity and meaty power in the Echézeax and Grands Echézeaux, perfume and seductive depths in the Romanée-St-Vivant and Romanée-Conti, and spice, substance, and packed fruit in the Richebourg and La Tâche. The Montrachet (of which there are but 3,000 bottles a year) is said to be a model of multi-layered concentration,

creamy charm, mineral depths plus, of course, the final, bewildering concentration of flavour that only Burgundy's greatest sites can deliver.

Joseph Roty
21220 Gevrey-Chambertin, Tel: 03 80 34 38 97, Fax: 03 80 34 13 59

Powerful, slow-ripening Gevrey-Chambertin (including Grand Cru Charmes and Griotte) and top-value red and rosé Marsannay from this traditional domain in Gevrey, run by philatelist and military historian Joseph Roty with help from his son Philippe.

Emmanuel Rouget ✿
21640 Flagey-Echézeaux, Tel: 03 80 62 84 56, Fax: 03 80 62 86 61

No late 20th-century burgundian winemaker enjoyed the same reputation as Henri Jayer – even though, like Gérard Chave in Hermitage, he claimed to do no more than take great care over what was in any case traditional. In retirement, Jayer continues to make a little Nuits-St-Georges and Echézeaux from his brother George's vines. Jayer's heir, however, is his nephew, Emmanuel Rouget, a tall yet bashful former mechanic. None of the lessons have been lost, and if you want to discover the sweet, lip-smacking, creamy, brambly pleasures of Vosne-Romanée and Echézeaux, then there are few better bottles than these with which to do it. The explosively deep and spicy Cros Parentoux, a tiny Premier Cru, is more expensive than the supple and expressive Grand Cru Echézeaux (Jayer remembers that during the Second World War it was used for growing jerusalem artichokes by a local carter). Fortunate is the drinker who can discuss, a glass of each to hand, the justice of this.

Jean-Marc Roulot
21190 Meursault, Tel: 03 80 21 21 65, Fax: 03 80 21 64 36

Fine Meursault estate (formerly named after Guy Roulot, Jean-Marc's father) producing light, limpid, uncluttered wines in which fresh fruit and soil are very much to the fore.

Christophe Roumier *see* Georges Roumier

Georges Roumier
21220 Chambolle-Musigny, Tel: 03 80 62 86 37, Fax: 03 80 62 83 55

Carefully made wines from scrupulously sorted fruit from this Chambolle estate, run by Christophe Roumier, include a fine Grand Cru spread peaking with tiny quantities of Musigny. The Premier Cru Les Amoureuses, though, can be just as good as some of the Grands Crus, and there is also a Corton-Charlemagne of lusher, more voluptuous style than many. Christophe Roumier also leases some Charmes-Chambertin and Ruchottes-Chambertin which, together with a parcel of village Chabolle and Premier Cru Les Cras, he sells under his own name.

Armand Rousseau
21220 Gevrey-Chambertin, Tel: 03 80 34 30 55, Fax: 03 80 58 50 25

Fifty years ago, Charles Rousseau was one of the pioneers of domain-bottling in the region, having taken over from his father Armand after the latter's death in a car accident in 1959; now Charles's own son Eric is at the helm. The 14-ha domain has some superb plots in the northern Côte de Nuits, including nearly 7 ha in the Chambertin Grands Crus. Viticulture and winemaking follow the restrained lines of Burgundy's best growers, though the domain's particular gift is its stock of old vines (the 2.2-ha parcel of Chambertin has an average age of over 60 years).

Aleth le Royer-Girardin
21630 Pommard, Tel: 03 80 22 59 69, Fax: 03 80 24 96 57

Pommard producer whose hands-off approach (fermentation in large oak *foudres*, long lees contact, low sulphur levels) results in a fine range of limpidly fruity, expressive wines from both Pommard and Beaune.

Etienne Sauzet ✿
21190 Mersault, Tel: 03 80 21 32 10, Fax: 03 80 21 90 89

Gérard Boudot acquired a négociant's licence after losing a third of his estate to his brother-in-law in 1990, so you will find both domain and non-domain wines here. They have become expensive, justifying these prices (perhaps) with great hare leaps in concentration, power, and electric force. Look out, among the fine Puligny Premiers Crus, for the honeyed, dense Combettes. The four whites Grands Crus betray their ambition with flavours of heavy-metal density, and ingot-like prices.

Mounir Sawma *see* Lucien Le Moine

Christian Serafin
21220 Gevrey-Chambertin, Tel: 03 80 34 35 40, Fax: 03 80 58 50 66

Exuberant, lavishly flavoured red burgundies are the speciality of Gevrey-based Christian Serafin, achieved by low yields, late harvesting and ample new oak. Serafin's Charmes-Chambertin (its quality improved by the acquisition of old vines in the 1990s) is a reference bottle.

Eric de Suremain
21190 Monthélie, Tel: 03 80 21 23 32, Fax: 03 80 21 66 37

The fittingly named de Suremain owns what are relatively modest vineyards in Rully and Monthélie (Château de Monthélie), yet his dark, sumptuously fruited results with the 1999 vintage prove that he can create wines of extraordinary depth and seriousness from these well-tended, low-yielding vineyards.

Jean Thévenet *see* Domaine de la Bongran

Tollot-Beaut
21200 Beaune, Tel: 03 80 22 16 54, Fax: 03 80 22 12 61

This large, 22-ha domain based in Chorey-lès-Beaune produces a range characterized for much of the 1990s by solidity and generous oaking; with the 1999 vintage, however, it seemed to move up a notch in terms of achieving sumptuous fruit quality. The basic Chorey-lès-Beaune offers excellent value; the sweetly expressive Corton-Bressandes is the domain's pinnacle.

Jean et Jean-Louis Trapet
21220 Gevrey-Chambertin, Tel: 03 80 34 30 40, Fax: 03 80 51 86 34

Improving Gevrey-Chambertin domain. Reduced yields, later harvesting, biodynamics and the discontinuation of fining and filtering have brought greater fruit density and meaty depths.

Domaine Valette
71570 Chainte, Tel: 03 85 35 62 97, Fax: 03 85 35 68 02

Low yields and late harvests produce rich, exotic, boundary-pushing whites from Mâcon-Chaintré and Pouilly-Fuissé made by former *coopérant* Gérard Valette and his son Philippe. One of the best of these (a 1994 Pouilly-Fuissé) beat 14 Montrachets of the same vintage in a 1997 Paris tasting. Like fellow Mâcon winemaker Jean Thévenet, the Valettes' late-harvesting practices have brought them into conflict with local AOC authorities, since some of their wines are fermented from such rich musts that, despite being technically dry, they taste slightly sweet; the Valettes also make use (like Thévenet) of botrytized Chardonnay grapes, another dangerous game to play with authority in this region. The top wines spend between 18 and 36 months in wood, and are bottled unfined and unfiltered. If you want to discover the floral power, rich orchard fruits and sheer voluptuousness of southern Burgundy, look here.

Verget ❂
71960 Sologny, Tel: 03 85 51 66 00, Fax: 03 85 51 66 09

Belgian Jean-Marie Guffens, the creator (with former business partner Jean Rijckaert; the two have now parted company) of this négociant house, is unique in the world of French wine. Underneath his radically informal, wise-cracking, roll-up-smoking, almost gangster-like appearance lurks intense energy, an obsessive attention to detail and a formidable winemaking curiosity. Guffens purchases grapes rather than must or wine, paying the best prices for low-yielding vineyards, harvesting manually using his own team, and sorting the fruit fanatically. In addition to pressing and vinifying all his purchases himself, he also separates each pressing into four staged lots in order to give himself maximum flexibility when it comes to crafting finished wines. Verget works the entire length of Burgundy; among his very best wines are those he makes in Chablis

(see separate chapter), a region where slap-dash local standards don't always do the superb terroir justice, and where the style of the wines suits Guffens' own tastes for crystalline fruit quality. Don't buy Verget wines looking for the kind of cheese paste, farm straw richness of traditional, "funky" white burgundy; these are white wines made with the kind of ravishing purity and compelling, sensual austerity more familiar among the greatest winemakers of the Saar, the Ruwer, or Alsace. (Guffens working with Riesling would be a treat.) The potential range of white wines produced by Verget (Guffens claims he doesn't understand red winemaking) is enormous; stars of past vintages have included fruit-dense Meursault Poruzots and Casse Têtes, a broad-hewn, spicy Chassagne-Montrachet La Maltroye Vieilles Vignes and multi-layered Chassagne-Montrachet La Romanée, and an unusually poised, vigorous, incisive, palate-searching Bâtard-Montrachet. His own base in the Mâconnais (see Guffens-Heynen) means that there is a wide selection of parcel-based Verget *cuvées* from this region including fascinating Pouilly-Vinzelles from 50-year-old vines (Les Quarts and a late-harvest Levrouté).

A&P de Villaine
71150 Bouzeron, Tel: 03 85 91 20 50, Fax: 03 85 87 04 10

Good Côte Chalonnaise wines (and an outstanding Bouzeron Aligoté) produced by Aubert de Villaine of Domaine de la Romanée-Conti. Given the care and skill that goes into them, the fact that these wines aren't better still is a conclusive argument for the truths of terroir, as de Villaine himself loves to point out.

Comte de Vogüé ❂
21220 Chambolle-Musigny, Tel: 03 80 62 86 25, Fax: 03 80 62 82 38

The finest holdings in Chambolle-Musigny belong to this estate, including a mouthwatering 70% of the Musigny vineyard and 2.5 ha of Bonnes Mares. Winemaker François Millet has, since his arrival in 1985, greatly improved the quality of what were often disappointing Grand Cru bottles during the 1970s and early 1980s, though this quiet, thoughtful, and fiercely reserved man is reluctant to assign this to a particular strategy. "Being absolutely non-systematic, I don't want to give you a recipe. Observation. The mood of the terroir...." The wines are neither highly extracted nor highly oaked; instead they are marked by grace, perfume, and silky breadth. The Bonnes Mares (a heterogenous terroir according to Millet) is packed with black fruits; the Musigny is more multi-dimensioned, the lightly tarry fruits thrillingly tenacious. Both exemplify the sheathed power of burgundy at its most classical.

Domaine de la Vougeraie
21700 Premeux-Prissey, Tel: 03 80 62 48 25, Fax: 03 80 61 25 44

Jean-Claude Boisset has been, in financial and acquisitive terms, unquestionably the most successful Burgundy négociant of recent years; all that has eluded him, as he has assembled his empire, is admiration and acclaim for the Boisset wines themselves. This is now coming, thanks to the outstanding winemaking supervision of recently installed Gregory Patriat. Boisset also owns Viénot, Chauvenet, Mommessin, Jaffelin, Pierre Ponnelle, Ropiteau Frères, Bouchard Aîné, and Thorin, as well as Moreau in Chablis and Varichon et Clerc in Savoie; it is the fifth largest wine company in France. The creation of this large (37 ha) domain based in Premeaux brings together the vineyard holdings of four previous domains owned by Boisset. Two thirds are in the Côtes de Nuits, and one third in the Côte de Beaune. The name Vougeraie relects the fact that a number of the 29 parcels are sited in or around Vougeot – where the Boisset family home is also to be found. Pascal Marchand (formerly of Comte Armand) has been given absolute control over winemaking; Bernard Zito is in charge of the vineyards, which are organically cultivated and mainly horse-ploughed. The wines I have tasted so far have included a fine, sweetly spicy 1999 Vougeot Premier Cru Les Cras from 35-year-old vines and a deliciously peppery 1999 Pommard Les Petits Noizons. The white *monopole* of Clos Blanc de Vougeot has more than mere curiosity value and is impressively scented; the red Clos du Vougeot parcel is in 50-year-old vines. Both vineyard holdings and ambition make this a domain to watch.

Beaujolais

Strange Fruit Beaujolais is an enigma. Its soils have fine potential, its best growers are skilled, yet its wines remain almost secret. Why? Gamay. The raw material of Beaujolais is hermaphrodite: the flavours of red wine, but often the texture and balance of a white.

The script could not have been more perfectly written. It was the end of the day, a day of travel and hurry; darkness was beginning to finger the still-bare spring vineyards. We drew into the courtyard of the Foillards in Morgon. Two customers were there already, travellers both, drinking and discussing the wines; one recollected how, in his Médocain youth, Beaujolais had been called the *vin de palefrenier*, the groom's wine. A third man appeared, the organizer of the local *fanfare*, the brass band: he drank too. I was given a glass. Everyone talked, laughed. And then came one of those cinematically familiar moments when, by the sheer force of sensual evocation, a noisy conversation seems to fade into silence and the spectacle of moving lips, while the wine itself grew huge, irrepressible, as hungry for attention as any crisis-struck three-year-old. It was, in short, an epiphany. I jotted a few, odd, unsatisfactory notes concerning mouth-perfume and surging, gliding movements; the word "jubilee" proved oddly tenacious, though it was hard to say why. In the end, I settled for three flat words, banal but straightforward, which I underlined with such force that I broke the lead in my pencil. "Absolute, pure deliciousness." Then I settled back to drink. So it was, this 2000 Côte de Py from Jean Foillard, made from vines of between thirty and seventy years old in the "rotten rock" of this hill-slope subzone of Morgon. It couldn't be anatomized; it couldn't be clothed in analogies; it couldn't, above all, be left undrunk.

"It's a drink," said Marcel Lapierre to me two days later, in describing his new Beaujolais-Villages called Château Cambon. "*Ça se bois sous la douche* (you can drink it under the shower); it's a wine you don't ask questions about." He was talking about one of his "lesser" wines, but the same can be said even of the greatest Beaujolais of all. If red wine can be nubile, this red wine is. To set about naming its parts is to demean its beauty. It has, if you like, a huge capacity for goodness, and almost none for greatness. It is the proof that happiness can sometimes be uncomplicated.

All of this is the consequence of the fact that Beaujolais is made from Gamay: a thin-skinned, prolific, early-ripening grape of fundamental inconsequentiality. The fact that this good-tempered but easygoing variety is still prized and championed here is one of the more unusual lessons of the New France. Beaujolais, after all, remains very much a region of small growers, many of whom are making exactly the same sort of decisions to pursue quality that can be found in the Rhône Valley or in Languedoc. The region has neither the indiscriminate local demand that acts as a disincentive to quality in Savoie (the traditional market of Lyons is more Rhône-obsessed today), nor are most of its wines made in giant négociant or cooperative cellars, as in Champagne, meaning that volume and regional origin are all. Yes, old vines are treasured; yes, the vines are harvested by hand. (Hand-harvesting,

indeed, is obligatory here, since Beaujolais vinification is almost always based on what is called carbonic maceration, which requires whole bunches of unsullied fruit; machines can't yet manage to pick grapes in this careful way.) The best growers, like Jean Foillard and his close neighbour Marcel Lapierre, use cold maceration, natural yeasts, minimum sulphur dioxide, and bottle their wines without fining or filtration. Eric Janin, a third of whose vines are over eighty years old, is experimenting with biodynamics and cover crops between the rows of vines, with destemming, with *pigeage*, and with barrique ageing. So, famously, does Château des Jacques, the Jadot-owned property run by Guillaume de Castelnau. Throughout the ten Beaujolais *crus*, the hunt is on for individual site definition; the names of *lieux-dits* are beginning to appear on labels. In Morgon, for example, wines from the Côte de Py attract a premium, and Corcelette and Clachet are beginning to win a name for stylistic differences, too; Fleurie, meanwhile, has no fewer than thirteen INAO-recognized *climats*, including La Madone, Grille-Midi, and the hopefully named Le Bon Cru.

There is, though, one big difference between the best of Beaujolais and the best of Châteauneuf or of Cahors, of Roussillon or of Richebourg: yields. "Gamay," says Guillaume de Castelnau, "is very different to Pinot Noir. There is almost no difference between a wine at fifty hl/ha and one at twenty-four hl/ha. The only real quality difference comes with old vines." Marcel Lapierre has made wines at fifteen hl/ha, but says that "there's no point: the fruit disappears. I got sixty hl/ha in 2000 and they were some of the best wines of my career." Eric Janin, too, has compared wines at thirty hl/ha with wines at fifty hl/ha and said he cannot find any difference between the two. "I don't attach too much importance to yields," says Agnès Foillard. "If you lower yields too much, you lose drinkability." I have listened to these intelligent and thoughtful growers on this subject, and have no reason to doubt the truth of what they are saying. Yet a lingering doubt remains – and the memory of another Gamay, too, produced from yields of thirty hl/ha at most. That Gamay was the legendary 1996 Anjou Gamay "*sur spilite*" of Claude Papin. Do low yields for Gamay make a difference in Anjou but not in Beaujolais?

Perhaps the truth, finally, is a question of aesthetics: what beauty do you wish to create? The sober, dark, bitter-edged beauty of ambition and intensity? Or the hilarious, quenching beauty of the boisterously drinkable? "*L'eclat de rire à la table*" reads the neck label of Château Thivin's Cuvée du Clos Bertrand, more useful than any tasting note or food-matching recommendation: "the peal of laughter at table". The beauty of Beaujolais has always resided somewhere in mid-swallow, in wide eyes and rosy cheeks, in the scents that rise from the throat, and the easy chuckle which follows.

"What I look for is maximum ripeness, which is hard work because Gamay rots easily. In the winery, my aim is to touch everything as little as I can. *C'est un vin de fainéant et de radin* (it's the wine of a do-nothing and a skinflint)."

MARCEL LAPIERRE

If any Beaujolais can outlast a dog and grow in stature with the years, it is the wine grown on the crunchy, rust-pink sands which anchor this windmill, this moulin à vent.

Guillaume de Castelnau

Seventeen years as a cavalry officer, finishing as a commandant, have left Guillaume de Castelnau with a palpable commitment to the task in hand. He only left the cavalry, indeed, because "there weren't any wars. No wars mean no advances." Vines claimed him by chance, and now he has thrown heart and soul into seeking out lines of advance for Louis Jadot in Beaujolais. A sense of terroir is the aim: "We're refinding our terroir in Beaujolais. We lost that in the past." Experiments with biodynamics are one way of achieving this, though de Castelnau says, "It's just an agricultural strategy; it's not my religion." With the Jadot holdings now encompassing twenty-seven ha (sixty-seven acres) of Moulin-à-Vent in which the company distinguishes five climats, nine ha (twenty-two acres) of Beaujolais Blanc planted with Chardonnay, and the new thirty-five-ha (86.5-acre) purchase of Château de Bellevue in Morgon bringing three more climats, the commandant is marshalling his forces.

The Adventure of the Land

Beaujolais is regarded, administratively, as part of Burgundy; geologically, however, it most definitely belongs to the northern Rhône. Great red burgundy is Pinot Noir grown on alkaline limestone; good Beaujolais is Gamay grown on acidic granite.

Beaujolais is divided into two: the northern or Haut-Beaujolais, and the southern or Bas-Beaujolais. Granite dominates the north; this is where Beaujolais-Villages comes from, and where you find all of the ten Beaujolais *crus* (whose AOC is their village name alone, and which provide a quarter of the Beaujolais production total). The landscape is roundly, softly hilly: comforting and mammary.

The main differences between the *crus* are those of height and mineral composition. **St-Amour** (310 ha/770 acres), furthest north, is on mixed granite, clay, and schist, while neighbouring **Juliénas** (600 ha/1,480 acres) has still more clay mixed in with its sandy granite. High, pungent **Chénas** (280 ha/690 acres), across the River Mauvaise, is the smallest of the *crus*, on relatively pure sandy granite with some gravel. Below it lies **Moulin-à-Vent** (650 ha/1,600 acres), certainly the best of the *crus*, whose lip-smacking depth and pungency, and relatively generous tannic structure, is said to be due to the presence of manganese in its salmon-pink granites and sands. At least as important as this, though, must be its superb, southeast-facing slopes. West of Moulin-à-Vent is **Fleurie** (860 ha/2,120 acres), whose propitious east-facing slopes and pink granite shingles seem to produce the fragrant, nose-teasing wine the name promises. **Chiroubles** (370 ha/910 acres), which lies between 250 and 450 metres (820-1,480 feet), is the highest of all the *crus*, which is the main factor behind its lightness and incisiveness; the soils are pure granite mixed with a fine, pale clay called smectite. **Morgon** (1,100 ha/2,720 acres) is geologically different: the grey-red soils in this large *cru* are called *roches pourries* or "rotten rocks". They are formed of a decomposed schist containing iron, and provide what is often the deepest *cru* wine after Moulin-à-Vent, and one whose cherry-like fruit has an eerie ability, when aged, to mimic Pinot Noir.

The Côte de Py sector of Morgon offers some superb slopes. **Régnié** (550 ha/1,360 acres) is part sandy granite, part schist, giving at best a clean, classic *cru* wine. The two southernmost *crus* are **Brouilly** and **Côte de Brouilly**, surrounding the 484-metre (1,587-feet) high peak of Mont Brouilly. The upper vineyards are those of the Côte (320 ha/790 acres)), the soils being composed of granite with blue diorite and schist: the fine aspects give wines with both perfume and alcoholic richness. Brouilly is the largest of the *crus* (1,300 ha/3,210 acres), and is geologically various, with granite, schist, and river alluvium, plus some more of that clayey smectite. The best Brouilly is generous and fruity. Good **Beaujolais-Villages** can be as good as the *crus*, though it can also be thin and tenuous.

An enigma, finally, before we leave the pretty Haut-Beaujolais. This region offers one of the most purely mineral of wine-growing environments: the vines' roots here bathe in granite, schist, and sand. It is rare, however, to find "mineral" flavours mentioned in Beaujolais tasting notes; the customary references are overwhelmingly to fruits and flowers. Compare this with the incessant references to mineral flavours in Chablis or Sancerre, where the vines' roots bathe in sticky, pale, and alkaline non-crystalline sediments. Why?

There are a number of possibilities. Perhaps what we call mineral flavours are in fact no such thing; we may be tasting something else altogether, and describing those flavours as "mineral". Perhaps mineral flavours are only ever transmitted by certain grape varieties (Chardonnay and Sauvignon Blanc but not Gamay). A third theory might be that mineral flavours are commoner when vines grow in sedimentary rocks; perhaps the structure of sediments renders minerals more accessible to root systems than harder crystalline rocks do. Yet the fact that Riesling in Alsace and Germany can be intensely mineral when grown in crystalline soils (as found in eleven of Alsace's Grands Crus) or slate (a metamorphic rock) fails to support this. One might consider that mineral flavours are more

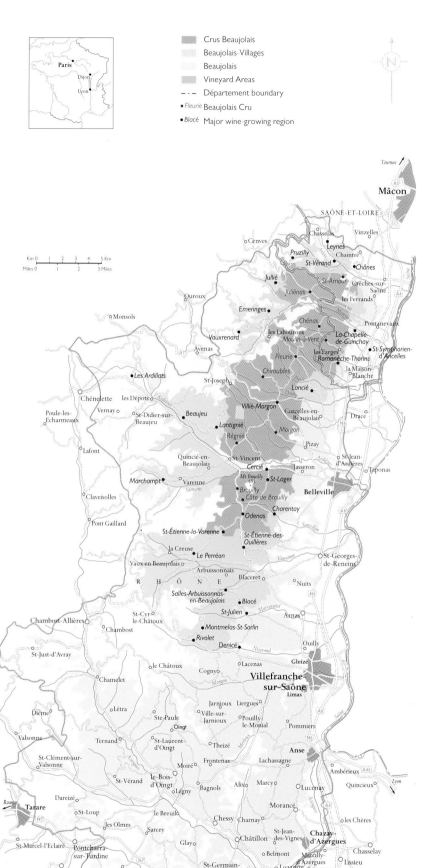

readily palpable when vines grow in alkaline rather than acidic soils, yet this theory would be subject to the same objections from Alsace and from Germany. Are mineral flavours quite simply easier to spot in white wines than red? Hardly. Red wine from the Graves, from the Médoc, or from many parts of the Languedoc often seem to contain a marked mineral residuum. Maybe mineral flavours only appear when yields drop below thirty hl/ha or so – yet Vincent Dauvissat in Chablis creates memorably mineral wines with yields twice as large as that. The subject, in sum, is the most mysterious of all in present-day wine scholarship.

Adieu granite, in any case, when you reach the Bas-Beaujolais, a total contrast to the Haut-Beaujolais. This is the land of *pierres dorées*, of golden limestones not dissimilar to those found in the English Cotswolds. Beautiful building stone – but not, in truth, as ideal for the Gamay as the granites further north. This is where ordinary **Beaujolais** (and **Beaujolais Supérieure**, not superior at all but merely slightly more alcoholic) comes from, much of which is sold as Beaujolais Nouveau. The **Coteaux du Lyonnais**, finally, is a small transition zone of AOC vineyards between Beaujolais and the Rhône. Gamay, Chardonnay, and Aligoté make the wines resemble the former more than the latter.

Beaujolais Flak

Nouveau: the fatal flaw

Beaujolais is the only wine region in France that manages to vinify, bottle, and sell between a third and a half of its crop within six months of harvest. What was initially a cunning sales initiative by Beaujolais growers for the Parisian market became, during the 1970s and 1980s, a giant international operation of great logistical sophistication. New wine drawn off fresh from the vat is perfumed, fresh, juicy, and heady – which, broadly speaking, is Beaujolais' profile in any case. It works well; it makes money; what's the problem?

The problem is that the new-wine tradition is essentially a local one. My happiest memories of it are in Germany, where the wine is brought to your table in brimming jugs, still milky with carbon dioxide and sometimes sweet with unfermented sugar. Start bottling it, start exporting it, and it just can't be like that any more. It's got to be "safe" and "stable".

Which, in sum, is why most Beaujolais Nouveau tastes disagreeably confected. Making and selling it is in fact an abuse of raw materials; no wine that is whipped through thermo-vinification and then thrashed through severe stabilization and filtration treatments will ever emerge comely and composed at the end. It becomes an industrial product made by chemists. It may be good for bank accounts, but it is bad for the region in a broader sense, since it limits quality aspirations. The sooner that Beaujolais Nouveau is forgotten (apart, of course, from out of deliciously illegal barrels in Lyon cafés), the better.

Beaujolais: People

Bellevue *see* Jadot

Christian Bernard ✪
69820 Fleurie, Tel: 04 74 04 11 27, Fax: 04 74 69 86 64

These ambitious, luscious, richly extracted wines from Fleurie and Moulin-à-Vent may not be typical but they make exciting drinking. The Fleurie Clos des Grands Fers is packed with creamy black cherry, while the Christian Bernard Moulin-à-Vent is truffley and exotic.

Jean-Marc Burgaud
69910 Villié-Morgon, Tel: 04 74 69 16 10, Fax: 04 74 69 16 10

Jean-Marc Burgaud's 13-ha domain is not only a source of unusually good Régnié, but this is also a good name to note if you want to compare the different terroirs of Morgon. Both the spicy, firm-fruited Côte de Py and the much softer, more seductive Charmes are typical.

Calot
69910 Villié-Morgon, Tel: 04 74 04 20 55, Fax: 04 74 69 12 93

Yet another highly consistent Morgon domain, the 12 ha of François and Jean Calot are supple, scented, and packed with cherry fruit. There are four *cuvées* including a voluptuous Vieilles Vignes and a "Tête de Cuvée"; even better, though, is the close-textured and lightly tannic Cuvée Jeanne.

Cambon *see* Marcel Lapierre

La Chanaise *see* Piron

La Chaponne ✪
71570 Romanèche-Thorins, Tel: 04 85 35 52 42, Fax: 04 85 35 56 41

Laurent Guillet's 10-ha Morgon domain is planted in two of the main appellation *climats*: Côte de Py and Grands Cras. Guillet's ripe fruit and long vatting times are producing superb wines: the 2000 Domaine de la Chaponne, with its 13% of natural alcohol, is packed with chocolate cherry fruit, while the 2001 Côte de Py is sweet and artlessly delicious.

Cheysson
69915 Chiroubles, Tel: 04 74 04 22 02, Fax: 04 74 69 14 16

Chiroubles can sometimes be a difficult call; its height means a perpetual struggle for ripeness, and its fugitive, piercing charm does not always travel well. This large 26-ha domain is one of the best sources of good Chiroubles, both in pungently fruity Tradition guise and in the rather riskier venture of the oak-aged Prestige.

Chignard
69820 Fleurie, Tel: 04 74 04 11 87, Fax: 04 74 69 81 97

Michel Chignard's 8 ha of Fleurie in the *lieu-dit* of Moriers produce benchmark wines of smooth, ripe, enticing fruit with a softly meaty edge. The Cuvée Spéciale, by contrast, is a lower yielding, old-vine selection which sees new wood, giving it a smoky darkness of burgundian style.

Clos des Grands Fers *see* Bernard

Clos du Fief *see* Tête

Diochon
71570 Romanèche-Thorins, Tel: 03 85 35 52 42, Fax: 03 85 35 56 41

There are only 2 ha of Bernard Diochon's Moulin-à-Vent Vieilles Vignes *cuvée*, but these 80-year-olds produce one of the appellation's star wines, packed with mouthfilling black fruit.

Duboeuf
71570 Romanèche-Thorins, Tel: 03 85 35 34 20, Fax: 03 85 35 34 25

For many of the world's wine drinkers, Beaujolais means Duboeuf. This négociant blends and sells an astonishing 30 million bottles a year – astonishing not in number but in the fact that quality levels are relatively high. They are rarely over-processed and some of the *cru* bottlings (in particular the Morgon) can be excellent. Duboeuf's domain bottlings (like the Fleurie Domaine des 4 Vents) are well differentiated, too.

Dubost
69430 Lantignie, Tel: 04 74 04 87 51, Fax: 04 74 69 27 33

The wines of this 13-ha domain are sold both under the Dubost name as well as Domaine du Tracot; most of the vines are Beaujolais-Villages, though there are also parcels in Morgon, Régnié, and Brouilly. Jean-Paul Dubost is now in charge, though look out, too, for the excellent wood-aged Villages Les Charmieux Tête de Cuvée bottled under father Henri's name. The Morgon is the best of the *cru* wines, though there is, alas, just half a hectare here.

Fines Graves
71570 Romanèche-Thorins, Tel: 04 85 35 57 17, Fax: 04 85 35 21 69

Jacky Janodet's well-sited 12-ha domain produces finely crafted, nourishing Chénas and Moulin-à-Vent.

Foillard ✪
69910 Villié-Morgon, Tel: 04 74 04 24 97, Fax: 04 74 69 12 71

Jean Foillard and his wife Agnès have an 8-ha estate mostly planted in Morgon including a fine 5 ha's worth of parcels on the Côte de Py. There is a long, cold maceration of up to four weeks here before fermentation, and the Côte de Py wines are stored in old wood. From 2000, Jean Foillard is trialling a separate *cuvée* from 50-year-old vines grown in the sandy soils of Corcelette, which makes a smoother, more velvety wine than the lusty, tar-edged cherries of the Côte de Py. Even better is the Cuvée Laure, the heart of the pressings of the oldest (80-year-old) vines, though this is never actually sold but just served to good friends and customers. Tasty refinement reaches its apogee here.

du Granit
69840 Chénas, Tel: 04 74 04 48 40, Fax: 04 74 04 47 66

Gino Bertolla's 8.5-ha domain is magnificently sited in the upper reaches of Moulin-à-Vent (at about 260 metres, planted in two parcels: the pink granite of La Rochelle and the more manganese-rich Les Caves); he works with 45-year-old vines and high densities. In poor years there is just one *cuvée*, Tradition, but in most vintages there is also a Vieilles Vignes *cuvée* which, with time, acquires enticing notes of liquorice, coffee, and chocolate (the 1989 is still going strong).

des Jacques *see* Jadot

Jadot ✪
71570 Romanèche-Thorins, Tel: 03 85 35 51 64, Fax: 03 85 35 59 15

American-owned Burgundy négociant Louis Jadot has three domains in Beaujolais: the 27-ha Château des Jacques in Moulin-à-Vent; the newly purchased 35-ha Château de Bellevue (once the property of cinema pioneer Louis Lumière and his brother Auguste); plus 9 ha sited near Chénas planted with Chardonnay. This, one of France's only Chardonnays grown (in part) on granite, is given barrel-fermentation in burgundian style for the Bourgogne Blanc Clos de Loyse, and is steel-fermented for the Beaujolais Blanc Grand Clos de Loyse; the former, unsurprisingly but perhaps disappointingly, is more

---

Star rating system used on producer spreads   ✪ Very good wine   ✪✪ Excellent wine   ✪✪✪ Great wine

interesting than the latter. In addition to the "château" red wine, a range of five single-*climat cuvées* is produced at Château des Jacques: the elegant Champ de Cour; the dapper and fleshy Clos des Thorins; the crystalline La Roche; the complex and rounded Grand Carquelin; and the earthy, powerful Rochegrès, produced on the purest granite. All are vinified in burgundian style, too: the fruit (which is sorted) is cold-macerated, destemmed, macerated for up to 30 days with *remontages*, and oak-aged. The plan is to do the same at Bellevue with its three *climats*: Côte de Py, Clos de Bellevue (in Corcelette), and Les Charmes.

Janin ✪
71570 Romanèche-Thorins, Tel: 03 85 35 52 80, Fax: 03 85 35 21 77

Eric Janin's 12.5-ha Moulin-à-Vent estate is run with great thoughtfulness along partly biodynamic lines; Janin is also experimenting with destemming and burgundy-style vinifications. Top *cuvée* is the Clos du Tremblay, made from 60- to 90-year-old vines: explosive and expansive, with earthy depths behind the fruit.

Joubert
69430 Quincié-en-Beaujolais, Tel: 0793 17 09 737, Fax: 04 74 69 05 83

This 10-ha domain produces elegant and expressive unfiltered, unsulphured Brouilly and Beaujolais Villages.

Lacoque
69910 Villié-Morgon, Tel: 04 74 69 16 52, Fax: 04 74 04 27 03

Joël Lacoque's Cuvée Marie Jeanne Morgon, made from 80-year-old vines on the Côte de Py given oak ageing, makes a wonderfully exotic mouthful of sweet, sexy black cherry and coffee.

Hubert Lapierre
71570 La Chapelle-de-Guinchay, Tel: 03 85 36 74 89, Fax: 03 85 36 76 69

Hubert Lapierre's 7.5-ha domain is an excellent source of Chénas (he is the appellation president): classicists will prefer the supple, fruit-splashed Vieilles Vignes *cuvée*, while modernists or burgundy fans might go for the successfully oak-aged Cuvée Spéciale. Lapierre also makes a Moulin-à-Vent from the fresher, higher-sited vineyards of his commune.

Marcel Lapierre ✪
69910 Villié-Morgon, Tel: 04 74 04 23 89

There may be vineyards elsewhere in France as impeccably tended as Marcel Lapierre's 11 ha in Morgon, but I haven't seen them; these vines would shame the vineyard managers of many classed growths in the Médoc. There is a long cold maceration here before fermentation, which begins in classic Beaujolais style, continues with *pigeage*, *délestage*, a submerged cap, and a basket press, and finishes in used *pièces* (from Prieuré-Roch). The resulting wine is dark and fruit-packed, the typical Morgon cherries of youth ageing slowly and rewardingly towards lighter, creamier strawberries with time; for a moment, tasting these wines blind, Pommard and even Pomerol doesn't seem a light year away. The 16-ha Château Cambon in the Villages area, co-owned with Jean-Claude Chamonard, produces lighter wines of exquisite scent.

La Madone
69820 Fleurie, Tel: 04 74 69 81 51, Fax: 04 74 69 81 93

The Madonna which keeps her supervisory eye on the little chapel that dominates the hill of Fleurie took a tumble after a recent storm, but this mishap doesn't seem to have knocked quality in Beaujolais' purest granite terroir. Jean-Marc Després' 9-ha domain is a reliable source for this deliciously soft and quenching wine. The Vieilles Vignes is especially good.

Nesme
69910 Villié-Morgon, Tel: 04 74 04 21 28

Morgon is buzzing with quality wines, and Jean-Pierre and Nicole Nesme's Fûts de Chêne *cuvée* is a wonderful, meaty benchmark for this style, 57-year-old vines and a manganese-rich subsoil giving the fruit seriousness and stony depth.

Piron
69910 Villié-Morgon, Tel: 04 74 69 10 20, Fax: 04 74 69 16 65

Not all of the wines of this large 22-ha domain are successful, but the

Morgon Côte de Py has clean, textured fruits and in good vintages the Beaujolais-Villages Vignes de Pierreux can be excellent value. The Moulin-à-Vent Vigne du Vieux Bourg and Régnié Domaine de la Chanaise need a little more flesh, while the white Roche Noire fails to make much impact.

Sornay
69910 Villié-Morgon, Tel: 04 74 04 23 65, Fax: 04 74 69 10 70

Noël and Christophe Sornay's 8-ha Morgon domain produces wines of strikingly pretty classicism, singing with elegant cherry fruit.

Terres Dorées
69380 Charnay de Beaujolais, Tel: 04 78 47 93 45, Fax: 04 78 47 93 38

Inheriting 20 ha in the south of Beaujolais is not the easiest route to winemaking notoriety, but Jean-Paul Brun's inventivity and passion has succeeded in creating a range that puts this limy clay terroir through its paces. In many ways, Brun's work with Chardonnay is his greatest achievement, from the unoaked but beautifully ripe, exotic, almost Alsace-like Beaujolais Blanc via a less successful barrel-fermented *cuvée* to the massive and creamy late-harvested Labeur d'Octobre. The best of the Gamay-based *cuvées* is the almost Pinot-like, perfumed l'Ancien, made from old vines. There is a beautifully labelled Pinot Noir, too, of light and modest authenticity, and a deeper Moulin-à-Vent sourced and sold on a négociant basis.

Tête
69430 Beaujeu, Tel: 04 74 04 82 27, Fax: 04 74 69 28 61

This is the reference domain for both Juliénas and St-Amour. The power of the former (7 ha) makes it the Nuits-St-Georges of Beaujolais, while the bitter-edged cherrystone fruit of the latter (just one ha, alas) has electrifying depth and pungency.

Jean-Paul Thévenet
69620 St-Vérand, Tel: 04 74 71 79 42, Fax: 04 74 71 84 26

Another of the many stars of Morgon, Jean-Paul Thévenet has just 5.5 ha from which he produces a Tradition of zesty brio and a Vieilles Vignes *cuvée*, based on centenarian vines, which perfectly exemplifies the graceful, elegant purity and softly gamey flavours which Gamay produces in the Clachet subzone.

Thivin ✪
69460 Odenas, Tel: 04 74 03 47 53, Fax: 04 74 03 52 87

This 26-ha domain nestles snugly under Mont Brouilly, with a spring trickling in its courtyard and a sunny garden on the hillside. Claude Geoffray always adds a little Chardonnay to his Gamay, as the regulations permit, "for finesse and complexity. I don't like pure varietal wine." Of the 26 ha, 15 are planted in Côte de Brouilly and 3 in Brouilly, giving wines (Cuvée du Clos Bertrand and Manoir du Pavé respectively) of refreshingly crunchy, sour fruit. The two top *cuvées* are the Cuvée de la Chapelle, from the highest (4-ha) parcel owned by the domain, where the cherry fruit seems ballasted by rare stony depths; and the dark, barrique-aged Cuvée Zaccharie, where the vanilla and tannin from the wood adds a sexy sheen to a lusher, darker style of cherry fruit.

de Tracot *see* Dubost

Vignes du Tremblay *see* Janin

Vissoux
69620 St-Vérand, Tel: 04 74 71 79 42, Fax: 04 74 71 84 26

Few Beaujolais growers are in a position to pronounce on the region's different terroirs with the authority of the affable Pierre-Marie Chermette, since he has 15 ha in the south of the region, 6 ha in Fleurie and a single hectare in Moulin-à-Vent. Conclusions? That climate and exposition may, in the end, be the most important factors of all, since Vissoux's southern Beaujolais Gamay is actually grown on granite rather than limestone – yet the differences between it and the *cru* wines are still stark. The Moulin-à-Vent here combines crunchy fruit with background meatiness, yet it is the pure fruit seduction of the Fleurie Les Garants, faintly wreathed in smoke, which provides the domain's greatest wine.

The Jura

The Secret Garden Small, rural, and peaceful, the home region of Louis Pasteur remains well outside the stockade of the conventional and the fashionable. Tradition is never more improbable, nor convention unconventional, than here among the yellow whites and coral reds.

There was half an hour to spare; my next appointment was at the Fruitière Vinicole at Voiteur. Across the road from this small cooperative, the little River Seille was busily gurgling and chuckling its way towards Burgundy. Up above, an easy sixty metres (200 feet) higher, the eagle's nest village of Château Chalon teetered on the edge of its limestone stump. I walked up through the vineyards that lie like skirts about the fissured, honey-coloured rock, counting twelve different varieties of wild flowers on this April afternoon as I did so – or thirteen, including the wild strawberries. A single wine-grower was scattering fertilizer like a biblical seedsman. There were cows on the pasture across the valley; the hollow knock of their bells floated in the still air. I sat and rested. An elderly peacock butterfly paused briefly on my knee, flexing its tired wings. Only a month to live: better make the most of it.

Bucolic? Sure. The charm of the Jura and its wines come from the sense that time has grown genuinely mossy and amnesiac here. Small vineyards, old vines, curious grape varieties seen and tasted nowhere else, vinification methods that would be regarded as obtuse or mad by the oenological conformists who pass judgement at international wine shows. If you are one of those people who long to escape from the shallowness and tedium of wine fashion, then the Jura is for you.

Its greatest wine takes six years to make and another ten in bottle before it acquires anything resembling charm. Even then, many would regard this wine, Vin Jaune, as a bizarre exercise in vinous brinkmanship. The majority of the region's white wines are deliberately and knowingly oxidized. The red wines are pale. Vivid and sometimes austere acidity runs like a motorway through all. New oak, high alcohol, extract, glycerous textures, sweet fruit: the Jura has almost none of these early twenty-first century creature comforts. If you want a glimpse of what good wine might have tasted like in the time of Shakespeare, though, look here.

Given all of this, the Jura's role in the New France is likely, you might assume, to be muted. If the Jura's chief appeal to the world's wine-drinking community is that of curious antiquity, what can the avant-garde do?

Much, as it happens. First, the market stimulus is there. In contrast to the situation in nearby Savoie, the Jura needs to sell its wines, and not just ration them by price to thirsty local tourists. The fact that the largest local négociant, Henri Maire, is France's largest direct-sales wine specialist is not coincidental. Secondly, any tradition worth pursuing needs constant invigorative reinvention. If a tradition freezes, it dies. "People work much more professionally now than they did back in the 1960s," says Jacques Puffeney. "Before,

people made wine on a DIY basis, and lots of those wines were botched. Nowadays almost all wine-growers are really serious." Nor have the philosophical changes so apparent in other French wine regions passed the Jura by. Michel Rolland's profound belief in the perfection of the oak barrel as a recipient for wine and in the vital importance of having fully ripe grapes finds its echo, for example, in the work of the Rolet brothers. The hyper-energetic Stéphane Tissot, like Michel Escande in Minervois or Gérard Gauby in Roussillon, takes nothing for granted and rethinks everything he does, even if it means foregoing the AOC for some of his wines (like his Vin de Paille). The quest for terroir so apparent in the work of Olivier Zind-Humbrecht MW or Jean-Michel Deiss also obsesses young Julien Labet, who challenges the axiom that the region's greatest wines will always be those *sous voile* (*voile* is the film of yeast that forms on ullaged wines here, and is a central element of Vin Jaune *élevage*). "For me, leaving wines on ullage and allowing a *voile* to form obscures rather than expresses terroir. It's a decision, an intervention, a sort of blockage. That's why almost all the wines I make, I keep topped up." Labet may or may not be right about *voile*; Bertrand Delanney of the Voiteur cooperative says that even his base wines for Crémant du Jura, made reductively and kept topped up at all times, begin to acquire a distinctive *jaune*-like tang

if kept as reserves. The Jura's terroir, in other words, may float in the air as much as it surges from the ground.

The Jura is also beginning to prove attractive to outsiders. Jean Rijckaert, the former partner of Jean-Marie Guffens in Verget and now a winemaker and négociant in his own right, is an enthusiast for what he has discovered here. He came to the region by chance, but the fact that Arbois is only eighty km (fifty miles) from Beaune and lies on the same latitude as Montrachet impressed him. So did the region's old vines (including Chardonnay); so, even more importantly, did the open-mindedness and lack of preciousness in the spirit of the local wine-growers. "If you want a grower with good parcels in Burgundy to do something special for you, you have to get down on your knees in front of him first and kiss his shoes. Here, they are just happy if you are interested." Rijckaert has even become a convert to the delights of Savagnin, though many find this thick-skinned, pulpy, juiceless, high-acid, later-ripening cousin of Gewurztraminer a challenge too far. "I think it can acquire a complexity that eludes even Chardonnay in the heavy clay soils you find here," he says. "The fruit is more confit (cooked) in style; it's got great concentration, and great acidity too. The skin is incredibly thick. If it was a red grape variety, it would make fantastic wines as well."

"Who killed all the old vines in France? Money. The Jura is an old vineyard region, and there was never enough money here to pull up the old vines and plant younger, more productive clones. That's one of its main attractions: it's a region of old vines."

JEAN RIJCKAERT

Viticulture is rarely as tranquil and pastoral as here – though the Jura's wine specialities can jolt by their strangeness.

Jacques Puffeney

Jacques Puffeney has travelled. His father was a vineyard worker; Jacques himself began, in the 1960s, with just 20 ares. He now has 7.5 ha (18.5 acres) – and a series of fine, pure, and exquisitely typical wines under his belt. More than that, he is a secret scholar, a quiet theorist, a practical researcher. "I spent eight days in Jerez," he told me, "but I was more struck by the differences between Vin Jaune and sherry than by any similarities. Then I travelled to Tokaji, and the wines I saw sous voile there were much closer to Vin Jaune, especially the Tokaji Szamorodni made from Furmint." He experiments ceaselessly himself – with skin maceration, with topping up, with new oak, and (for his Rouge Vieilles Vignes) with mixed plantings. "I've only got one ambition left that I haven't realized yet," he says, "and that's to plant ungrafted Savagnin. I've had to tussle with INAO over this for two years. But soon...."

The Adventure of the Land

There are two ways to look at the Jura. You can either see it as Burgundy's twin, or as the first step on the Alpine staircase.

Why Burgundy's twin? Because it occupies the hills on the other side of the broad Saône Valley from those of the Côte d'Or. The Saône has not carved itself a true river valley, but rather squats in a graben, a trench dropped between two parallel faults. (The same is true of the Rhône, which takes advantage of a graben to survey, from a languid distance, both the vineyards of Alsace and those of Baden.) Burgundy's vines echo across the valley, too: Chardonnay accounts for forty-five per cent of Jura plantings, and Pinot Noir for a further ten per cent.

And why the first step to the Alps? Because, when you are in the Jura, that is the way the hills look, the air smells, the road signs point. The "Vignoble du Revermont", they call it: the "vineyard of the back-mountain". The hill-line here is broken by a series of side valleys or *reculées*: travel up any of them and the roads will take you first of all to woods and high pastures, then to steep mountain valleys (including that of the Bienne where you will find an entire town, Morez, busy manufacturing spectacles), and finally to snug ski resorts and airy summer hiking centres.

Is there, after "Jurassic Park", a better-known geological period than that which takes its name from this region? Far more significant than its dinosaurs, though, were the warm, quiet seas of the Jurassic, its lagoons of sea-lilies and its blizzards of oysters, its constellations of starfish and its catacombs of coral. Their legacy is a great sickle of limestone that arcs through France. Ironically, however, there are many French vineyard areas where "the Jurassic" is far more gleamingly evident than in the Jura. In general terms, this is a vineyard region of heavy clay, the Madiran of the north. (The Jura's wines, though in register so different, can sometimes share a kind of brutal quality with those of Madiran. My own belief is that the distinctive use of controlled oxidation in this region developed in part as a softening

device, to mitigate that acidic hardness.) The lime may leave its chemical legacy in the occasionally shelly and fossil-hardened soil, but the pure stone itself lies deeply buried here.

The biggest AOC in the Jura is that of **Arbois**, with 850 ha (2,100 acres) gathered about the town; **Pupillin** is a *cru* that can add its name to that of the overall AOC, despite no evident distinction of taste. Arbois may be the epicentre of Jura wine-growing, but the vineyards themselves stretch, often sparsely, far to the northeast and southwest of Arbois, following the hill-line; the overall AOC for this long fillet of land is **Côtes du Jura** (650 ha/1,600 acres under vine). These two appellations cover the full spectrum of Jura winemaking, which is... complicated.

Arbois is the Jura's red wine heart, first of all; very few red wines are made in the Côtes du Jura. These reds can be based on Poulsard (sometimes described as a rosé grape, so uniformly pale are its wines, though in truth the local term "coral" is more apt: wines based on Poulsard often seem to glow like sacramental blood); Trousseau (slightly deeper and meatier); and Pinot Noir (which resembles a mountain cousin of Savigny up here). Varietal names (especially Pinot Noir) may be used on labels, though Poulsard and Trousseau are often blended, too. White wines, meanwhile, are mostly based on Chardonnay, though this could either be made in a classic, reductive manner, often now fermented in new oak, burgundy-style; or in the local manner, with controlled oxidation. Whites may also be made from Savagnin, the Vin Jaune grape, and these are more likely to appear in semi-oxidized guise; indeed if a Vin Jaune is not performing too well during its six-year *élevage*, it is often blended or declassified into a varietal Savagnin. Some producers, however, will vinify and bottle Savagnin as a classic varietal, with no controlled oxidation: it can then resemble a nervier, more sinewy Viognier, provided it is made from fully ripe fruit. Blends are permitted, too; Chardonnay tends to be the majority partner in these, though a minority of Savagnin can often prove dominant in flavour terms.

Now on to the Jura's great specialities. **Vin Jaune** (no more than four per cent of the Jura's total production) is made from Savagnin alone, usually grown on dark marl soils and late harvested. It is late-ripening anyway, and withstands the rigours of early autumn rains thanks to its thick skin. After fermentation, the new wine is put into oak casks already used for Vin Jaune, and thus containing a population of local ambient yeasts in its wood pores. An air space is left at the top of the cask, and the cask is not topped up. After a while, a film of yeast grows over the wine, known locally as *voile* or "veil" and visually similar (though greyer and thinner) to the flor that grows on casks of fino and manzanilla sherry. The wine is left alone for six years and three months, though its health is monitored regularly. It is then decanted into unique, dumpy bottles called *clavelins*. These contain 62cl, this amount being said to be all that remains of a litre of wine after six years' slow evaporation. The scent of Vin Jaune can resemble sherry, though with further bottle age it can also take on notes of wild mushroom and walnut. In flavour, however, the wine has absolutely nothing in common with sherry at all. Sherry is made from Palomino, one of the world's least acidic white wine grapes; Vin Jaune, being based on Savagnin, always carries a forceful acidic charge which can fall across the tongue like a blow from an axe. It is for this reason that Vin Jaune is usually far more enjoyable as a food partner (particularly for rich, creamy dishes) than on its own – though great Vin Jaune can, at around its twentieth birthday, balance out this acidity with a wealth of countryside and forest allusions. There's no denying, however, that it can be a difficult wine to like at first, in the same way that a classic French cheese like Munster, Maroilles, or Crottin de Chavignol can challenge the uninitiated.

The other great Jura speciality is **Vin de Paille**. "Straw wine" is made in a number of French regions (Gérard Chave's is magnificent). The Jura tradition is to base it on Poulsard, Savagnin, and Chardonnay; after hanging and drying the grapes, the wine is generally made in the early months of the new year before being cask-aged for three years (the casks are topped up this time). It is rarely as succulent and unctuous a wine as it can be in warmer regions, but the acidity of the Savagnin gives the Jura's versions a refreshingly lively, tangy, Tokaji-like balance. **Macvin** is fortified grape juice made in the same way as Pineau des Charentes, though the use of local *marc* instead of a polished brandy gives it a rustic style. The Jura is also the source of some surprisingly good sparkling wines, the best of which are sold as **Crémant du Jura**.

There are, though, two further AOCs to log. **L'Etoile** is an eighty-ha (198-acre), white wine zone of five hills around the village of the same name planted with ninety per cent Chardonnay and just ten per cent Savagnin. There is some Vin Jaune production here, but Etoile is best known for Chardonnay-based whites that combine allusive finesse with some of the local Jura tang. Sparkling wines can be very good here, too (in pre-AOC days, buyers from Champagne made substantial purchases in Etoile).

Finally, **Château-Chalon** is an AOC for Vin Jaune alone; other wines made there are sold as Côtes du Jura. This has always been one of the most strictly administered AOCs in France, with a commission visiting each parcel prior to harvest to check quality and yield, and in the case of very poor years (like 2001) all the growers agreeing not to use the appellation at all. There are just fifty ha (124 acres) in cultivation – not simply around the rock on which the eponymous village perches, but also in some neighbouring communes (especially the well-sited Ménétru le Vignoble).

- AOC Arbois
- AOC Château-Chalon
- AOC l'Etoile
- Vineyard areas

Jura Flak

The "O" word

It's a welcome problem, but it's a problem nonetheless. What aromas and flavours await you when you open a bottle of white wine from the Jura? Will the wine turn out to be a classic, barrel-fermented Chardonnay, its character marked only by the distinctively forceful, acidic quality of the local terroir? Or will it be a wine whose tangy, oxygen-informed style is clearly modelled on the Vin Jaune ideal? These wines provide very different drinking experiences, yet the labels will not help you distinguish them. As more and more of the younger generation turn away from the tangy, semi-oxidized style, appreciated locally but often incomprehensible outside the region, this hazard will become more common. Vinification information is ideally suited to back labels, so no one need change the law. We just need to know what's in the bottle.

Jura: People

d'Arlay
39140 Arlay, Tel: 03 84 85 04 22, Fax: 03 84 48 17 96

The Château d'Arlay, owned by Alain de Laguiche, is the grandest and most aristocratic property in the region – though not necessarily the most propitiously sited from a viticultural point of view. Blending is very much the *modus operandi* here, with the Corail offering one of the most bizarre *assemblages* in French winemaking: Pinot Noir, Trousseau, and Poulsard with Chardonnay and Savagnin. The plain white Côtes du Jura is often the best wine.

Aviet
39600 Montigny-lès-Arsures, Tel: 03 84 66 11 02

Lucien Aviet is one of the Jura's greatest characters. A visit to the "Caveau de Bacchus", with its stove, its player-piano, its alluringly draped mannequin ("*à consommer, de préférence chambré, sans modération*" reads a notice on her arm), and Gorki the mongrel, is an essential detour for anyone passing near Arbois. You will quickly learn to call Chardonnay "Melon à Queue Rouge", to call Poulsard "Ploussard", and to join Aviet in castigating Pinot Noir here as a "dangerous product". Behind the humour there is a serious range from this small 6-ha domain, with the Trousseau-based red Cuvée des Géologues wines and the unusually mellow Arbois Vin Jaune both noteworthy. Son Vincent does the hard work these days.

Berthet-Bondet
39210 Château-Chalon, Tel: 03 84 44 60 48, Fax: 03 84 44 61 13

The red wines here are dull, but the balanced, full-flavoured Château-Chalon takes age well, while the Côtes du Jura Tradition (a Savagnin-Chardonnay blend) offers some of the same nutty complexities for much less outlay.

Croix d'Argis *see* Henri Maire

Durand-Perron
39210 Voiteur, Tel: 03 84 44 66 80, Fax: 03 84 44 62 75

Old vines and a long tradition of Vin Jaune-making are two of the reasons why Jacques Durand's Château-Chalon is often one of the region's best. Buy it if you want the best, for long storage (you will be told not to put it in the fridge when you eventually come to drink it); if not, the Côtes du Jura wines here (a Savagnin and a village Chardonnay from Voiteur) are very nearly as good for less than half the price.

Fruitière Vinicole de Voiteur
39210 Voiteur, Tel: 03 84 85 21 29, Fax: 03 84 85 27 67

This small cooperative opposite and below Château-Chalon has just 75 ha to its name (45 ha of which is Chardonnay) belonging to 50 members; only eight are full-time viticulturalists. All of the wines are carefully made and satisfying; perhaps the best is the mouthfilling Chardonnay-Savagnin, full of fresh almondy substance, while the Vin Jaune and Château-Chalon are drivingly and challengingly typical.

Grange Grillard *see* Henri Maire

Labet ✪
39190 Rotalier, Tel: 03 84 25 11 13, Fax: 03 84 25 06 75

This 9-ha domain near Rotalier was created by Alain and Josie Labet, but their three children, Julien, Romain, and Charline, all now work with them; the thoughtful and talented Julien is the winemaker. Like many of the younger generation in the Jura, his finest wines are produced using fully filled casks, since he believes that it is in that way that the stamp of terroir emerges most articulately. These wines include the assertive Fleur de Chardonnay and two single-parcel alternatives, Les Varrons (a rich, creamy Chardonnay grown in red limestone soils) and La Bardette (more perfumed: the essence of the Jura countryside, grown in typical blue marl soils). Labet's Vin de Paille is superbly balanced, and the Vin Jaune memorably nutty. "We don't fully understand Vin Jaune and I think it's a good thing," says Labet. "There should be some things which remain beyond our understanding."

Ligier ✪
39380 Mont-sous-Voudray, Tel: 03 84 71 74 75, Fax: 03 84 81 59 82

The large, 14-wine range from this 9-ha Arbois domain includes a Chardonnay Vieilles Vignes *cuvée* and a pure Savagnin in Vin Jaune style. Best of all, though, is the super-ripe, almost Viognier-like Cuvée des Poètes, a pure Savagnin produced in the best years only and given a classic burgundy-style *élevage*. The Cuvée des Princes, a 50/50 Chardonnay-Savagnin blend, is made in the same way, with fastidious topping-up. Ligier's reds are well worth trying, too, particularly the glintingly fleshy Poulsard.

Lornet
39600 Montigny-lès-Arsures, Tel: 03 84 37 44 95, Fax: 03 84 37 40 17

Frédérique Lornet's home is the abbey at Montigny-lès-Arsures from where he runs this 15-ha Arbois domain. The oaked Trousseau les Dames is Lornet's best wine; the Chardonnay les Messagelins can be intense and rewarding, too.

Macle ✪
39210 Château-Chalon, Tel: 03 84 85 21 85, Fax: 03 84 85 27 38

The courteous Jean Macle is widely regarded as the master of Château-Chalon, and his son Laurent is now carrying forward the fine tradition of this craftsmanlike domain. There are 11 ha altogether: 8 ha of Chardonnay planted in Côtes du Jura, and 3 ha in Château-Chalon itself (a single hectare in steep and stony soils at the base of the rock, and 2 ha in Ménétru-le-Vignoble). The average vine age here is 30 years, and yields are around 40 hl/ha for the Côtes du Jura and 25 hl/ha for the Savagnin. The wines are fermented using wild yeasts in enamel-lined tanks, then aged in casks under voile. The Côtes du Jura, here, can be every bit as good as the Vin Jaune and in some vintages makes a more accessible, less austere wine, full of typical forest-plant and morel mushroom complexities. Great, well-aged Château-Chalon from Macle, like the 1989 now coming into early maturity, is magnificently dense and complex, one of those wines that seems to riffle through a repertoire of the natural world as you sniff and sip.

Henri Maire
39600 Arbois, Tel: 03 84 66 12 34

This company is the giant of the Jura, selling almost half of the region's production direct to French customers in their homes, via a network of 360 salesmen. (Restaurant sales go under the name Marcel Poux.) It has 300 ha of its own vineyards, including four domains: Grange Grillard, Sorbief, Montfort, and Croix d'Argis, where the company is trialling organic production. The unusual sales strategy is perhaps one reason why these wines are not competitive with the region's best, though the example of Rolet shows that quality and size are not necessarily incompatible. Reds and pinks from Sorbief are the pick of the bunch.

Star rating system used on producer spreads	✪ Very good wine	✪✪ Excellent wine	✪✪✪ Great wine

Montfort *see* Henri Maire

Overnoy
39600 Pupillin, Tel: 03 84 66 14 60, Fax: 03 84 66 14 60

This tiny Arbois-Pupillin domain of just 2 ha is run by one of France's legendary pioneers of organic cultivation and non-interventionist winemaking, Pierre Overnoy, now assisted by Emmanuel Houillon. The wines are hard to find, but both the lees-rich, unsulphured red Poulsard and the powerfully aromatic whites are among the region's most memorable bottles.

La Pinte
39600 Arbois, Tel: 03 84 66 24 58

When I first visited this large 30-ha Arbois-Pupillin domain over 10 years ago it had rather a mournful air, as if founder Roger Martin's grand ambitions were beginning to founder. Under Philippe Chatillon, however, the domain is holding its own with some impressively ripe whites made in non-*typé* style with fully topped-up casks; Poulsard finds its evangelist, too, in the enthusiastic Chatillon.

Poux *see* Henri Maire

Puffeney ✪
39600 Montigny-lès-Arsures, Tel: 03 84 66 10 89, Fax: 03 84 66 10 89

Jacques and Monique Puffeney's 7.5-ha domain in Arbois is, Jacques claims, one of only half a dozen or so in the region to harvest the entire crop by hand; Puffeney works his soils, uses wild yeast, ferments almost everything in *foudres* and gives all the wines at least two years' *élevage* after which, he says, they don't need filtering. This is a fine, pure, and clearly differentiated range, based on fully ripe fruit; Puffeney is one of the latest harvesters in Arbois (he didn't begin until October in 2001). The Chardonnay is complex, intense, with lots of apricot fruit and just enough of the local "Jurassic" tang to make it much more than a mere varietal. The Cuvée Sacha (the name signifies SAvagnin plus CHArdonnay) has lots of chew and tang, the Savagnin component having been aged under *voile*. Puffeney's aim with his pure Savagnin, by contrast, is to make a floral style of wine aged in fully topped-up smaller casks. This is one of the best red wine ranges in the region, too, from the pretty, glowing, lightly nutty Poulsard, the gamey Trousseau and the ripely perfumed Pinot Noir to the faintly meaty yet delicate Rouge Vieilles Vignes with its Assam-tea tannins (this wine is a vineyard blend of Poulsard, Trousseau and Pinot with a little Chardonnay, planted in 1929 and 1945). Puffeney's Vin Jaune is pure, smooth, harmonious, and unusually mellow. "If you make a proper Vin Jaune, it's indestructible," says Puffeney. "It's difficult to make; there are lots of hazards; but once it's there, it's there."

Rijckaert
71570 Leynes, Tel: 03 85 35 15 09, Fax: 03 85 35 15 09

Burgundy-based Belgian winemaker and négociant Jean Rijckaert now owns 4 ha of his own in Buvilly in the Côtes du Jura and in Arbois; he also buys from local growers with a further 7 ha in the region (you'll find the growers' names on labels). This is a subtle, carefully crafted range of white wines made in classic burgundy style (ie using barrel fermentation and without controlled oxidation); Rijckaert says that they need a longer *élevage* than his Mâcon wines, and for maximum articulacy they need some bottle age, too. In youth, all is clean lime purity.

Rolet ✪✪
39600 Arbois, Tel: 03 84 66 00 05, Fax: 03 84 37 47 41

This immaculate, 65-ha domain is run with astonishing meticulousness and care by the four Rolet siblings (Pierre and Elaine, plus winemaker Guy and vineyard manager Bernard). Like the domains of the Bunan family in Bandol and the Laplace brothers at Aydie in Madiran, it proves that family ownership at its best is unbeatable for creating the very highest levels of viticultural achievement. Fully ripe grapes, brilliantly judged use of wood,

and delicate use, too, of controlled oxidation to create what Guy calls "*une petite inflection noisette*" ("a little hazelnut note") are all hallmarks of the domain's wines, the consistency of which is impressive for such a cool-climate vineyard region. Among the stars is a scented, graceful, and spicy Arbois Pinot Noir, a persistently floral and intense l'Etoile, and some of the most ageworthy Chardonnay-Savagnin blends the region can offer, both for the white Arbois Tradition and for the Côtes du Jura. The Vin de Paille is full of typical woodland enchantment, and the Vins Jaunes are benchmark classics.

Sorbief *see* Henri Maire

Tissot ✪
39600 Montigny-lès-Arsures, Tel: 03 84 66 08 27, Fax: 03 84 66 25 08

This domain, which has 20 ha in Arbois and another 10 ha in Côtes du Jura, still bears the name of André and Mireille, but it is their son Stéphane who is turning it at bone-breaking pace into one of the region's most forceful, innovative, and occasionally controversial. Like Julian Labet, Stéphane Tissot worked in both South Africa and Australia prior to starting work with his father in 1990; he has converted the entire domain to organic cultivation. "As a means and not an end," he stresses. "For all that, it's the future of viticulture." Around half the domain lies on propitious hill slopes in four separate parcels (Les Bruyères, La Mailloche, Les Graviers, and En Barberon), and the single-parcel barrel-fermented Chardonnays he produces from these are the most "burgundian" and terroir-orientated of his wines. As good are Tissot's graceful Trousseau reds, aged in *demi-muids*; a fine varietal Savagnin of unusual ripeness and glycerousness; scented Vins Jaunes; and an extraordinary Vin de Paille dried for so long and thus so sweet that it no longer qualifies for the AOC. Tissot sells it as PMG – *pour ma gueule* (my gobful).

Savoie

Checked by Success Savoie is France's most fortunate wine region: it enjoys bouyant and undiscerning local demand. Easy pickings, though, don't necessarily make for great wines, and those growers struggling to make great *vins de terroir* here can often feel lonely.

The very idea seems improbable. Wine here, in the mountains? Here, where tourists are still returning home on crutches in mid-April? Here, where you have to cut corridors through the forest just to give the avalanches somewhere to go? Vines, after all, don't just need a sunny week or two in summer; they need the sort of heat that turns grass brown, that bleaches fence posts, that makes you think twice before stepping out at lunchtime. Here?

Yes, here. Remember, after all, the effect of a well-positioned slope on a vineyard: it lifts vines up towards the sunshine. Even in fringe latitudes, a well-directed slope can put the sun in the centre of the sky, and with it, increase the heat at a summer noon by roasting margins. When that vineyard is backed by a mountain, and its valley closed at one end by another mountain, the furnace factor can increase still more dramatically.

Viticulture here is also ancient (there were vineyards in Chignin in the eleventh century), and travel around the region in the past was difficult and slow. Before telephones and cars, a mountain valley was a kingdom to itself. This is the reason for what can seem today to be the oppressive complexity of Savoie's wines. Production here is small (the AOC of Corbières alone produces almost four times as much wine as the whole of Savoie), yet it is atomized between four AOCs and a VDQS, all of which encompass more than twenty *crus* and well over a dozen grape varieties of both colours. The region's long, slow evolution has given rise to a wine culture of jewel-box intricacy.

There is a strong case for simplifying Savoie's appellation system, and if the region was ever faced with the pressing need to sell its wines to the world, then it would surely have to consider doing so. The fact is, though, that production is so tiny, and consumption so local, that the incomprehensibility of its appellations to non-locals scarcely matters. (Over eighty per cent of the wines of even a top producer like Michel Quénard is sold in the Rhône-Alps.) Most drinkers will only ever encounter these wines during a holiday, and then their refreshment value, and their flavours of orchard fruits, of mineral salts, of sap, and of nuts will matter far more than the significance of their strange forest of names.

The adventure of the land

Half the sky, in Savoie, is often filled with rock. In fifteen minutes on a twisting road, you can leave vineyards whose vines are just coming into leaf and travel upwards through freshly green mixed woodland, bright with sunbeams; and then on to budding birch groves in which cowslips and primroses are still blooming; and finally up to leafless cool copses, fingering mists, and conifer plantations in which patches of tired snow lie like grubby cushions on the still-frosty earth. The

vertical dimension is every bit as important as the horizontal dimension for plant life in Savoie. It's the Médoc's antithesis.

Geologically, Savoie as a whole is every bit as complex as it looks on the ground or on the map. Yet agricultural land occupies a tiny majority of Savoie's terrain – and vines occupy a mere two per cent of the region's agricultural land. Viticulture here is pure opportunism, which means that Savoie's vines are generally rooted either in scree or in glacial deposits, since these tend to be what is found at the base of mountains where the hot spots accrue. This rubble is generally limestone, like the mountains from which it has been ground or prised.

The overall regional AOC is that of **Vin de Savoie**, though this may be (and usually is) followed by the name of one of fifteen *crus*. The wines can be red or white, and produced from a number of different grape varieties; these are often (though not always) stated on the label. Where the wine is white and no variety is stated, assume it will be based on Jacquère. There is a second overall regional AOC, too: that of **Roussette de Savoie**. This is for white wines only, produced from the indigenous grape known locally as Roussette or Altesse. It, too, has its own *crus*, though there are only four of these.

In volume terms, the two most important Vin de Savoie *crus* are **Apremont** and **Abymes**, for light white wines based on the Jacquère grape variety. The names hark back to a doom-laden night in November 1248 when, after copious rain, a huge portion of Mont Granier crashed down onto the village of St-André and several nearby hamlets, burying 5,000 humans "and innumerable animals" as they lay sleeping. The rubble-filled necropolis was left alone for centuries, but eventually planted with vineyards whose names recall the "bitter mountain" and the "ruins" of their birth. The northeast-facing aspects and low relief mean that these are, at best, light, fresh, salty, nettle-brisk whites, the Muscadet of the Alps.

Facing them are the steeper, warmer vineyards of **St-Jeoire-Prieuré**, **Chignin**, **Montmélian**, **Arbin**, **Cruet**, and **St-Jean-de-la-Porte**, which together constitute the vineyards of the Combe de Savoie, lying beneath the Massif des Bauges. This boomerang-shaped stretch of limestone scree vineyards produce what are probably the greatest of Savoie's wines, in particular the fragrant Roussanne-based whites of **Chignin-Bergeron** (Bergeron is the local name for Roussanne), full of haunting quince fruit and mayflower fragrance. This is also a fine zone for the weightier, more succulent Roussette de Savoie wines, though there are no specific Roussette *crus* here. All the whites are marked by striking mineral-salt complexities. The indigenous red variety Mondeuse is at home here, too, especially in Arbin. These *crus* lie within easy reach of Chambéry. The tiny

"Twenty years ago everyone said we were mad when we planted vineyards on the steep slopes at Torméry. Those slopes were so steep that we needed terraces. The easy money back then lay in planting Jacquère on the lower vineyards. Now it's a different story. Now they're all trying to plant up on the slopes."

MICHEL QUENARD

The best vineyards of the Lac du Bourget lie hidden to its west, overlooking the
◀ *River Rhône: the crus of Jongieux, Marestel, and Monthoux.*

Michel Quénard

You need sturdy legs and a strong heart to be a wine-grower in Savoie. Stroll into the vineyard where Jason Lowe photographed Michel Quénard (they lie adjacent to the cellars), and you'll see a towering rock wall. The Massif des Bauges disappears, as often as not, into swirling cloud. The Chignin vineyard soils are constituted by the rubble which wind, sun, and frost has prised off these slabs and chimneys, and sent tumbling hundreds of feet below. Michel Quénard and his father André are masters of the Bergeron grape, known in the Rhône Valley and elsewhere as Roussanne. They argue it should be limited to the best and steepest local sites where it can ripen fully, like the Coteaux de Torméry, giving wines of real texture and perfume as it does so. Others, less exigent, feel that there is a role for lighter, slighter Bergeron, grown on flatter, richer soils and providing higher yields. Both sell well.

Roussette de Savoie *cru* of **Monterminod**, finally, lies tucked away next to Chambéry, wedged beneath the striking peaks of the Croix du Nivolet and Mont Peney.

There is another stretch of vineyards near Aix-les-Bains, to each side of the Lac du Bourget. The *crus* of **Jongieux**, **Marestel**, and **Monthoux** are entirely screened from the lake by the feline spine of the Mont du Chat; they face west across the peaceful pastureland of the Upper Rhône Valley. The stony Jongieux is a *cru* of Vin de Savoie, but Marestel and Monthoux are both Roussette de Savoie *crus*; the Altesse thrives on these sunlit, limestone marls and screes to give some of the most complete and subtle wines of Savoie, without the mineral-salt notes of the Combe de Savoie but with tantalizing hints of honey, marzipan, and lime blossom. Other white varieties, including Jacquère and Chardonnay, can be very good here, too; the reds, though, are much less impressive.

There are a few scattered vineyard sites over the mountain and across the lake, sharing space with Aix's grander lakeside suburbs, but the next Vin de Savoie *cru* is found about five km (3.1 miles) to the north of the Lac du Bourget, beside the Rhône: **Chautagne**, chiefly used for light, Gamay-based reds. Further north still, in the Vallée des Usses (a tributary of the Rhône), lies **Frangy**, another Roussette de Savoie *cru*, though smaller and less successful than either Marestel or Monthoux.

Entirely separated from the rest of the *crus*, in what is called the Côte d'Arve above Bonneville, is the Vin de Savoie *cru* of **Ayze**. This is one of the highest in the AOC; the speciality here is light, incisive sparkling wines based on a local grape called Gringet (related to the Jura's Savagnin), blended with Mondeuse Blanche (or Roussette d'Ayze), Marsanne (locally called Grosse Roussette), and Chasselas (locally called Bon Blanc).

The final Vin de Savoie *crus* lie on the shores of Lake Geneva: these are **Ripaille**, **Marin**, and **Marignan**, specializing in Chasselas grown on glacial deposits, giving distinctively light, fresh white wines of buttery, salty flavour. Nearby **Crépy**, for no good reason, has an AOC of its own; it is similar in style to the three local Vin de Savoie *crus*.

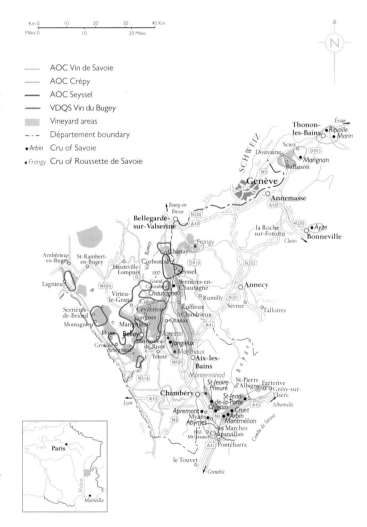

| Km 0 | 10 | 20 | 30 | 40 Km |
| Miles 0 | | 10 | | 20 Miles |

- AOC Vin de Savoie
- AOC Crépy
- AOC Seyssel
- VDQS Vin du Bugey
- Vineyard areas
- Département boundary
- **Arbin** Cru of Savoie
- **Frangy** Cru of Roussette de Savoie

The final AOC of Savoie is that of **Seyssel**, an eighty-two-ha (203-acre) vineyard zone that lies on each side of the Rhône Valley about ten km (6.2 miles) north of the Lac du Bourget, between the Roussette *cru* of Frangy and the Vin de Savoie *cru* of Chautagne. The Altesse grape variety is widely planted here for still white wines (which can be called either Seyssel or Roussette de Seyssel); it is also used to bolster the rather neutral wines of the indigenous white Molette grape variety when making the pleasant sparkling wines of Seyssel.

That's not all, folks. The neighbouring *département* of Ain has the VDQS of **Bugey**, whose extensive though sparsely planted growing zone stretches away to the west of Savoie's AOC areas. There are eleven different *crus* for **Vin du Bugey** and **Roussette du Bugey**, though all except three are now defunct. (Savoie, too, has defunct *crus* such as Sainte-Marie d'Alloix and Charpignat.) The three surviving Bugey *crus* are **Cerdon**, **Manicle**, and **Montagnieu**. The vines of Montagnieu grow on propitiously sited, limy glacial deposits a little further down the Rhône river valley from Savoie's Jongieux, Marestel, and Monthoux; it specializes in Roussette-based sparkling and still wines. Manicle (the birthplace of France's most celebrated literary epicure, Brillat-Savarin) is near Virieu-le-Grand, and produces whites based on Jacquère and Chardonnay, as well as some light reds. Cerdon, by contrast, is the nearest wine-growing region to France's poultry capital of Bourg-en-Bresse, and specializes in sparkling rosé based on the Jura's Poulsard variety. Bugey wines without these *cru* names are likely to be light, graceful, and fugitive at best.

Savoie Flak

Downhill quality

After the bright intoxication of snow and the adrenaline surge of an unbroken descent, visitors to the French Alps may not be picky about the quality of what they drink with their evening fondue. Indeed merely to be offered a local wine, rather than have to endure the tedium of yet more internationally marketed products of somnolent familiarity, is a delight. So it is perhaps not surprising that the basic quality of wine in Savoie is among the sloppiest in France. In visiting the region, I drank Apremont and Abymes of genuinely abysmal quality: wine that tasted weak, dilute, and coarse, like an alcoholic soft drink. This should worry the INAO, since the tasting panels responsible for administering the Vin de Savoie AOC are obviously ceding quality standards to commercial pressure. The region's best growers, by contrast, are often appalled by the race for yields which they see in the vineyards around them, and lament the fact that their own stocks are so quickly exhausted that they have to bottle their finer wines too soon in order to avoid breaking supply to the market. The truth is that Savoie needs more vineyards so that the region's best growers can expand their production, and so that the region itself can begin to compete on the national and international stage. Local growers confirm that there are many good or even great sites which are still unplanted, and which could produce wines to rival the best in present-day Savoie once the vines have reached maturity.

The problem is that vineyard policy in France is decided nationally, and it is hard to get new "plantation rights" here as it is in the Languedoc. Perhaps the disappointing quality of much "ordinary" Savoie wine also acts a disincentive to the bureaucrats to look favourably on Savoie's case. For the foreseeable future, thus, it seems likely that Savoie's wine will remain a sometimes disappointing local curiosity. The lost souls of St-André deserve better.

Savoie: People

Pierre Boniface
73800 Les Marches, Tel: 04 79 28 14 50, Fax: 04 79 28 16 82

Pierre Boniface's Les Rocailles range includes some of the most carefully crafted Jacquère from Apremont. In addition to the domain sources, Boniface also buys fruit for this small négociant business.

Bouchez
73800 Cruet, Tel: 04 79 84 30 91, Fax: 04 79 84 30 50

Gilbert Bouchez's domain in Cruet produces consistently good Roussette de Savoie as well as lingering Jacquère whose grapefruit and lime flavours can acquire a smoky edge on occasion.

Bouvet
73250 St-Pierre-d'Albigny, Tel: 04 79 28 54 11, Fax: 04 79 28 51 97

Like many growers in Fréterive, the Bouvets are nurserymen first and foremost, using the soft and fertile silt of the valley floor. Up on the slopes of the Combe de Savoie, however, this domain has made a speciality of red varieties, with pleasant, oak-aged Pinot Noir and tasty Mondeuse.

Eugène Carrel
73170 Jongieux, Tel: 04 79 44 02 20, Fax: 04 79 44 03 73

This, one of the two Carrel domains in the outstanding *cru* of Jongieux, is a good source of concentrated old-vine Gamay as well as subtle, pear-fruited Roussette de Savoie.

Charlin
01680 Groslée, Tel: 04 74 39 73 54, Fax: 03 74 39 75 16

Patrick Charlin's domain in the Bugey *cru* of Montagnieu makes a good case for this VDQS as a fine source of sparkling wines. Charlin's Pinot Noir-based red is one of the region's best, too.

Cave de Chautagne
73310 Ruffieux, Tel: 04 79 54 27 12, Fax: 04 79 54 51 37

For anyone touring the region, this small, friendly and easily accessible co-op is well worth a visit. Chautagne is best known for its Gamays, but the Mondeuse makes a satisfying glassful here, too.

Claude Delalex
74200 Marin, Tel: 04 50 71 45 82

The Chasselas-based wines of this Marin domain are worth seeking out for those who want to see what differences a blocked malolactic fermentation can make to these otherwise salty, biscuity white wines (you may find a little extra peachy fruit). Clos de Pont is the top *cuvée*.

Dupasquier ✪
73170 Jongieux, Tel: 04 79 44 02 23, Fax: 04 79 44 03 56

Few domains in Savoie are run with the attention to detail of Noël Dupasquier's 12.5-ha estate in the quiet backwater of Jongieux, its west-facing vineyards stretching up spectacularly to 450 metres on the slopes behind the cellar. There are some small plantings of Gamay, Pinot Noir, and Mondeuse, but the site and its clay-lime soils are best suited to white grape varieties and particularly Altesse, of which Noël and his son David have 4 ha. The Dupasquiers work with very ripe fruit, using as many non-interventionist strategies as they can: natural yeast, minimal sulphur, no forced fermentations (including malolactic – about half the wines do it), and bottling with a light filtration only (which their restaurant customers demand). All of the white wines are superb. They include a deliciously sappy Jacquère; a startlingly distinctive Chardonnay produced from 50-year-old vines, and packed with soft honey and nuts; a rich, chewy, satisfying Roussette de Savoie (from the less well-sited Altesse parcels) and the memorable *cru* Roussette de Savoie Marestel, from the mid-slope vineyards: voluptuous, rich, and perfumed, with touches of pear, ginger, cream, spice, and honey, and a finish that almost hints at sake. This wine ages gracefully, acquiring nuttiness with the years. Of the reds, the light yet balanced Pinot Noir (grown on gravel parcels) is probably the most successful; Mondeuse is less rich, ripe and resonant here than in the Combe de Savoie sector.

Michel Grisard
73250 Fréterive, Tel: 04 79 28 54 09, Fax: 04 79 71 41 36

This Fréterive grower, Savoie's leading exponent of biodynamics, has separated his domain from that of his father and brother Jean-Pierre and Philippe Grisard, though the family remain on good terms and there are some shared vinification facilities. The two specialities here are fine, well-crafted Mondeuse, including a Prestige version in the best vintages; and lingering, close-grained Roussette de Savoie made with Burgundian techniques (including barrel-fermentation).

Marjorie Guinet et Bernard Rondeau
01640 Boyeux-St-Jérôme, Tel: 04 74 37 12 34, Fax: 04 74 37 12 34

Sweet pink sparkling Cerdon from Bugey, made by the *méthode ancestrale*, will never trouble Laurent-Perrier or Krug, but if you want to find out what fun it can be, try the Guinet-Rondeau version.

de l'Idylle *see* Tiollier

Jacquin
73170 Jongieux, Tel: 04 79 44 02 35, Fax: 04 79 44 02 35

Edmond Jacquin's domain in Jongieux is a good source for the haunting richness of its Roussette *cru* Marestel, as well as for one of the deepest, best-balanced red wines (based on Mondeuse) of this quiet, half-hidden area. Even the Gamay has plenty of perfumed interest at this constantly reliable property.

Lucey
73170 Lucey, Tel: 04 79 44 01 00

The imposing medieval Château de Lucey belongs to the founder of Casino supermarkets, Charles Defforey. Its small, 3.5-ha parcel of vines, however, was only planted (with Roussette and Mondeuse) in the early 1990s, and Defforey put a young Burgundian, Michaël Grosjean, in charge. The style is very much based on the burgundy model, with extensive use of wood, *bâtonnage*, and long *élevage*: untypical but impressive.

Magnin
73800 Arbin, Tel: 04 79 84 12 12, Fax: 04 79 84 40 92

This 5.5-ha domain, run with great passion by Louis Magnin and his wife Béatrice, has now uprooted almost all of its Jacquère to concentrate more fully on Mondeuse-based red wines (4 ha) and a little Bergeron and Altesse. The Chignin-Bergeron smells of mountain plants and is full of firm apricot fruit; the Altesse-based Roussette is bigger and chunkier, with flavours of honey and nougat. The Mondeuse Tradition is a light, zippy wine; the Vieilles Vignes *cuvée* is richer and meatier; while the new oak-aged "La Brova", bottled without fining or filtration, is textured and deep, its vivid fruits resonant and long, like a distant mountain cousin of St-Emilion.

Star rating system used on producer spreads   ✪ Very good wine   ✪✪ Excellent wine   ✪✪✪ Great wine

Mollex

01420 Seyssel, Tel: 04 50 56 12 20, Fax: 04 50 56 17 29

Good Seyssel producer whose concentrated, dense still white Seyssel and crisp, refined sparkling wines (given long lees-ageing) are both among the best of this Rhône-side AOC.

André et Michel Quénard ✪

73800 Chignin, Tel: 04 79 28 12 75, Fax: 04 79 28 09 60

This 21-ha domain is run with great application by Michel Quénard; his smiling and energetic father André may be retired, but continues to play a major role. Their vineyards lie on the southern (and sunnier) parts of the Combe de Savoie sector, and include some fine, steep scree slopes of perfect exposure used for Bergeron, Altesse, and, especially where the soils become richer in clay, Mondeuse. The less well-sited slopes are used for Jacquère, Gamay, and Pinot Noir. The whole range is reliable. Outstanding wines include the Vieilles Vignes *cuvée* of Chignin (made from 40-year-old Jacquère): a wine whose discreet pear fruit and salty, sappy depths would put most Abymes and Apremont to shame; and the exotic, haunting, peachy Roussette de Savoie, picked on the edge of over-ripeness, giving it a fugitive resemblance to a mountainside Pinot Gris or even Viognier. The Chignin-Bergeron is graceful and concentrated, again packed with soft, ripe fruits, while there is also a single-parcel selection called Les Terraces in which these fruits are bolstered an arresting mineral backbone and extra luscious richness. With time, these Bergerons acquire notes of nougat, limeflower, and honey, while the fruits metamorphose from pear and apple to apricot and peach. The Mondeuse, here, begins with lots of lively red fruit, and modulates towards mineral and liquorice notes with time; there is a fine Vieilles Vignes *cuvée* from the high-sited Coteaux de Torméry.

Jean-Pierre et Jean-François Quénard

73800 Chignin, Tel: 04 79 28 08 29, Fax: 04 79 28 18 92

Jean-François Quénard's studies in Bordeaux and California have given him perspectives few others in Savoie have; he uses these to good effect in a well-crafted and accessible range. The domain lies in one of the most beautiful spots in Chignin, next to the Tour Villard (part of the ruined Château de Chignin); the best wines are a ripe and rounded Chignin-Bergeron Vieilles Vignes, and the Jacquère-based Anne de Biguerne Chignin.

Raymond Quénard

73800 Chignin, Tel: 04 79 28 01 46, Fax: 04 79 28 16 78

Raymond Quénard has handed over 5 ha of his 7.5 ha domain to his son Pascal, whose domain is run separately. The Chignin Vieilles Vignes remains a compelling example of Jacquère, based as it is on 100-year-old vines; Raymond Quénard's Bergeron, too, is based on old vines (70 years old this time), and has more of the white-flower perfume so typical of this variety in the Rhône than most of its Savoyard rivals. Quénard has experimented with oak unsuccessfully, concluding that "you lose out both in terms of varietal character and local style".

de Ripaille

74200 Thonon-les-Bains, Tel: 04 50 71 75 12, Fax: 04 50 71 72 55

This magnificent (and much-visited) property occupies a sun-baked tongue of gravels protruding into Lac Léman (Lake Geneva); its 21 ha of vineyards constitute the totality of the *cru* Ripaille which, with the nearby AOC of Crépy and the other Vin de Savoie *crus* of Marignan and Marin, mark France's most serious attempt to get to grips with the Chasselas grape variety. French Canadian Paule Necker, having married owner Louis Necker, now makes the wines, all of which go through the malolactic, Swiss-style, to produce wines which smell of butter yet taste crisply tantalizingly, almost biscuity with mineral salts, hinting enigmatically at mango, dried peach, grilled almond, and lime blossom. Evian water is bottled just down the road, and there is something no less tonic, no less refreshing in the wine of this beautiful spot.

Les Rocailles *see* Pierre Boniface

Tiollier

73800 Cruet, Tel: 04 79 84 30 58

The high-sited domain of Philippe and François Tiollier is the *cru* leader for the Combe de Savoie zone of Cruet, and the brothers produce a wide range. Jacquère, here, is invigorating, with more substance than it tends to have from the flatter "ruins" across the valley; in addition to the vintage-dated varietal, there is also the non-vintage, young-vine Cuvée l'Orangerie, crisply thirst-slaking; and the deeper, more sinewy Vieilles Vignes *cuvée*. The Roussette Cuvée Emilie is rich and succulent; the light Mondeuse, though, is a disappointment.

Trosset

73800 Arbin, Tel: 04 79 84 30 99, Fax: 04 79 84 30 99

Fleshy, pungent Mondeuse reds are made at this small domain in the Combe de Savoie *cru* of Arbin.

Vullien

73250 Fréterive, Tel: 04 79 28 61 58, Fax: 04 79 28 69 37

Another of the pack of good growers based around Fréterive at the eastern end of the Combe de Savoie zone, the Vulliens produce typically subtle, soft, and almondy Roussette.

The Rhône Valley

Rising in the East The Rhône, a watery narrative linking two deeply dissimilar wine families, is the story of the moment. Drinkers increasingly accustomed to perfumed seduction, glycerous textures and the warmth of ripe fruit are taking to Rhône wines with unprecedented enthusiasm.

It's March; there are grey skies to the south of Lyon. The city's fringe is industrial, chemical, electrical. This part of France resembles a human wrist: the lines of communication (veins, arteries, sinews) are jumbled together in prominent fleshlessness here. The TGV route clamps itself to the river, while motorways duck and weave about both; power lines tramp the hills. Every town hereabouts now has its spawn of cheap matchbox hotels, ready to gather in the fugitives of the night. Agriculture, as always in France, tries to compete, though it does so here in an industrial kind of way: greenhouses fill the valley floor, forcing the pace, screening growth from view.

There is an alternative, but at this chilly, leafless time of year you might not notice, and especially not if your gaze is fixed hurriedly north or south, blurring the intermediate world. There are high hills at the valley's edge here. Look carefully in March, and you will see little pegs of life forming a mycelium on them, waiting for the return of light and warmth. Vine stumps – but not only vines; a forest of stakes, too, forming a thick superstructure for the vines. (Germany's Mosel wine-growers would not feel out of place. They too need to stake every vine on their tumbling slate slopes.)

The hills are stony: a rubble of granite; lumps of muddy quartz; boulders, above all, of softer schist. As you climb, you skid. Few roots hold these minerals in place, which is why men have built terraces here. The paste of minerals is moist and dark. Mist, on this cool morning, slides through breaks in the hill line.

At the top of the slopes, the soil grows richer. Beehives steal into the vines. And then the country opens up, leaving the restless, monochrome valley behind. Fruit trees begin to infiltrate the vines, and eventually take over completely. They shake their blossom at the sky. The vines slumber on.

The second image is as saturated with colour as the first is drained of it. It is now September; harvest time. As in March, a mist opens the day, but here in the southern Rhône it is filled with rose and ochre, thinning as the sunlight grows. The pickers move through it with the time-dissolving stealth of ghosts. They might have spent the night in bed; they might, though, have just stepped from a fresco.

To my eye, there are no more beautiful vineyards in France than those of the southern Rhône. Culturally, we are already in Provence, a land of tangy speech, of lavender, of old songs. It's not hard, in the intricate walled village of Séguret, to lose five hundred years; to read a few lines of Villon and clothe them with the flesh of today – a sparrow's rustle, a creaking door, a voice through an open window. The sun burns brightly here, and seems to set slowly, drawing colour osmotically out of the landscape as it does so: orange stones, grey cypresses, white houses, silver olives, green vines, purple lavender.

The landscape here romps away for miles. Peak succeeds peak; underneath each, a village of impractical, medieval glory, cascading with flowers. At night, their stones glow; they become places of peace, moths, and warm dust. The vineyards themselves lie below the villages, ample and rangy. Barely a hundred metres passes without a rise, a dip, a fold in the landscape; the vines perch on a gentle chaos of terraces. In few parts of France, indeed, do vineyards succeed and follow each other as ubiquitously as here, gathered like wheatstraw into a bale of appellations that tumble down towards the heart of Provence. The river is miles away, all but forgotten. The higher you go, the more ubiquitous becomes the scrubby, crackling, all-enfolding woodland with its pines, its stunted oaks, its sprawling thyme.

These two scenes are, if you like, Rhônes apart. The river itself is born in the cold wet mud of an Alpine glacier and tumbles into France via the spectacular mountainside vineyards of the Valais. The first wine region it meets is Savoie (Seyssel grows on its banks) after which it meanders west towards Lyon. Once the river has settled for the south, it flows swiftly, eddying down a narrow corridor (this is not a river to fall into) between Vienne and Valence before making more leisurely progress towards Avignon's famous bridge and the delta country beyond. The thread of vineyards clinging to the river's northern section is called the Côtes du Rhône Septentrionales; the

blanket of vineyards surrounding the river further south is the Côtes du Rhône Méridionales. They have, in truth, little in common.

Beaujolais knocks on Lyon's door from the north, and Côte Rôtie does so from the south. Compare these two wines. They are closer than you would think. Both Côte de Brouilly and Côte Rôtie are born in quartz, in schist, in granite; they have a glinting, acidic hardness to them. Crystal-rooted Syrah and Gamay are tenors (indeed Gamay might be called a counter-tenor); limestone-anchored Grenache and Mourvèdre are Russian basses. Let's mix more metaphors. Rich, fat, lazy Châteauneuf, with its belly-fat tannins, is as different from Côte Rôtie as a bulldog is from a greyhound. Part of Côte Rôtie's classicism is the fact that it teeters fragrantly along the edge of ripeness; part of Châteauneuf-du-Pape's appeal is that it is built on a roar of alcohol, a roar that only the skilled can tame and taper into melodic grace. The northern Rhône is highly vintage-sensitive, and wines from cool or rainy years can be a trial to drink; wines from the south are much more forgiving, less marked by inclemency.

Another profound difference is that of size. The northern Rhône, in this respect as in others, continues the Burgundy theme. It is not unusual for growers to make a living from three or four hectares here. Look at a map of the *lieux-dits* of Côte Rôtie or Hermitage, and you'll see the same kind of subdivisions of these hills as you find in Burgundy,

"I don't like the word 'winemaker'. It doesn't mean anything to me. You make shoes; you don't make wine. I prefer to call myself a 'wine helper'. You help wine to make itself. That's how I consider my job. That's the way to keep a low profile – under nature, under the climate, under the fruit. Wine is a great gift. We didn't make it. It took 2,000 years. We are just here for a while."

LOUIS BARRUOL

◀ *A long day of sunshine ahead for Tavel: unsurprisingly the town's orange-hued rosé is the world's headiest. Siestas should be scheduled.*

Michel Chapoutier

Brash, outspoken, and confident, the young Michel Chapoutier has taken what was a somnolent and under-performing négociant company and galvanized it into creating some of France's greatest modern-day wines. Chapoutier has been helped in this quest by his quieter elder brother Marc, as well as the talented oenologist Albéric Mazoyer; his inspiration, tellingly, came in part from the Alsace avant-garde of Jean-Michel Deiss and André Ostertag and in part from two local masters, Marcel Guigal and Gérard Chave. The company's eighty-five ha (210 acres) of Rhône Valley vineyards have been converted to biodynamics, as have its properties in other regions; yields for its greatest wines (like the white Hermitage Cuvée de l'Orée) are as low as those of Leroy in Burgundy. The wines have the same intense concentration — and killer prices. In contrast to Leroy, though, the huge Chapoutier range also includes cheaper alternatives: there are wider perspectives here, as the use of Braille labels proves.

Yves Cuilleron

Passion, enthusiasm, and energy bubbles from the optimistic Yves Cuilleron — and for all that he was originally going to pursue a career in industrial draftsmanship. It was only when a childless uncle's vines seemed as if they would have to be sold that he reprogrammed his career, and from 3.5 ha (8.6 acres) back in 1987 he now has no less than thirty ha (seventy-four acres). Not only that, but as one of the three partners in the Vins de Vienne enterprise he has recreated a "lost" vineyard to the north of Côte Rôtie, crafted some beautiful micro-négociant wines, and, latterly, set off to explore a great terroir in the Languedoc. (The Vins de Vienne team now has four ha (ten acres) of prime schist vineyard in Faugères, though it will be a year or two before the newly planted vines -- Syrah, Grenache, and Mourvèdre -- are fruiting.) The Sotanum vineyards above Vienne are, in some ways, typical of Cuilleron, who both travels widely and is also fascinated by the history of wine. "I love to get hold of old books," he says, "and find out how things were done in the past. In the northern Rhône, some people talk about de-leafing and the use of new oak as modern developments, but I've found references to both in books which date from a century ago. There is very little which is truly new." He has proved this in his own work with his sweet, late-harvest Condrieu wines: another nod to history. Cuilleron claims he has enough work in hand to keep him occupied for the next year or two. May be he has. But then again....

Rémi Klein

It's hard not to enjoy life in the company of Rémi Klein. His distant family roots may lie in Alsace, but the Kleins' North African background (his father left Morocco in the early 1960s) seems to have left more of a stamp on this easygoing and friendly wine-grower and his enthusiastic wife Ouahi. There's nothing laissez-faire about his work, though: one reason why the Domaine de Réméjeanne makes such beautiful Côtes du Rhône wines is that Klein is constantly researching, trialling, and testing new techniques and approaches. "I like to move forward by little stages," he says, describing himself as an evoluatif; much of his "evolutionary" work has been done with other key local wine-growing friends like André Romero, Marcel Richaud, and Denis Alary. Lengthy extractions, micro-oxygenation (he visited Patrick Ducournau personally to learn about the technique), lees work, malolactic in barrique: all of these are practiced here, but always thoughtfully and never routinely. The result is a range of wines that, like their creator, combine finesse with friendliness.

Louis Barruol

The Château de St-Cosme can trace its history back to the year Columbus made his celebrated expedition to America, though the cellar itself includes stone tanks first lowered into position by Roman wine-growers (and identified by Barruol's uncle, a well-known local archaeologist). The softly spoken Louis took over his maternal family domain in 1992, its 500th anniversary year, but by 1997, he says, he felt "his brain getting smaller and smaller" – so he decided to set off up and down the valley to craft a range of micro-négociant wines as well as continuing to make St-Cosme. The relationships he has built as he's done this, he says, have been as "enriching" as the wines he's created: "I work with young people, old people, easy people, difficult people. My aim is to create wines that express their origin above all; for me that is the value of wine. To be reminded of a place on earth, especially when you are 10,000 kilometres away, is something fantastic for me. But there's no doubt that human methods, and human beings, are very important as well."

Winemaking according to Guigal

"The first aim is to harvest very ripe grapes. Not over-ripe, but just at the moment when the grape is about to become over-ripe. You know there are two maturities: the one that can be measured in terms of sugar and acidity, and then the maturity of the stems. Cabernet Sauvignon stems never really ripen; Syrah stems, by contrast, can ripen completely." Guigal has a machine that enables him to use between one per cent and one hundred per cent stems – and he goes to both extremes. And then? "I put the grapes in a tank, and the laws of physics tell me that whatever is solid will float, and whatever is liquid will sink. My job is to make everything good in the solid part migrate to the liquid part. I can do this by washing the juice over the cap; another technique is to push the cap down into the must twice a day. It has been done that way with feet in our part of the world for 2,400 years; but there are problems. In three weeks or a month you will lose two degrees of alcohol. You won't get many people telling you that, especially not Burgundians, because it means they have to chaptalize. That's the first thing. The second thing is that you lose aroma. For Syrah, it is best to keep as much aroma as you can. This is why we have invented a closed vat within which we can pump down the cap." Guigal always uses wild yeasts; fermentation is initially at between 28°C and 30°C (82.4°F and 86°F), rising to 33°C or 34°C (91.4°F or 93.2°F). As fermentation finishes, when there is about five g/l sugar left in the wine, the bunches are pressed. The press wine is immediately mixed with the free run, and fermentation finishes in cask at about 18°C (64.4°F). There is much speculation as to how Guigal is able to age his red Syrah in cask for forty-two months without the wine becoming woody. The stems, the press wine, finishing alcoholic fermentation and carrying out malolactic fermentation in wood, he says, are the keys. "The malo in wood helps give the wines roundness and volume. If I destemmed everything and didn't add the press wine, it would dry out."

Guigal admits to having a passion for élevage: "It's the house obsession. Why does extended élevage interest us? It's like cheese. Everyone knows that with ripening you can give it an extra dimension. Wine's the same." Rigour is needed, since "we work with very low acidities. Looking after a wine with high acidity is very easy; anyone could do it. When acidity is low and the pH is high, by contrast, you have to top up two or three times a week, you have to use top quality wood, you have to work meticulously – and we like that." He also points out that long ageing means that he has to interfere very little with his wine: two or three rackings in the first year, one or two in the second, none in the third. He uses low levels of sulphur, and no fining or filtering. "Long ageing means we can sleep quietly."

---

the only difference between them being that they haven't been hierarchized and given the sanction of a confetti of different AOCs.

And the south? In an average year, the southern Côtes du Rhône will produce over twenty-five times as much wine as the northern Côtes du Rhône. If Hermitage, Côte Rôtie, and its neighbours resemble Burgundy, the southern Côtes du Rhône is a kind of aspirant Bordeaux. Just as the Rhône itself fans out and dissolves, via the wan swamp of the Carmargue, into the bright blue of the Mediterranean, so the thin trickle of granite vineyards which constitute the northern Côtes du Rhône billow out into the ample, russet, sun-soaked stonefields of the south.

In the context of the New France, the northern and the southern Rhône each have a different story to tell. Let's begin in the north.

Given the quality of Côte Rôtie, of Hermitage, of Condrieu today, it is hard to imagine that these were once struggling wines dealt bitter blows by phylloxera, and the frosts of 1956. The future seemed, in the early 1960s, to lie in the more productive viticulture of the plains. Why should wine-growers slide on the treacherous granite rubble filling little ledges above the river, remake their terrace walls every ten years, and carry medieval basketfuls of grapes on their backs uphill fifteen metres (fifty feet) to a tiny roadway in the late twentieth century? Why should they persist with a difficult, shy-cropping, and degenerate grape variety like Viognier? Life could be much easier.

Many did, indeed, abandon their vineyards; a few, like the now-celebrated Georges Vernay in Condrieu, persisted. At present, history is repaying their persistence with interest. The propitiousness of these vineyards is evident; some consider Côte Rôtie, indeed, to be one of the most perfect vineyard sites anywhere in the world. Moreover the slow recovery of past vineyard glories continues. Three northern Rhône growers – Yves Cuilleron, François Villard, and Pierre Gaillard – have set about clearing and replanting the slopes that once produced the "Vins de Vienne", at Seyssuel. "We'd always known that those terraces existed, and we often drove past them," says François Villard. "Then one day Yves said 'What about replanting Seyssuel?', as casually as one might say 'Do you want a cigarette?' In fact, we think it might prove to be one of the greatest sites in the whole region." Some seven ha (17.3 acres) have been replanted so far, six (14.8) with Syrah (the soil is schist rather than granite) and one (2.47) with Viognier.

The wine, called Sotanum, is a Vins de Pays des Collines Rhodanniennes, since the entire vineyard had been abandoned by the time the local AOC regulations were formulated.

In other appellations, too, the same work of slow, patient vineyard recovery is well underway. St-Joseph, in particular, is an enormous vineyard area with many pockets of great potential: it marks the southerly continuation of the same granite slopes that gave birth to Côte Rôtie and Condrieu, though the fact that the river has stopped flowing southwest and now flows south means that the fundamental aspect (east rather than southeast) is less propitious. This makes it the perfect area, in other words, to set about elaborating a *cru* system (la Côte Ste-Epine, opposite Hermitage, is already well-known). Crozes-Hermitage is not dissimilar.

The temper of those working the vineyards, as these details suggest, is in many ways also Burgundian in outlook. Parcels, pockets, morsels, *crus*: great northern Rhône wine-growers are all on a quest for particularity of terroir. The grape variety mix, having a near-burgundian simplicity to it, provides few distractions from this quest. For red wines, Syrah stars, producing reds of perfume and of slender vivacity. (The idea that Hermitage and even Cornas are heavy, thumping, gutsy wines is utterly mistaken.) Whites, meanwhile, fall into two camps. Viognier from Condrieu and elsewhere (generally though not ubiquitously unwooded) rivals Alsace Gewurztraminer as the world's most exotically and lusciously scented white wine, while the combination of Marsanne and Roussanne (often wooded) gives whites of structure, sinew – and fat. As in Burgundy, négociants (Chapoutier, Jaboulet, and the outstanding Guigal) rival the greatest growers. As in Burgundy, too, wine "finishers" are beginning to make their appearance (Dominique Laurent has his Rhône partner in Michel Tardieu, who in turn is inspiring the younger generation like Louis Barruol), and the Vins de Vienne team has spotted the opening for a quick-footed, lightweight micro-négociant business. The work of consultant Jean-Luc Colombo is no less influential.

The southern Rhône, by contrast, faces different challenges, and offers a different sort of appeal to drinkers. The problems of the past here were not physical difficulties leading to total eclipse, as at Condrieu or Seyssuel; but the dead-end of low quality, low price, and high volume. Cooperatives continue to dominate here (there are 114

in the Rhône Valley); many of today's outstanding growers were *co-opérants* just ten years ago. There is still an ocean of indifferent wine on offer in the Côtes du Rhône, much of it sold *en vrac*, *à la tireuse* (out of the end of a pump nozzle). The mentality that lies behind this kind of production, too, is still much in evidence. In the middle of a recent harvest, between Tavel and Bagnols, I saw two trailers full of grapes sitting in the open under a burning sun while their drivers took a couple of hours' lunch break. Maybe there was another explanation; maybe someone's wife was giving birth prematurely, and needed a lift to hospital. But maybe, too, they just didn't realize that leaving a trailerful of fresh grapes under the midday sun mattered that much. Or maybe they didn't care.

The southern Rhône's leading wine-growers are no less interested in terroir than their counterparts in the north, though the site-research has not advanced to the same degree here yet. Châteauneuf-du-Pape is the only AOC where internal *crus* are likely to play a prominent role in the coming decade, and even there the wide spectrum of grape variety possibilities (thirteen, famously, in theory) means that the game of difference can be played with less objective finality than it can in regions where a single variety holds sway. The Hommage à Jacques Perrin from Beaucastel is certainly very different to Rayas, but is one comparing the difference between *crus* or the difference between a wine built preponderantly on low-yielding, old-vine Mourvèdre and one founded on low-yielding, old-vine Grenache? Growers like Yves Gras, Louis Barruol, Serge Férigoule, and André Roméro are proving just how outstanding Gigondas, Vacqueyras, and Rasteau can be, but another dozen or two vintages and a community of rival growers of similar expertise are needed before the differences between these wine-growing sites begin to watermark the wines.

Despite all these differences, the Rhône is one of France's most flourishing wine regions at present. It is well administered and promoted, with only Châteauneuf-du-Pape riven by the pointless internal divisions which characterize so many other French regions. Its greatest wines are now beginning to be as sought-after internationally as the finest clarets and burgundies (though they are as yet available in smaller quantities, and their labels are often ugly). There is a growing sense, too, that the supporting cast in the Rhône will, in the long run, furnish ordinary, everyday wine of greater volume and appeal than

Burgundy can ever manage, and of greater consistency and stylistic affability than Bordeaux. The region's future seems bright.

Motorway madness

"We learnt about it a bit late, but it's often like that," said Marcel Guigal. "I immediately went up to Paris and asked my INAO colleagues to vote a resolution against the motorway. I was surprised by my colleagues. They did more than vote; they came down to Ampuis to protest, high and loud, in the vineyards. Côte Rôtie is a museum appellation; it's the oldest, the steepest in France. It's a rare patrimony; we have to protect it."

So what was at issue? As I stressed at the beginning of this chapter, the vineyards of the northern Rhône overlook the most significant transport bottleneck in France. The vines don't complain; the inhabitants of Lyon do. At present, the A6/A7 motorway thunders right through the middle of town and then on past Vienne and Ampuis. Lyon's former mayor, Raymond Barre, wanted to shift the motorway further west, well clear of the city; this would have the further advantage, according to prefect Michel Besse, of bringing the Saône-Rhône axis closer to the *département* of the Loire (and thereby linking France's two most important river valleys). But guess where the new route of the motorway will rejoin the old? At Ampuis.

"If this project goes ahead," says Besse, "no AOC parcel, even those unplanted at present, will be touched." Maybe not; but the fact is that the new motorway will tunnel right underneath Côte Rôtie, emerging at the site of a quarry between the parcels of Côte Rozier, La Landonne, and Neve. AOC president Gilles Barge says that the quarry zone should have been classified as AOC back in 1964, but wasn't since the region was relatively obscure back then. Moreover there is the problem of the pollution from the tunnel and motorway, and the damage to the vines' roots, which rummage deep into the rock of the hillside. The wine-growers of Côte Rôtie remain adamantly opposed to the motorway route, despite Besse's reassurances. "For the moment," says Guigal, "we're talking. If we have to take to the streets later, we will."

The Adventure of the Land

Before we tackle soils and slopes, a word about wind. In this corridor, it never stops. And you only have to look at the stooped trees and shrubs of the hilltops to know which way it blows: from north to south. This is the penetrating mistral: cooling yet health-bringing, chasing away the fugs and fungal diseases which can beset Bordeaux or Champagne, yet at its most demonic, enough to tear tender young shoots clean off the vines. Most of the Rhône's greatest vineyards, thus, are in sites which offer some protection from the worst blows, hidden behind bluffs and shoulders of rock, or in the lee of a turn in the river. The mistral is most acute in the northern Rhône where it is funnelled along the river along with all the human traffic – which is yet another reason why this vineyard area is cooler than its latitude and its popular image might suggest. The continental climate of the northern Rhône is a third. The influence of the Mediterranean – lazy days, warm nights – begins only beneath Valence and Montélimar.

The recently replanted vineyards of Vienne (which lie on the east rather than the west bank of the river) still have to prove themselves before they emerge from beneath the dark and often promising cloak of the Vin de Pays des Collines Rhodaniennes. When and if they do, they will be the Rhône region's most northerly *cru*. Until then, this is **Côte Rôtie**'s distinction. The river here carves its way through a rift of crystalline rocks (these form the eastern edge, in fact, of the Massif Central, France's hard old heart). The 200 ha (494 acres) of vineyards are all found on the steeper, western side of the river, thanks to the south or southeastern exposure they get there; the less steep eastern bank of the river looks northwest, and is therefore wholly unsuited to vines. The hazardously steep slopes of this sunflower-like vineyard (or, as the French name has it, "roasted slope") were first eyed by the Romans, who knew immediately that it was worth sending slaves to terrace them and plant them with vines. They're formed of mica-rich schist and gneiss, and are internally subdivided into a wide number of *crus*, most of whose names are not yet used on labels (though this may soon change as interest in this fine AOC grows). What you will see on labels, by contrast, is mention of the Côte Brune and the Côte Blonde. This reference is to the central part of the AOC, above Ampuis, where the best wines of all are to be found: Brune lies to the northeast, its dark schists exclusively planted with Syrah; Blonde lies to the southwest, and its lighter, greyer soils contain more Viognier (up to fifteen per cent of this white grape if wished).

South of Côte Rôtie lies the ninety-eight-ha (242-acre) AOC of **Condrieu**, for Viognier-based whites only. Why the sudden shift from red wine to white? There is a subtle modulation of soil type: granite and sand takes over from the mica-schist. The honey blonde, in other words, turns platinum. More importantly, perhaps, is the marked southern swing of the river, which means that south-facing slopes become much rarer here than in Côte Rôtie; growers hunt them down on the northern halves of side valleys. Whatever happens here, at any rate, pleases Viognier enormously: this grape is now widely travelled both in France and abroad, but no one has yet come close to replicating the aromatic power and glycerous fullness it achieves on these tiny (and all-too-collapsible) terraces. Great Condrieu makes a plausible case to be both the world's most powerfully scented white wine, and its most sensually overwhelming (its textural richness matches its embedded scents). Everything, though, comes at a price, and in Condrieu's case, it is that the wine loses all this charm and appeal within about three years. Whatever

the local producers say, the fact is that Condrieu is the only one of France's unquestionably great wines that is best drunk as soon as the bottles come into your possession. (Unsurprisingly, therefore, there is more in restaurant cellars than underneath private homes.) Within Condrieu is the little four-ha (9.9-acre) **Château Grillet**, the Rhône's answer to the Loire Valley's Coulée de Serrant. This property is sited in an unusual, Bandol-like amphitheatre; it should produce the most show-stopping Viognier of all. Under present ownership, the bottled evidence fails to make the vineyard's case.

St-Joseph overlaps with the southern end of Condrieu, and then runs for some sixty km (thirty-seven miles) down to Cornas, peeking across the river at Hermitage and Crozes-Hermitage as it does so. This long and spindly chain of opportunist vineyards (870 ha/2,150 acres planted) is perhaps the most intriguing AOC in the northern Rhône, and may eventually produce wines to rival the best of both Côte Rôtie and Cornas. Not, though, without much hard work in reclaiming the most suitable sites (as in Condrieu, the south-facing slopes of side valleys) from the hungry scrub. Once again, the soils are preponderantly granite and schist, giving Syrah-based reds of great purity and intensity. The whites, however, mark a contrast with vineyards further north: they are based on Marsanne and Roussanne, rather than Viognier, and resemble those of Crozes-Hermitage but with added finesse. Laudably, this is an AOC whose growers have decided to reduce rather than expand its boundaries, ensuring that the vines don't spread too far on to the flat plateau land at the top of the hill where they don't belong. The ninety-one ha (225 acres) of **Cornas** might almost be seen as the greatest (and most southerly) *cru* of St-Joseph – or, if you prefer, as a kind of giant red version of Château Grillet. It is, in other words, another amphitheatrical basin stretching back from the river just northwest of Valence. The soils, however, are a relatively fine granitic sand and clay with a seasoning of limestone scree (unique in the northern Rhône) from the nearby Arlettes hills, and the sheltered, saucepan-like site is a hot one – hence the sturdiness of the Syrah-based wines produced here. ("Sturdy", as ever, should be placed in the northern Rhône context: even Cornas, with its tumbling tannins, will seem fragrant and fugitive alongside a stone-dense Bandol or Coteaux du Languedoc.) Jean-Luc Colombo, who knows Cornas as well as anyone, describes it as "an island of the south in the north".

Meanwhile, across the river, **Hermitage** has happened. It's a spectacular hill, as those who take the TGV between Paris and Avignon will know (motorway travellers miss out on this view, but are compensated with a tour of Crozes-Hermitage instead). As with Côte Rôtie, Hermitage's 134 ha (330 acres) are unofficially subdivided into a number of different *crus*; in contrast to Côte Rôtie, these are based on quite markedly different soil and rock types. The western end of the hill (generally thought to be the best) is granite; its mineral origins in the Massif Central reveal that it's a misplaced lump of the porphyry normally found across the river. (Les Bessards is the name to look out for here.) The eastern side of the hill is formed chiefly of river deposits cemented together and piled high, seasoned with clay and loess (Méal, Chante Alouette, Rocoules, and others). All well and good, but it's chiefly the fact that they sit one hundred metres (300 feet) above the river, perfectly exposed to the summer sun swinging like a crane jib across the sky, that make the vines so happy to be here. Syrah (above all on the granite) produces grand, authoritative yet

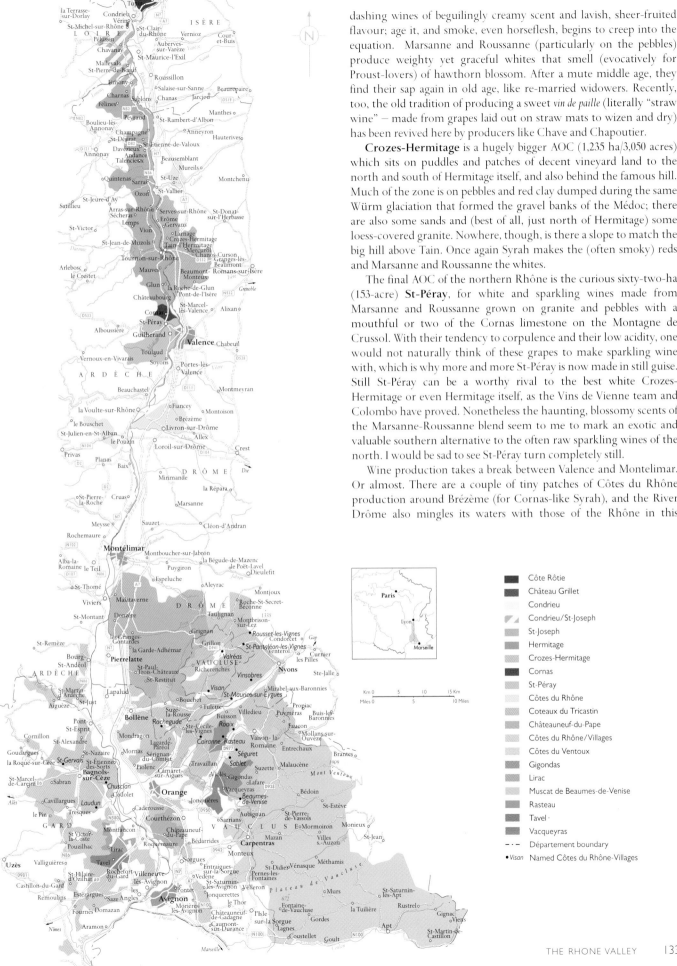

dashing wines of beguilingly creamy scent and lavish, sheer-fruited flavour; age it, and smoke, even horseflesh, begins to creep into the equation. Marsanne and Roussanne (particularly on the pebbles) produce weighty yet graceful whites that smell (evocatively for Proust-lovers) of hawthorn blossom. After a mute middle age, they find their sap again in old age, like re-married widowers. Recently, too, the old tradition of producing a sweet *vin de paille* (literally "straw wine" – made from grapes laid out on straw mats to wizen and dry) has been revived here by producers like Chave and Chapoutier.

Crozes-Hermitage is a hugely bigger AOC (1,235 ha/3,050 acres) which sits on puddles and patches of decent vineyard land to the north and south of Hermitage itself, and also behind the famous hill. Much of the zone is on pebbles and red clay dumped during the same Würm glaciation that formed the gravel banks of the Médoc; there are also some sands and (best of all, just north of Hermitage) some loess-covered granite. Nowhere, though, is there a slope to match the big hill above Tain. Once again Syrah makes the (often smoky) reds and Marsanne and Roussanne the whites.

The final AOC of the northern Rhône is the curious sixty-two-ha (153-acre) **St-Péray**, for white and sparkling wines made from Marsanne and Roussanne grown on granite and pebbles with a mouthful or two of the Cornas limestone on the Montagne de Crussol. With their tendency to corpulence and their low acidity, one would not naturally think of these grapes to make sparkling wine with, which is why more and more St-Péray is now made in still guise. Still St-Péray can be a worthy rival to the best white Crozes-Hermitage or even Hermitage itself, as the Vins de Vienne team and Colombo have proved. Nonetheless the haunting, blossomy scents of the Marsanne-Roussanne blend seem to me to mark an exotic and valuable southern alternative to the often raw sparkling wines of the north. I would be sad to see St-Péray turn completely still.

Wine production takes a break between Valence and Montelimar. Or almost. There are a couple of tiny patches of Côtes du Rhône production around Brézème (for Cornas-like Syrah), and the River Drôme also mingles its waters with those of the Rhône in this

Côte Rôtie
Château Grillet
Condrieu
Condrieu/St-Joseph
St-Joseph
Hermitage
Crozes-Hermitage
Cornas
St-Péray
Côtes du Rhône
Coteaux du Tricastin
Châteauneuf-du-Pape
Côtes du Rhône/Villages
Côtes du Ventoux
Gigondas
Lirac
Muscat de Beaumes-de-Venise
Rasteau
Tavel ·
Vacqueyras
- - - Département boundary
• *Visan* Named Côtes du Rhône-Villages

▲ *Gigondas is sited higher than Châteauneuf-du-Pape; you can taste as much in its brisker, more assertive style of tannins.*

viticultural intermission. The banks of the Drôme, further upriver, are home to another member of France's little club of unusual sparkling wines: **Clairette de Die**. This wine has a long, artisanal history not dissimilar to that of Gaillac's *méthode rurale* sparkler: these were prickle-fresh wines whose fermentation had stopped naturally. Since the early 1990s, however, this name has been used to refer exclusively to semi-sweet, Muscat-based sparkling wines with low alcohol levels (ironically, since it means that Clairette is a grape variety now no longer used in Clairette de Die). Ordinary dry sparkling wine genuinely made from Clairette grapes is called **Crémant de Die**. There are also two deeply obscure AOCs for still wine here: **Coteaux de Die** (from the same zone as Clairette de Die) and **Châtillon en Diois** (from a slightly higher, cooler neighbouring zone).

The southern Rhône, roly-poly young brother to the beanpole of the North, has a much more diverse patchwork of appellations than its elder sibling. Grenache takes over from Syrah; the sun burns more brightly; vineyard densities thin from as much as 10,000 vines per ha to as few as 3,000. The all-embracing AOC is of course **Côtes du Rhône** itself – France's second biggest after AOC Bordeaux. As with Bordeaux, the principle is that all the most promising vineyard land within this huge, 42,000-ha (103,740-acre) area is entitled to a superior AOC from among those outlined below. Côtes du Rhône on its own generally means an easygoing, lightly coloured red wine with the soft sweetness of the Grenache grape running through it, or a fullish white wine of muted personality. The grape variety spectrum is wide here, however, which means that a Syrah-based, Mourvèdre-based, or Viognier-based surprise is always possible. And indeed not infrequently a talented grower with a parcel or two of promising, well-exposed land can produce a strawberry-red Côtes du Rhône of such perfume and grace that, for a happy moment or two, you are certain that it is the finest wine in France. It is an AOC of potential surprises.

Promotion has been available since the mid-1960s in the form of the **Côtes du Rhône-Villages** appellation. There are two sorts of *village*: ninety-six communes have the right to use the AOC as it stands, and sixteen of the best villages have the further right to append their own name to the AOC. (Note that there are more vineyards in the sixteen named communes – over 4,000 ha/9,880 acres – than in the eighty unnamed communes, where just 3,000 ha/7,410 acres are cultivated.)

The overall Villages AOC resembles a pair of lungs of a mildly assymetrical sort, the right ventricle being larger than the left. On the right (the east), you'll find an amphitheatre of villages crouching beneath Mont Ventoux, their circularity interrupted by the ivory dagger of the Dentelles de Montmirail. Small rivers, somnolent in summer and springing briefly into urgent life in the winter, trickle down from the Alps, steal across the stonefields, and lose themselves in the much-managed embrace of the Rhône. On the left (the west), there is a less geometrically coherent group of villages lounging beneath the uplands of the Ardèche; beneath them, the sandier flatlands of the Rhône Gardoise drift south towards Nîmes. Huge heterogeneity, in other words – though there are some outstanding vineyard sites within this vast area. Almost the only soil you can be certain not to find here is the acidic, crystalline glitter so typical of the northern Rhône; dust-raising limestone, sand, marl, and pebbles (either loose or as conglomerate) are all more typical here. The heights vary from forty metres (130 feet) at Laudun to around 300 metres (985 feet) for the higher villages like Rousset or St-Pantaléon. Steep slopes are rare, but most of the vineyards are lifted off the floor of the river valley and set on gentle hills. There are significant climatic differences between the villages of the southeast like Cairanne, Rasteau, Séguret, Sablet, and Beaumes de Venise, and those of the northeast like Vinsobres, Valréas, and St-Maurice. The southern villages are, in Louis Barruol's words, "Grenache-land; Syrah works much better in the northern villages. They form, if you like, the northern Rhône of the south." Were you disposed to bet on the next villages to achieve *cru* status, my tips would be for the marl and pebble hot spots of Cairanne and Rasteau, where the wines of the best producers are already entirely competitive with Gigondas and Vacqueyras. But remember that the AOCs of **Rasteau** and **Muscat de**

Vines at the top of Côte Rôtie's steep slopes soak up the sunshine. Some consider this the world's most propitious vineyard site. ▶

Beaumes-de-Venise are for sweet, fortified Vins Doux Naturels — grapey and wheat-gold in the latter case, dark red and Grenache-rich for the former (though paler versions theoretically exist).

It's hard, verbal association being what it is, not to assume that **Gigondas** is a gigantic wine (although etymologically the name evokes joviality rather than raw size). The red marls, sands, and pebbles on a limestone base which sunbathe beneath the Dentelles offer a snug bed for Grenache to ripen lavishly in here, though the fact that the vineyards climb up to 400 metres (1,310 feet), and that a number of them are north-facing, mean that the wine rarely has the bass-note fat of lower-lying Châteauneuf. The tannins are brisker and more piercing here, too. As always with Grenache-dominated wines, too, don't assume that pale colours mean light wine; Gigondas is always heady. **Vacqueyras** is a newcomer among the *crus* (since 1990 only), but its 1,100 ha (2,720 acres) are already proving themselves with wines that are both a little softer and a little fleshier than neighbouring Gigondas (the vineyards are slightly lower and flatter, though the geological mix is similar; the Grenache here ripens up to two weeks earlier than at Gigondas). They can, too, have a stone-fruit scentedness that sometimes eludes the rather fiercer, more fiery, more spicy Gigondas.

And so to the southern Rhône's iconic vineyard area: **Châteauneuf-du-Pape**. It's big (3,200 ha/7,900 acres), gently contoured, and hot; and so visually tempting a spectacle is offered by the giant rolled boulders with which some of its vineyards are carpeted that the world assumes that these *galets roulés* are "the secret". If only it were so simple. Many vineyards in Châteauneuf (including Rayas, one of the very greatest) do not have monster surface pebbles in them at all, but sand and fine stones; and where the river-rolled boulders do exist (to the east of the AOC), they are much less important to the vines than the clay and iron-rich sands that lie beneath. (The Bruniers of Vieux Télégraphe reckon that there is a year's moisture stored in the clay beneath the stones in the great plateau parcel of La Crau.) There is gravel, finally, in the southernmost part of the AOC, between Fortia and the river. The wide range of permitted grape varieties (thirteen in all) also adds to the diversity of the AOC. Despite the low maximum yield (35 hl/ha) and the fact that mechanical harvesting is outlawed here, there is some feebly flavoured Châteauneuf on sale, hidden inside the grandiose bottle the AOC has adopted. Some unskilfully vinified Châteauneuf, too, can be bothersomely hot and strong, like an energetic infant of adult size waving its arms and bawling. The best, by contrast, is unique within French wine: a grandly soft wine, deliciously burdened with sweetness and spice like a cedar whose branches are laden with snow. It's a wine ready to welcome drinkers at two or three years, yet its flurry of goosedown tannins and meaty extract will hold two decades at bay. White Châteauneuf is no less heady than red, and sometimes merely that. The best, though, is a glycerous, apricot-fruited wine of such richness that one is surprised to find, as the flavours tumble like autumn leaves after you swallow, that it is in fact dry.

The two *crus* that lie to the west of the river are **Lirac** and **Tavel**. The geology here is not greatly dissimilar to that of Châteauneuf-du-Pape, though it is sand and limestone slabs rather than clay which lies beneath rolled pebbles. For this reason, these vineyards are dryer and more open still. Lirac and, especially, Tavel have for long made a

speciality of strong and heady rosé (indeed the Tavel AOC is for rosé alone). It may be saleable, but red wines produced here offer beefier delights, as the best domains of Lirac have conclusively proved.

All of the regions we have described so far constitute what we might call the heart of the southern Rhône. Clustered around this central area are six satellite AOCs: Côtes du Vivarais and Coteaux du Tricastin to the north; Côtes du Ventoux, Côtes du Lubéron, and Coteaux du Pierrevert to the southeast; and finally Costières de Nîmes to the southwest.

Côtes du Vivarais, which only became an AOC in 1999, is sited to each side of the Ardèche gorge to the west of the Rhône, created by the river gobbling deeply into the pure limestone here. These are fresh, light, simple upland wines growing on clay over chalk in rather cooler, damper conditions than are typical further south. **Coteaux du Tricastin**, by contrast, across the Rhône on its east side, is a mistral-prone vineyard area actually better known for its truffle oaks than its relatively light, dilute, often rather stringy red wines. Syrah stands a better chance than Grenache of ripening fully in both Vivarais and Tricastin, though the AOC regulations oddly require a blend. The **Côtes du Ventoux** has two quite distinct vineyard areas: the large horseshoe of vineyards behind Carpentras, snug under the bulk of Mont Ventoux; and the long corridor of vines on the northern side of the Apt Valley. Although we have moved well to the south of villages like Rasteau and Gigondas by now, there remains a kind of mountain coolness and freshness to the red wines of Ventoux. Nights can be cold here, and the mountain brings more rain than the open Rhône Valley will ever see. **Côtes du Lubéron** is another large, oyster-shell-shaped vineyard area in the heart of Provence south of Apt; its vineyards are found to both the north and the south of the Montagne du Lubéron. It's an area of great natural beauty, which the wines (grown on the perhaps unpropitious terroir of gravel over sand) always seem to struggle to match. White wines, indeed, have often been more impressive in general here than the slight, vaguely tangy reds, which is one reason why a white wine specialist like Jean-Marie Guffens was attracted to the area. Finally, further east from the Rhône and indeed well on the way to the Alps, is **Coteaux de Pierrevert**. This is a kind of easterly continuation of the Côtes du Lubéron. Like the Lubéron, its best wines are lighter, elegant, fresher, and more Provençal than the sweet, heady classics of the Rhône, grown once again in a landscape of lavender-dark beauty.

The opposite is true of the **Costières de Nîmes**. We are, by now, in Rhône delta country, half-way into Languedoc already, and the landscape is flat and dreary, expiring as if exhausted at the marshy, reedy sea edge of the Petite Carmargue. The quality of the red wines here, by contrast, can be startlingly good, with an authoritative stamp of character to them, and some of the soft, beefy flesh and power of better-than-ordinary Châteauneuf. Both Grenache and Mourvèdre can ripen well here, which is not true of either Ventoux or Lubéron, though interestingly most producers favour lushly fruited Syrah with plenty of bottom to it. In terroir terms, Costières de Nîmes is not dissimilar to the sand and gravel sectors of Châteauneuf, and it also reminds me of the sands and gravels in some parts of the promising Languedoc zone of La Méjanelle, also favoured for gutsy reds. It's low (150 metres/490 feet at the highest spot) and mostly covered with a gigantic carpet of river-rolled small quartz pebbles up to ten metres (thirty-three feet) deep in places, seasoned with sands and occasionally clearing to leave patches of red clay.

Rhône Flak

The cooperative challenge

Many of the cooperatives in the southern part of the valley have not yet made the mental and practical leap required for quality wine production. These, indeed, are some of the poorest cooperative-produced wines in France. Until the worst co-ops begin to emulate the best (like Cave de Clairmonts in the north or the Caves of Rasteau or Cairanne in the south), the basic Côtes du Rhône appellation will not be able to capitalize on its extraordinarily broad potential appeal.

Overdue *crus*

INAO should recognize the "best of the rest" among the leading named Côtes du Rhône Villages (like Cairanne and Rasteau) by giving them a red wine AOC of their own. This would provide the incentive for growers to further refine the stamp of terroir in their wines.

No more prestige, please

In some southern Rhône appellations (especially Châteauneuf-du-Pape and Gigondas) there has been a mania for *cuvées de prestige* (special selections of the total crop) over the last few years. It's understandable, and in some ways laudable: the best of these wines from the 1998 and 2000 vintages are certainly among the greatest southern Rhône wines ever vinified, and it is a privilege to be alive at this moment and to drink them. Yet it is equally certain that these selections are depleting and impoverishing the quality of the "ordinary" *cuvée*, the wine which bears the name of the property alone.

There are two possible solutions. One is the Bordeaux model: the property's main wine becomes the *grand vin* or the *cuvée de prestige* itself, with less good wine being used for a "second wine" sold under a different name. This requires much discipline, but will pay long-term dividends, and is probably best suited to areas like the southern Rhône where multi-variety blends are the norm. It is the route taken by Vieux Télégraphe among others. The other is the northern Rhône model, whereby the property's main wine is a blend, and other, smaller production wines are *cru* or single-parcel bottlings (which may or may not be better than the blend). This works well in single-variety areas, but is less suited to areas where greatness is always created by a little judicious varietal (and thus site) blending.

Serine: disappearing genes

Many winemakers believe that the greatest vine material in Côte Rôtie is not Syrah, but a closely related, autochthonous variety which they call Serine. "It always gives you very low yields of thirty-five hl/ha at most," François Villard told me, "and the berries are always small." Alain Paret, confirming that Serine's natural yield is around half that of Syrah, points out that while Syrah has round grapes, Serine has elongated, olive-like grapes. Its stems, however, according to Villard, mature much more regularly than the stems of Syrah ever do – which is why destemming (Guigal excepted) is now almost ubiquitous. "It's the ancient clone of Syrah," according to Louis Barruol. "It usually has less weight and less colour than the Syrah, but a lot more complexity, a lot more expression, a lot more finesse. That is where that classic smoke comes from, that fat, that bacon. It's dangerous because when it doesn't work it can be terrible. But when it works, it's the best thing you can grow in Côte Rôtie." It is, though, becoming rarer with every year: Barruol reckons at most twenty per cent of the vineyard area is now planted with Serine. Why? "All these plants are ill," sighs Louis Barruol. "They have diseases. You have to replant Serine every thirty years. So the nurserymen have given up with them. They just sell clones of Syrah." Villard confirms that the only way to ensure the survival of Serine is for growers to carry out their own selections and propagations; this is a difficult, time-consuming, and only intermittently successful activity. Yet the very idea that we might lose prized traits of genetic diversity within the bloodline of one of the most popular grapes in the world seems incredible.

▼ *The Romans knew well that vines loved open hillsides – so it's small wonder that they pioneered Côte Rôtie.*

▼ *The sun seems to have roasted the Champet family's hoarding as effectively as it does the vineyards behind.*

Rhône: People

Alary

84290 Cairanne, Tel: 04 90 30 82 32, Fax: 04 90 30 74 71

The quietly spoken Denis Alary and his father Daniel run this 25-ha Cairanne domain with great thoughtfulness. The Font d'Estevenas white (65% Roussanne with 20% Viognier and 10% Clairette) is a clever blend, the Clairette bringing a little acidity to add edge to the hawthorne and orange blossom of the other two grapes. The red Font d'Estevenas (40% Syrah, 60% Grenache) was, at least in 1999, one of those wines that made an almost unanswerable case for Cairanne's elevation to *cru* status: aromatic scents of spiced beef, and intense, dry-herb flavours of bay, cypress, and thyme. An old vine (65-year) parcel of Grenache provides the mouthfilling La Jean de Verde *cuvée*.

Thierry Allemand ✪

07130 Cornas, Tel: 04 75 81 06 50, Fax: 04 75 81 06 50

A mere 3.4 ha here, alas, which means that Allemand's dense, fragrant, tight-grained Cornas Chaillot and top *cuvée* Reynard, aged without new oak, are little seen. A part of Allemand's domain is old-vine stock from Noël Verset; this, combined with a supremely gentle approach to extraction, gives the Allemand wines their hallmark depth and finesse within this sometimes rough-shod AOC.

Aphillanthes

84850 Travaillan, Tel: 04 90 37 25 99, Fax: 04 90 37 25 99

Small production but excellent quality from this "villages" domain based in Travaillan. The Cuvée Trois Cépages brings together equal quantities of Grenache, Syrah, and Mourvèdre; the Cuvée du Galets ups the Grenache; while the showstopping Cuvée du Cros is a pure Syrah.

Gilles Barge

69420 Ampuis, Tel: 04 74 56 13 90, Fax: 04 74 56 10 98

Straightforward Côte Rôtie made the traditional way (all the stems are included, and old wood is used) by the appellation president. In ripe vintages the Cuvée du Plessy makes a thumpingly good case for Côte Rôtie in sturdy mood.

Beaucastel ✪

84350 Courthézon, Tel: 04 90 70 41 00, Fax: 04 90 70 41 19

With 100 ha under vine on both sides of the motorway in the northeast of the Châteauneuf appellation, this grand estate both looks and feels like the Latour or the Lafite of its AOC. Run by brothers François and Jean-Pierre Perrin, Beaucastel is for some drinkers the greatest Châteauneuf, while others consider the bottle variation of its wines unacceptable, and their ageing trajectory eccentric. Beaucastel was a pioneer of organic cultivation as early as the 1970s, under François and Jean-Pierre's father Jacques Perrin; it was Jacques Perrin, too, who "perfected" the technique used here of heating the grapes briefly on arrival at the winery to 80°C before allowing them to cool for fermentation. (It is, apparently, only the skin which reaches 80°C; the heat does not last long enough to bring all of the grape pulp up to this temperature.) The benefits are said to include better extraction, slower fermentation, and an anti-oxidizing effect, enabling the Perrins to use very low levels of sulphur subsequently. What is undeniable is that this is a violent intervention on what should be first class raw materials, and as such is perplexing at an estate whose philosophy is otherwise geared towards absolute respect for nature's gifts. This is one of the few estates that uses the complete spectrum of 13 grape varieties, and Mourvèdre, too, is more important here than elsewhere, with around 30% in the estate red, and up to 70% in the Hommage à Jacques Perrin, (produced in the best years only). The Perrins also rate the black grape Counoise highly, and value the obscure Muscardin and Vaccarèse, too. Grenache, by contrast, whose sweet unction is in many ways the dominant note in most Châteauneuf, is reined back here to a mere 30%. Large wooden *foudres* are used throughout, with the exception of the small Syrah component which undergoes some barrique-ageing. And the results? Great Beaucastel is a fine and unique wine, combining savoury depths with unusually vivid fruit for Châteauneuf and elegant, subtler spices, too, than are found in many of its peer wines. With age, it can take on becoming meat, coffee, tobacco, truffle, and incense notes (the Havana-scented 1989 is paradigmatic). The Hommage à Jacques Perrin is deeper, more herbal, more acidic, more tannic, almost frighteningly intense in youth, requiring many years to reach a digestible balance. Too many bottles of red Beaucastel, however, prove to be in a reduced, stinky state when opened, perhaps because of the very low sulphur levels used. (Historically, too, gamey brettanomyces characters have played a leading role in Beaucastel's profile in certain vintages.) It seems to me that the Beaucastel style swings and veers more widely from year to year than the Châteauneuf norm (though vintage variation was one problem that the grape-heating technique was meant to overcome). This unpredictability also applies to the Coudoulet de Beaucastel, the Côtes du Rhône produced from just across the motorway, though at its best this is a red of captivating articulacy and pure-fruited impact. The white Châteauneuf, by contrast, is a remarkably consistent wine, nutty and succulent, and the *spéciale cuvée* Roussanne Vieilles Vignes seems to me to be the greatest of all the wines produced at this estate: fatty yet vivid and shapely, apricot-saturated yet full of mineral complexities.

Beaurenard

84231 Châteauneuf-du-Pape, Tel 04 90 83 71 79, Fax: 04 90 83 78 06

This large, 50-ha Châteauneuf domain owned and run by Paul, Daniel, and Frédéric Coulon produces pure, sweet-fruited wines in the modern idiom but with plenty of old-fashioned depth. The Boisrenard luxury *cuvée* (Grenache with a little Mourvèdre from vines at least 65 years old) sees up to 20% new barriques, and is a deep, gutsy yet subtle wine full of southern forest warmth.

Bois de Boursan

84230 Châteauneuf-du-Pape, Tel: 04 90 83 51 73, Fax: 04 90 83 52 77

The fastidious Jean-Paul Versino is one Châteauneuf producer whose special *cuvée* (Cuvée des Félix) does not seem to result in a minor-key "classique": both are fat, glowing red wines, while the Félix seems to have extra texture and depth. There are just 13 ha here, and everything (down to bottling without filtration) is done to maximize quality.

Henri Bonneau

84230 Châteauneuf-du-Pape, Tel: 04 90 78 13 81

I have tried to visit Châteauneuf's Henri Bonneau but was told that "Monsieur Bonneau doesn't receive English journalists". Those who know him well describe unforgettable visits to one of the Rhône's great right-wing eccentrics (perhaps the greatest, now that Jacques Reynaud is no more). Nor, alas, have I been able to taste Bonneau's wines, though once again those with long experience of these speak of them in reverential terms. They come from a small, Grenache-dominated holding of under 6 ha on La Crau plus a morsel near Courthézon, and total production is a mere 1,500 cases. The special *cuvées*, Cuvée Marie Beurrier and the legendary Réserve des Celestins, are considered appellation landmarks; among the greatest of all Châteauneufs. I will keep trying.

Star rating system used on producer spreads   ✪ Very good wine   ✪✪ Excellent wine   ✪✪✪ Great wine

Bosquet des Papes ✪

84230 Châteauneuf-du-Pape, Tel: 04 90 83 72 33, Fax: 04 90 83 50 52

Don't be put off by the folksy labels; this 27-ha estate produces Grenache-rich Châteauneuf of length, elegance, and tantalising herb and *garrigue* scents. The ordinary *cuvée* can be dry; try to get hold of the endearingly named "Cuvée Essentiellement Grenache" (luscious, sweet, and full) and the dense, concentrated Cuvée Chante Le Merle Vieilles Vignes.

La Bouïssière ✪

84190 Gigondas, Tel: 04 90 65 87 91, Fax: 04 90 65 82 16

This 8-ha domain is one of the new stars of Gigondas. The village wine has been a magnificent bottle in both 1998 and 1999: dark, sweetly meaty, and packed with dense extract which contrives to avoid the dryness and pinched heat that traps some other Gigondas producers. The selection La Font de Tonin mingles Grenache with Mourvèdre to provide even more depth, power, and surging black fruit; it wears its new oak lightly. Brothers Gilles and Thierry Faravel are a force to be reckoned with.

Brusset

84290 Cairanne, Tel 04 90 30 82 16, Fax: 04 90 30 73 31

Huge 87-ha domain run by father Daniel and son Laurent Brusset, with vines in four appellations. The basic wines in this extensive range are pleasant, well-made, unspectacular; the Cairanne Coteaux des Travers has a juicy, carbonic maceration quality. The top wines, by contrast, are outstanding, made with low yields, wild yeasts, cool pre-fermentation maceration, "*robopigeage*", use of lees, and no filtration: all the cossetting a wine could want, in other words. The Cairanne Vendanges Chabrille (made with over-ripened 80-year-old Grenache and Syrah) is packed with spice yet balanced by lively natural acidity, while the Cairanne Hommage à André Brusset, a new prestige *cuvée* beginning with the 1999 vintage, is dense and tight-sewn, needing time for the components to settle and meld into articulacy. There are two Gigondas *cuvées*: the gutsy, slightly raw Grand Montmirail (around 70-75% Grenache, 20-25% Syrah, and 5-10% Cinsault), dusty with tannin and white pepper; and the Hauts de Montmirail (55-60% Grenache plus around 25% Mourvèdre and 15% Syrah), a dark, oak-aged *cuvée* with greater sweetness and fleshier fruit characters.

du Caillou

84350 Courthézon, Tel: 04 90 70 73 05, Fax: 04 90 70 76 47

The tragic death of Jean-Denis Vacheron in March 2002 means that his widow Sylvie continues the work of her father Claude Pouizin in making this improved Châteauneuf, though this is one of those domains where two special *cuvées* can leave the "normal" *cuvée* tasting disappointingly simple and eviscerated. Les Quartz is one of the two selections; perhaps it's auto-suggestion, but this *cuvée* really does seem to taste tautly mineral, and less broad-bellied than the AOC norm. The Réserve Clos du Caillou, meanwhile, is a powerful, dense Châteauneuf (including 40% Mourvèdre) packed with smoke and fire.

Les Cailloux ✪

84230 Châteauneuf-du-Pape, Tel: 04 90 83 73 20, Fax: 04 90 83 77 24

André Brunel is another Châteauneuf producer lucky enough to have parcels of 100-year-old Grenache among his holdings (the main part of which lies near Mont Redon); these are used for the magnificent Cuvée Centenaire, a wine of such depth and richness that the 1998 took over a year to complete its fermentation. The "ordinary" Châteauneuf is outstandingly good, too (indeed price-wise it offers better value): real hedonist's wine, full of notes and allusions (tobacco, cep, coffee, herbs) and marked by succulent drinkability.

la Canorgue

84480 Bonnieux, Tel: 04 90 75 81 01, Fax: 04 90 75 82 98

This 30-ha property in Lubéron owned by Jean-Pierre Margan is already organic, and part biodynamic. Its south-facing slopes are warmer than many in the AOC (Mourvèdre does ripen here, according to Margan), and the Syrah-dominated red wine (balanced with 20% Grenache and

10% Mourvèdre) is one of the best structured and most articulate wines of the AOC, with bright, pure herb-cherry scents and flavours.

du Cayron

84190 Gigondas, Tel: 04 90 65 87 46, Fax: 04 90 65 88 81

Michel Faraud's 15-ha domain is one of the best sources for Gigondas which combines, as few do, weight with finesse. The wines are bottled without fining or filtration after a slow *élevage*.

M Chapoutier ✪✪

26600 Tain-l'Hermitage, Tel: 04 75 08 28 65, Fax: 04 75 08 81 70

Until the mid-1980s, the wines of Chapoutier were often disappointing. Since 1987, when Michel and Marc Chapoutier took over from their father Max, the improvement has been dramatic: almost all of the wines have acquired more concentration and depth. Indeed initially they acquired too much depth, a kind of manic depth based on late-harvest frenzy and forests of new oak; in the late 1990s and early years of the new century Michel Chapoutier has been looking for more finesse, and sometimes (as in 1999) harvesting a little earlier than his fellow growers. All of the domains (over 80 ha up and down the valley as a whole) owned by Chapoutier have been converted, or are in conversion, to biodynamics, making this the first of France's great merchant houses to follow leading private domains down this route. Chapoutier claims he is now beginning to reap the full benefits of this, with, for example, the 1999s ripening earlier than in neighbouring vineyards due to biodynamics and his fastidiously low yields.

The domain wines account for 30% of production, and négociant wines for 70%, the former often being markedly superior to the latter. In St-Joseph, for example, the Domaine Les Granits white (a barrel-fermented pure Marsanne) is excitingly rich and ripe, brimming with apricot; the Deschants négociant equivalent, by contrast, is merely a pleasant, aniseed-soft white. The contrast between the red versions of these wines is even more marked. Much the same is true of the comparison between the négociant Crozes-Hermitage Les Meysonniers and the domain version Les Varonnières. The "prestige" philosophy is one which has been wholeheartedly embraced by the Chapoutier brothers, with "luxury" *cuvées* (made from parcels of old vines) for almost all of the wines coming from the greatest *crus*. These can be superb; indeed a wine like the 1999 Côte Rôtie La Mordorée, with its pure-fruited intensity and richness, challenges its rivals for the "wine of the vintage" crown. This selectivity has also enabled Chapoutier to be more successful than either Guigal or Jaboulet in Châteauneuf-du-Pape, with the superb Barbe Rac (made from a small parcel of centenarian Grenache) and the fine, single-vineyard Croix de Bois. But in Hermitage (or Ermitage, as the Chapoutiers prefer for their *cru* wines), the existence of the three magnificent luxury *cuvées* Méal (the swishest), Pavillon (the most powerful), and l'Ermite (the most mineral) is to the detriment of La Sizeranne, which is a good but seldom great wine. Even the luxuriousness itself can be overdone, as in the lavishly oaked white Ermitage l'Orée, a pure Marsanne from Le Méal which is sometimes smothered (as it was during the lesser vintages of the early 1990s) under the oppressive embrace of wood. There are, nonetheless, some great successes here, and the house style is laudably concentrated, exuberant, and expressive, and at best an intoxicating stylistic whirlwind. The top wines are terrifyingly expensive, but some of the southern Rhône selections (in particular the generous reds from Rasteau, Vinsobres, and Valréas) provide excellent value.

La Charbonnière

84230 Châteauneuf-du-Pape, Tel: 04 90 83 74 59, Fax: 04 90 83 53 46

Much-improved Châteauneuf-du-Pape estate run by Michel Maret; unusually for this appellation, which in general has some of the ugliest labels in France, the bottle is a handsome one. The "*classique*" is sound but unexceptional; as so often here, the excitement begins with the *cuvées de prestige*. There are three of these: Mourre de Perdrix is a fiery wine from a parcel near Courthézon, given a cunning 10% of new wood; the Vieilles Vignes (with its attractive orange peel scents and exuberant, glycerous fruit) is an old-vine selection; while Les Hautes Brusqières is a selected Grenache-Syrah blend of great concentration.

J-L Chave ✪✪
26600 Tain l'Hermitage, Tel: 04 75 07 42 11, Fax: 04 75 07 47 34

The Chave line, which stretches back astonishingly to 1481, could make a fair claim to be France's winemaking royal family: in no other of France's great terroirs is the largest individual landholder so deeply rooted in time and place, so supremely competent, and so modest a custodian of the insights and the craftsmanship of the past. Gérard Chave has been in charge for the past few decades; he is now joined by his intelligent and articulate son Jean-Louis (the first son of every second generation is called Jean-Louis); standards at this domain, which produces only Hermitage, a little St-Joseph and the Côtes du Rhône Mon Coeur, have never been higher. Chave, like Vieux Télégraphe in the south, has no truck with the modern fashion for picking the eyes out of the crop to make *cru* wines or luxury *cuvées*. (Or almost no truck: he has, not without misgivings, made just 200 cases or so of a luscious, oaked Cuvée Cathelin, based on his parcel in Bessards, in 1990, 1991, 1995, and 1998; there is a *vin de paille*, too.) In most years, thus, all of the fine raw materials (whites from Roucoules, Maison Blanche, l'Ermite, and Péleat; reds from Roucoules, Beaumes, Dionnières, l'Ermite, Méal, and a 2-ha helping of the granitic Bessards) are blended into the two plain Hermitage *cuvées*; any wine which is not worthy of the Chave name (about 20% of the crop after most vintages) is sold in bulk to négociants who, one imagines, fight for the privilege. Chave's white (usually around 80% Marsanne and 20% Roussanne) is a wine of burgundian complexities: scented, honey-laden, and charming in early youth, then needing 10 or more years to open up again and reveal its mineral depths. The red is less showy than some of its rivals, particularly in youth (no new oak here, though well-armed with extract, tannin, and ripe fruit), but as the years progress it reveals more nuances than any, and is a model of controlled grandeur. Low yields, late picking (the chestnuts, Gérard says, must fall first), minimum handling, no filtering: no tricks. Other than the existence of Hermitage itself.

Jean-Louis Chave
07300 Mauves, Tel: 04 75 08 24 63, Fax: 04 75 07 14 21

Gérard Chave's son Jean-Louis is putting his skills and energy to good use with a micro-négociant range of northern Rhône wines (especially St-Joseph) which stamp the tongue with the smoky minerality unique to Syrah grown in this area.

Chèze
07340 Limony, Tel: 04 75 34 02 88, Fax: 04 75 34 13 25

Vivid and urbane St-Joseph made by one of Jean-Luc Colombo's Rhône Vignobles group, Louis Chèze. The red Cuvée Prestige de Caroline (Louis' daughter) is pungent and deep.

La Citadelle
84560 Ménerbes, Tel: 04 90 72 41 58, Fax: 04 90 72 41 59

This 40-ha Lubéron estate, belonging to *Emmanuelle* film producer Yves Rousset-Rouard, is internally varied (65 parcels, 14 grape varieties, and 4 soil types) and run with great ambition (alongside an extensive corkscrew museum). There are three ranges: the young-vine Chataîgnier, the classic Domaine wines, and the selected Cuvée du Gouverneur red. The first two feature bright, juicy, lively reds and soft whites; the Gouverneur is deeper, softer, and spicier.

Cave des Clairmonts
26600 Beaumont-Monteaux, Tel: 04 75 84 61 91, Fax: 04 75 84 56 98

This small, family-run cooperative owns 86 ha scattered throughout Crozes-Hermitage, and usually produces some of the best value in the appellation: perfumed, lunging, and energetic wines.

Auguste Clape ✪
07130 Cornas, Tel: 04 75 40 33 64, Fax: 04 75 81 01 98

There are now three generations working together at this celebrated 11-ha Cornas domain: Auguste, his son Pierre and youngster Olivier. Chewy, spicy, tight-sewn, compressed, long-lasting: these "typical" attributes of Cornas can be hard to find in some producers' wines, but not in that of Clape (who gives his

crop twice-daily *pigeage*). Young-vine fruit is now used for the Renaissance *cuvée*, while there is also an exuberant Côtes du Rhône and pure-Syrah Vin des Amis.

Clos des Papes
84230 Châteauneuf-du-Pape, Tel: 04 90 83 70 13, Fax: 04 90 83 50 87

Despite its name, this estate actually draws fruit from 18 separate parcels covering about 32 ha scattered about Châteauneuf (one of which is the Clos des Papes). Paul Avril and his Burgundy-trained son Vincent produce a consistently powerful, intense yet soft-textured Châteauneuf aged in large wood and bottled without filtration.

Clos Petite Bellane
84600 Valréas, Tel: 04 90 35 16 45, Fax: 04 90 35 19 27

Pétrus-trained Thierry Sansot is producing beautifully perfumed, silky wines which perfectly exemplify the elegance of Valréas. Les Echalas is a pure Syrah, offering a warm southern echo of a fine St-Joseph.

Clusel-Roch ✪
69420 Ampuis, Tel: 04 74 56 15 95, Fax: 04 74 56 19 74

Tiny 4-ha domain run by Gilbert Clusel and Brigitte Roch with great sense of finesse. The top Côte Rôtie *cuvée*, Les Grandes Places, is one of those exclusively planted with the low-yielding Serine Syrah (see page 137), which helps to create a wine of impressive length, earthy textures, and spicy, animal classicism. The ordinary Côte Rôtie can have (as in 1999) devastating purity in youth: an essence of perfumed red fruits, almost more burgundian than burgundy itself. Time draws smoke mysteriously into the wine.

du Colombier
26600 Tain-l'Hermitage, Tel: 04 75 07 44 07, Fax: 04 75 07 41 43

The wines of Florent Viale's 15-ha domain prove, as few others do, just how different Syrah grown in the northern Rhône is from Syrah grown elsewhere: pure fruit perfumes lick from them like flames from a bonfire, while the wines themselves are vivid and quenching. The Hermitage here is vastly more structured than the Crozes (including the top *cuvée* Gaby), proving the hill's case.

Jean-Luc Colombo ✪
07130 Cornas, Tel: 04 75 40 24 47, Fax: 04 75 40 16 49

With his love of new oak, emphasis on cellar cleanliness, and his belief in total destemming, Marseille-born oenologist Jean-Luc Colombo upset traditionalists when he first arrived in the village he chose to make his base, Cornas. Yet what his style has done is help place the wines of this lesser-known northern Rhône *cru* in the international context they merit, to render them intelligible to those who found their harsh acidity, dry tannins, and occasional lack of hygiene simply too much to take in the past. He is also an astute marketeer. His work with great individualists like Georges Vernay, Jean-Michel Gerin, and Yves Cuilleron shows that, like Michel Rolland, he is a sensitive rather than a dictatorial consultant; his own carefully measured and crafted wines, meanwhile, are essential references for their AOCs, though they rarely seem to me to be supreme expressions of terroir. (The work of this self-proclaimed "hyperactive epicure" in other regions like Roussillon, Languedoc, and Provence is perhaps one reason why his own wines have not always been as consistent as one would wish. Colombo says he drives 60,000 km a year.) There are three Cornas wines from Colombo's own 17-ha domain of which the old-vine, single-parcel Les Ruchets is the finest: dark, resin-scented, with explosive fruit, stealthy spice, meaty extract, and firm backing tannins. La Louvée (another parcel) and the blended Terres Brûlées are lighter and more lyrical, while the young-vines Collines de Laure is a declassified Cornas, offering excellent value in good vintages. The super-spicy Cornas Les Méjeans, finally, is from purchased fruit. The St-Péray La Belle de Mai is blossom-cream scented, lively, and graceful – one of the best of the new generation (and one of the few to be 100% Roussanne). Like Michel Tardieu, he has also worked successfully with cooperatives such as the Cave de Cairanne (for its Cuvée Antique, Cuvée Temptation, and Réserve des Voconces).

Pierre Coursodon
07300 Mauves, Tel: 04 75 08 18 29, Fax: 04 75 08 75 72

Jérôme Coursodon is one of those who can see that the future of an appellation as extraordinary as St-Joseph has to be that of *cru* research, and accordingly you will find a wide range of single-parcel wines here (together with lavish but intelligent use of new wood). Not everything, naturally, is wholly successful, but a wine like the 1999 L'Olivaie, an old-vines parcel of plunging depth, should act as an alarm clock for other producers.

Yves Cuilleron ✪
42410 Chavanay, Tel: 04 74 87 02 37, Fax: 04 74 87 05 62

The talented, dynamic yet affable Yves Cuilleron is one of the great northern Rhône success stories of the last few years. He took over his uncle Antoine's vines in 1987, just as they were about to be sold for want of a successor, and rapidly made an enviable reputation for himself. (His 1994 Chaillets Vieilles Vignes was the wine which first showed me that Viognier grown in Condrieu can even eclipse the greatest Alsace Gewurztraminers for sheer, overwhelming, and improbable aromatic power.) There are three Condrieu *cuvées*: the richly fruited La Petite Côte, the heavily scented Chaillets Vieilles Vignes (from 35- to 55-year-old vines) and a semi-sweet Les Eguets harvested (as Cuilleron says his grandfather did) around All Saints' Day. The white St-Joseph Le Lombard can be excellent, too, albeit in a very different style to the Condrieu *cuvées* (hawthorn rather than gardenia); and Cuilleron's Les Serines red St-Joseph can on occasion outclass his Côte Rôtie Bassenon and Terres Sombres, which are sometimes too oak-dominated (though both were superbly balanced in 1999). (See also Vins de Vienne.)

Delas ✪
07302 Tournon-sur-Rhône, Tel: 04 75 08 60 30, Fax: 04 75 08 53 67

Until recently, this négociant and domain-owner (12 ha of its own), owned by Champagne house Deutz (itself owned by Roederer), produced traditional, often impressively forceful but rather harsh and austere wines. Under the direction of Jacques Grange, a Chapoutier-trained Burgundian, the wines have acquired a richer fruit style with much greater sensual appeal. New oak was once frowned on here; it is now used enthusiastically. Destemming, pre-fermentation macerations, lees contact, and the abandonment of fining and filtration have all filled the wines out towards amplitude. A Chapoutier-style proliferation of *cuvées* makes it a difficult range to summarize succinctly, but look out for the best mid-range wines like the crunchy, palate-rousing St-Joseph Cuvée François de Tournon or the finely drawn Crozes-Hermitage Clos St-Georges if you want value. For absolute quality, the Hermitage Les Bessards or the Côte Rôtie La Landonne are striding giants of explosive depth and power. There is much in between, and past disappointments should not put you off re-trying: the Côte Rôtie Chante Perdrix, for example, which was in the past a modest wine produced in 30,000 bottle quantities is now much improved at between 5,000 and 10,000 bottles. The whites lag behind the reds.

de Deurre
26110 Vinsobres, Tel: 04 75 27 62 66, Fax: 04 75 27 67 24

Hubert Valayer left the unimpressive Vinsobres cooperative in 1987 – and also left the country for a couple of years, partly to get experience in California and Australia (with Penfolds) and partly because his plans for a private cellar ran into depressing bureaucratic problems (the local mayor was also the cooperative president). The wines of his 46-ha domain are steadily improving (Valayer works with consultant Jean-Luc Colombo). They include a spicy Villages from St-Maurice and a fresh fruited Vinsobres Fûts de Chêne. The Cuvée des Oliviers is a savoury, bay-perfumed Syrah, while best of all is the pure-Grenache Cuvée des Rabasses: powerful and rich, packed with chocolate and earth.

Pierre Dumazet ✪
07340 Limony, Tel: 04 75 34 03 01, Fax: 04 75 34 14 01

Pierre Dumazet is an artist of Viognier whose brilliant Côtes du Rhône Cuvée du Zénith (from vines just outside the Condrieu AOC) would cost twice as much if vines grew just a little further up the hill, and whose Vin du Pays Viognier, too, is made with absolute seriousness and instinctive skill. The secret, he claims, is low yields. Dumazet is adept at walking the tightrope between the exotic aromatic extravagances for which Condrieu is so famous while maintaining a lemony tautness often overlooked in appreciations of the wine, but which is vital in making it a success – as countless flabby Viogniers grown further south prove. His Côte Fournet is an old-vine (70 years+) masterpiece.

Entrefaux
26600 Chanos-Curson, Tel: 04 75 07 33 38, Fax: 04 75 07 32 27

Charles and François Tardy's 25-ha domain continues to evolve and give Crozes-Hermitage some of its most vivid and exuberant wines. Oak is now used here more than it was in the past, to particularly impressive effect for the old-vine Les Machonnières. The white Les Pends is a well-judged blend of 80% Marsanne and 20% Roussanne.

des Espiers
84190 Vacqueyras, Tel: 04 90 65 81 16, Fax: 04 90 65 81 16

This Gigondas domain is run by Philippe Cartoux whose Cuvée des Blaches is dense and weighty yet built with becomingly sweet tannins. It's made from a parcel of 35-year-old vines on the slopes of the Dentelles, up behind the village.

des Estubiers
26600 Tain-l'Hermitage, Tel: 04 75 08 28 65, Fax: 04 75 08 81 70

This 50-ha, pebble-scattered Tricastin estate was purchased by Chapoutier in 1998, and immediately began the conversion to biodynamics. La Ciboise is a lightweight Grenache, ideal for chilling; the Château des Estubiers is Syrah-led and mountain fresh, with deft tannins.

Ferraton
26600 Tain-l'Hermitage, Tel: 04 75 08 59 51, Fax: 04 75 08 81 59

This was once a domain with fine vineyards but rustic wines. The vinification has now been handed over to Chapoutier's Albéric Mazoyer, and is much improved, making the most of the choicely sited 10 ha in Hermitage and Crozes-Hermitage. There are also some wines vinified and sold under this name on a micro-négociant basis (the use of the word Domaine distinguishes the two).

Font de Michelle ✪
84370 Bedarrides, Tel: 04 90 33 00 22, Fax: 04 90 33 20 27

Like Vieux Télégraphe, Font de Michelle (run, as it happens, by the Brunier's cousins Jean and Michel Gonnet) is a Châteauneuf domain whose wines have surged in quality in the late 1990s. The 30 ha are sited near to the Crau vineyards of Vieux Télégraphe; Grenache also dominates the blend, and the red wine is forthright and unapologetic, packed with deliciously comely jam-fruits. Rather than making a second wine, though, the Gonnets have chosen the *cuvée de prestige* route. This wine (Cuvée Etienne Gonnet) is a cellar selection rather than a parcel, and offers similar style to the "ordinary" wine but with extra tannic power, fruit concentration, and ageing potential.

Font Sane
84190 Gigondas, Tel: 04 90 65 86 36, Fax: 04 90 65 81 71

Véronique Peyesson's two finest wines are her rich, spicy classic Gigondas and the denser, smokier barrique-aged Gigondas Cuvée Fûtée, a cellar selection.

Fortia
84321 Châteauneuf-du-Pape, Tel: 04 90 83 72 25, Fax: 04 90 83 51 03

After a dismal period between the late 1970s and the early 1990s, this historic 30-ha estate, where the rules for the ground-breaking Châteauneuf AOC were first drawn up, is now producing much improved wines under Bruno Leroy, with consultative advice from Colombo. This is forthright, mid-weight Châteauneuf, with no special or selected *cuvées* to eviscerate the single bottling.

Pierre Gaillard ✪
42520 Malleval, Tel: 04 74 87 13 10, Fax: 04 74 87 17 66

Pierre Gaillard's association with Yves Cuilleron and François Villard in the Vins de Vienne project seems to have given his own winemaking more consistency:

the standard achieved by this 16-ha domain is now outstanding across a surprisingly wide range. Gaillard has a masterly hand for Viognier, as his blossomy white Côtes du Rhône shows. His is one of the examples of Condrieu in which a mineral grittiness underlies the scented exoticism of the surface; the late-harvest Fleurs d'Automne and *vin de paille* Cuvée Jeanne-Elise suggest exotic new horizons for this AOC as one of the great dessert wines of the world. Don't miss Gaillard's Roussanne St-Joseph white: pure, fleshy white peach and apricot. The ordinary red St-Joseph is full of soaring blackcurrant, while the *cru* Clos du Cuminaille adds more granitic intensity; Les Pierres turns on the oak and power-hammer fruit. The Côte Rôtie, finally, is svelte and sexy, full of chocolate and truffle (15% Viognier); the pure-Syrah Côte Rôtie Rose Pourpre is no less rich, but far smokier. There are also three *cru* wines: the sweet-scented Le Cret (Côte Blonde); the meaty, powerful Les Viallières; and the dense, sombre Côte Rozier.

Gangloff
69420 Condrieu, Tel: 04 74 59 57 04, Fax: 04 74 59 57 04

The unforgettably tangle-haired Yves Gangloff and his wife Mathilde have, alas, very small holdings, but the finely crafted, mouthfilling Condrieu and the two smoky, vividly curranty Côte Rôtie *cuvées* (the young-vine La Barbarine with 10% Viognier, and the pure, older vine La Sereine Noire) are memorable.

La Gardine
84230 Châteauneuf-du-Pape, Tel: 04 90 83 73 20, Fax: 04 90 83 77 24

This large Châteauneuf estate is one of the advocates of new barriques for ageing its impressive special *cuvée*, La Cuvée des Générations (and its white equivalent, Marie Léoncie) This is a welcome stylistic experiment, since the raw materials are dense and vivid enough to support the wood's added tannin and vanillic richness. The "*classique*" Tradition is consistently and satisfyingly brawny.

Gerin ✪
69420 Ampuis, Tel: 04 74 56 16 56, Fax: 04 74 56 11 37

Rugby-playing Jean-Michel Gerin's domain is small (7 ha in Côte Rôtie and just 1.5 ha in Condrieu) but his red wines are outstanding. Champin le Seigneur is a blend of different parcels on Côte Rôtie, and includes 10% Viognier: the 1999 was lush and perfumed. There are two *crus*, both pure Syrah: La Landonne is as forthright as its reputation suggests, steaming with tarry warmth; while La Grande Place (a high-sited parcel) is hauntingly scented and velvety, full of chocolate and flowers rather than smoke. The Condrieu La Loye is improving, with more glycerousness than in the past, and in the best years Gerin makes an exotic Vendanges Suprêmes from November-picked fruit.

Alain Graillot
26600 Pont l'Isère, Tel: 04 75 84 67 52, Fax: 04 75 84 79 33

Self-taught former agricultural machinery salesman Alain Graillot stormed onto the Crozes scene in the mid-1980s, and by the end of the decade seemed to be producing some of the best wines in the AOC. A dip followed in the early 1990s, but in the second half of the decade the wines have settled down into a steady rhythm, with the Crozes-Hermitage La Guiraude (a barrel selection) often being surprisingly better than his small parcel of Hermitage.

Gramenon ✪
26770 Montbrison, Tel: 04 75 53 57 08, Fax: 04 75 53 68 92

Michèle Laurent has succeeded magnificently in taking over the work of her husband Philippe (killed in a hunting accident) at this 24-ha Vinsobres domain. There are now more *cuvées* than ever, but with even stranger and more evocative names, but the Gramenon hallmarks of great finesse, grace, perfume, and depth of flavour remain. Those, too, who think that "secure" winemaking is necessary should try these wines, the best of which (like the Ceps Centenaires, made from two parcels of 100-year-old Grenache, a Rhône classic of absolute purity) are made with no added sulphur dioxide and bottled without any fining or filtration. The perfumed poise of Hauts de Gramenon, the lush floral qualities of Sierra du Sud, and the simple deliciousness of Poignée de Raisins are close to the heart of the Rhône's appeal.

Grands Devers
84600 Valréas, Tel: 04 90 35 15 98, Fax: 04 90 37 49 56

The Bouchard family (having sold Bouchard Père et Fils in Burgundy to Joseph Henriot) thought about moving to Bordeaux, but decided that the "cultural differences" would be too great. Instead they chose René Sinard's old domain: 25 beautiful hectares in the cooler, northern section of the Villages zone (20 in Valréas, 5 in Visan). No wood is used, and the range is elegant, floral, graceful, silky, charming. Even the bigger wines (like the Valréas 1998 or the Syrah 1999) are perfumed, with the wines' substance based on fruit rather than tannic mass.

Bernard Gripa
07300 Mauves, Tel: 04 75 08 14 96, Fax: 04 75 07 06 81

This 10-ha estate is one of the most reliable of all sources for St-Joseph, and there is remarkable consistency across the range from the light and lively white, full of woodland blossom, to the vivid, deep "classique" and the gratifyingly lush and juicy Les Berceaux, made from a parcel of 50-year-old vines in the heart of the appellation. Long-lasting St-Péray, too.

Guigal ✪✪✪
69420 Ampuis, Tel: 04 74 56 10 22, Fax: 04 74 56 18 76

Winemaking genius comes in all shapes and sizes. Marcel Guigal's authority is quiet, that of a senior cardinal or unobtrusive spy-master rather than a bayonet-rattling brigadier. He is small, almost slight; he dresses unshowily (the occasional bright beret aside); he speaks in little more than a whisper. Yet there is no more successful négociant in France today, and as a winemaker, too, his touch is as assured as any fifth-generation Burgundian or First Growth "director of production". His techniques have proved hugely influential both in his own and other regions. The success of the business was initially based on the acumen of his own father Etienne, who began as a worker for Vidal-Fleury and ended, in his 75th year, by buying the company with Marcel. If the best wines of the northern Rhône are today as sought-after as the greatest Grand Cru burgundies (which, in so many ways, they resemble), then much of the credit must go to Etienne and Marcel Guigal. Marcel's own son Philippe appears to share the same modesty, seriousness of purpose, and commitment to the region his father has always shown. With the recent acquisition of Jean-Louis Grippat and de Vallouit, the family faces new challenges.

It is important, in writing about Guigal, to distinguish between the négociant side of the business (enormous: Guigal buys from 67 growers in Côte Rôtie alone, and from nearly 400 growers for his Côte du Rhône) and the domain itself and its celebrated Côte Rôtie and Condrieu vineyards (tiny: just 14 ha in 2000, though recent purchases are expanding the holdings). The outstanding three-star rating for Guigal is based on and merited by his domain wines; the négociant wines can on rare occasions rise to these heights, but in general deserve a one-star rating.

Guigal's methods are described on page 130: his copious and extended use of new wood, yet the remarkable way in which his wines seem to digest this wood, is an enduring source of fascination to other winemakers and drinkers alike, and at times seems almost magical. This enchantment can be smelled and tasted by the lucky few who are ever in a position to purchase his domain wines. Condrieu La Doriane is voluptuously rich yet informed and given gravity by pure, liquid mineral notes. Look out for the new (ex-Grippat) St-Joseph Vigne de l'Hospice, a model of subtly oaked purity. The rest of the domain is in Côte Rôtie, and comprises three single vineyard sites (La Mouline, La Landonne, and La Turque) plus the Château d'Ampuis, an assembly of six different vineyard sites (La Garde, La Clos, La Grande Plantée, La Pommière, Pavillon Rouge, and Le Moulin). La Mouline, based on 60-year-old vines with 11% of Viognier sited in the Côte Blonde, is scented, silky, intensely concentrated yet seamless, too; La Landonne, by contrast, made from steep vineyards in the Côte Brune and with no Viognier component, is slower to unfold, brooding, coffee-dark, earthy, truffle-laden. La Turque (from the Blonde side of the Côte Brune) is vigorous, ripe, at times floral, at other times suggesting roast meats. The Château d'Ampuis is always a fine summary of the vintage, yet Guigal's late-harvesting techniques give it a becoming fleshiness behind its curranty purity.

What of the négociant wines? The Côte Rôtie, the Condrieu, and the white Hermitage can all be outstanding, particularly after fine vintages, while the red Hermitage is sound; the southern Rhône wines, by contrast, often show perhaps a little more northern reserve than one might wish. The Côtes du Rhône, despite being produced in enormous quantities, often offers superb value: the 1995 and 1998 vintages, for example, were both gratifying wines and a fine advertisement for the valley as a whole. (See also de Vallouit, and Vidal-Fleury.)

Paul Jaboulet Aîné ✪
26600 La Roche-de-Glun, Tel: 04 75 84 68 93, Fax: 04 75 84 56 14

Together with Guigal and Chapoutier, this was until 2005 one of the three great family-owned merchant houses in the northern Rhône. Jaboulet has 91 ha of its own vineyard, including 26 ha in various parts of the hill of Hermitage itself (5 ha used for white wine and the rest for red). The 40-ha Thalabert domain in Crozes-Hermitage is also one of what the French call the "lighthouses" of the AOC (despite being on flat gravels to the south of Tain), while the 3.7-ha Domaine de St-Pierre in Cornas is a newer star, producing wine of impressively sweet, sustained fruit to contrast with the more animal négociant version. (Jaboulet's commitment to Cornas has been long-standing; back in the early 1980s the company sold 95% of the AOC's production.) Jaboulet has also acquired the old-vine 5-ha Crozes domain of the late Raymond Roure (in whose cobwebby cellar I enjoyed an unforgettably bacchanalian tasting in 1996); this is sited on the Hermitage-like south-facing granite slopes to the north of Tain. Land has been purchased in St-Joseph and Condrieu, and there is a joint-venture project in hand with the town hall of St-Péray. Quality has until recently been high through the domain range, with the red Hermitage La Chapelle in particular being a legendary wine of remarkable consistency, creamy aromatic power, and exquisite fruit qualities: vivid and seductive. Perfectly poised, in other words, between the fragrance and finesse of the north and the substance and matter of the south. The merchant wines (including a willowy Côte Rôtie Les Jumelles, the juicy St-Joseph La Grande Pompée and the gamey Hermitage Le Pied de la Côte) are less consistent, but worth following in good vintages. It's hoped that the new owner Jean-Jacques Frey will restore Jaboulet to its past position of eminence.

Jean-Paul et Jean-Luc Jamet ✪
69420 Ampuis, Tel: 04 74 56 12 57, Fax: 04 74 56 02 15

Just 6.5 ha here, but quality is consistent year after year (the unctuous red 1978 was one of the greatest Côte Rôties I have ever tasted), and the style, too, could hardly be more typical: scents of currants and smoke, and brisk, fresh, vivid flavours subsiding into a ripe-tannined, silky finish.

La Janasse ✪
84350 Chourthézon, Tel: 04 90 70 86 29, Fax: 04 90 70 75 93

This splendid 47-ha estate is situated in the Courthézon sector of Châteauneuf, near to Beaucastel, though it has a number of scattered parcels on the different internal terroirs of the AOC. Father Aimé Sabon looks after the vines, while son Christophe is in charge of winemaking, which is contemporary in style (Colombo advises; there is some destemming, a little small and new oak, and no fining and filtering). In addition to the Tradition, there is also a Prestige, a Cuvée Vieilles Vignes (vines over 80 years old) and the Cuvée Chaupin (whose vines are also around 80 years). Both the Vieilles Vignes, the Chaupin, and the Prestige can be superb, absolutely classic and beautifully defined, sweetly luscious without ever sinking into soupiness. The effect of all this selection, though, is to make the Tradition a simpler, less penetrating bottle than it might otherwise be. The Les Garrigues Côtes du Rhône offers excellent value.

Robert Jasmin
69420 Ampuis, Tel: 04 74 56 16 04, Fax: 04 74 56 01 78

Robert Jasmin's premature death in 1999 meant that his son Patrick was on his own from that vintage onwards. It was a fine one to start with. This is Côte Rôtie of great purity and elegance, the kind of wines which remind drinkers just how stylistically close Burgundy and the northern Rhône are.

Laurus *see* Gabriel Meffre

Patrick Lesec (Lesec Selections)
75018 Paris, Tel: 01 44 70 62 90, Fax: 01 44 70 62 93

Broker Patrick Lesec runs a Tardieu-like "finishing" operation using good or top-quality raw materials given fastidious *élevage* and bottled without fining or filtration, with an emphasis on the southern Rhône. His greatest wine is probably the Châteauneuf Les Galets Blonds (from Crau), a luscious old-vine Grenache, but the barrique-aged Gigondas Les Espalines-Les Tendrelles is a success, too. Lesec has also worked to great effect with Remizières and St-Cosme.

Marcoux
84230 Châteauneuf-du-Pape, Tel: 04 90 34 67 43, Fax: 04 90 51 84 53

This 16-ha Châteauneuf domain was one of the pioneers of biodynamics in the Rhône Valley under Philippe Armenier; his sisters Sophie and Catherine are carrying on his work in the same spirit. The vineyards include parcels in many different zones (including Crau), and the wines are sweet, tangy, glycerous, and rich. The Vieilles Vignes *cuvée* (70-100 years old, sited in Charbonnières, and other parcels) stiffens this sweetness with thrashing extracts.

Mas Neuf
30600 Gallician, Tel: 04 66 73 33 23

Former sensory analyst and wine enthusiast Luc Baudet bought this 33-ha Costières de Nîmes domain in 2000, and immediately made an excellent start with a superb Cuvée Prestige, packed with sugar-dusted blackberries and with a rich tannin structure. This 75% Syrah and 25% Grenache and Mourvèdre was aged in second-hand barriques from Lafite and Smith Haut Lafitte.

Gabriel Meffre
84190 Gigondas, Tel: 04 90 12 30 22, Fax: 04 90 12 30 22

Large négociant whose Laurus range offers sound, occasionally excellent examples of 18 leading southern and northern Rhône AOCs. All are aged in what Meffre calls "the Laurus barrel", a larger-than-usual 275-litre barrique. Meffre's "Chasse du Pape" Côtes du Rhône brand ably demonstrates the kind of consistent warmth this region can provide, though the embossed bottle and the name certainly engenders public confusion with Châteauneuf itself.

Monteillet
42410 Chavanay, Tel: 04 74 87 24 57, Fax: 04 74 87 06 89

Promising newcomer Stephan Montez has, like so many young Frenchmen of his generation, travelled to see how things are done in California and Australia; indeed he even worked at the English vineyard Denbies. He has come back to hone traditional French techniques towards perfection by greater cleanliness and scrupulousness with raw materials. This is an impressive range, albeit available in very small quantities. The Côte Rôtie Les Grandes Places is packed with sweet, enticing coffee and toast. With under half a hectare, though, there isn't much to go around. The St-Joseph offers a little more to chose from, with the juicy-sweet Cuvée Papy being the best buy.

La Mordorée ✪
30126 Tavel, Tel: 04 66 50 00 75, Fax: 04 66 50 00 75

By some margin the best producer in Lirac, Christophe Delorme's 55-ha biodynamic estate also includes some unusually fresh Tavel and sadly tiny quantities of the rich, meaty Châteauneuf Reine des Bois (the Reine des Bois name is used for all Réserve-level wines at Mordorée). As with France's other great biodynamic estates, these wines have superb definition and focus, as palpable in the soft-fruited basic Rhône as it is in the unusually spicy, smoky Reine des Bois Lirac.

Mourgues du Grès
30300 Beaucaire, Tel: 04 66 59 46 10, Fax: 04 66 59 34 21

François Collard managed a *stage* at Lafite, and a period as a wine journalist, before settling in to this 35-ha family domain situated on the typical small rolled stones of the Nîmes AOC (these stones are locally called Grès or Gress). Les Galets (red, white, and rosé) is the basic *cuvée*, for drinking young and fresh; even the red has bright acidity and juicy fruit. Terre d'Argence is a deeper, chewier red (based on 80% Syrah and 20% Grenache, both from 35-year-old vines) and a Roussanne-dominated, gently perfumed white. Finally there is a red and rosé Capitelles des Mourgues, the rosé being barrel-fermented and containing 60% Mourvèdre, while the red has the same *assemblage* as the Terre d'Argence but sees a year in wood, perfuming its fruit attractively. Collard has now abandoned filtration.

de Nages
30132 Caissargues, Tel: 04 66 38 44 30, Fax: 04 66 38 44 21

Négociant Michel Gassier runs this 70-ha Nîmes domain side by side with Domaine de Molines, whose vineyards lie in Vin de Pays land. Gassier claims that there are no less than 13 metres of pebbles at Château de Nages itself, with a little sand and marl which keep moisture within the stones. The two best wines here are the Cuvée Joseph Torrès white (pure barrel-fermented Roussanne), full of lushly smoky apricot; and the Cuvée Joseph Torrès red (pure Syrah), which gets a year in barrique, one third new: the 1998 has chocolate truffle scents and a wealth of blackberry jam and spice flavours. It's bottled unfiltered.

La Nerthe
84230 Châteauneuf-du-Pape, Tel: 04 90 83 70 11, Fax: 04 90 83 79 69

Large, even magnificent property in Châteauneuf which gives its name to its own locality, sited a little way southwest of Crau. The acquisition of La Terre Ferme in 1991 made it, in effect, contiguous with Crau, though there are a number of different terroirs within the property (sand, clay, and giant pebbles over clay). The 1990s have seen slow, steady improvements here, and the fact that blends tend to be at most only 50% Grenache gives the wine a fresher, more brambly style of fruit than some of its peers, and slightly brisker tannins. The Cuvée des Cadettes is the red selection, based on a Grenache-Mourvèdre plot planted in 1900: denser fruit, of which 50% goes into barrique.

Niero-Pinchon
69420 Condrieu, Tel: 04 74 59 84 38, Fax: 04 74 56 62 70

Banker Robert Niero took over his father-in-law's domain in the 1980s, expanding it to 3 ha of steep-sloped Condrieu. The basic *cuvée* is mainly steel fermented (plus a small amount in old barriques) to give a cleanly peachy wine with elegant acidity; the Coteau du Chéry is richer and more glycerous, its fruit from older vines. Niero also has a small parcel of Côte Rôtie (in Les Viallières) from which he makes a sturdy, peppery wine.

Oratoire St-Martin
84290 Cairanne, Tel: 04 90 30 28 82 07, Fax: 04 90 30 74 27

Yet more proof of the worthiness of Cairanne from this scrupulously run 25-ha domain. Frédéric and François Alary's most concentrated wines are the Réserve des Seigneurs and the Prestige.

Les Pallières *see* Vieux Télégraphe

Alain Paret
42520 St-Pierre-de-Boeuf, Tel: 04 74 87 12 09, Fax: 04 74 87 17 34

Alain Paret owns vineyards in Condrieu and St-Joseph (and also has a Vin de Pays domain in the Hérault where he grows Syrah and Viognier). He is also a friend of Gérard Depardieu – who is his partner for the Condrieu wines. (The friendship dates from the day that Depardieu drank a bottle of his wine in a restaurant and enjoyed it so much he telephoned him afterwards to say so.) The range includes the fiery, intense singe-vineyard Lys de Volan Condrieu and the more fragrant, multi-site Ceps du Nebadon, as well as an occasional late-harvest Condrieu, Sortilèges d'Automne. The wood-aged Larmes du Pierre St-Joseph (both red and white) comes from a single granite and blue clay site, and shows haunting mineral qualities; Les Pieds Dendés is a lighter and simpler wine. The top St-Joseph, 420 Nuits, is made from Serine planted in a site called Rochecourbe; it is then aged for 420 nights (or 14 months) in new oak (from

five forests). The result is indeed sweetly oaky, yet in the mouth there is a meteor shower of crisp, spicy fruit and vivid pepper.

Pégaü ✪
84230 Châteauneuf-du-Pape, Tel: 04 90 83 72 70, Fax: 04 90 83 53 02

This 20-ha Châteauneuf domain has vine parcels, the vast majority between 40 and 70 years old, in a number of different zones of the AOC. The style of wine produced by Paul Feraud and his daughter Laurence is rich, sometimes rustic but always powerful and beefy, based preponderantly on late-harvest Grenache. The "*classique*" is rather misleadingly called the Cuvée Réservée, and a barrique-aged version of this produced in the best years only is called Cuvée Laurence. In 1998, a monumental, storm-trooping wine baptized Cuvée da Capo was created containing all of the 13 authorized varieties, harvested very late and allowed to ferment gently at its own pace for two years before ending up at over 16.5% alcohol. The name is no doubt a musical reference, but for a wine of this insolent power the Mafia overtones don't go amiss. There is no fining or filtering here, and the wines age superbly.

Perrin
84100 Orange, Tel: 04 90 11 12 00, Fax: 04 90 11 12 19

The Domaine Perrin name is used for micro-négociant wines made in various Rhône appellations by the Perrins of Beaucastel (especially Pierre Perrin, the son of Jean-Pierre). They offer good value and authenticity.

André Perret ✪
42410 Chavanay, Tel: 04 74 87 24 74, Fax: 04 74 87 05 26

Perret's wines have pushed the St-Joseph appellation to its limits, using super-ripeness to create wines of succulence and depth; the red Les Grisières, from 50-year-old vines, is outstanding. Perret also produces good Condrieu, especially the juicy, exotic Coteau de Chéry.

Pesquié
84570 Mormoiron, Tel: 04 90 61 94 08, Fax: 04 90 61 94 13

The Quintessence, a site selection combining 55-year-old Grenache with 20% Syrah, is one of the most intense of Côtes du Ventoux's wines, needing only slightly more sweetness of fruit and wealth of tannin to be outstanding. There is also a Cuvée Terrasses and a Cuvée Prestige produced at this 72-ha domain, owned by Paul and Edith Chaudière.

Le Pigeoulet *see* Vieux Télégraphe

Pignan *see* Rayas

Rabasse Charavin
84290 Cairanne, Tel: 04 90 30 70 05, Fax: 04 90 30 74 42

Corinne Couturier's Cairanne domain produces a wide range of wines from Cairanne (14 ha) and Rasteau (8 ha); there are also 25 ha of ordinary Villages and 18 ha of Vins de Pays, too. The Rasteau is based on a blend which includes 40% Mourvèdre balanced with Grenache, giving it a spice-and-prune character. The Cairannes are more Grenache-rich, and are full of the sweet unction of this grape at full ripeness but without the sometimes biting tannins of Gigondas or the fierce alcoholic heat of Châteauneuf. The Cuvée d'Estevenas is pale yet succulent, layered with perfumed cherry fruit.

Rayas ✪✪
84260 Sarrians, Tel: 04 90 65 41 75, Fax: 04 90 65 38 46

Jacques Reynaud, who died in the mid-1990s, was celebrated for two things: his sometimes misanthropic eccentricity, and his ability to create brilliant Châteauneuf out of the apparent squalor of the Rayas cellar. Under his nephew Emmanuel, things have changed. A little. More consistency is the aim, but eccentricity and apparent squalor are still treats on offer for those lucky enough to visit Rayas. Grenache remains king here (Jacques Reynaud claimed never to have clapped eyes on Mourvèdre) – and Grenache grown from old, low-yielding vines, picked very late, on sandy or clay-lime soils, but not from the pebblefields of the Châteauneuf photo-myth. The wines are light in colour but hauntingly beautiful in character, and remarkably durable in time: fat, sweet yet savoury too, the strawberry and cherry characters of youth modulating towards a softly licking fire of spices in maturity. There are, as one might expect, no *cuvées de prestige* here; the *classique* is the *grand vin*. Pignan is a kind of second wine, coming from the parcel of that name sited near Courthézon, plus less successful Rayas vats (or barrels, or *foudres*, or *demi-muids*). Fonsalette is a Côtes du Rhône from the edge of the Châteauneuf zone which, by dint of its ferociously low yields, can often be better than many lesser Châteauneufs; the slightly cooler climate gives it a darker colour and brisker tannins than Rayas, but it lasts just as well. The white Fonsalette, indeed, is often more successful than Rayas's own white. At Fonsalette the Reynauds prove that they are not Grenache monomaniacs with a Syrah *cuvée*, taken from a single, north-facing vineyard and full of gamey, truffley, boar-hunting appeal. Pialade is a *cuvée* made from the leftovers of everything else. (*See also des Tours.*)

Réméjeanne ✪
30200 Sabran, Tel: 04 66 89 44 51, Fax: 04 66 89 64 22

This 35-ha estate, run with enormous enthusiasm by Rémi and Ouahi Klein, proves two things. The first is that, for simple, artless, delicious, and supremely drinkable red wine, almost nowhere in the world can match the Côtes du Rhône at its best. The second is that there are still many secrets of terroir to discover, even in an area as extensively and lengthily cultivated as the Rhône. No one, in other words, ever paid much attention to the wines of the out-of-the-way village of Sabran – until a careful, thoughtful winemaker like Rémi Klein came along. *Et voilà*: a new terroir in which Syrah can achieve a tissue-soft lyricism seldom seen elsewhere. Les Arbousiers (which means "the strawberry trees") is the "*classique*" *cuvée*, including a citrus-scented white, a vinous rosé, and a sweet-fruited red made from equal parts of Syrah and Grenache grown on loess. Les Chèvrefeuilles (the honeysuckle) is a young-vine blend stiffened with a little old Carignan and Counoise. Les Genevrières (the juniper bushes) is mainly Grenache with some Syrah and Mourvèdre, providing an enchanting mix of grace and power, while best of all is Les Eglantiers (the dog roses), an almost pure Syrah grown on limy sands and given a year in barrique on lees with micro-oxygenation: pure, perfumed, with exquisitely judged, sweet, cocoa-dusted fruits.

Remizières ✪
26600 Mercurol, Tel: 04 75 07 44 28, Fax: 04 75 07 45 87

Careful, fastidious winemaking characterises this 27-ha domain run by Philippe Desmeure where standards seem to rise with every year which passes. The St-Joseph is full of crisp fruit and mineral depths, while the Crozes wines, too, have great purity and vividness of flavour. The unfiltered, oak-aged Cuvée Christophe red achieves a thrilling balance between oak richness and elegant fresh fruit, while the white is honeyed and haunting. These are not always easy wines, but they track the land with sensuous fidelity.

Richaud
84290 Cairanne, Tel: 04 90 30 85 25, Fax: 04 90 30 71 12

Another of the many up-and-coming Cairanne stars, Marcel Richaud produces a convincing range from his 41-ha estate. The white wine, part-barrique-fermented, is much better than its modest Côtes du Rhône AOC would suggest, while the Cairanne "classique" is round, long, and fatly satisfying. There are two top *cuvées*, the richly oaked Ebrescade (from high-sited vineyards near Rasteau) and the dark and fleshy Estrambords.

la Roquette *see* Vieux Télégraphe

René Rostaing ✪
69420 Ampuis, Tel: 04 74 56 12 00

The self-critical René Rostaing is slowly refining his art (decreasing the already modest input of new oak, picking later, bottling without filtration) and in so doing has made himself into one of the very finest producers of Côte Rôtie. There are three *cuvées*: the Classique (now benefiting from the previously separated Viallière parcel), the dense and saturated Landonne, and the scented, soaringly seductive Côte Blonde, the only one of the Rostaing *cuvées* to contain

a dash (under 5%) of Viognier. Rostaing's Condrieu La Bonette is unoaked, shimmering with honeysuckle scent.

Roger Sabon
84230 Châteauneuf-du-Pape, Tel: 04 90 83 71 72, Fax: 04 90 83 50 51

Roger Sabon's holdings are scattered in different sectors of Châteauneuf (including Crau and Nalys) and the wines are based on a solid core of Grenache – including, for the Cuvée Prestige, fruit from 100-year-old vines. Apart from the simple Tradition, these are fragrant, well-structured classics, bottled without filtration.

St-Cosme ✪
84190 Gigondas, Tel: 04 90 65 80 80, Fax: 04 90 65 81 05

The ambitious and articulate Louis Barruol (who speaks excellent English: his wife is from Newcastle) is one of the new stars of the southern Rhône – and of the northern Rhône too, since the wines he has "signed" from Condrieu and Côte Rôtie are superb. Grace, purity, and singing fruit are three of the Barruol hallmarks; it is almost as if he is making Gigondas (always potentially a bruising wine) in the spirit of Côte Rôtie itself. The Côtes du Rhône "Les Deux Albion" is a masterpiece of floral enchantment when young (this red wine includes 10% Clairette); even Barruol's celebrated prestige Gigondas Valbelle has an almost Pinot-like aromatic finesse, with beautifully restrained oak influence.

Sang des Cailloux ✪
84260 Sarrians, Tel: 04 90 65 88 64, Fax: 04 90 65 88 75

Serge Férigoule's 16-ha domain is one of the stars of Vacqueyras. No herbicide, no pesticide, no stainless steel, no fining, no filtration: like many of France's greatest modern day winemakers, Férigoule's success is defined as much by what he doesn't do as what he does. The barrel-fermented white has memorable floral intensity, although it is produced in tiny quantities. There are two reds. The standard *cuvée classique* bears (in annual rotation) the name of one of Férigoule's three daughters Floureto, Doucinello and Azalaïs. There is also an old-vines cuvée whose name is invariably Lopy. This takes the flower and citrus fragrances of the classic cuvée and compresses them memorably into saturated cherry fruit supported by soft, sweet tannin. Sang des Cailloux proves just how different Vacqueyras is from neighbouring Gigondas.

Santa-Duc ✪
84190 Gigondas, Tel: 04 90 65 84 49, Fax: 04 90 65 81 63

Yves Gras' 22-ha domain has been one of the AOC leaders in Gigondas for a decade or more now, and the *cuvées* (including an exuberantly full-fruited Côtes du Rhône and, in good years, the oaked Gigondas Hautes Garrigues, made with late-harvested old-vine Grenache plus 20% Mourvèdre) seem to acquire new chocolatey, earthy depth and density with every year which passes. The challenge in Gigondas is to extract depth and texture of fruit with the same facility as tannin; few do this as successfully and consistently as Gras. How? Lees work is important here; Gras exchanges ideas with Pascal Verhaeghe and Luc de Conti. There is also a pre-fermentation maceration. The *élevage* is very slow, and the wines are bottled unfined and only lightly filtered. The Hautes Garrigues *cuvée* is a selection of older vines from the zone of the same name which actually lies below the village on clay-rich limestones.

Marc Sorrel
26600 Tain l'Hermitage, Tel: 04 75 08 59 51, Fax: 04 75 08 81 59

With just 4 ha at his disposal, there isn't a great deal of Marc Sorrel's precise, tightly constructed red and white Hermitage and Crozes-Hermitage to stock cellars worldwide. The standard is consistent and the style one of classical purity. There are two *cru* *cuvées* of the Hermitage: Le Gréal red is a blend of Méal and Greffieux, while the outstanding white comes from Les Roucoules alone.

La Soumade ✪
84110 Rasteau, Tel: 04 90 46 11 26, Fax: 04 90 46 11 69

André Roméro, the self-proclaimed "madman of Rasteau", has the brand of insanity which every French appellation needs somewhere in its midst: the furious pursuit of every drop of flavour, ripeness, and expression which wine grapes are capable of surrendering in this spot on earth. The domain, at 26 ha, is sizeable, and the range (from Vins de Pays up to the magnificent Confiance, made in the finest years only from a single parcel of 100-year-old Grenache grown on blue clay) is outstanding. In addition to his magnificent "normal" wines, Roméro also makes Vins Doux Naturels under the Rasteau AOC including a pure Grenache Blanc Doré, aged towards unusual complexity in *foudres*. This is full-bodied, full-blooded winemaking in an area which deserves an appellation of its own.

Jean-Michel Stephan
69420 Tupin et Semons, Tel: 04 74 56 62 66, Fax: 04 74 56 62 66

Promising young Côte Rôtie grower whose Vieilles Vignes *cuvée* is based on 100-year-old vines: elegant, pure, concentrated style. Stephan formerly worked for Guigal, and the polish of his wines reflects that apprenticeship.

Cave de Tain l'Hermitage
26601 Tain-l'Hermitage, Tel: 04 75 08 20 87, Fax: 04 75 07 15 16

This cooperative's top Hermitage *cuvées*, Gambert de Loche and Nobles Rives, are well worth trying: sleek and articulate.

Tardieu-Laurent ✪✪
84160 Lourmarin, Tel: 04 90 68 80 25, Fax: 04 90 68 22 65

The principle is simple enough: buy the best grapes (paying, of course, the highest prices), then treat them like royalty. The suppliers make the wine; Tardieu's work is to coax and tease them through two leesy years of low-sulphur time, keeping reduction at bay, in first class barrels before hand-bottling them without fining or filtration. The range covers the whole of the valley, from a Lubéron made in conjunction with the Cave Lourmarin that genuinely seems to smell of lavender and a thumpingly beefy Costières de Nîmes to exquisitely floral Côte Rôtie "*classique*" and barely less perfumed Hermitage. Disappointments are gratifyingly hard to find here, though the ordinary Crozes-Hermitage can be a little under-ripe and the white Côtes du Rhône Cuvée Guy Louis struggles under its weight of oak. Outstanding wines, by contrast, are plentiful. Those hunting for value should focus on wines like the spice-bomb Côtes du Rhône Vieilles Vignes red (made from 80-year-old Grenache grown near Châteauneuf), the coffee and mocha Vacqueyras Vieilles Vignes, or the violet-scented St-Joseph Vieilles Vignes. Up among the summits, you'll find a magnificent articulate, resonant Cornas Vieilles Vignes (from 100-year-old vines at Sabarotte); the typically mineral, profoundly blackcurranty St-Joseph Les Roches Vieilles Vignes; and, above all, Tardieu's Côte Rôtie Cuvée Spéciale Vieilles Vignes: pure mouth-perfume.

Tourettes
71960 Sologny, Tel: 03 85 51 66 00, Fax: 03 85 51 66 09

Jean-Marie and Maine Guffens' Château des Tourettes near Apt is the source of the Verget du Sud wines. (Apt itself now also has a Guffens grocery, wine shop, and restaurant called Le Carré des Sens.) Why? "*Le terroir, c'est la chose qu'on aime*," said Guffens at a 2001 press conference in Lubéron – the terroir is what you have to love... like your children, he pursued. When he saw a pure limestone plateau at 400 metres orientated towards the north, he knew he could produce good whites there – though with Chardonnay in the blend ("I can't live without Chardonnay") the wines are sold under Vins de Pays legislation. Le Plateau de l'Aigle is the name he has chosen for the best of these (barrel-fermented, naturally). There are also Verget du Sud whites from both Lubéron and Ventoux, and Tourettes reds from Lubéron. The 1998 and 1999 vintages of these were dark, spicy, elegant, with lush tannins: promising wine in a fresh style.

des Tours
84260 Sarrians, Tel: 04 90 65 41 75, Fax: 04 90 65 38 46

Emmanuel Reynaud produces a pale and toothsome Vacqueyras Grande Réserve here from over 90% Grenache filled out with a stroke of Syrah: soft, ripe, and long (though quarrels with the Vacqueyras tasting panel means that the 1998 emerged under the Côtes du Rhône AOC). There is also a lighter,

simpler Vin de Pays de Vaucluse which blends Grenache and Syrah with Cinsault, sold as Domaine des Tours.

de la Tuilerie
30900 Nîmes, Tel: 04 66 70 07 53, Fax: 04 66 70 04 36

The Comte family's 70-ha Nîmes estate has north-facing vineyards which gives the wines of Château de la Tuilerie an edge and definition in great years which some of its rivals don't have (whereas in lesser years the acidity levels can be over high). There are three *cuvées*, all Syrah-dominated: the fresh and perfumed Carte Blanche (up to 40% Grenache), a Vieilles Vignes *cuvée* based on 25-year-old Syrah (oldish rather than old vines) and the oak-aged Cuvée Eole.

du Tunnel
07130 St-Péray, Tel: 04 75 80 04 66, Fax: 04 75 80 06 50

Stéphane Robert's domain was founded in 1996, and in addition to clean, fresh St-Péray produces two fine Cornas *cuvées*, a gutsy, vivid Prestige from 80-year-old vines, smelling of black pepper and violets, and an only marginally less exciting "*normale*" from 50-year-old vines.

Pierre Usseglio
84230 Châteauneuf-du-Pape, Tel: 04 90 83 72 98, Fax: 04 90 83 72 98

Jean-Pierre and Thierry Ussgelio's 23-ha domain has turned heads in the late 1990s not only for their satisfying fiery, olive-scented "*classique*" but also for two new selected *cuvées*, the Cuvée de Mon Aïeul (from 1998) and, in 1999, the Cuvée Cinquantenaire, to celebrate the domain's 50th anniversary. The outstanding qualities of these (the Aïeul is based on 80-year-old Grenache) bode well: a domain to watch.

de Vallouit
26240 St-Vallier, Tel: 04 75 23 10 11, Fax: 04 75 23 05 58

This latest Guigal acquisition has some fine vineyard holdings in the northern Rhône (such as Hermitage Les Greffières and St-Joseph Les Anges) which will be turned to good account. The négociant wines, too, should improve, though the Vidal Fleury example suggests that this may take time.

Verget du Sud *see* **Tourettes**

Georges Vernay ✪
69420 Condrieu, Tel: 04 74 56 81 81, Fax: 04 74 56 60 98

George Vernay was the man who saved Condrieu, who refused to give up with his cussed, low-yielding Viognier vines and his inaccessible, unmechanizable Condrieu terraces when everyone else thought that the wine-growers' life hereabouts should be an easier, more "modern" one. It must be gratifying to him to see not only that this AOC now has one of the highest average prices in France, but also that Viognier is now a grape of honour in most of the world's warmer wine-growing regions. The ebullient Vernay himself has now retired, and the 7-ha domain is run by his daughter Christine and her husband Paul Amsellem. The ordinary Condrieu here is correct, vinous and long, but unshowy; for the fireworks, you need to find one of the two *cru* wines, Les Chaillées de l'Enfer and the Coteau de Vernon, both barrique-fermented (though with a maximum of 20% new oak). These are both magnificent wines, dripping sensuality from every pore yet at the same time with a serious mineral backbone to them. Honey and honeysuckle characterize the Coteau de Vernon, whereas the Chaillées has a spicier, more fiery quality. There are also two Côte Rôtie wines: an elegant, chocolatey Classique (with 10% Viognier) and a pure-Syrah Maison Rouge, full of glowing charcoal embers.

Vidal-Fleury
69420 Ampuis, Tel: 04 74 56 10 18, Fax: 04 74 56 19 19

Historic (none more so) négociant company owned since 1994 by Guigal. Despite this, the Guigal magic has yet to show itself in the Vidal-Fleury range which can be over-lean and dry. Improvements are beginning to be apparent in the northern Rhône selections, particularly Côte Rôtie La Chatillonne.

Vieille Julienne
84100 Orange, Tel: 04 90 34 20 10, Fax: 04 90 34 10 20

Jean-Paul Daumen's domain is another of Châteauneuf's many fast improvers. As so often, the domain wine itself is pleasant, supple, and unexceptional; get hold of either the Cuvée Reservée or the Vieilles Vignes *cuvée*, by contrast, and you will find them powerfully sweet and succulent, built on around 80% Grenache (Daumen is a big fan of Rayas). Both need time to settle down and stop swinging their arms about. The Côtes du Rhône is spicy and warm.

Vins de Vienne ✪
38200 Seyssuel, Tel: 04 74 85 04 52, Fax: 04 74 31 97 55

This partnership between Yves Cuilleron, Pierre Gaillard, and François Villard has two aims. The first is to try to recreate the historic (but long since abandoned) Seyssuel vineyard sited above Vienne, at which point the river, Rheingau-like, jinks west. (Is it chance or connection that its name is so similar to Seyssel, the Savoie vineyard which is also sited on the banks of the Rhône much further north?) It was Gaillard who first found reference to this vineyard in a 17th century text by Olivier de Serres, and the *"idée un peu folle"* (slightly crazy idea) to replant it took form with the creation of Vins de Vienne in February 1996, the south-facing, schist slopes being cleared later in the year. Despite lying on the east of the river, the site is protected and hot: cactus and cicadas normally only found 200 km further south exist here, and the slope has its own unique flower, called *la gagée du rocher*. There will be three reds, all pure Syrah: Sotanum (the *"classique"*), Taburnum (a parcel selection) and Heluicum (a super-selection made in the best years only). There will also be a Sotanum Rosé and a white Vionnier (sic), all of these wines being sold as Vins de Pays des Collines Rhodanniens, since Seyssuel is outside any present AOC area. The initial releases of Sotanum (which is given 18 months in new barriques) are promisingly rich and fleshy for a wine produced from baby vines.

The other role of the Vins de Vienne is to act as a micro-négociant for Rhône valley wines, and here the team has got off to a flying start with some brilliant 1999 and 2000 releases including a fresh and creamy St-Péray Les Bialères, the splendidly succulent and well-balanced Condrieu La Chambée, and the exotically spicy, sexy Côte Rôtie Les Essartailles. The inspiration of Michel Tardieu isn't too hard to spot here, since these are all intricately worked in vinification terms, using copious new oak (sometimes too much, as for the 1999 white St-Joseph l'Elouède) and lees input. The minimalist packaging makes the wines a restaurant hit, and private buyers are likely to covet them soon, too.

Le Vieux Donjon
84230 Châteauneuf-du-Pape, Tel: 04 90 83 70 03, Fax: 04 90 83 50 38

Classic, sweet, warm Châteauneuf of pebble-rounded substance, made with old vines of 80 years or more, on the rolled pebbles of the Pied Long sector in the northwest of the AOC; yields are well-below the 35 hl/ha AOC maximum.

Vieux Relais
30126 Tavel, Tel: 04 66 50 36 52, Fax: 04 66 50 35 32

Pierre Bardin's domain seems to have one of the best terroirs in the AOC, and the two *cuvées* produced by the now elderly Bardin have a long, fine track record. The deeply flavoured and tangy Tradition is a 50/50 Syrah-Grenache blend; the Sélection is (most unusually for Costières de Nîmes) mainly Mourvèdre balanced with Grenache, packed with olive and liquorice flavours.

Vieux Télégraphe ✪✪
84370 Bedarrides, Tel: 04 90 33 00 31, Fax: 04 90 33 18 47

This Châteauneuf, one of the Rhône's greatest estates, is brilliantly run by Frédéric and Daniel Brunier, the great-grandsons of the founder Hippolyte Brunier. Vieux Télégraphe itself occupies 70 ha entirely sited on the hot and stony plateau of La Crau, to the east of the appellation; indeed the *galets* were at 37°C on the day I called, which is certainly hot enough to cook eggs on. The Bruniers now also own the 28-ha estate of La Roquette (whose red comes from three different terroirs, including some of the sands of Pignan), and are part-owners (with their American importer Kermit Lynch) of the 25-ha Domaine les Pallières in Gigondas. The Vieux Télégraphe style has

deepened becomingly since the sons took over from their father Henri, even though, according to Daniel *"on ne fait pas la course à l'extraction ici"* ("we don't chase extraction here") and the estate is still a firm believer in big wooden *foudres* rather than barriques for *élevage* – of the red wine; a portion of the white does spend time in barrique. The wine is racked every three months for two years, and then bottled without fining or filtration. One reason for the increasingly high quality of Vieux Télégraphe has been the admirable decision to produce a second wine called Vieux Mas des Papes (from 1994); yields are always low, and the vines are aged between 40 and 70 years old. The style is classically Grenache-led, giving a wine of relatively light colour but powerful scents (roast meat, herbs, and sweet plums) and generous though soft and svelte tannic depths behind the roar of spicy flavour. Roquette is scarcely less impressive (40-year-old vines, also Grenache-dominated) with its bubbling, creamy-sweet fruits, while the Pallières offers the fine-grained, sweet, and perfumed fruits of Gigondas backed by the typical fiery boot of warmth. (It is a wine which, even more than Châteauneuf, seems to taste of hot stones.) Le Pigeoulet is a light, pretty and perfumed Vin de Pays de Vaucluse from the edge of the Châteauneuf appellation: both colours are ideal for chilling.

François Villard ✪
42410 St-Michel-sur-Rhône, Tel: 04 74 56 83 60, Fax: 04 74 56 87 78

Former chef François Villard's domain is not yet a large one (just 6.5 ha), but the waves that his intense, dense wines have created have put his wines at the top of many Rhône-lovers' shopping lists. There are four Condrieu *cuvées* (Grand Vallon, Terrasses du Palat, Deponcins, and the late-harvest Quintessence), the Côte Rôtie La Brocarde, and red (Reflet and Grand Reflet) and white (Mairlant) St-Josephs. Late harvesting, lees contact and very low yields are all in evidence here, which means that the relatively lavish oak the wines receive is swiftly subsumed into the wines' overall wealth of flavour. The Condrieu wines are all showy and flamboyant, though some can lack subtlety; for me the smoky aromatic expressivity, fruited sumptuousness, and exquisite tannins of the Brocarde and Reflet wines suggest that Villard is becoming an even more impressive red winemaker than white.

Viret
26110 St-Maurice, Tel: 04 75 27 62 77, Fax: 04 75 27 62 31

This fascinating domain in the Rhône village of St-Maurice, run by former cooperative member Alain Viret and his son Philippe, claims to practice not organics, not biodynamics... but "cosmoculture", an agricultural system inspired by Mayan civilization. The cellar, or "cathedral of the wines", is made of large blocks of stone weighing between three and six tonnes arranged according to the "golden number", an architectural formula derived from study of Greek and Roman temples. The wines reflect the "unique biotope" in which they come into being. As you might have guessed, they are hand-harvested, fermented with natural yeasts, see minimum sulphuring, and are bottled without filtration. There are six of them, the best being the three single-parcel wines from St-Maurice. Maréotis is light and perfumed; Les Colonnades (which uses old Carignan, Mourvèdre, and 100-year-old Grenache) is textured and chocolate-rich; Emergence (Grenache, Carignan, and the domain's oldest Syrah) has animal scents and is the most powerful and mineral of the three. A fourth *cuvée* is in preparation, ageing in ex-Margaux barriques.

Voge
07130 Cornas, Tel: 04 75 40 32 04, Fax: 04 75 81 06 02

Grandfather Alain Voge has named his unoaked, pure-Marsanne St-Péray Cuvée Mélodie-William after his *petits enfants*: it's a fascinating wine in which minerals and blossom, pleasingly, have the upper hand over fruit. Less successful, to my mind, is the Cuvée Boisé, where oak (half new) clouds these more fugitive characteristics. Voge's Cornas, meanwhile, is a dark, smoky, perfumed, and pure classic. There is also a barrique-aged Vieilles Vignes *cuvée*, and in great years the rousingly animal Cuvée Les Vieilles Fontaines, made with the oldest vines of all, planted in the 1920s. He has 7 ha in each appellation.

Provence

In Search of a Soul   At first glance, Provence seems to have it all: beauty, stonefields, sun, a wide spread of varieties, and (thanks to the mistral) an aptitude for organic cultivation unmatched anywhere else in France. Bandol aside, though, great wines are rare here. Why?

France's AOC system gives its wine edifice a look of solidity and permanence. Who could doubt, gazing up at the porticos of Bordeaux, that the synthesis of Cabernet Sauvignon and Merlot is right for Pauillac? Who could question the perfumed rectitude of Pinot Noir for Nuits, the flinty contentment of Sauvignon Blanc in Sancerre, or the heavy-lidded passion Viognier shows for Condrieu?

Look a little closer, though, and you will discover that this beautiful system is riddled with inconsistencies and uncertainties. We have already seen, in other chapters, how geographical delimitations vary from the absurdly precise (in Burgundy) to the inadequately vague (in Champagne or the southern Rhône). Politics has, in theory, no role to play in the appellation system, yet in areas like the Languedoc (with the segmentation of Corbières or Fitou) it spuriously substitutes for the realities of terroir. With Provence, we come to an entire region in which the AOC system is evidently a work in progress. Were the AOCs of Provence to remain immutable, their boundaries unchanged and their varietal specifications frozen as they are at present, it would be a tragedy for the region. Provence produces many good wines and a few great wines, but it also produces a vast amount of undistinguished wine. At least part of the blame for this must lie with its broad-brush appellation boundaries and its muddled schema of varietal specifications. Provence could do better and Provence will

do better – provided INAO is ready to allow the most talented producers the freedom to experiment, and providing the AOC framework here is regularly revised to take account of their achievements. To date, sadly, this has not always been the case. INAO regulations have often promoted mediocrity in Provence, and made life difficult for those trying to make great wine here.

Let's start, though, with the one great certainty of Provence: its beauty. Is there a motorway anywhere in the world which has cut its roaring path through finer landscapes than the A8 in Provence? The ceaseless rising and falling of the hills, a production of three successive deformations during a troubled Tertiary period here, gives the very structure of Provence a mesmerizing sinuousness. At least three different limestones gleam in the extravagant sunlight; elsewhere there are glittering, mica-rich schists; elsewhere, too, throbbingly red oxide-laden soils unfold contrastingly under pool-blue skies. The untrodden shoulders and haunches of white stone which soar above the A8 swarm with scented trees. These wild Aleppo pines sometimes make Provence resemble Greece's resin-fresh and winter-watered Ionian islands; sometimes, though, they achieve the intricate, stunted perfection of a Japanese landscape brushed into being by a Masanobu or a Tohaku. Off the main routes, the ever-present *garrigue*, with its thyme and fennel, its juniper and oak, seems almost Tuscan. In a

breeze, the silver-backed olive leaves in the groves glimmer like shoals of herring turning on a bank. Later, the night songs of the *cigales* build a warm, thick wall of sound around each sleeper. It is as if all the hallmark Mediterranean beauties are gathered together in Provence. Even the landmark peaks – the molars of the Alpilles, the brooding bulk of Mont Ste-Victoire, the ragged highlands of the Maures – mark the landscape with an impeccable, painterly rhythm. And who, in the end, could wish for a finer prevailing wind than the mistral? In winter, its penetrating persistence may prove exhausting for those out pruning in its teeth; in summer, though, it makes Provence's inland heat the dryest and most sprightly of the south. As it chases hazes and smogs out into the sea, it leaves the air gaspingly bright and brilliant. Nowhere in southern Europe does the clarity of light come closer to the limpidity of South Africa's Stellenbosch or of New Zealand's Marlborough than in Provence. Vines love it. A casual glance at the vineyards of Bandol or Les Baux might lead you to conclude that it is here, rather than in Pomerol or Pommard, that France's greatest natural vineyard assets are to be found.

Vines like it; so do people. Hence one of the paradoxes of Provence, and perhaps one of the reasons why its viticulture has not undergone the slow and steady evolution seen in other regions. Provence at the beginning of the twentieth century was "poor, isolated, and miserable," in the words of Marielyne Pouchin of Château Bas. "People died of hunger here. You made a living with a few sheep, with small-scale polyculture. We weren't on any of the great routes like Bordeaux, Burgundy, or the Rhône. This was Jean de Florette country. It's only since Brigitte Bardot that we have sold our products more expensively." Her husband Philippe Pouchin points out that the Avignon-Marseilles-Aix-Nîmes connurbation is now the second largest *bassin de consommation* (consumer area) in France after Paris; Aix is France's Silicon City. "We're now a suburb of Paris," smiles Marielyne. The pressure on land grows continually. "We don't," continues Philippe Pouchin, "have our backs to the wall; that's our problem. Our wine-growers have large local markets, a huge tourist market and the possibility of making money with real estate, too. In backwoods Languedoc, they can't count on that. They have no tourists and lots of mosquitos. Their wine-growers have to try; ours don't."

The relatively comfortable role of viticulture in local economic life can often be a curse in disguise; the dismal quality of wine in Germany's Württemberg, to cite another European example, is due to the undemanding and prosperous local market of Stuttgart, with its Mercedes and Porsche factories. This phenomenon is made worse in Provence by the fact that many locals and tourists drink wine not with their noses and mouths but with their eyes. "*Les consommateurs de*

"Carignan? I love it because it's so difficult. The most boring grape variety I've ever worked with is Cabernet Sauvignon; it's so easy. All you do is decide what yield you want. You can make some nice wines with it, but I think this is really Syrah or Mourvèdre or Carignan country. It's tough country – and you need tough varieties."

LARS TORSTENSON

A cornflower sky and clear, breezy air, seen here over Bonnieux, makes living in Provence a four-season pleasure.

rosé," says France Carreau Gaschereau of Château du Seuil, "*sont surtout des consommateurs de robe,*" ("rosé drinkers drink colour above all").

It's 9.30 on a late August morning, and I'm walking though the little village of Eguilles. The sun is, of course, shining; people are allowing their dogs to defaecate on the pavement, buying newspapers, carrying bread home for breakfast. I pass a café, open to the street. At the nearest table, a brawny, silver-haired man sits looking out, cigarette in hand; we exchange meaningless glances. In front of him sits a small, café glass half-full of pale rosé wine. The condensation on its side indicates that it has been recently poured. I walk on. Five minutes later, I return by the same route. The same man sits in the same place; there is now a new glass in front of him, beaded yet again with condensation, and filled again to the brim with the same pale, chill rosé. He looks glumly content.

Rosé, rosé, rosé: this is still the backbone of regional production, accounting for as much as eighty per cent of the wines of Côtes de Provence, seventy per cent of Coteaux Varois and fifty per cent of Coteaux d'Aix en Provence. There are, of course, some great rosés produced in Provence, including (perhaps surprisingly) a number of barrique-fermented and barrique-aged rosé wines. There is nothing mysterious about this: if you are going to go to the trouble and expense of barrel-fermenting your rosé, then you will be wasting your money unless the fruit is intensely flavoured and produced with restricted yields. Densely fruited rosés can acquire added structure and depth by clever use of wood (one- or two-year-old barriques are a better idea than new wood), producing what Guy Négrel calls "*rosé d'hiver*", or "winter rosé". Yes, it works.

Most of Provence's rosé, by contrast, is as dreary to drink as it is pretty to look at. At no point during the research for this book did I struggle as hard to find interest in French wine as I did when tasting rosés in Provence. If they sell easily (as they do), one can hardly blame the producers for producing them; the profits on these high-yielding, rapidly sold wines are doubtless comforting. It is undemanding consumers who are culpable, though since most are just there to

have a good time on their summer holidays the notion of "culpability" is in itself a silly one. The fact is that there will be no dramatic improvement in the general quality of Provence's wine as long as rosé continues to play the role it does there. All of the region's great wines are either red or white, yet for most producers, these wines represent a minority (whites an often tiny minority — just four per cent of Côtes de Provence) of their production.

I alluded at the opening of this chapter to the uncertainties which lie beneath what seems to be a settled system of appellations here. Problems connected with appellation boundaries will be discussed in The Adventure of the Land. Let's, though, consider here what we might call the case of the muddled grapes.

The greatest and happiest match between grape variety and terroir in Provence is unquestionably that of Mourvèdre in Bandol. This late-ripening variety, so gruff and inarticulate elsewhere, blossoms in the limestone and sandstone cauldron of Bandol to produce dark, dense wines packed with blackberry fruits, beef, toffee, and minerals. Mourvèdre, though, "needs its feet in the water, its head in the sun, and with a clear view of the sea," according to Philippe Pouchin ("like Parisians on holiday," adds Marielyne). In other words, it is a non-starter for many of Provence's vineyards, sited as they are at around the 300 metre (985 feet) mark; both Christian Double at Château de Beaupré and Eloi Dürrbach of Domaine de Trévallon report that Mourvèdre in their vineyards rarely climbs above eleven per cent alcohol by volume. Wholly unripe, in other words. If you're not in Bandol or in the hotter, coastal parts of Côtes de Provence, therefore, what varieties do you build your red wine on? Grenache, Syrah, Cinsault, Cabernet Sauvignon, and Carignan all play an important role, with Cabernet Sauvignon (officially limited to thirty per cent of each vineyard's total plantings) being in many ways the most controversial. What is Cabernet doing in Provence, and does it belong there?

Its origins in Provence date back to the post-phylloxera period; it is not a late arrival, swung into the vineyards to capitalize on the variety's last thirty years of international celebrity. Cabernet, moreover, is

Lars Torstenson

It would be hard to look less Provençal than this tall Swede, inevitably blond, inevitably fluent in English as well as French. Fourteen years in the south, though, have given him a permanent tan – and a sunny sense of humour. He runs two properties: Domaine Rabiega, owned since 1986 by Vin & Sprit, the former Swedish drink monopoly; and Château d'Esclans, a property leased by Vin & Sprit. There are also some négociant wines, sold as "Rabiega". Torstenson is a novelist as well as a winemaker – and has written wine books in Swedish, too. ("Those wine books are very boring. I tried to make them funny, but I couldn't.") A winemaker with imagination, then?

Just so. Everything that comes out of this domain seems almost purposely designed to give the appellation authorities a headache. Torstenson's entire winemaking oeuvre is an endless experiment – which is why, in my opinion, he is such a valuable figure in a region like Provence which is still finding its way forward. To decode the labels, it helps if you know a little English. The "Carbase" of d'Esclans, for example, is code for a pure Carignan (produced by taking ten hl/ha off sixty-year-old and seventy-year-old vines, with a year in barrique); "Mourbase" is pure Mourvèdre. In theory, pure varietals are not allowed in Côtes de Provence – though Henning Hoesch of Richeaume has never had any difficulty with this restriction, and the official line seems to

be that it is vineyard plantings which are what matters, not what is in an individual bottle. So long as there is an appropriate blend of varieties in your vineyards, you can bottle what you like? No one is quite sure.

Single varietals, anyway, are just the beginning for Torstenson. More typical of his creative ways are two wines officially categorized as Vin de Table – Recinsaut and the one-off Rabiega Vin Toussaint. For Recinsaut, Torstenson took Cinsault from d'Esclans and made a recioto-style wine with it, allowing the bunches to dry before fermentation. Why Cinsault? "Because I didn't know what to do with that bloody grape." The Vin Toussaint takes experiment out to the very fringes of eccentricity – or parsimony. It is a multivintage (1991, 1992, and 1993) assembly of rotten-ripe Carignan picked after All Saints' Day, in November, then aged oxidatively in new Limousin oak before being blended and bottled in July 1995. The fruit was rotten-ripe, Torstenson says, because at that stage the vines were still recovering from the excess nitrogen left in the soil by years of "conventional" viticulture (all the vineyards are now cultivated organically); the vineyards also needed further drainage work. The final bottles of this last-ditch salvage operation now sell for 106 Euros per half-litre, and are apparently sought-after. There is method in his madness.

Raimond Villeneuve

Most of France's biodynamic winemakers are mid-life converts to the cause, often for the most pragmatic of reasons. They have, in other words, put it to the test against conventional viticulture, seen the improvement in their wines, and converted to it as a farming technique. Not so Raimond Villeneuve (far left).

Rudolf Steiner is far more widely known for his educational theories than for a system of agriculture developed (by others) from a series of semi-visionary lectures he gave in the year before his death. Raimond Villeneuve attended one of Steiner's schools during ten years in Germany (his mother is Bavarian), and has an instinctive understanding of the principles underlying biodynamics. The principle of the biotope, for example: a farm considered as a functioning and self-sustaining environment rather than a production unit. The importance of polyculture – which remains an ideal; Château de Roquefort is not yet polycultural. In a personal sense, too, Villeneuve has pursued the rounded Steiner ideal rather than the narrow career progression most children are forced into. This is a

family domain (since 1812), yet Villeneuve began his working life by training as a cabinetmaker and worked at that craft in Italy for three years before commercial training in Paris and a spell as a négociant in Mâcon. He finally returned in 1995 – and found Roquefort "healthy". "It had been well looked after, by just one family, in the ancestral manner. They only bought sulphur, and didn't use too much for reasons of expense. A bit of Bordeaux mixture also went on every other year, in August; not every year since that cost too much, too. I learned a lot from our old workers, Louis and François Rigaud – they had many years of observation in their heads. Observation is the basis of all organic culture. Anyone can buy biodynamic preparations, but that is only the first step."

Like many of the best growers in Provence, Villeneuve has problems with the appellation authorities: in this case, he has discovered (by observation and tasting) that his best parcel of vines is actually on land considered as poor by INAO. He is considering making all his reds and whites as Vins de Pays in future, and only producing

rosé under the Côtes de Provence banner. "The problem is that INAO doesn't understand southern environments; the pedological considerations are very different here from those in the Loire or Burgundy." And for his own vineyard – sited in the south of the appellation not far from Bandol – he is convinced that Grenache (and, to a lesser extent, Carignan) are the ideal varieties. "The base for me here is Grenache since when it's fully ripe it gives my wines the jovial quality of the south. It's the meat. Everything else is a seasoning, a vegetable."

Roquefort was a jovial place on the day I called – Raimond was talking to some German wine enthusiasts; his wife Florence was looking after their playful daughter Anastasia (whom Raimond calls "poupette"); the dogs were playful, too, despite the heat. Finally a boisterous ex-Army captain called Max arrived to taste, buy, and exchange jocund insults with the man who, he quietly confided to me later, was "the best in the region". I had a feeling le Capitaine (a bachelor gallant for whom biodynamics meant nothing) spoke from a position of extensive, and enthusiastic, research.

popular with many of the growers I talked to, though I am tempted to say for the wrong reason – because it is unproblematic. In the quotation on page 149, Lars Torstenson of Domaine Rabiega sums up both the appeal and the danger of Cabernet Sauvignon in Provence. Guy Négrel of Mas de Cadenet provides another typical response to Cabernet. "I want Cabernet Sauvignon because it brings structure – but I absolutely don't want wines which smell and taste of Cabernet." In some ways, the Cabernet debate has been skewed a little by the fact that two of the region's greatest producers, Eloi Dürrbach at Trévallon and Henning and Sylvain Hoesch at Richeaume, have both achieved outstanding results with it. Neither Trévallon nor Richeaume is wholly typical of Provence in terms of either terroir or winemaking technique, though; and in my view Cabernet Sauvignon is one of the reasons why many red wines in Provence still taste oddly bitter, sour, and austere, lacking in textural depth. Sugar ripeness is achieved too swiftly with Cabernet here, while full physiological ripeness often lags behind; Cabernet likes a slow, maritime season. The hugely experienced René Rougier of Palette's Château Simone says that Cabernet should be no more than "the salt and pepper in reds in Provence," while for Bernard Teillaud of Château Sainte Roseline the use of Cabernet is "intellectually as well as strategically a bad idea. We will always make a second-rate Cabernet by comparison with Bordeaux." Whether the core of each estate's red wine is built on Grenache or Syrah, though, depends on warmth and altitude. Even Grenache can have problems ripening fully in some of Provence's higher vineyards. The impetus for change, experiment, and further observation needs to be kept up. Remember, after all, that Mourvèdre itself was initially limited to just twenty per cent in Bandol, whereas today's greatest Bandols are pure Mourvèdre.

If anything, the situation regarding white grape varieties is still less satisfactory. Rolle, Ugni Blanc, and Clairette are the three main "native" varieties, with Grenache Blanc, Sauvignon Blanc, Sémillon, and Marsanne playing subsidiary roles. Each has its own supporters, and there is no doubt that skilled growers can make some creamy, subtle, and elegant white wines using carefully constructed blends of these permitted varieties. The Cuvée du Temple Blanc which Philippe Pouchin produces at Château Bas using Sauvignon Blanc, Rolle, and Grenache Blanc is a persuasive example, while the white wines of Château Simone in Palette make a singular case for the value and worth of Clairette. Many of Provence's white wines, however, are mild, characterless, and inconsequential – despite the fact that the height of the vineyards and their limestone soils seem unusually propitious for whites. (When Alain Combard of Domaine St-André de Figuière came to Provence from Chablis, he was expecting to make excellent reds – but it was the potential quality of the white wines that surprised him.)

If not Rolle, Ugni Blanc, and Clairette, then what? Eloi Dürrbach points out that his vineyards at Trévallon are less than ten km (six miles) from the boundaries of the Rhône region – yet a Marsanne/Roussanne white blend is forbidden for AOC whites in Provence, while the mediocre Ugni Blanc is given the run of the vineyards. Gilles Meimoun of Château Real Martin is another grower who is convinced that Marsanne and Roussanne is the right combination for Provence's whites – the proof being that he has taken Ugni Blanc as far as it can go for his existing white (based on low-yielding fifty-year-old vines picked both early and late and with "fresh" component later blended with the super-ripe component). It's pleasant wine, but evanescent; Meimoun would love to do better.

As in the southern Rhône, another key debate in Provence concerns the use of barriques. There is a "modernist" school which believes strongly that barriques can lend a depth and sensuality to the sometimes austere wines of Provence. Those who favour barriques include Richeaume, Rabiega, Courtade, Bas, and the Burgundian Luc

▲ The Alpilles – the "Alplets" – provide the raw, limestone food, shattered in colder times, for the vineyards of Les Baux.

Sorin in Bandol. "For me," says Philippe Pouchin of Château Bas, "foudres are the past. They belong to another epoch." Ranged against the use of barriques are most other Bandol producers, agreeing with Cyrille Portalis of the historic Pradeaux domain that "les tisanes de bois, ce n'est pas le Bandol" ("Bandol wines aren't oak tea"). Eloi Dürrbach and his follower Rémy Reboul of Château d'Estoublon also prefer not to use barriques for red wines. "Barriques," says Dürrbach, "make the reds round here taste too civilized. With foudres, the wine flavours are more pure; I can keep the savage character of the Alpilles in my wine." Henri de St-Victor of Château Pibarnon, a life-long wine enthusiast who is convinced that Pomerol was greater in the days before producers could get hold of copious new wood, says that "with barrique-aged Bandol you always know what you are going to get. With foudres, the wines age in a more surprising and suggestive way."

Finally, no discussion of Provence should omit the fact that this is France's leading region for the production of organic wine. "It's nothing spectacular here," said Rémy Reboul; "we can produce wines easily without chemicals, so why not?" "It's easy here," agrees Dominique Hauvette. "Most of our properties are isolated, surrounded by garrigue, and we all have the mistral." This is a superb opportunity for Provence – and yet few producers actually go to the trouble of seeking organic certification, and the region itself does not appear to use this "green" dimension in its limited marketing strategies. Why not? The producers themselves appear to think, quite misguidedly, that if they seek organic certification they will no longer appeal to "normal" wine drinkers looking for high quality vins de terroir. This view of the role of organic wine within the greater wine marketplace is now a superannuated one, as the growers and regional committees need to realize. Were Provence to replace pink with green, it would be entirely to its advantage.

The Adventure of the Land

Where does Provence begin? The wine bureaucrat's answer is likely to be very different to the man in the olive grove's answer. When I asked Serge Férigoule, who makes superb Vacqueyras at Domaine du Sang des Cailloux, where he came from, he told me he was a Provençal – from Avignon. If you drive among the villages of the southern Côtes du Rhône, you will smell lavender and see little girls wearing brightly patterned fabrics. Côtes du Ventoux might conceivably be considered (and tasted) as high-country Rhône, but Côtes du Lubéron to its south is certainly Provençal in terms of culture, landscape, and wine flavour, just like Coteaux de Pierrevert a little further east. The texts of Bosco and Giono provide delicious literary confirmation of this. For the INAO administrator, however, all of these regions hold hands under the Rhône parasol. Since in promotional terms, the Rhône is far better organized than Provence, they may be well advised to stay there; nonetheless it is a cultural impoverishment of Provence to regard it as merely beginning south of the Durance.

As you leave Avignon, the first AOC you will come to is the most recent, **Les Baux de Provence**. Les Baux only came into being as a separate AOC for red and rosé wines in 1995; prior to that, it had been a subsection of Coteaux d'Aix (whites produced here are still sold as Coteaux d'Aix). Anyone who has ever set foot in the streets of Les Baux will not forget the forbidding sight of its ruined castle walls soaring above them, nor the tales of cruelty which seep from their stones. The fastness of Les Baux is grafted onto one of the spurs of Les Alpilles ("the Alplets"), a heavily weathered and deformed limestone massif – thus most of the vineyards of this AOC are not in its high centre, but in the lower foothills to the north, south, east, and west. The vines in general grow in the limestone rubble shattered from the Alpilles during the deep chills of the Ice Ages mixed with varying amounts of clay. Even within this relatively small area, though, ripening times vary considerably: ripening at Mas de la Dame in the south, for example, is up to fifteen days ahead of Domaine de Trévallon in the north. Do the two zones therefore merit separate AOCs? If this was Burgundy, there would probably be four. Regulations for Les Baux are a little stricter than for Coteaux d'Aix in general – lower yields, denser plantings, twelve months' ageing for red wines before sale.

Lourmarin and the Lubéron hills may badge themselves as part of the Rhône
▼ *Valley, but their scents and accents are decidedly Provençal.*

Coteaux d'Aix en Provence is one of the two major catch-all AOCs of Provence. It includes a wide variety of terroirs from the eastern end of the Alpilles to the Durance river valley, from back-country high lands to the flat, developed and industrial land around the Etang de Berre. As you fly into Marseille Airport, it is the vineyards of Coteaux d'Aix which you will see below you. Limestone provides the dominant soil type throughout. Sometimes this takes the form of blindingly white rubble and scree; sometimes it melts into richer, darker clays and marls; sometimes it is mixed with sands and gravels. In terms of flavour impact, soils are much less important here than height and the diurnal temperature differences which height brings. Once again, it has to be stressed that the higher parts of Coteaux d'Aix, at between 300-400 metres (985-1,310 feet) where many of the leading domains are sited, constitute relatively cool wine-growing environments. James de Roany of Fonscolombe and Calavon, for example, has relatives in Crozes-Hermitage. By comparing notes, he has noticed that their Syrah always buds and ripens earlier than his. As I toured Provence in August 2001, the daytime temperature was in the mid-30°Cs (mid-90°Fs). At night the temperature at Château Calissanne, a property sited close to the Etang de Berre at sea level, was barely cooler. At Château Revelette, by contrast, owner Peter Fischer said that the morning temperatures were about 7°C (45°F). Once again, this is not an AOC which makes a great deal of unitary sense.

Côtes de Provence, of course, is worse. This AOC covers a vast area (about 20,000 ha/49,400 acres), and has no less than six different zones in different locations, not one of which touches another. Like Coteaux de Languedoc, it cannot be regarded as any more than a temporary and transitional appellation, though since it came into being in 1977 the situation is obviously one which INAO is not minded to resolve swiftly. We discovered with Coteaux d'Aix that in soil terms there was some homogeneity, even if the differences in height led to very different wine styles; Côtes de Provence does not even have that. At the very least, it includes three fundamentally different soil types, and the variations in height noted in Coteaux d'Aix are just as acute here. The eastern and the coastal parts of Côtes de Provence are crystalline: granite, schist, and quartz have been weathered to provide notably acidic soils. To the northwest, by contrast, there are limestone soils of the type found in Coteaux d'Aix and Les Baux, while red sandstones tend to dominate in the southwest. There are also sizeable transition zones where soils of each type are commingled. Given that

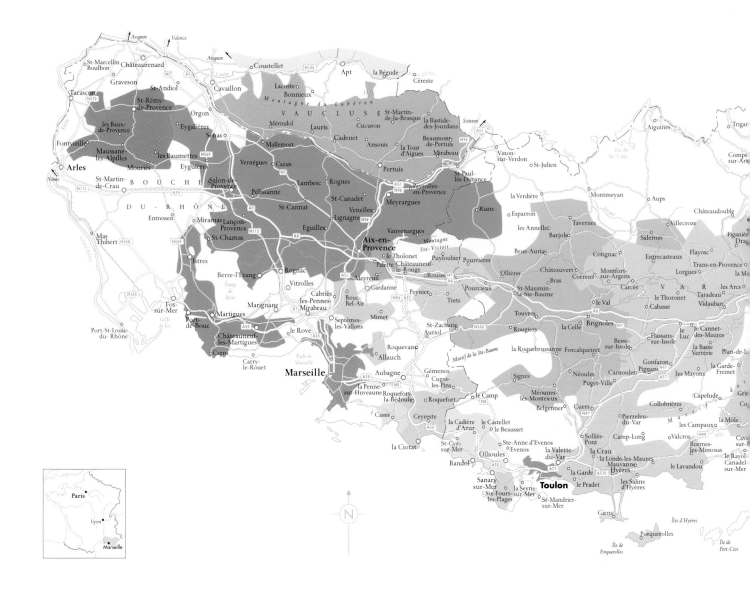

eighty per cent of production is rosé, I am tempted to say that of all French appellations, this is the one where terroir counts for least.

The small western and large eastern lobes of Côtes de Provence are interrupted by the **Coteaux Varois**. Once again, this is a large AOC containing widely dispersed vineyards; the fact that it is sited further inland, though, means that they are generally higher still (300-400 metres/985-1,310 feet is not uncommon) and cooler than many others in Provence. The annual weather pattern, too, is more continental than in other parts of Provence, with cold winters and more abrupt autumn and spring seasons. Microclimate counts for a lot here, with many vineyards nestling in hollows and dips between wooded hills.

We have now covered ninety per cent of Provence's vineyard areas. What remains are three tiny appellations of largely historical interest – plus the vineyards which constitute Provence's one true Grand Cru. This is **Bandol**. In contrast to Provence's biggest AOCs, Bandol has as clear and unitary an identity as any lonesome pine. It's comprised by the hill slopes of eight villages which lie to the hinterland of the chic

little holiday resort of Bandol itself. These form a natural amphitheatre whose highest vines lie at 400 metres (1,310 feet) or so. Many (though not all: there are internal bowls within the amphitheatre) of the slopes face due south, and the AOC gets a full 3,000 hours of sunshine a year. Compare this with Burgundy: even a sunny year like 1985 provides just 2,010 hours (and a dim year like 1965 can deliver as little as 1,583 hours). If any slopes in France deserve to be called *côtes rôties*, it is in truth those of Bandol. Geologically, it is preponderantly limestone and marl; there is some sandstone, and some red clay, too. Gruff Mourvèdre loves it here: this late-ripening variety soaks up the light and heat over the fierce summer, with the result that it behaves more amicably and generously than it does elsewhere. Low yields (a limit of 40 hl/ha with 35 hl/ha agreed for Mourvèdre) and obligatory hand-harvesting help maintain quality.

Between Bandol and Marseille lies the little AOC (just 200 ha/490 acres) of **Cassis**. Geologically it is on much purer limestone than Bandol, which is perhaps why white wines outnumber red here. The

Provence Flak

All these issues have been mentioned in the introduction; here is a final summary of Provence's three biggest problems.

Provence is ill-served by its appellation system

One of the recurring themes of this book is appellation inconsistency. Some areas (like Burgundy) have far too many appellations; others (like the southern Rhône) have too few. Some appellations (like those of the Bergerac region) cater for a past which has disappeared; some (like Côtes du Vivarais or Coteaux du Tricastin) for a future which has yet to appear. Provence, so lucky in many respects, is unlucky in that its appellation system is perhaps the least satisfactory of any major French region. Almost the only appellation which makes perfect sense at Provence at present is Bandol, though eventually Les Baux de Provence might qualify. The others are either wild generalizations, lunging sweeps of land which contain multiple and often hugely differing terroirs (Côtes de Provence is the worst case, but this is also true of Coteaux d'Aix and Coteaux Varois); or they are ant-like appellations of anecdotal interest only (Bellet, Palette, and Cassis). Reform is urgent, yet the impetus for it nowhere evident.

Provence has a grape problem

Provence does possess the treasure which every region needs: a grape to call its own. Alas, that grape is Mourvèdre, which needs furnace-like conditions to ripen. At Bandol, it finds its furnace. But most of Provence's vineyards are up in the hills, where it is much, much cooler, and where Mourvèdre is a no-hoper. Then what? Then we have Syrah, Grenache, and Cabernet Sauvignon, a thoroughly unsatisfactory partnership, with handfuls of Carignan and Cinsault thrown in to muddy the waters further. Bordeaux doesn't want to allow Provence to major on Cabernet Sauvignon or even to have Merlot to play with at all, while the Rhône valley doesn't want to let Provence concentrate on Grenache and Syrah. In the case of white wines (for which Provence has a much greater aptitude than most drinkers appreciate) the situation is similar. "Rival" regions (though no part of France should rival any other) want it to employ fundamentally dull Mediterranean grapes like Vermentino, Clairette, and Ugni Blanc with a little Sémillon and sometimes Sauvignon thrown in for luck. Bordeaux won't let it concentrate on Sémillon and Sauvignon, and the Rhône Valley won't let it have Viognier, Marsanne, and Roussanne at all. Grape wise, Provence is shafted.

In the end, evolution will have the final say, as it always does. My own belief is that one has only to look at the wider cultural situation to understand the viticultural one. As I wrote earlier in this chapter, what we wine drinkers think of as "the southern Rhône" is in fact part of Greater Provence. Wine-growing Provence should have exactly the same grape varieties as the southern Rhône – and Bordeaux varieties here should gradually be edged towards Vins de Pays status (outstanding wines from a few outstanding individual growers, but regionally a gross mistake).

Rosé: happily problematic

For books like this, the famous rosé of Provence is a problem. From the taster's point of view, most of it is (as the French might graphically put it) *nulle*: zero, void. Yet most drinkers don't read books like this. Most drinkers like the way it looks, and they don't much mind the way it tastes, either. Most drinkers enjoy it, and it makes money. Which is why the problem, for the growers of the region, is a happy one.

	Bandol
	Les Baux de Provence
	Bellet
	Cassis
	Coteaux d'Aix en Provence
	Coteaux Varios
	Côtes de Provence
	Côtes de Lubéron
	Côtes de Ventoux
	Palette
	Département boundary

Km 0   5   10   15 Km
Miles 0   5   10 Miles

fact that Ugni Blanc is the main variety used, supplemented by Clairette, Marsanne, and Sauvignon Blanc, means that the wines rarely rival the landscape in terms of beauty and memorability. **Palette** lies between Marseille and Aix-en-Provence, and is even smaller still, with just thirty-five ha (eighty-six acres) under vines at present, and in quality terms is a single-property AOC: the immaculate, jewel-like Château Simone. Once again, the base rock is limestone, though this is a very different site from Cassis: it is north-facing, and hidden in the woods. Everything about Palette is unique, including its seemingly haphazard collection of grape varieties (*see* page 152); the white is a more memorable and distinguished wine than the red. Finally, many miles to the east on Nice's doorstep, comes **Bellet**. Like Cassis and Palette, this is another tiny (thirty-eight ha/ninety-four acres) and picturesque AOC producing footnote wines from a selection box of grape varieties – mainly Rolle for the white, with Folle Noire and Braquet coming into play for the red. The vines are planted on steep slopes of gravel, sand, and clay.

Provence: People

des Alysses
83670 Pontevès, Tel: 04 94 77 10 36, Fax: 04 94 77 11 64

Late harvesting (towards the end of October) gives the red Cuvée Angelique a supple ripeness unusual in the Coteaux Varois. Proprietor Jean-Marc Etienne, a former teacher and friend of Eloi Dürrbach, also makes a Cuvée Prestige given both barrique-ageing and then an extended period in *foudres* (in 2001 the 1997 and 1998 were still in *foudres*). The raw materials for this wine are evidently superb, and both the 1994 and 1996 are balanced, full, and subtle.

Barbanau
13830 Roquefort-la-Bédoule, Tel: 04 42 73 14 60, Fax: 04 42 73 17 85

This 20-ha Côtes de Provence estate, almost adjacent to Roquefort and even closer to Bandol and Cassis, is run by Sophie Cerciello-Simonini and Didier Simonini in tandem with another estate, Clos Val Bruyère, sited in Cassis. The white wines have fine fresh citrus characters, especially the Barbanau Cuvée Classique, a blend of 80% Rolle picked slightly over-ripe with 20% Clairette.

Bas
13116 Vernègues, Tel: 04 90 59 13 16, Fax: 04 90 59 44 35

The Paris-Marseilles TGV line may have destroyed the peace and tranquillity of Georges de Blanquet's Château Bas, but under Philippe Pouchin's administration the wines of the Coteaux d'Aix property have improved dramatically. There are three levels: l'Alvernègue is the name used for the jolliest, simplest wines; Pierres du Sud are "gastronomic" wines; and the Cuvée du Temple is the top range, "a work of art and an expression of terroir," according to the ambitious Pouchin. The rosé Cuvée du Temple is one of the most successful of the new oaked versions produced by Provence's try-harder estates: it has just 40% barrel-fermentation, which fills out the palate and smooths in a little cream without losing the liquorice and peppery spice from the fruit. The Cuvée du Temple red (55% Syrah with 30% Cabernet and 15% Grenache) is suave and expressive, with some chocolate softness. Best of all to my mind, though, is the Cuvée du Temple white, perhaps the finest white wine in the AOC: elegant, subtle, creamy, and full of finesse, its delicate tangerine fruit is beautifully balanced by lemony lees richness and oak from barrel-fermentation.

Bastide Blanche
83330 Le Beausset, Tel: 04 94 32 63 20, Fax: 04 42 08 84 84

Louis and Michel Bronzo's 23-ha domain is another Bandol landmark where the Longue Garde *cuvée* (which here includes around 25% Grenache) provides wonderfully sturdy, beefy wine for the long haul. There are also two more-or-less pure Mourvèdre *cuvées*: Estagnol (grown on clay-limestone and gravel) and Fontanieu (grown on red clay).

des Béates ✪
13410 Lambesc, Tel: 04 42 57 07 58, Fax: 04 42 57 07 58

This 25-ha biodynamic domain in Coteaux d'Aix is part owned by the Chapoutier brothers; its red wines are among the biggest and most powerful in the appellation. Truffle and underbrush characters dominate the domain wine, while the Cuvée Terra d'Or is darker and oakier still, combining the bright, herb-strewn purity of fruit so typical of Provence with a richer, sturdier, and more extractive style than that either sought or achieved by others.

la Bégude
83330 Camp de Castellet, Tel: 04 42 08 92 34, Fax: 04 42 08 27 02

Guillaume Tari's 11 ha lie at one of the highest points in Bandol, at around the 400 metre mark, on marl and clay soils. The red wine contains up to 10% Grenache, and is gentler, lighter, with more fragrant in expression than some.

Bunan ✪✪
83740 La Cadière, Tel: 04 94 98 58 98, Fax: 04 94 98 60 05

Brothers Paul and Pierre Bunan were two of the great pioneers of Bandol; when they arrived at Moulin des Costes back in the 1960s, Paul remembers, "we were alone on the mountain". Now every morsel of vineyard land in the AOC is fought over. The domain is run today by Paul, his son Laurent (who worked for a while for Mondavi and Phelps in California) and long-serving cellarmaster Robert Gago, with the help of 25 employees. They now have 85 ha spread over four estates: Moulin des Costes, Mas de la Rouvière, Château de la Rouvière, and Domaine de Bélouvé. The range is exceptionally consistent, and the best wines (such as the Moulin des Costes Charriage 1998) take Bandol to new heights – or rather depths. Black in colour, with quiet yet promising scents of truffle, earth, and prune, this wine's flavour is one of the few to truly justify the symphonic metaphor. Packed with mineral fire, too, it contrives to taste (glory to France) like the abstract of a mountain.

Calissanne
13680 Lançon-de-Provence, Tel: 04 90 42 63 03, Fax: 04 90 42 40 00

This spectacularly large (1,000 ha, of which 100 ha are planted to vines) estate is sited close to the Etang de Berre, making it atypically hot for Coteaux d'Aix; a recently planted parcel of Mourvèdre, surrounded by *garrigue*, is already giving fine results. The top wine is the Clos Victoire: the white version (based on Clairette) is rich, southern, and honeyed; the red (60% Syrah and 40% Cabernet Sauvignon) is a big wine for Provence, with lots of smoke and fat and less herbal austerity than many of its AOC *confrères*.

la Calisse
83670 Pontevès, Tel: 04 93 99 11 01, Fax: 04 93 99 06 10

The unforgettable Patricia Ortelli, a passionate mid-life convert to viticulture, has brought this 10.5-ha vineyard in Coteaux Varois back to life with characteristic energy and determination. "I want people who drink the wine," she says, "to have the impression that they're biting a grape," and this freshness of fruit characterizes the three-tier range: Tradition, Patricia Ortelli, and Etoile.

la Courtade
83400 Ile-de-Porquerolles, Tel: 04 94 58 31 44, Fax: 04 94 58 34 12

Expensive and ambitious Côtes de Provence wines grown on 25 ha of the car-free island of Porquerolles, off Toulon. The barrel-fermented, Rolle-based white is long and lemony, but lacks aromatic definition; the Mourvèdre-based red is oaky and intense, with prominent acidity and sharp tannins: impressive, but slightly violent in composition. L'Alycastre is the name used for the second wines.

Duvivier
83670 Pontevès, Tel: 04 94 77 02 96, Fax: 04 94 77 26 66

Fascinating Coteaux Varois property owned by 4,500 Swiss and German shareholders organized by Karl Scheffer, a distributor of organic wines, and run by Antoine Kaufmann. The best wine is Les Mûriers, one of the earthiest and densest wines in the AOC.

d'Estoublon
13990 Fontvieille, Tel: 04 90 54 64 00, Fax: 04 90 54 64 01

This old property sited to the southwest of the Coteaux des Baux appellation is in mid-renovation at present. The handsome Rémy Reboul, his welcoming

---

Star rating system used on producer spreads   ✪ Very good wine   ✪✪ Excellent wine   ✪✪✪ Great wine

wife Valérie and her father, Ernest Schneider (owner of Breitling watches), are restoring the estate, with viticultural and vinification advice from Eloi Dürrbach of Trévallon. There are 17 ha of vines planted at present and will eventually be 20 ha, most on rough gravel soils; the 1999 and 2000 red wines (aged in 30-hl foudres rather than barriques) are both relatively light, but full of sweet, comely fruit. The blend is Grenache-dominated, with small percentages of Syrah and Counoise and a pinch of Cinsault. The Ugni Blanc/Grenache Blanc white is over-weighty, but Reboul has planted Marsanne and Roussanne which he hopes will come on stream for 2003 and improve matters (despite the fact that the INAO has trained its guns on these varieties in Provence).

Jean-Pierre Gaussen ✪
83740 La Cadière-d'Azur, Tel: 04 94 98 75 54, Fax: 04 94 98 65 34

This 15-ha domain, the best parts of which are sited at the bottom of a long, clay-limestone slope near La Cadière d'Azur, is another Bandol domain with a fine tradition for its Longue Garde cuvée (produced, from pure Mourvèdre, in the best years only). They are vinified, unusually, in roto-fermenters, and aged in old foudres. Youthful aromas of blackberry and blackcurrant give way to a brooding taciturnity after a few years, in turn resolved into aromas of meat, tobacco, and tapenade. The tannins are dense and mouth-coating, and there is the true pounding fire of this sun-roasted AOC in the wine's core.

Gros' Noré ✪
83740 La Cadière-d'Azur, Tel: 04 94 90 08 50, Fax: 04 94 98 20 65

Rough diamond Alain Pascal has 13 ha of vines on the same fine clay-lime hillside stretch in Bandol as Lafran-Veyrolles and Jean-Pierre Gaussen; the terroir comes surging through in red wines of typically gruff power and meaty depth with (at present) a smoky-sweet sheen from new foudres.

Dominique Hauvette
13210 St-Rémy de Provence, Tel: 04 90 92 03 90, Fax: 04 90 92 08 91

Dominique Hauvette is a skilled winemaker, working with 14 ha of her own and a further 6 rented ha, all in Les Baux. She believes (unlike many) in Cinsault, and makes a wine called Amethyst (90% of which is 35-year-old Cinsault) to prove her point: soft, drinkable, soothing, and perfumed. The domain wine, meanwhile, based on 50% Grenache with Syrah and Cabernet, is long, tangy, and subtle.

Lafran Veyrolles ✪
83740 La Cadière-d'Azur, Tel: 04 94 90 11 18, Fax: 04 94 90 11 18

Claude Jouve-Ferec's 10-ha domain produces, in addition to worthwhile Clairette-based white wines and a lightly fruited rosé, two deep Bandol reds, the "classique" in which the Mourvèdre is mixed with Cinsault, old-vine Carignan, and Grenache; and a pure Mourvèdre cuvée called Longue Garde. The classique is a sturdy blackberry-scented wine; the Longue Garde, by contrast, is more brooding, with its scents of earth and ash and its blend of fire, stone, and vivid plum.

Mas de Cadenet
13530 Trets, Tel: 04 42 29 21 59, Fax: 04 42 61 32 09

Father Guy and son Mathieu Négrel's 40 ha of Côtes de Provence vines produce wines divided into two ranges: Mas de Cadenet for foudre-aged wines, and Mas Négrel Cadenet for old-vine selections which are aged in barriques. The blends in principle are similar: preponderantly Rolle for the whites, giving wines of whispering aniseed softness; while the reds are based on Grenache (45%), Syrah (40%), and Cabernet Sauvignon (15%). Both cuvées of the red are supple and ripe, but the Mas Négrel Cadenet version makes a persuasive case both for old vines and barriques: it is here that the distinctive gravel terroir of the estate comes to the fore in a wine of gratefully earthy finesse.

Mas de la Dame
13520 Baux de Provence, Tel: 04 90 54 32 24, Fax: 04 90 54 40 67

Pleasingly, the Mas de la Dame (mentioned by local seer Nostradamus in one of his less gnomic predictions) is now owned by two dames: Anne Poniatowski and Caroline Missoffe. The estate, which lies in the warmer southern half of Les Baux, is advised by Jean-Luc Colombo, who has instituted full manual harvesting

and helped rethink the range. The Coin Caché white (based on 80% Sémillon balanced by Clairette) is one of Provence's best oaked white wines – a rich, creamy, lush mouthful. Among the three red wines, the Réserve de Mas Rouge is most typically Provençal: relatively light and dry, full of herbed stonefruit. The red Coin Caché (based on a single parcel of Grenache with 20% Syrah) is a delicious glance towards Châteauneuf from Les Baux, spicy and jammy though with a typical Provençal lightness of touch. Top of the range is La Stèle (the name refers to the pyramidal gatepost – at which point, according to Nostradamus, the invading sea will one day stop). The 40% Cabernet seems to stamp the wine more forcefully than the 60% Syrah.

Mas de Gourgonnier
13890 Mouries, Tel: 04 90 47 50 45, Fax: 04 90 47 51 36

This traditional, carefully run domain in the warm, southern sector of Les Baux is now into its fifth generation. The Réserve du Mas is the best wine: a meaty red whose Grenache, Syrah, and Cabernet components have a spicy quality entirely unrelated to new oak (the Cartier brothers prefer the "managed oxidation" of foudres).

Mas de la Rouvière *see* Bunan

Moulin des Costes *see* Bunan

Ouillières
13410 Lambesc, Tel: 04 42 92 83 39, Fax: 04 42 92 83 39

Large domain (78 ha in Coteaux d'Aix with a further 22 ha as Vins de Pays) whose best red wines, the Dame des Ouillières and the Réserve Louis Charles, both combine intense prune fruit with intelligent use of oak. This is also one of the few domains to persist with the Provençal tradition of vin cuit (simmered must which is then barrique-fermented and aged).

Pibarnon ✪
83740 La Cadière-d'Azur, Tel: 04 94 90 12 73, Fax: 04 94 90 12 98

Determination and vision have built Pibarnon from 3.5ha of Bandol vineyards surrounding an ugly little house to 50 ha of vineyards surrounding what appears to be an 18th-century manor. The almost boyishly enthusiastic Henri de St-Victor was the driving force behind the creation of the vineyard, and is still very involved, though his son Eric is taking over the relay. The white wine here is based on nearly as many varieties as Simone, and is subtle and nuanced. The red, almost pure Mourvèdre with just a dash of Grenache, is one of the subtler and less bruising Bandols, too, memorably combining savoury and sweet notes (soft plum, tobacco, violet, and pine).

Pigoudet
83560 Rians, Tel: 04 94 80 31 78, Fax: 04 94 80 54 25

Look out for the flower-and-herb-scented Cuvée la Chapelle, whose length and purity indicates careful viticulture. Sabine Rabe and Elke Schmidt's 70-ha property near Rians is the most northerly of Coteaux d'Aix.

Pradeaux
83270 St-Cyr-sur-Mer, Tel: 04 94 32 10 21, Fax: 04 94 32 16 02

If any estate seeps history in Bandol, it is this one: the estate was acquired in 1752 by Jean-Marie-Etienne Portalis, one of the co-authors of the Napoleonic civil code; later generations of the family, in particular Countess Arlette Portalis, helped get the AOC off the ground back in 1941. The relaxed and affable Cyrille Portalis is now in charge of the antique cellars with their mountains of ancient (and occasionally seeping) foudres. Everything is done traditionally: harvesting is late; there is no destemming; there are certainly no barriques, and the wines remain in foudres for three or four years. The 20 ha of vines are sited much lower than most of the other great domains in the AOC, at about 30 metres. The wines are relatively pale in colour, tannin-dredged (and thus almost Nebbiolo-like), with flavours of mushrooms, earth, and olives. The site of the estate is much coveted by transport planners: having lost land to the 1956 Paris-Nice rail link and only just avoided the Marseille-Toulon motorway, Pradeaux is now under threat from the Marseille-Toulon rail link.

Rabiega

83300 Draguignan, Tel: 04 94 68 44 22, Fax: 04 94 47 17 72

Provence's most inventive and experimental domain was bought by the Swedish drinks company (and then monopoly) Vin & Sprit in 1986, and has been run by Lars Torstenson since 1988. They go to market as Côtes de Provence, Vin de Pays, and even Vin de Tables, depending on which side of the local rules and regulations they fall. It's not an easy domain to describe succinctly, since Torstenson hardly ever does the same thing twice. In any case, there are two domains: Domaine Rabiega (10 ha, high-sited, and open to the mountains), and the leased Château d'Esclans (35 ha, low-sited, and open to the sea at La Motte); wines simply labelled Rabiega are part of the estate's micro-négociant business. Lead bottles include the white Clos Dière, a wine of reticent peachiness made from Sauvignon Blanc (60%), Chardonnay (30%), and Viognier; the Clos Dière red, meanwhile, comes in two versions (I is Syrah-based; II is built on Grenache and Carignan with a seasoning of Cabernet). Clos Dière I is a sensual, fragrant, subtle wine with creamy fruits; Clos Dière II is less outstanding, though its sweet oak and jolly, juicy fruit is enjoyable enough. Recinsaut is an intriguing *recioto*-style Cinsault from d'Esclans, while the Carbase and Mourbase wines from Esclans are both monovarietals (Carignan and Mourvèdre respectively); the former has more fiery depth and pruney intensity; the latter is correct but gentle.

Real Martin

83143 Le Val, Tel: 04 94 86 40 90, Fax: 04 94 86 32 23

Some 33 ha of this 200 ha estate, sited high (350-400 metres) on the borders of Côtes de Provence and Coteaux Varois, are planted to vines – but none of them, interestingly, are Cabernet Sauvignon. The wines are made by owner Jacques Clotilde's son-in-law, Gilles Meimoun, with advice from Jacky Coll (who helped create La Courtade). Meimoun insists that what he wants above all is the Mediterranean character in his wines. The white is as characterful as Ugni Blanc can ever be; the red, an unwooded blend of Syrah and Grenache, is balanced and elegant. The L'Optimum version is not, Meimoun insists, a prestige *cuvée*, but simply an alternative red in which a proportion of the Syrah component has spent a year in barriques.

Revelette

13490 Jouques, Tel: 04 42 63 75 43, Fax: 04 42 67 62 04

Peter Fischer's domain (in contrast, for example, to Calissanne) is one of the highest in Coteaux d'Aix, with vineyards at 400 metres. The stamp of this altitude can be tasted in the purity and elegance of the wines, including one of Provence's best Chardonnays (the Grand Blanc, a Vin de Pays des Bouches du Rhône) and the Syrah-Cabernet Grand Rouge, a wine of depth and incision but grace and purity, too.

Richeaume ✪

13114 Puyloubier, Tel: 04 42 66 31 27, Fax: 04 42 66 30 59

This superb 60-ha red-soiled Côtes de Provence estate (with 25 ha under vines) nestles like a fox cub beneath the motherly Mont Ste-Victoire, and has been run for 30 years now by historian Henning Hoesch. He has recently been joined by his son Sylvain, who trained with Paul Draper at Ridge in California, and with Penfolds in Australia, too. Despite the necessity of replanting in 1989 after a fire, the wines are far denser and more succulent than in the past, partly thanks to later and later harvest dates. The Cabernet is beautifully crafted, with mingled currant and cinder flavours, while the Syrah achieves a perfumed lyricism closer to the northern Rhône style than the south. The Cuvée Columelle is one of Provence's great wines: a complex, finely detailed selection of the estate's best Cabernet, Syrah, and Merlot over which the perfume of sweet thyme seems to blow. The Viognier is successful, too, with its scent of nougat and haunting flavour of flower oils.

Rimauresq

83790 Pignans, Tel: 04 94 48 80 45, Fax: 04 94 33 22 31

This 37-ha Côtes de Provence domain, well run by the honest and intelligent

Pierre Duffort, is owned by a Scottish family of tea planters called Wemyss. (You can see a bottle of 1858 Lafite, embossed with the name Wemyss Castle, in the cellar reception area.) The terroir is unusual: sandy granite, quartz, schist, and rocks with a verdigris appearance which Duffort thinks might be due to the presence of bauxite. Both the white (pure Rolle in 2000) and the red (Cabernet, Syrah, Mourvèdre, Grenache, and a little Carignan, *foudre*-aged) are not so much herb-strewn as mineral-infused, giving them an impressive purity and distinction; with lower yields, they could be better still.

Romanin

13210 St-Rémy-de-Provence, Tel: 04 90 92 45 87, Fax: 04 90 92 24 36

This 54-ha biodynamically-run Les Baux estate has been created by Jean-André Charial, the chef-owner of the Les Baux restaurant l'Oustau de Baumanière, on behalf of a Parisian couple called Colette and Jean-Pierre Peyraud. The red is a blend of Syrah, Grenache, and Cabernet Sauvignon to which Counoise and Mourvèdre are occasionally added; there is also a selection of the best fruit called Coeur, which is part-barrique aged. These are not fleshy wines; elegance and vivacity are their hallmarks, with slighty bitter, herbal finishes.

La Roque

83740 La Cadiere d'Azur, Tel: 04 94 90 10 39, Fax: 04 94 90 08 11

With Grande Reserve, the Bandol cooperative shows that it can compete with some of the AOCs better private domains: this 30hl/ha wine with 5% each of Grenache and Carignan to balance the Mourvèdre evolves relatively swiftly, yet has an appealingly harmonious, creamy style with wild-mushroom notes.

de Roquefort ✪

13830 Roquefort La Bedoule, Tel: 04 42 73 20 84, Fax: 04 42 73 11 19

Raimond Villeneuve's 27-ha Côtes de Provence domain is sited behind the hill from Bandol and Cassis: it combines height (350 metres) and proximity to the sea (under 5 km away) with reddish clay-limestone soils and a warm, bowl-like position underneath the ruined fortress of Roquefort. Villeneuve's balanced approach to his land is the very model of biodynamic thinking (as opposed to biodynamic fashion): above all, he wants it to function as a biotope, a sustainable, balanced organism, and in this respect wages an ongoing struggle against a pony club who enjoy a lease on some of the land and who have different priorities. He makes two whites: a pure Clairette Vin de Pays des Bouches du Rhône, crisp and liquorice-flavoured; and the richer, creamier Les Genêts, a blend of Clairette and Rolle with a little barrel-fermentation. Les Mûres, a blend of all of his red varieties, has bright, come-hither fruit scents, vivid pungency, and a clean, ripely bitter end; Rubrum Obscurum Ex Veteribus Vitibus (the "dark red from old vines") is a *foudre*-aged blend of Grenache, Mourvèdre, and Carignan with splendidly dense plum fruit layered with sweet herbs. The *saignée* from Rubrum Obscurum is used for a fine, salty rosé called Semiramis. Finally, in certain years Villeneuve produces La Pourpre, the Le Pin of Provence: a spicy, exotic, and lush blend of Syrah and old Carignan given wood ageing in young *demi-muids*.

Routas

83149 Châteauvert, Tel: 04 94 69 93 92, Fax: 04 94 69 93 92

The energetic Philippe Bieler, Wall Street refugee and ex-cranberry tycoon turned wine producer, creates a wide range of wines from this 45-ha domain under both Coteaux Varois and Vin de Pays du Var legislation. Pyramus is a typical Provençal white blend of Ugni Blanc, Rolle, and Clairette, while Coquelicot is a Viognier (80%) and Chardonnay blend. Infernet (named after an astonishingly deep sink-hole found on the property) is a typical Provençal blend of Grenache, Syrah, and Cabernet, and Agrippa is a straight Syrah-Cabernet blend. There are also three red varietals: The Cabernet Sauvignon That Wild Boars Prefer (sic), Cyrano (a pure Syrah), and Carignane (a pure Carignan from 60-year-old vines). In general the style is light, elegant and pure.

Rouvière *see* Bunan

St-André de Figuière

83250 La Londe-les-Maures, Tel: 04 94 00 44 70, Fax: 04 94 35 04 46

This 20-ha domain in maritime, granite-and-schist-soiled Côtes de Provence is owned by Alain Combard, who worked for 20 years with Michel Laroche in Chablis before returning to his roots. Contrary to what he expected, Combard found that his white wines were more impressive than his reds: the luscious and pear-fruited Grande Cuvée Delphine puts Rolle through its paces with 100% barrel fermentation. The red wines are pure and elegant.

Sainte Roseline
83460 Les Arcs-surs-Argens, Tel: 04 94 99 50 30, Fax: 04 94 47 53 06

No expense has been spared by Bernard Teillaud in restoring this beautiful Côtes de Provence domain which, ten centuries ago, was in monastic hands, and which stands next to a church in which you can see the mummified body of a saint, minus one eye (it was stabbed by a curious bishop). There has been much replanting and many of the 37 ha of vines are still young, but advice from Michel Rolland is already helping to produce the creamy white Cuvée Prieure (based on Rolle and Sémillon) and the warm and curranty red Cuvée Prieure (based on Mourvèdre, Syrah, and Cabernet Sauvignon).

du Seuil
13540 Puyircard, Tel: 04 42 92 15 99, Fax: 04 42 92 18 77

The exquisitely labelled Château Grand Seuil wines include a honeyed, sumptuous white, an over-oaked rosé (12 months in barriques) and a plump, soft, comforting red whose majority Cabernet component (60%) is late harvested for full ripeness. This beautiful Coteaux d'Aix 55-ha domain belonging to the Carreau Gaschereau family lies around the 350 metre mark.

Simone
13590 Meyreuil, Tel: 04 42 66 92 58, Fax: 04 42 66 80 77

The little vineyard in the big woods is immaculately looked after by René Rougier and his son Jean-François, musicians and winemakers both; it's worth a visit for the spectacular ride along its hillside drive alone. For the time being, Simone is the only vineyard in Palette producing serious wine, though Crémade under its new Parisian owner may soon compete. The Simone vineyards are unusual in almost every respect: they are planted on north-facing limestone rubble on the side of the Arc Valley in a woodland location. "I've never ripped up a vine in my life," says René Rougier; some of the vines here are 150 years old, and there is a huge spectrum of varieties planted including Muscat, Furmint, and Bourboulenc among the whites and Castet and Manosquin among the reds. Nonetheless the white is mostly Clairette (80%), and the red is 50% Grenache and 25% Mourvèdre. Both receive a long *élevage* (the red actually spends two years in *foudre* before going into barrique), and make most sense after further bottle age. The white acquires a strange and eerie allusiveness, suggesting wax and incense, though it is kept lively at all times by its vivid acidity: is this the world's best Clairette? The rosé, both vinified and aged in *foudres*, is vinous and adult; the reds are relatively light, slender, and elegant. The Bordeaux bottles with their beautifully old-fashioned labels add to this estate's uniqueness.

la Suffrène ✪
83740 La Cadière-d'Azur, Tel: 04 94 90 09 23, Fax: 04 94 90 02 21

Cédric Gravier is a recent arrival on the Bandol scene, having left the cooperative, with impeccable timing, just before the 1998 harvest, but his early domain releases confirm him as one of the new stars of the AOC. For a début vintage, the superb old-vine Cuvée Les Lauves showed beautifully judged rich tannins, chestnut and earth flavours and a sustained acid balance, too.

Tempier ✪
83330 Le Castellet, Tel: 04 94 98 70 21, Fax: 04 94 90 21 65

With Pradeaux, Tempier is one of the two grand old warhorses of the Bandol AOC. The Peyraud family succession has been interrupted for the time being, but Savoyard Daniel Ravier is getting into his stride with the wines on behalf of the owning family, and the last few vintages have marked a return to historic form. There are no fewer than five separate red *cuvées*. Two cover the entire domain: the light and cherryish Classique (20-year-old vines in which Mourvèdre is joined by Grenache, Carignan, and Cinsault) and the more succulent Cuvée Spéciale (35-year-old vines, with 80% Mourvèdre and 20% Grenache). Three

single-vineyard wines then follow. La Tourtine is based on a 6-ha parcel at 170 metres, and Cabassou is a 1.2-ha parcel underneath La Tourtine. La Migoua, meanwhile, is a 5-ha parcel sited at about 270 metres, though a full southerly exposition and an amphitheatrical aspect turn up the heat. The proportion of Mourvèdre varies: 95% for Cabassou (plus a little Grenache, Cinsault, and Syrah); between 70 and 80% for La Tourtine (plus Cinsault and Grenache); and just 50% for La Migoua (plus 30% Cinsault, 18% Grenache, 2% Syrah). Cabassou, as you might expect, is the beefiest, spiciest, and earthiest; Migoua is long and animal, full of bay leaf and calfskin; La Tourtine can be slightly austere, though its *garrigue* and olive nuances are pure and provoking.

Tour du Bon ✪
83330 Le Brûlat du Castellet, Tel: 04 98 03 66 22, Fax: 04 98 03 66 26

Well-run 12-ha Bandol domain producing a harmonious, vivid, and svelte Classique ready to drink relatively swiftly (55% Mourvèdre with 35% Grenache and 10% Cinsault) as well as the superb St-Ferréol, packed with concentrated black olive and dry cocoa, for long keeping.

Trévallon ✪
13103 St-Etienne du Gres, Tel: 04 90 49 06 00, Fax: 04 90 49 02 17

It is somehow typical of the muddle and fragmentation which characterize wine-growing in Provence that the greatest of all wine producers in Les Baux, Eloi Dürrbach of Domaine de Trévallon, is forced to sell his wine as Vin de Pays. Dürrbach's disputes with the authorities, historically based on his use of Cabernet, has even meant that he has been refused permission to expand his 15-ha vineyard – so new plantings have to be compensated for by uprooting some of his old vineyards. Trévallon lies in the far north of Les Baux, on 30 tiny parcels of bright white limestone rubble, giving wines with lots of finesse but not necessarily huge power (it's too cool here, says Dürrbach, to ripen either Mourvèdre or Grenache fully). The white wine, a defiant barrique-fermented Roussanne/Marsanne blend, is sumptuously honeyed; the red (nowadays a 50/50 Cabernet/Syrah blend) is poised and balanced, full of herb and bay. It unfolds slowly in time. Back in 1985, Dürrbach bottled experimental versions of the red aged in both barrique and *foudre*; with time, he says, the *foudre* wines were "purer; they kept the savage character of the area better." Trévallon, therefore, is entirely aged in *foudres* today.

les Valentines
83250 La-Londe-les-Maures, Tel: 04 94 15 95 50, Fax: 04 94 15 95 55

Ex-Parisian computer entrepreneur Gilles Pons' Côtes de Provence 23-ha domain is now producing one of Provence's best Ugni Blanc-based whites (from 70-year-old vines). Pons uses a similar technique to Gilles Meimoun at Real Martin and others whereby a portion is picked early for freshness and another portion harvested very late for rich lushness. The red is no less carefully constructed from 35% each of Grenache and Syrah plus 15% of Cabernet and Mourvèdre; the two latter varieties are vinified in wooden conicals for structure, while the former varieties are vinified in concrete for a fruit emphasis. Some 30% of the final blend goes into barrique. The result is fresh, lively, and peppery.

Vannières
83740 La Cadière-d'Azur, Tel: 04 94 90 08 08, Fax: 04 94 90 15 98

This handsome 32-ha estate on the boundary of Bandol (20 ha) and Côtes de Provence (10 ha, with 2 ha for Vin de Pays) produces a pretty, peachy white wine and a red Bandol of remarkable floral aroma in youth, with fresh spice and smooth tannins, ageing gracefully towards a sweet and creamy old age.

Vignelaure
83560 Rians, Tel: 04 94 37 21 10, Fax: 04 94 80 53 39

Few estates in France have had quite such a colourful ownership history as this one in Coteaux d'Aix; it merits a book of its own. The owner today is former Irish racehorse-trainer David O'Brien, and the estate is settling down with a pretty, mid-weight, tobacco-scented and cherry-fruited domain wine as well as Cabernet and Merlot varietals sold as Vin de Pays.

Bordeaux

Rewriting the Classics Bordeaux has changed. This was once a region where conservative precedent was all; it is now a region of experiment, ambition, and grand stylistic diversity. The dilute and inarticulate will no longer suffice.

You'd think you were in a glass lift at first, moving up a few floors in the open air. But the lift doesn't stop. You move up a swift forty floors in the bright sunlight. The lift shakes, unshackled. Then it tilts forward, the horizon slides upwards, and you're looking down through the glass walls to the dusty, blade-blown patch of earth you've left below. But you don't fall. The patch of earth, and its neighbouring trees, begins to trail backwards. The helicopter shudders off through the warm air.

At first the Médoc reveals only its history of quiet pasture, its cast of somnolent brown cows. Their grass sinks into the great avenue of muddy water that defines this land's eastern boundaries. Then, one by one, white patches stitched with green brocade begin to appear. They are never as uniform as you'd think when you drive along the region's roads; woodland and pasture, ditch and dyke, interrupt the vineyards with boggy breaks. Only in St-Julien and Pauillac, after the resurgence of pastureland which succeeds Margaux, is there anything to approach the monocultural.

Many vineyards look toothless, scattered with missing vines. There are stretches of empty earth, tortured with herbicide: brown, lifeless. Hills? There's only one: Lafite's, rising up from its marsh and its gardens, overseen by Cos d'Estournel to the north and shared by Mouton to the south. The rest, from up here in the lark air, are no more than caresses of pale sand and pebble, moulded like snow over which the faintest of

night breezes has shimmered. With our bird's eyes the châteaux, so portentous on the ground, seem mere cairns – neat piles of stones left by travellers to make sense of a senseless place. After St-Estèphe, the thread of symmetrical viticulture is lost. The white patches grow intermittent; the neat rows occasional. The forest gnaws into the land.

Then it's a Saturday evening, and this is a Belgian bicycle: sturdy, comfortable, middle-aged. There's been rain, leaving the air washed clean; the spring sun is now sinking over Libourne, over Bordeaux, over the Atlantic, leaving Pomerol flushed faintly with russet gold. The pointed finger of the church steeple cuts into the cooling sky. I pedal off from Le Pin and Catusseau – hamlet of vegetable plots, of vineyard worker's houses, of secret ambitions – towards Trotanoy. It looks Tuscan, with its drive of cypresses. They're replanting a parcel next to the road. I study the bare earth, idiotically looking for traces of visible magic, and finding none. Just stones, million upon million of them, water-rolled and water-sucked from the distant hills of Périgord, of the Limousin. The sticky tile-orange molasse clutches them meaninglessly.

I bike on – to the church, Pomerol's pip. The war memorial *tricolore* flutters bravely in the evening breeze. There's a school, a playing field, a few houses; you can't really call it a village. Even the cemetery lies elsewhere, across the vineyards, next to Eglise-Clinet. I bike out that way, then turn right, to head for the Gays and the Fleurs. It's looking

stonier still up here; and the vineyards slope off visibly to my left, dipping down to the River Barbanne. Pétrus is easy to find: the *chaufferettes* line the vineyards (March and April means frost danger), and the gilded P at the top of the flagpole catches the evening sun. I'm riding gently uphill, now: this is the highest zone in the appellation. It's said to sit on a buttonhole of clay which pushes up through the gravel and molasse, this sacred monster of a vineyard, but to the cyclist's eye the vineyards look no different from those of Vieux Château Certan next door. I then turn left, and left again: past La Conseillante, past Evangile – and then across the strange appellation boundary for a little detour into St-Emilion. Cheval Blanc and the Figeacs proclaim themselves with typical Bordelais discretion; there are no Hermitage-style painted walls here. I retrace my *trajet*, and head back past Petit Village and Beauregard to Catusseau. I've seen the best of the best, and it took just half-an-hour. Had I set out to pedal up the Médoc, I'd have barely begun. Le Pin, Trotanoy, L'Eglise-Clinet, Lafleur, Pétrus... yet next to them properties like Haut-Tropchaud, Guillot, Chêne Liège. The world-famous next to the utterly obscure: that's Bordeaux, too.

Bordeaux: wine giant

Suppose, if you will, that the wine map of France was based not on topography but on emotion and aspiration. The position of Bordeaux would swiftly change. It would no longer constitute a flat red puddle lying at the base of the country's green and mountainous southwest, marked by a deep marine incision; it would lie somewhere very close to the country's heart. Bordeaux not only constitutes France's biggest AOC area; its success also furnishes the scale by which all other French regions measure themselves. Indeed every producer who has ambitions to make great red wine anywhere in the world looks to Bordeaux. It is to French wine what Shakespeare is to English drama, what Verdi is to Italian opera, or what Tolstoy is to the Russian novel: inexhaustible, containing multitudes, defining not merely itself but the whole culture in which it exists.

A few facts and figures illustrate the point. The great Rhône Valley appellation of Hermitage, for example, occupies 134 ha (331 acres) in total; a leading Hermitage grower like Jean-Louis Chave cultivates just ten ha (25 acres) of that geologically complicated hill. There's only ninety-eight ha (242 acres) of Condrieu in total, and even the recently extended AOC of Côte Rôtie covers just 200 ha (494 acres). In Burgundy, parcels are smaller still. A large négociant like Louis Jadot grows wines under thirty-eight appellations – yet that still means only seventy ha (173 acres). Of those marketing and bottling Grand Cru Montrachet, the majority possess well under a single hectare of vines. There are just twenty-five cases of Leflaive's Montrachet to satisfy the whole world.

"If you play finesse on a great terroir, you have the classics of Bordeaux. Power is not a natural element in Bordeaux, because we don't have the same amount of sun as California or Australia. When we play in that field, it is like a boxer who is boxing above his weight. When you box above your weight, you know how it will end. Sadly."

CHRISTIAN MOUEIX

"Trop de finesse tue la finesse."

JEAN-LUC THUNEVIN

It's been a long march to the top for Angélus. Having arrived, it's easing back on sheer weight for stylistic refinement.

Contrast Bordeaux. Château Lafite-Rothschild, one of Bordeaux's five first growths, has ninety ha (222 acres) under vine, and produces up to 19,000 cases a year; the biggest of the classed growths, Château Lagrange, has no fewer than 113 ha (279 acres) to its name – more than the whole AOC of Condrieu. Most Médoc châteaux have at least fifty ha (123 acres) planted; four châteaux, therefore, would occupy the entire surface of Côte Rôtie. The Médoc has hundreds of such châteaux. Properties are, admittedly, smaller in St-Emilion and Pomerol (Cheval Blanc has thirty-six ha/eighty-nine acres and Pétrus just eleven ha/ twenty-seven acres), yet the appellations themselves are still huge by comparison with others elsewhere in France: St-Emilion occupies over 5,000 ha (12,350 acres, or, if you prefer, thirty-seven whole AOC Hermitages). Not all of this wine is great, of course; indeed plenty of it is dull and dilute. But there are still enough superb vineyard sites to provide a deep pool of several colours, and of various degrees of sweetness. Bordeaux is the only region of France to produce red, dry white, and sweet white wine at the very highest levels. You could drink Bordeaux wine on most occasions without any sort of privation at all; all the region is missing is a good source of sparkling wine.

This size, the notion of the "château", and the fact that different regions of Bordeaux have long-standing and officially accepted classification systems has helped Bordeaux's prosperity enormously. It means, in effect, that a stock market exists for fine Bordeaux wine. No other region in France (or, as yet, the world) benefits from this. There is enough fine wine from Bordeaux for stock to be comfortably acquired, held and traded internationally; and châteaux names which make no reference to ownership lend this stock an air of permanence and continuity which is altogether missing, for example, from notoriously mutable Burgundian family domains. The core of every fine wine or wine brokerage business, therefore, is fine Bordeaux. This brings wealth to the region, and keeps the world's attention focused on it.

It also disguises the fact that, historically speaking, Bordeaux as we know it today is a relatively young wine region. It is much younger than Burgundy, and is junior, too, to local rivals such as Cahors, whose grandeur was once so envied by Bordeaux that it resorted to underhand protectionism to steal its markets. There was some viticulture here in Roman times – most notably in St-Emilon, whose steep south-facing escarpment would immediately have triggered Roman viticultural instincts. (They never wasted a hill, either for defence fortifications or a decent vineyard.) The Médoc, by contrast, was a dreary and inaccessible marshland prone to flooding until the seventeenth century. The Dutch water engineers then drained it, and the great gravel banks thus liberated proved, with time, to be extraordinarily welcoming for Cabernet Sauvignon vines. A terroir was discovered; with it came mushrooming prosperity. A short drive up the D2 which threads its intricate way northwards through the Médoc takes you past an unrivalled concentration of portentous masonry. This was the Napa Valley of the eighteenth century.

Bordeaux's fortunes in the twentieth century have been mixed, though no more so than any other of France's major wine regions. The economics of wine, after all, are intimately linked to two things: nature's gifts (the quality of vintages, particularly important in a maritime climate like Bordeaux's), and the social context in which the wines are consumed. Two world wars and a global economic depression were not the ideal backdrop for viticultural prosperity in the first half of the last century; poor vintages in the 1930s and mixed vintages in the 1960s and 1970s, too, depressed potential interest. Bordeaux was in any case complacent, living on its historical

It was in backstreets like these, in the picturesque and wholly impractical town of St-Emilion, that the garage movement was born. ▶

reputation; those who make wine in the region today shudder when they see the mediocrity to which great properties were allowed to sink. They open many of their own museum bottles with trepidation.

The year that changed everything was 1982. It was a glorious, hot, and generous vintage, and the winemaking advances put in place by Professor Emile Peynaud (most notably the selection of the best part of the harvest alone for the *grand vin* which bears the château name) were beginning to have their effect. Since 1982, the top 300 properties in Bordeaux have experienced a period of prosperity unmatched since the mid-nineteenth century. What's brought this about?

Demand, first of all. The world has grown more peaceful and more prosperous during these years, and cultures which once took little interest in wine, and the European cuisine in which it plays such a key role, have now learned to prize both. Up until 1982, Bordeaux's customers were essentially the European middle class, plus a few wealthy Europhile Americans. It is now the whole of an increasingly moneyed world. Indeed it was almost hysterical demand from new Asian markets which drove up the en primeur price of 1996 Bordeaux, and which encouraged the Bordeaux château-owners to offer the amiable but weakly constituted 1997 vintage at unsustainably high prices. There is a deep pool of top Bordeaux, but it is finite.

The second major factor has been the rise of the wine media and the wine critic. In March of each year following the vintage, the critics arrive and make their initial assessment of the wines. This is a hazardous business, since the wines are unfinished, the blends not yet finalized, and the hurdle of bottling still over a year away. Not only are assessments made hastily, but allegations of doctored samples, of the *cuvée du journaliste*, regularly surface. Pascal Delbeck of Château Belair claimed, at the time of the 2000 en primeur tastings, that "percentage scores given to the new vintage [are] often based on doctored samples", while a leading Pomerol proprietor assured me that American oak is often used to "sweeten" the samples shown at en primeur tastings. The proprietors price their wines based on the reaction of the critics, and in particular the vintage report of Robert Parker. The wines are then released; a flurry of speculative purchases ensues. This has created a culture of winner wines or trophy wines that, a decade or more from maturity and often before they are even bottled, attain astonishingly high prices. As I write, the infant 2000s of some châteaux are opening at higher prices than the great (and now semi-mature) 1990s from the same properties. The avalanche of cash for the winners acts as a magnetizing incentive to other producers to up their game – creating in turn a bigger pool of winner wines. The net result is increased standards of viticulture and winemaking, and increased revenues for the growing band of proprietors who play this game.

The benefits have not affected all in the region equally, though. The first to suffer were the négociants – the great "merchant princes" of the past. Historically, it is hard to come to any conclusion other than that their past role is now over. They were there to support the proprietors through difficult vintages, and to sell their wines to sometimes reluctant, indifferent, or otherwise distracted customers. Winemaking advances and global demand means that there are no more difficult vintages in the old sense; and wine critics have taken over the job of being the sales force for top Bordeaux. The system of château proprietors releasing their wines onto the market via the top fifteen or twenty négociant companies continues, for the time being, largely because of the greedy miscalculation by the proprietors about the worth of the 1997 vintage. In 2001, the négociants are still carrying the stocks of 1997, and financing the proprietors' error – thus earning their continuing loyalty. Eventually, however, there will be no economic reason for this three-tier sales system to continue. What is to stop, for example, Châteaux Le Pin, Léoville-Poyferré, or Lafaurie-Peyraguey

▲ *This small ecclesiastical statue is a modest attempt to beautify what is one of the ugliest chais in Bordeaux: that of Château Pétrus.*

organizing an internet auction for en primeur sales? It would assuredly be in the proprietors' interests to do this, with increased direct revenues more than compensating for the administrative costs involved.

You will have noticed that I mentioned "the top 300 properties" a few paragraphs earlier. There are around 12,500 producers altogether in the whole of Bordeaux; ninety-five per cent of these produce relatively simple, straightforward wine with no ageing or investment potential whatsoever. The surge in recent prosperity has passed these wine-growers by. Indeed at this level, Bordeaux is regarded as an increasingly uncompetitive wine region, over-endowed with laxly administered AOCs that are rapidly losing whatever allure they once held for the consumer. Even the current President of the Comité Interprofessionel des Vins de Bordeaux, Eric Dulong, admits that it is "crazy" to have fifty-seven different AOCs in Bordeaux – though he is against the idea of a Vins de Pays alternative for Bordeaux, since it would mean the rise of varietal wine in the region. "There are already too many varietals. The only solution for Bordeaux is to keep the AOC system but to simplify our communication, and try to do some lobbying to change the regulations of the AOC to be more competitive."

There has been another side effect of Bordeaux's recent surge in prosperity, too. Some welcome it; others feel that its consequences may be catastrophic. This is that the taste of Bordeaux itself is changing.

Style games

Last night, here in Oxford, I understood something. I was with my parents; we were about to eat. I pulled a bottle out of a case of assorted

Count Stephan von Neipperg

Stephan von Neipperg is the fifth of eight children. His father, Count Joseph-Hubert von Neipperg, bought Canon-la-Gaffelière in St-Emilion in 1971; the vineyard land which became Clos de l'Oratoire, La Mondotte, and d'Aiguilhe was purchased later. Since the mid-1990s, Neipperg has worked with Stéphane Derenoncourt, and the wines they have crafted together are now some of the most admired in the region. "My aim was always clear: I wanted to make the best wine possible in each terroir. To start with, though, I didn't know my terroir. It took me a lot of years to discover it, and I don't know everything yet. Also I am not a scientific guy, and to start with I was making wines in the wine school way. Today, we are very far from all those things; we are making wine the way they did eighty years ago, and it is much more interesting than the way wine was made in the last twenty years. Getting closer to nature, sorting the fruit, using wild yeasts, working with wooden tanks and not steel, working with whole berries, using pigeage, working with the lees, reducing sulphur, fermenting very slowly: all these things are very important. You have to respect the grape and the grape skin. I am very selective in the skins. With a very good skin you can make a big wine; a bad skin cannot make a big wine. I am a producer of skins."

Michel Rolland

Michel Rolland is not simply the most influential winemaking consultant in Bordeaux; he has become the world's foremost shaper of wines. "I don't transform wines," he told me, "I try to make them as good as they can be within the context in which they are produced. That's the first point and I think it's very important. Secondly, I drink wine; I like wine. I am the first drinker in principle, and when I drink I like the notion of pleasure. I like supple wines made from ripe grapes, and I think perhaps that that is also what the consumer is looking for."

Picking at full ripeness is the most important of all Rolland's innovations. This was often regarded as dangerous in Bordeaux, since it meant risking the autumn rains. Rolland's own father, he told me laughingly, routinely picked the harvest at the family property, Le Bon Pasteur in Pomerol, before the fruit was fully ripe. "He taught me loads of things, but he didn't teach me about maturity. In fact I'll tell you how this whole maturity business came about. When I began in 1970, I had a look at the wines that had already been made in the region. The vintages everybody talked about in Bordeaux were 1928, 1929, 1945, 1947, 1955, and 1961. Only six great vintages in seventy years. I began to think I'd chosen rather a boring career. I then wondered why those vintages were so good. If you look at their

profile, you'll see that they are all high in alcohol, low in acidity, with small crops, so evidently those were ripe crops. Look at the 1947 – I was born in 1947, so I take a great deal of interest in that vintage – and you'll find that the wines often have more than fourteen per cent alcohol, with a pH of above 3.6, and with a total acidity of less than three g/l, giving them a suave, rounded, silky quality. They were ripe; very ripe. I'm an epicurean; I like pleasure. To make the wines that I liked, I had to harvest ripe grapes."

Rolland has been identified with certain techniques – including the troublesome one of carrying out the malolactic fermentation in new oak casks. "I feel that great wine needs to be 'raised' in wood. Yet you can also end up spoiling a wine with wood. So what do we have to do? We have to try to integrate as fully as possible the taste of new wood. The best way to do this is to put the wine into barriques when it is still warm, just after vinification, at a temperature of 77 or 79°F (25/26°C). You can do the malo there, too, but it's not essential. It's running the wine very quickly into wood which counts." Another key Rolland innovation has been the willingness to "permit" wines to have what were previously regarded as dangerously low levels of acidity. "Acidity helps wine travel through time but without necessarily adding much in terms of quality.

In other words the wine remains austere, a bit rigid and closed, and that's not much fun for drinkers. I repeat, all the great vintages in Bordeaux except 1945 are vintages with low acidity." It is actually this readiness to embrace low-acid balances in wine that has given Rolland his fearsome reputation for cellar hygiene. "It's true that low acid wines are dangerous wines: they might be attacked by bacteria or yeast infections. Low acidity means that sulphur dioxide is less active, so you have wines which are more difficult to preserve in a good state. To avoid these problems, you need a clean cellar."

Another key feature of the wines of those properties for which Rolland consults is their supple tannins. "That's linked to my ideas about maturity. When you have truly ripe grapes, you have silky, soft tannins, so you can extract a great deal from them."

Some critics, though, claim that Rolland-influenced wines are over-simple and formulaic. "I'm not an intellectual, so I don't know how to make intellectual wines. Wine is business. Wines aren't made for wine journalists, or for intellectuals who drink twice a year. It's made for daily drinking. There are 300 million hectolitres of wine produced in the world every year, and we have to make sure they're drunk. It's not intellectuals who are going to drink them. If giving pleasure is a failing, then I'm full of failings."

Gérard Perse

Gérard Perse is, together with Count Stephan von Neipperg, perhaps the most influential of Bordeaux's present-day proprietors. His work at Monbousquet, Pavie, and Pavie Decesse in St-Emilion (in collaboration with Michel Rolland, Alain Raynaud, and vineyard manager Laurent Lusseau) serves as a model for all those wishing to maximize the potential of their terroir. How is it done?

"We rethought our pruning techniques; we retrellised our vineyards to have a higher, more open canopy; we redrained the whole vineyard so that the roots could go deeper. We swopped a yield of sixty hl/ha for one of twenty-five hl/ha: six bunches per vine, and not one grape more. For vinification, I took my inspiration from the best practices everywhere, including Burgundy. Sorting tables, maximum maturity, temperature control, and work on the lees. We save all the fine lees from fermentation and add them to the wine in barrique: they bring depth, fat, aroma, structure. Cold fermentation of the fruit before fermentation was not really inspired by Burgundy, but more by my own thinking. I noticed that the later a fermentation begins, the purer the aromas were. In the past, fermentations began as soon as possible to avoid potential problems. I decided to do the opposite. And we got much finer, purer aromas as a result."

How typical, though, are these wines of the classic Bordeaux style? "Listen: we've been overproducing in Bordeaux for thirty years. If you do that, you lose the terroir. The more you bring yields down, the more chance you give to the terroir to speak. The type of wines we are making now are closer to what was produced before 1939. All the modern methods – tractors, fertilizers, chemicals – gave a lot of dilution. It was a period of short cuts."

Jacques Thienpont

Jacques Thienpont is a Belgian country wine merchant. His family had links with Pomerol: his grandfather Georges Thienpont bought Vieux Château Certan in 1924. It is now run by his cousin Alexandre. Another cousin, Nicolas Thienpont, owns properties in the Côtes des Francs, and runs Pavie Macquin and Bellevue; his brother Luc owns and runs Labégorce-Zédé and Clos des Quatres Vents in Margaux. He is also the man who has created the most celebrated two-ha (five-acre) vineyard in the world: Le Pin. The initial one-ha (2.47-acre) parcel came up for sale in 1979; his uncle Léon wanted to buy it for VCC, but the shareholders didn't, so Jacques bought it. Since then he has doubled its size "by flirting with the neighbours". As a winemaker, Jacques Thienpont is the opposite of a garagiste. His philosophy is terroir and vintage above all. "I look after the grapes. I try to make the wine as simply as possible. In the cellar of Le Pin there are no machines, no computer. Everything is done by hand." There is no cold maceration, there is no long extraction, there is no use of 200 per cent new oak. Thienpont does carry out malolactic fermentation in barrique; indeed it was in his cellars that its advantages were discovered – by accident. "At the beginning, I only had one vat to make the wine. So I had no option but to run the wine into barrels after fermentation, and to warm the place up so it would take place. My oenologist was Dany Rolland, the wife of Michel Rolland, and she said 'That's a good experiment'. And it has now become fashionable – but in my head, I was just doing things the way my grandfather did them. In the old days at VCC, they used to say, 'Oh, the barrels are talking to each other'. No one knew why." Thienpont is bemused by Le Pin's extraordinary success. "My philosophy used to be vivons caché, vivons heureux (live quietly, live happily). Now I'm at the front of the pack, and it's embarrassing because everyone is always looking at you. But I make my wine my way. It's sold in about thirty minutes. No one has refused it yet. The market does the rest, and what people think about the wine is their opinion. I don't care."

wine samples: 1998 Château Cluzan, a simple AOC Bordeaux, selected and sold (and sent to me as an unsolicited sample) by Maison Sichel. For the record, it had won a bronze medal at the Concours Générale Agricole at Paris in 1999.

Cork out; wine into glass. I sipped. I sipped again, though this time I pulled much more of the wine into my mouth than I would normally do. It was cool, limpid, resonant; balanced. Balanced... I thought of the black-headed gulls I had seen landing on the flood waters of the River Cherwell that afternoon, buffeted by the equinox, trembling on the wind's edge, yet still easing themselves in the sheeting water with soft poise. I took three long draws, filling my mouth with the wine and sliding it down my throat. No burn; no fire; pure refreshment. It wasn't that I was dying for a drink; we'd drunk wine at lunch. But I knew that this wine would slip down with the gratifying ease of a billiard ball rolling serenely towards its pocket. There were three of us; but under other circumstances I knew I could finish this bottle on my own. No, of course it would never win any more than a bronze medal anywhere, and it was lucky to win bronze; it wasn't that sort of a wine. But it was a satisfying, balanced, supremely digestible drink. Bull's-eye claret.

I then understood what Christian Moueix (the man who has made Château Pétrus since 1971) had told me six days earlier. We were talking about the pros and cons of the new Bordeaux. "I'm a traditionalist, even if I'm not very old yet. Which is to say that I respect the terroir, I respect the weather. I'm against those new technologies, which I think have the big danger of losing the finesse and the elegance and the subtlety which for me make Bordeaux unique. And the easiness of drinking a great Bordeaux when, as a couple, you can easily drink a bottle without becoming tired. These new technological wines are so thick that you really have trouble swallowing them. We are entering the competition of the muscles rather than the brain. So, for me, that new approach in Bordeaux is a big mistake. Which does not mean that the new school will not win. I fear that they will win. Which will be to Bordeaux's disadvantage."

Moueix is by no means alone in thinking this way. In the summer of 1999, Anthony Barton of Château Léoville-Barton told me that "the new, big-extraction wines are very obvious. Whether they will age or not remains to be seen. My palate's used to a softer, more subtle style of wine." I thought, too, of Paul Pontallier at Château Margaux, enthusing about the style of the 1999 Margaux. "All our efforts here at Margaux go towards producing something like 1999: all the suppleness, all the delicacy... where the strength is hidden behind the suppleness, hiding its power behind the subtlety. The 1999 has now been five months in one hundred per cent new oak. Where is the oak? Digested by the wine. That's the proof of the strength of the wine. Behind the gentleness, there's an iron fist. That's the particular genius of Margaux." Or the great taster and critic Michael Broadbent MW, writing in *A Century of Wine* (ed. Stephen Brook): "There is nothing to match claret at table. It has the right weight, is rarely too alcoholic, and appeals to the senses – also, in the case of the finer wines, to the intellect. Claret is refreshing... Is it too much to hope that the oenologist will be persuaded to back off, to leave Pomerol to its naturally fleshier style, the Médoc to its mixture of masculine and feminine styles, both of which benefit from bottle-ageing?"

So what are they worrying about? "A terrific effort, and one of the stars of the vintage, the 1998 boasts an opaque, thick looking, black/purple color in addition to gorgeous aromatics consisting of blackberries, blueberries, smoke, minerals, and vanillin. Extremely full-bodied and rich... this blockbuster effort is one of the great surprises of the vintage." That is Robert Parker's tasting note for the 1998 Péby Faugères, a St-Emilion which he scores (in 2001) higher than the wines of either Cheval Blanc or Ausone. "A dense purple color is followed by scents of jammy black fruits intermixed with smoke, licorice, and truffles. Deep, full-bodied, textured, and super pure as well as harmonious, this terrific offering should drink well for ten to fifteen years." Thus Parker on the 1999 Clos du Jaugueyron Margaux, scored higher in 2001 than the 1999 Cos d'Estournel, Ducru-Beaucaillou, Léoville-Barton, or Léoville-las-Cases. It would be inaccurate and misleading to say that Parker is incapable of appreciating subtle and quiet forms of beauty in wine (as his reviews of Haut-Brion prove), but he also greatly enjoys ripeness, richness, and thick, soft textures, and rewards wines that deliver these things with enthusiastic notes and scores. And Robert Parker makes the market in fine Bordeaux. Wines constructed in this style sell well; they make fortunes.

Of course Pétrus, Léoville-Barton, and Margaux are widely appreciated, too, and thus amply profitable. For other properties, though, especially for those who do not believe in lush and luscious Bordeaux, the battle is a more difficult one. The Lurton family, for example, have had a long struggle to get Châteaux Brane-Cantenac

Denis Durantou

Perhaps the fact that Denis Durantou's house and the Eglise-Clinet cellar lie next to Pomerol's cemetery is not coincidental: few seem to have learned more from the spirit of the ancestors than this nimble and mischievous master, about to embark on his twentieth vintage. No fads, no frills, no fetishes: just the attentive formula of great gravel, old vines, and low yields, with eighty per cent new oak for the wines that make the cut.

Durantou is married to the painter Marie Reilhac, and the pair have three talented daughters, Alix, Noémie, and Constance. Rather than throw himself into garagiste posturing, Durantou is building up a sizeable négociant business from his newly built chais in nearby Catusseau – over which Marie Reilhac has a light-filled studio. Wine sits happily, here, between commerce and art. ▶

Jean-Luc Thunevin

Jean-Luc Thunevin may be the man who, more than any other, has given the anthill of St-Emilion the kick it was longing for, but he's far from being an outsider: one of his classmates was Ausone's Alain Vauthier and the two men remain close friends. Family, too, is as important here as it is for any traditional Médoc estate: Thunevin's wife Murielle Andraud (pictured with him) is intimately involved in the business and vinifies in her own right at Marojallia in Margaux, while daughter Virginie works with them, too. Her own daughter, Axelle, has already given her name to a cuvée of 2000 Valandraud. Thunevin's good-humoured enthusiasm for the work of other wine-growers who, like him, began with nothing is as much of an inspiration as Valandraud itself. Michel Puzio, for example, at Croix de Labrie acknowledges the help of Thunevin – and Puzio in turn is now a consultant to other châteaux. Thus the network expands.

and Durfort-Vivens appreciated. The same is true of Laurent Vonderheyden's work at Château Monbrison; of the efforts of John Kolasa on behalf of the Wertheimers of Chanel at Châteaux Rauzan-Ségla and Canon; or of the work of Pascal Delbeck at Château Belair. Consider Parker's often muted enthusiasm for wines such as Magdelaine or Vieux Château Certan, thought by many to be two of the finest properties in St-Emilion and Pomerol respectively; consider his frank unenthusiasm for the Moueix-produced wines of Moulin du Cadet or Fonroque.

You'll have noted Christian Moueix's phrase "technological wines".

What does he mean?

In the old days in Bordeaux, pruning, winemaking, and wine-raising (élevage) were standard, time-honoured procedures. Yields varied, of course, depending on the generosity of a summer; so, too, did the quality of the wines. "Historically," as Moueix puts it, "there have always been, out of ten vintages in Bordeaux, two great ones, three good ones, three average ones and two poor ones. For centuries."

And now? There are many ways of reducing yields to ferociously low levels of thirty hl/ha or less (yields of between fifty and sixty hl/ha were typical of Bordeaux throughout most of the second half of the twentieth century). Such yields would once have been uneconomical; but with a Parker score of ninety or over, they are uneconomical no longer. The old consensus, too, about ripeness has disappeared; today's ripe wines are yesterday's over-ripe wines. The new economics of superstar Bordeaux makes the obsessive sorting of perfect from imperfect grapes possible, the grand vin (or the micro-wine) being made from impeccable grapes alone.

Once the grapes are crushed, other possibilities present themselves. The Burgundian technique of a cold, pre-fermentation maceration, for example, is now widely used in St-Emilion to create fresh fruit flavours. At Château Pavie, 600 kg of dry ice (carboglace) is emptied into

Stéphane Derenoncourt

"I came to Fronsac in 1982. For a girl. Hitch-hiking; I didn't have a job, so I did the grape harvest. Before 1982, I had never seen a vine. I noticed the weather was good here, so I decided to stay."

Uniquely among Bordeaux's great winemakers, Stéphane Derenoncourt is self-taught. He grew up in Dunkerque, but settled, as he describes above, in Aquitaine. Even then, his love affair with wine took a while to take off. Initially, he preferred music. "I did odd jobs in the vineyard. But I didn't like vineyard work; it was so difficult. Spiritually, too, because Bordeaux has a feudal mentality. I preferred playing the blues. But I needed to eat, so I learned pruning. At the end of the 1980s, Madame Barre, who was in charge at Pavie Macquin, asked me to work with her. When I saw it, I accepted directly. I began to love viticulture when I experienced the whole cycle."

Derenoncourt is utterly different from Bordeaux's other key figures: he dislikes the limelight; he distrusts wealth; his philosophy may involve technical innovation, but it is led by intuition, observation, and a deep respect for nature. He wears sandals. I have never yet seen him in a suit.

"Everything I have learned, I have learned myself. I learned biodynamics via my own vegetable garden, and afterwards in vineyards. My passion is working with something living, with love. To work biodynamically, you need observation and closeness to the vines. You can't have two weeks off; you need to be there. That's why they've been so suspicious of biodynamics in Bordeaux – the base of everything here is always a lie. The owners are never wine-growers; they're businessmen. The vineyard workers are always in the shadows. We have far fewer vine

disease problems in Côtes de Castillon than in St-Emilion. Why? There's less money here for chemical treatments, therefore they have killed life less. People talk about la lutte raisonée; it just means using fewer products, but the philosophy is the same. When you treat, you kill. It's not a philosophy of life, it's a philosophy of death. All of life is a chain. When you remove a link from the chain, nothing works."

His techniques? "The first revolution was the taste of the grape. The second revolution was gentle handling. Afterwards, I work with micro-oxygenation. The tradition in Bordeaux is to rack every three months. Why? I don't know; that's just the tradition. But why rack the wine if it doesn't need it? I only want to do something to the wine if it needs it. To work in the most natural way possible, that is my winemaking philosophy."

▲ Grass growing between the rows in this St-Emilion vineyard marks a modest step forward towards sustainable viticultural practices.

each wooden fermenter, holding the temperature of the harvest at 8°C (46°F) for one week before fermentation begins. The most notorious of the recent techniques, meanwhile, is "concentration", now beginning to be the preferred alternative to chaptalization. Chaptalization meant the sugaring of must to achieve higher final alcohol levels than the grapes were capable of delivering on their own; it was practised, even by the greatest châteaux, in most years. For example, 1999 was the first year since 1961 that no chaptalization of Cabernet Sauvignon whatsoever took place at Château Palmer. "We have always chaptalized at least half of our Cabernet Sauvignon," Paul Pontallier of Margaux told me in 1999, "even in the greatest vintages." Concentration means the removal of water, by reverse osmosis or vacuum evaporation, to provide richer, denser musts. These in turn not only deliver higher alcohol levels, but richer flavours also; though even the enthusiasts for this technique admit that if there are any unwanted or off-flavours in the wine, then concentration will amplify these unhappily. The traditional technique of "bleeding" (*saignée*) continues to be practised, sometimes with savage ferocity; the ambitious St-Emilion micro-property Croix de Labrie drained away forty per cent of its harvested juice in 1999, thereby greatly diminishing the proportion of juice to skins and increasing the resulting wine's concentration to prodigious levels.

Enzymes can be used to affect the nature of the matter extracted from the grapes, and temperature control, too, enables extraction to continue lengthily and comprehensively. Selected yeasts can be used to create particular aromas. The wine can be run off into new oak to finish its fermentation, and the troublesome business of carrying out malolactic fermentation in new casks is now widely practised; both of these techniques promote suppler, richer new-oak integration than did traditional practices. Wines can be given "200 per cent" new oak; in other words, they can be racked from a brand new oak barrel into another brand new oak barrel, trowelling copious oak-vanillins, toast and tannins into the wine at the same time. Both in vat and in cask, wines can remain on their lees for extended periods, using the technique of micro-oxygenation to prevent them acquiring the stinky, "reduced" aromas they might otherwise do. Lees from the initial fermentation, indeed, are even added to the wines in barrel. The lees can be stirred, especially prior to malolactic fermentation. This period

of lees contact adds further texture, flavour, and richness, as well as keeping colours deep and opaque. Finally, after an extended period in cask, the wines are bottled without fining or filtration.

These are some of the ways in which, for example, a wine like Château Monbousquet is able to exceed the apparent potential of its modest St-Emilion terroir; by which a wine like La Mondotte is able to dazzle the world in its first two vintages (1996 and 1997) from a standing start; by which a wine like Château Valandraud, composed from a number of parcels scattered about St-Emilion, is able to sell at higher prices than Médoc first growths; by which a wine like Château Cos d'Estournel is able to produce deep and full-flavoured wines in moist or rain-affected vintages like 1997, 1998, and 1999. This is the New Bordeaux, and it is this that makes traditionalists like Christian Moueix fearful for the future.

Is he right?

I put it to Moueix that the results of these different efforts mean that, overall, the quality of the best Bordeaux is much improved. He may regret the stylistic developments, but he cannot regret the qualititive improvements. The game has been raised.

"It's clear," he agreed. "Thanks to the new technology in viticulture and winemaking, the two great vintages [out of ten] are still the two great vintages; the three good vintages are now very good vintages; the three average vintages have become, probably, three good vintages; and the two disastrous vintages have become two average vintages. That's a serious difference." Moueix's fear, though, is that the charms of the new lush, black Bordeaux will prove transitory and superficial.

One of wine's beauties is that it cannot be hurried. These dense, saturated, vintage-defying clarets have only been produced since the mid- to late 1990s; we will not be able to evaluate the experiment that they represent until 2020 or so. I remain sanguine. Why?

All of the recent developments in Bordeaux have been the consequence of greatly increased efforts in both vineyard and cellar. Yields have been lowered, ripeness is more regularly and fully achieved,

Spirit of the garage

The association of the words "garage" and "wine" began when Jean-Luc Thunevin, one-time forestry worker, disc jockey, bank employee, and wine merchant, began to vinify in the premises of a former garage in the back streets of St-Emilion. Using fruit from different parcels of vineyard, he created a wine that had initially no name and no reputation; he therefore put all his effort and energy into making the best wine he could. "To begin with," says Thunevin, "the garagistes were people like me who, without any money, managed an amazing success. Without money, because we didn't have any. We made hand-sewn wines, if you like, because we didn't have any alternative. Since then there are lots of people who have attached themselves to this movement, including well-known classed growths who make their own garage wines, and with amazing success, too. Look at La Mondotte from Canon-la-Gaffelière, La Gomerie of Beau-Séjour Bécot, l'Hermitage from Matras, or St-Dominique from La Dominique. It's often INAO which has created those garage wines, by refusing to allow a separate parcel to be classified within a property. So the producer says, 'Merde to INAO, we'll do what we want and make a great wine.' And, of course, now there is a third category: people who want to jump on the bandwagon. But the true garagiste is someone who has no other possibilities than to make the greatest wine he can because he has no money, no big vineyards, and he just has to live off the sale of 3,000 bottles. For me, that's a garagiste. That's the pure spirit of the garage."

How, I asked Thunevin, is it done? What's the garage recipe? "It's not complicated. It consists of doing the opposite of what you normally do when you're small. You invest a lot of work; you sacrifice everything to please the vine. So:

1. Small yields. We're allowed sixty hl/ha. Great wine equals thirty hl/ha at most. It's an essential rule.
2. You work organically. You use physical work in the vineyard to solve problems, rather than chemicals.
3. You use leaf plucking.
4. You harvest absolutely ripe grapes, even with all the risks of losing everything which it entails. By hand, of course, sorting each bunch and each berry.
5. You carry out serious vinification, which I would define as using wild yeasts only; using good wooden vats in a clean cellar; and using good new oak casks. Great wines aren't frightened of new oak. You have to do serious élevage, which can either be on lees with no racking or as I do it, the traditional way, with racking. (In the fine detail, every garagiste has totally different techniques.) You have to make a second wine, even if you're small; or sell off what isn't good enough. And then you have to show the wine to tasters who might fall in love with it."

I put the most frequent criticism of garage wine to Thunevin: the fact that the garagiste's fastidious technical work obscures terroir. He disagreed. "You can't turn a donkey into a racehorse. Impossible! The terroir is always far more important than all human techniques. I know the fact that it's me that is saying it may seem paradoxical, but it's true. If you have a bad terroir, a garagiste can make a correct wine. From an average terroir, a garagiste can make a good wine. And from a great terroir, a garagiste can make a very great wine. The garagiste is a catalyst for quality; that's all."

Isn't what the garagistes do merely replicating an international, New World influenced style of wine in Bordeaux? "Whatever our techniques, whatever our ambition, you cannot pick a ripe grape in Bordeaux and make a Californian wine. But if anyone wants to compare Valandraud to a Harlan, or a Grange, then that's a fine compliment for me."

And what of Bordeaux's hallmark elegance and finesse? Can you really find that quality in garage wines? "Too much finesse kills finesse. Finesse shouldn't be about thinness. The truth is that the great vintages of the past weren't marked by elegance and finesse; they were marked by the generosity of nature. That is what the garagistes have understood; it is that which we struggle to achieve within the limits of what nature allows."

fruit quality is subject to severe selection, and the winemaking process itself is both understood and scrutinized far more completely than at any time in the past. Let's be quite clear: these are not the conditions which produce bad wines. Bad wines are produced when corners are cut, when yields are raised, when traditions go unexamined, when flavour is created by chemical adjustments in the winery rather than hard work in the vineyard, when the act of high agriculture which winemaking represents becomes an industrial process in order to maximize profits for shareholders.

Two major advances have happened in Bordeaux during the 1990s. The first is that the majority of those owning top châteaux are trying much harder than they ever did in the previous five decades to produce great wine, year after year. The second is that the aesthetic possibilities of what fine Bordeaux wine might look, smell, and taste like have broadened. Bordeaux is perhaps the most favoured spot on the earth's surface from which to make red wine; nowhere else in the world has this large an expanse of evidently outstanding terroir. It is not far-fetched to make a comparison between what is happening at present to wine production in Bordeaux with what happened to Italian painting in the Renaissance, or what happened to English literature in the Elizabethan age. The possibilities suddenly look much larger, much more exciting, much more diverse than they have ever looked before. A stale and confined world has become a broad and adventurous one. Of course there are sillinesses and excesses, but the fundamental truth is that Bordeaux has never produced as much good, exciting and aesthetically diverse wine as it is producing at present.

▼ *Vines on death row at Château Pavie. New owner Gérard Perse intends to use less herbicide than its former owners, happily.*

The Adventure of the Land

Bordeaux, as we have already discovered, is the world's largest fine wine region. If its geology was as complicated as that of Burgundy or Alsace, then the sheer scale of the area would mean unwieldy volumes of explanation, and hundreds of different appellations. It's not like that, fortunately. This is an area of large properties, extensive appellations and broad differences. Of one difference, indeed, above all.

Rive gauche is a ringing phrase, with its evocations of bohemian Paris and artistic indigence. In its Bordeaux context, the "Left Bank" has another meaning altogether: it means all the land found on the western side of the River Garonne and the Gironde Estuary: the Médoc, Graves, and (if you like) Sauternes. The "Right Bank", by contrast, refers to the vineyard areas found to the east of the Dordogne and the Gironde: St-Emilion, Pomerol, Fronsac. (I list here only the main areas: Bordeaux has no fewer than fifty-seven individual appellations.) You'll have worked out, by looking at the map and reading this, that the Gironde is the waterway found downstream of

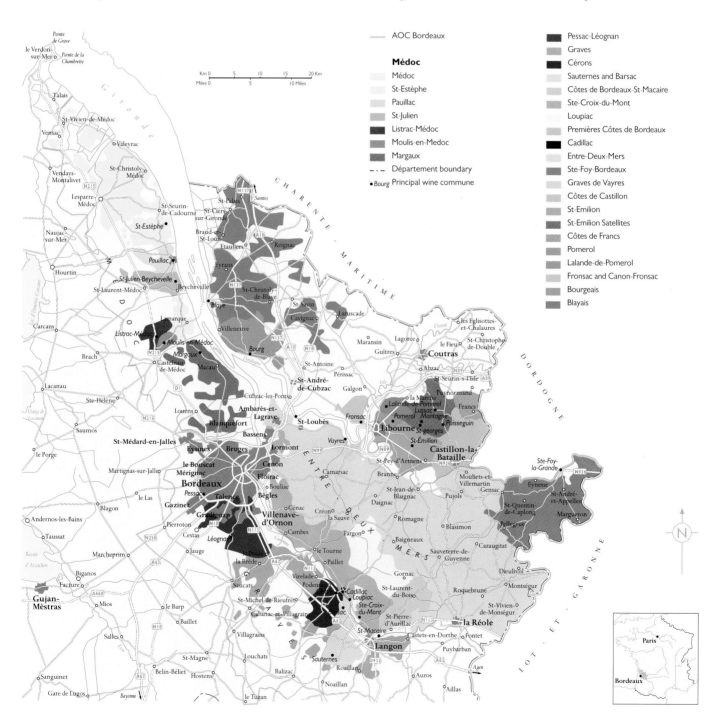

Médoc
- Médoc
- St-Estèphe
- Pauillac
- St-Julien
- Listrac-Médoc
- Moulis-en-Medoc
- Margaux
- Département boundary
- Bourg Principal wine commune

AOC Bordeaux

- Pessac-Léognan
- Graves
- Cérons
- Sauternes and Barsac
- Côtes de Bordeaux-St-Macaire
- Ste-Croix-du-Mont
- Loupiac
- Premières Côtes de Bordeaux
- Cadillac
- Entre-Deux-Mers
- Ste-Foy-Bordeaux
- Graves de Vayres
- Côtes de Castillon
- St-Emilion
- St-Emilion Satellites
- Côtes de Francs
- Pomerol
- Lalande-de-Pomerol
- Fronsac and Canon-Fronsac
- Bourgeais
- Blayais

the confluence of the Dordogne and the Garonne. Between those two rivers is the area called, with a little poetic licence, the Entre-Deux-Mers, the "Between-Two-Seas".

The Left Bank/Right Bank distinction is fundamental to an understanding of the adventure – one might almost call it a battle – of this land. Not only does it often correspond to a fundamental change of terroir, but it also signifies the one major switch in grape variety in Bordeaux, between the Cabernet Sauvignon of the Left Bank and the Merlot of the Right Bank. When tasters sit down to a plain decanter of fine red Bordeaux, the first thing they will set about guessing is whether it is Right Bank or Left Bank. Appellation, property, and vintage come later.

Let's begin on the Left Bank. Geologically, this is the youngest of all France's vineyard areas; like human beings themselves, this vineyard is the product of the Quaternary era. The dinosaurs were already long extinct by the time the key geological element of these vineyards took form. Not only that, but our Stone Age ancestors had learned to use fire. They needed to: this was the Great Ice Age. Ice fields covered much of Britain and all of Scandinavia. The effect of these was to lock water in the north and the south, lowering sea levels in between these expanded Polar regions. During the Würm glaciation, the coldest and longest geological winter of the Great Ice Age, the course of the Gironde was some sixty metres (200 feet) lower than it is at present (and, by the way, the Channel separating present-day Britain and France did not exist). That ancient, chilly river bed is now long lost and deeply buried.

Rivers wander as time passes. Provoked by catastrophic events such as floods, they move their courses to wherever resistance to their force is weakest. At the same time, they ceaselessly usher water forwards to the sea, and in the process roll stones and dump mineral debris. This process is the key to the geology of France's greatest vineyard area. The truth is that Châteaux Latour, Lafite, Haut-Brion, Yquem, and all the rest of the Left Bank giants grow on the rolled, dislocated, and discarded stones of the Massif Central, of the Pyrénées, of Périgord, and Limousin. The snow, the rain, and the floods of the Great Ice Age, with its freezing glacials and watery interglacials, washed and tumbled mountainside on mountainside of stone down into the Aquitaine basin. The rising, the falling, and the wandering of the Garonne, Dordogne, and Gironde scattered these pebbles in great shoals and banks, much as a gardener might push autumn leaves into deep pre-bonfire drifts. The gravel banks on which most of today's vineyards are sited are those of the Günz glaciation, the early Stone Age, formed just under a million years ago; the same is true of the best sector of Pomerol. Sometimes there were calmer periods, and finer deposits: if you could X-ray these gravel banks, you would find that they are interspersed with lenses of dense, moist clay and tight sand. As the sea retreated, indeed, it left mile after mile of lonely dunes running out into what we know as the Atlantic. The wind blew hard in the Great Ice Age, and much of this sand went winging its way inland to form aeolian (wind-borne) deposits. During the Riss glaciation, these wind-borne sands almost buried the gravels of the Médoc. Had humans not planted, later, one of France's largest pine forests on the sandy sea-side of the Médoc, those gravels would be dune-covered now, and we would never have known the taste of Lafite or Latour.

Underneath the gravel, of course, there is bedrock. Typically for France, which over the course of geological history has been a much-submerged and watery nation-to-be, it is limestone. This is not the limestone of the tropical dinosaur period that one finds in Burgundy, but younger limestone, deposited in a series of sea invasions during the Tertiary period. The characteristic fossil of these seas is that of a starfish which lived and died by the million – hence the French name of this bedrock limestone: *calcaire à astéries* ("starfish limestone"). The fossil,

alas, is generally found in parts and not wholes. Even so, one might consider Bordeaux a wine sandwiched between stars.

Broadly speaking, the Left Bank is a terroir of gravel over limestone, while on the Right Bank, the limestone emerges at the surface, and gravel is less prominent. Much of the higher land in St-Emilion, of Bourg and Blaye, of Côtes de Castillon, and of Canon-Fronsac is sited on pure (though much weathered) starfish limestone. The lower parts of these appellations mingle recent river alluvium with copious sand and occasional gravels. The plateau of Pomerol is the only major exception to this Right Bank generality; in a way, you might consider it a mini-Médoc. Here the River Isle (today a minor tributary of the Dordogne, but a river with a mightier Ice Age past) has dumped millions of tons of its own gravel, sourced from the high country of Périgord and Limousin. Significantly, the bedrock here is not starfish limestone but the soft, sandy-clay (marl) deposits known as Fronsadais molasse. Clay, famously, pushes towards the surface in the "buttonhole" of Pétrus. Another characteristic of Pomerol is a layer of what is called in French *crasse de fer*, or "iron filth": iron-rich, wind-blown sands.

It's not gravel alone, remember, which is Bordeaux's secret; gravel alone would have little to offer the vine, as New Zealand's wine-growers have discovered. It is the rich mixture of mineral elements that are found inside the gravel banks, with their secret caches of clay and of sand, and the lure of limestone or molasse beneath. All of this sends the vine's roots on a subterranean mineral treasure hunt.

As always, too, terroir is more than geology alone; site, aspect, and weather patterns play their role. It's no use coming to Bordeaux and expecting to see another Côte d'Or, Côte Rôtie, or Hermitage. The only place in Bordeaux where you can see a south-facing hillside of this sort, the kind of place that you know just has to be a vineyard, is in St-Emilion and its southern Côtes de Castillon continuation, where the limestone plateau drops away steeply towards the Dordogne river plain. It's an exception. Bordeaux in general is built more along Châteauneuf-du-Pape lines: this is Big Sky country. The vines, in other words, sometimes curve imperceptibly up or down a gentle knoll (*tertre* or *croupe*), but in general they lie more or less flat on their beds and blankets of gravel, facing out the meterological dramas above.

And dramas there can be. The latitude of Bordeaux, just tucked beneath the 45th parallel, puts it into the warmer meridional half of wine-growing France (rather than the cooler septentrional half), yet it is the Atlantic Ocean, and the warm downcurving currents of the Bay of Biscay, which are in the end more important than its rung on the north-south ladder. The Médoc itself, indeed, is a tongue of gravel and sand lapping the salty Atlantic; if global warming does bring higher sea levels, then Latour and Margaux will be some of the very first vineyards anywhere in the world to sink beneath the incoming rollers. Bordeaux's climate is profoundly maritime: year-round mildness, year-round changeability. (Vinexpo 2001 began cold and wet, and finished five days later in Arabian heat.) The prevailing westerlies skate in off the sea; they often bring rain, and often at the wrong time. If one had to nominate one single factor which makes the difference between a great Bordeaux vintage and the merely good, it would be harvest rain. In general, too, this climatic changeability means that the precise nature of each vintage is more important than one might imagine in a vineyard area at this latitude. In Bordeaux, vintages count.

So much for the general picture. What of the specific appellations? **Bordeaux** is the basic AOC that encompasses the entire region; it covers 38,551 ha (95,221 acres, or three times the size of Coteaux du Languedoc, seventeen times larger than the entire Bourgogne AOC, and thirty-five times larger than all of the vineyards in the Jura). As you might imagine, with such a huge area, quality and style are variable.

Now let's slice Bordeaux into four quarters: Médoc; Graves and Sauternes; Entre-Deux-Mers, and the Right Bank.

The Médoc itself, that famous stranded tongue between the Atlantic and the Gironde, is internally subdivided. Its most northerly section (the tip of the tongue) is AOC **Médoc**; the better, southern half is the nominally illogical AOC of **Haut-Médoc**. Within Haut-Médoc, you find the communal AOCs of (from north to south) **St-Estèphe**, **Pauillac**, **St-Julien**, **Listrac**, **Moulis**, and **Margaux**. It is from these six AOCs, and especially from St-Estèphe, Pauillac, St-Julien, and Margaux, that most of the greatest Left Bank wines come, based on a preponderance of Cabernet Sauvignon, balanced by smaller proportions of Merlot, Cabernet Franc, and sometimes Malbec and Petit Verdot. There are few places in France where the complex truths of terroir are explored with subtler articulacy than here. In principle, all of the best sites are similar: well-drained gravel banks set back from the marshy lowland at the water's edge. (I have walked down to the river from both Château Margaux and Château Latour: within seconds, you leave priceless vineyard for worthless pasture.) Yet everyone who has ever set about blind-tasting wines from these communes will know that the differences between them are incontrovertible. Margaux is light, floral, graceful, and fragrant; St-Julien is fruity, intense, and refined; Pauillac is beefy, fat, and powerful; St-Estèphe is sterner and stonier. The geologically curious cast around for explanations – iron in St Estèphe's gravel; limestone and marl closer to the surface in Margaux – but the precise reasons are hidden inside the complex sub-surface mineral architecture of each of the gravel banks, and change from property to property. Moulis and Listrac are less gravelly: the limestones and marls push up to the surface here, and the gravels thin. The wines are tougher and less refined than in the four great Médoc communes, but satisfying and comforting.

The Graves (the word means "gravel") begins in the city of Bordeaux – or it did. For some odd, unfathomable, and misguided reason, in 1987 the growers of the northern part of the Graves decided to abandon this old, descriptive, and resonant name and call themselves by the turgid, dual-commune name of **Pessac-Léognan**. Visit the great city-centre vineyard of Haut-Brion and you will see the vines nestling in splendid, glinting, quartz-brilliant gravel defilades: how could this area not be called Graves? Indeed Haut-Brion, with its Günz gravels lying over starfish limestone, has arguably the most impeccably gravelly terroir of any property in the entire region. The red wine itself is the archetype of fragrant, medium-bodied, magnificently concentrated finesse. We can say with certainty that the city of Bordeaux, itself built on gravel over limestone, has obliterated for all time some fine vineyards; wine-growers have no less a reason to shed tears over these lost wines than music lovers do over Bach's two lost Passions.

Most of Pessac-Léognan now sprawls in and out of the suburbs, and is set amongst the woods that take over at the southern end of the city. (Pine trees are the main source of income for many farming families in both the Graves and Sauternes to the south; wine, especially wine which requires as many gambles as Sauternes does, is thought of as a *danseuse* – an amusing frivolity on which to lavish surplus income without hope of return).

The present-day AOC of **Graves** lies to the south of Pessac-Léognan. Its best wine-growing sites are, once again, on gravel mounds; there are fewer of them than in Pessac-Léognan, and the quality of the wines rarely reaches the same level. Pessac-Léognan and Graves both produce good white wines as well as red, reflecting the fact that the gravel is beginning to thin through these appellations, and sand and limestone play more and more of a role in the soils. The forest backdrop, too, has its own effect, muting the bright light found out on the exposed gravels of the Médoc, and increasing humidity.

Cérons, which lies between Graves and Barsac, is one of Bordeaux's many struggling AOCs. Its dry red and white wines are sold as Graves. The sweet wines of this transition zone do not enjoy the renown of Barsac and Sauternes – yet producing great sweet wine is an expensive and sacrificial business. The less remunerative the return, the harder quality is to attain.

With **Barsac** (whose producers may, if they wish, also use the Sauternes appellation) and **Sauternes** itself, we reach sweet white wine country. Yet again, Bordeaux succeeds in trumping its world rivals. These are not just any sweet wines, but perhaps the most sensorially overwhelming of all: heady, unctuous, glycerous, deriving glorious reciprocality of flavour from their new oak barrels. Terroir, to tell the truth, is less important in creating them than human intervention – or, to put it another way, these sweet wines exist thanks to a man-made terroir.

Prior to the seventeenth century, this was just more Graves red wine country, though the quality of the red wines (some of which are still produced today under the simple AOC Bordeaux) was rarely glorious. The gravel banks here are intermittent, occasionally deep, but often mixed, too, with sand, lime, and marl. Barsac, indeed, has almost no gravel at all, just limestone and red sands; the greatest property of the area, Yquem, is sited on a low dome of sandy gravels sprinkled over limy clay. The uniqueness of the area, though, is its watery T-junction.

It is at this point that a secret little river meets the Garonne. It's called the Ciron. This shy watercourse has rarely seen the sunlight until now, winding as it does through the quiet, resinous, needle-strewn shade of a million pine trees planted by human beings to turn sand to economic use. Its waters, thus, are cool; colder than those of the Garonne. The trees attract moisture in any case (as they famously did on uninhabited, primeval Madeira), and the mingling of the two waters provokes mist, particularly in early autumn. When a morning of mist and an afternoon of sunshine gets to work on ripe Sémillon and Sauvignon Blanc grapes, the result is *Botrytis cinerea* or "noble rot" – and the glory of Sauternes. The Left Bank vineyards continue after Langon, but for AOC Bordeaux only.

Now we cross the Garonne. Between the two "seas" of the Garonne and the Dordogne is the biggest area of vines in Bordeaux, but the one with the fewest great wines: general farming country which happens, for cultural reasons, to be set to viticulture. It has also been subdivided into a confusing mass of little-known appellations whose reputations were often originally made with cheap sweet white wines in which the market no longer has much interest. **Cadillac, Loupiac,** and **Ste-Croix-du-Mont** all sit opposite Sauternes on the north bank of the Garonne, and offer the best of these; the steeper slopes on this bank means less gravel, though, and less mist too. Yields are higher here. **Premières Côtes de Bordeaux** is a long strip of vineyard running from the Bordeaux suburbs across the River Garonne down to Langon; it is for red and sweet white wines. The sweet whites of **Côtes de Bordeaux-St-Macaire** and the dry whites of **Entre-Deux-Mers-Haut-Benauge**, both resoundingly obscure, neighbour the Premières Côtes at their southeastern end. **Entre-Deux-Mers** itself is a giant AOC for dry whites; reds and rosé wines produced here are sold as AOC Bordeaux. **St-Foy-Bordeaux** is a tongue of the Bergerac and Montbazillac region which finds itself in the *département* of the Gironde rather than the Dordogne, and is thus attached to Bordeaux: it produces reds and both dry and sweet whites. **Graves de Vayres** finally, is a red and white AOC for the low-lying, relatively rich-soiled gravel vineyards found to the south of the Dordogne.

And so to the Right Bank. The terroirs of the two leading appellations, **St-Emilion** and **Pomerol**, have been described above. The gravel plateau of Pomerol is more homogenous than is St-Emilion

– although, as I discovered (as it happens) in running around it on the day before I am writing this text, there are still a number of relatively poorly drained Pomerol vineyards sited on sand and on marl rather than gravel. Another factor worth noting is that the gravels of the Günz glaciation – always considered to be the best in Bordeaux for wine – dominate the zone between Pétrus, La Conseillante, and the church (at around the thirty-five-metre/110-feet mark). The AOC then slopes gently down through the Mindel glaciation gravels (each side of the N89, at around twenty metres/sixty-five feet) to Riss glaciation gravels near the railway line and the appellation borders (fifteen metres/fifty feet or less). The quality of the wine slopes with them. If this was Burgundy, Pomerol would be at least three separate AOCs.

What is true of Pomerol is even more true of St-Emilion, which has a minimum of four clearly differentiated terroirs. The best sites are often thought to be those on the edge of the limestone escarpment on which the medieval town, certainly the prettiest in the Bordeaux region, is sited: loam derived from starfish limestone, superbly drained, with a fine south-facing aspect. Properties here include Ausone, Belair, and Magdelaine. Properties at the foot of this escarpment, and in the flat land which runs down to the Dordogne, are thought to be less favourably situated, on marl, sand, and some gravel, though much depends on the ambitions of the producer: Monbousquet shows what can be achieved. Vines on the gently sloping plateau to the north side of the town itself are rooted in loams based on weathered starfish limestone, seasoned with more recent wind-drift silts: these are in general slightly cooler sites. Finally, the northwestern corner of St-Emilion is, in effect, a mini-Pomerol: Günz gravel terraces over limestone. This is where the extraordinary Cheval Blanc is sited, along with the cluster of Figeac properties and La Dominique (though it is a transition zone: Cheval Blanc itself has three internal terroirs). These properties have terroir in common with their neighbours Evangile, Petit Village, and Beauregard.

Côtes de Castillon includes a genuine continuation of the limestone escarpment vineyards of St-Emilion, and is an AOC whose best sites have great things to offer, as the coming years will certainly prove. **Lalande-de-Pomerol** and the "satellite" St-Emilion AOCs (**Montagne-St-Emilion**, **St-Georges-St-Emilion**, **Puisseguin-St-Emilion**, and **Lussac-St-Emilion**) are all separated from their big brothers by the little River Barbanne. Lussac is on post-Ice Age alluvial terraces of less interest than Pomerol's Ice Age gravels; the St-Emilion satellites, though, have occasional fine outcrops of starfish limestone which can give good results with Merlot. **Bordeaux-Côtes de Francs** has sandy soils. Across the Isle from Pomerol are the hilly vineyard areas of **Fronsac** and **Canon-Fronsac**, whose clay, limestone and sandy marl soils, combined with high percentages of Cabernet Franc and Malbec, give relatively sturdy wines: they are the Listrac and Moulis of the Right Bank, if you like. Finally, facing the Médoc across the Gironde, are a couple of vineyard areas that can never seem to make up their minds what they should be called: **Blaye**, **Blayais**, **Côtes de Blaye**, or **Premières Côtes de Blaye** and, to its south, **Côtes de Bourg**. Côtes de Blaye is an AOC for white wines only, but the rest are for wines of both colours, with Bourg generally producing the better reds. Note, though that from the 2000 vintage the Blaye AOC implies red wines produced with a lower yield than Premières Côtes de Blaye: fifty-one hl/ha rather than sixty-one hl/ha. The soils here are hugely various, since the limestone of the plateau has been weathered and mixed with sand, gravel, loam, and iron-rich clays.

Should global warming raise sea levels, this will be a sight to terrify Médoc proprietors: a surging Gironde.

Bordeaux Flak

Bordeaux is a divided society

Bordeaux, the cliché runs, is two worlds. This is the longest chapter in this book, yet the subject matter is a mere five per cent of Bordeaux's entire output. The Bordeaux the world talks about is a tiny band of celebrity wines within the region, made by the wealthy for the tables of the rich. Ordinary Bordeaux winemakers, producing basic Bordeaux for impecunious drinkers, bask but faintly in the reflected light that falls from the windows of the great châteaux. Basic Bordeaux is a medium-bodied red wine of no great distinction. Indeed were it not for that distant glow (all Bordeaux AOC wine must by law now bear the portentous legend "Grand Vin de Bordeaux"), it might not even find a market. The prices of the great and the modest move further apart each year. "A century ago," says Anthony Barton, "an ordinary generic Bordeaux sold for two-thirds of the price of the first growths." Today, that prospect is risible. Yet at the same time, the family of ordinary Bordeaux wines suffers with inappropriate expectations because of its overachieving sibling. "We need to give Bordeaux wines a new image, to try to democratize the consumption of Bordeaux wines," says Eric Dulong of the CIVB. "We need to have fun with Bordeaux wines. I want to see people drinking Bordeaux as they might drink a beer at a bar, or during a picnic, or sitting around with friends." Is calling an ordinary supermarket red a "*grand vin*" the way to do this? I doubt it. However you look at it, the situation of a tiny elite of world-famous

winner wines and a vast mass of obscure, loser wines is unhealthy. Bordeaux needs to find some way of bringing its family closer together.

Bordeaux's appellations don't make sense

Bordeaux's appellations are packed with anomalies. Some of the fifty-seven are utterly obscure: when did you last drink a bottle of Haut-Benauge or Ste-Macaire? Why should these areas be distinguished from the basic Bordeaux or Entre-Deux-Mers AOCs? Other Bordeaux appellations, by contrast, are transparently inadequate. At the very least, the AOC of St-Emilion contains four entirely separate terroirs: the Günz gravels near Pomerol; the limestone plateau behind the town; the limestone slope itself; and the flatter, sandy land beneath the slope. According to studies carried out by the University of Bordeaux, there are no fewer than seventeen soil types within St-Emilion and its satellites. Much of Côte de Castillon, too, is closer in terroir terms to classic St-Emilion than are parts of the existing St-Emilion AOC. Even little Pomerol should be, from a pure terroir point of view, at least three different AOCs: one for each glacial terrace (Günz, Mindel, and Riss). In the Médoc, there is a strong case to be made for a knoll-by-knoll delimitation of terroir rather than the existing blunderbuss system of communal AOCs. Were such a study to be undertaken, the puzzle of why world-renowned properties such as Château Latour are found next to properties of almost subterranean obscurity like Château St-Mambert Bellevue within the Pauillac AOC would be instantly solved. It is the knoll, and not the commune, which counts. These appellation

▼ *Have bottling line, will travel. Few French wine domains are large enough to justify the expense of permanent facilities.*

anomalies, of course, are what Bordeaux's various classification systems attempt to rectify, though they do so ineffectively. The geological work has all been done; so, too, has the pragmatic vineyard work, and the cellars of the wealthy around the world contain the bottled evidence. Why does INAO not recategorize Bordeaux from scratch?

The Bordelais are greedy

Greed is perceived as being the oldest problem of all in Bordeaux. The wines of Bordeaux may be much admired, but the public perception of those who produce those wines is of a rapacious and arrogant elite. The price of Bordeaux's great bottles is often four or five times the price of the greatest bottles from the Rhône or from Burgundy – yet even a cursory look at production figures will reveal that in most cases the Bordeaux wines are produced in far larger quantities than their Rhône or Burgundy equivalents. Who is to blame?

The answer is simple and obvious: it is those who pay the prices, rather than those who ask for them, who are to blame. Markets make prices, not producers. There is plenty of wine in the world; no one has to drink Bordeaux. If the price is too high (as it was in 1997), the wine will go unsold. Yet the community of world wine drinkers is still in no doubt whatsoever that the greatest red wines in the world are those produced in this region following a successful vintage like 1990, 1995, 1996, or 2000. Since the "developed" world is generally a peaceful and prosperous place at present, it contains many very wealthy individuals who consider 1,667 Euros a reasonable amount to pay for a case of great wine. "If somebody's prepared to pay you 23 Euros a bottle for your wine," says Anthony Barton, who has always priced Léoville-Barton modestly, "you're not going to say 'Oh my dear fellow, I'll give it to you for 15 Euros'." "It's a big problem," Jean-Luc Thunevin told me when I asked about the high prices of his wine. "Offer and demand, always. Lots of money has been made via the stock market. The Japanese study the French Paradox, and want to drink our wine. There are Russian millionaires; there are Texan millionaires. Lots of people want the same boxes of wine. It's a shame. But I'm happy to take the money. It's helped me buy top-quality vineyards, and to pay over half my workers double the minimum wage for a thirty-five-hour week. We were one of the first companies in France to introduce the thirty-five-hour week. And I'm happy to fly Business Class rather than Economy Class. That's life. No one is obliged to buy. If it's too expensive, the customers will disappear. It happens every ten years in Bordeaux, and life goes on."

Great Bordeaux is sold fraudulently

It is a bewildering paradox that the most expensive wines in the world are sold in an unfinished state. Here is what happens. A harvest, in September. Fermentations, in the autumn. Result? By February, a dozen parcels, atomized into hundreds of barrels of wine, of various qualities, new and unfinished, needing a year and a half's rest before bottling, and all of them different from one another and becoming more so with every day which passes.

It is at this point that those executing production must decide which barrels will make the cut for the *grand vin*, and which will be scuttled into the second (and perhaps third) wines. They have to decide how much press wine to include. Then they have to put samples of the blend together – and make them taste nice. Then, in March, the world's tasters arrive. And the world's scorers. Well, let's be honest, the world's scorer. Most of the tasters provide what one château proprietor calls

▼ *It may look like an inner-city building lot, but in fact this is precious Günz gravel. It's a plot of Trotanoy, awaiting replanting.*

"the noise"; for price, though, only one taster counts. The châteaux await their scores. They price (in most cases) at as high a level as they feel their scores merit. Sales are concluded by July. And the wines? They're still unfinished, lying in a hundred different pieces in the barrels.

The system, of course, is wide open to abuse. Samples can be coaxed, cosseted, and massaged into shape; no one superintends their authenticity. If a wine obtains a better score than expected, proprietors might well be tempted to make less second wine than they had originally planned. Whatever happens, there are decisions (and hazards) ahead before the wine is bottled. If a finished wine doesn't match the quality of the March sample, then the taster, and the noise, may revise their scores. No one, though, ever asks for a refund. The deals are done; the money's in the bank.

There's only one solution, but it's a distant one, requiring a common front among all Bordeaux's leading properties. The solution is to follow the example of what is quite possibly the world's greatest property, Yquem, offering tasting samples and selling only after the wine is bottled and finished. Depressingly, Yquem offered its 2000 vintage for the first time en primeur in the sales frenzy of May and June 2001. But this would mean a huge loss of income for all those involved: to be paid early is to be paid more. So it won't happen; the fraud will continue.

Classifications: do they matter?

I once attended a blind tasting of Bordeaux red wines at which "an official", one of the wine world's genuine civil servants, was present. The official insisted that it would be completely inappropriate to muddle up St-Emilion Grand Cru wines with St-Emilion Grand Cru Classé wines; they were of a different order of merit altogether. Five minutes spent tasting offered conclusive proof to the contrary. This kind of hierarchical stalinism is both amusing and pitiful.

Bordeaux has many classifications; all are ignored in *The New France* (there are specialist books available in which they are reproduced faithfully). All classifications are, in the end, only tenuously useful, for the following two reasons. The first is that Bordeaux classifications are based not on terroir alone, but on the boundaries of private property. Châteaux swop, sell, or buy parcels continuously, thus changing their

▼ Bordeaux's great châteaux may be owned by rich men, but those who do the hard work see little of this wealth.

boundaries (which were drawn up based on considerations other than terroir in the first place). There are assuredly very great terroirs all over Bordeaux, but classifying châteaux is an inefficient means of hunting them down.

The second reason is that classifications imply qualitative differences, yet they only ever reflect a historical assessment, and the quality of some properties changes with the same speed at which the Gironde flows into the sea. Even where classifications are subject to revision, the lag time between quality being achieved by an assiduous producer and its recognition in a classification is usually no less than a decade. Changes have come with cheetah-like speed to Bordeaux in the late 1990s. The result? Bordeaux's classifications have never been less useful than at present.

Of course classifications are fun as a debating point for enthusiasts; and some – most notably the 1855 classification of the châteaux of the Médoc – are regarded as a signpost towards the assessment of where a region's best terroirs are to be found. Whether or not a château is performing at the level of its original 1855 classification is sometimes taken as a measure of the skill of present-day management – yet this only makes sense if one assumes that all managers were equally skilled (or unskilled) in 1855, which seems most unlikely. The truth is that the 1855 classification was just a snapshot, too.

Second wines, third wines... and *grands vins*

Compare, for a moment, a typical Bordeaux château with a typical Burgundian domain. The château sits surrounded by its vineyards, usually sited entirely within one appellation; the domain, by contrast, has a little Grand Cru land, half a dozen Premier Cru sites, and lots of "village" vineyard, scattered up and down a forty-eight-km (thirty-mile) strip and covering a dozen or more AOCs. Utterly different, then?

On the surface, yes. In another sense, though, the differences are deceptive. The proprietorial borders of Bordeaux châteaux were not decided by geologists, or by wine brokers, or by the CIVB. They were decided by multiple accidents: speculative land drainage, a switch from stock-rearing to viticulture, or the decision to uproot a few peach trees as well as, of course, centuries of chaotic family succession. In terroir terms, property boundaries may make little sense. Almost all Bordeaux châteaux (and in the Médoc such properties routinely cover sixty ha/150 acres or more) possess good parcels, average parcels, and poor parcels. They will have old vines and young vines. They grow up to four different grape varieties, some of which perform well in one year and some in another. They therefore find themselves each June with the previous year's harvest segmented into lots whose quality varies greatly. They could, of course, bottle it all under the château name and make, quite literally, an average wine. Or they could do what Professor Emile Peynaud urged them to do half a century ago, and separate their wine into the very best fraction (which goes out under the château name, known as the *grand vin*) and the rest (which may all be sold as "second wine", or may be further subdivided to make a good "second wine" and a less good, possibly generic "third wine"). All large, ambitious properties now produce second wines; smaller properties in general do not (though this does not stop them selling off inadequate wine as a bulk disposal when necessary). The hallmark of mediocre Bordeaux properties of any size is the refusal to make a second wine.

Most second wines are excluded from the following section, since their general profile usually shadows that of the property from which they come. Readers should note, however, that these wines often offer excellent value and drinking qualities. It will generally be apparent which property a second wine comes from by its name. Famous examples include Les Forts de Latour, Carruades de Lafite, or Réserve de la Comtesse. Others, perplexingly, adopt a more opaque naming policy.

Bordeaux: People

Domaine de l'A
33500 Castillon, Tel: 05 57 24 60 29

Côtes de Castillon is one of Bordeaux's most promising new AOC areas, and Stéphane Derenoncourt (see page 167) and his wife Christine are two of the foremost vineyard and winery thinkers in the region today. Domaine de l'A is the Derenoncourts' own 4-ha property, sited in the west of the AOC near the St-Emilion border, cultivated biodynamically. The vineyard is planted to old vines (60% Merlot); and the wines are wood-fermented, barrique-aged with lees nourishment, and bottled without fining or filtration. The first two vintages, 1999 and 2000, were promisingly rich and fleshy; look for more backbone as the years pass.

d'Aiguilhe
33350 St-Philippe d'Aiguille, Tel: 05 57 40 60 10, Fax: 05 57 40 63 56

This large, 30-ha Côtes de Castillon property was purchased from the Cava-producing Raventós i Blanc family in 1998 by Comte Stephan von Neipperg, the owner of Canon-la-Gaffelière, Clos de l'Oratoire, and La Mondotte. The improvements have been rapid, with the 1999 and 2000 vintages both providing some of the best value for money in all of Bordeaux. This is exuberant, articulate, gratifying red wine with a firm Right Bank stamp to it. In vintages like 2000, it provides gorgeous drinking balance and sumptuous, soft-textured tannins.

Ampélia
33500 Castillon, Tel: 05 57 25 19 94

Small (4.5 ha) promising Côtes de Castillon property owned by François Despagne. The 2000 vintage offered a graceful, violet-perfumed mouthful.

d'Andréas
33330 St-Emilion, Tel: 05 57 55 09 13, Fax: 05 57 55 09 12

This is a 2-ha St-Emilion estate. The wine is made with the consulting help of Jean-Luc Thunevin in fiery, fierce, and extractive style, needing time to calm in bottle.

Angélus ✪
33330 St-Emilion, Tel: 05 57 24 71 39, Fax: 05 57 24 68 56

This 23.5-ha St-Emilion property is situated on the gentler slopes to the west of the town itself, and has been one of the appellation leaders since the mid-1980s. Vigorous, energetic, concentrated, and deep, the labrador-like Angélus usually needs time to incorporate its lavish, chocolatey oak. Hubert de Boüard de Laforest of Angélus was one of the pioneers of *effeuillage*, green harvesting and late picking in the appellation. The necessity to pick earlier in 1999, however, because of an untimely hail storm seems to have opened up new aesthetic possibilities, and the 2000 was marked by an exciting freshness, liveliness, and purity.

d'Angludet
33460 Cantenac, Tel: 05 57 88 71 41, Fax: 05 57 88 72 52

This 34-ha Margaux backwoods property, well run by the Sichel family, produces wines of gentle, country style.

l'Archange
33330 St-Emilion, Tel: 05 57 51 31 31

This St-Emilion is the family property (a former vine nursery) of Michel Rolland's right-hand man Pascal Chatonnet, also a leading international consultant in his own right (he works with Vega Sicilia among others). L'Archange lies close to Cheval Blanc, La Dominique, Rol Valentin, and Figeac. Its début vintage for the international market was the 2000, a wine of dreamily soft, voluptuous fruit.

d'Arche
33210 Sauternes, Tel: 05 56 61 97 64, Fax: 05 56 61 95 67

Much improved 30-ha Sauternes property producing lushly peachy wines in the late 1990s.

d'Armailhac
33250 Pauillac, Tel: 05 56 59 22 22, Fax: 05 56 73 20 44

The *cadet* member of the trio of closely sited properties owned by Philippine de Rothschild, daughter of Baron Philippe. It's been through a series of name changes (Mouton d'Armailhacq, Mouton Baron Philippe, Mouton Baronne Philippe, and since 1989 plain d'Armailhac); this latest, simplest name is worth remembering since the property often (1995, 1999) offers some of the best classic value in Bordeaux. Soft, comely, accessible, fine-sewn, yet full of meaty Pauillac class nonetheless.

l'Arrosée
33330 St-Emilion, Tel: 05 57 24 70 47

The well-sited St-Emilion escarpment vineyard of l'Arrosée means that fine results are possible and intermittently achieved here; the wines have a graceful, lyrical, light-textured style. The cellar, however, requires investment and renovation, and one must assume that the vineyards are maintained in approximately the same state.

Aurelius
33330 St-Emilion, Tel: 05 57 24 70 71, Fax: 05 57 24 65 18

A new, 4,000-case "garage" wine from the hangar-like St-Emilion cooperative, lush and affable in style.

Ausone ✪✪✪
33330 St-Emilion, Tel: 05 57 24 70 25, Fax: 05 57 74 47 39

Together with Cheval Blanc (though utterly different in both terroir and wine style), Ausone has historically always been considered one of St-Emilion's two finest wines. Indeed Ausone is, in a way, the soul of St-Emilion. This is the town's eagle's-nest property: its 7 ha are sited high on the limestone escarpment, grafted into ancient ruins and picturesquely mortared rubble, the wines traditionally having been aged in a series of spectacular cave cellars (though problems with humidity have meant much recent renovation of these). Its old vines, too, express a kind of reduced essence of St-Emilion, with much of the appellation's flamboyance stripped away to leave only the raw, tight, dense, black hole concentration of low-yielding, sun-roasted, limestone-grown Merlot itself. Yet Ausone has underperformed for much of the second half of the 20th century, begging just too much indulgence of its drinkers and giving them, in return, just too little pleasure for too long. After traumatic ownership and management changes in the mid-1990s, there have been dramatic improvements, beginning with the 1996 vintage. Owner Alain Vauthier, working with Michel Rolland, has taken the minerality and density of Ausone and clothed it with flowers, spice, and flesh. None of the authority, gravitas, or age-worthiness has gone; instead they have helped Ausone to emerge from its crabby shell and charm, even seduce, with its black liquid fire.

Axelle de Valandraud *see* Valandraud

Balestard
33750 St-Quentin de Baron, Tel: 05 57 24 28 09, Fax: 05 57 24 18 76

This 9.5-ha property in Entre-Deux-Mers produces one of the finest red AOC Bordeaux on the market, proving the worth of an unsparing, quality-driven "garage" philosophy. There are many classified properties of various sorts across Bordeaux that produce inferior wine to that of Balestard.

Star rating system used on producer spreads   ✪ Very good wine   ✪✪ Excellent wine   ✪✪✪ Great wine

Balestard la Tonnelle
33330 St-Emilion, Tel: 05 57 74 62 06, Fax: 05 57 74 59 34

Chunky 11-ha St-Emilion, offering solid drinking rather than ravishing concentration and finesse.

Barde-Haut
33330 St-Christophe-des-Bardes, Tel: 05 56 64 05 22, Fax: 05 56 64 06 98

This 17-ha St-Emilion property emerged from absolute obscurity with a fine 1997 vintage, championed by Robert Parker; at that point one leading London broker thought the name might even be a punning allusion to the wine's pneumatic delights (a liquid Brigitte Barde-Haut, so to speak), and that the joke would quickly fade. Not so. Solid performances in 1998 and 1999 led to its sale to the ambitious Cathiard-Garcin family, and the 2000 vintage suggests that this property, sited near Trottevieille, will continue to scrap among the St-Emilion avant-garde. Expect dark colours and lush succulence.

Bastor-Lamontagne
33210 Preignac, Tel: 05 56 63 27 66, Fax: 05 56 76 87 03

Once a royal property, the 58 ha of Bastor-Lamontagne, sited near Suduiraut, is now owned by Crédit Foncier, the owner of Beauregard in Pomerol. Its wine is steady in quality, full of chunky pineapple fruit, ageing well, and offering, like most of the best properties in Sauternes, superb value for money.

Batailley
33250 Pauillac, Tel: 05 56 00 00 70, Fax: 05 57 87 48 61

This 55-ha Pauillac château is set well back from the river, producing a relatively restrained, round-shouldered wine of satisfying balance.

Beaulieu
33540 Sauveterre-de-Guyenne, Tel: 05 56 61 55 21, Fax: 05 56 71 60 11

Try-harder Bordeaux red (sold under the appealing Comtes des Tastes name).

Beauregard
33500 Pomerol, Tel: 05 57 51 13 36, Fax: 05 57 25 09 55

With 17 ha to its name, this is one of Pomerol's largest properties, owned since 1991 by Crédit Foncier; the château building has one of the most beautiful wisteria plants in the Gironde curling round its courtyard walls. This is soft, creamy Pomerol of satisfying classicism, soon ready yet holding well.

Beau-Séjour Bécot ✪
33330 St-Emilion, Tel: 05 57 74 46 87, Fax: 05 57 24 66 88

Close to Angélus in both geography and style, the 16.5 ha of this leading St-Emilion produce a poundingly fruited, tannin-dredged, lavishly oaked red wine which needs plenty of time for its clenched flavours to ease and modulate.

Beauséjour Duffau Lagarrosse
33330 St-Emilion, Tel: 05 57 24 71 61, Fax: 05 57 24 66 88

This is the smaller (7-ha) part of the once-unified property of Beauséjour, and its wines are made in a less ebullient, rather nervier style than those of the Bécot family. In great vintages (1990, 2000), everything comes together to produce a wine of remarkable density, purity and intensity.

Beau-Site
33250 Pauillac, Tel: 05 56 00 00 70, Fax: 05 57 87 48 61

Firm St-Estèphe from as much as 70% Cabernet Sauvignon. The *beau site* itself is next to Calon-Ségur.

Beau Soleil
33750 Pomerol, Tel: 05 56 68 55 88, Fax: 05 56 68 55 77

The 3-ha Pomerol property, run by GAM Audy, is late harvested to give a dark, almost fiercely chewy style.

Bel-Air la Royère
33390 Cars, Tel: 05 57 42 91 34, Fax : 05 57 42 32 87

Xavier Loriaud's 45-ha Côtes de Blaye property is producing taut, meaty, vivid reds using low yields (around 30 hl/ha) and careful winemaking (including new oak and *élevage* on lees). Fine value.

Belgrave
33290 Parempuyre, Tel: 05 56 35 53 00, Fax: 05 56 35 53 29

Improving 55-ha Haut-Médoc property from St-Laurent, set back behind St-Julien and adjacent to Lagrange. It shares a knoll with Camensac and La Tour Carnet. As with a number of such properties, its 2000 vintage was the best for many years: vivid, full, glowing with rounded and balanced black fruits.

Bellefont-Belcier
33330 St-Laurent-des-Combes, Tel: 05 57 24 72 16, Fax: 05 57 74 45 06

The 12 ha of this St-Emilion property are sited on relatively flat land, but standards have been rising throughout the late 1990s under the guidance of the former winemaker for Larmande, and this is now a wine of satisfying density.

Bellegrave
33500 Pomerol, Tel: 05 57 51 20 47, Fax: 05 57 51 23 14

This 7-ha Pomerol doesn't have the best location (it lies in the northwest, near de Sales) but produces clean, fresh, unpretentious, and modestly priced wine.

Bellevue
33330 St-Emilion, Tel: 05 57 74 41 61

"*Un terroir de rêve*" is how Stéphane Derenoncourt describes this 6-ha St-Emilion property sited close to Angélus, Beau-Séjour Bécot, and Beauséjour Duffau. It's had an elegant but quiet track record; all that began to change in 2000, when Nicolas Thienpont took over as manager and Derenoncourt as advisor. They found 40-year-old vines, and were quickly able to make a handsome, pure-plum wine by bringing down yields dramatically and coaxing the wine into greater richness via lees nourishment techniques.

Bellevue Mondotte
33530 Arveyres, Tel: 05 57 24 87 87, Fax: 05 57 84 93 70

New, port-like, St-Emilion microcuvée from the energetic Gérard Perse: extravagant yet controversial. Is this Bordeaux or Barossa?

Bellile Mondotte
33330 St-Laurent-des-Combes, Tel: 05 57 74 41 17

Well-sited 4.5-ha St-Emilion property between Troplong Mondot, La Mondotte, and Tertre Roteboeuf. With neighbours like that, the challenge to improve standards is lighthouse-clear; Jean-Luc Thunevin has been called in to supervise vinification; this will be a name to watch. The 2000 turns on the fruit.

Berliquet
33330 St-Emilion, Tel: 05 57 24 70 48, Fax: 05 57 24 70 24

For many years, this 9-ha St-Emilion property, owned by Parisian investment banker Vicomte Patrick de Lesquen, was made by the cooperative, and the qualities of its fine terroir (close to Ausone, Canon, and Magdelaine) and 40-year-old vines were hidden. Under the guidance of Patrick Valette, son of the former owner of Pavie, the wine has greatly improved. The 2000 vintage is deep, classical, and resonant, superbly balanced and delicately oak-spiced, without the caricaturial qualities of some contemporary St-Emilions.

Bernadotte
33250 St-Sauveur, Tel: 05 56 59 57 04, Fax: 05 56 59 57 04

Much improved 8-ha Pauillac backwoods property, sited near Lynch-Moussas, in the same ownership as Pichon-Lalande. Don't look for driving meaty depths; well-managed, tapered blackcurrant fruit characterize the wine.

Beychevelle
33250 St-Julien-Beychevelle, Tel: 05 56 73 20 70, Fax: 05 56 73 20 71

Large (90 ha), beautiful and well-sited St-Julien property admired more for its elegance and finesse than for concentration and flesh.

Bonalgue
33500 Libourne, Tel: 05 57 51 62 17, Fax: 05 57 51 28 28

Robust, chunky, farmhouse-style Pomerol sited on the outskirts of Libourne offering unpolished good value.

Bonnet
33420 Grézillac, Tel: 05 57 25 58 58, Fax: 05 57 74 98 59

This enormous, 225-ha estate is bigger than the whole of the AOCs of Côte Rôtie or Condrieu. Owned by the Lurton family, it produces both white Entre-Deux-Mers and red Bordeaux, with the cream of the crop going into special Réserve and "Cuvée Divinus" bottlings.

Le Bon Pasteur
33500 Pomerol, Tel: 05 57 51 23 05, Fax: 05 57 51 66 08

Michel Rolland's portfolio of consultancies is so extensive that one wonders just how much time he is able to devote to his family property, but Le Bon Pasteur maintains enviably high standards. Its position on the St-Emilion border is promising, the ripeness and low-yield depth of the wines.

Bourgneuf Vayron
33500 Pomerol, Tel: 05 57 51 42 03, Fax: 05 57 25 01 40

This 9-ha Pomerol property has improved its concentration, though the style is burly and rustic.

Boyd-Cantenac
33460 Margaux, Tel: 05 57 88 90 90, Fax: 05 57 88 33 27

One of the outlying Margaux châteaux, Boyd-Cantenac has an unimpressive track record, though the depth and elegance of the 2000 vintage suggests better is to come.

Branaire
33250 St-Julien-Beychevelle, Tel: 05 56 59 25 86, Fax: 05 56 59 16 26

Few efforts have been spared in recent years at this 52-ha St-Julien property. It shares with nearby Beychevelle an almost Margaux-like floral finesse and elegance, though Branaire often exhibits better depth of sweet currant fruit. It may be a quieter, less showy Médoc performer than some, but its balance and urbane classicism make it an insider's choice, with 1996 and 2000 both fine.

Branda
33570 Puisseguin, Tel: 05 57 74 62 55, Fax: 05 57 74 57 33

One of the welcome benefits brought by Bordeaux's "garage" revolution has been the dramatic rise in the quality of wines of modest origin – like the toothsome reds from this 5-ha Puisseguin-St-Emilion property. Michel Puzio of Croix de Labrie makes the wine for owners Arnaud Delaire and Yves Blanc; Michel Rolland and Pascal Chatonnet consult. The medieval château, a tourist attraction, boasts a "sensory garden" (aren't they all?).

Brane-Cantenac
33460 Cantenac, Tel: 05 57 88 83 33, Fax: 05 57 88 72 51

It takes a long while to renovate an 85-ha château, but that's what Henri Lurton has been doing over the past decade for this Margaux grandee. The 2000 vintage provided a new benchmark: aromatic, svelte, expressive, mouthfilling, and fresh, the very model of restrained yet articulate elegance.

Branon
33850 Léognan, Tel: 05 56 64 05 22, Fax: 05 56 64 06 98

A super-soft microcuvée from the Garcin-Cathiard stable, the 250 cases of this 2000 Pessac-Léognan from 2 ha of vines (and with a pH of 4.12) made under the auspices of Michel Rolland are, sure enough, impressive, packed with meat and cream and with a long, smoky-bacon finish. A further 4 ha have been planted.

Brisson
33220 St-André et Appelles, Tel: 05 57 46 10 79

Another leading Côtes de Castillon contender, Brisson combines some of the lush fruit of Lalande-de-Pomerol with the meaty depth of classic St-Emilion.

Broustet
33720 Barsac, Tel: 05 56 27 16 87, Fax: 05 56 27 05 93

Small, 16-ha Barsac property whose wines, full of balanced, lemon-cream finesse, have improved steadily throughout the 1990s.

Brown
33850 Léognan, Tel: 05 56 87 08 10, Fax: 05 56 87 87 34

Improving, 25-ha Pessac-Léognan property owned by Bernard Barthe sited in the north of the appellation: midweight reds with the true earthy stamp of the AOC.

La Cabanne
33500 Libourne, Tel: 05 57 51 04 09, Fax: 05 57 25 13 38

Many-parcelled 10-ha Pomerol property (though its château is close to Trotanoy) producing rustic, tough though durable wines.

Calon-Ségur ✪
33180 St-Estèphe, Tel: 05 56 59 30 08, Fax: 05 56 59 71 51

This handsome 74-ha property is the most northerly of the Médoc's classed growths. Impressive wines in 1995, 1996, and 2000 marked a leap forward from the disappointing wines of the 1960s, 1970s, and 1980s. Its gravel over marl soils, and its long history of outstanding wines (including many great vintages in the 1920s and 1940s), show that this can be one of the most classic St-Estèphes of all: thick-textured, dark fruited, and slow to evolve.

Cambon la Pelouse
33460 Macau, Tel: 05 57 88 40 32, Fax: 05 57 88 40 32

Haut-Médoc property sited close to Giscours and Cantemerle on the Margaux border producing ripe, accessible, and lyrical wine in recent vintages, giving the lie to the myth that all good Bordeaux is overpriced.

Camensac
33112 St-Laurent-Médoc, Tel: 05 56 59 41 69, Fax: 05 56 59 41 73

Over-achieving 75-ha Haut-Médoc from one of the best zones of this extended AOC (close to Belgrave and La Tour Carnet in St-Laurent), Camensac's most successful wines (like the 2000 vintage) combine vigorous, pencilly depths with vivid blackcurrant fruit.

Canon (Canon-Fronsac)
33500 Libourne, Tel: 05 57 55 05 80, Fax: 05 57 55 79 79

Tiny 1.5-ha property overlooking the Dordogne in Canon-Fronsac formerly owned by Christian Moueix but now transferred, with Moueix's other Fronsac concerns, to Jean Halley of Carrefour. In good vintages like 1998, this is one of the appellation's outstanding wines: textured, firm, and earthy. The 4-ha Canon de Brem and the 4.3-ha Canon-Moueix are sited close by, providing more solid, affable wine (see also La Croix-Canon). Is it too much to hope that Halley will change these confusing names?

Canon (St-Emilion) ✪
33330 St-Emilion, Tel: 05 57 55 23 45, Fax: 05 57 24 68 00

Distinguished St-Emilion property owned since the mid-1990s by the Wertheimer family of Chanel fame, its 18 ha have recently been extended by a 3.5-ha purchase from nearby Curé-Bon. This will help sustain the château through an extensive replanting programme of 7 ha out of its original 18 ha (like a number of St-Emilion properties, Canon has to combat the effects of what is called *pourridié* – root problems caused by planting vines on the sites of former fruit orchards which had been imperfectly cleaned). There was also an unhappy period in the early 1990s where many wines suffered from TCA taint caused by pentachlorophenols in roof timber treatments: another problem that the new owners have had to surmount. The 2000 vintage showed the way forward: this is a wine of grace, warmth, concentration, and a classic St-Emilion meatiness, promising much for the future.

Canon-la-Gaffelière ✪
33330 St-Emilion, Tel: 05 57 24 71 33, Fax: 05 57 24 67 95

This 19.5-ha St-Emilion property sited towards the bottom of the celebrated limestone escarpment has been German-owned since 1971, when it was purchased by one of Württemberg's leading winegrowers, Comte Joseph-Hubert von Neipperg. However it is since Comte Stephan von Neipperg (*see* page 164), the son of Joseph-Hubert, took over in 1985 that the property has come into its own with steadily rising quality, intensity, depth, and concentration, making it today one of the most consistent of all St-Emilions. This is stout, chewy, meaty, stomach-filling wine, built on a core of old-vine Cabernet Franc (40-45%). Neipperg says that this is a much warmer site than La Mondotte, and almost too warm for successful Merlot.

Cantemerle
33460 Macau, Tel: 05 57 97 02 82, Fax: 05 57 97 02 84

The forest park of Cantemerle, sober behind its railings, marks the beginning of Médocain grandeur as one drives northwards out of Bordeaux. This 85-ha property is now owned by the mutual insurance company SMABTP; the wines are relatively light but tasty.

Cantenac-Brown
33460 Cantenac, Tel: 05 57 88 81 81, Fax: 05 57 88 81 90

The 42 ha of this distinguished Margaux site and its extraordinary Victorian château have presented the wine division of the insurance company AXA with one of its biggest challenges. Margaux is the hardest commune in Bordeaux from which to produce immediately showy, impressive wine, since its virtues and delights lie in discreet nuance and subtle inflections; over-exuberant extractions can easily collapse into rusticity and gawkiness. From 1997, however, this property has been producing delicious wine, marked by flowers, spice, and pencil box classicism.

Cap de Faugères
33350 Ste-Colombe, Tel: 05 57 40 34 99, Fax: 05 57 40 36 14

Promising Côtes de Castillon property initially purchased in 1987 by film producer Péby Guisez and his wife Corinne together with the neighbouring St-Emilion property Château Faugères (qv: the two châteaux are found each side of the St-Emilion/Castillon border). Péby Guisez died in 1997, but Corinne continues his outstanding work. The wine is dark, intense and meaty, better than many underperforming St-Emilions.

Caprice d'Angelique *see* Rocher Bellevue

Carignan
33360 Carignan, Tel: 05 56 21 21 31, Fax: 05 56 78 36 65

Despite its unfortunate name, this has been one of the outstanding properties in the Premières Côtes de Bordeaux since owner Philippe Pieraerts took over in 1981. Low yields, 100% new oak and sensitive winemaking advice from Louis Mitjavile combine to make the grand vin (based on just 12 ha out of 65) an intense and vigorous wine, though without the supple unction that its Merlot-dominated blend (70%) might imply.

de Carles
33141 Saillans, Tel: 05 57 84 32 03, Fax: 05 57 84 31 91

This fine 20-ha Fronsac property is sited on a commanding position above the River Isle; its odd, squat, pugnacious château building is classified as a historical monument. Some of the deepest, most ambitious wine in the AOC is produced here, packed with the chunky, satisfying depth so typical of Fronsac. Haut-Carles is the prestige *cuvée*, and La Preuve par Carles was a wine produced in 2000 which, like L'Interdit de Valandraud and Le Défi de Fontenil, was declassified to table wine status due to the fact that it was produced from vineyards which had been covered with protective plastic sheeting against possible rainstorms.

Les Carmes Haut-Brion
33600 Pessac, Tel: 05 56 93 23 40

Tiny 4.7 ha parkland Pessac-Léognan is surrounded by the city of Bordeaux. Unlike the other nearby Haut-Brion properties (Les Carmes is owned by the Furt family, not the Dillon descendants), red wine alone is produced here, combining much of the pencilly finesse of Pessac with tapered, creamy fruit.

Carsin
33410 Rions, Tel: 05 56 76 93 06, Fax: 05 56 62 64 80

This 40-ha Finnish-owned property in Premières Côtes de Bordeaux has been run along "Australian" lines since 1991 under Australian winemaker Mandy Jones. The wines are solid and cleanly crafted.

Certan de May (de Certan)
33500 Pomerol, Tel: 05 57 41 53, Fax: 05 57 51 88 51

This small, 5-ha property lies just across the road from Vieux Château Certan, which with it was originally unified, and produces wine of similarly graceful, milky, stealthy style, though with perhaps even finer grained tannins.

Certan Guiraud *see* Certan Marzelle, Hosanna

Certan Marzelle
33500 Pomerol, Tel: 05 57 51 78 96

Small parcel of pure Merlot acquired by Moueix with the former Certan Guiraud. It will be made (at the new Hosanna winery) and bottled separately.

de Chambrun
33500 Libourne, Tel: 05 57 51 18 95, Fax: 05 57 25 10 59

This tiny, 1.5 ha property in the fast-improving AOC of Lalande-de-Pomerol is owned by the ambitious de Janoueix family. The 2000 vintage was a wine of astonishingly deep colour, filled with rippling, truffley blackberry fruit.

Chantegrive
33720 Podensac, Tel: 05 56 27 17 38, Fax: 05 56 27 29 42

Enormous 92-ha Graves estate whose oaked white Cuvée Caroline can be sumptuous and whose red is increasingly impressive, too.

Charmail
33180 St-Seurin-de-Cadourne, Tel: 05 56 59 70 63, Fax: 05 56 59 39 20

Fine value wine from a 22-ha property sited, like Sociando-Mallet, on the knoll of St-Seurin-de-Cadourne, just north of St-Estèphe. This is one of the leading Médoc experimenters with the Right Bank (and burgundian) technique of cold pre-fermentation maceration.

Les Charmes Godard
33570 St-Cibard, Tel: 05 57 56 07 47, Fax: 05 57 56 07 48

This 6-ha property is sited in the Côtes des Francs, just north of Castillon, and is owned by Nicolas Thienpont of Puygueraud; the Thienpont family (members of which also own Vieux Château Certan, Le Pin, and Monbrison) helped pioneer this pretty, hilly area of mixed farms. In addition to the vivid, mineral-stiffened red, there is also a lush, exotic barrel-fermented white wine with notes of peach and lemon, made from a blend of Sémillon and Muscadelle with Sauvignon Gris.

Chasse-Spleen
33480 Moulis-en-Médoc, Tel: 05 56 58 02 37, Fax: 05 57 88 84 40

Well made and memorably named (the disappearing spleen was not that of Baudelaire but Byron), this 80-ha Moulis estate, now owned by the Merlaut family, produces wines with more elegance and balance than the appellation's reputation normally suggests.

Cheval Blanc ❍❍❍
33330 St-Emilion, Tel: 05 57 55 55 55, Fax: 05 57 55 55 50

Together with Ausone, Cheval Blanc is one of St-Emilion's two legendary properties – though it is utterly different from Ausone in every sense. Geographically, it lies well away from the town of St-Emilion and its famous limestone Côte, instead abutting Evangile and La Conseillante; it is, in effect, a Pomerol sited outside Pomerol. There are three separate soil types on the 36-ha property: one is classic Pomerol gravel; another is a gravel-clay mixture; the third is sand and clay. No less noteworthy is the high percentage (57%) of Cabernet Franc in the vineyards. Whereas Merlot is king over the Pomerol border, in this eccentric, Far West zone of St-Emilion, the Cabernets play a key role (at Figeac just across the road, it is Cabernet Sauvignon which matches Merlot hectare for hectare). Cheval Blanc changed hands in 1998, when Bernard Arnault and Baron Albert Frère bought it from the previous owners, the Fourcaud-Laussac family; no expense has been spared since to make it not only the greatest property on the Right Bank of Bordeaux, but one with ambitions to be the greatest property in the entire region. In the 1998, 1999, and 2000 vintages, Cheval Blanc was outstanding; the quiet, confident director

Pierre Lurton is making fine use of the qualitative freedoms he has been given, helped by vineyard consultant Kees van Leeuwen. It is never the biggest or meatiest red wine in Bordeaux, and those who measure wines in their youth by weighing tannin in one hand and fruit in the other may wonder what all the fuss is about. Give it time, though, and it seems to draw silk garments out of some invisible drawer, increasing in textural sensuality and soft, dropping weight with each year; its allusive mixture of chocolate, raspberry, cherry, and cream, polished with the finesse of cedar, is hard to resist. Those whose only experience of Cabernet Franc has been through the red wines of the Loire will find little to recognize in this sweet and sumptuous mouthful. The historical record, moreover, is conclusive: as at Haut-Brion, great wines have been produced here repeatedly, and in spite (if one can put it like that) of the winemaking innocence of the past. There can only be one conclusion: Cheval Blanc occupies one of Bordeaux's finest terroirs.

Domaine de Chevalier
33850 Léognan, Tel: 05 56 64 16 16, Fax: 05 56 64 18 18
This 35-ha Pessac-Léognan property set amidst woodland to the extreme west of the AOC produces both red and dry white wines which, from great vintages, evolve slowly in bottle to produce wines of allusive finesse. The site is prone to both frost and hail problems, so it is not an easy vineyard to run; and its style has sometimes seemed rather old-fashioned during the 1990s, with inconsistent results.

Cissac
33250 Cissac-Médoc, Tel: 05 56 59 58 13, Fax: 05 56 59 55 67
Well-known 50-ha property from one of the less favoured Haut-Médoc communes (Cissac-Médoc), the wines of Cissac were austere and slender for many years, but are now made in a richer, rounder style.

Citran
33480 Avensan, Tel: 05 56 58 21 01, Fax: 05 57 88 84 60
This large, 90-ha Haut-Médoc property on the edge of Moulis benefited from 9 years of Japanese investment, during which the vineyard was greatly improved by unsexy but vital new drainage schemes (poor vineyard drainage remains the biggest single factor preventing quality improvements for many modestly financed properties in Bordeaux). It's now owned by the Merlaut family, and produces fleshy, attractive wines for drinking young.

Clarke
33480 Listrac-Médoc, Tel: 05 56 58 38 00, Fax: 05 56 58 26 46
This 53-ha Listrac property owned by Baron Edmond de Rothschild should produce some of the Médoc's finest wines, since no expense is spared in its production. The truths of terroir are the same for all, however; this is polished wine and often a very good buy (especially now the vines are older), but Listrac cannot provide the plunging depths of the greatest gravel sites in nearby Pauillac or Margaux.

Clément-Pichon
33290 Parempuyre, Tel: 05 56 35 23 79, Fax: 05 56 35 85 23
This 25-ha property just to the north of Bordeaux is owned by the proprietor of La Dominique, Clément Fayat, who (with help from Michel Rolland) produces atypically sweet-fruited, rich-textured wine here.

Clerc Milon
33250 Pauillac, Tel: 05 56 59 22 22, Fax: 05 56 73 20 44
Mouton-owned, the 32-ha Clerc Milon has superbly situated vines, and its dense, taut, and stately style provides some of the best value in Pauillac.

Climens ✪✪
33720 Barsac, Tel: 05 56 27 15 33, Fax: 05 56 27 21 04
The 29-ha of Climens form one of the highest and finest parcels of Barsac. Each vintage is carefully and unhurriedly composed by Bérénice Lurton, and for pure fruited finesse (as opposed to lush unction) this property has few rivals.

Clinet ✪
33500 Pomerol, Tel: 05 57 51 27 87
The 9-ha Pomerol property of Clinet holds a special place among the pantheon of Right Bank châteaux that have catapulted themselves into prominence in the last decade of the 20th century. Clinet managed it not by slow annual increments, but with two sensational wines: the 1989 and 1990. These thick, dark, unctous, saturated mouthfuls form points of reference for each vintage, as well as monumental Merlots. How were they achieved? Low yields and super-ripeness are the keys (though fruit sorting, 100% new oak, and the absence of fining and filtration are also important). In other words, these great wines were the triumphant vindication of the theories of Michel Rolland, a close friend of the man who made them: Jean-Michel Arcaute. Throughout the 1990s, Arcaute refined but never compromised his late-harvesting techniques, making Clinet into one of the darkest and most succulent wines of this dark, succulent appellation. It didn't always work, of course; in vintages like 1998 and 1999, late-season rain made life difficult. Yet Clinet kept its style and, in truth, succeeded far more often than it failed. The wines were never dilute; critics of Clinet's style pointed out that acid levels this low tend to give rather corpulent, adipose wines which lack freshness and drinkability. Arcaute left Clinet in 2000 and died in 2001, but the style print remains under new owner Jean-Louis Laborde (with Michel Rolland continuing to consult).

Clos Badon Thunevin
33330 St-Emilion, Tel: 05 57 55 09 13, Fax: 05 57 55 09 12
"Clos" – a term originally signifying a walled vineyard, and with strong burgundian connotations – is one of the key markers for "garage" wines in present-day Bordeaux. This 6.6-ha vineyard in St-Emilion is sited on slope-bottom land, just to the north of the Castillon road, beneath Pavie, and is made by the King of the Garagistes, Jean-Luc Thunevin, from a blend of Merlot and Cabernet Franc. It is, as you might expect, lush, and offers better value for money than many garage wines.

Clos Chaumont
33550 Haux, Tel: 05 56 23 37 23, Fax: 05 56 23 30 54
Ambitious, Dutch-owned Premières Côtes de Bordeaux producing sumptuous reds, a barrel-fermented dry white Bordeaux, and small quantities of sweet Cadillac.

Clos du Clocher
33500 Pomerol, Tel: 05 57 51 92 14
This 6-ha Pomerol property is sited near Beauregard, and its lyrical, tongue-caressing style echoes that of its much larger neighbour. Reduced yields and advice from Michel Rolland are upping the concentration levels.

Clos Dubreuil
33330 St-Emilion
Minuscule quantites of rich, dense St-Emilion made with the help of consultant Louis Mitjavile.

Clos l'Eglise (Castillon)
33350 St-Magne-de-Castillon, Tel: 05 57 40 06 75
One of two Castillon properties jointly owned and run by Gérard Perse of Pavie and Dr Alain Raynaud of Quinault l'Enclos, the other being Château Ste-Colombe. The ambitions are highest at this 16-ha property: 35 hl/ha, hand-harvesting, 100% new oak, this blend of 60% Merlot with 20% each of the two Cabernets gives one of Castillon's firmest, densest, tightest-meshed wines, bottled without fining or filtration.

Clos l'Eglise (Pomerol)
33500 Pomerol, Tel: 05 56 64 05 22, Fax: 05 56 64 06 98
This 6-ha property sited close to Clinet, Eglise-Clinet and Rouget is run with limitless commitment by the Cathiard-Garcin family. The result is a Pomerol of almost parodic depths, packed with oak, vanilla, and cocoa.

Clos Fourtet
33330 St-Emilion, Tel: 05 57 24 70 90, Fax: 05 57 74 46 52

A superb, 20-ha site next to the old town of St-Emilion makes Clos Fourtet one of the leading properties of the plateau. Philippe Cuvelier bought Clos Fourtet from the Lurton family in 2001, and ambitious improvements can be expected to what is already a much denser, richer wine than in the past.

Clos Haut-Peyraguey
33210 Bommes, Tel: 05 56 76 61 53, Fax: 05 56 76 69 65

Good value, vanilla scented, vividly balanced Sauternes from a well-sited 15-ha property between Yquem and Rayne-Vigneau.

Clos du Jaugueyron
33460 Arsac

Margaux is a much bigger AOC than the others in the Médoc, thanks to the inclusion of the communes of Soussans, Arsac, Cantenac, and Labarde within its boundaries. It's no accident, then, that it is in Margaux that the garage spirit has settled first – at Marojallia, at Clos des Quatre Vents, and here at Clos du Jaugueyron, a tiny 2.5-ha old-vine parcel which straddles the Margaux/Haut-Médoc boundary. Owner Michel Théron believes the vines predate phylloxera. The wines are packed with layered blackcurrant and spice – should you ever come across one. There are only 100 cases of the Margaux; this is Bordeaux on a Burgundy scale.

Clos Nardian
33330 Vignonet, Tel: 05 57 84 64 22, Fax: 05 57 84 63 54

Ambitious white wine produced by Jonathan Maltus of Château Teyssier from just half a hectare of vines on the northeastern edge of the Entre-Deux-Mers. Fifty-year-old vines and a yield of 25 hl/ha plus barrel fermentation in new oak gives sumptuous results for this 50/50 Sauvignon-Sémillon blend.

Clos de l'Oratoire
33330 St-Emilion, Tel: 05 57 24 71 33, Fax: 05 57 24 67 95

Sited on the cooler plateau land north of the town of St-Emilion, this 10-ha property is, in terroir terms, perhaps the least interesting of the three Neipperg St-Emilions (the other two being Canon-la-Gaffelière and La Mondotte). Drinkers who discover its consistency, concentration, balance, and succulence, however, allied to its reasonable price may have reason to consider it the greatest achievement of the three. As at La Mondotte, Stephan von Neipperg says, Merlot ripens very well here, though it is texturally different: less vivid and lush.

Clos Puy Arnaud
33350 Belvès-de-Castillon, Tel: 05 57 47 90 33, Fax: 05 56 90 15 44

This 8.5-ha Côtes de Castillon property, recently purchased by jazz singer Thierry Valette and made with the help of Stéphane Derenoncourt, produced an elegant, spicy 2000. Look for further improvements and a possible transition to biodynamics.

Clos des Quatre Vents
33460 Soussans

Of the 2 ha in this Margaux parcel, one, planted with very old vines, is used for this vividly fruited, complex, and finely embroidered wine made by Luc Thienpont of Labégorce-Zédé.

Clos René
33500 Pomerol, Tel: 05 57 51 10 41, Fax: 05 57 51 16 28

There are no great Pomerols in the northwestern sector of the AOC, which is where Clos René's 12 ha are situated, but this is generally a well-made, easygoing, supple mouthful of rich red wine.

Clos St-Martin ✪
33330 St-Emilion, Tel: 05 57 24 71 09, Fax: 05 57 24 69 72

Just 1.4 superbly sited hectares, picked as late as possible, provide a St-Emilion of spoon-standing concentration and profound tannic grip.

Clos de Sarpe
33330 St-Emilion, Tel: 05 57 24 72 39, Fax: 05 57 74 47 54

Another St-Emilion where the garage challenge has not passed unnoticed, this 4-ha property sited near Trottevieille to the east of the town is largely planted with older vines. Yields are tiny (just 25 hl/ha), there is no fining or filtration, and the wine is made in an exuberantly extracted, teeth-coating style. Salt it away.

La Clotte
33330 St-Emilion, Tel: 05 57 24 66 85, Fax: 05 57 24 79 67

La Clotte has a fine sand-and-gravel site near to Pavie-Macquin, and its 3.7 ha are beginning to reveal the class of the terroir with recent tasty, sweet-fruited offerings. Stéphane Derenoncourt consults.

La Clusière
33330 St-Emilion, Tel: 05 57 55 43 43, Fax: 05 57 24 63 99

This 2-ha St-Emilion micro-property within Pavie is not a marketing strategy of owner Gérard Perse, since the site was separated under the Valette family also; it lies a little further east along the ridge. It does not have the same strapping power as Pavie, but its surging purity and chocolate depths are impressive nonetheless.

La Conseillante ✪
33500 Pomerol, Tel: 05 57 51 15 32, Fax: 05 57 51 42 39

Superbly sited 12-ha Pomerol property lying on St-Emilion's northwestern border, close to Evangile, Cheval Blanc, La Dominique, and the Figeacs. La Conseillante, like Cheval Blanc itself, is often a wine which begins life so copiously clad in baby fat that one suspects it will never make old bones. Wrong. It lingers impressively, becoming more savoury and Havana-wreathed with the years, though a second wine might improve its concentration.

Corbin
33330 St-Emilion, Tel: 05 57 25 20 30, Fax: 05 57 25 22 00

The group of Corbin properties (there are almost as many Corbins as there are Figeacs) lies in an intriguing sector of St-Emilion at its far northwestern tip, within easy strolling distance of La Dominique and Cheval Blanc. This is still the zone of soft, billowing, Pomerol-like St-Emilion, mouthfuls for hedonists and sensualists, without much if any of the sometimes frightening tannins of the Côte. Fruit-packed Corbin itself fits the bill.

Cos d'Estournel ✪✪
33180 St-Estèphe, Tel: 05 56 73 15 50, Fax: 05 56 59 72 59

The wines of this well-run 64-ha second growth (now owned by Geneva-based food manufacturer Michel Reybier) are sumptuous, spicy, and consistent. It has a fine position, on deep gravels looking across the little Chenal du Lazaret to the "marsh" of Lafite. Stylistically, it is less typical of St-Estèphe than either Calon-Ségur or Montrose: no tough tannins, in other words, and rarely the same need for long ageing. One reason for this may be the readiness to adopt the latest technical innovations here: Jean-Guillaume Prats is one of the Médoc's pioneers in using concentration techniques, and ample new oak and malolactic in *barriques* adds to the sumptuous, fine-grained textures of this wine. Prats is one of the few Médoc managers to openly welcome the "kick in the butt" which the Right Bank garagistes have given the Médoc; having studied their methods, he is cutting yields (though the 40-hl/ha he is aiming for is still well above typical "garage" levels) and working in the vineyards to improve the quality of the grape skins. The 2000 Cos reflects this new philosophy with a wine which combined floral aromas with dense, tight-packed cinder and meat flavours.

Cos Labory
33180 St-Estèphe, Tel: 05 56 59 30 22, Fax: 05 56 59 73 52

The 18-ha St-Estèphe neighbour of Cos d'Estournel produces worthy but rarely outstanding wines; Cos d'Estournel has the best of the gravel mound which the two properties share with Lafon-Rochet.

Côte de Baleau
33330 St-Emilion, Tel: 05 57 24 71 09, Fax: 05 57 24 69 72

This 17-ha property on the St-Emilion plateau is the largest of the three owned by the Reiffers family (the other two are Grandes Murailles and Clos St-Martin). Hugely improved on its past performances, this is now a dense, taut wine sold at an attractive price.

Coufran
33180 St-Seurin-de-Cadourne, Tel: 05 56 59 31 02, Fax: 05 56 59 32 85

The 75 ha of Coufran are doubly unusual for the Haut-Médoc, first of all for occupying a superbly sited, prominent gravel knoll within a stone's throw of the Gironde, just north of St-Estèphe, and secondly for the high percentage of Merlot in the vineyard plantings (85%). The results are, as you might expect, lusher, rounder, and spicier than the Médoc average.

La Couspaude
33330 St-Emilion, Tel: 05 57 40 15 76, Fax: 05 57 40 10 14

The 7 ha of this St-Emilion property (a genuine clos) are sited on the plateau behind the town. During the mid- to late 1990s the wine has been made in an almost parodically new wave, low-acid style; the fruit seems to disappear in a welter of fudge and toffee-like sweetness. Fascinating, exotic, and odd.

Coutet ✪
33720 Barsac, Tel: 05 56 27 15 46, Fax: 05 56 27 02 20

Together with Climens, the 38-ha Coutet is one of the two great properties in Barsac: the epitome of light-fingered, lemony finesse.

Couvent des Jacobins
33330 St-Emilion, Tel: 05 57 24 70 66, Fax: 05 57 24 62 51

The vineyards of this former monastery in the heart of St-Emilion (a ravishingly beautiful building beneath which stretch cellars of mysterious intricacy) are found just outside the town. For long a light, well-made but unexceptional wine, the 2000 showed promising depth.

La Croix-Canon
33126 Fronsac, Tel: 05 57 25 90 81, Fax: 05 57 25 11 74

At 14 ha, this is the largest of the group of closely sited Canon-Fronsac properties formerly owned by Moueix and now owned by Jean Halley of Carrefour; it was originally called Charlemagne. Old vines (some centenarian) and 70% Merlot provide an unusually rich Canon-Fronsac.

La Croix de Gay
33500 Pomerol, Tel: 05 57 51 19 05, Fax: 05 57 74 15 62

The well-sited 12 ha of Croix de Gay owned by Alain Raynaud and his sister Chantal Lebreton produce one of the lightest, most delicately stated of all Pomerols. See also Fleur de Gay.

Croix de Labrie
33330 St-Emilion, Tel: 05 57 24 64 60

Tiny flat-land St-Emilion property (initially 125 cases, now 750) made by garagiste Michel Puzio with what even his advisor Jean-Luc Thunevin recognizes is an eyebrow-singing commitment to excellence; Puzio, for example, drained off no less than 40% of the juice of his 1999 wine in what was not so much a saignée as a haemorrhage. Thunderous depths, here, for those that can lay hands on the wine.

La Croix du Casse
33750 St-Germain-du-Puch, Tel: 05 57 34 51 51, Fax: 05 56 30 11 45

This 9-ha property is not sited in a favoured part of Pomerol; it lies to the south of the AOC, near the railway line which coincides with the appellation boundary. Nonetheless the recent record of La Croix du Casse is excellent: these are deep, late-harvested, lavishly extracted, tannic, amply oaked, low acid reds, bottled without fining or filtration, whose only failing is the lack of core grandeur of fruit which terroir alone can contribute. Owner Jean-Michel Arcaute and his son Alexi both died, prematurely, in 2001.

La Croix St-Georges
33506 Libourne, Tel: 05 57 51 41 86, Fax: 05 57 51 53 16

Turnaround 5-ha Pomerol property not far from Le Pin whose 1999 and 2000 vintages have been made in a new wave, steamroller style full of earth, tannic depth, and crushed black fruits.

Croizet-Bages
33250 Pauillac, Tel: 05 56 59 01 62, Fax: 05 56 59 23 39

One of the Médoc's most long-standing underperformers, given the quality of its terroir, this 29-ha Pauillac property at the heart of the Lynch-Bages plateau continues to machine-harvest and make no second wine. The wines, though, are better vinified than was once the case.

Les Cruzelles
33500 Lalande-de-Pomerol, Tel: 05 57 51 79 83

Lalande-de-Pomerol recently launched by the ambitious Denis Durantou of Eglise-Clinet. The 2000 vintage was fresh, soft, and lissom, for swift drinking.

Dassault
33330 St-Emilion, Tel: 05 57 55 10 00, Fax: 05 57 55 10 01

This well-resourced 24-ha St-Emilion property, run by the grandson of the aviation industrialist Marcel Dassault, is sited in the north of the AOC on plateau land. It produces straightforward, unexceptional but carefully made wines.

La Dauphine
33126 Fronsac, Tel: 05 57 25 90 81, Fax: 05 57 25 11 74

Formerly in Moueix ownership and now owned by Jean Halley of Carrefour, this 10-ha Fronsac property offers excellent value for money. It is sited close to Canon de Brem and Canon-Moueix on the border with the AOC of Canon-Fronsac, overlooking the Dordogne; its wine has more charm than either.

Dauzac
33460 Labarde-Margaux, Tel: 05 57 88 32 10, Fax: 05 57 88 96 00

This 45-ha property lies close to the estuary, its vines on the gentlest of mounds, towards the far south of the Margaux AOC. Under the ownership of insurance company MAIF, it produces soft, supple wines for mid-term ageing.

Doisy-Daëne
33720 Barsac, Tel: 05 56 27 15 84, Fax: 05 56 27 18 99

The three Doisy properties lie between Coutet and Climens in Barsac. This 15-ha estate (part-owned by the celebrated Bordeaux white-wine researcher Denis Dubourdieu) produces a pure Sémillon of luscious, thick-textured sweetness, almost more Sauternes than Barsac in style.

Doisy-Dubroca
33720 Barsac, Tel: 05 57 83 10 10, Fax: 05 57 83 10 11

A tiny, 3-ha strip between its two larger siblings, this property is Lurton-owned and made at Climens: scented citrus qualifies its sweetness.

Doisy-Védrines
33720 Barsac, Tel: 05 56 27 15 13, Fax: 05 56 27 26 76

At 27 ha, this is the biggest of the three Doisy properties. Its wines are consistent and carefully made, but lack the wild grandeur and steamroller unction of the very best Barsac and Sauternes.

Le Dôme ✪
33330 Vignonet, Tel: 05 57 84 64 22, Fax: 05 57 84 63 54

Tiny, 1.7-ha parcel of St-Emilion, sited between Angélus and Grand Mayne, planted with 72% Cabernet Franc and owned by Englishman Jonathan Maltus of Château Teyssier, whose aim is to produce "a garage or icon or trophy wine" here. Le Dôme is made by Neil White, with advice from Gilles Pauquet (who also consults to Cheval Blanc and Figeac): the 1998 and 2000 vintages produced dark, brooding wines filled with rich and relatively unshowy raspberry and plum fruits. The 150% new wood does not mark the wine exaggeratedly, boding well for its bottle evolution.

La Dominique
33330 St-Emilion, Tel: 05 57 51 31 36, Fax: 05 57 51 63 04

This superb 18-ha St-Emilion site is adjacent to Cheval Blanc, and was one of Michel Rolland's first consultancies (Bon Pasteur is not far away). The wines are lush, soft, and blackberryish, almost echoing those of La Conseillante on the other side of Cheval Blanc, though perhaps with a little less complexity and milky depths to their fruit. In addition to the *grand vin* and *second vin* (St-Paul de Dominique), a microcuvée called St-Domingue has been produced here from unclassified parcels which ups the concentration levels still further and provides exotic, late-harvest fruit characters and the sweetness of lavish oak.

Ducru-Beaucaillou ✿
33250 St-Julien-Beychevelle, Tel: 05 56 73 16 73, Fax: 05 56 59 27 37

St-Julien grandee whose name refers to its 50 ha of "beautiful" gravelstones, sited in the southern, Beychevelle sector of the appellation, fronting the Gironde. (Not directly, of course, since there are the usual fields of grazing pasture to cross before you reach the water's edge.) This is classic Bordeaux of almost understated beauty, like an impeccably tailored suit; it is medium-bodied, never over-extracted, garishly fruited or over-oaked, but always a model of balance and harmony, blackcurrant purity, and pencil-box class. Standards have been consistently maintained since the Borie family bought the property in 1941, with the only difficulties coming with cellar-related TCA problems between 1988 and 1990.

Duhart-Milon
33250 Pauillac, Tel: 05 56 73 18 18, Fax: 05 56 59 26 83

This 65-ha Lafite-owned property (vineyards only; there is no château building) produces wines of elegance and nuance. In place of classic Pauillac beefiness, you'll find liquorice, pepper, aniseed, allied to increasing ripeness under the assiduous administration of Charles Chevalier throughout the 1990s. Just as Lafite rivals Mouton for grandeur, so Duhart-Milon rivals Clerc Milon for value.

Durfort-Vivens
33460 Margaux, Tel: 05 57 88 31 02, Fax: 05 57 88 60 60

As with all the Lurton-owned properties (this one belongs to Gonzague Lurton), the emphasis at this 30-ha Margaux property is on elegance, finesse, and classicism rather than modish extraction.

Domaine de l'Eglise
33330 St-Emilion, Tel: 05 56 00 00 70, Fax: 05 57 87 48 61

Another Pomerol property clustered around the landmark church, this improving 7-ha estate is producing increasingly well-structured, amply fruited wines.

L'Eglise-Clinet ✿✿
33500 Pomerol, Tel: 05 57 25 99 00

Denis Durantou's 6-ha Pomerol estate produces one of the most consistently outstanding wines of the AOC, thanks to a fine stock of old vnes (some centenarian) and deep roots, too, in the winemaking culture of this sun-lit plateau. Durantou resists winemaking fashions, eschewing the late harvesting, lavish oak, and micro-oxygenation techniques of the garagistes; his firm Pomerols are often unyielding and darkly fiery in their youth, but with time seem to build and broaden into rich-toned, enduring thoroughbreds.

L'Evangile ✿
33500 Libourne, Tel: 05 57 51 15 30, Fax: 05 57 51 45 78

Evangile's 14-ha occupy a superb site between Pétrus, La Conseillante and Cheval Blanc. The intermittent greatness of the past looks like being achieved more regularly under Lafite-Rothschild ownership (since 1990). In style, Evangile has little of the milky charm of La Conseillante; instead it seems to combine the raspberry seduction of Cheval Blanc with some of the chewy depths of Pétrus.

Faizeau
33570 Montagne, Tel: 05 57 24 68 94, Fax: 05 57 24 60 37

This 10-ha Montage St-Emilion property is noteworthy partly because of its stock of 80-year-old Merlot vines (used to make a Vieilles Vignes *cuvée*), and partly because it is jointly owned by Alain Raynaud of Quinault l'Enclos and his sister Chantal Lebreton, who makes these wines as well as helping her father Noël Raynaud make Croix de Gay and Fleur de Gay. They are earthy and full.

Falfas
33710 Bayon-sur-Gironde, Tel: 05 57 64 80 41, Fax: 05 57 64 93 24

This biodynamically run, American-owned 22-ha property in Côtes de Bourg produces unshowy yet dense and carefully crafted wines.

de Fargues
33210 Fargues-de-Langon, Tel: 05 57 98 04 20, Fax: 05 57 98 04 21

This property is one of a sizeable number in Bordeaux to "prove" beyond doubt the truth of terroir. Terroir writes the melody in wine; the rest is mere performance. De Fargues is owned by the Lur-Saluces family of Yquem fame; indeed it has been in this family's ownership for over 500 years, rather longer than Yquem was. It was always produced in the same way, with the same care, and with what was often a lower yield (it lies to the east of Yquem and generally has a later harvesting date). The quality (and value) of the wine is outstanding – but Yquem it isn't. The reason is that its 15 ha lie on a different gravelly knoll with another network of clay veins, a little further from the Garonne and the cool, forest-shaded Ciron.

Faugères
33330 St-Etienne-de-Lisse, Tel: 05 57 40 34 99, Fax: 05 57 40 36 14

Unpromisingly sited 20-ha St-Emilion estate in the far east of the AOC – yet under its former owner Corinne Guisez producing deep, seductive red wine of the sort which only the appellation leaders once produced. See also Cap de Faugères and Péby Faugères. Investments by new owner Silvio Denz look set to raise quality still higher.

Ferrand-Lartigue
33330 St-Emilion, Tel: 05 57 74 46 19, Fax: 05 57 74 46 19

Tiny 3-ha St-Emilion property run on perfectionist lines, with winemaking help from Louis Mitjavile. The style is smooth, supple, and pure.

Ferrière
33460 Margaux, Tel: 05 57 88 76 65, Fax: 05 57 88 98 33

The minnow of the Médoc, little Ferrière (just 8 ha) is now producing classically fragrant Margaux under the direction of Claire Villars-Lurton.

Feytit-Clinet
33500 Pomerol, Tel: 05 57 25 51 27, Fax: 05 57 25 93 97

This 7-ha Pomerol may lie next door to Latour-à-Pomerol, but its taste, under Moueix management, has been a contrast: light, soft and easygoing. Moueix is no longer involved, and owner Jeremy Chasseuil's aim is to make a deeper and more resonant wine.

de Fieuzal
33850 Léognan, Tel: 05 56 64 77 86, Fax: 05 56 64 18 88

This 48-ha property sited to the south of Pessac produces increasingly sumptuous red wines (both 1999 and 2000 were lusher than many in the AOC, thanks to work from Jean-Luc Marchive, formerly of Evangile) and vivid, fresh whites, both offering good value. It was acquired by the Irish banking millionaire Lachlann Quinn in 2001.

Figeac ✿
33330 St-Emilion, Tel: 05 57 24 72 26, Fax: 05 57 74 45 74

Large 40-ha property at the Pomerol end of St-Emilion, just across the road from Cheval Blanc. As with Cheval Blanc and the Corbin properties, there is a significant continuation of the Pomerol gravel plateau here. Vintages like 1982, 1990, and 1998 prove that Figeac's potential is magnificent; the fact that it is planted with 70% of Cabernet Sauvignon and Cabernet Franc compared with just 30% of Merlot never makes it wholly typical of St-Emilion or Pomerol, however. (Nor, of course, with 57% Cabernet Franc, is Cheval Blanc itself.) Consistency is a problem here, and barrel samples from Figeac are harder than most to judge, but at its best these are masterful wines of rigour and power.

Filhot

33210 Sauternes, Tel: 05 56 76 61 09, Fax: 05 56 76 67 91

Large, 60-ha Sauternes property sited below Guiraud, producing underachieving, unoaked wines.

La Fleur

33230 St-Emilion, Tel: 05 57 51 75 55

"La Fleur" is one of the most confusing names in Bordeaux. The word itself means "flower" – hence its widespread though soft-minded appeal for proprietors. In addition to being or forming part of the primary name of a large number of Right Bank properties (both as two words and as one), it is also widely used to describe both the second wines of a number of properties and a super-selection *cuvée* from many properties. Small wonder consumers are confused: *chers amis Bordelais,* no more flowers, please! La Fleur on its own is the name of a small, 6-ha Moueix run estate in the unpromising far north of St-Emilion, producing easygoing, swiftly evolving wine.

La Fleur de Boüard

33330 St-Emilion, Tel: 05 57 24 77 31

There are in fact three flowers emerging from this new Lalande-de-Pomerol operation, owned by Hubert de Boüard of Angélus: the second label is La Fleur St-Georges, and the top *cuvée* carries the embarrassing name of "Le + de la Fleur de Boüard". These dark, lush, sweet-fruited wines have huge early appeal; it remains to be seen whether or not alluvial terraces of Lalande-de-Pomerol can produce wines whose spine lasts the test of time.

La Fleur Caillou *see* La Grave (Fronsac)

La Fleur de Gay

33500 Pomerol, Tel: 05 57 51 19 05, Fax: 05 57 74 15 62

Special *cuvée,* produced in the best years only, from La Croix de Gay in Pomerol. The construction (high tannin plus sweet fruit, but without supercharged lees-derived extraction) is traditional rather than New Wave.

La Fleur de Jaugue

33500 Libourne, Tel: 05 57 51 51 29, Fax: 05 57 51 29 70

Inexpensive, top-value St Emilion made in low-yielding, concentrated, tough-guy style.

La Fleur-Pétrus

33500 Pomerol, Tel: 05 57 51 78 96, Fax: 05 57 51 79 79

This 13-ha Pomerol property may face Pétrus across the road, but in style it is utterly different: this is tiptoe, ballerina-like wine of fine, stealthy, sometimes clove-like fragrance, silken textures and powdery, drifting fruit.

La Fleur St-Georges *see* La Fleur de Boüard

Fombrauge

33330 St-Emilion, Tel: 05 57 24 77 12, Fax: 05 57 24 66 95

Fombrauge occupies a whopping 52 ha, making it the largest vineyard in St-Emilion. It dominates the commune of St-Christophe-des-Bardes: gently rolling plateau land in the northeast of the appellation. This sector has never been associated with high quality – but that looks as if it is about to change, now that Bernard Magrez of Pape-Clément and La Tour Carnet has taken over from the Danish consortium (it included a 10% Lego share) which previously owned the property. The 2000 was a dramatic improvement on previous vintages, made with reduced yields and greater selectivity: it's a ripe, vivid, toothsome, fleshy St-Emilion with flavours of coffee and black cherry fruit. There is better to come, one assumes. (See also Magrez-Fombrauge.)

Fonplégade

33330 St-Emilion, Tel: 05 57 74 43 11, Fax: 05 57 74 44 67

This 18-ha St-Emilion occupies a superb, mid-slope site on the Côte. Many years of disappointing wines look to be drawing to a close with the 2000 vintage, overseen by Christian Moueix, in which Fonplégade produced a classic Côte-style wine with mineral depths qualifying its calm black fruits.

Fonroque

33500 Libourne, Tel: 05 57 51 78 96

This 19-ha property on St-Emilion's plateau produces a relatively stern wine with sometimes forceful tannins. Unfashionable, yet its beef and spice are enjoyable and the value is good too. Changes are underway so look for further improvements.

Fontenil

33500 Pomerol, Tel: 05 57 51 23 05, Fax: 05 57 51 66 08

Michel Rolland's home-made wine from his and his wife Dany's 8.5-ha property in the northeastern part of Fronsac, facing Lalande-de-Pomerol across the little River Isle. This is lush, ripe, sleek wine of clinging unction, a thousand sips distant from the characteristic earthy brusqueness of the appellation.

Fougas Maldoror

33710 Lansac, Tel: 05 57 68 42 15, Fax: 05 57 68 28 59

An 11-ha Côte de Bourg property, the top *cuvée* is the Maldoror, its name evoking for the literary drinker a nightmare glass. Dark it certainly is; cruel perhaps not; indeed its sweet, gypsy richness is soothing and exotic. Owner Jean-Yves Béchet also owns the more frighteningly tannic Riou de Thaillas.

Franc Maillet

33500 Pomerol, Tel: 06 09 73 69 47, Fax: 05 57 51 96 75

Obscure but improving Pomerol property, sited in the promising northeast of the AOC near Bon Pasteur; Cuvée Jean-Baptiste is especially good. Recent vintages have shown plenty of plum and pepper.

Franc Mayne

33330 St-Emilion, Tel: 05 57 24 62 61, Fax: 05 57 24 68 25

The two Maynes (Franc and Grand) dominate the gentle slope which stretches down from the limestone town of St-Emilion towards the gravels of the Figeac properties; La Gomerie is the other key wine in this zone. Of the two, Franc (at 7 ha) is much the smaller; having passed through AXA ownership between 1984 and 1996, it now belongs to Georgy Fourcroy and his associates, with advice from the ubiquitous Michel Rolland and a corresponding increase in density and depth of flavour.

de France

33850 Léognan, Tel: 05 56 64 75 39, Fax: 05 56 64 72 13

With its 34 ha of vines close to those of Domaine de Chevalier, Fieuzal and Haut-Gardère, former sugar beet magnate Bernard Thomassin, helped by Michel Rolland, is coaxing de France towards making what should be an excellent Pessac-Léognan.

Gaby

33126 Fonsac, Tel: 05 57 51 24 97, Fax: 05 57 25 18 99

Improving 9.5-ha Canon-Fronsac property owned by Antoine Khayat, and made with consultancy help from Gilles Pauquet.

La Gaffelière

33330 St-Emilion, Tel: 05 57 24 72 15, Fax: 05 57 24 69 06

This 22-ha St-Emilion property on the lower part of the Côte includes one of the most important archaeological finds in St-Emilion – the remains of a large, 10-room Roman villa. The wine of La Gaffelière, too, is classical in its restraint and fragrant meatiness; no over-extraction here.

Gamage

33350 Castillon-la-Bataille, Tel: 05 57 40 52 02, Fax: 05 57 40 53 77

This 36-ha property in Entre-Deux-Mers is part-owned by the British wine writer Steven Spurrier. The white is fresh and sustained (thanks to 60% old-vine Sémillon); the red Bordeaux Supérieure is balanced, supple, and full.

La Garde

33650 Le Brede, Tel: 05 56 81 58 90

Well-positioned 45-ha Pessac-Léognan property between Latour-Martillac and Haut-Nouchet, owned since 1990 by CVBG Dourthe-Kressman. These are consistent and reliable wines, though neither deep nor powerful.

Garreau

33710 Pugnac, Tel: 05 57 68 90 75, Fax: 05 57 68 90 84

Prominent Côtes de Blaye property whose ripe reds from low-yielding vines offer outstanding value for money. Look for the Cuvée Armande, a selection of the best fruit aged in 100% new oak to give a darkly lustrous, smoky wine.

Le Gay

33500 Pomerol, Tel: 05 57 51 12 43, Fax: 05 57 51 67 99

Small but well-sited 5-ha Pomerol property perched above the little River Barbanne in the north of the AOC; sternly tannic wines.

Gazin

33500 Pomerol, Tel: 05 57 51 07 05, Fax: 05 57 51 69 96

Superb 24-ha parcel of vines in Pomerol, adjacent to Pétrus and Evangile, giving wines of forceful, meaty, sometimes rather rough-and-ready style.

Gigault

33390 Blaye, Tel: 05 57 42 34 34, Fax: 05 57 42 34 35

Together with Grands Maréchaux, Gigault (especially the Cuvée Viva) proves that even in the unheralded vineyards of Premières Côtes de Blaye, fine, pleasure-giving red wine can be produced: this is dark, sweet-fruited, and winsome, made by owner Christophe Reboul-Salze with the help of shareholder Stéphane Derenoncourt. The Cuvée Viva is 95% Merlot, mainly matured in new oak.

Gilette

33210 Preignac, Tel: 05 56 76 28 44, Fax: 05 56 76 28 43

"Do different" might be Gilette's motto. Christian Médeville, the owner of this 4.5-ha Sauternes estate sited almost on the Garonne waterfront, ferments all his wine in steel tanks rather than *barriques*, then stores them in concrete for 15 years or more before bottling. The results are fresher and creamier than expected, but it is telling that his example has gone unfollowed in the region.

Girolate

33420 Naujan-et-Postiac, Tel: 05 57 84 55 08, Fax: 05 57 84 57 31

This 10-ha parcel in Entre-Deux-Mers is planted with Merlot at the super-high density of 10,000 vines per ha; the wine is entirely vinified in barriques. Jean Louis Despagne is the man behind this ambitious project.

Giscours

33460 Labarde, Tel: 05 57 97 09 09, Fax: 05 57 97 09 00

Large 83-ha vineyard at the southern end of Margaux whose quality has fluctuated greatly down the years. Under the Dutch ownership of Eric Albada Jelgersma, there have been marked improvements, and the 2000 vintage was the best here for two decades: rich, deep, and textured, its components beautifully marshalled and disposed.

Gloria

33250 St-Julien-Beychevelle, Tel: 05 56 59 08 18, Fax: 05 56 59 16 18

A number of widely scattered plots comprise St-Julien's 48-ha Gloria; the wine is usually accessible, juicy, and fragrant, though without any concentration.

La Gomerie

33330 St-Emilion, Tel: 05 57 74 46 87, Fax: 05 57 24 66 88

Walloppingly oaky, pure Merlot made by Gérard Bécot from a small, unclassified 2.5-ha St-Emilion plot sited beneath Grand Mayne; it is the Mondotte, if you like, of the Beau-Séjour Bécot family, flaunting its unabashed sweetness like a feather boa.

Gracia

33330 St-Emilion, Tel: 05 57 24 70 35, Fax: 05 57 74 46 72

Tiny St-Emilion estate owned by Michel Gracia whose dark, taut, sinewy garage-style wine is made with the help of Ausone's Alain Vauthier.

Grand-Corbin-Despagne

33330 St-Emilion, Tel: 05 57 51 08 38, Fax: 05 57 51 29 18

This 27-ha St-Emilion property sited northeast of Cheval Blanc has greatly improved over the last half-decade of the 1990s under François Despagne; the 2000 vintage was packed with Pomerol-like blackberry fruit, and offered superb value for money.

Grandes Murailles ✿

33330 St-Emilion, Tel: 05 57 24 71 09, Fax: 05 57 24 69 72

Tiny 2-ha St-Emilion property just behind the town itself whose "big walls", now somewhat reduced in size, were once those of a monastery. As with the other two wines of the Reiffers family (the even tinier Clos St-Martin and the more spacious Côte de Baleau), these are now wines of extraordinary tightness and close-textured saturation, looking for a long sleep before maturity.

Grand Mayne

33330 St-Emilion, Tel: 05 57 74 42 50, Fax: 05 57 24 68 34

At 19 ha, this is the larger of the two properties on the handsome Mayne hillside, and is run with great care by the Nony family. There were some TCA problems with the 1993 and 1994 vintages, but apart from those difficulties this is a wine of breadth, combining typical meaty classicism with great purity.

Grand-Pontet

33330 St-Emilion, Tel: 06 85 83 08 65

This 14-ha property on the northern edge of the town of St-Emilion is another example of the vastly improved quality which the final years of the 1990s brought: lowered yields and increased ripeness have revealed a round, limpid, rich-fruited wine.

Grand-Puy-Ducasse

33042 Bordeaux, Tel: 05 56 11 29 00, Fax: 05 56 11 29 01

This 40-ha Pauillac property, its *chai* on the quayside in Pauillac, combines a number of scattered vineyard parcels. There have been slow, steady quality improvements under Mestrezat ownership (the abandonment of machine harvesting, more selectivity, up to 50% new oak for the grand vin), and the wine is a good buy for those who don't want to wait too long. (Mestrezat, like Cordier, is now owned by the Languedoc-based Val d'Orbieu group.)

Grand-Puy-Lacoste

33250 Pauillac, Tel: 05 56 73 16 73, Fax: 05 56 59 27 37

Set well back from the river, the 52 ha of Grand-Puy-Lacoste may not provide the beefiest and burliest of Pauillacs, but this Borie-owned property turns its gravel banks into a deep, vivid, slowly evolving wine packed with singing blackcurrant fruit.

Les Grands Chênes

33340 St-Christoly Médoc, Tel: 05 56 41 53 12, Fax: 05 56 41 35 69

This Haut-Médoc property now belongs to Bernard Magrez of Pape-Clément and Fombrauge; the Rolland team consults. 2000 was fleshy, long, and savoury.

Grands Maréchaux

33920 St-Girons d'Aiguevives, Tel: 05 57 42 49 08

This Premières Côtes de Blaye property co-owned by Christophe Reboul-Salze and Etienne Barre proves, as does the Gigault Cuvée Viva, that low yields and contemporary techniques (cold pre-fermentation maceration, long alcoholic fermentation, oak ageing with lees contact) can give the wines of this region an entirely new articulacy.

La Grave (Fronsac)

33126 Fronsac, Tel: 05 57 51 31 11, Fax: 05 57 25 08 61

This 4-ha estate is biodynamically run by Paul Barre and produces straightforward, soft, pleasantly rustic wines. The 4.4-ha La Fleur Caillou in Canon-Fronsac is in the same ownership. This was Stéphane Derenoncourt's first training ground in Bordeaux, between 1985 and 1987.

La Grave à Pomerol, Trignant de Boisset

33500 Pomerol

This cumbersomely named, Moueix-owned 8.4-ha property in the north of the appellation produces blackcurrant-cream wines of grace and finesse.

Gree Laroque
33910 St-Ciers-d'Abzac, Tel: 05 57 49 45 42, Fax: 05 57 49 45 42

Just 1.6 ha of Bordeaux Supérieure (sited 8 km from Fronsac) makes this wine, based on 40-year-old vines, a garage-scale proposition. With the help of Stéphane Derenoncourt, the proprietors (Patricia and Arnaud Benoit de Nyvenheim) produce a wine of deliciously sweet, intense fruit.

Greysac
33340 Bégadan, Tel: 05 56 73 26 56, Fax: 05 56 73 26 58

This 80-ha Haut-Médoc property sited north of St-Estèphe produces wines of elegance rather than girth, ready soon.

La Griffe de Cap d'Or
33330 St-Emilion, Tel: 05 57 55 09 13, Fax: 05 57 55 09 12

Relatively inexpensive pure-Merlot, lavishly oaked garage wine from St-Georges-St-Emilion: juicy and toothsome.

Gruaud-Larose ✪
33250 St-Julien-Beychevelle, Tel: 05 56 73 15 20, Fax: 05 56 59 64 72

Massive, stately 82-ha property sited just inland from the hamlet of Beychevelle in St-Julien, Gruaud-Larose is now owned by Jean Merlaut of the Taillan group though the wines have been made since 1970 by Cordier's Georges Pauli. This gentle rise of red gravels has historically surrendered one of the commune's most massive, craggy, and tannin-laden wines, Gruaud-Larose's greatest successes coming when those tannins are woven most seamlessly into dark blackcurrant fruit (as in 1986, 1990, and 2000).

Guiraud ✪
33210 Sauternes, Tel: 05 56 76 61 01, Fax: 05 56 76 61 01

The sober black label of this 84-ha Sauternes property conceals a colourful history, during which the property has soared and sunk repeatedly under a succession of eccentric owners. Since 1981, the Canadian Narby family have been in charge, and their skilled manager Xavier Planty has slowly raised Guiraud to be one of the most consistently rewarding and unctuous of all Sauternes. Saturated apricot and apricot kernel flavours are a hallmark.

La Gurgue
33460 Margaux, Tel: 05 57 88 46 65, Fax: 05 57 88 98 33

Calm, quiet, thrilling fruit is produced from this 10-ha Margaux, owned by the Merlaut family.

Haut-Bages Averous
33250 Pauillac, Tel: 05 56 73 24 00, Fax: 05 56 59 26 42

Not a property in its own right, but the second wine of Lynch-Bages.

Haut-Bages Libéral
33250 Pauillac, Tel: 05 57 88 76 65, Fax: 05 57 88 98 33

The 28 ha of this Pauillac are superbly situated, with most adjacent to Latour and Pichon-Lalande. It's a lovely drink and a fresh-flavoured classic; could it be more? The site suggests it could.

Haut-Bailly ✪
33850 Léognan, Tel: 05 56 64 75 11, Fax: 05 56 64 53 60

This 28-ha estate next to Larrivet Haut-Brion is one of the finest in Pessac-Léognan; Robert Wilmers, a New York banker, is the new owner, though former proprietor Jean Sanders and his granddaughter Véronique continue to run the estate. You could call it the Conseillante of Léognan: cherry-cream fruit sings out of Haut-Bailly in the early years, yet it ages superbly, building and then retaining flesh, before unfolding into a gracefully milky old age. It's the apogee of Bordeaux balance and digestibility.

Haut-Batailley
33250 Pauillac, Tel: 05 56 73 16 73, Fax: 05 56 59 27 37

This 22-ha backwoods Pauillac estate is owned by the Borie family who produce simple, straightforward wines of fresh elegance and memorable blackcurrant purity.

Haut-Beauséjour
33180 St-Estèphe, Tel: 05 56 59 30 26, Fax: 05 56 59 39 25

A 19-ha property in St-Estèphe owned by Louis Roederer. Not yet wholly successful: the 2000 vintage was less fleshy than most of its peers.

Haut-Bergey
33840 Léognan, Tel: 05 56 64 05 22, Fax: 05 56 64 06 98

Both Michel Rolland and Jean-Luc Thunevin advise at this 26-ha Pessac-Léognan property, owned since 1991 by the sister of Smith Haut Lafitte's Daniel Cathiard, Sylviane Garcin-Cathiard. No expense is spared in either vineyard or cellar, and since 1998 the wine has rapidly acquired density, flesh, and an impressive fantail of smoke and black fruit flavours. As these vintages of the late 1990s age, the true potential of the terroir should become apparent.

Haut-Brion ✪✪✪
33602 Pessac, Tel: 05 56 00 29 30, Fax: 05 56 98 75 14

So, here we are, in the middle of suburban Bordeaux, yet the gravel banks of this superb 50-ha property, glittering with quartz as the sun chases away the rain, rival anything you will find under the sweeping sea-skies of Pauillac or St-Estèphe. The château itself is warm, wainscotted, smoky, lived-in; there is room for a park; the city bustle continues on the other side of high walls. This is one of the five "first growths" of Bordeaux; historically, indeed, it is the first of the firsts, since this wine was causing the rich to fumble for their wallets in Paris and London long before any Dutch drainage engineer had ever set foot in the Médoc. Even today, the style of wine produced here in the city, by Haut-Brion and its four close neighbours, is uniquely refined. The pencilly scents and flavours so typical of Bordeaux are rarely sharpened to a finer point than here; cedar and Havana rarely combine so suggestively in a glass of red wine. The classic earthiness of the Graves is there too, lending a reduced, savoury, pan-scraped, *jus*-like quality to the wine. Fruit, of course, is the core of all, yet in some ways fruit is less important, less simple, less evident in Haut-Brion than in other, more open-hearted rivals. Truffle-like, it needs unearthing. Hot vintages (the most memorable example is 1989) can give the wine an astonishing and tenacious density as well as an unheralded and unexpected sweet succulence. There is a white, too, produced in tiny quantities: lemon and grapefruit-packed in youth, age seems to drip softening cream into its pores.

Haut de Carles *see* de Carles

Haut-Chaigneau
33500 Néac, Tel: 05 57 51 31 31, Fax: 05 57 25 08 93

This relatively large (20 ha) Lalande-de-Pomerol property, sited in the eastern (Néac) sector of the AOC, is owned and run by oenologist André Chatonnet, the father of Michel Rolland's collaborator Pascal Chatonnet. Like most wines in Lalande-de-Pomerol, it does not have a great deal of sinew and structure, yet its cherry-chocolate fruits make it a fine early drinking buy.

Haut-Condissas
33340 Bégadan, Tel: 05 56 41 58 59, Fax: 05 56 41 37 82

This Haut-Médoc is made from a selected micro-parcel of Rollan de By: the 2000 is dark, fruity, and packed with ripe tannin.

Haut-Gardère
33850 Léognan, Tel: 05 56 64 75 33, Fax: 05 56 64 53 64

The 25-ha Haut-Gardère is owned by Irish banker Lochlann Quinn, and produces good value, smoky reds, and balanced, well-oaked whites.

Haut-Marbuzet
33180 St-Estèphe, Tel: 05 56 59 30 54, Fax: 05 56 59 70 87

The 50-ha St-Estèphe property of Haut-Marbuzet produces relatively soft, richly oaked wines containing more Merlot than most properties in the AOC.

Haut-Nouchet
33650 Martillac, Tel: 05 56 72 69 74

Louis Lurton's 38-ha Pessac-Léognan, cultivated organically, is sited near Latour-Martillac. Its red and white wines are slowly increasing in depth and richness.

Haut-Sarpe

33506 Libourne, Tel: 05 57 51 41 86, Fax: 05 57 51 53 16

This 11-ha property near Sansonnet and La Couspaude is another outpost of the rapidly improving Janoueix empire.

Haut-Troquart la Grâce Dieu

33502 Libourne, Tel: 05 57 51 78 96, Fax: 05 57 51 79 79

Tiny 2.5-ha St-Emilion in Moueix stable planted to 90% Merlot, making soft, light-textured wines.

Haut-Villet

33330 St-Emilion, Tel: 05 57 47 97 60, Fax: 05 57 47 92 94

Like Faugères, the 7-ha Haut-Villet is sited on the far eastern edge of the St-Emilion appellation. Its wines are no less ambitious, especially the densely extractive Cuvée Pomone; they need age.

L'Hermitage

33540 St-Martin du Puy, Tel: 05 56 71 57 58, Fax: 05 56 71 65 00

Small, 4-ha property in the same ownership as Matras, and sited just above it, between Berliquet and Angélus. This is a pure Merlot wine, two-thirds of which comes from 70-year-old vines; the wine is dark, sweet-fruited, ripe, and lush.

Hosanna ✪

33500 Pomerol

The former Certan Guiraud has been renamed Hosanna by Christian Moueix, who has also sold off the property's 4-ha "Clos du Roy" parcels to Nenin (see also Certan Marzelle); a new winery is being built at present. Designed by Herzog and de Meuron, it will make the Pétrus *chai* look dowdier than ever by comparison. Hosanna is superbly sited near Vieux Château Certan, Lafleur, and Pétrus, and the 2000 vintage produced a dark wine of arresting grace and milky sweetness, its Merlot balanced with 30% Cabernet Franc.

d'Issan

33460 Cantenac, Tel: 05 57 88 35 91, Fax: 05 57 88 74 24

The 52-ha Margaux property of d'Issan is all that remains of the once mighty Cruse empire. If an empire must be reduced to a single property, one can understand the desire for it to be this one: the fairytale elegance of the 17th-century château captured on this wine's label (the most beautiful in the world?) is an accurate depiction of reality. The wine is light, elegant, and fragrant, applauded by the European rather than the American school of criticism. Both the 1996 and 1999 here were exceptionally vivid and fine-drawn, and the 2000 was outstanding, too.

Jacques Blanc

33330 St-Emilion, Tel: 05 57 56 02 97, Fax: 05 57 40 18 01

This 20-ha St-Emilion property is named after a celebrated 15th-century St-Emilion figure; it has been cultivated biodynamically since 1989. A number of different *cuvées* are produced, of variable quality, the best being l'Apogée; Jean-Luc Thunevin is advising.

Jonqueyres

33750 St-Germain du Puch, Tel: 05 57 34 51 51

This 45-ha Bordeaux Supérieure is part of the GAM Audy group, advised by the late Jean-Michel Arcaute and Michel Rolland; its wine is much more firmly structured than the appellation norm, with tarry depths.

Karolus

33290 Le Pian-Médoc, Tel: 05 56 70 20 11, Fax: 05 56 70 23 91

This wine is made from a small, 3.5-ha parcel of the vines of Sénéjac. It's deeper and more broad-shouldered than Sénéjac in style, with a richer tannin structure, but no shortage of perfumed blackcurrant fruit.

Kirwan

33000 Bordeaux, Tel: 05 57 87 64 55, Fax: 05 57 87 57 20

Few properties in the Médoc have improved the quality of their wine so dramatically as this 35-ha property in Margaux; the 1998, 1999, and 2000 vintages are all resonant, perfumed, and rich-textured, rivalling the very best of this much-improved commune. Rolland consults.

Labégorce

33460 Margaux, Tel: 05 57 88 71 32, Fax: 05 57 88 35 01

This 33-ha Margaux property is one of the few to have admitted to using American oak to make its rough-hewn though sweet-scented wines. These are now showing more polish (especially 1995 and 1998).

Labégorce-Zédé

33460 Soussans, Tel: 05 57 88 71 31, Fax: 05 57 88 72 54

Elegant, classic Margaux made from 25.5 ha of vines long-separated from Labégorce itself. Like Le Pin and Vieux Château Certan, this property is owned by the Belgian Thienpont family; Luc Thienpont, the brother of Le Pin's Jacques, runs it with great attention to detail and fidelity to terroir.

Lafaurie-Peyraguey

33300 Bordeaux, Tel: 05 57 19 57 77, Fax: 05 57 19 57 87

This fine 40-ha Sauternes property is sited just to the west of Yquem, on slightly lower gravels, close to the Ciron. It's been the property of Cordier – now owned by Val d'Orbieu – since 1917, and Georges Pauli oversees vinification, producing consistently rich and slow-evolving wine.

Lafite-Rothschild ✪✪✪

33250 Pauillac, Tel: 01 53 89 78 00/05 56 59 01 74, Fax: 01 53 89 78 01/
05 56 59 26 83

Lafite, by 4 ha the largest of the "first growths" (it has 94 ha compared to Margaux's 90 ha), is also unusual in that it has more relief in its gravels than its peers. The château itself sits at the lowest (and least viticulturally useful) part of the property; indeed its neighbour Cos d'Estournel looks down onto the "marsh" of Lafite, drained for fields and gardens. South of the château, however, the banks of gravel rise steeply up like a giant stone wave, soaring to all of 25 metres in a knoll shared with Mouton; parcels of Lafite stretch east almost as far as Pauillac's former oil refinery, too. It is no surprise that a mere third of Lafite's production is actually bottled as grand vin. Under the ownership of Eric de Rothschild and, since 1994, the management of Charles Chevalier, Lafite has experienced one of the most glorious vintage runs in its history. Elegance and finesse summarize the classical qualities of Bordeaux, and it is these intrinsically reticent qualities which Lafite paradoxically manages to amplify and exemplify. The wines are as finely drawn as a Doré engraving, full of telling detail and suggestive articulacies, yet never overstated or over-extracted. It is a wine built of whispers, yet they can swell, in one glass, towards a chorus of hair-turning harmony.

Lafleur ✪

33240 Mouillac, Tel: 05 57 84 44 03, Fax: 05 57 84 83 31

Which of Pétrus's five distinguished neighbours has a terroir to match the celebrated clay buttonhole? The vote generally goes to Lafleur's 4.5 ha of deep gravel stiffened by iron. It's not the same, of course, and nor is the 50% of Cabernet Franc in the vineyards, but at its best this is a beast with the sinew and muscle to match Pétrus. The plunging, panther-like 2000 vintage, packed with cream and wizened plums, looks like evolving into just such a wine.

Lafon-Rochet

33180 St-Estèphe, Tel: 05 56 59 32 06, Fax: 05 56 59 72 43

Lafon-Rochet's 40 ha should, by all surface estimates, rival the vineyards of its St-Estèphe neighbour Cos d'Estournel and even glance, as the château itself does, towards Lafite. They don't, despite the care which owners Alfred and Michel Tesseron put into their wine. Yet another secret, therefore, of the enigmatic lenses hidden within the Médoc's gravel mounds? Perhaps. Nonetheless Lafon-Rochet has provided, during the mid- and late 1990s, some delicious, spicy, full-flavoured, and increasingly deep wines sold at attractive prices.

Laforge

33330 Vignonet, Tel: 05 57 84 64 22, Fax: 05 57 84 63 54

This is one of three St-Emilion properties owned by ambitious British producer

Jonathan Maltus. It is far from unitary: the 6 ha are widely separated, with some parcels (there are five in total) on the plain near Monbousquet, some on the plateau near Larmande, and the best vineyards next door to Clos Fourtet, close to the town of St-Emilion itself. This is the most sweet-fruited and Merlot-rich of Maltus's wines, packed with cherry-plum cream.

Lagrange (Pomerol)
33500 Libourne, Tel: 05 57 55 05 80, Fax: 05 57 51 79 79

This centrally situated, 8-ha property is Moueix-owned. It produces pure-fruited wines, though the substance and depth of these rarely matches the quality of its great stablemates like Pétrus, Trotanoy, or, more recently, Hosanna.

Lagrange (St-Julien)
33250 St-Julien-Beychevelle, Tel: 05 56 73 38 38, Fax: 05 56 59 26 09

The 113 ha of Lagrange make it the Médoc's largest "classified" property; it passed into Suntory ownership in 1983. Lagrange has been well run for the Japanese by administrator Marcel Ducasse, a former consulting oenologist, and yields, selection, and vinification have given classic, elegant, limpidly blackcurranty wines in good vintages such as 1989 and 1990. Ducasse, though, is not one of those who is prepared to run what he sees as the risks inherent in bottling his wine without fining or filtration. The excitement and depth of barrel-tastings is sadly not always duplicated in the "correct" wines that one finds in bottle.

La Lagune
33290 Ludon-Médoc, Tel: 05 57 88 82 77, Fax: 05 57 88 82 70

The nearest of the Médoc's major châteaux to Bordeaux, the 72-ha La Lagune produces easygoing, gentle, well-rounded, and unchallenging claret. Improving under ownership of Jean-Jacques Frey.

Lamothe-Bergeron
33460 Cussac Fort Médoc, Tel: 05 56 58 94 77, Fax: 05 56 58 98 18

Satisfying and inexpensive 66-ha Haut-Médoc property, promisingly sited near the estuary in Cussac, in the same ownership as Grand-Puy-Ducasse (Mestrezat/Val d'Orbieu).

Lamothe Guignard
33210 Sauternes, Tel: 05 56 76 60 28, Fax: 05 56 76 69 05

This 17-ha Sauternes property adjacent to La Tour Blanche has produced some glycerous, full-flavoured, lushly botrytized wines and age-worthy wines in the 1990s, offering fine value.

Lanessan
33460 Cussac-Fort-Médoc, Tel: 05 56 58 94 80, Fax: 05 57 88 89 92

This 40-ha property is another leader in the thread of villages that separate St-Julien from Margaux (grouped together under the catch-all Haut-Médoc appellation); it lies on a promising bank near to Gruaud-Larose. This is exuberant, blackcurrant-packed wine aged without new oak.

Langoa Barton
33250 St-Julien-Beychevelle, Tel: 05 56 59 06 05, Fax: 05 56 59 14 29

This, the smaller sister of Léoville-Barton (15 ha), has less favourably sited vineyards; its wines are lighter, though full of scented classicism nonetheless.

Larcis Ducasse
33330 St-Emilion, Tel: 05 57 24 70 84, Fax: 05 57 24 64 00

Superbly sited St-Emilion property whose 11 ha lie on mid-slope next to Pavie. Given this plum site, the wines should be much better than they are.

Larmande
33330 St-Emilion, Tel: 05 57 24 71 41, Fax: 05 57 74 42 80

This 25-ha property is sited on the cool, northern plateau behind the town of St-Emilion, yet impressively dense wines are being made here at present thanks to investment from insurance company La Mondiale.

Larose-Trintaudon
33112 St-Laurent-Médoc, Tel: 05 56 59 41 72, Fax: 05 56 59 93 22

Monstrous, 172-ha property (France has many entire appellations smaller than

this) set well back from the river in St-Laurent producing easygoing, softly fruity wines. La Tourette, a special *cuvée*, is more exciting. It is the property of yet another insurance company, AGF, and produces over a million bottles a year.

Larrivet Haut-Brion
33850 Léognan, Tel: 05 56 64 75 51, Fax: 05 56 64 53 47

Well-sited 42-ha Pessac-Léognan estate next to Haut-Bailly (and thus nowhere near Haut-Brion itself), this is another property that has undergone a renaissance in quality during the latter half of the 1990s, with consultative help from Michel Rolland. Both red and white are smooth, soft, luscious, and debonair. The property is owned by the Andros group (which makes Bonne Maman jams), and run with great attention to detail by Philippe Gervoson.

Lascombes
33460 Margaux, Tel: 05 57 88 70 66, Fax: 05 57 88 72 17

Big changes are underway at Lascombes, a 50-ha Margaux property which, unsurprisingly, languished under the ownership of British brewer Bass. The new American owners (investment company Colony Capital) have appointed the former winemaker of Montrose, Bruno Lemoine, to oversee the vineyard and cellar, while there is Right Bank management influence, too, from Alain Raynaud of Quinault l'Enclos and Yves Vatelot of the outstanding Bordeaux Reignac. The 2000, produced from much-reduced yields and with severe selection (just 30% of the total harvest used), marked a shimmering and sumptuous leap forward.

Latour ✪✪✪
33250 Pauillac, Tel: 05 56 73 19 80, Fax: 05 56 73 19 81

Pauillac has no fewer than three of the five "first growths", classified in 1855, within its boundaries; the 65 ha of Latour are the closest of these to the river itself. From the château tasting room, indeed, you can look down across a strip of quiet pastureland to the vast, turbid mass of water – and sense, as the vines themselves doubtless do, how bright the summer light becomes when the sun bounces off the water and shimmers through the open, treeless vinescape. Latour's mounded gravels are a sort of giant raised beach beside the estuary; the oldest vines rooted in this beach are the 45-year-olds of the plot which surrounds the château, called l'Enclos. Since 1993, Latour has been owned by François Pinault, a leading French industrialist whose fortune was made in the wood business; it is run, with palpable ambition, by the intelligent and committed Frédéric Engerer. Huge investments in a new underground cellar are underway at present, and there is no doubting the determination of the present team to make Latour the Médoc's greatest wine. Its ability to transcend the vagaries of vintage suggest that the terroir, at least, has no peers. What of its style? Latour is the most baronial of the first growths. The very greatest Latours are wines of extraordinary resource, of profound depths, of dark and distant riches which take many years to slide into the light and scented warmth of maturity. Is there, under Pinault and Engerer, a "new Latour"? If anything, recent vintages have begun to build an unexpected charm into the equation. Latour in the past was, one might almost say, the Madiran of the Médoc; it was grand, and gave little away in terms of accessibility and seduction prior to eventual maturity. The great Latours of the last decade (1995, 1996, 1999, 2000) have shown a new sweet-fruitedness and creaminess in youth without any loss of subterranean power, a consequence, perhaps, of Engerer's thoughtful work on the press wines. All of the first growths are now producing exemplary second wines, but Les Forts de Latour is particularly good, rivalling other top Médoc châteaux's *grands vins*.

Latour-Martillac
33650 Martillac, Tel: 05 57 97 71 11, Fax: 05 57 97 71 17

This 38-ha Pessac-Léognan belonging to the Kressman family has in the past produced richer white wines than red, though the rotund 1998 red marked a change of pace; its site (south of Martillac) lies towards the border with Graves.

Latour à Pomerol
33500 Libourne, Tel: 05 57 51 78 96

This 8-ha property comprises several differently positioned parcels. Profoundly rich wines have been produced here in great vintages in the past, but it is an inconsistent performer, sometimes spoiled by over-brisk acidity and grouchy tannins; 1998 is the best of recent vintages.

Laville Haut-Brion
33602 Pessac, Tel: 05 56 00 29 30, Fax: 05 56 98 75 14

This, the tiniest of the Haut-Brion family (just 3.7ha), produces white wine only; the vineyards are sited in the least gravelly, southern sector of this group of five suburban properties. In its early youth, it is crisper and more floral than the white wine of Haut-Brion itself, yet it has great tenacity in time, gradually unfolding towards a rich-fruited and intricate maturity.

Léoville-Barton ✪✪
33250 St-Julien-Beychevelle, Tel: 05 56 59 06 05, Fax: 05 56 59 14 29

This 45-ha St-Julien property is much loved among wine drinkers everywhere for its honest, high-effort pursuit of traditional Médoc-making aesthetics – and its generally modest and realistic pricing policies. The credit for both must go to one of the Médoc's grand seigneurs, Anthony Barton, who resisted firmly when AXA offered a "crazy price" for his château during the 1980s. Barton's methods are classic; the changes he has implemented during the 1990s include picking later than in the past and increasing selectivity for the *grand vin*, but he is opposed to anything "which makes the wines thicker and blacker than they were before" and he is "not fond of over-oaked wines... my palate's used to a softer, more subtle style of wine." Léoville-Barton has turned in some magnificently dense and finely woven performances in 1995, 1996, 1999, and 2000, and in many ways of all the St-Julien properties this is now the appellation model for impeccable balance and currant-fresh breed.

Léoville-las-Cases ✪✪
33250 St-Julien-Beychevelle, Tel: 05 56 73 25 26, Fax: 05 56 59 18 33

The biggest of the three Léoville properties, the Las Cases vineyards (97 ha in total) echo and abut those of Latour, just a little further north. There are stylistic similarities, too: Las Cases is every bit as portentious a wine as the lion-capped stone arch which marks the entrance to its vineyards suggests it will be, and Las Cases is certainly the most "Pauillac" of all the St-Juliens. This is one of the Médoc properties which has the first growths avowedly in its sights: throughout the 1980s and 1990s under Michel Delon its concentration and depth was ratcheted up, vintage by vintage, towards wines of thunderous power and explorer-like qualities of endurance. The chief means of doing this was the dispatch (to the fine second wine Clos du Marquis and third wine Bignarnon) of those vats which were even marginally off the pace, even in great vintages (67% was demoted in 1990). The lofty price of Las Cases was another way in which the challenge to the first growths was issued. Michel Delon died in 2000; his son Jean-Hubert is now in charge, though the ambitions remain unchanged.

Léoville-Poyferré ✪
33250 St-Julien-Beychevelle, Tel: 05 56 59 08 30, Fax: 05 56 59 60 09

The 80 ha of Léoville-Poyferré occupy a number of scattered parcels intermingled with both Barton and Las Cases. Historically, it has lagged behind its very different though equally successful siblings; since the early 1980s the property has lived up to the promise of its terroir. Thanks to the advice of Michel Rolland, Poyferré is rather fuller, softer, and fleshier than either Las Cases or Barton, with vividly perfumed, oak-sweetened fruit. Almost 10% Petit Verdot in the vineyard plantings, though, gives it plenty of pepper and spice, too.

Lezongars
33550 Villenave-de-Rions, Tel: 05 56 72 18 06, Fax: 05 56 72 31 44

This 45-ha property in the Premières Côtes is beginning to turn out exciting, vivid red wine under the ownership of the British Iles (Philip, his wife Sarah and son Russell); winemaker Samuel Mestre is advised by the passionate Michel Puzio of Croix de Labrie. L'Enclos du Château Lezongars uses finest parcels.

Lilian Ladouys
33180 St-Estèphe, Tel: 05 56 59 71 96, Fax: 05 56 59 35 97

Rejuvenated 48-ha St-Estèphe property, promisingly sited behind Lafon-Rochet and now owned by Alcatel (and vinified by Georges Pauli).

Liot
33720 Barsac, Tel: 05 56 27 15 31, Fax: 05 56 27 14 42

Fine value, 20-ha Barsac sited near Climens producing supple sweet whites for drinking young.

Liversan
33250 St-Sauveur-Médoc, Tel: 05 56 41 50 18, Fax: 05 56 41 54 65

This 50-ha Haut-Médoc property sited behind Pauillac (and near the outstanding Bernadotte) produces softly meaty red wine.

Loudenne
33340 St-Yzans-de-Médoc, Tel: 05 56 73 17 80, Fax: 05 56 09 02 87

Superbly sited 48-ha Médoc property sitting on its own knoll next to the Gironde north of St-Estèphe. Loudenne is probably better known for its residential wine school than for its perplexingly light wines. 1998 suggested improvements are on the way.

La Louvière
33420 Grézillac, Tel: 05 57 25 58 58, Fax: 05 57 74 98 59

A magnificent château building sits at the centre of this 48-ha Pessac-Léognan estate, well-sited between Haut-Bailly and Carbonnieux. Both red and white are well-made, satisfying classics for early drinking rather than long storage.

Lynch-Bages ✪✪
33250 Pauillac, Tel: 05 56 73 24 00, Fax: 05 56 59 26 42

This huge, 90-ha property on the outskirts of Pauillac is, like Léoville-Barton, always high up on the list of everyone's favourite Médoc wines. Why? A charismatic proprietor (Jean-Michel Cazes, ably assisted by Daniel Lhose) and a wine whose character seems to combine depth, meaty Pauillac classicism and a warm, ripe, open-hearted affability. The great successes of 1989 and 1990, in which Lynch-Bages is among the top 10 Médoc wines of the vintage, looks like being repeated in 2000: this terroir is one which comes into its own in hot years. Lesser years, however, are rarely mean and never forbidding; even when the concentration is lacking, there is always plenty of curve to this comely wine.

Lynch-Moussas
33250 Pauillac, Tel: 05 56 00 00 70, Fax: 05 57 87 48 61

Not an easy terroir to work with, the 35 ha of Lynch-Moussas are set well back from the river; Grand-Puy-Lacoste and Batailley are nearby. These are supple, soft wines of sweet fruit in warm years, for relatively swift drinking.

Magdelaine
33330 St-Emilion, Tel: 05 57 51 75 55, Fax: 05 57 25 13 30

This 28-ha St-Emilion property (planted with 90% Merlot), perched on the slope beneath Canon, is made with maximum attention to finesse and delicacy by Christian Moueix; fruit from the younger vines is now made into a wine called Château St-Brice. Stylistically, it is much closer to its neighbour Belair than it is to the post-1996 Ausone or to nearby Angélus: this is chiffon St-Emilion, though the old vines (50 years) give the wine great length. The tradition of tending the vines by horse continues: Camilla has now taken over from Reveuse (who had succeeded Pompon).

Magrez-Fombrauge
33330 St-Emilion, Tel: 05 57 24 77 12, Fax: 05 57 24 66 95

This ambitiously priced wine is based on selected fruit from the Fombrauge vineyards in St-Emilion: there are under 500 cases available. The vines are in early middle age (25 years), and the Rolland touch is evident in its black fruits of glossy ripeness and its lavish oak. Time will tell how good this terroir truly is.

Malartic-Lagravière
33850 Léognan, Tel: 05 56 64 75 08, Fax: 05 56 64 99 66

The 44 ha of this Pessac-Léognan property are sited close to the town of Léognan itself. Following a desultory period under the ownership of Champagne house Laurent-Perrier, this property has passed to the Bonnie family, and the wines are much improved, the red in particular being full of mid-weight, savoury depths.

Malescasse
33460 Lamarque, Tel: 05 56 58 90 09, Fax: 05 56 59 64 72

This 37-ha Haut-Médoc, owned by Alcatel Alsthom with winemaking supervised by Georges Pauli, produces fresh-fruited, vivid red wines for medium-term drinking.

Malescot-St-Exupéry
33460 Margaux, Tel: 05 57 88 97 20, Fax: 05 57 88 97 21

This smallish (23 ha planted out of 45 ha) central Margaux property, its vineyards close to those of Margaux itself, has put on a turn of speed during the late 1990s – as, of course, has the commune of Margaux in general. The charm of this graceful, stealthy, aerial, and fragrant wine owes little to fashionable extraction and everything to terroir.

de Malle
33210 Preignac, Tel: 05 56 62 36 86, Fax: 05 56 76 82 40

This grand 200-ha estate (27 ha are under vines for Sauternes), together with its beautiful, listed château, lies nearer to the River Garonne (and further from the vital Ciron) than most of the appellation greats; indeed half lies in Graves, where the red Cardaillan is produced. In fine vintages this can be lightly and hauntingly classic Sauternes – honeyed fruit, burnt cream, and lanolin richness.

Marbuzet
33180 St-Estèphe, Tel: 05 56 73 15 50, Fax: 05 56 59 72 59

Small 7-ha property once serving as the name for the second wine of Cos d'Estournel, but now once again a property in its own right. Normally an affable, well-rounded claret, though the deeper, more ripely tannic 2000 vintage suggested that improvements were imminent.

Margaux ✪✪✪
33460 Margaux, Tel: 05 57 88 83 83, Fax: 05 57 88 83 32

Visitors who have strolled (with audible dignity) up the long, tree-shaded, gravel-strewn drive leading to this effortlessly aristocratic château, with its four-columned portico, cannot fail to be struck by a sense of the calm assurance that exudes from every stone, every branch, every obediently trembling leaf. This much-visited place seems to sum up the serene supremacy of Bordeaux – as does (for those lucky enough to taste it) the wine. If any red Bordeaux could be said to encapsulate everything that makes this region unique in the wine world, it would have to be Margaux, since it is endowed more amply than any other rival with scented finesse, with power allied to poise, with compressed, mid-weight beauty. Young Margaux (the 1996 and 2000 were both typical) seems a compost of flowers. Mature Margaux is vivid, balanced, quenching, and warmly reverberative red wine. Old Margaux contains more inflections and nuances than a Henry James novel, and can last as long, too (though the weak vintages of the 1960s and 1970s have been largely swallowed by time). There are 90 scattered hectares all told, some of them several kilometres distant from the château itself – yet none, says administrator Paul Pontallier, "are incapable of contributing to Margaux one day or other." Selection rather than extraction is the way that Margaux's density and complexity is built; both 1999 and 2000 represented just 40% of production, with the balance either going into the exemplary second wine Pavillon Rouge, or being sold off in bulk. All the *grand vin* is aged in new oak for up to two years, yet you'd be hard pressed to pick it out among the fruits and flowers of this synopsis of the natural world. The property is jointly owned by the Agnelli family of Fiat fame, and the Mentzelopoulos family – who purchased it from the Ginestets in 1977.

Marjosse
33420 Tizac-de-Curton, Tel: 05 57 55 57 80, Fax: 05 57 55 57 84

AOC Bordeaux property owned by Pierre Lurton, the administrator of Cheval Blanc: a deliciously soft red wine, drinking well from the off.

Marojallia
33330 St-Emilion, Tel: 05 57 55 09 13, Fax: 05 57 55 09 12

Much excitement was caused by the 1999 arrival of Marojallia, made from just 2 ha in Margaux by Murielle Andraud, the wife of Jean-Luc Thunevin,

since it was perceived to fire the starting gun for the garage wine movement in the Médoc. Yields as low as 20 hl/ha produce a vivid and intense wine, yet those who claim that the garage approach negates terroir should note the pure-fruited freshness in Marojallia, utterly different to anything produced in St-Emilion by the same team. The (young) vines are owned by property developer Philippe Porcheron and, despite its tiny size, there is also a second wine called Clos Margalaine. It is sited between Le Tertre and Monbrison.

Marquis d'Alesme Becker
33460 Margaux, Tel: 05 57 88 70 27, Fax: 05 57 88 73 78

This 10-ha Margaux belongs to the same family which own Malescot-St-Exupéry (the Zugers), but is a less impressive wine: slender and ungiving.

Marquis de Terme
333460 Margaux, Tel: 05 57 88 30 01, Fax: 05 57 88 32 51

This steady Margaux performer of 40 ha generally produces light, spicy wines – though the 1996 was unusually deep and tannic.

Marsau
33570 Francs, Tel: 05 57 40 67 23, Fax: 05 57 40 67 23

Wannabe Pomerol, dark and sweetly oaky, produced from pure Merlot grown on this 9-ha Côte des Francs estate by the boss of négociants CVBG Dourthe-Kressman, wine merchant Jean-Marie Chadronnier.

Matras
33330 St-Emilion, Tel: 05 57 51 52 39, Fax: 05 57 51 70 19

Small 10-ha St-Emilion property, sited beneath Berliquet, in the same ownership as neighbouring l'Hermitage. In contrast to the pure-Merlot Hermitage, Matras is produced from a third each of Merlot, Cabernet Sauvignon, and Cabernet Franc to make a more sinewy wine.

Maucaillou
33480 Moulis, Tel: 05 56 58 01 23, Fax: 05 56 58 00 88

Much expanded 85-ha Moulis property with an oddly unforgettable château which the proprietor, Philippe Dourthe, describes as "half Renaissance and half Arcachon villa". The wine of Maucaillou has become increasingly chunky, spicy, and serious over the vintages of the late 1990s, culminating in an impressively dark and tight-knit 2000.

Mazeris
33126 St-Michel-de-Fronsac, Tel: 05 57 24 96 93, Fax: 05 57 24 98 25

This 15-ha Canon-Fronsac property made under the Moueix banner generally produces satisfying wine marked by peppery spice.

Mazeyres
33500 Libourne, Tel: 05 57 51 16 69

Improving though unpropitiously sited 20-ha Pomerol property run by Alain Moueix. The 2000 vintage was impressively close-textured and incense-scented.

Méaume
33230 Marasin, Tel: 05 57 49 41 04, Fax: 05 57 69 02 70

Briton Alan Johnson-Hill's 28-ha Bordeaux property produces satisfying and balanced early drinking reds.

Meyney
33180 St-Estèphe, Tel: 05 57 57 25 50, Fax: 05 56 11 29 01

The 49 ha of Meyney sit just north of Montrose in St-Estèphe, looking out across the Gironde with a superb view of the Blayais nuclear power station; the terroir is unusual in that the vine's roots grasp ample blue clay as well as gravels. This Cordier-owned property generally produces a full-flavoured, sturdy, smoky wine offering fine value and impressive consistency.

Milens
33330 St-Hippolyte, Tel: 05 57 55 24 47, Fax: 05 57 55 24 44

This St-Emilion is inauspiciously sited in the flatter, southern part of the AOC, but is producing a fleshy and pleasurable wine with consultative help from Jean-Luc Thunevin and Louis Mitjavile.

La Mission Haut-Brion ✪✪
33602 Pessac, Tel: 05 56 00 29 30, Fax: 05 56 98 75 14

La Mission faces Haut-Brion, railings to railings, across Bordeaux's Avenue Jean Jaurès, though the disposition of its 20 ha are less confrontational; the southernmost plots of these two great Graves wines (the AOC is Pessac-Léognan) are actually commingled, with La Mission's being planted to a higher density than Haut-Brion's (10,000 vines/ha rather than 8,000 vines/ha). The two properties have been in the same ownership since 1983. Some deplore this, claiming that La Mission more regularly eclipsed Haut-Brion itself when the two properties were direct competitors. According to Jean Delmas, though, the two properties are managed in an identical way, with identical yields and identical winemaking, providing a rare opportunity to foreground minute differences in terroir. La Mission has, in the past, been a more richly constituted and tannic wine than Haut-Brion; it now shares much of Haut-Brion's elegance, finesse, pencil-perfect balance, and aromatic complexity. In hot vintages (such as 1989 and 2000) some of that old tannic power seems to surge back, and the wine can go head-to-head with its northern neighbour; it also has a fine record for depth of flavour in weaker years, and is regarded as one of the most consistent of all great Bordeaux wines.

Monbousquet ✪
33330 St-Sulpice-de-Faleyrens, Tel: 05 57 55 43 43, Fax: 05 57 24 63 99

A cause célèbre among modern-day Bordeaux properties, since it was this 34-ha château more than any other which showed by just what margin achievement could exceed expectation. When, that is, the necessary funds and driving ambition were available from the proprietor (in this case, former hypermarket owner Gérard Perse). Monbousquet was once an obscure St-Emilion property sited well away from the majestic slope at the top of which the town sits, and on the sides of which most of the great terroirs are generally thought to be situated. Its soils are flat, a mixture of sand, clay, and some gravel: nothing special. Yet from 1995 onwards (Perse bought in 1993) Monbousquet has contrived to send to market a wine whose sumptuous fleshiness, whose lush fullness, whose dark and softly extracted fruit succeeds in seducing all those who lay lips on it. If Monbousquet can do it (as it repeatedly has), why not others? This is the challenge which has led to the explosion of garage wines in the region, and to a revision of thinking about St-Emilion's terroirs in general.

Monbrison
33460 Arsac, Tel: 05 56 58 80 04, Fax: 05 56 58 85 33

This smallish 21-ha property in the Arsac sector of Margaux now shares with du Tertre the distinction of being the best property in this inland commune. Monbrison (run by Laurent Vonderheyden) is a model of purity and elegance, with a lighter tannic structure than du Tertre.

La Mondotte ✪✪
33330 St-Emilion, Tel: 05 57 24 71 33, Fax: 05 57 74 67 95

This extraordinary wine owes its existence to a quarrel. It's a 4.5 ha parcel of St-Emilion sited between Troplong Mondot and Tertre Roteboeuf which its owner, Comte Stephan von Neipperg, originally wanted to include within Canon-la-Gaffelière. There is a history of widely separated parcels which are allowed to compose "unitary" properties throughout Bordeaux (see, for example, Gloria, Prieuré-Lichine, or Valandraud); the authorities, though, said that if Neipperg did this, Canon-la-Gaffelière would have to be demoted from a Grand Cru Classé to a Grand Cru. "Right," said Neipperg, piqued. "Now I will show you what I can do there." He built what he calls a "special cellar" to make a "special wine", and he and his cellar master Stéphane Derenoncourt set about their "garden work" in the vineyard, plucking leaves, slashing yields, working with biodynamic methods, and making severe fruit selections. The wine is fermented very slowly, with very little sulphur, run into new oak before malolactic, and left unracked, nourishing itself on the lees (with micro-oxygenation to keep reduction at bay). The front label bears none of the "official" AOC wording; that is all banished to the back. The result is a pure

Merlot (the vineyard includes Cabernet Franc but it is generally excluded) of huge concentration, succulence, and sweet-fruitedness which has been rapturously received by Parker – and millionaires worldwide. Alas for the price.

Montrose ✪
33180 St-Estèphe, Tel: 05 56 59 30 12, Fax: 05 56 59 38 48

This superb, 68-ha parcel of St-Estèphe is capable of producing some of the grandest, most tannin-drenched wines in the Médoc; Montrose can keep time at bay as few others can. There is considerable vintage variation, however, and some wines have been lighter and more "accessible" over the last two decades; the 1999 and 2000 vintages suggest a return to dark, former form.

Le Moulin
33500 Pomerol, Tel: 05 57 51 77 69

Tiny and formerly obscure Pomerol property producing clean, soft, vivid, lush, and pure wines.

Moulin du Cadet
33500 Libourne, Tel: 05 57 55 05 80, Fax: 05 57 51 79 79

This minuscule 5-ha St-Emilion property is where owner J-P Moueix has experimented with biodynamics. Like many Moueix wines, it is made in a lighter and fresher style than the contemporary norm – a part of Christian Moueix's campaign to defend the elegance and finesse he feels is threatened by the New Bordeaux's more extravagantly extracted wines.

Moulinet
33330 St-Emilion, Tel: 05 57 74 43 11, Fax: 05 57 74 44 67

Large 18-ha Pomerol sited on the unpromising northwestern edge of the AOC, Moulinet has traditionally produced innocuous, easygoing reds. Moueix management (from 2000) may improve matters.

Moulin Pey-Labrie
33126 Fronsac, Tel: 05 57 51 14 37, Fax: 05 57 51 53 45

Well-run 7-ha Canon-Fronsac domain producing sturdy, chunky wines.

Moulin St-Georges
33330 St-Emilion, Tel: 05 57 24 70 26, Fax: 05 57 74 47 39

Sitting in a fine spot underneath the town and close to the original parcels of Valandraud, this 6.5-ha property (owned by Ausone's Alain Vauthier) is producing articulate wines which combine dense lushness with the pure-fruited elegance that is Ausone's own hallmark.

Mouton Rothschild ✪✪✪
33250 Pauillac, Tel: 05 56 59 22 22, Fax: 05 56 73 20 44

The 75 ha of Pauillac occupied by Mouton Rothschild sit, set back from the estuary, on the plateau and the southern side of the knoll which this first growth – so promoted, singularly, in 1973 – shares with Lafite. (The larger Lafite has a few parcels of its own on this southern side, too.) Is it, then, like Lafite? Hardly. Lafite is characterized by aristocratic restraint and debonair elegance; Mouton is voluptuous, rotund, opulent – the Falstaff of the first growths. This great swell of gravels is certainly very special, but perhaps the differences between the two properties are chiefly accounted for by the fact that Lafite slopes markedly to the north down to 5 metres or so, whereas almost all of Mouton is openly exposed at between 20 and 25 metres. The property's great champion was the creative and far-sighted Philippe de Rothschild, pioneer of estate bottling, artist's labels, and (with Mouton Cadet) branded Bordeaux. The property seemed to stagger a little after his death in 1988, but since the mid-1990s has been firmly back on track with some caressing, arresting, and typically showy red wines (even if nothing yet to match the black dynamite of 1986).

Myrat
33720 Barsac, Tel: 05 56 27 09 06, Fax: 05 56 27 11 75

This 22-ha Barsac property, owned by the descendants of the de Pontac family which first sold Haut-Brion in London in Pepys' day, was entirely replanted in 1988. The wines are slowly deepening and improving.

Nairac ✪
33270 Barsac, Tel: 05 56 27 16 16, Fax: 05 56 27 26 50

Few Sauternes properties are run with the single-minded dedication which Nicolas Tari puts into the 16-ha Nairac, sited near to the town of Barsac itself. This wine is produced along the same patient, non-interventionist lines as the greatest wines of Alsace are – not a common practice in conservative and sometimes underfunded Sauternes – using dense, supersweet musts expressed from grapes picked as late, and as carefully, as possible. These slowly evolving wines combine the vivid fruit spectrum of classic Barsac with the weight and unction of the greatest Sauternes.

Nenin ✪
33500 Libourne, Tel: 05 57 51 00 01, Fax: 05 57 51 77 47

This Pomerol property lying just outside the hamlet of Catusseau was purchased in September 1997 by the Delon family of Léoville-las-Cases in St-Julien, and its 25 ha have since been swelled by other land purchases (including the "Clos du Roy" parts of Certan Guiraud which Christian Moueix didn't want for Hosanna) to a total of 34 ha. The 1998 and 1999 vintages were unexceptional, but in 2000 Nenin produced exactly what long-term spectators of the Delon approach had expected: a dense, powerful, and flavour-wealthy wine which was among the appellation leaders in the vintage. Reduced yields, full ripeness and selection (including the creation of a new second wine, Fugue de Nenin) had the desired effect – and, interestingly, Jean-Hubert Delon doesn't rule out the future creation of "other types of wine like a microcuvée or a third wine". Will Nenin be where Jean-Hubert Delon builds his garage? We'll see.

Olivier
33850 Léognan, Tel: 05 56 64 75 16, Fax: 05 56 64 54 23

As so often in the Graves, the château itself at this 48-ha property (moated and fortified, of medieval origin) is built on a far grander scale than the wine. Nonetheless Olivier has been making increasingly impressive wines during the late 1990s from its single parcel of vines, and the smoky, tobacco-and-plum-fragrant 2000 was among the best reds in the AOC.

Les Ormes de Pez
33180 St-Estèphe, Tel: 05 56 73 24 00, Fax: 05 56 59 26 42

Fine value 35-ha St-Estèphe property owned and run by the Cazes family of Lynch-Bages, situated inland from the Gironde around the hamlet of Pez. The style is open and accessible, with lots of pure-drawn blackcurrant fruit; the old vines add depth.

Les Ormes Sorbet
33340 Couquèques, Tel: 05 56 73 30 30, Fax: 05 56 73 30 31

The mixed agricultural land which dominates the northern Médoc is scattered with hundreds of little-known vineyards; thanks to high plantation densities, low yields, and a refusal to cut corners with oak, this 21-ha château is one of the best of the crowd.

Palmer ✪✪
33460 Margaux, Tel: 05 57 88 72 72, Fax: 05 57 88 37 16

Palmer is a wine whose quality tends to weave according to the strength of the vintage, but at its best this is Margaux's main challenger within the AOC of the same name. The 45-ha property is situated further south than Margaux itself, sandwiched by d'Issan and Rauzan-Ségla. When it's good (as it unquestionably has been in 1999 and 2000), this is the fleshiest, slinkiest, most sumptuous wine in the commune, packed with sweet blueberry fruit.

Pape Clément ✪
33600 Pessac, Tel: 05 57 26 38 38, Fax: 05 57 26 38 39

Like the Haut-Brion properties (though situated a few kilometres to their southwest), the 32-ha Pape Clément is a wholly suburban vineyard, swallowed by Bordeaux itself. Seven-league strides have been made here during the 1990s under the ownership of Bernard Magrez and Léo Montagne, and Pape Clément now produces some of the most memorable reds and whites in the AOC. As at Haut-Brion, the soil is intensely gravelly, though here it seems

to give more yielding, soft-textured, and user-friendly red wines tasting less of graphite and gravy and more of cherry fruit and coffee cream. That same creaminess, too, is apparent in the whites.

Patache d'Aux
33340 Bégadan, Tel: 05 56 41 50 18, Fax: 05 56 41 54 65

Produced towards the northern tip of the Médoc, this 43-ha property produces wines of juicy appeal, particularly after warmer vintages.

Pavie ✪
33330 St-Emilion, Tel: 05 57 55 43 43, Fax: 05 57 24 63 99

This beautifully situated 37-ha property, whose original cellar was dug into the hillside of St-Emilion's spectacular escarpment, passed out of the ownership of the Valette family in 1998 – and into the hands of the ambitious Gérard Perse, who "sold everything" to buy it. Perse immediately built a spectacular new *cuverie* and *chai* (the old troglodytic one, though picturesque, was over-damp), and the wine changed dramatically. Under the former régime, it had been round, expressive, and gracefully typical in good vintages yet lean, short, and unyielding in less successful years; Perse (working with Alain Raynaud and Laurent Lusseau) has managed to give it a striking coal-seam depth and force, yet without sacrificing any of its sweet-edged lyricism.

Perse's tools have been dramatically reduced yields, leaf-plucking, late harvesting, fanatical fruit sorting, cold pre-fermentation maceration, impeccable cellar hygiene, lavish new wood, and the refusal to fine or filter. He employs, in other words, a mixture of the new and the old to recreate his ideal of the "*cuisine de grandmère*" – wines of saturated depth of flavour, delicious in youth yet ageing well, too, and reflecting their place of origin with maximum articulacy.

Pavie Decesse ✪
33330 St-Emilion, Tel: 05 57 55 43 43, Fax: 05 57 24 63 99

Pavie Decesse is a much smaller property than Pavie (10 ha) and lies above it on plateau land rather than the slope. Since both of these St-Emilion properties are owned by Gérard Perse and made by similarly painstaking means, the comparison between them is instructive. Pavie Decesse does taste cooler, tauter, and in some ways more intense, with more pepper amongst its plum; it lacks the sheer power and moist, chewy depth of Pavie. This, despite the fact that plantings at Pavie Decesse are 90% Merlot and 10% Cabernet Franc, whereas Pavie has 30% Cabernet Franc and 10% Cabernet Sauvignon.

Pavie Macquin ✪
33330 St-Emilion, Tel: 05 57 24 74 23, Fax: 05 57 24 63 78

This 15-ha property sited above Pavie and overlooking the deep little valley at the bottom of the town of St-Emilion belongs to the Corre-Macquin family. It is run by Nicolas Thienpont, a cousin of Jacques Thienpont of Le Pin and Alexandre Thienpont of Vieux Château Certan, and cultivation here is very much in the biodynamic spirit. Stéphane Derenoncourt (whose first job in Bordeaux was at the biodynamic Château la Fleur Caillou in Canon-Fronsac) acts as consultant, and his minimal handling, lees contact, and micro-oxygenation techniques have lent the sometimes stern Pavie Macquin an improving succulence. If anything, however, the colours, fruit, and tannin structure are deeper still – the property has a fine stock of old vines – making this one of the chief *vins de garde* in the appellation.

Péby Faugères ✪
33330 St-Etienne-de-Lisse, Tel: 05 57 40 34 99, Fax: 05 57 40 36 14

This is the name Corinne Guisez gave to the super-cuvée she produced at Château Faugères in the far east of St-Emilion following the death of her husband Péby; it's made from a small parcel of Merlot with a seasoning of Cabernet Franc. Like Monbousquet, it shows what can be achieved from St-Emilion's "unpromising" terroirs: saturatedly dark in colour, it has powerful black-fruit scents and flavours with bubbling, seething tannins. Now owned by Silvio Denz.

Petite Eglise
33500 Pomerol, Tel: 05 57 51 79 83

Not, as some have assumed, a pure second wine of Eglise-Clinet (though it does include all the second wine of this great Pomerol: 70 out of 120 Eglise-Clinet casks in 2000, for example, and half of those in new wood). Denis Durantou's high class blended Pomerol, thus, offers a taste of the real thing.

Petit Village
33500 Pomerol, Tel: 05 57 51 21 08, Fax: 05 57 51 87 31

This well-sited 11-ha Pomerol sandwiched between Vieux Château Certan and Beauregard has been Médoc-run for 30 years – at first by Bruno Prats of Cos d'Estournel, and latterly by the AXA Millésimes team of Pichon-Longueville. It's always a well-made, dark, sumptuous, and black-fruited Pomerol without having the power and tenacity of the very finest – though the new owner Gérard Perse seems likely to change that.

Pétrus ✪✪✪
33500 Pomerol, Tel: 05 57 51 17 96, Fax: 05 57 51 17 96

Of the two legends of Pomerol (the other one begins with "P", too), this 11.5-ha property is the older, its record for excellence running back to the 1920s before the historical thread of what was then considered a very humble wine region is lost. Great vintages of Pétrus loiter in time like solidified lava: dense, powerful, multi-layered, packed with coffee, spice, earth, and roasted black fruits. What is gratifying about Pétrus, moreover, is that it is not a modern, hi-tech wine which transcends vintage variation; instead it always gives a compelling account of vintage, albeit seen through its distinctively dark lens. What is galling about Pétrus is that it is unobtainable for non-millionaire wine lovers. Why is this brooding diplodocus among Pomerols so different from its graceful neighbours like La Conseillante, Vieux Château Certan and La Fleur-Pétrus? If you walk the road from VCC to Pétrus the fine-pebbled Günz gravels and iron-bearing sands of the surface do not seem to change at the vineyard boundaries; underneath, however, the layer of clay-like Fronsadais molasse blisters towards the surface here. Is less gravel and more clay the answer? So far as anyone knows. Pétrus is also almost pure Merlot – yet so is the utterly different La Fleur-Pétrus. In any case the Merlot-mimicking Cabernet Franc performance of nearby Cheval Blanc suggests that grape variety here is subordinate to the stamp of terroir. What is beyond all doubt is that, after an uncertain period in the mid-1980s, Pétrus is now performing as well as it has ever done, coaxed towards contingent perfection by Christian Moueix. The habitually self-critical Moueix himself is in no doubt that 1998 is the outstanding recent vintage.

Peyrou
33350 St-Magne-de-Castillon, Tel: 05 57 40 06 49, Fax: 05 57 74 40 03

Promising though small (5 ha) Côtes de Castillon property on the very edge of St-Emilion, close to Faugères.

de Pez
33180 St-Estèphe, Tel: 05 56 59 30 26, Fax: 05 56 59 39 25

This 24-ha property in inland St-Estèphe has been owned since 1985 by Champagne house Louis Roederer. The wines are dark and full-fruited, but not yet dramatically different from their past performances.

Phélan Ségur
33180 St-Estèphe, Tel: 05 56 59 74 00, Fax: 05 56 59 74 10

Handsome 64-ha property in St-Estèphe between Meyney and Calon-Ségur. More elegant, pure-fruited wines than the AOC profile leads one to expect.

Piada
33720 Barsac, Tel: 05 56 27 16 13, Fax: 05 56 27 26 30

This 9.5-ha Barsac property once formed part of Coutet, whose knoll it shares. Good quality and value, though the terroir suggests more still might be possible.

Pibran
33250 Pauillac, Tel: 05 56 73 17 17, Fax: 05 56 73 17 28

A well-situated 10-ha neighbour of Pontet-Canet, Pibran is part of the AXA

Millésimes portfolio and provides classically meaty, muscular, boisterous, and uncomplicated Pauillac. Great value in generous vintages.

Pichon-Longueville Baron ✪✪
33250 Pauillac, Tel: 05 56 73 17 17, Fax: 05 56 73 17 28

At 68 ha, this is the smaller of the two Pichon estates, though the château building and modern, Egyptian-inspired *chai* are the grandest in Pauillac, and rival Margaux's own buildings for architectural opulence. Its vineyards form the middle sector of a steadily rising knoll which begins at Latour and carries on, retreating from the estuary, towards Haut-Batailley. Of the two Pichons, it is the Baron that shadows the Latour style most convincingly, with a combination of dense, pressed black fruits and sheathed, meaty power. It has been well-run since the late 1980s by AXA Millésimes, both the 1989 and the 1990 being outstanding successes in those vintages.

Pichon-Longueville Comtesse de Lalande ✪✪
33250 Pauillac, Tel: 05 56 59 19 40, Fax: 05 56 59 26 56

The Comtesse, at 75 ha, is bigger than the Baron, though the vines growing on two sides of the property itself are those of Latour while just across the road lie the Baron's parcels. Aside from a small plot just to the north of the château, almost all the Pichon Lalande vines lie some distance inland from the buildings, between Pichon Baron's parcels and those of Haut-Batailley. This is the most graceful and least forceful of the great Pauillacs, with a creamy sumptuousness in the best vintages; the higher sited gravels may have something to do with this, as does the sizeable percentage of Merlot (35%). However there is also a 10% stock of old-vine Petit Verdot (planted in 1932) which can be called on, as in 2000, to stiffen the Comtesse's sinews and pepper its sheeny wine.

Picque Caillou
33700 Mérignac, Tel: 05 56 47 37 98, Fax: 05 56 97 99 37

This 20-ha property is the last survivor of the vineyards of Mérignac, site of Bordeaux's airport. A unique and stony terroir within Pessac-Léognan, then – though the weather station at Mérignac also shows that this is the rainiest spot in Bordeaux, and Picque Caillou can suffer badly in wet vintages. At its best, this is light and flavoursome Pessac-Léognan of easydrinking grace. It's owned by Paulin Calvet, export manager for J-P Moueix; Jean-Claude Berrouet consults.

Le Pin ✪✪
33500 Pomerol, Tel: 05 57 51 33 99

Alongside Pétrus, Le Pin is Pomerol's second legend. Bottles from this tiny 2.1-ha vineyard became, during the 1990s, the ultimate "trophy wine" of worldwide collectors, to the utter bemusement of its down-to-earth owner, Belgian "country wine merchant" Jacques Thienpont. Thienpont bought the first hectare back in 1979; it was sited near some of the outlying plots of Vieux Château Certan, a property purchased by Thienpont's grandfather back in 1924. It was good land, just north of the hamlet of Catusseau, composed of deep, well-drained Günz gravels over Fronsadais molasse. (It's astonishing to note, by the way, the splendidly obscure properties which neighbour Le Pin: Haut-Tropchaud and Grate-Cap, for example, which if re-drained and viticulturally improved could surely produce far more exciting wine than they do at present.) Thienpont ran the vineyard almost on a hobby basis at first, but the quality of the soil and his own "keep it simple" winemaking philosophy meant that the wine shone, not only in great vintages like 1982 but also in lesser vintages like 1987 and 1993. As revealed on page 165, this was also the property where the benefits of putting the wine through malolactic in new oak casks were first appreciated – by accident and by necessity. The wine's style is, yes, exotic, voluptous, and sumptuous, just as Pomerol should be, but it is also pure, lyrical, and accessible. It is not, in other words, difficult for drinkers to enjoy its greatness, no matter what their background. The name was memorable; the label classically simple (designed in two minutes on the counter of the local printer's). The wine caught on. Its rarity value (there are just 500 or so cases for the world) fuelled collector's imaginations as much as its scents and flavours, and at the height of the speculative market in summer 1997, Le Pin 1982 was trading for as much as £30,000 a case. Jacques Thienpont had sold it for less than £100 a case; he felt, he says, "a little like Van Gogh, who sold his paintings cheap, while on the market they made other prices." This fame has also led to misunderstandings about the style of the wine, many expecting it to be – like the garage wines of Thunevin and others – black, tannic, and powerfully extractive. In fact the family resemblance to Vieux Château Certan (which Jacques Thienpont feels is often just as good as Le Pin) is clear: this is pure, singing Pomerol, sumptuous yet svelte, too.

Le Pin Beausoleil
33420 St-Vincent-de-Pertignas, Tel: 05 57 84 02 56, Fax: 05 57 84 02 56

This 6-ha Bordeaux Supérieure property, sited just across the Dordogne from Côtes de Castillon, has been completely restored by owner Arnaud Pauchet since 1994, and is now producing concentrated, soft textured, blackcurrant-deep wines that wildly outperform the AOC standard. Nicolas Thienpont and Stéphane Derenoncourt lend a hand.

de Pitray
33350 Gardegan, Tel: 05 57 40 63 38, Fax: 05 57 40 66 24

This 30-ha property is one of the grandest in Côtes de Castillon, and has a long tradition of making sound, well-balanced, classically styled wines.

La Pointe
33500 Pomerol, Tel: 05 57 51 02 11, Fax: 05 57 51 42 33

Another neighbour of Nenin, this fine 22-ha Pomerol estate could surely produce better wine with greater viticultural efforts and reduced yields.

Pontet-Canet ✿
33250 Pauillac, Tel: 05 56 59 04 04, Fax: 05 56 59 26 63

Take a look at the terroir of Pontet-Canet, and it's hard to reach any other conclusion but that this should be one of the very greatest wines in Pauillac; this large, 79-ha property occupies the southern sector of the giant gravel bank on which Lafite and Mouton also have their vineyards. It looks a perfect spot, most of it at exactly the same height as some of Mouton's greatest plots. Pontet-Canet was shabbily run by its former owners the Cruse family, however, and it took new owners Guy and Alfred Tesseron some time to begin to make the necessary improvements (including an end to machine harvesting, strict fruit sorting and the creation of a second wine). Since 1994, however, Pontet-Canet has begun to realize its potential with bigger, more richly textured wines packed with pencil, spice, and earth flavours.

Potensac
33340 Lesparre-Médoc, Tel: 05 56 73 25 26, Fax: 05 56 59 18 33

This 51-ha Médoc property is not the most fortunately sited of the many that scatter the landscape north of St-Estèphe, but its ownership by the scrupulous Delon family, and its stock of old vines, means low yields (35 hl/ha), crop selection, 20% new oak and bottling without filtration. Potensac is best in warm vintages, when you can expect a dense, blackcurrant-saturated, earthy red wine which evolves slowly and expressively.

Poujeaux
33480 Moulis-en-Médoc, Tel: 05 56 58 02 96, Fax: 05 56 58 01 25

This well-run 52-ha property is one of the best in the backwoods commune of Moulis, producing grippy, chunky, intense red Bordeaux which needs a few lost years in a cellar to overcome its often raw youth.

La Prade
33570 St-Cibard, Tel: 05 57 56 07 47, Fax: 05 57 56 07 48

Small 4.5-ha Côtes de Francs property sold by Patrick Valette to appellation specialist Nicolas Thienpont in 2000. The cool, clay soils give an elegantly mineral, earthy mouthful.

Preuillac
33340 Lesparre Médoc, Tel: 05 56 09 00 29, Fax : 05 56 09 00 34

This 30-ha backwoods Médoc is now jointly owned by the Mau family

and its Dutch agents: the 2000 vintage was a great improvement on past performances. The property also has a wine school.

Prieuré-Lichine
33460 Cantenac, Tel: 05 57 88 36 28, Fax: 05 57 88 78 93

The fact that this 70-ha Margaux property has parcels scattered throughout every commune within the AOC (purchased, at various times, from Brane-Cantenac, Durfort-Vivens, Palmer, Ferrière, Kirwan, Giscours, d'Issan, and others) makes it difficult to generalize about – and difficult to manage, too. In its present-day form, the property was created by Alexis Lichine and his son Sacha. Sacha Lichine sold in June 1999, however, to Groupe Ballande (large shareholders in Sovex, a mining company with interests in New Caledonia) – who imaginatively put Stéphane Derenoncourt in charge. The wine has subsequently acquired a new grace, subtlety, and textural wealth thanks to Derenoncourt's minimal handling and lees-contact work, with the 2000 being an outstanding success, full of soft, flower-wrapped fruits.

Prieurs de la Commanderie
33330 St-Emilion, Tel: 05 57 51 31 36, Fax: 05 57 51 63 04

Small, unpromisingly sited 4-ha Pomerol property in the same ownership as St-Emilion's lush La Dominique.

Puygueraud
33570 St-Cibard, Tel: 05 57 56 07 47, Fax: 05 57 56 07 48

Excellent Côtes de Francs property owned and run by Nicolas Thienpont producing wines with brisk, bitter-edged raspberry fruits. The Cuvée Georges, produced in the best years only (such as 2000), is a fascinating blend of 35% each of Malbec and Cabernet Franc, complemented by 20% Merlot, and just 10% Cabernet Sauvignon: long and vivid, full of peppery spice and liquorice.

Quinault l'Enclos
33500 Libourne, Tel: 05 57 74 19 52 fax : .05 57 25 91 20

Will this prove to be Libourne's Haut-Brion? It's a 15-ha walled clos lying within the city limits and planted to 50-year-old vines, bought in the mid-1990s by Alain and Françoise Raynaud. The wines are made in contemporary style, with low yields, fastidious fruit sorting, cold pre-fermentation maceration, long cuvaisons, malolactic in barriques, and 15 months in 100% new wood. The result, of course, tastes nothing at all like Haut-Brion: it's a dark, thick-textured, exotically fruity (blackberry and blueberry) St-Emilion, slick with smoky-sweet oak.

Rabaud-Promis
33210 Bommes, Tel: 05 56 76 67 38, Fax: 05 56 76 63 10

This 33-ha Sauternes estate occupies a fine site, close to the little River Ciron and adjacent to Rayne Vigneau and Sigalas-Rabaud (with which it has formed a unitary property on two occasions). The 1988-1990 trio of vintages were excellent, and vintages since have kept up these ample, elegant standards.

Rahoul
33640 Portets, Tel: 05 56 67 01 12, Fax: 05 56 67 02 88

This 31-ha Graves property owned by Champenois Alain Thiénot (who also owns the excellent Loupiac property Château de Ricaud) produces a soft, medium-bodied, currant-and-tobacco-flavoured wine.

Rauzan-Despagne
33420 Naujan-et-Postiac, Tel: 05 57 84 55 08, Fax: 05 57 84 57 31

This is a well run 40-ha property in the east of the Entre-Deux-Mers, near the small town of Rauzan. The Merlot-rich Cuvée Passion is a ripe, spicy mouthful.

Rauzan-Gassies
33460 Margaux, Tel: 05 57 88 71 88, Fax: 05 57 88 37 49

This 30-ha Margaux property offers, like its sibling Croizet-Bages in Pauillac, conclusive proof that terroir remains largely mute if viticultural and winemaking efforts are inadequate. Machine harvesting and the refusal to make a second wine are just two of the reasons why, at best, Rauzan-Gassies makes modestly successful, short-lived wines, lacking in pronounced personality.

Rauzan-Ségla ✪

33460 Margaux, Tel: 05 57 88 82 10, Fax: 05 57 88 34 54

The 51-ha Rauzan Ségla, now owned by the Wertheimer family of Chanel, proves that Rauzan-Gassies could do better; the two vineyards are adjacent. Major investments have been made here in vineyards, cellar, and in the pretty château buildings, and the result is a swan-like wine of depth, elegance, and finesse, full of tapered blackcurrant fruit.

Raymond-Lafon ✪

33210 Sauternes, Tel: 05 56 63 21 02, Fax: 05 56 63 19 58

This 18-ha Sauternes property is owned by the former Yquem manager, Pierre Meslier; it sits underneath Yquem; its average yield is the same as Yquem's (around 10 hl/ha); it is made in the same way as Yquem. The message, in other words, is clear: although hard to find, this is one of the greatest of all Sauternes.

Rayne Vigneau

33210 Bommes, Tel: 05 56 01 30 12, Fax: 05 56 01 30 27

This large, 80-ha Sauternes property occupies a superb hill directly above the Ciron, its vineyards rising from 25 metres to over 60 metres; nearby La Tour Blanche has a similar profile though is less extensive. The gravels of this great rising bank are said to include semi-precious stones like agate and topaz. Rayne Vigneau has, though, produced disappointing wines for much of the 20th century; the improvements instituted by Mestrezat during the 1980s have taken the property towards a correct, light, and lemony style, though not all the way towards the challenging unction which the terroir – and the property's 19th-century reputation – suggest is possible.

Reignac

33450 St-Loubès, Tel: 05 56 20 41 05, Fax: 05 56 68 63 31

Large, 63-ha property in the St-Loubès sector of Entre-Deux-Mers where Stephanie and Yves Vatelot produce superb red AOC Bordeaux with a seriousness of approach which would shame many leading Médoc properties. Cuvée Spéciale is, perhaps confusingly, a step up from Cuvée Prestige; there are fine white versions, too.

Reynon

33410 Béguey, Tel: 05 56 62 96 51, Fax: 05 56 62 14 89

38-ha near Cadillac is where Denis Dubourdieu, Bordeaux University's leading white-wine researcher, and his wife Florence live, producing a range of reds and whites which peak with the carefully crafted and fragrant Reynon Vieilles Vignes.

Rieussec ✪

33210 Fargues-de-Langon, Tel: 05 56 62 20 71, Fax: 05 57 98 14 10

Few Sauternes have a recent record to match that of the 75-ha Rieussec, first under Albert Vuillier and latterly under the Lafite umbrella of Domaines Barons de Rothschild. The property occupies a splendid hill just east of Yquem, at around the same 70 metre mark. More new oak is used than under the Vuillier regime, with the result that Rieussec – always one of the very richest Sauternes – is now creamier and more thickly textured than ever. The high percentage of Sémillon and Rieussec's warm microclimate puts the emphasis on orange, caramel, honey, and rich, gardenia-like floral scents rather than the fresh lemon and crème anglaise of lighter peers.

Riou de Thaillas

33330 St-Emilion, Tel: 05 57 68 42 15, Fax: 05 57 68 28 59

Oddly labelled and powerfully extracted St-Emilion from a tiny 2.5-ha estate near the Pomerol border run by Jean-Yves Béchet (see Fougas Maldoror) with garage levels of commitment and ambition. Stow it and see.

Ripeau

33330 St-Emilion, Tel: 05 57 74 41 41, Fax: 05 07 74 41 57

This 15-ha St-Emilion sited close to Cheval Blanc and Figeac has begun to realize its potential with the scented and lively 2000 vintage, made with the help of Alain Raynaud of Quinault l'Enclos.

de la Rivière

333126 Fronsac, Tel: 05 57 55 56 56, Fax: 05 57 24 94 39

Fronsac's most impressive château (including 8 ha of cellars) produces typically chewy, frank wines.

Roc de Cambes

33330 St-Laurent-des-Combes, Fax: 05 57 74 42 11

Just as (at Tertre Roteboeuf) François Mitjavile anticipated the present-day St-Emilion quality revolution by a decade or more, so at Roc de Cambes he set the example for all those now making great Bordeaux in modest appellations. He bought this 10-ha Côte de Bourg property in the mid-1980s, no doubt reminded of Tertre Roteboeuf by its old vines and natural, amphitheatrical setting above the town of Bourg and the final kilometres of the Dordogne. By dint of low yields, late harvesting, and careful use of oak, Mitjavile has been able to create a delicious and sweet-fruited red wine (from 65% Merlot) which, in great vintages, could easily come from St-Emilion itself.

Rocher Bellevue

33350 St-Magne-de-Castillon, Tel: 05 57 40 08 88, Fax: 05 57 40 19 93

Well-sited 15-ha Côtes de Castillon property on the continuation of the St-Emilion slope. It's here that the talented Umbrian winemaker Riccardo Cotarella made a fat and fleshy garage wine from pure Merlot in 2000 called Caprice d'Angelique.

Rocher Figeac

33500 Libourne, Tel: 05 57 51 36 49, Fax: 05 57 51 98 70

This 7-ha member of the large Figeac cluster of properties lies on the outskirts of Libourne, producing soft, gentle, Pomerol-like wine.

Rol Valentin

33330 St-Emilion, Tel: 05 57 74 43 51, Fax: 05 57 74 45 13

Tiny 3.5-ha property on the plateau of St-Emilion where former Lille footballer Eric Prisette makes a tight, dense, lavishly extracted garage wine for long ageing. The terroir was improved by selling a sandy parcel and buying a clay-limestone parcel in 1999.

Rollan de By

33340 Bégadan, Tel: 05 56 41 58 59, Fax: 05 56 41 37 82

Ambitiously run 23-ha Médoc estate whose quality has risen markedly in the late 1990s. See also Haut-Condissas.

Romer du Hayot

33720 Barsac, Tel: 05 56 27 15 37, Fax: 05 56 27 04 24

This 16-ha Sauternes property lies next to de Malle, though you'd have to cross a motorway to go from one vineyard to the other. The wines are light, honeyed, and soft-fruited, for swift drinking.

Rouget

33500 Pomerol, Tel: 05 57 51 05 85, Fax: 05 57 55 22 45

Large, 16-ha property on the northern edge of the Pomerol appellation, where the fine plateau parcels around the church begin to slope down towards the Barbanne. Historically, this has been considered a promising terroir, though under its previous owner the wines were rarely exciting. Under new owners the Labruyère family, changes are apparent, and Rouget's chunky, four-square style is beginning to show greater subtlety of fruit and increased richness.

Roylland

33330 St-Emilion, Tel: 05 57 24 68 27, Fax: 05 57 24 65 25

This small 10-ha St-Emilion property is sited beneath Angélus, producing pure, sweet-fruited wines backed by supple tannins and oak spice. Owner Bernard Oddo calls on winemaking advice from Jean-Michel Dubos of Beauséjour Duffau.

Saintayme
33500 Pomerol, Tel: 05 57 51 79 83

This St-Emilion produced by Denis Durantou of Pomerol's Eglise-Clinet is a selection of fruit purchased from properties near Figeac, Tertre-Daugay and Monbousquet given classic barrel-ageing in Durantou's newly built merchant cellars in the Pomerol hamlet of Catusseau. The debut 2000 vintage was soft, lush, and sweetly stylish.

St-Brice *see* Magdelaine

St-Domingue *see* La Dominique

St-Pierre (Pomerol)
33500 Libourne, Tel: 05 57 51 06 07, Fax: 05 57 51 59 61

Tiny, well-sited 3-ha property next to the village's prominent church. Like many of Pomerol's small properties, though, the wines fail to fulfil the soil's potential.

St-Pierre (St-Julien)
33250 St-Julien-Beychevelle, Tel: 05 56 59 08 18, Fax: 05 56 59 16 18

This 17-ha property sited near Branaire and Beychevelle produces robust, earthy, exuberant though unsubtle wines.

Ste-Colombe
33500 St-Magne-de-Castillon, Tel: 05 57 40 06 75

Of the two Côtes de Castillon properties owned and run by Gérard Perse and Alain Raynaud, the wine of Ste-Colombe is produced with higher yields (50 hl/ha) from machine-harvested fruit, and is fined and filtered (c.f. Clos l' Eglise). It's a lively, crunchy straightforward red wine requiring little or no ageing.

de Sales
33500 Pomerol, Tel: 05 57 51 04 82, Fax: 05 57 25 23 91

At 47.5 ha, this is easily the biggest property in Pomerol – but it's also one of the least well-sited, in the low-lying northwest sector of the AOC. The property produces, in good vintages, sound though unambitious wines.

Sansonnet
33330 St-Emilion, Tel: 03 26 88 75 81, Fax: 03 26 88 67 43

This 7-ha walled property is sited near to La Couspaude, on the plateau of St-Emilion; it was bought in 1999 by the d'Aulan family, who formerly owned Piper-Heidsieck. As vinified by the late Jean-Michel Arcaute, the wine has been made in a lush, late-harvest style, packed with dark fruit and smoky oak.

Sénéjac
33290 Le Pian-Médoc, Tel: 05 56 70 20 11, Fax: 05 56 70 23 91

This 28-ha property at the southern end of the Médoc has recently been bought by Thierry and Loraine Rustmann of Château Talbot. Its previously light and softly curranty wine has deepened impressively – and this is one of those Médoc properties which has chosen to cherry-pick its best vineyards to make a microcuvée (called Karolus, see also page 188).

Sigalas-Rabaud
33210 Langon, Tel: 05 56 11 29 00, Fax: 05 56 11 29 01

This is the smaller, 14-ha part of the divided Rabaud estate; the vines are slightly more elevated than those of Rabaud-Promis and have been historically considered superior. Cordier and its skilled winemaker Georges Pauli administer the estate on behalf of its owners, and this is a carefully made, accessible, lavishly fruited, and appealingly perfumed Sauternes.

Siran
33460 Labarde, Tel: 05 57 88 34 04, Fax: 05 57 88 70 05

Siran is a 25-ha Margaux estate lying in the south of the AOC on a well-exposed site close to the river. It's been well-run for three decades or more, and its 12% dollop of Petit Verdot plus advice from Michel Rolland helps give it a more robust and full-flavoured style than one might expect from the location.

Smith Haut Lafitte ✪
33650 Martillac, Tel: 05 57 83 11 22, Fax: 05 57 83 11 21

Few properties in the entire Bordeaux region have received more care than Smith Haut Lafitte under the ownership of former ski champion Daniel Cathiard and his unforgettably enthusiastic wife Florence. Eleven of the 55 ha are given over to white wine (generally pure Sauvignon Blanc; the vineyard contains just 5% each of Sémillon and Sauvignon Gris), combining vivid fruit with rich, sumptuous oak. The red wine, meanwhile, is a finely nuanced midweight. It's less mineral and gravelly in flavour than the Haut-Brion group of properties, but more than compensates with ample svelte, smoky-sweet fruit and a chocolate-cedar finish. There is also a therapeutic spa on the premises, utilizing grape products and run by the Cathiard's daughter Mathilde, and the Cathiards are moving towards biodynamic cultivation. They cooper their own oak, and have even made kosher Pessac-Léognan in the past.

Sociando-Mallet ✪
33180 St-Seurin-de-Cadourne, Tel: 05 56 73 38 80, Fax: 05 56 73 38 88

The classification-defying Sociando-Mallet, whose 45 Haut-Médoc hectares are found in a superb gravel mound close to the river just north of St-Estèphe and Calon-Ségur, is a tribute to the skills and efforts of proprietor Jean Gautreau, who bought the property in 1969 as a ruin. High planting densities, manual harvesting at full ripeness, long macerations, between 80 and 100% new oak and the refusal to fine or filter are some of the reasons behind the success of this powerfully constituted and slowly evolving wine.

de Sours
33750 St-Quentin de Baron, Tel: 05 57 24 10 81, Fax: 05 57 24 10 83

This 50-ha property in Entre-Deux-Mers, owned by Briton Esmé Johnstone, produces wine of all colours, but is chiefly known for its outstanding rosé, one of France's best, and the red La Source, based on 65-year-old vines.

Suduiraut ✪
33210 Preignac, Tel: 05 56 63 27 29, Fax: 05 56 63 07 00

This 87-ha property is one of the three grand neighbours of Yquem (the other two being Rieussec and Guiraud). Its wines have been steadily improving in quality and growing in consistency since it was purchased by AXA Millésimes in 1992, with the 1999 in particular being outstandingly good, one of the wines of the vintage. The Suduiraut style is, at its best, an appellation heavyweight: thick, glycerous, and burnished, packed with melting lemon butter, honey, and lanolin.

Taillefer
33500 Libourne, Tel: 05 57 25 50 45, Fax: 05 57 51 50 63

This 11.5-ha Pomerol property sited in the far south of the appellation produces unexceptional though pleasant Pomerols.

Talbot
33250 St-Julien-Beychevelle, Tel: 05 56 73 21 50, Fax: 05 56 73 21 51

This massive, 102-ha estate is the largest in St-Julien, and one of the biggest in the entire Médoc; most of the vineyards lie on a gravel bank set back from the river, adjacent to parcels of Léoville-las-Cases and Léoville-Poyferré. It remains in the possession of members of the Cordier family: Lorraine Rustmann and Nancy Bignon (though Cordier itself now belongs to the Languedoc group Val d'Orbieu). Talbot had a reputation for tannic depth when made by Cordier's Georges Pauli (who told me he loves the taste of tannin); it is now made in a softer, more voluptuous, and more accessible style.

du Tertre
33460 Arsac, Tel: 05 57 97 09 09, Fax: 05 57 97 09 00

The 50-ha du Tertre is one of the two leading properties in the Margaux commune of Arsac; it occupies a sandy gravel knoll (*tertre*) of its own, just to the west of Monbrison, with (unusually) its vineyards in one contiguous parcel. It's been in slow renovation since 1961, at first by the Capbern-Gasqueton family of Calon-Ségur, and more recently by Eric Albada Jelgersma, and this work is finally coming good with superb vintage successes in 1996 and 2000. This is now one of Margaux's most densely knit and brooding wines.

Tertre Roteboeuf ✪

33330 St-Laurent-des-Combes, Fax: 05 57 74 42 11

This brilliantly run, south-facing 5-ha jewel in St-Emilion is, in many ways, the forerunner and inspiration for today's "garage" wine movement, since from the early 1980s it has managed to utterly eclipse its previous form and reputation and challenge the appellation's finest and grandest wines, vintage after vintage. Not that the terroir is disappointing: it occupies a superbly protected, amphitheatrical site at the point where the St-Emilion Côte horseshoes round between St-Laurent and St-Hippolyte. The property is owned and made by François Mitjavile, whose warm-hearted and voluble affability conceals a fierce and unremitting dedication to quality. Harvesting is as late as possible, yields are no higher than 35 hl/ha, and the wines spend up to 18 months in new oak. The result is red wines of magnificently sweet, spicy unction – the Châteauneufs of St-Emilion, if you like. The only disappointment is the wine's self-effacing label.

Teyssier

33330 Vignonet, Tel: 05 57 84 64 22, Fax: 05 57 84 63 54

This 11-ha St Emilion is Englishman Jonathan Maltus's home property, sited in the lowest and least exciting sector of the AOC (unlike his Le Dôme and Laforge). This is, though, a well-made, juicy, early drinking red.

Thieuley

33670 La Sauve, Tel: 05 56 23 00 01, Fax: 05 56 23 34 37

Modestly sited 60-ha Bordeaux property between Créon and Targon where the skilful Francis Courselle makes a fine white Bordeaux Sec as well as the oak-fermented Cuvée Francis Courselle.

La Tour Blanche

33210 Bommes, Tel: 05 57 98 02 73, Fax: 05 57 98 02 78

This 30-ha Sauternes estate, whose relatively steeply sloping vineyards overlook the little River Ciron, has been a wine school since 1911. Its final private owner was the memorably named Daniel Osiris, an umbrella manufacturer, who left it to the French state in his will provided it became a "free and open" agricultural college. The terroir is a fine one, once considered second only to Yquem, and since the arrival of Jean-Pierre Jausserrand in 1983 it has begun a slow ascent back up the quality hierarchy (the students, perhaps disappointingly, are not involved in making the wine). Vintages since 1988 have seen the new oak which great Sauternes needs, and in fine vintages like 1990 or 1997 this is now a powerfully honeyed, unctuous wine, packed with pineapple and orange.

La Tour de By

33340 Lesparre Médoc, Tel: 05 56 41 50 03, Fax: 05 56 41 36 10

Large, 74-ha Médoc property sited on a knoll next to the estuary (the *tour* was once a lighthouse) which produced solid, chunky, benchmark claret during the 1980s and early 1990s. Recent vintages, though, have disappointed.

La Tour Carnet

33112 St-Laurent-de-Médoc, Tel: 05 557 22 28 00, Fax: 05 57 22 28 05

This 42-ha Haut-Médoc property lies close to Belgrave and Camensac, all three offering fine value for money at present. La Tour Carnet is now in the ownership of the skilled and ambitious Bernard Magrez of Pape Clément and Fombrauge with consultation from the Michel Rolland team; the 2000 vintage immediately revealed reduced yields and riper fruit with a vivid, lyrical yet dense wine backed by promising tannins.

La Tour Figeac

33330 St-Emilion, Tel: 05 57 51 77 62, Fax: 05 57 25 36 92

When two of your neighbours are Figeac and Cheval Blanc, it would be surprising if you couldn't make an exciting wine, and since the arrival of Otto Rettenmaier in 1994, this has been what has begun to happen at this 12-ha St-Emilion property. It's run (biodynamically) for Rettenmaier by Christine Derenoncourt, the wife of Stéphane Derenoncourt, with single-minded

dedication and impressive results, beginning with the 1998 vintage. Christine Derenoncourt's great dislike in wine is "unripeness", which she considers even today to be a big problem in many Bordeaux wines. The 1998 and 2000 vintages are both lushly expressive, sweet-fruited St-Emilions of grace and delicacy: more Cheval Blanc, in other words, than Figeac.

La Tour Haut-Brion

33602 Pessac, Tel: 05 56 00 29 30, Fax: 05 56 98 75 14

La Tour Haut-Brion's miserly 5 ha of vines lie to the south of La Mission, interspersed with parcels of La Mission and Laville; almost 80% of Cabernet Sauvignon and Cabernet Franc in the vineyard gives this wine the potential to be one of the sternest of this little suburban community, though the vines are still relatively young. (Prior to 1983, this served as the second wine of La Mission Haut-Brion.) Blackcurrants and earth are both prominent in the scents and flavours of La Tour Haut-Brion, and the final blends are often very different to the vineyard plantings (the 2000 vintage, for example, was 53% Merlot) giving the wine a sweeter sheen than you might expect.

Tour de Mirambeau

33420 Naujan-et-Postiac, Tel: 05 57 84 55 08, Fax: 05 57 84 57 31

Large 60-ha property owned by Jean-Louis Despagne in the east of Entre-Deux-Mers producing outstanding red Bordeaux and white Entre-Deux-Mers. The basic *cuvées* are among the best in the appellation; the two Cuvée Passion wines challenge Pessac-Léognan (white) and St-Emilion (red – based on 70% Merlot) peers: fine value throughout. See *also* Girolate.

La Tourette see Larose-Trintaudon

Troplong Mondot ✪

33330 St-Emilion, Tel: 05 57 55 32 05, Fax: 05 57 55 32 07

This 30-ha St-Emilion property, run by Christine Valette with advice from Michel Rolland, occupies a commanding position to the west of the town of St-Emilion. A clue to the fact that this is one of the highest spots in the vicinity is the presence of an inelegant water tower next to the driveway; this lies some 100 metres above sea level. (Contrast Monbousquet at 5 metres and Cheval Blanc at about 35 metres.) Perhaps it's the height that gives these dark wines their firmness and briskness, or perhaps it's the old-vine fruit; evident new oak is sometimes stiffly prominent in their youth. Not, in other words, the kind of St-Emilion one could ever confuse with Pomerol; succulence and lushness are many cellar years away.

Trotanoy ✪✪

33500 Pomerol

This 7-ha Pomerol estate occupies a commanding position in the centre of the appellation, just at the point where the plateau begins to slope away towards the north and west; the terroir combines gravel and clay. The château lies at the end of an Italianate, cyprus-lined drive; it is the home of Jean-Jacques Moueix, Christian Moueix's cousin. Historically, Trotanoy has been one of the greatest of all Pomerols, tugging at the coat-tails of Pétrus itself; it is a wine of coal-seam density and tight-strapped tannin, needing many years to unfold and yield its meat-and-chocolate treasures. After a disappointing patch in the 1980s, it has swung excitingly back on form in the 1990s and in 2000.

Trottevieille

33330 St-Emilion, Tel: 05 56 00 00 70, Fax: 05 57 87 48 61

This 10-ha St-Emilion property lies just to the north of the lofty Troplong Mondot. It's a promising site, though the wines have often failed to live up to this promise, lacking richness and depth.

Valandraud ✪

33330 St-Emilion, Tel: 05 57 55 09 13, Fax: 05 57 55 09 12

This St-Emilion is the ultimate garage wine, made by the king of the garagistes, Jean-Luc Thunevin. It won its name in the poor vintages of the early 1990s, during which it came from nowhere to challenge the top wines of the appellation, by dint of Thunevin's fastidious viticulture and winemaking techniques (see page 169). Where is Valandraud? Look on a map, and it will be marked in the centre of historic St-Emilion where, down a narrow side street, Thunevin has his astonishingly neat and tidy cellar, tasting room, house, aviary and swimming pool; a stream runs through the property. The wine was composed of three parcels up until 1997, the best of them sited in the little valley at the bottom of the town (to which Thunevin gave his wife's maiden name, Andraud, though historically it was called Franc Fongaban); and the other two in less exciting, sand and gravel sites in the flatter south of the AOC. "Since 1997," Thunevin told me, "we have earned lots of money, so I bought a 6.5-ha parcel between Pavie and the Castillon road, at the bottom of the Côte, for a property I call Clos Badon Thunevin; and in 1999 I bought 5.5ha in the very best part of the appellation, a parcel called Belle Air Ouÿ." This parcel lies on the plateau, in the far west of the AOC (so perhaps not in truth the "very best" zone), next to Fleur Cardinale. In 2000, most of the blend of Valandraud came from Belle Air Ouÿ, making it (in principle) very different from previous Valandrauds: less fleshy, more aquiline. Until Thunevin finally decides on the boundaries of the property, it will be hard to generalize about the wine's character, though its quality is always serious, dark, intensely fruited, and sumptuously oaked. The second wine is called Virginie de Valandraud (Virginie is the name of Jean-Luc Thunevin's daughter). In 2000, meanwhile, the best single barrels of Merlot, Cabernet Sauvignon, Cabernet Franc, and Malbec were kept aside, blended, and given the name of Jean-Luc Thunevin's granddaughter Axelle (the daughter of Virginie) to create a black wine of truffle-laden exoticism.

Valrose
33370 Fargues St-Hilaire, Tel: 05 56 68 33 83
This 5-ha St-Estèphe was the co-project of the late Jean-Michel Arcaute and Gérard Neraudau: quality improvements were in hand at the time of Arcaute's tragic death.

Verdignan
33180 St-Seurin-de-Cadourne, Tel: 05 56 59 31 02, Fax: 05 56 81 32 35
Like Coufran, a superbly sited property on a deep gravel mound owned by the Miailhe family; Sociando-Mallet is a neighbour. Fine value.

La Vieille Cure
33141 Saillans, Tel: 05 57 84 32 05, Fax: 05 57 74 39 83
This American-owned, 40-ha Fronsac estate overlooks the River Isle, facing Lalande-de-Pomerol; and in some ways its soft, lush style is more typical of Lalande than boisterous, chewy Fronsac. It is justly popular for its value.

Vieux Château Certan ❍❍
33500 Pomerol, Tel: 05 57 51 17 33, Fax: 05 57 25 35 08
Situated next to a dangerous fiveways crossroads in Pomerol, this 13.5-ha property is run with quiet acuity by the retiring Alexandre Thienpont. Before Pétrus' ascent to stardom, VCC was considered to produce the greatest wine in the AOC. Its vineyards are adjacent to those of Pétrus and La Conseillante among others; two separate parcels lie near Le Pin. It is rarely one of the lusher, showier Pomerols, partly due to its varietal mix (the two Cabernet varieties account for 40% of plantings), partly due to its well-drained gravels, and partly due to the Thienpont's traditional approach to vinification and reluctance to use 100% new oak. At its best (in 1998 and 2000), this is a wine of spellbinding grace and charm, soft yet intense raspberry fruit, and seductive floral perfume. If Pétrus is the Latour of Pomerol, then VCC is its Margaux.

Vieux Château Champ de Mars
33350 Castillon
This 17-ha property in the middle of Côtes de Castillon has a fine stock of old vines which, combined with low yields and new wave St-Emilion techniques, is producing excitingly dense, concentrated wines. The Cuvée Johanna is not a selected parcel, but the same blend as the main wine given the Burgundy techniques of pre-fermentation maceration and fermentation in small vats with *pigeage* (punching down of the cap of skins and pips).

Vieux Robin
33340 Bégadan, Tel: 05 56 41 50 64, Fax: 05 56 41 37 85
Médoc property, half the production of which goes into the scented, complex, and impressive Cuvée Bois de Lunier.

Villa Bel-Air
33650 St-Morillon, Tel: 05 56 20 29 35, Fax: 05 56 78 44 80
This 46-ha property in the forested tranquillity of the Graves is owned and run by Jean-Michel Cazes of Lynch Bages. The 2000 red was soft, creamy, charming, and precocious, offering fine value.

Vray Croix de Gay
33500 Néac, Tel: 05 57 51 64 58, Fax: 05 57 51 41 56
Small, 4-ha property, enviably sited next to Lafleur and Croix de Gay, and in the same ownership as Siaurac in Lalande-de-Pomerol. The winemaking seems to lack delicacy, with sometimes obtrusive, abrasive tannins.

Yon Figeac
33330 St-Emilion, Tel: 05 57 74 49 59, Fax: 05 57 74 47 58
This well-sited, 24.5-ha estate is the top Bordeaux property of Bernard Germain who, at Fesles, Varennes, and Chamboureau, has accomplished so much in the Loire Valley in recent years. The smoky, thick-textured 2000 vintage suggested that this may be a name to watch in future. The Germain group also owns 10 other Bordeaux properties.

d'Yquem ❍❍❍
33210 Sauternes, Tel: 05 57 98 07 07, Fax: 05 57 98 07 08
No property in France dominates its appellation in the way that Yquem dominates Sauternes. At 113 ha, Yquem is the biggest property in the AOC; it sits in the centre, at the highest point; it produces what is its unquestionably its greatest wine. When wine lovers get together to reminisce about "the greatest bottle I have ever drunk", Yquem (from a wide spread of vintages) seems to be spoken about more frequently and more passionately than any rival. It is one of the most difficult wines on earth to make, yet the tradition of quality and selectivity is such here that it is one of the most consistent of all great wines (poor vintages are declassified altogether). This was the property that, having been in the Lur Saluces family since 1785, was finally swallowed up by the LVMH luxury goods conglomerate in 1999. Not without rancour: Comte Alexandre de Lur Saluces, who had made the wine with such success and determination since 1968, fought the sale in the courts against his brother and other family members, but lost. Under LVMH, he continues to make the wine.

So what's so special? Terroir, of course, yet this is a terroir which humans have had to assist. The hilltop dome on which Yquem sits is composed of sandy gravels over limy clays, and the clay means that the water table is high here. In the 19th century, over 10 km of drainage pipes were installed; Yquem would not be Yquem without these. Its position at the top of slopes above the distant Garonne and the nearby Ciron is ideal for bathing its vines rhythmically in autumn morning mist and afternoon sunshine. Tiny yields (10 hl/ha or, famously, one glass per vine) and immense patience in waiting for the perfect moment to pick each bunch of grapes (150 harvesters can spend up to six weeks each autumn at the château) mean that the raw materials are as perfect as nature permits; the wines are then fermented in new oak, and spend a leisurely three-and-a-half years in cask before being bottled unfiltered. The long period spent in cask means that up to 20% of each vintage of Yquem is lost as what distillers call "the angel's share"; there is further elimination of unsatisfactory casks at the final blending stage, even after great vintages. The result of all these efforts is a golden sweet wine of dazzling concentration, complexity, and unction capable, in most vintages, of ageing for 50 years or more. In great vintages like 1986 and 1988, it seems to acquire extra dimensions of subtlety and flavour beyond those of other properties; a vintage like 1983, by contrast, impresses because it is more beautiful than its appellation rivals — and perhaps than any other wine on earth.

Southwest France

In Search of Lost Wine No part of France is further from Paris and access to overseas markets than this "high country", a fact which nearly snuffed out the lives of its dark, thunderclap wines. Now they're back – though with a softer, sheenier style than in the past.

The train slid slowly into Cahors railway station. I stood with my rucksack on my back, ready to alight. (A small pleasure of train travel: the chance to alight.) There in front of me was a long, still line of open freight carriages, extravagantly laden. Not coal, not sand; still less grapes or wine. This was the fruit of the *causses*: wood. Massive trunks, deposited into hefty cradle-cars, the whole train forming a giant battering ram.

I had rattled through the wild woods to get here; more wild woods lay further and beyond. The weather was as rough and rude as the forested hills. It was the end of April, yet the sky was grey, cold, and blustery, shaking chill rain over the small city from time to time. The woman who ran the railway buffet told me, more sympathetically than accurately, that today was one of the ice saints' days. My drinking companions, this Sunday morning, were all north Africans, well-wrapped against the cold, sipping coffee, smoking and calling to each other across the room, lifting their hands with an indolence suited to hotter climates. Company, of course, creates its own warmth.

I walked the narrow streets of the empty, quiet town, squeezed like toothpaste onto a peninsula in the serpentine Lot. The *ruelles* were full of jokes: a mesmerizing clock, powered by shuffling ball-bearings; a musical fountain on which one could play tunes, by covering the small water apertures with one's fingers. These delicious mechanical delights were the work of a man called Michel Zachariov. My own mind, so weakly mechanical, saluted his delightedly.

By dinner time, the rain was drenching. Few restaurants were open; the Auberge du Vieux Cahors was one. I ordered a bottle of 1998 Château Lagrezette. It was dark, balanced, and thick-textured, tasting like minced railway lines with powdered stones sprinkled over the top; if there was fruit in it, it was prunes, and coffee too, and smoke. Wild wine. The food was average but the meal was great: just fifteen euros to include a thick slice of foie gras, and then duck breast with tagliatelle and beans and the rest; no sooner have I finished one dish than the next arrives. The chef is upstairs – I imagine him watching television, maybe football, and cooking for his small, half-empty restaurant with one eye on the screen. For pudding I chose Île Flottante and the waitress (who has hair the colour of treacle pudding) calls up the shaft of the dumb waiter "*Une Île!*", and down it comes in no more than thirty seconds. I eat every morsel of this meal.

Afterwards I walk again to the Pont Valentré which only those on foot can now use, though carts in their millions have trundled across it, incising its stones, in times past. It's floodlit on this cold, wet night; I am the only one on the bridge. The roar of the weir beneath draws me towards it. Using my umbrella to shield the glare from the floodlights, I look down one hundred feet to the water and see

countless illuminated raindrops seethe on the Lot like a Doré engraving of medieval despair. The water is black, as black as the wine once was. As black as the wine is once more.

Overcoming history

The wines of Southwest France have been, over the last two centuries, through a second Dark Age. In Roman times, these lands were swiftly colonized (by 50 BC) for wood and for wine. Bordeaux's early prosperity was based not on its own wine production, but on tolls: a form of commercial extortion. The Lot, the Aveyron, the Viaur, the Tarn, and the Garonne all flow through Bordeaux, with the Dordogne but a short journey away. Throughout the Middle Ages, wines from this "high country" region, the Haut-Pays, were considered superior in quality to those from Bordeaux; indeed "Bordeaux wine" was often blended with the "black wine" from Cahors and other nearby regions in order to give it the body and stuffing which wealthy northern European clients valued. By the mid-nineteenth century, the production of Cahors and Gaillac rivalled that of Bordeaux itself. Yet Bordeaux consistently used – or, to modern eyes, abused – its position, by insisting that wines from the Haut-Pays could not leave Bordeaux's famous Port de la Lune before Christmas, or by insisting that Cahors used smaller barrels than

Bordeaux... yet paid the same duty per barrel. These discriminations continue to rankle with growers today. You will not hear much good of Bordeaux spoken in the vineyards of Cahors or Madiran.

Phylloxera, when it came, devastated the Haut-Pays. Regions such as Bordeaux or Burgundy had the international renown to recover as swiftly as viticultural advances allowed. Cahors and Gaillac, by contrast, were remote and agriculturally challenging; when the vines sickened and died, the wine-growers left for the cities – or for a new life in South America. By the 1950s, mere fragments of vineyard remained, in the hands of ageing growers whose only hope lay in the cooperative movement. Twenty years of AOC production had passed the Southwest by. The bloodline had almost been lost.

Almost. Three elements, though, have combined over the last decade to make the Southwest one of the New France's most startlingly improved wine regions: great grape varieties, forgotten terroirs of outstanding quality, and the burning desire to prove a point. There is still some way to go, and in terms of raw size the Southwest will never recapture its past grandeur. Cahors, for example, has around 6,000 ha (14,800 acres) under vine today. This may expand a little, but it will never again have the 40,000 ha (99,000 acres) it had planted in the middle of the nineteenth century. The Southwest will, though, make great wines again; indeed it is already doing so.

"My formula is simple. Every morning, I ask myself if I can try to improve the quality of my wine. To do that, I use the most searching and the most reliable tool: tasting. That's how you detect what works and what doesn't, what needs changing, what could be improved. Tasting brings you closer to your terroir. The work you carry out year-round in the vineyard can immediately be detected – in the glass."

ALAIN BRUMONT

The twists and turns of the serpentine Lot provide fine bedroom views as well as
◀ *superb river-gravel vineyards.*

This is not an easy region to understand: no other region of France can rival the Southwest for sheer heterogeneity. Before taking a systematic look at the wine-growing terroirs of the Southwest in The Adventure of the Land, though, here are a few snapshots from the region to convey that diversity – and that point-proving passion.

Snapshot one: Luc de Conti

I was at Bordeaux's trade fair Vinexpo; this was my favourite stand. All the others were tailored confections, perspex wonderlands, brand-builders' pleasure domes, bottom-line pavilions; this was just a primitive, functional, disgracefully unsightly, and heavily wine-stained stand. It belonged to the bunch of producers who call themselves the Vinarchistes. Among them, Luc de Conti.

He found me a chair and we sat down together. In the middle of the Vinexpo hurly-burly, he seemed remarkably calm, slightly built, with smiling eyes. "Don't class me as a biodynamicist," he said; but his concerns were those common to all of France's greatest wine producers outside the hierarchical and conservative world of Bordeaux. "The soil is a cadaver. It's lost its capacity to digest dead leaves. Steiner's ideas were adapted to what were fundamentally healthy soils; ours have been bombarded with chemicals for fifty years. I won't begin to make Steiner preparations for another ten years; our soils won't be healthy enough until then." He calls himself an "agrobiologist", and is slowly nursing his forty ha (ninety-nine acres) back to life with compost, with seaweed, with silica.

His other great concern, almost an obsession, is with lees – one of wine's life forms which school-book oenology has little time for, discarding them like sewage. After fermentation, de Conti sorts his lees and makes what he describes as a kind of mayonnaise with them using a mixer; this is then reintroduced back into the wine to nourish it. He does no racking, relying exclusively on micro-oxygenation to avoid reduction problems; the lees help in this process, too. Little or no sulphur means that everything in the cellar must be spotlessly clean. Each year, he makes a starter barrel to check his yeast populations; in an "agrobiological" domain like his, he claims, there are up to 300 different yeast strains, whereas conventionally farmed domains have no more than twenty or so. We taste his wines together: they are cashmere-soft, gathered and folded together with the delicacy of a nurse bandaging a wound. Another originality, in these days of a red wine aesthetic entirely predicated on darkness and power: four *pigeages* only, and a 25°C (77°F) fermentation temperature. "*On cherche la sous-extraction* (we look for under-extraction) – I want to avoid anything hard or brutal." Under-extraction? A *vinarchiste* indeed.

Snapshot two: Clos Triguedina

It was a shame Jean-Luc Baldès wasn't around when I called; he's the eighth generation of his family to grow vines and make wine at Clos Triguedina in Cahors, a historical continuity few others can match. The enthusiastic Arnaud Bergeron, his *chef de culture*, gestured towards a scruffy white car. "Let's take a look at the vines," he said.

We drove up. And up – winding through the pretty forest scrubland, strewn with shrubby oaks. From time to time, among the trees, Arnaud would point out the remains of old dry stone walls. These were the tombstones of pre-phylloxera Cahors: long-abandoned terraces for ghostly vineyards, now consumed by leaf, thorn, and twig. The journey skywards taught me a lesson in terroir I was to see repeated all over the Southwest: most of the vines grow on former river terraces left dry and vacant by a restless watercourse.

Higher still, though, and we came to a white vineyard: blanched pebbles gleamed in the late afternoon sun. This was the *causse* itself: the limestone upland which lies above the terraces, and which forms

Alain Brumont

Alain Brumont is the Citizen Kane of Madiran. That, at any rate, is my little contribution to an ongoing debate. Riffle through his glowing press pack, and you'll see that he's also been called the Philippe de Rothschild of Madiran, the Garibaldi of the Southwest, the Che of the vines, and the Louis XIV of the vines. Hard to be both Che and Louis XIV at the same time, you'd think, yet we're dealing with a complex character.

He is, though, not an easy man to get on with; he began by falling out with his father, and has continued by falling out with almost everyone else he has come across. "He lives on Planet Wine," said his second wife Caty to me. "Not on Planet Earth. And that's difficult for terrestrial relationships...." The result of a lifetime of profound disagreements is that Brumont does everything on his own. He has built the largest domain in Madiran, with over ten per cent of the AOC and more than 150 ha (370 acres) of superb vineyard sites. He green-harvests three times. He vinifies everything his way: no micro-oxygenation here. He has developed his own system of auto-pigeage. He is a passionate believer in new wood. He has high-density vineyard plantings of more than 8,500 plants per ha. He makes his own compost (with horse, sheep, and cow manure, pomace, and ground stones). He's building his own four-star hotel; his own château. He even tries to sell much of his harvest himself to 60,000 private clients. "For me, to make wine, I have to refuse everything which comes from outside." And this is why, in what must sometimes be a lonely over-achieving grandeur, he reminds me of Citizen Kane.

Pascal Verhaeghe

Mathematics was Pascal Verhaeghe's first love. "I wasn't," he remembers, "interested in wine. I was the son of a wine-grower, but it just seemed to me to be a lot of hard work." And then? A friend was working with Jean-Marie Guffens in Burgundy; Verhaeghe was invited over. "I was planning to be there for an hour or two; I stayed three days. After that I gave up my maths. Jean-Marie helped me to discover a lot about wine, and about the pleasure of wine." Verhaeghe worked with Guffens, and also with Saintsbury in California's Carneros, before taking over the family domain in Cahors with his brother Jean-Marc in 1987; Luc de Conti has been another friend and mentor. Understanding how to achieve full ripeness with Malbec; deriving richness from lees contact; barrel-fermenting red wines to get texture and complexity without woody notes; a Charter of Quality for Cahors – Verhaeghe has done much for this brilliant but forgotten terroir. Now, with Marcevol in Roussillon, a new chapter begins.

The Laplace Family

Château Aydie sits high on a hillside. François Laplace put two chairs out at the head of the vineyard. We sat down; the afternoon was growing cool. He showed me his place on earth. Madiran, he said, was constituted by four side valleys tucked away in an elbow of the River Adour, and we could see most of them spreading away in front of us. Occasionally the French Air Force would make deafeningly low passes over the region, but in the silence that sandwiched this carbon thunder, we could hear church bells ringing in the distance, and dogs barking. This is dog country: everyone has dogs, big Pyrenean shepherd dogs which come bounding out to meet you, brave and dim, slavering appreciatively at sight of your calves and buttocks. There are tractors, too; there are cows; there is maize. Until recently, there were more of all these things than vines. Just look at that soil: pale, rich clay. It doesn't look like vine soil at all: too lush, too stoneless. The surface, though, can be deceptive; underneath huge limestone boulders "float in it," as Alain Brumont says, "like clouds in a summer sky".

I have never met wine-growers of greater seriousness than the three Laplace brothers. François is in charge of commerce; Jean-Luc looks after all the winemaking; and the rugged, handsome, and taciturn Bernard is in charge of the vineyards. Their sister Marie administers the domain, and their father Pierre still helps around the place. Everything is impeccably clean, minutely organized, deeply considered, exhaustively refined. They smile little; they think much. Perhaps Tannat, clay, and an outlook of stern Victorian industriousness all go together.

The late-ripening Tannat has certainly been a challenge for Madiran's growers, despite its fine quality potential. (A curiosity of Tannat, François Laplace told me, is that it is impossible to machine-harvest: the machine's percussion shakes all the leaves off the plant, but the grapes remain firmly attached to the vine.) As its name suggests, Tannat is ferociously tannic, a sabre-toothed tiger among grape varieties. The traditional way of taming it was to put it into big wooden vats for some years before broaching it. When the AOC was first established, back in 1948, the wines had to be aged for three years before release (it's now just one year). In the 1980s, as in most French regions, stainless steel tanks began to replace the old wooden vats, partly for reasons of hygiene and partly to emphasize the increasingly sought-after fruit flavours. Disaster! Tannat not only kept its sabre-toothed tannins, but it also proved to be a variety hugely prone to reduction; the wines began to stink. They then had to be ceaselessly racked, moved, and oxygenated, which in turn left them bruised, battered, and fleshless; just as tannic, save now rather more dryly so.

This being Madiran, everyone put their furrowed brows together to try to find a solution. And they found one. It's called micro-oxygenation: the streaming of tiny beads of oxygen through the wine at different stages of its development, and its inventor was a cousin of the Laplaces called Patrick Ducournau. Much of the development work was done at Aydie, and the original patent was a joint one shared by Ducournau and the Laplaces. Jean-Luc Laplace gave me a crash course in

micro-oxygenation. My layman's understanding of it is found on page 205.

As it turned out, this was probably the most significant French development in vinification techniques of the 1990s, and micro-oxygenation is now practised in almost all of France's red wine regions. In Bordeaux, its effect has been enormous; little Madiran has changed the way that France's greatest red wine tastes. Before this breakthrough, there was much talk of reducing the level of Tannat in Madiran below the sixty per cent stipulated by the AOC; on the day I called on the Laplaces, there was a commission from INAO in the region to study proposals to raise the proportion of Tannat to eighty per cent. Many already use one hundred per cent Tannat anyway.

We tasted. "These are truly wines for food," stressed Jean Luc. "They're not made for sipping in front of the TV. They're very difficult to taste on their own. It's essential to decant them." The black samples looked gorgeous in the plain, shapely, low-bottomed decanters which, I don't doubt, have been personally designed after rigorous late-night taste tests by the Laplaces. And the wines?

If you could taste a winter night, this is what it would taste like. Smoke from fires, the blackness of cloudy night skies, fruits as shocking as the north wind, tannins with the power of storm-torn earth: it's all here. Sweetened – yes, that was another Laplace discovery, that barriques soften rather than intensify the tannins of Tannat – by oak. And, improbable as it may seem, delicious. You just need to know what you're in for. "Our wines are," as Jean-Luc says, "the absolute opposite of burgundy."

Cahors' second major terroir. From here, the valley of the Lot opened up before us in remarkably perfect silence, the nearest press of people now many miles distant. A hoopoe bounded off into the blue air; purple orchids poked from the grasses at the vineyard's edge.

Baldès not only has a sense of history, but he is ready to experiment, too. He makes impressive Cahors – especially Prince Probus, which moves through the mouth with stately taurean power, all flank and dewlap; yet he's also created fine white wines from his highest vineyards in this overwhelmingly red wine area, including a superb Chenin Blanc-based dessert wine. Historical meditation has also led him to make "The New Black Wine".

What was the old black wine? André Jullien's 1816 description of this antique curiosity is fearsome. The grapes were put in the oven and baked, or alternatively crushed and the resulting must poured into a saucepan and boiled. After what must on occasion have been a troublesome and lengthy fermentation, the wine was often fortified, turning it into a kind of dry port. "Very useful," said Jullien, "for adding colour, body, and strength to feeble wines;" he also added, perhaps superfluously, that "they survive transportation well." The English name "black wine" was commonly used for these because they were popular with English clients.

Baldès's modern version is different (as, of course, it has to be in order to qualify as AOC Cahors). Arnaud Bergeron explained how the wine is made, using technology from the local prune industry. The Auxerrois grapes are picked, by hand, with a little *surmaturité*; they are then put into wooden boxes with grills at the bottom, and warm air is blown into the bottom of the box. The warm air rises; the grapes shrivel. The grapes are then pressed and fermented, before being aged in new oak barriques for eighteen months. "Black" in its modern sense is perhaps a misnomer (young Probus is blacker), but it makes dark, expressive, smoky wine with agreeable bitterness and sweetness.

Snapshot three: Robert Plageoles

Gaillac occupies a handsome, ramped horseshoe of vineyards up above the River Tarn. When I called in to see Robert Plageoles at his hillside domain, he was talking to a customer – or rather an acolyte, a slightly unhinged enthusiast who stayed with us all afternoon, gradually becoming more inebriated and more animated with each hour that passed. Plageoles himself is ostensibly a winemaker; it would be more accurate, though, to call him a viticultural archaeologist who happens to make wines in order to put certain theories and researches to the test. (His son Bernard, by contrast, is a

Widely spaced rows like these in Bergerac may be easy for machines, but they ▼ *make it harder to create quality wine.*

man of far fewer words and greater practical expedition.) Plageoles, his acolyte, and I passed our afternoon in some of the most abstruse wine speculations I have ever engaged in. Perhaps, I thought at one point, I had fallen back in time three or four centuries; Plageoles spoke of the Romans as if they had left just a year or two earlier. He described the *passerillage d'Hesiod* (grape-drying, Hesiod-style – which means, it turns out, a pinching of the stems on the vine, used for his sweet Ondenc) as if Hesiod was teaching at the local oenology school. Only the arrival of a disorientated Danish lorry driver brought us back to the twenty-first century.

Gaillac, according to Plageoles, rivalled Hermitage and Côte Rôtie as the greatest of Gallo-Roman vineyards. He has spent the last twenty years searching for the Gaillac grape varieties of the past: Mauzac Vert, Roux, and Noir, Ondenc, Duras, Prunelart (Cot à Queue Rouge). The rise of the "international" grape variety fills him with horror. "When I taste Merlot in Corbières it makes my hair stand on end and my stomach sick. We're in the process of betraying 2,000 years of history." Lots of his wines (and not just his *vin jaune*-like Mauzac Vin de Voile) have deliberate notes of oxidation. "Oxidation is a fault? Excuse me, but stupidity is a fault, too." The whites are green-fruited; the reds are pale and light, for serving chilled. In most ways they are untypical of Gaillac – yet Gaillac is an AOC with so many personalities that they seem perversely typical, too. Plageoles likes it like that. "*Le jour où on sait, on est deçu,*" he tells us ("the moment you finally know something, you are disappointed"). The acolyte rocks with laughter.

Snapshot four: Patrick Germain, Frédéric Ribes, and Marc Penavayre

Black wines in Cahors, historical wines in Gaillac, and then... well, what exactly? What is the Côtes du Frontonnais, with its Négrette grape variety, all about? Patrick Germain, evicted from his huge family estates in Algeria and Morocco, bought Bellevue la Fôret in 1974, and knew what he wanted to do there. "I didn't want to create a *grand vin*," he says, "but a *vin sympathetique*." As it turned out, he couldn't have chosen a better spot than Fronton or a better grape variety than Négrette with which to do exactly that. Its pepper-and-tobacco scents and its sour-fresh fruit make it the Beaujolais of the south, perfect for serving cellar-cool on a hot evening in Toulouse. Gulpable, heady: an aria. Pure joy of wine.

That, anyway, is what Négrette mixed with a little Syrah, Cabernet Franc, Cabernet Sauvignon, and Gamay gives you, with yields just the other side of fifty hl/ha, and machine-friendly vineyards planted with under 5,000 vines per ha. But then, of course, you want to do a little more. Having created a *vin sympa*, you begin to think that maybe it might be fun to make a *grand vin* after all.

Which is where Frédéric Ribes of Domaine Le Roc and Marc Penavayre of Château Plaisance come in. Ribes' top *cuvée* is a Négrette/Syrah blend called Don Quichotte produced from his best parcels, softly extracted by *pigeage* and given a year in older barriques and a year in tanks. In Don Quichotte, Fronton succeeds (analogically speaking) in moving south from Beaujolais towards the northern Rhône: this is a wine in which fresh flowers meet roasted coffee. Penavayre, by contrast, takes Fronton further north, towards Burgundy, with his Thibaut de Plaisance. It's also an oak-aged Négrette/Syrah blend, but this time it's an essay in dancing elegance, in liquorice-washed fresh fruit.

The simple country pleasures of Fronton, though, will never be far away. I arrive to meet Ribes an hour or so before sunset, and along with the taste of his cool, fresh, grateful *"classique" cuvée* I remember seeing the hams hanging from the cellar ceiling, their parchment-fawn fat lent a rich gold by the setting sun. When I arrived at Château Plaisance, meanwhile, I was late; I felt flustered. Penavayre's mother Simone smiled with broad and unhurried sympathy. *"Nous vivons dans une monde de précipitation* (we live in a hurried world)," she said, shaking her head, and we both chuckled over the folly of it all.

Snapshot five: Jean Casaubielh and friends

Daniel Craker, an young English winemaker who works with Jean-Bernard Larrieu at Clos Lapeyre, met me at Pau railway station in his aged silver Clio. We chugged out of town, and up into the hills. The Pyrénées gleamed in front of us. Cyclists were out and about, rolling through the newly warm air. I suddenly longed to be on a bike myself, to feel the bite of the gradient, the rush of the breeze, the scent of the fresh leaves, and to feed on the hypnotic snow-lure of those mountains.

We arrived at Domaine Guirardel. It's an old house, roomy and well-used, perched on a hillside and sheltered by a snug snood of woodland. We were met by a group of producers, all of whom had brought their wines to taste. First, though, we walked down into Jean Casaubielh's vineyards, which fall off the side of the hill beneath his garden. "The vines look at the Pyrénées and the sun," explained Jean; we did both ourselves. Jurançon's is a classic viticulture of opportunism: tiny parcels snuggled onto propitiously sunny, sheltered spots. In the right site, you can make vivid white wine of arresting intensity; in the wrong site, you won't get your maize ripe and even the cows will shiver. Each autumn the foehn wind comes billowing up out of Spain, pushing the rain away and ripening the tough, enduring Gros Manseng and Petit Manseng grapes. We walked up to Jean's garden: he wanted to show me, by way of proof against my snow-dazzled incredulity, the lavender, the palms, the orange tree, and the oleander, all of which survive, tubless and stationary, the sub-Pyrenean winter.

We tasted in the cellar, and talked among ourselves: Daniel, Jean, Pascal Labasse, the bear-like Charles Hours and the fastidious Henri Ramonteu. Outside the cellar door, the sunshine continued to cascade. Then Jean Casaubielh invited us in for lunch: into his bachelor living room (his wife died some years ago), dominated by its squat television set onto which the sunbeams tumbled. We ate a hilarious, joke-strewn lunch with lots of wine and plastic boxes of food from the local *traiteur*; its climax was a 1938 Bi de Prat from Guirardel. As we tasted this long-lost autumn and its stowed, secret fruits, still fresh after a fifty-year hibernation, we fell silent.

Micro-oxygenation: invented here

Wines need to breathe. Just as fish do. Which is to say that too much air is fatal (they become oxidized and spoil), but too little is very nearly as bad (they become reduced and spoil, too); like fish, they need just a little oxygen to keep them fresh and healthy. How do you

▲   *The black wines of Cahors have been warming old bones for far longer than the garnet wines of the Médoc.*

give wines the air they need? Traditionally, the answer is by keeping them in wooden containers (which are porous) and by moving them from one container to another every month or two (this process is called racking). A huge amount of thought and experiment has gone into the way that wines are vinified over the last thirty years, but very little into the way that wines are dosed with oxygen. Until, that is, the wine producers of Madiran ran into colossal reduction problems after they began to put their Tannat-based red wine into stainless steel.

Thus the idea of micro-oxygenation was born. The technique addresses wine's need for oxygen; using it, you can stabilize colour, improve the structure and texture of a wine, and avoid the stinky characters which come from reduction. Wines can be micro-oxygenated during alcoholic fermentation to improve yeast performance and avoid the risk of stuck fermentations. After alcoholic fermentation and before malolactic fermentation, micro-oxygenation will help fix colour, provide rounder, juicier tannins, and provide richer and more articulate flavours; during barrel-ageing the benefits are much the same, with improved aromatic complexity and further rounding out of the tannic mass. This, of course, is not the result of the oxygen alone, but also of the fact that the wine can nourish itself on its lees (uncommon in the past for red wines, which were almost always racked off their lees).

The amounts of oxygen dribbled into the bottom of the wine are very small (hence the term *micro-bulleur* or micro-bubbler to describe the equipment which does this); indeed the oxygen itself is "eaten" by the wine and never actually reaches the surface. The oxygen doses can be computer controlled and automatically administered, day and night. Manual micro-oxygenation, for individual barriques of wine, can be carried out via a wand-like piece of equipment called a *cliqueur*, because of the clicking noise it makes as the oxygen is trickled into the wine.

The Adventure of the Land

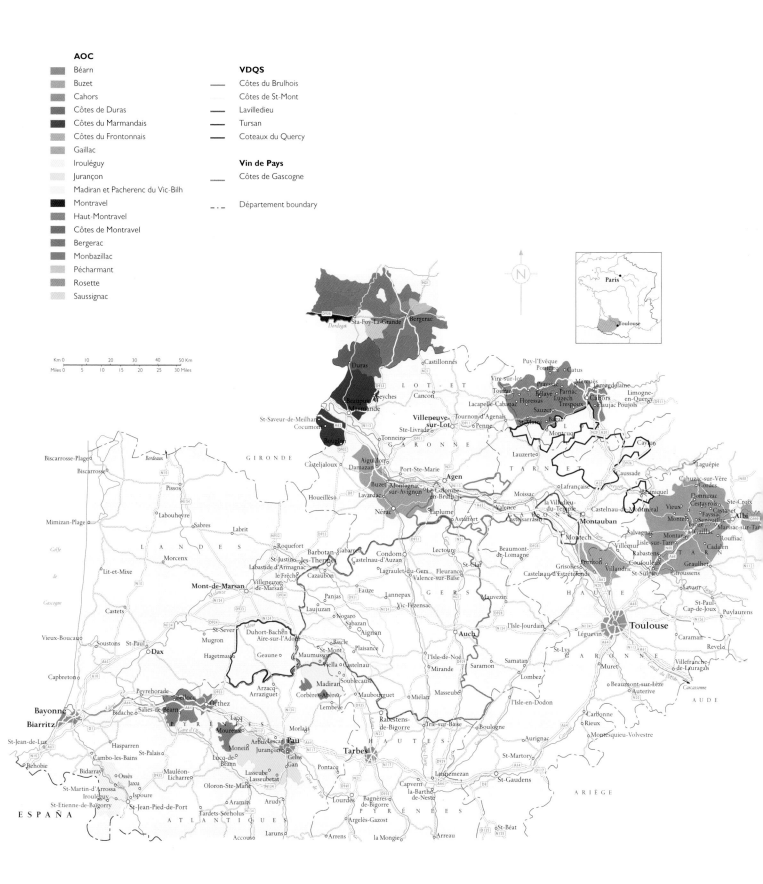

AOC
- Béarn
- Buzet
- Cahors
- Côtes de Duras
- Côtes du Marmandais
- Côtes du Frontonnais
- Gaillac
- Irouléguy
- Jurançon
- Madiran et Pacherenc du Vic-Bilh
- Montravel
- Haut-Montravel
- Côtes de Montravel
- Bergerac
- Monbazillac
- Pécharmant
- Rosette
- Saussignac

VDQS
- Côtes du Brulhois
- Côtes de St-Mont
- Lavilledieu
- Tursan
- Coteaux du Quercy

Vin de Pays
- Côtes de Gascogne

- - - Département boundary

Geologically and administratively, the Southwest is a mess. A delicious mess, admittedly, but a mess nonetheless. The region begins by hanging on the coat-tails of Bordeaux: Bergerac is under an hour from the centre of St-Emilion. By the time we get to Gaillac and the Côtes du Frontonnais, we are knocking on the door of the Languedoc. The region finishes in Basque country, with the mysterious green-sloped Irouléguy. Grape varieties, soils, and climates all vary hugely; it's a region, if you like, of convenience. Or inconvenience. We're deep in the countryside here; most journeys unravel down meandering lanes.

Let's begin in **Bergerac**. Why, first of all, is this not part of Bordeaux? The present-day answer is political; the historical answer has more to do with religion. *Département* boundaries change here: Bordeaux belongs to the Gironde; Bergerac to Dordogne. Bergerac was a Protestant area, whereas Bordeaux was Catholic; Bergerac, too, enjoyed an exemption to the *privilège de Bordeaux*, which meant that it alone among the wines of the Haut-Pays could get its wines downriver and off towards foreign markets (especially, in Bergerac's case, Holland) without the let and hindrance of the Bordelais. The fact is, though, that in pure terroir terms Bergerac is still part of greater Bordeaux: the starfish limestone and Fronsadais molasse of Bordeaux's Right Bank continues upstream here, interspersed with the sands, gravels, and slope wash brought down by the river in its steep tumble from the Auvergne. Montravel is adjacent to the Côtes de Castillon; Saussignac is embroidered into Entre-Deux-Mers.

As these barely familiar names suggest, the appellation system here descends into one of its periodic flurries of complication. Bergerac and **Côtes de Bergerac** are the fundamental regional appellations for both red and white wine; there is no delimitational difference between them, merely a theoretical fillip of alcohol. (Côtes de Bergerac is for red wine only, whereas Bergerac is for red and white.) Sweet wines from this general area are sold as **Côtes de Bergerac Moelleux**. There are also a number of *cru* appellations, mainly for dry white or sweet white wines. Why not red? For marketing reasons as much as the aptitude of the terroirs: the Dutch loved sweet whites. Nowadays this vocation makes much less sense, and growers in **Montravel**, for example, have recently won the long overdue right to begin making some of the increasingly fleshy reds for which the Côtes de Castillon is now well-known. **Pécharmant** is the other exception to this red-less rule (its dry whites are mere Bergerac and most of its sweet whites Rosette); iron in the sands over the limestone base favour the lightly structured reds specified by the AOC regulations. The sole dry white wine *cru* in the rest of the region is Montravel. Sweet wines, by contrast, can be produced in the *crus of* **Rosette, Côtes de Montravel, Haut-Montravel, Saussignac**, and, most famously of all, **Monbazillac**. Of these different appellations, it is Monbazillac which has the biggest stamp of personality about it: this can be a prodigiously sweet white wine which may not quite have the finesse of Sauternes or Barsac, but which more than makes up in honeyed volume and succulent, thrashing power. It is often, indeed, the very sweetest of all France's sweet wines. The vines do not grow, as those of Sauternes do, on sandy gravel mounds, but on a kind of mineral sandwich in which the slices of bread are composed of limestone while the filling is a richer marl and moist clayey sand. Monbazillac marks the highest point within Bergerac; it is here that the autumn river mists clear first, favouring both botrytis and the shrivelling, baking, and roasting which great sweet wines need. Throughout the Bergerac region Bordeaux grape varieties are used.

Côtes de Duras continues the Bergerac theme: it lies adjacent to both Saussignac and Bergerac, sharing the same soils and Bordelais grape varieties. You might think it had a hard job differentiating its whites (sweet and dry) and reds from those in the rest of the *peloton*

hereabouts, and you'd be right. Things are marginally easier for the **Côtes du Marmandais**, whose two zones flank the Garonne, because at least it has some genuine Southwestern grape varieties to play with including Fer Servadou, Abouriou, and Malbec (Cot). These are often mixed with Bordeaux varieties; indeed the over-flexible AOC regulations also permit Gamay and Syrah. Of the two terroirs, that which lies north of the Garonne resembles Duras and Bergerac (limestone, shale, and molasse), while the more promising southern sector offers some tasty gravel terraces not dissimilar to those of Sauternes and Graves downriver.

Further upriver and further southeast, meanwhile, lie **Buzet** and **Côtes du Brulhois**, facing the prune country of Agen across the dragonfly-patrolled water. The former is a muddle-soiled AOC, cursed yet again with the sweet pain of growing Bordeaux varieties and making a duller job of them than Bordeaux does, despite great efforts by the local co-op. The latter, a 250-ha (620-acre) VDQS with two co-ops and four individual producers, resumes the work on Southwestern varieties begun in the Marmandais: Tannat, Cot, and Fer Servadou are permitted along with the Bordeaux classics, and Brulhois lays claim to a "black wine" tradition. That's the theory, anyway; for the time being it outruns practice by a half-marathon. Perhaps the involvement of French singer Francis Cabrel here will help.

We are, though, getting ahead of ourselves. Just downstream of Agen, the Lot couples with the Garonne. Trace the green Lot back upstream, and during its most serpentine stretches you will find **Cahors**. The odd element in this much-improved AOC is that it is a dual-terroir region. You would expect, therefore, to find two entirely different styles of wine, corresponding to those two terroirs. There are indeed two styles of Cahors: serious, dark, close-textured, minerally meditative wines and lighter, easygoing quaffing wines. Everything to do with viticultural ambition, in other words, and almost nothing to do with terroir. For that, we may have to wait another fifty years.

So what are they, these two terroirs? The Lot cuts its winding way through an arid limestone plateau at this point: the *causse*. Some vines are up on that stony, oak-scattered, truffle-nursing plateau. The rest, the most, are down in the valley, rooted into the multimineral gravel terraces left by the river as it has pushed its way into greater and greater convolutions. Wine-growing is easier in the valley (less drought, less frost) but great wines can be produced in both locations – and they do have one mineral component in common. The river gravels are full of ironstones, and up on the *causse*, too, long-term weathering has created numerous sinks in which iron oxides precipitated from ground waters have gathered. Iron was once smelted here. The AOC is for reds only (whites go to market as Vins de Pays) based on at least seventy per cent of Cot (Malbec, here paradoxically called Auxerrois), with Merlot and Tannat among the complementary varieties. Stretching away south on the *causse* is the new VDQS of **Coteaux du Quercy**: look out for good things from those prepared to work hard on this challenging terroir.

Further east up the Lot are the two little VDQS zones of **Vins d'Entraygues et du Fel** and **Vins d'Estaing**, and the AOC of **Marcillac**. The first two are minute (just ten ha/twenty-five acres in Entraygues et du Fel), and gloriously complicated. Fel has schist, while Entraygues has granitic sand: the former favours reds based on Fer Servadou, Cabernet, and Gamay, while the latter suits Chenin-based whites. Estaing's tiny limestone terraces (just seven ha/ seventeen acres) are planted with Arboriou, Moussaygues, and Gamay for reds, and Chenin and Rousselou for whites. Marcillac, meanwhile, where the 150 ha (370 acres) of present-day vineyards are all that is left of an astonishing 5,000 ha (12,350 acres) of vines in 1870, continues the ferrous theme of Cahors with reds made from Fer Servadou (locally

called Mansois) grown on terraces of an iron-rich red clay called rougier. There are some limestone *causse* vineyards, too. Marcillac's original role was to slake the thirsts of the coal-miners of nearby Decazeville.

Let's return to the Garonne as it makes its way down from Toulouse, picking up the waters of the Tarn, the Viaur, and the Aveyron as it does so. The VDQS of **Lavilledieu** and the AOC of **Côtes du Frontonnais** keep Toulouse well-watered with their light, peppery, lip-smacking reds, grown on modest, gently raked river terraces whose mineral elements include clay, silt, sand, gravel, and pebbles. They owe their character more to the Négrette grape (balanced by a huge range of complementary varieties including both Cabernets, Gamay, and Syrah) than to any particular distinctions of terroir.

Further up the Tarn comes **Gaillac**, an AOC with a long and proud historical record, but one whose multiple complications act as a check on its modern-day progress. Gaillac is positioned midway between the Atlantic and the Mediterranean, between Bordeaux and Languedoc, between the past and the present. A lot of wine is produced here, but only a third is AOC (another third is Vin de Pays and the rest is Vin de Table). "This is the first time in living memory," Alain Boulanger, the *président* of the local Interprofession told me, "that wine-growers here have been paid more for producing less." The AOC itself straddles the river, though most of the vineyards are sited on the north bank, which rises steadily through sand and gravel terraces to clay-limestone hillsides and finally to the wood-shaded limestone plateau around Cordes. These are often deep, rich (though varied) soils, and it is not uncommon to see vineyards next to fields of grain or of maize; mechanical harvesting dominates. There is also some alluvial land under vines near the river, while south of the river there are gravel terraces and gravelly clay soils near Cunac, too. Most of the AOC's production is of disappointingly easygoing and unambitious red wines based on Duras, Fer Servadou (locally called Braucol), Syrah, and Gamay. The whites are more interesting thanks to two indigenous varieties, the appley Mauzac and the more vegetal Len de l'El (also spelt Loin de l'Oeil), though neither of these is ever likely to·have much international appeal. Prettier wines, in truth, are made with Muscadelle. The great viticultural archeologist Robert Plageoles works hard at producing wines from permitted though rare varieties such as Ondenc and Prunelart, though none follow his lead. In addition to dry and sweet white wines, there are also two sorts of sparkling wine. Perlé (or Fraîcheur Perlée) has a bare prickle created by gas from the malolactic fermentation. Gaillac Mousseux, by contrast, is a fully sparkling wine made either by the Champagne method,. or by the *méthode Gaillacoise* or *méthode rurale*, where the termination of the initial alcoholic fermentation creates the sparkle in the bottle. Further up the Tarn, finally, is the VDQS area of **Millau** or **Côtes de Millau**. Gamay and Syrah are the principal varieties used for the reds and Chenin Blanc for the whites; these are generally light and slender wines, not dissimilar in style to those of the Côtes d'Auvergne on the other side of the Massif Central.

Almost all of the Southwestern vineyards we have examined so far owe their existence to the action of a congregation of rivers. The astonishing truth is that every single drop of water in all of those rivers will end up flowing past Château Latour and the Blayais nuclear power station. The vast area, in other words, forms just part of the drainage basin which eventually meets the sea in the Gironde Estuary; little wonder that the Bordelais were able to strangle these vineyards into commercial submission in the past. The remainder of the Southwest's vineyards, by contrast, belong to a different story. We now join a second drainage basin: that which meets the sea at Bayonne. We cross the pastoral spiritland of Armagnac, and approach the Pyrénées. We begin to hear the strange jangle of Basque.

The transition is marked by the most successful and impressive of all of the Southwest's VDQS wines: **Côtes de St-Mont**. Like the hugely successful Vins de Pays denomination of **Côtes de Gascogne**, this owes its existence to the determination of Gascony's grape growers to find new means of expressing their vineyards in a world which drinks less Armagnac than it used to. Côtes de Gascogne's success has been chiefly based on whites produced from Armagnac grape varieties (Ugni Blanc and Colombard) given cunning market appeal by cool fermentation and clever use of residual sugar – in other words, by winemaking strategies rather than by any notable expression of terroir. Côtes de St-Mont, by contrast, is a VDQS in which terroir does speak clearly. It booms out of the sands and loamy clays of the southern Bas-Armagnac, adjacent to Madiran and not dissimilar to the soils and slopes of Madiran itself. Some seventy per cent or more of Tannat for the red wines, and the use of Arrufiac, Manseng, and Courbu balanced with Sémillon and Sauvignon for the white wines, reinforces the kinship. These non-brandy grape varieties, in other words, make of St-Mont a mini-Madiran, a junior Pacherenc.

Madiran itself, and its white wine alter ego **Pacherenc du Vic-Bilh**, occupy a single AOC zone on the left bank of the Adour as it makes its way down to Bayonne, basking in lush rural countryside between the Landes and the Pyrénées. The combination of rich clay-loams concealing limestone boulders, and a rippling series of gentle valley slopes, has proved ideal in particular for the red Tannat grape variety (balanced with the two Cabernets and Fer Servadou). Madiran's reds are a French ultimate. No other French reds (not Cornas, nor Hermitage, nor Gigondas, nor Bandol) can truly match them for sheer tannic power and dark, smoky, battlefield force. They are Mephistolean – sometimes problematically so. Yet the ingenuity and energy of local producers has produced astonishingly impressive results from this AOC over the last decade. In 1945 just a few hectares were cultivated here; now it produces some of France's most challenging yet rewarding red wines. The drastic improvement in Pacherenc is more recent still, with some finely detailed and gratifyingly complex dessert wines to rival those of Jurançon emerging in the last few years. Next to Madiran lies the VDQS of **Tursan**. Tannat, too, is used here, together with the two Cabernets and Fer Servadou, as is the rarely seen Baroque variety for white wines

(complemented by Manseng and Sauvignon Blanc). The wines from this agriculturally rich Landes vineyard, however, are much lighter and less ambitious in style to those of Madiran and Pacherenc (aside from those of Michel Guérard at Château de Bachen).

Closer still to the Spanish border lie France's three last vineyards, all of them AOCs: Béarn, Jurançon, and Irouléguy. **Jurançon** is unquestionably the outstanding region of the three, though the AOC is for white wines only, based on Gros Manseng, Petit Manseng, and Courbu. These are cramponed into a long loin of hilly clay, jewel-studded with the usual clatter of water-rolled and ice-dumped mountain quartzes, and crusted with ironstone. This soil can be lusciously hard to work. Just as important as the soil medium itself, though, are the individual, sunflower-like dispositions of each opportune vineyard – and the distinctive high-training and staking of the vines themselves. The crystalline, snowfield sweetness of the greatest Jurançon has nothing to do with botrytis and everything to do with languid autumn sunshine dehydrating and buckling the low-yielding, shrivel-prone Petit Manseng.

Béarn (and its recently acquired subzone **Béarn-Bellocq**) lies downsteam of Jurançon, between the two *gaves* (rivers) of Pau and Oléron. The vineyards are sited on clay-limestone hill slopes, and produce both sweet and dry whites as well as light, tangy reds and locally celebrated rosés. Tannat and the two Cabernets are the main source of the reds; the whites, by contrast, are based on a local variety called Raffiat de Moncade (as well as the two Mansengs).

And so to the final frontier: **Irouléguy**. Thus modern map-readers see it, though the truth of course is that it lies at the heart of the Basque country, and it is only the present-day Franco-Spanish border that has made it any sort of an outpost. These are, once again, vineyards of fortune interrupting a green pastureland. You find vines here on widely scattered south-facing slopes, often steep, their roots fumbling in red sandstone and schist mixed with clay. Tannat and the Cabernets give red wine, while the whites are based on the two Mansengs and Petit Courbu. Irouléguy tends to produce difficult red wines, packed with searing acidity, fierce ferrous overtones, and bitter edges; the whites are more civilized and accessible, bright with mountain freshness.

Southwest France Flak

The Southwest isn't yet a region

What do Bergerac and Irouléguy have to do with each other? Very little, in truth. Why do Bergerac and Cahors refuse to work with each other, and both refuse to work with Madiran? Because they all see each other as rivals. Which is the only one of France's so-called regions to contain two entirely different river systems at its heart? This one.

It's obvious, really: the wine-growing zones of the Southwest only form a "region" because they have no alternative; they have nowhere else to go. Sometimes, though, a flag has to be sewn from disparate threads. All French wine-growing regions, in any case, need to realize that they are not each other's rivals, but rather colleagues with common cause. One of the biggest handicaps France imposes on itself in today's wine world is its chaotic, fragmented, and ineffectual promotion structure. The Southwest, of all French wine regions, is the one which most challengingly resembles a box of chocolates: every wine inside is a different shape, size, and made of different ingredients. A committed, unified front is badly needed if these often superb wine-growing regions are ever to emerge from obscurity.

The Southwest is inconsistent

Anyone setting out to research quality standards in today's Bergerac, in Cahors, in Madiran, or in Jurançon will be dazzled by what he or she discovers. Few AOCs have moved forward in quality terms over the last decade as swiftly as these. By contrast, general quality standards in Buzet, in Brulhois, in Lavilledieu, in Tursan, and even in Gaillac remain unexciting. It's tempting to blame unadventurous and over-dominant cooperatives for this state of affairs, but it would be wrong to do so: the superb work of the Producteurs Plaimont in Gascogne and in Côtes de St-Mont, or the spirit of adventure pushing forward a cooperative like the Union CVG in Gers, show that communal work is no bar to quality. What is essential, though, is honesty. Unless producers in these failing regions measure their wines against the highest standards achieved by individual growers in other local AOCs, they will have little future. "Cellar palate" – becoming so used to one's own wines that one is incapable of seeing their faults – has always been one of the wine world's greatest problems; the tragedy is that it is so easy to remedy.

Southwest France: People

l'Ancienne Cure
245600 Colombier, Tel: 05 53 58 27 90, Fax: 05 53 24 83 95

The best wines of energetic Christian Roche's 38-ha Bergerac domain are the Cuvée l'Abbaye (including a marzipan Monbazillac and a subtle, sumptuous Bergerac Sec) and the meaty, spicy red L'Extase.

Arretxea
64220 Irouléguy, Tel: 05 59 37 33 67, Fax: 05 59 37 33 67

Irouléguy, the mysterious AOC of France's Basque country, tends to produce difficult wines, packed with searing acidity, fierce ferrous overtones, and bitter edges. Thérèse and Michel Riouspeyous' small, 6-ha domain, entirely planted on south-facing terraces, is one of the few to manage to balance these challenging facets of the terroir with the kind of ripeness and richness needed to show them at their best, especially the white Hegoxuri, a blend of the two Mansengs and Petit Courbu given part-barrel fermentation.

Aydie ✪✪
64330 Aydie, Tel: 05 59 04 08 00, Fax: 05 59 04 08 08

This is one of the most immaculately and professionally run domains in the whole of France, with 68 ha of Madiran land and a further 20 ha in Gascogne. It is very much a family affair, in the hands of the three sons and the daughter of Pierre Laplace – whose own father, Frédéric, was one of the pioneers of the Madiran revival (when the AOC was created in 1948, there were only 50 ha of vines in cultivation; now there are 1,650 ha). Every aspect of wine production here is subject to scrutiny, research, experiment; not only were the Laplaces in at the birth of micro-oxygenation (see page 203), but they have also carried out extensive research into the ideal materials in which to vinify Tannat (wood or fibreglass – thanks to the variety's thirst for oxygen). *Délestage* is preferred to *pigeage* or *remontage* for extraction (since it breaks the cap of skins more comprehensively); they are experimenting with cold pre-fermentation macerations. For ageing the wines, they feel that 250-litre barriques are ideal for great years, but in less good years the wines perform better in 400-litre barrels. The use of lees is a science here, too: "They help build the fruit," Jean-Luc Laplace says – but they must be selected first, and stirred, and they work better with micro-oxgenation in large wooden vessels than in barriques. The result of this frenzied curiosity is a range of model Madirans. Mansus Irani is the "*classique*": 60% Tannat with 40% Cabernet Franc gives a violet-scented yet strong wine with shocking squeezed-sloe fruit. Odé d'Aydie (a first parcel selection) brings the Tannat component up to 80 and sometimes (as in 2000) 100%, with a combination of barrique and *foudre*-aged components: it's a sweeter and richer wine, the sloes now plums, and the tannic structure broader. Château d'Aydie, finally, is the *grand vin*: a strict, parcel-selected 100% Tannat with greater power and energy still than either of its siblings: ducal power of fruit (blackberries, blackcurrants), but also a gratifying allusiveness with age (tobacco, wild mushroom). The Pacherenc Sec is brilliantly vinified: bottled nettley with gas and packed with dry grapefruit and pineapple. The Moelleux is magnificently concentrated, but has less hedonistic appeal than some.

Bachen
40800 Duhort-Bachen, Tel: 05 58 71 76 76, Fax: 05 58 71 77 77

The fact that Michel Guérard's celebrated Eugénie-les-Bains lies within the AOC of Tursan means that the wines he makes there are inevitably the best known in the area; Guérard is almost the only producer, too, to make a white (based on the rare Baroque). Baron de Bachen is the top *cuvée*; Château de Bachen the "ordinary" version. The wines are pleasant, but little more.

Barréjat
32400 Maumusson-Laguian, Tel: 05 62 69 74 92, Fax: 05 62 69 77 54

Those who find much Madiran just too tough should look out for the wines of Denis Capmartin and his 20-ha estate Château Barréjat. There are three red *cuvées*, all of them rich-fruited and deeply sensual; indeed the middle *cuvée* (a 50% Tannat, 50% Cabernet blend) is actually called Séduction. The basic Tradition (60% Tannat) is soft, accessible, and finely balanced, with a touch of *surmaturité* in the fruit. The glory of this domain is its old-vine stock, some of which are ungrafted, pre-phylloxera vines around 200 years old; these are used for the superb, 80% Tannat Vieux Ceps *cuvée*. The 1999 vintage has rich, smoky scents and an elegant, toothsome flavour which combines blackberries and black cherries with burnt brown sugar. The dry white Pacherenc is unexceptional, but may improve when its Arrufiac component (a variety described by Denis Capmartin as "useless" though at one stage obligatory) is replaced by Petit Manseng. The Moelleux (pure Petit Manseng, and with one unoaked and one oaked version) are concentrated though monodimensional.

Beaulieu
47180 St-Sauveur-de-Meilhan, Tel: 05 53 94 30 40, Fax: 05 53 94 30 40

Robert and Agnès Schulte's 30-ha Marmandais domain produces elegant, carefully crafted wines, the best of which is the oaked Cuvée L'Oratoire. If Elian da Ros's inspiration seems to look further south towards the terroir-dominated profundities of the new Languedoc, these wines glance northwest, towards the finesse of classic Bordeaux.

Beauportail
24100 Bergerac, Tel: 05 53 24 85 16, Fax: 05 53 61 28 63

Young Fabrice Feytout has catapulted himself to the front of the small Pécharmant *peloton* with a series of graceful and expressive reds beginning with the plump 1998.

Bellegarde ✪
64360 Monein, Tel: 05 59 21 33 17, Fax: 05 59 21 44 40

Pascal Labasse' 15-ha Jurançon domain produces a clean, crisp, sappy, mineral-tinged Sec from pure Gros Manseng, as well as a barrel-fermented Sec Cuvée Bois which includes 30% Petit Manseng: it's softer and plumper. It's with the three sweeter wines, though, that Labasse's skills shine. The basic Jurançon has impressive richness for a non-oaked wine, while the oaked Cuvée Thibault memorably combines lushness and precision. The 2000 vintage Cuvée DB, meanwhile, picked on December 23rd has essence-like levels of concentration and extraordinary allusiveness, suggesting flowers, fruits, honey, spices, and fresh spring undergrowth: a magnificent wine. The 1995 Cuvée DB, packed with tangerine and orange, shows how well this wine can age, too, softening yet still retaining its explosive power. (Pascale Labasse also produced a version of this wine with zero sulphur: aromatically, it now shows tangy oxidative characteristics, and the fruits are more apricot than citrus.)

Bellevue la Forêt
31620 Fronton, Tel: 05 34 27 91 91, Fax: 05 61 82 43 21

The wide open spaces of Patrick Germain's single-parcel Fronton estate, with a massive 115 ha under vine, have an Australian or Californian look to them, and the considerable quantities of wine available here have helped put this rather

---

Star rating system used on producer spreads   ✪ Very good wine   ✪✪ Excellent wine   ✪✪✪ Great wine

shyly expressive, Toulouse-slaking AOC on the international map. The estate contains a number of different soils within its boundaries, sited on the first terrace of the Tarn: some are sandy; some stony. These differences are reflected in a wide number of cuvées; another focus is continual experiment by Partrick Germain and his long-term cellar master Christian Ivorra with the Négrette variety. (At the moment, they are working out whether micro-oxygenation will help it cope with wood more successfully than normally vinified Négrette does.) The classic red cuvée is a blend of 50% Négrette with 15% each of Syrah and Cabernet Franc, and 10% each of Cabernet Sauvignon and Gamay: it smells of pepper and tobacco leaf, and tastes sour-fresh with lots of cherry-plum, smooth tannin and a peppery finish. It's an ideal red for chilling. The pure Négrette Ce Vin, made from the best parcels, is light, tarry, and floral, while there are two oaked cuvées: La Sélection (30% Négrette, 40% Cabernet Sauvignon, 20% Cabernet Franc, and 10% Syrah) and Prestige (just 10% Négrette, with 50% Cabernet Sauvignon, 25% Cabernet Franc, and 15% Syrah). Cuvée Or (20% Négrette with 30% each of Cabernets Sauvignon and Franc, and 20% Syrah) is unwooded, but made in a slightly more extractive style. None, though, has any great depth or texture: they are pleasant, fruity, well-made wines offering uncomplicatedly easy drinking.

Berthoumieu ✪
32400 Viella, Tel: 05 62 69 74 05, Fax: 05 62 69 80 64
Didier Barré's 26-ha domain is well up to the generally high standards of the Madiran appellation. The Cuvée Tradition contains 55% Tannat, though you might guess there is more by its substance and depth. The Cuvée Charles de Batz, with 90% Tannat, is a typical Madiran powerhouse needing at least five years before it begins to open up. Its ample tannins are impressively fat and unctuous, rather than hard and dry. Barré has 3.5 ha of white varieties for an old-vine Pacherenc Sec and the sweet, luscious, oaked Symphonie d'Automne.

Bouscassé see Brumont

Bru-Baché
64360 Monein, Tel: 05 59 21 36 34, Fax: 05 59 21 32 67
Claude Loustalot, the nephew of Georges Bru-Baché, produces an extravagantly fruited range of wines from his 8 ha of Jurançon vineyards, including the carefully judged, wooded Sec Casterrasses, but above all the sweet La Quintessence, capable of acquiring lushly buttery overtones with age. L'Eminence, the top wine, does show more power and push but not, perhaps, quite the level of intricate detail the price difference with Quintessence would suggest.

Brumont ✪✪✪
32400 Maumusson-Laguian, Tel: 05 62 69 74 67, Fax: 05 62 69 70 46
Alain Brumont is a driven man; indeed no wine-grower in France sets about his work with a greater and more restless ambition than this fierce over-achiever. He claims there are 22 good hills in Madiran, and he appears to be busy acquiring vineyard sites on all of them. Bouscassé, Montus, and Meinjarre are the three domains with which Brumont's name has been longest associated. More recently, these have been joined by La Rosée ("a little bowl, very hot"), and the high-sited, unusually stony La Tyre, perhaps the greatest of all. Each has a different terroir, since Madiran is far from homogenous: Bouscassé, for example, is a relatively rich clay-limestone with iron intrusions; Montus is a classic hillside gravel terrace of glacial origin. With his autumn series of late-harvested, Pacherenc wines (Vendemiaire, harvested in October; Brumaire in November, and Frimaire in December – the names are taken from the French Revolutionary calendar), Brumont has provided a real challenge to Jurançon and given the world sweet wines of remarkably new balance and flavour.

Oak provides the style key for all of Brumont's Tannat-based reds; indeed his special Millennium Cuvée was a 1994 vintage given 2,000 days in barrique. The results, though, are far from plank-juice; oak is the key which seems to unlock their full range of expression. The 1990 Bouscassé Vieilles Vignes, for example, is a genuinely sensual Madiran with a rich garbure of aromas (soft fruits, cedar, cigars) and an unctuous, swimming flavour of spice and minerals.

The 1990 Montus Cuvée Prestige, by contrast, is a more masculine, thrusting wine with thicker tannins and more plunging acidity; even here, though, there is no sense of oak dominating but rather providing a brazier in which the wine's flames can flicker and dart. In youth, the Bouscassé (there is an ordinary version as well as a Vieilles Vignes) sings with blackcurrants and prunes, while Montus (in ordinary and Cuvée Prestige guise) takes similar fruits but cloaks them in incense- and spice-smoked tannic drapes. The 12-ha La Tyre promises to be deepest of all. Samples of the 2000 vintage taste like young, dry vintage port, alive with plant sap and hammered stonefruit, seemingly made not just of grapes but of whole crushed vines. None of the reds are filtered. "The best filter," says Brumont, "is the barrique." The latest experiments of this inveterate researcher are with 400-litre barriques armagnacaises, now used to give a little more softness to the the the Cuvée Montus XL. Brumont has followed his own vinification star entirely up until now (which means auto-pigeage and no micro-oxygenation but regular rackings). He is now beginning to work with the Bordelais Pascal Chatonnet, in part to overcome some brettanomyces problems; it will be interesting to see whether the affable Chatonnet's relationship with the famously difficult Brumont actually lasts – and if so, whether the wines will become more softly succulent and a little less ferocious.

For his dry white wines, Brumont is a great believer in the potential of the Petit Courbu ("petit around here means grand"), a variety he feels could eventually be the Viognier of the Southwest, and his scented dry Pacherenc Jardins de Bouscassé, all apricots and honeycomb, supports the theory. The white Montus is pure Petit Courbu, barrel-fermented and aged for 18 months (after being raisined in little boxes for a few post-picking days): it's a succulent, exotic, white Rhône-like wine which almost teeters into parody yet is finally both toothsome and compelling. The dessert Pacherencs all have two or more years in new barriques (the Frimaire only gets made in about two years out of five, since it requires exceptional autumn weather) and can be magnificently complex and detailed, though the risks entailed makes them a more variable success than the rest of the Brumont wine family. At their best, they are true autumn symphonies, magnificent composts of leaves, berries, orchard fruits, and warm winds, given the vanilla glycerine of oak.

Capmartin
32400 Maumusson-Laguian, Tel: 05 62 69 87 88, Fax: 05 62 69 83 07
Guy Capmartin's small 8-ha Madiran domain produces a consistently impressive range of wines led by the deep and spicy Cuvée du Couvent.

Cauhapé ✪✪
64360 Monein, Tel: 05 59 21 33 02, Fax: 05 59 21 41 82
Jurançon may be well off the beaten track for most wine lovers, but in the intelligent perfectionist Henri Ramonteu, France has one of its greatest winemakers. Ramonteu describes himself, with medieval relish, as a "grammarian of wine". This is partly a nod at the kind of clean, neat, precision winemaking in which he specializes, but also reflects the nature of the game in Jurançon: you wait, you gather; you wait some more, you gather again; you wait still further, gather a little more, and once again wait…. The grammarian's wines are divided into "declinations of Gros Manseng" (two Secs, the oaked Sève d'Automne and the unoaked Chant des Vignes, plus a sweet wine called Ballet d'Octobre) and "declinations of Petit Manseng" (just one Sec, the oaked Noblesse, plus three sweet versions picked as the autumn proceeds: Symphonie de Novembre, Noblesse du Temps, and finally the midwinter Quintessence du Petit Manseng). It is worth quoting Ramonteu's own writings on these two grapes (he has 17 ha of each), since he understands them intimately. He describes the "fresh sappiness" and "muscularity" of Gros Manseng, and says that its "lines of force" can be extracted to make "architectural wines" in which aromatic exuberance and formal grace are perfectly balanced. Petit Manseng, by contrast, comes together like woven threads towards a "taut, pressed, dense point" of flavour, with its extraordinary sugar-acid balance creating not so much architecture as a magnetic field. As I have already indicated, cleanliness and precision are key elements of

Ramonteu's winemaking, and the cleanliness is all the more striking since he is working with plenty of wine-feeding lees contact. His wines also have superb intensity, though his yields are not fanatically low and the vines are, on average, 20 years or so old. Finally, the Sève d'Automne and the Noblesse are for me probably the most successful of the oaked dry Jurançons: again, Ramonteu seems to have an intrinsic understanding of what is required to knit the wine's elements together into a seamless whole. The oak component of the Quintessence, too, is a glorious success, lending the intense and vivid fruits an irresistable succulence and a roasted quality which almost mimics the absent botrytis notes. A reference domain, in sum.

du Cayrou
46220 Prayssac, Tel: 05 65 22 40 26, Fax: 05 65 22 45 44

This is the largest of three properties belonging to the family of Jean Jouffreau, one of the pioneers of the revival of Cahors; the other two are Clos de Gamot, where there is a 2-ha parcel of 116-year-old Malbec, and the recently acquired Clos St-Jean, a historic property being replanted with high vine densities. Both Cayrou and Clos de Gamot are very much river-terrace vineyards: they sit snugly in two of the Lot's most serpentine bends, south of Puy l'Evêque and Prayssac respectively. Clos St-Jean, by contrast, is a hill-slope vineyard found near Sals, to the west of Cahors. The wines are rather old-fashioned in style, with relatively light colours, light textures, and a cool, elegant fruit style; most memorable is the Cuvée des Vignes Centenaires, produced at Clos de Gamot in the best vintages, which has some succulence and depth.

du Cèdre ✪✪
46700 Vire-sur-Lot, Tel: 05 65 36 53 87, Fax: 05 65 24 64 36

The 24-ha estate of Pascal and Jean-Marie Verhaeghe has done as much as any to improve the recent quality of Cahors and provide the challenge it should be giving to the most profound Malbecs of Argentina – and some of the other great wines of France. Not only does the domain lead by example, but Pascal Verghaeghe has also been the driving force behind the Cahors "Quality Charter". There are four different *cuvées* produced here. The first is the classic du Cèdre, packed with meaty fruit and made with a softening 20% Merlot added to the Malbec; there is also a barrique-aged Prestige version in which the Merlot is replaced by 10% Tannat, giving the wine a taut, smoky, ham-stock character. The best Malbec goes into Le Cèdre, entirely aged in new oak: flower-perfumed in youth, it then turns smoky; its explosive black plum-prune fruits and thick-textured, leonine tannins age slowly towards the ripe softness of age. The Verghaeghe brothers have worked with Patrick Ducournau since the early 1990s, and also shared much of the lees-contact research undertaken by Luc de Conti in Bergerac. Like de Conti, they have produced a new *cuvée* in 2000 called GC which has been entirely vinified in 500-litre new oak *demi-muids*, with long subsequent lees contact; the samples which I have tasted were strikingly soft, lush, and richly fruited, a kind of Pomerol among Cahors. (See also Haut-Monplaisir.)

Chante Coucou *see* Elian da Ros

Chapelle l'Enclos *see* Mouréou

Clos de Gamot *see* Château du Cayrou

Clos Lapeyre ✪
64110 Jurançon, Tel: 05 59 21 50 80, Fax: 05 59 21 51 83

This 12-ha family domain based near La Chapelle de Rousse (the highest part of Jurançon) is run today by Jean-Bernard Larrieu in association with Englishman Daniel Craker. The Cuvée Vitatge Vielh Sec is one of the region's outstanding dry wines, made from a small 1.5-ha parcel of 60-year-old vines, including 50% Petit Manseng: it has a taut, perfumed, intense flavour backed by vivid acidity: an authentically shocking taste of high-country Pyrénées. There are three late-harvest wines, meanwhile: the ordinary *cuvée* is based on 80% Gros Manseng, mainly tank-aged, while the Sélection is 100% Petit Manseng, picked by *tries* in November and barrel-fermented in new oak. As with all the great Jurançon estates, don't despise a wine just because it contains Gros Manseng;

the basic Clos Lapeyre is superb, full of lingering apricot. The Sélection ups the intensity, mixing notes of lemon verbena and mint to the vivid, bright fruits, and the 12 months spent in new oak casks on fine lees adds a buttery richness, too. Finally, there is the Vent Balaguèr (the Occitan name for the warm southern wind of autumn): an extraordinary wine made in suitable years only from raisined Petit Manseng picked in December then left outdoors in small boxes if the sun continues to shine and dried indoors if not. It is pressed at the beginning of January, and slowly fermented in new wood at its own pace. The début 1998 vintage was both sweet and liquorous yet fiery and roasted too, with a magnificent architecture of fruit flavours giving it 30-second length. There is also an entirely unrelated domain of the same name in Béarn producing a fresh, mountain-crunchy red Béarn and a wooded white Béarn based on Gros Manseng and Arrufiac.

Clos St-Jean *see* Château du Cayrou

Clos Triguedina ✪
46700 Puy-l'Evèque, Tel: 05 65 21 30 81, Fax: 05 65 21 39 28

This 60-ha Cahors domain has 48 ha on the river terraces, and a further 12 ha up on the *causse* (used for white varieties, sold as Vin de Pays du Comté Tolosan). The Clos Triguedina is produced from 75% Malbec (with 20% Merlot and 5% Tannat), aged in used oak for 18 months: this is delicately clinker-scented, soft, lush, full, and subtle, yet it still manages to convey the iron and roast meat flavours which typify serious Cahors. It ages well: a 1967 was still graceful and sweet-fruited in 2000. Prince Probus, meanwhile, is the top *cuvée*, produced exclusively from old-vine Malbec (50 years+) aged in newer oak: black in colour when young, with aromas of coffee and smoky prunes and a deep, ripe, beefy style, flower-eged (iris, peony) in extreme youth. It matures slowly towards notes of cream, wild mushroom, and truffle (as the 1990 has in 2000). "The New Black Wine", produced from pure, semi-dried Malbec since 1994, is paradoxically slightly lighter than Prince Probus, with more smoke, liquorice, spice, and bittersweetness about it. The white Vin de Lune wines are good, too: the barrel-fermented dry white (full, textured, honeyed) is based on Chardonnay and Viognier, while the impressive Chenin-based Moelleux (18 months' oak) is suprisingly unctuous, full of apricot and peach flesh yet with poised, plunging acidity, too – quite literally half-way between Jurançon and Sauternes. Domaine Labrande is a neighbouring property also owned by Jean-Luc Baldès, and Balmont de Cahors a third brand.

Clos Uroulat
64360 Monein, Tel: 05 59 21 46 19, Fax: 05 59 21 46 90

Charles Hours is everyone's image of the ideal Pyrenean winegrower: jolly, fleshy, strong, with a head perfectly fashioned for a beret and a name homonymous with the region's most celebrated wild animal. Don't be misled, though: this skilled and consistent winemaker is much more than a postcard stereotype. The Jurançon Sec, Cuvée Marie, comes from a 3-ha vineyard planted almost wholly to Gros Manseng with a little Courbu. It's barrel fermented (just 10% new oak) and lees-aged for 11 months, and can be both the creamiest and smokiest of all dry Jurançons. Uroulat is the sweet version: 4 ha planted with Petit Manseng harvested in October and November. This wine needs age. In youth, it is solid but gruff; after a decade or so, it opens up into buttery yet fresh-fruited articulacy.

La Colombière
31620 Villaudric, Tel: 05 61 82 44 05, Fax: 05 61 82 57 56

Baron François de Driesen (who spent 20 years working with margarines, soaps, and fatty acids before becoming a winegrower) and his daughter Diane are the leading practitioners of carbonic maceration for the Négrette in Fronton at their 17-ha estate. The wines are light, tender, and strawberry-fresh.

Coss-Maisonneuve
46140 Carnac Rouffiac, Tel: 05 65 24 22 36

Vivid floral scents and pure spiced prune fruits characterize the impressively elegant Cahors Les Laquets from this biodynamic domain.

Côtes d'Olt

46140 Parnac, Tel: 05 65 30 71 86, Fax: 05 65 20 17 71

This cooperative is producing much better wines than in the past. The Impernal, in particular, is a fine old-style Cahors. It lacks the colour and extraction of the modern AOC leaders, but makes up in terms of warm, prune-and-ham-stock characters: a country soup wine from the French backwoods.

du Cros

12390 Goutrens, Tel: 05 65 72 71 77, Fax: 05 65 72 68 80

Philippe Teulier's Domaine du Cros is the largest in its little-seen AOC of Marcillac. Lo Sang del Païs has a clean, fresh-fruited style, like Beaujolais with a little extra grip; the Cuvée Vieilles Vignes, by contrast, is a rustic and energetic wine which finishes with a jangle of minerals.

Ducournau *see* Mouréou

Escausses

81150 Ste-Croix, Tel: 05 63 56 80 52, Fax: 05 63 56 87 62

Denis Balaran's clean, fresh, and expressive Gaillac wines are some of the best in this often unfocused AOC.

Grand Chêne

82340 Donzac, Tel: 05 63 39 91 92, Fax: 05 63 39 82 83

Pleasant, light red based on 40% Cabernet Franc and 30% Tannat (the balance from Merlot and Cabernet Sauvignon), produced by the Cave de Donzac, is one of the better wines in the generally uninspiring Côtes de Brulhois.

Guirardel

64360 Monein, Tel: 05 59 21 31 48

Jean Casaubielh's small, traditional domain produces two carefully vinified Jurançons. The domain wine is based on Gros Manseng, while the Bi de Prat is more intense, built on Petit Manseng.

Haut-Bernasse

24240 Bernasse, Tel: 05 53 58 36 22, Fax: 05 53 61 26 40

Cellist Jacques Blais' wines have more finesse, balance, and delicacy than many in the Monbazillac; honey, banana, and crystallized lime peel combine with peach-skin acidity to provide gratifying drinking.

Haut-Monplaisir ✪

46700 Lacapelle Cabanac, Tel: 05 65 24 64 78, Fax: 05 65 24 68 90

This Cahors property, owned by the Fournié family, lies just above Château du Cèdre on slightly stonier soil; Cathy Fournié and Daniel Salinié are helped by the Verghaeghe brothers of Château du Cèdre. There are three *cuvées*: the comely, soft-tannined Haut-Monplaisir; the richer, more deeply textured Prestige Haut-Monplaisir; and finally a new "Charte de Qualité" *cuvée*, also oak-aged but with more intense, explosive fruit than the Prestige. Haut-Montplaisir is obviously a promising terroir, making this a name to watch.

Herri Mina

64220 Ispoure

Jean-Claude Berrouet, winemaking overseer for the Moueix estates in Bordeaux (and thus the man who helps Christian Moueix craft Pétrus) has his own domain at Ispoure in Irouléguy. His white wine, with its scents of angelica and green-shock of intense celery-lemon freshness, is a mouth-watering treat.

Jolys

64290 Gan, Tel: 05 59 21 72 79, Fax: 05 59 21 55 61

The 36 ha of Château Jolys make it one of the largest properties in Jurançon. The Sec has a bright mineral freshness to it. The four sweet wines have a slightly softer style than some of their peers, with the most interesting comparison being between the December-harvested Petit Manseng Vendange Tardive and the January-harvested Gros Manseng Epiphanie; both have 18 months in barriques. The Epiphanie is weightier, but the Vendange Tardive has more finesse and nuance. Cuvée Jean is a November-harvested Petit Manseng full of lush pear fruit.

K de Krevel

33220 Porte-Ste-Foy-Ponchapt, Tel: 05 53 24 77 27

Belgian Guy-Jean Kreusch (Kreusch + Montravel = Krevel), a mayonnaise magnate, is behind these two good red and white wines, produced at Domaine de Métairie (he also owns Domaine Puy de Grave in Pécharmant). The white Montravel, made with consultative help from Denis Dubourdieu, is soft, dry yet honeyed; the red has the characteristic fresh-fruitedness of the best Bergeracs.

Labranche Laffont

32400 Maumusson-Laguian, Tel: 05 62 69 74 90, Fax: 05 62 69 76 03

Another typically competent domain within rapidly improving Madiran. The Vieilles Vignes *cuvée* (based on 50+ year old vines, and some which pre-date phylloxera) is deep and expressive, full of moist dark fruits.

Labrande *see* Clos Triguedina

Laffitte-Teston

32400 Maumusson, Tel: 05 62 69 74 58, Fax: 05 62 69 76 87

Jean-Marc Laffitte's 40-ha domain produces solid, reliable Madiran and impressive Pacherenc. The dry white Ericka, two-thirds fermented in new oak, is a wonderfully pithy mouthful, while the *moelleux* is scented and lush.

Lagrezette ✪

46140 Caillac, Tel: 05 65 20 07 42, Fax: 05 65 20 06 95

This 65-ha showcase property is one of the new stars of Cahors; it belongs to Alain-Dominique Perrin, who runs the luxury goods company Richemont, owner of Cartier and other marques. Perrin bought the property in 1980 and at first took his grapes to the Côtes d'Olt cooperative; he left the co-op in 1992, and is now building up a négociant business as well as bottling his own wines. Michel Rolland consults – which means late-picking by hand (many in Cahors still harvest by machine), with a cold pre-fermentation maceration, long *cuvaison* with soft extraction techniques including *pigeage*, minimum sulphur dioxide, no pumping of the must or wine, and extensive use of oak. There is also a multi-tiered selection process, with a third wine (Moulin Lagrezette) and a second wine (Chevalier Lagrezette) used to build quality in the Château Lagrezette. Above this come two prestige *cuvées*: the Cuvée Dame Honneur, which is a selection of the best parcels, and Pigeonnier, made from a third-terrace, 2.7-ha parcel by the château building itself. Moulin and Chevalier are both pleasant, easy-drinking Cahors which see some softening oak; the three top wines, by contrast, are splendidly deep and varied expressions of the intrinsic qualities of dark, smoky Cahors. Lagrezette itself is around 82% Malbec with the balance provided by Merlot and a tiny seasoning of Tannat, given 18 months in oak of which a third is new each year: it strikes a fine balance between succulent prune fruit and the smoky, ferrous, spark-raising grind of this stony, iron-strewn terroir. Dame Honneur (without Tannat) is sweeter, more chocolatey, more oak-sumptuous; while the pure-Malbec Pigeonnier (for which the yield is no more than 20 hl/ha) is sloe-intense and livid in its youth, all fire and pepper and ground stones, needing extended ageing.

Masburel

33220 Ste-Foy-la-Grande, Tel: 05 53 24 77 73, Fax: 05 53 24 27 30

Neil and Olivia Donnan's 25-ha Bergerac property is run with considerable ambition and with the curious delight of those who have discovered wine-growing later in life (as Neil did, after 30 years working for Mars). "What fascinates me about wine is the 10,000 variables," says Neil. "Nothing ever happens twice." The irrepressible Olivia is the driving force behind the Château Masburel, working with cellarmaster Eric Combret, previously at Sigalas-Rabaud. "Lovely gooey clay," is Olivia Donnan's description of her soils, "with a lot of limestone beneath." The wines are powerful and impressive, but lack harmony and subtlety: the pure Sauvignon is honeyed and weighty; the red is wild and smoky, more Madiran in style than Bergerac. Lady Masburel is the second label.

Jean-Luc Matha

12330 Clairvaux, Tel: 05 65 72 63 29, Fax: 05 65 72 70 43

Fourteen hectares cleared from the red-earthed Marcillac slopes since 1975 by Jean-Luc Matha produce one of the sweeter, fresher wines of the region for the "*cuvée générique*". The oaked Cuvée Spéciale, meanwhile, is brisker and deeper, with ironstone complexities, like a distant southern echo of Bourgueil.

Meinjarre *see* Brumont

Montauriol
31340 Villematier, Tel: 05 61 35 30 58, Fax: 05 61 35 30 59

The mineral-charged Tradition (60% Négrette, 40% Syrah and Cabernet Franc) and the oakier Mons Aureolus (from 50% Négrette with 25% each of Syrah and Cabernet) are two of Fronton's more impressive wines. The domain, purchased in 1998 by Nicolas Gélis, includes 35 ha in two parcels.

Montus *see* Brumont

Moulin des Dames *see* Tour des Gendres

Mouréou ✪
32400 Manmousson-Laguian, Tel: 05 62 69 78 11, Fax: 05 62 69 75 87

Patrick Ducournau is probably the most influential winemaker in the entire Southwest – though not so much for his 18-ha Madiran domain as for his development and consultation work which nowadays takes him on almost as many air miles as Michel Rolland. He is Monsieur Micro-oxygenation (see page 205) – a technique developed to tame the ferocious tannins of Tannat without either creating the reduction problems this variety is prone to, or pumping the wine too full of wood. "The effect of wood without the taste of wood," is Ducournau's simple summary. The result is genuinely sumptuous and soft wine: Domaine Mauréou can be drunk with pleasure almost immediately, while La Chapelle l'Enclos in denser and wilder, slower to unfold. The Pacherenc from Chapelle l'Enclos is honeyed, waxy, and limpid, almost Loire-like.

Pichard
65700 Soublecause, Tel: 05 62 96 35 73, Fax: 05 62 96 96 72

René Tachouères' 12-ha south-facing parcel of Madiran, inherited from his uncle who was one of the first to bottle in the region, is planted with 50% Tannat, 40% Cabernet Franc, and 10% Cabernet Sauvignon. Why so much Cabernet? "In good years, Tannat is sublime, but in difficult years it can disappoint. And in any case these are some of the oldest Cabernet vines in the region, so it would be a shame to uproot them." Tachouères is the guardian of the old, traditional style of Madiran: all his wines are given long ageing in old wooden *foudres* and then in bottle; no messing about with barriques and micro-oxygenation here. The results are less showy wines than those produced by the AOC vanguard, but in good vintages (like 1995, 1994, and 1990) can acquire appealing incense-like aromas and rounded, almost creamy flavours of liquorice, prune, and blackcurrant pastille. There is, in short, something almost clarety about them, perhaps as a consequence of the Cabernets. There was a Prestige Cuvée in 1994 with 60% Tannat and ageing in two new-wood *foudres* acquired in that year; a one-off barrique-aged 1990 was a landmark bottle, too.

Robert et Bernard Plageoles
81140 Cahuzac-sur-Vère, Tel: 05 63 33 90 40, Fax: 05 63 33 95 64

The wines of this unique Gaillac domain (composed of two separate properties, Roucou and Très Cantous) are a challenge; nothing quite like them is produced anywhere else in France. As I stated in the introduction, they should be seen as a mind-challenging exercise in aroma- and flavour-archaeology, rather than being wines of simple hedonistic appeal. The low-alcohol, sparkling Mauzac Nature is a yeasty, orchard mouthful; the Mauzac Vert (which Plageoles calls a Sec Tendre, a "softened dry") is a still wine in which the apples and pears acquire a faintly bittersweet edge. The Mauzac Roux, by contrast, is a smooth, sweet mouthful in which the same fruits have been crystallized into succulence. Plageoles' most obviously appealing wine is his sweet Muscadelle, produced from very low yields (around 12 hl/ha) from grapes which he describes as "*bletti sur souche*" (rotten-ripe): liquid honey. From the Ondenc ("the grape which gave Gaillac its past glory"), Plageoles makes a bitter-edged Moelleux, as well

as the truly impressive Vin d'Autan ("a wine of the wind and of the spirit"), collected later in the season, lightly oxidized, packed with autumn leaf, honey, walnut, and quince flavours and with vivid acidity, too: a kind of Tokaji of the Southwest. Plageoles' celebrated Vin de Voile ("veil wine" – in other words, made with a kind of flor film on it, as the Jura's *vins jaunes* are) is based on Mauzac Roux, and tastes sharp, oxidized, and mouth-scouring; there is also a pretty little Mauzac Nature ("*à boire à l'esprit libre*" – for glugging, as we might more vulgarly say in English). Plageoles' reds, too, have more than a touch of the Jura about them, being in general light, fresh, unwooded, and tannin-free: I tried the coolly tarry Prunelart (aka Cot à Queue Rouge) and the nutty Mauzac Noir.

Plaisance
31340 Vacquiers, Tel: 05 61 84 97 41, Fax: 05 61 84 11 26

Marc Penavayres, a former viticultural researcher for INRA at Angers, has taken over this family domain in Fronton from his parents Louis and Simone. Le Grain de Folie is an almost pure Négrette mixed with 10% Gamay: a "*vin de plaisir, de copains, de comptoir*" as Penavayres puts it (a wine for pleasure, for friends, for drinking at the bar), with its vivid acidity and juicy, peppery fruit. His other red *cuvées* are more serious: Château Plaisance (65% Négrette mixed with 22% Syrah and the balance Cabernet Sauvignon) is poised, vivid, and floral; and Thibaut de Plaisance is a selection of his best *cuvées* of Négrette and Syrah, barrique-aged, which give a wine with an almost burgundian style of liquorice-brocaded fruit. Tout Ço Que Cal is the name of a new blend (Négrette, Syrah, and Cabernet Sauvignon) inspired by the great Languedoc reds of Mas Jullien and others. The researcher in Penavayre hasn't quite given up work either, though; he's using a new variety called Liliorila (a Baroque x Chardonnay cross) together with Chenin Blanc and Sémillon for a semi-sweet white blend called Maëlle, and he's also experimenting with botrytized Chenin Blanc for a wine inspired by Alsace's Sélection des Grains Nobles wines.

Primo Palatum ✪
33190 Morizès, Tel: 05 56 71 39 39, Fax: 05 56 71 39 40

Xavier Coppel is, if you like, the Dominique Laurent of the South. He produces a range of hand-vinified wines from purchased fruit right across Languedoc, Roussillon, Southwest France, and Bordeaux (his home patch). It is with his Madiran, Cahors, and Jurançon *cuvées* that some of his greatest successes have come, partly because the quality potential of these AOCs is so high, and partly because these wines lend themselves to his showy, extractive, richly oaked style. Both the Cahors and the Jurançon are available in Classica and Mythologia versions, the latter being still more concentrated and lavish.

Producteurs Plaimont
32400 St-Mont, Tel: 05 62 69 62 87, Fax: 05 62 69 61 68

This enormous and astutely managed group of cooperatives is a model for other regions of France – both in terms of its drive for quality, and its readiness to innovate within the terroir-based genius of the French wine tradition. There are over 1,000 members, and it has 1,200 ha in Côtes de St-Mont, another 1,200 ha in Côtes de Gascogne, and 250 ha in Madiran and Pacherenc, too. The wine range is large and inevitably various; the best are produced within the Côtes de St-Mont AOC, including the crisp and vivacious white Les Bastions (40% Gros Manseng, with 30% each of Arrufiac and Petit Courbu) and the fresh, mineral red Les Bastions (70% Tannat, with 15% Cabernet Sauvignon, 10% Pinenc, and 5% Cabernet Franc). There is also an intense, barrique-aged old-vine *cuvée* Esprit de Vignes and the perfumed, 7.5-ha single parcel Monastère de St-Mont. Top of the range red from Côtes de St-Mont is Le Faite, an adventurously packaged selection of the best parcels and *cuvées*: deep, leathery, smoky. The Arte Benedicte Madiran is an iron-clad red of sturdy typicity.

Henri Ramonteu *see* Cauhapé

Le Roc
31620 Fronton, Tel: 05 61 82 93 90, Fax: 05 61 82 72 38

Frédéric and Jean-Luc Ribes' 26-ha Fronton domain is scattered over five parcels on the typical mixed, glacial soils of the second and third Garonne terraces. In addition to a fine rosé (produced by "bleeding" of the red varieties after a cold pre-fermentation maceration, and with up to five months' lees contact), the Ribes brothers also produce some of the AOC's best reds. The "classique" is a fresh and crunchy mouthful based on 60% Négrette with 25% Syrah and 15% Cabernet. The Cuvée Reservée, by contrast, has 25% Cabernet and just 50% Négrette; this selection of the best fruit parcels has longer maceration and a year in barrique (of which around 20% are new) followed by six months in tank. This keeps its fresh, floral "Frontonnais" personality, while giving the wine a softer, richer flavour. More ambitious still is the Cuvée Don Quichotte, a half-Négrette half-Syrah cuvée extracted by pigeage to give greater fruit and soft-tannin density, with a year in barrique (none new) and a year in tank and bottling without fining or filtration. The floral notes are joined by coffee; the palate is milky-soft, faintly smoky, full of vivid fruit.

Elian da Ros ✪
47250 Cocumont, Tel: 05 53 94 72 29, Fax: 05 53 94 72 29

The wines created by the brilliant Elian da Ros, who trained and worked for five years with Olivier Zind-Humbrecht, have managed to give the Côtes du Marmandais the personality and the impact it needs to put it on the world's drinking map. (He is one of only four producers in the AOC who are not members of the two local cooperatives.) The benefits of his low-yield, non-interventionist approach are evident from the mainly Merlot Vin de Pays de l'Agenais "Vignoble du Cocumont", full of tobacco-road warmth, up to the finest cuvée Clos Bacquey, a Côtes du Marmandais made from da Ros' best sites and with a higher than usual percentage of Abouriou. This gives the wine a challenging tautness, riveting its clattering minerals and soft liquorice together with black-chocolate acidity. The seductively named Chante Coucou is a wine of great loveliness and sustained depth, its understated raspberry fruit charged with the glitter of iron and firm, coating tannins.

La Rosée see Brumont

Rotier
81600 Cadalen, Tel: 05 63 41 75 14, Fax: 05 63 41 54 56

This well-run 28-ha domain is one of the leaders in Gaillac, slowly edging towards wines of concentration, depth and pungent character. Renaissance is the top range.

Roucou see Plageoles

St-Guilhem
31620 Castelnau-d'Estretefonds, Tel: 05 61 82 12 09, Fax: 05 61 82 65 59

Philippe and Arlette Laduguie's small 7-ha vineyard produces three cuvées: the straightforward Tradition, the oaked Renaissance and the slightly less oaky Amadeus, described by Laduguie as the "quintessence of my best parcels". It is this wine (late-harvested, given cold pre-fermentation maceration and aged in older barriques) which is most successful, its pure fruits lent a violet sheen. Laduguie also has 25 ha of woods; "we keep nature company," he says.

Tariquet
32800 Eauze, Tel: 05 62 09 87 82, Fax: 05 62 09 89 49

Yves Grassa is one of the most skilful and commercially astute producers in Côtes du Gascogne, and this is the name of his "home" domain. The most successful of the wide range of wines he produces here is the Tête de Cuvée Chardonnay, rather subtler in style than the toffee-oaked "ordinary" Chardonnay; there is also a sweet-edged, softly grassy Ugni Blanc-Colombard blend.

Tirecul la Gravière ✪
24240 Monbazillac, Tel: 05 53 57 44 75, Fax: 05 53 24 85 01

Bruno Billancini's 10-ha domain produces some of the showiest of all Monbazillacs. With 50% Muscadelle and 42% Sémillon, however, they are hardly the most typical (Sauvignon accounts for a mere 8%). The system of picking by tris is pursued with great rigour; fermentation is entirely in barrique, half of them new. In addition to the "classic" cuvée, outstanding in its own right, there is also the extraordinarily viscous, sugar-laden Cuvée Madame.

Tour des Gendres ✪
24240 Ribagnac, Tel: 05 53 57 12 43, Fax: 05 53 58 89 49

Luc de Conti runs this innovative 40-ha Bergerac estate with his brother Jean and his cousin Francis (who looks after the vines). "On cherche l'anti-vin-moderne par excellence," says Luc de Conti, in discussing his ideals ("We're looking for everything unmodern"). In addition to Tour des Gendres itself, Moulin des Dames is also produced here – a limestone and marl parcel which the de Contis are moving towards biodynamic cultivation; 6 ha are planted with white varieties and 8 ha with red. The white is subtle, pure, and linen-textured; the red dark, curranty, rich-tannined yet soft – the de Conti hallmark is a supple breadth and smooth, expressive drinkability. Best of the limestone-grown Tour des Gendres wines is the Cuvée La Gloire de Mon Père: a creamy, tissue-soft red of lingering depth and presence. Together with Pascal Verghaeghe of Château du Cèdre in Cahors, de Conti has been experimenting with barrel-fermenting red wines in 500-litre casks. Whereas Verghaeghe upended the barrel, removed the head, and carried out pigeage as if the barrel was a micro-vat for his "GC", de Conti achieved his extraction by rolling the barrels once a day for eight days. The result is a wine called Anthologia: lushly fruited and perfumed, poised and silk-textured – the Margaux of Bergerac.

Tres Cantous see Plageoles

La Tyre see Brumont

Les Verdots ✪
24560 Conne-de-Labarde, Tel: 05 53 58 34 31, Fax: 05 53 57 82 00

David Fourtout's wines go to market under a variety of different names (Clos des Verdots, Château Les Tours des Verdots, Les Verdots Selon David Fourtout, Grand Vin Les Verdots): the reason for this playfulness is the pun offered by the word "Verdots" (which in French sounds identical to verres d'eau, meaning "glasses of water"). His latest name for what was previously the Grand Vin is simply Le Vin, enabling him to say to customers "Avant je faisais les verres d'eau [Les Verdots]; maintenant je fais Le Vin" ("Before, I used to make glasses of water; now I make wine"). My apologies for this necessarily laborious explanation. Beneath all of this fun is a serious, thoughtful, and inventive winemaker – he has designed his own conical vats, for example, to provide micro-pressure which aids extraction during the cuvaison period. The less ambitious wines (Clos des Verdots and Château Les Tours des Verdots) are fresh and delicious. Top of the range is the Grand Vin (or, from 2000, Le Vin). The white, from 80-year-old vines yielding less than 20 hl/ha, is 40% Muscadelle (including some botrytized fruit), 30% Sauvignon Blanc, 20% Sauvignon Gris, and 10% Sémillon). Scents of celery and flowers barely prepare the drinker for the explosive crushed fruits, lent unctuousness by oak, which follows. The Merlot-dominated red is less exciting, but a fine wine nonetheless, with sweet, poised, crunchy fruit. Fourtout also makes some of the best Côtes de Bergerac Moelleux, from vineyards a mere 50 metres from the Monbazillac AOC boundary: sumptuous, complex and multi-fruit-faceted. There is, too, a Monbazillac from rented vines; the 1999 had delicately mentholated aromas and tangy, steamroller sweetness.

de Viella ✪
32400 Viella, Tel: 05 62 69 75 81, Fax: 05 62 69 70 18

Slightly built Alain Bortolussi's 23-ha domain is now producing some of the finest (and the best value) wines in the outstandingly competitive AOC of Madiran. Look out for his pithy, barrel-fermented dry Pacherenc and buttery, unctuous Moelleux; he also manages to find the extra sweetness which Tannat begs for in his carefully crafted Madiran. Tradition is the unoaked cuvée, made with 40% of the two Cabernets to balance the Tannat. The "Vieilli en Fûts de Chêne" is the prestige version, from a 5-ha parcel planted with 30-year-old Tannat. Not only does the concentration reveal low yields, but the wine is also beautifully vinified, combining the stuffing of the terroir and the grape with remarkably smooth, soft, yielding textures.

Languedoc-Roussillon

Return to the Light Cheap, rough wine may remain statistically significant in Languedoc-Roussillon, but the region's best growers have long since left that past behind. Their dark wines of stone and sun, new and strange, have a disconcerting Mediterranean beauty.

It's mid-September: harvest's edge. We've been driving, my guide and I, south to the sea. France has two corridors to link its Lyonnais heart, Parisian head, and Bordelais nose to the Mediterranean: the Rhône descends from the north, and the Toulouse-Carcassonne corridor, since the seventeenth century occupied by the Canal du Midi, meanders in from the west. Between lie mountains and uplands, and at the water's edge, linking all, is a plain. Nowadays, this part of the Mediterranean is a cul-de-sac, the sea in gentle retreat.

As La Clape proves. This long, bright lobe of limestone was once an island protecting the Roman port of Narbo (today's Narbonne); now it's bedded into the mainland by the lagoon-mothering coastal bars that characterize this stretch of the Mediterranean coast. The afternoon sunlight glitters on the water, dissolving the horizon into a dance of bright motes.

We pull up a debris-strewn drive, and come to a stop in a courtyard next to a well-worn old house: the Château de Négly. From the upper level of what looks like an old barn, a man talking into a mobile phone eyes us. He disappears.

We go inside, and upstairs. A gaggle of workers cluster round a pneumatic press. We are ignored. The main man has moved away, into the next room, where he continues talking on his mobile phone while gazing down into his still-empty vats.

Time passes. We look out from the barn towards the sea. Palm trees wave like fond aunts in the distance.

Eventually the call ends. Jean Paux-Rosset has got the rough good looks of a working-class film star; his accent, and the quick-fire abruptness of his speech, makes him hard for me to understand. What do we want to know? He hasn't really got time to see us; his winemaker, Cyril Chamontin, will look after us. Yet in the end he finds time to show us around, and when he does hand us over to Chamontin for the tasting, he constantly returns and interrupts. He's prickly; he's joky; he fingers his stubble; his piercing blue eyes interrogate us. His language is salty, provocative. There are more mobile phone calls. I can't understand the orders he seems to be issuing, but compromise appears to play little role among them. The place is a mess, and everyone is grumpy. He has a relationship of bantering disaffection with Cyril, who reciprocates in kind. Dyspepsia reigns.

Then we taste. The contrast between the chaotic surroundings and the ordered intensity in the glasses is astonishing. His yields, we learn, are minute; as low as fifteen hl/ha. It was his parents' property; after his father's death, his mother ran it. She refused to accept any advice from her son, so he had to leave her alone to run it her way. Hers were the old ways. She used to take 4,500 hl a year from the fifty ha

(123 acres) – an average yield of ninety hl/ha; he takes 1,500 hl (thirty hl/ha). He pushes the grapes to absolute ripeness, no matter what the climatic risks. Not a single damaged grape, he tells us, goes into the vats: you can see him sorting his fruit, berry by berry, on page 221. For his finest wine, the evocatively named Porte du Ciel ("gateway to the sky"), he buys a new open wooden fermenter every year. The *cuvaison* lasts between October and Christmas, with *pigeage* three or four times a day. "It's like soup at the end." The wine then spends up to two years in barriques, with a flexible programme of micro-oxygenation, lees contact, and racking, according to what Rosset and Chamontin, and consultant Claude Gros, feel the wine needs.

We taste its detonating concentration, its plunging intensity, while looking out at the peeling walls and the distant sands, remembering a mother who believed in quantity above all. We taste how Languedoc's changed.

Close encounters in high lands

Narbonne to Carcassonne, Carcassonne to Toulouse, Toulouse to Agen, Agen to Bordeaux: this water-veined corridor from the Mediterranean to the Atlantic is the most important single topographical feature of Languedoc-Roussillon. When the Canal du Midi was built, it was Europe's Suez or Panama, saving sailors hazardous weeks of labouring across Biscay, around jutting Iberia and through the Straits of Gibralter. Nowadays, the canal, with its somnolent lines of plane trees, serves chiefly to nourish the watery holiday dreams of the stockbrokers of Surrey and Sussex. Even the French seem to find it a little slow. The English love it.

To each side of the canal, the hills mount and then the mountains rise. South lies Corbières, into which we are driving as dusk falls. I have been here once before; I went to visit an English anthropologist-turned-wine-grower called Nick Bradford of Domaine des Pensées Sauvages, at Albas, who served me a salad over which was flaked shards of dried liver. I remember thinking that this wild, survivalist's food marked the measure of the landscape; if Scotland were to be dragged south, herb-sown and sun-blistered, it would look rather like this. As we drive further and further into the lost hills, a car comes hurtling over a blind brow towards us, lurches wildly to avoid the imminent collision, and fantails away into the dusk. Just a moment's lapse in the anonymous precipitator's concentration, and someone else would be writing this book. He had probably travelled this road thirty times before, and never yet met a car coming the other way.

Night falls as our pulses slow again. Human lights are scarce among these tumbled, craggy, chaotic hills of stone and thorn.

"We're at the end of a story. When wine-growers empty tanks of wine at Sète as they did ten days ago, it's the end of a story. Those people have no future; they are no longer recognized by anyone. I've got great confidence in the quality wines of this region. Stylistically we're a bit massive at the moment, but we'll find more finesse. It hasn't been a tranquil journey, but I always had confidence that it would turn out like that."

JEAN CLAVEL, DECEMBER 2001

Sun, sea, and schist: everything needful to make great Banyuls and Collioure. Grenache, Syrah, and Mourvèdre all love it here.

▲ *A few producers still keep stalks in their vats, but most – like the Maury cooperative – destem before crushing.*

scented prettiness; searching out the best sites (four local terroirs have been defined, corresponding to schist, limestone, alluvial, and gravel terrace soil types, though as yet without any legal recognition); selecting the best parcels from a total of 760; reducing yields. The aim is to produce an "estate" wine for the twelve major members; similar systems are already in operation, for example, for the gigantic Val d'Orbieu.

Most significant of all, though, was a phone call back in April 1998 from Michel Tardieu. The Corbières authorities had, thoughtfully, asked Rhône-based Michel Tardieu and his Burgundian partner Dominique Laurent, specialists in fostering and finishing wines (*see* pages 103 and 146), to work on an advisory project in the region. The reason was that in 1997 many Corbières winemakers had thrown their wines into new wood with abandon, and the results had been unbecoming: a little outside help was needed. Of the twelve cooperatives that volunteered for the project, Castelmaure was one of the four to be chosen; the 2000 vintage, about to be picked as we talked, was the third in which they had worked with Tardieu. The wines the two partners have created together have not only sold very well (and at prices that would have been considered unthinkable ten years ago), but also opened up startling quality possibilities. Now the idea is to develop a system of internal Grands Crus, and to go even further in lowering yields and achieving super-ripeness.

We sipped the 1998 Cuvée No 3 (number three, they told me, since it's the cooperative's third wine, made by three partners from three varieties – and sold for three figures) as the night nestled down into the hills about us. It was unusually graceful, fleshy, and expressive for a Corbières, built on a warm core of ripe (fourteen per cent) fruit. Our eyes gleamed. "What do they think of this in Paris?" I asked. "It will be sold in Paris," they told me. "But first, we want it sold in Bordeaux."

The sailor's return

And then there are the outsiders, the *illuminés*, the moonstruck. Michel Escande stood in his cellar, his hands on the bar top in front of him; he smiled mischievously. His feet were planted widely, I now recall; he looked as if he was expecting the cellar to develop a swell, and the bar top to metamorphose into a ship's wheel. "I was handsome back then," he was reminiscing, "and I looked after myself. It was a good life." These were his early sailing years, the years when he met his wife who had just cruised back from Casamance, the years when he bought his own catamaran and set up a sailing school. Which went bust. "I only had one client, and when he dropped me, that was it."

Perhaps it's not entirely fair to call Escande an outsider; his father, who ran a heavy-plant hire company, owned ten ha (24.7 acres) here, in what is now Minervois La Livinière. He cleared the land with his machines for fun when business was quiet. "My wife and I decided to work in vineyards, which was as close to nature as sailing was," Escande explained. "There are astonishing parallels between the two, in fact. What I do now is what I used to do when I sailed, which is to make the best of natural conditions. If you're going out sailing, you have to check the weather forecast, to gauge what's ahead, to make the best of the sea. Viticulture, too; you have to optimize the natural conditions that exist. And then there's the friendship. When you're in a port, that's extraordinary, that comradeship among men of the sea, that sympathy, that common passion. It's the same with vine-growing, with people who taste wine – we all have the same philosophy of life. There was no problem as a transition."

It is conclusively and saturatingly dark by the time we reach our destination: the little village of Embres et Castelmaure in Termenès, the most southerly of the eleven "terroirs" of Corbières. Surrounded by shadowy massifs, this seemed truly *le fin fond du monde*, the back of beyond. I have the impression (though memory may be playing tricks) of gloomily operatic street lamps, of stray dogs, of dusty dented vehicles, of someone playing a trumpet outside, and then of strange, Moorish singing from an upstairs room. The village clock strikes eight; the cooperative cat mews to be let in. Let in to prowl, fastidiously, among the pools of water, and the vats of dark, scented must.

The president of SCV Castelmaure, the village cooperative, comes out to meet me, reaching for my hand with uncomplicated curiosity. He's called Patrick de Marien. He's unshaven, and smells at this mid-harvest moment of hard work; yet there's something artistic and bohemian about him, too – he could be a film-maker, maybe, or a trusted restorer of musical instruments. There's a smile playing about his face as he tells me, dramatically, semi-teasingly, about everything the cooperative has managed to achieve. With him is Bernard Pueyo, the co-op's director, his straighter foil, concerned and industrious.

Like many of France's best cooperatives, Castelmaure's advantage is that it isn't too big. There are ninety members and 300 ha (740 acres) all together, but just twelve members account for ninety per cent of the harvest. "Only twenty years ago," says de Marien, "we were considered as good for nothing but Vins de Table." The cooperative has moved forward with all the Languedoc's innovations: carbonic maceration as a way of lending Carignan a

▲ *The high Corbières is rough country with a violent past; the mist can descend at any time on its lonely vines.*

Escande's inspiration was Jacques Raynaud of Château de Rayas in Châteauneuf-du-Pape whom he met, admired, and learned much from. "It was Raynaud who made me taste what one can do with grapes, when I was a young wine-grower. He was very welcoming. You have to have an idea of where you're going, and he gave me that." Like Raynaud, though, Escande works intuitively. He's given up organic production, for example, having tried it for two years. "It didn't work. These things can't be imposed. Rules, charters, systems – none of that is very interesting. You have to feel it, work it out for yourself. You have to go where the wind pushes you." He also has Raynaud's teasing approach to questions. When asked how he gauges his extractions, for example, he will tell you that he takes a horseshoe and puts it on top of the wine. If it floats, he's extracted enough. If it sinks, he hasn't.

What is so winning in Escande's wines is their sensual appeal. "I used to plough barefoot," he says, "just for the physical and sensual pleasure of it. You have to feel things." He describes his Esprit d'Automne as a "consensual" wine; in La Féline, he says, "nothing should stick out; there should be lots of depth underneath." He takes enormous pleasure in the Languedoc's wine ferment, and particularly in that of La Livinière ("Minervois is a bus, but La Livinière is a racing car"). This is not, you'd guess, a winemaker who would be happy in Bordeaux. "We're just insects. It's a *vivier* here, an adventure; everything is up for rediscovery. It's an effervescence; it's a mayonnaise; it's extraordinary. Wine is energy. This is driving me crazy with pleasure at the moment. The vine is an antenna between the sky and the earth. The horizon of possibilities is immense."

Way to go

The three scenes just described are being repeated across Languedoc at present. Not ubiquitously: it's still more common, at harvest-time, to see the big beetle-like machines wrestling the fruit off mile after mile of flat-land vineyard. The trailers of bruised and broken grapes are then trundled back through the heat of the afternoon to the co-op, where they're carelessly vinified into the thin, petrol-pump red that, mysteriously, older French consumers still hold in high regard. This market, though, is in steep decline. There were over four million hectolitres of wine from the Languedoc without a ready buyer in 2000 and 2001, and up to 100,000 ha (247,000 acres) of vines still need to be uprooted in the region. For Chantal Lecouty of Prieuré de St-Jean de Bébian, the Languedoc's weakest cooperatives are "our biggest problem: they're a dead weight." Sylvain Fadat of Domaine d'Aupilhac says the cooperative system in Languedoc is "totally obsolete." When Alexandre Pagès outlined a project for a top wine to the cooperative to which he belonged, they refused to give him the go-ahead, and he was left with no option but to leave and found his own domain (Clos Ste-Pauline).

But little by little this low-initiative, low-expectation world is changing. What people like the Castelmaure cooperative members and Michel Escande are beginning to do is what we have already seen Jean-Michel Deiss do in Altenheim de Bergheim, or the Zind-Humbrechts in Rangen, or Claude Papin with his *pierre bise*, or the Vins de Vienne team with their Sotanum, or Elian da Ros with his Clos Baquey: to peel back the skin of the land. Any place hereabouts could produce grapes to make wine: an automatic process of historical drudgery. To peel back the skin of the land, though, requires grape growing of monastic devotion, grape growing as a kind of geological research; the fierce sense of historical inferiority which the Languedoc has traditionally felt has meant this has been a long time coming here. That is why, at Castelmaure, they want their wine to jolt Bordeaux before Paris.

Those determined to produce quality wine in the Languedoc have two means of doing so: Vins de Pays and AOC wines. During much of the 1990s, it was Vins de Pays that seemed to offer the brightest prospects: varietal wines made in a New World style, with varietal and vinification characteristics dominating their scents and flavours. In international terms, though, there is intense competition in the marketplace for wine of this sort, and production costs in France will always be higher than in the flat, irrigated, highly mechanized vineyards of Australia, South America, or South Africa. French consumers, moreover, take it as axiomatic that non-appellation wines are inferior to appellation wines, and in a way they're right: Vins de Pays are often based on inappropriate varieties for the region, rooted in second-rate soils. It is a bizarre fact that Merlot is the second most widely planted grape variety in the Languedoc, yet I tasted only one great Languedoc Merlot in the course of researching this book: Alain Chabanon's La Merle aux Alouettes. In most cases this sensitive variety, whose exact ripening point is often a difficult call, seems to be uncomfortable in this hot, rough, and stony region, though a final verdict must perhaps wait until the vines are older. Cabernet Sauvignon is better able to deal with the rigours of life in

Jean-Marie Rimbert

I looked around the cellar. There was a stuffed badger, an antique petrol pump, the rusting carcasses of a whole peloton of bicycles, glass demijohns, roadsigns, and a large plastic spider. Jean-Marie Rimbert, I had been told, collected old sardine cans. It was all beginning to make sense.

He's a tall man, with the brawny forearms that characterize both coopers and vine-pruners. He'd worked at Flaugergues as vineyard manager for five years before scraping together enough money to buy himself some land in St-Chinian, attracted by the old Carignan vines and the schistous terraces (locally called travers). His spirit of fun extends to printing the vintages on his labels using Roman numerals, and naming his estate wine La Mas au Schiste, "the house in the schist". Nothing so droll about that, of course, until you hear it pronounced in French: it's a homonym for masochiste. You need to be one to take on, as Rimbert did, his twenty ha (fifty acres) of steeply sloped terraced vineyards without even owning a tractor.

Rimbert is typical of what we might call the New Carignanistes. "Carignan," he told me, "is my Pinot. With small yields, it is a cépage noble. It's difficult, but it's got real finesse. It's a much more efficient vehicle for terroir than Syrah and Grenache, at least here, where the schist gives you relatively low-acid wines."

Rimbert makes three wines: a cuvée gourmande called Les Travers de Marsau; la Mas au Schiste itself; and finally Le Chant de Marjolaine, "my free expression": a 14.5 per cent, pure-Carignan Vin de Table made from tiny yields and very late-harvested fruit. The greatest wines of the Languedoc never taste easy or comfortable; they taste as if handfuls of stones had been stuffed into a liquidiser and ground down to a dark pulp with bitter cherries, dark plums, firm damsons, and tight sloes. This, at any rate, is pretty much what you will discover in Le Chant de Marjolaine, a song that no one has sung during the dark post-phylloxera century.

the Languedoc, yet the wines it produces here are not the region's most vivid, articulate, or exciting (*see* Jacques Lesineau's remarks under Moulin de Ciffre in the "People" section). Chardonnay, outside the cool heights of Limoux, is no more successful; Sauvignon Blanc, meanwhile, produces uniformly confected, lifeless wines throughout Languedoc. The unsurprising result is that sales of Vins de Pays, at the beginning of the twenty-first century, are flat. The latest scheme to revive the fortunes of Vins de Pays is the "Grand Oc" designation. This scheme is based on selecting outstanding wines in tastings, and giving them a minimum of twelve months' ageing. Probably more helpful to the reputation of Vins de Pays is the fact that some of the more expensive wines from the Languedoc, such as Mas de Daumas Gassac and Grange des Pères, are at present produced within the Vins de Pays legislation. Others (like Terre Inconnue) see little difference between Vin de Pays and Vin de Table, and if they want total freedom opt for the latter.

Yet even this situation is changing. Already the region's most expensive wines of all are AOC (the Roussillons of Gérard Gauby and the Coteaux du Languedoc wines of Négly), and in general the Languedoc's appellation wines are prospering. Over the last twenty years, regional production in the region has halved, yet AOC production has risen fivefold. The reasons are not hard to find. Great wine is always the consequence of the following equation: propitious vineyard soils plus well-adapted grape varieties plus fastidious viticulture and non-interventionist winemaking. The vast majority of Languedoc-Roussillon's most propitious vineyards are already classified as AOC, and in general the AOC rules favour the varieties that are best adapted to the region. Of course, errors occur, like over-zealously trying to chase Carignan out of St-Chinian, or – according to the Parcé family of Domaine de la Rectorie – of over-promoting Syrah in Roussillon; as Gérard Gauby has repeatedly pointed out, the idea of having a maximum alcohol level for Roussillon's white wines is also mad. No legislative system is perfect, and it is to be hoped these anomalies will be rectified in the years ahead.

My own belief, based on tastings during the course of three visits to the region for this book, is that the wines of Languedoc are surging in quality at present, and that the best of them are overwhelmingly AOC; good terroir-based zonal Vin de Pays, like those of Côtes de Thongue, may well become AOC in time. Vin de Pays, meanwhile, is proving very useful for lesser *cuvées*, for range extensions, for a bit of fun on the side. The example of Gilles Chabbert at Domaine des Aires Hautes is typical. His greatest wine, Clos de l'Escandil (magisterial in 1998), is AOC Minervois La Livinière, made from old Grenache plus more recently planted Syrah and Mourvèdre. He also, though, happens to have a fascinating parcel of thirty-five-year-old Malbec with which he makes an excellent Vin de Pays. The two are perfectly complementary.

Jean Paux-Rosset

"My mother Lucette," says Jean Paux-Rosset, "comes from an old Narbonne family. This property, Château de Négly, was where we all came to spend the weekends. During years, decades even, whatever we did here was just to keep the property going. Wine was just part of the picture, a way of making a little money. I felt twenty-five years ago that there was an alternative, that we had a great site, that we could make great wines, and I asked the family to be allowed to take over the property. They refused, for many years. 'Listen, petit, don't think you're going to run all that, you really haven't understood how it all works.' That was the message." The yields stayed high; the old ways remained the same; the grapes carried on going to the cooperative.

"So, since my family didn't understand my quest, I had to do other things. I got involved in promotion, housing developments, a garage for heavy goods vehicles – lots of other things, in the hope that one day I would be able to get back to my roots, my genes, and the family property. I was thrilled when my parents finally understood the challenge and let me take over. I knew what I wanted to do. Quality costs a lot of money, and today things are very difficult, I won't deny, but you have to keep going, and the journey is an interesting one. Everyone was against me ten or fifteen years ago, but events have proved me right. In the end I think my parents regretted not having let me do what I wanted earlier. My father is no longer alive, and I'm really sad that he isn't around to appreciate the wines we are making now. I have a son, Bastien, who's interested in the property, and his little sister loves it too. I hope I won't make the error that my parents made with me. If they want to grow up in it all, they'll be welcome."

What, I wondered, had made Paux-Rosset think that he could produce great wine in La Clape? After all, twenty-five years ago this was table wine country, survival farming, a few vineyards near the beach with little reputation beyond Béziers. He strokes his stubble.

"You know I always believed in the potential of La Clape; I always believed I could do something here. The inspiration didn't come from outside; I haven't been parachuted in. I was cradled in this culture; it was just that people didn't understand the challenge like I did. Men count for a lot, you know." He pauses. "For me, the notion of men is even more important than that of terroir." This is an unusual point of view for France, even in an area with as little historical fat to live off as the Languedoc, and Paux-Rosset isn't one of those who have made a point of working outside the AOC system. Indeed it's rumoured that La Clape could be one of the first parts of the Coteaux du Languedoc to get its own AOC, which surely Paux-Rosset would welcome. He shrugs. "It's all the same to me. For me, the future is La Négly."

The Adventure of the Land

It would be wrong to regard the present-day AOC system in the Languedoc as fixed and final. It isn't: it's evolving. Many of the present AOC boundaries are the result of political squabbles rather than the realities of soil, slope, and sky.

To simplify grossly, we could say that Languedoc-Roussillon has three types of AOC: hill sites, plain sites, and the sites of the Atlantic corridor. The hill sites are grafted into the chaotic foothills that tumble off the Massif Central and the Pyrénees (Minervois, St-Chinian, and Faugères, plus parts of the Coteaux du Languedoc, Roussillon, Banyuls, Corbières, and Fitou's western sector). The plain sites are constituted by most of the Coteaux du Languedoc, parts of Corbières and the coastal sectors of Fitou and Roussillon. Cabardès, Malepère, and Limoux are the AOCs of the Atlantic corridor, subject to Atlantic influences and often planted with Bordeaux varieties.

Let's begin with the biggest. In terms of size, **Corbières** is the giant of the Languedoc, producing almost half as much wine again as the second biggest AOC, Coteaux du Languedoc; it's also France's fourth largest appellation after Bordeaux, Bordeaux Supérieure, and Côtes du Rhône. It received its AOC in 1985, having been a VDQS wine since 1951. As an AOC, Corbières is too big, which explains the huge variations in wine quality you'll find under this name. The growers themselves realize this, and since 1991 they have segmented the AOC into eleven different "terroirs" (from east to west: Sigean – now renamed La Mediterranée – Fontfroide, Durban, Lézignan, Boutenac, St-Victor, Lagrasse, Montagne d'Alaric, Serviès, Termenès, and Quéribus). These have no legal status at present; the aim is to study the results they give, with a view to coming up with seven or eight official *crus*. As I write, it looks as if the first of these to receive *cru* approval will be the predominantly sandstone-soiled Boutenac, in every sense the hottest zone in the AOC, with Durban, Lagrasse, and La Mediterranée to follow. It is difficult to make many generalizations about these at present, owing to the fact that they have a wide variety of soils (limestone, schist, sandstone, and marl), heights (from sea level in La Mediterranée and Lézignan up to 500 metres/1,640 feet in Termenès), and exposures (countless valleys, slopes, hillsides, plateaux, and plains). James Wilson, in his book *Terroir*, speaks of the "geological cacophony" of this area, and anyone visiting Corbières cannot fail to be struck by the evident violence of local geological history, a many-million-year battle between stone and sky, laid out in all its fractured fury around your car, your bicycle, or your boots. Sounding out the wine voices of this chaos will provide wine drinkers with great enjoyment over the next several hundred years. The grape variety tools are Carignan (a maximum of fifty per cent, though it is rumoured Boutenac will be allowed up to sixty-five per cent, since Carignan performs well there), Syrah, Grenache, and Mourvèdre, the last three in unlimited proportion provided there are two or more varieties used.

Fitou, a wild and remote subzone on the Corbières-Roussillon frontier, is the oldest appellation in the Languedoc, dating from 1948, and is for red wines only (white and rosé wines can be sold as Corbières, and the region also includes vineyards classified for Rivesaltes and Muscat de Rivesaltes Vins Doux Naturels). It owes its early AOC recognition to politics – and the fact that high yields (and therefore the very worst quality wines) are impossible to achieve here. Oddly, though, its cultivated 2,560 ha (6,320 acres) are divided into

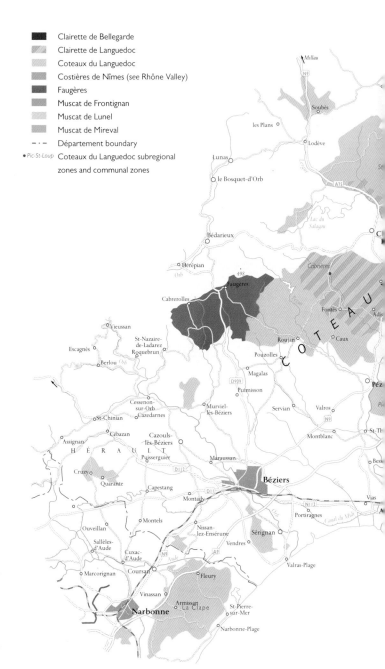

Clairette de Bellegarde
Clairette de Languedoc
Coteaux du Languedoc
Costières de Nîmes (see Rhône Valley)
Faugères
Muscat de Frontignan
Muscat de Lunel
Muscat de Mireval
– · – Département boundary
• *Pic-St-Loup* Coteaux du Languedoc subregional zones and communal zones

two very different sectors. The coastal sector of Fitou Maritime (made up of the five communes of Caves, Fitou, Lapalme, Leucate, and Treilles), adjacent to the lagoon-like Etang de Salses, is hot and low-lying, its soils composed of France's most typical wine-growing medium, clay-limestone. The wilder hill sector of Fitou Montagneux (the communes of Cascatel, Paziols, Tuchan, and Villeneuve) is predominantly schist, though with some clay-limestone sectors in Paziols and Tuchan. (Mont Tauch itself is a limestone peg.) Of the two sectors, Fitou Montagneux produces the best and deepest wines: just like the high Corbières, it is a kind of geological scrapyard, a stony wilderness where ravens and boars feel more at home than human

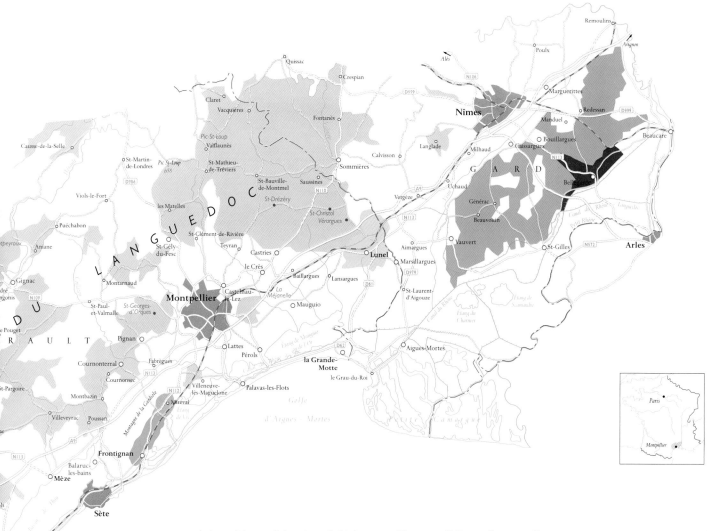

beings. Many of the vines (which grow at an average height of 300 metres/984 feet) are bent southwards by the ferocious prevailing winds. Fitou must be a three-variety blend, and this is the only AOC in France at present trying to promote Carignan, with a minimum thirty per cent requirement. Syrah, however, will have to furnish between ten and thirty per cent of blends by 2007; and the minimum ageing period before sale is no less than nine months (it is just four in Corbières). There is talk of extending the AOC to include white wines based on Grenache Blanc and complemented by Vermentino.

South of Corbières and Fitou lies **Roussillon**. Wherein the differences? *Appellation contrôlée* is supposed to concern terroir and terroir alone; the boundary between Cucugnan, Paziols, and Embres on the Corbières/Fitou side and their neighbours on the Roussillon side prove that this is not always true. You'll find the same rock-strewn wilderness of chaotic hills; the same blast of northern wind; the same desiccating summers. In terroir terms, schist is becoming more common as we go south, but schist has already established itself firmly in Fitou Montagneux and is, for example, the dominant rock type in Faugères and the north of St-Chinian. What's changed is a political border: we have left the Aude and entered the Pyrénées-Orientales. Nor is politics all. When I asked those in Corbières the difference, they told me that it is cultural, too. "We are Languedociens; they are Catalans."

The overall Roussillon appellation occupies 118 communes and around 4,800 ha (11,850 acres) ; within it lies the smaller appellation of **Côtes du Roussillon-Villages** (for thirty-two communes); the wines are eighty per cent red. The best wines of the Villages appellation come from the upper reaches of the three main valleys which stretch into the hills from the sea: that of the Agly, the Têt, and the Tech. Geologically speaking, schist is by no means the whole story; there is also gneiss, granite, and limestone here. Indeed in places the limestone is pure enough to quarry. To some extent, these geological differences are picked out in the four *crus* that can add their name to the Villages appellation. **Caramany**, from the village of the same name, is grown on gneiss; **Latour-de-France** is on brown schist; **Lesquerde** is granite; and **Tautavel** (for Tautavel and Vingrau) is on clay-limestone. Grenache and Carignan have traditionally been the dominant grape varieties, while Syrah and Mourvèdre have more recently come to join them. (Some local producers, such as the Parcé brothers of Domaine de la Rectorie, believe that Syrah is a dangerous outside interloper threatening the blissful hegemony of Grenache in Roussillon; others, by contrast, like Gérard Gauby, welcome it with open arms.)

This is also, of course, one of France's greatest areas for Vins Doux Naturels, and thereby hangs an explanation. The red wines of the general Roussillon zone, from producers such as Clos des Fées, Gardiès, Gauby, Lhéritier, and Marcevol, are perhaps the most dramatically improved wines in the New France, just as their Catalan neighbours further south in Priorato have thrown down a gauntlet for the New Spain. (There is an evident kinship in the baked, sweet, sometimes faintly medicinal fruit, mineral overtones, and dense textures of these remarkable Grenache-based wines.) Quality in Roussillon, from those who work with low yields, is often astounding. Yes, of course terroir has something to do with it: there are many superb (though labour-intensive) vineyard sites here, and both schist and limestone make appropriately difficult, austere soils. But the real answer as to why the red wines are now so good is found in the vogue for sweet fortified wine in France which followed the privations of the Second World War. Total production of Vins Doux Naturels peaked in 1964 at 712,690 hl; nowadays it rarely passes 500,000 hl. Yet the vines, and in particular Grenache, are still there. Some fifty years older. The Vin Doux Naturel heritage, in other words, with its old-vine patrimony, has given Roussillon something of a head start over much of the Languedoc, which had to uproot its Aramon before the serious search for red wine quality could begin. (Old-vine Carignan is common to both sectors.)

There are six Vins Doux Naturels appellations in Roussillon. Quantitatively, the most important is **Rivesaltes**, grown on almost 10,000 ha (24,700 acres) across the region (it also stretches into Corbières and Fitou). This is the AOC that has suffered the most over the last two decades, since Rivesaltes was historically a branded wine sold by négociants – and when the going got tough, the négociants got out, leaving the growers to fend for themselves. Both red and

	Cabardès
	Corbières
	Coteaux du Languedoc
	Côtes de la Malepère
	Fitou
	Limoux
	Minervois
	Muscat de St-Jean-de-Minervois
	Rivesaltes
	St-Chinian
- - -	Département boundary
SUB	Terroir of Corbières
La Clape	Coteaux du Languedoc subregional and communal zones
La Livinière	Minervois Cru
CLAMOUX	Minervois bioclimatic zone

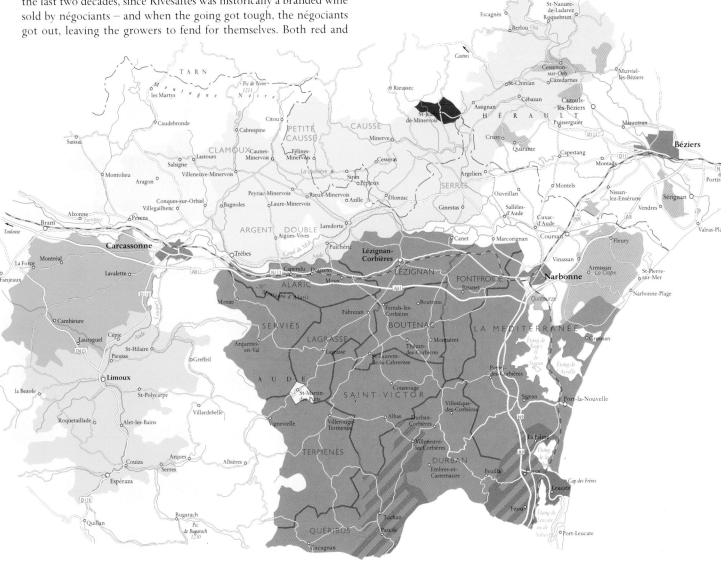

white grapes can be used (Grenaches Blanc, Gris, and Noir are dominant); the wines are fortified part-way through fermentation, and finish at 21.5% abv. Rivesaltes is sold as Rouge (young, red, and unoxidized), Ambré (oxidatively aged for two years), and Tuilé (the same, with at least fifty per cent Grenache Noir); Hors d'Age on a bottle of Rivesaltes means it has been aged for at least five years. The Rivesaltes version of the top-of-the-range "Vintage" style (bottled young, and based on seventy-five per cent Grenache Noir) is Grenat. It's worth noting, for all those who pay £200 a bottle to drink Echézeaux or St-Emilion cropped at twenty hl/ha, that the average yield for Rivesaltes in 1998 was 16.5 hl/ha.

The two *crus* for Roussillon's Vins Doux Naturels are **Maury** and **Banyuls**. Maury is a corridor of schist surrounded by limestone sited up near Corbières; the fortress of Quéribus can be seen, perched like a falcon, in the distance. Maury is overwhelmingly a Grenache-based red VDN which, if bottled young, can have some of the thunderous power of vintage port – though the name "Vintage", in use here for a while, has now been outlawed. Look out for the French words "Vendange" or "Récolte" instead. Banyuls, grown on a patchwork of pure schist slopes hard by the Spanish border, has traditionally been an oxidatively aged wine marked by the swashbuckling and insouciant tang locally called *rancio*. Traditionnel, Blanc, Doré, and Ambré wines will all be of this type. The more exciting and expressive (Vintage-style) alternative is called Rimage in Banyuls, and is supposedly made in great years

only. **Banyuls Grand Cru** is a silly AOC that merely means seventy-five per cent Grenache and at least thirty months ageing, and the little used AOC of **Grand Roussillon** is for blends of Rivesaltes, Banyuls, or Maury. **Muscat de Rivesaltes**, finally, is the sizeable Muscat Vin Doux Naturel appellation that also covers the three AOCs of Rivesaltes, Banyuls, and Maury. Banyuls producers who wish to use their Grenache (or Syrah, Mourvèdre, Carignan, or Cinsault) to make a schist-grown red table wine, as they might sensibly also want to do on these startlingly steep, terraced slopes within sight of the sea, can use the AOC of **Collioure**. This has identical boundaries to Banyuls.

So much for France's Deep South. With Limoux, suddenly, everything changes. Just like Corbières, it occupies the high, wild hills to the south of the Canal du Midi; yet it lies further west than Corbières, crucially a little closer to the Atlantic, and this makes all the difference. Welcome to Languedoc's Champagne. It's not just that its 1,800 ha (4,450 acres) produce the leading sparkling wine of the region (which it does), but it also produces the kind of cool, crisp, still white wines more typical of vineyards further north. The soils here are lime-rich and stony, though there are also admixtures of sandstone, marl, and conglomerate; their aptitude for white wine production is underlined by their long history. The Abbey of St-Hilaire is said to have bottled cork-stoppered sparkling wine from 1531, well before the technique was widely used in Champagne. **Blanquette de Limoux** is an AOC for sparkling

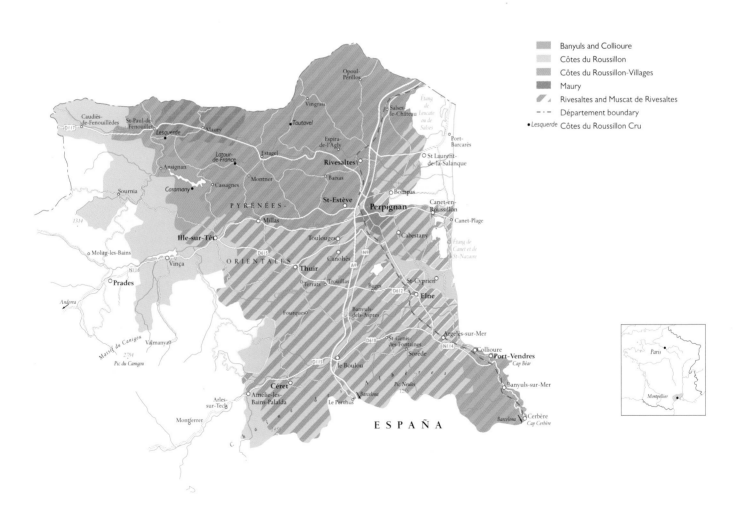

▲ *Durban, one of the eleven terroirs of Corbières, is tipped to receive the official accolade of "cru" status before long.*

more meaningful to younger wine drinkers but without trashing tradition altogether, and without disfiguring the soil's potential. A red wine version of the AOC has been approved from the 2003 vintage, moreover, and is the first AOC in Languedoc to permit fifty per cent Merlot (marking a sizeable concession on Bordeaux's part). The other permitted varieties are Cabernet Sauvignon, Cabernet Franc, Malbec, Syrah, Grenache, and Carignan (the last until 2010 only).

Underneath Limoux lies **Côtes de la Malepère**. This new red and rosé AOC is, like its smaller sibling Cabardès which lies just across the Canal du Midi, a kind of Bordeaux-Languedoc hybrid: Bordeaux varieties mixed with Grenache, Cinsault, Syrah, and Lladoner Pelut (a close relative of Grenache). Like Limoux, most of the Malepère vineyards are blocked from the Mediterranean by the Corbières uplands, making them cooler and rainier than the Languedoc norm. The vineyards surround the flattened limestone cone of Mont Naut and the Bois de Malepère ridge; they combine classic lime-clay with a mixture of sands and pebbles washed down from the Pyrénées.

Tiny **Cabardès** has just 400 ha (988 acres) in cultivation for its red and rosé wines. Whereas Malepère could be said to be Limoux's red shadow, Cabardès is a cooler, Atlantic interpretation of Minervois. Like Minervois and St-Chinian, it's wedged up against the long dark belly of the Montagne Noire, in a little amphitheatre cut by six rivers. This, though, is the cooler, breezier, damper end of the Montagne Noire. The grape variety mix looks in both directions: Bordeaux varieties (Merlot, Cabernet Sauvignon, Cabernet Franc) account for a minimum of forty per cent of the blend, and Languedoc/Rhône varieties (Syrah and Grenache) for another forty per cent. The balance is made up by an interesting seasoning of Malbec, Fer, and Cinsault. The soils are complex, reflecting the geological lucky dip of the Montagne Noire itself: granite, quartzite, limestone, and schist are all found here. These are some of the coolest, freshest, and often most perfumed red wines of the Languedoc.

With 4,500ha (11,115 acres) in cultivation, **Minervois** is the Languedoc's third biggest appellation after Corbières and Coteaux du Languedoc; like them, it has a huge internal variety of growing sites, and it's hard to see it maintaining its unitary integrity over the next hundred years. Indeed with the granting of a separate appellation for **Minervois La Livinière** in 1998, this AOC has beaten its two larger rivals in terms of winning official approval for the debut of a system of internal *crus*; more seem likely to follow. Is it the hare of the Languedoc?

It's certainly got a lot going for it. Some superb sites, for a start, as the Montagne Noire tumbles down in river-cut terraces towards the River Aude itself. The growers themselves have divided the appellation up into five internal "bioclimatic" zones, some of which are further subdivided, indicating the typical shuffled-card complexity of Languedoc AOCs. Les Côtes Noires is the first of these, sited in the northwest of the appellation, in whose schistous soils marble veins are found; Clamoux is to the south of Les Côtes Noires, on the western edge of the AOC. Both of these zones are almost Cabardès-like in nature, subject to Atlantic rather than Mediterranean influences, with some summer rain; they produce the freshest, lightest, and least alcoholic Minervois wines. What's called the Zone Centrale includes a little bit of everything, from the low-lying Balcons de l'Aude which surround the drained Etang de Marseillette, producing wines of often mediocre quality; to Le Petit Causse, a high-sited marl-and-limestone area with a superb south-facing exposition. It's in Le Petit Causse where the Minervois La Livinière AOC is to be found. The extensive terraces of the Argent

wines made by the traditional method based preponderantly upon Mauzac, a late-ripening variety of musky apple scent, blended with up to ten per cent of Chenin Blanc and Chardonnay. There is also a curious but precious pure-Mauzac alternative made by a single fermentation, terminated in sealed bottles (called the *méthode ancestrale* here). The wine is not disgorged before being sold, with the result that it is sweet, cloudy, and relatively low in alcohol: a refreshingly soft mouthful of wine foam. **Crémant de Limoux** is the region's third sparkling AOC, for traditional method wines made with a higher percentage (up to thirty per cent) of Chardonnay and Chenin Blanc.

It is the still wines, though, that have made **Limoux** one of the Languedoc's most successful regions. They're AOC, but they contain enough Chardonnay to make varietal labelling possible. This is, moreover, the only white wine AOC in France with compulsory whole-bunch pressing and barrel-fermentation; and the Chardonnay vines themselves are older than usual for Vins de Pays, thanks to the modifications made to the Blanquette AOC which sanctioned Chardonnay back in 1975. However, the wines still have to contain at least fifteen per cent Mauzac; Chenin Blanc can be used as an alternative to Chardonnay if wished (although it isn't, generally). This is a good example of how appellation regulations can be sensibly and successfully modified to become

Double in the west and the rocky austerities of the Mourels in the east complete the Zone Centrale. The highest vineyards of all are sited in the jagged white limestone Causse itself to the northeast of the AOC (an upland plateaux, often gorge-cut), with harsh winters and bright, austere summers. This dry, stony landscape is in part given over to Muscat production for **St-Jean-de-Minervois**, the Muscat with more finesse than any other. Cool air tumbles off the Montagne Noire, and the vines are grown in sheltered pockets and scrapes. It's here that the town of Minerve itself is found where, in 1210, Simon de Montfort's seven-week siege ended with the burning to death of 140 of its Cathar peasants, who were already dying of thirst: history is as ferocious as the landscape here. De Montfort got what he deserved at Toulouse: the hard end of a cannon ball. Finally, Les Serres in the far east of Minervois is the warmest and most Mediterranean zone of all. Its vineyard sites vary from low-lying, deep-soiled riverside terraces to marly hillsides and steep limestone slopes. The grape variety rules allow a maximum of forty per cent Carignan, with Grenache, Syrah, Mourvèdre, and Lladoner Pelut (or any combination thereof) accounting for a minimum of sixty per cent of blends. The La Livinière regulations are slightly more stringent, stipulating that the wines (made from slightly lower yields than Minervois itself) should be tasted three times by the AOC's tasting commission, and must be aged for a year before sale.

St-Chinian, like the eastern sector of Minervois, clambers up out of the Languedoc plain (the Atlantic corridor has, by now, been left behind); the Montagne Noire continues to furnish its mountain backdrop, together with the Caroux and Espinouse mountains. Its 3,000 cultivated hectares (7,410 acres) are divided into two subzones: schist and sandstone in the north and east; limestone in the south and west. The higher, schist slopes give pungent, intense,

concentrated red and rosé wines; the lower limestone sites provide softer, often more alcoholic wines. Grenache, Syrah, and Mourvèdre account for sixty per cent of blends, but old-vine Carignan is championed by the best growers, too. The appellation now includes white wines, too.

Faugères is a ramp of pure schist which climbs up from the Languedoc plain and the outskirts of Béziers to the foothills of the Cévennes; 1,800 ha (4,450 acres) of vineyard produce red and rosé wines based on (as usual) a maximum of forty per cent Carignan and a minimum of sixty per cent Syrah, Grenache, and Mourvèdre. Recent innovations include extending the AOC to include white wines, and a plan to launch something called Fine Faugères. The word "Fine" normally connotes a brandy, and indeed there is a tradition here of producing a pot-still brandy which dates back to the nineteenth century; a few producers continue to distil a Fine de Faugères. The plan, interesting if potentially confusing, is to extend this to connote a prestige range of wines based on old vines: forty years for Carignan, twenty years for Syrah and Grenache, and fifteen years for Mourvèdre.

The white wine **Clairette de Languedoc** AOC has existed since 1948, though the reputation the wines enjoyed then has been eclipsed. Clairette is certainly not a white grape of choice any more in the Languedoc: its low acidity and torpid weight make whites of much less contemporary appeal than the aromatic Roussanne, the lush Grenache Blanc, or even the crisp, acidity-retaining Bourboulenc. Clairette du Languedoc can be made in a number of ways, dry and sweet, fortified and unfortified; most are dry, though the historically important sweet version is making a modest return. A mere seventy ha (173 acres) are in cultivation, occupying terraces of mixed geological origin in two zones set back about thirty km

▼ *Machine harvesting in the rain makes it certain that this wine will be less good than it could be.*

▼ *Banyuls' quality of light is no less attractive to artists – and Sunday sailors – than it is to grape vines.*

(nineteen miles) from the sea. Even more insignificant is **Clairette de Bellegarde**, a tiny, sparsely used AOC sited in the southeastern part of the Costières de Nîmes. (For Costières de Nîmes itself, *see* the Rhône Valley chapter.)

And so to the most confusing appellation in France today, though one that is also the source of some of France's best-value wines: **Coteaux du Languedoc**. This AOC is best viewed as a kind of finishing school for the individual appellations of the future. At present each is dressed up in the same school uniform, but all are keen to leave as soon as possible, set off into the world and prove their individual merits. St-Chinian, Faugères, and, theoretically, Clairette du Languedoc have already made their escape into AOC adulthood and are regarded as established *crus* (thus wines from these AOCs can also be sold as Coteaux du Languedoc if wished).

In principle, any worthwhile vineyard site of the coastal zone that isn't yet an AOC on its own has been gathered together under the umbrella of Coteaux du Languedoc. Less good sites, or those with no historical viticultural tradition, are classified as **Vin de Pays**. There are exceptions to this rule: some producers (like those at Aniane) are on AOC land but prefer to work within the Vins de Pays framework since they want to use non-local grape varieties. Furthermore, growers in the Béziers area (where there are some excellent terroirs, such as the **Côtes de Thongue** midway between Béziers and Pézenas) were offered the chance to have their best sites classified by INAO but refused, since at the time the Vins de Pays route (and international varietals) seemed to offer a swifter journey away from the misery of the past than did AOC wine production and its use of local varieties. This decision is often a cause of present-day regret.

Perhaps the best way to understand the Coteaux du Languedoc patchwork is to think of it as analogous to the celebrated Burgundy pyramid. The fat and spreading bottom of the pyramid is provided by the regional AOC, Coteaux du Languedoc itself.

Half way up the pyramid are seven subregional zones (sometimes called "climatic regions"), all of which have the potential to become AOCs in their own right. From southwest to northeast, these are La

Clape, Terrasses de Béziers (which is much smaller than it should be, for the reasons mentioned above), Pézenas, Terrasses du Larzac, Grès de Montpellier, Pic-St-Loup, and (near Nîmes) Terres de Sommières.

Finally, at the top of the pyramid are twelve communal zones (sometimes called "terroirs"), all of which also have the potential to become AOCs on their own. Once again from southwest to northeast, these are Quatourze, Pinet, Cabrières, St-Saturnin, Montpeyroux, St-Georges d'Orques, La Méjanelle, St-Drézery, Vérargues, and St-Christol. For the record, La Clape and Pic-St-Loup double as both subregional zones and communal zones. You may see all of these names used on labels at present, though the AOC is always Coteaux du Languedoc.

If you like a bet, the insiders' tips for early promotion to AOC are on Pinet (for Picpoul de Pinet, a lemony monovarietal white wine), Montpeyroux (which would include the well-known Aniane), Pic-St-Loup, Grès de Montpellier, and the coastal, limestone tongue of La Clape (approved from the 2002 vintage).

This catch-all AOC includes a huge variety of different vineyard sites. Some, like St-Saturnin, Montpeyroux, and Pic-St-Loup, are classic terraced vineyards of calcareous marl grafted into the foothills of the Cévennes. Others, like La Méjanelle, Vérargues, and St-Christol, are lower-lying gravelly terraces of river-borne material providing vineyard sites similar to that of Costières de Nîmes. Cabrières, like Faugères, is schistous. La Clape, a hilly island of limestone once separated from the mainland, is different again, by reason of its markedly maritime climate; for bizarre political reasons a finger of Corbières reaches up to grab the southernmost part of La Clape. Quatourze is a flat and pebbley vineyard on the outskirts of Narbonne. It would be a great mistake to assume that the hill sites of the Coteaux du Languedoc are all superior to the flatter, more low-lying sites. Le Méjanelle within Grès de Montpellier, for example, is capable of producing superb, profound red wines from its river pebble and red clay soils, though sadly the voracious city of Montpellier is gobbling up its vineyards and slicing roads and motorways through them.

Muscat de Frontignan, **Muscat de Mireval**, and **Muscat de Lunel** are all very flat, coastal AOCs for Muscat-based Vins Doux Naturels: fat, honeyed, and gratifying, though without the edge and perfumed finesse of the very different **St-Jean de Minervois**, high-sited on its bright white limestones.

▼ *The refusal to separate red and white grape varieties reduces quality further for this cooperative consignment.*

Languedoc-Roussillon Flak

L'affaire Mondavi

The events that have come to be known as "*l'affaire Mondavi*" seem to have cast a questionable light on the Languedoc. Briefly, the Californian wine producer Robert Mondavi wished to acquire or create a wine domain to grow Syrah in the Languedoc at Aniane, a commune which – thanks to the presence of Mas de Daumas Gassac, Grange des Pères, and Capion – had developed a reputation for outstanding Vins de Pays. A persistent local rumour has it that Mondavi discussed the purchase of Mas de Daumas Gassac itself, but that agreement on the price proved impossible. (I have also been told that the Australian company Southcorp had six-month negotiations about the purchase of Mas de Daumas Gassac; these foundered for the same reasons.) Mondavi therefore decided to create his own domain from scratch, using what Aimé Guibert described as virgin forest within Aniane, and what Mondavi's man in France, David Pearson, described as "scrub land that had been used for grazing and agriculture for more than fifty years." Aniane town council, under mayor André Ruiz and with the active support of Montpellier's mayor Georges Frêche, approved Mondavi's plans on July 25th, 2000. The scheme was to plant small five-ha (twelve-acre) plots in the *garrigue* in an identical manner to the way in which Aimé Guibert had planted Mas de Daumas Gassac itself.

A local election then took place in which "Mondavi versus the forest" featured largely. Ruiz lost. The winner, Manuel Diaz, came from the anti-Mondavi (or pro-forest) camp, and Mondavi abandoned his project the following May, pulling out entirely from France and offloading his Vichon Méditerranée label shortly afterwards. Laurent Vaillé of Grange des Pères called it "a catastrophe. We've blown a unique opportunity of getting Languedoc known right around the world." The balance of opinion among French consumers on the French wine enthusiasts' website MagnumVinum.fr also came down against the "immobilism" that Mondavi's withdrawal represented. It made the Languedoc seem unwelcoming and uncouth to outsiders.

But it strains credibility to believe that Mondavi couldn't find any existing viticultural land with which to create outstanding Syrah in the whole of Languedoc-Roussillon. Syrah can be magnificent in St-Chinian, Faugères, and Minervois La Livinière, to name just three other zones; Gauby's Muntada and Négly's Clos des Truffiers are both astonishingly good Syrah-based wines grown nowhere near Aniane. "The problem was," said one local observer, "that Mondavi wanted to be between Mas de Daumas and Granges des Pères. He could have installed himself a thousand times in other places that are just as good. But he wanted to be next to Guibert, *contre* Guibert." We should also recognize that the decision was a remarkable (and unusual) example of local democracy proving more effective than outside capital aligned with local political power. For better or for worse, local people had the final word.

Up in arms

As the twentieth century becomes the twenty-first, Languedoc is the only region of France where wine – and specifically the over-production of mediocre wine – is still a cause of social unrest. Vats have been emptied, motorway toll booths trashed, and the premises of Midi négociant Daniel Bessière subject to 3.8 million euro's worth of damage shortly before the company was due to celebrate its one hundredth anniversary. Those who carry out such actions see them as being in the tradition of the celebrated 1907 uprising, but most observers agree that whereas the entire market was in chaos in 1907, the problems of the present day are, in Jean Clavel's words, simply "a crisis of bad quality wine. Half of Languedoc's wine is unsellable." Jean Clavel worked administratively for forty years to guide the Languedoc towards full AOC and Vins de Pays competitivity; his own belief is that this is the last gasp of those beyond reform. "Wine producers and cooperatives who make good quality wine don't have any sales problem, but a good third or more of our cooperatives haven't made the necessary advances. They won't change. But many of their members are old, and they don't have successors. They will finish their work," believes Clavel, "and the problem will diminish of its own accord."

Languedoc-Roussillon: People

Abbotts

34000 Montpellier, Tel: 04 67 91 31 00, Fax: 04 67 91 31 07

Australian Dr Nerida Abbott and Briton Nigel Sneyd are the couple behind this venture, producing wine in the Limoux, Minervois, Coteaux du Languedoc, and Côtes du Roussillon AOCs, preponderantly from purchased fruit. The wines are enjoyable and consistent, though not yet outstanding (in contrast to the grandiose packaging); oak is liberally used, with the best wine being the Minervois Cumulonimbus – a lush, sweet "Shiraz". Abbott is a great believer in the region, claiming it has "the most amazing potential in the world"; she chooses to work within the AOC system rather than the Vin de Pays system because "the AOC areas are where the best vineyards in the south of France are found."

de l'Aigle

11300 Roquetaillade, Tel: 04 68 31 39 12, Fax: 04 68 31 39 14

This leading Limoux estate of 22 ha now belongs to Burgundy's Antonin Rodet. Rodet's skilful and energetic winemaker, Nadine Gublin, says she is "thrilled" by the climatic conditions in Limoux: "Warm days, cool nights, clay-limestone soils, it doesn't rain too much, the ripeness is very good." Yields are reined back to 40 hl/ha, and the results are a range of accurately defined varietal wines with more subtlety than most – though as yet no profundity. (The previous owner, Champenois Jean-Louis Denois, was a casualty of France's wine bureaucracy: he planted Riesling and Gewurztraminer; another wine producer informed the INAO of this "crime"; he was prosecuted; he sold up in disgust.)

Aiguelière

34150 Montpeyroux, Tel: 04 67 96 61 43, Fax: 04 67 44 49 67

The best wines from this carefully run Montpeyroux domain are its two Syrah cuvées, Côte Dorée (grown on gravel) and Côte Rousse (grown on limestone). They are pliant, pure, and elegant.

Aiguilloux

11200 Thezan des Corbières, Tel: 04 68 43 32 71, Fax: 04 68 43 30 66

This 37-ha Corbières domain is sited on some of the only limestone soils in Boutenac and produces warm, ripe, deliciously fruited red wines sensibly rounded out in old wood.

Aires Hautes

34210 Siran, Tel: 04 68 91 54 40, Fax: 04 68 91 54 40

The range produced by Gilles Chabbert at his 28-ha Minervois La Livinière domain includes a worthwhile Malbec Vin de Pays d'Oc based on 35-year-old vines and both Minervois and Minervois La Livinière cuvées. The grandest wine by far, though, is the Clos de l'Escandil – a genuine walled vineyard in La Livinière planted with youngish Syrah and Mourvèdre and 50-year-old Grenache. Recent vintages haven't quite matched the quality of the legendary 1998 (produced with yields of 16 hl/ha), but this is still a ripe, coffee-scented wine of texture and distinction.

Alquier

34600 Faugères, Tel: 04 67 23 07 89

The wines bottled under the name Gilbert Alquier by this leading Faugères domain are rather slender and disappointing. The JM & F Alquier wines (Maison Jaune and Bastides) are better, though late bottling and late release does not necessarily work in their favour.

Aupilhac

34150 Montpeyroux, Tel: 04 67 96 61 19, Fax: 04 67 96 67 24

The outspoken Sylvain Fadat's 30-ha domain is one of the Montpeyroux vanguard; Fadat also produces wines under the Mont Baudile zonal Vin de Pays (for a pure Carignan and a "vin de plaisir" called Lou Badet) and uses Vin de Pays de l'Hérault, too, for a Cinsault from 101-year-old vines (Les Servières) as well as for his new Aniane venture, Les Plôs de Baumes – a toothsome Bordeaux blend grown on land his maternal grandfather cultivated. It is nonetheless d'Aupilhac itself, and its single-parcel selection Le Clos, which provides the densest, most tightly meshed flavours here (the challenging blend in 1999 was 40% each of Mourvèdre and Carignan, with just 20% Syrah).

les Aurelles

34720 Caux, Tel: 04 67 98 46 21, Fax: 04 67 09 32 58

Karl Mauguin and Basile Saint-German, both mid-life converts to wine production, established this 11.5-ha Coteaux du Languedoc domain near Pézenas in the mid-1990s by buying up old parcels of vines on gravel ridges just to the north of the town. The elegant, refined Solen is based on 65% Carignan and 35% Grenache, while the slightly plumper though still nimble Aurel is 45% Grenache, 30% Mourvèdre, and 25% Syrah. The inspiration is Bordelais (both spent time there working at Haut-Brion and Latour), hence the hunt for gravel. There is, though, a big difference: no wood is used here for the red wines. Grace and purity are the hallmarks.

Baron'arques

11250 Gardie, Tel: 04 68 69 77 77

This ambitious red wine is produced in Limoux by Baron Philippe de Rothschild working in conjunction with the Sieur d'Arques cooperative. It's a combination of 60% "Atlantic" varieties (Merlot and the two Cabernets) and 40% "Mediterranean" varieties (Grenache, Syrah, and Malbec) given Bordeaux-style vinification and oak ageing, making it similar in style to a Cabardès or a Malepère. The parcels used for the first three vintages come from the Mediterranée and Haute Vallée terroirs of Limoux (the villages are Villar-St-Anselme, St-Polycarpe, Gardie, and Villebazy), though until Limoux acquires its red wine AOC the wine is sold as Vin de Pays de la Haute Vallée de l'Aude. The results are complex, elegant and more urbane than the Languedoc norm, while the depth of fruit is steadily increasing; 1999 marked a step forward from 1998, and Vincent Montigaud claims that 2000 and 2001 are deeper and more resonant still. However the price, which is on parity with d'Armailhacq in Pauillac, is over-ambitious. The same partnership also produces a range of unexciting varietal wines sold under the Rothschild name. Domaine de Lambert, meanwhile, is a Limoux domain personally owned by Baroness Philippine de Rothschild; it is currently being replanted, under the supervision of energetic Californian Tod Mostero, to meet the expected requirements of the Limoux red wine AOC.

La Baume

34290 Servian, Tel: 04 67 39 29 49, Fax: 04 67 39 29 40

Australian company BRL Hardy's Languedoc enterprise specializes in producing adept though unambitious varietal wines. The Sélection Chardonnay and Cabernet Sauvignon are winery choices of the best contract fruit given barrique-ageing; the top wines, meanwhile, are the softly spicy Domaine La Baume barrel-fermented white (70% Viognier,

30% Chardonnay for 1998) and the clean, fresh Domaine La Baume red (55% Merlot and 45% Cabernet Sauvignon in 1998).

La Bégude *see* Comte Cathar

Belles Eaux
34720 Caux, Tel: 04 67 09 30 95, Fax: 04 67 09 30 95

This large, 50-ha Coteaux du Languedoc domain has traditionally sold on much of its production to regional négociants, but it is beginning to bottle more under its own name. The Tradition has lots of soft fruit; oak is well-handled and unobtrusive in the Fûts de Chêne *cuvée*, and there is also a selected Cuvée Sylveric of deeper, spicier fruit (it is based on 70% Syrah).

Bergé
11350 Paziols, Tel: 04 68 45 41 73, Fax: 04 68 45 41 73

Bertrand Bergé is one of the rising stars of the often disappointing AOC of Fitou: look out for his *garrigue*-scented, generously textured Fitou Ancestrale.

Borie de Maurel ✪✪
34210 Félines-Minervois, Tel: 04 68 91 68 58, Fax: 04 68 91 63 92

Michel Escande's 28-ha domain is the source of some of the greatest wines to come out of Minervois and the new Minervois La Livinière AOCs so far. The Cuvée Aude white wine is a crisp, salty, perfumed blend of Marsanne and small amounts of Muscat. Esprit d'Automne is supple and earthy, while La Féline is svelte and rich; both of these *cuvées* are Syrah-dominated. Cuvée Maxim is Escande's Minervois glance towards Bandol: this pure Mourvèdre is grown on sandstone, aged in *demi-muids*, and has stony scents and a powerfully leathery, mineral flavour lashed into place with rich, throbbing tannins. The unoaked, pure-Syrah Cuvée Scylla is a magnificent effort, and makes a fascinatingly aerial comparison to Négly's Porte du Ciel: the scents are almost Hermitage-like, while the flavours are graceful and layered, packed with cherry and liquorice. This is grown in Escande's highest parcels, at around 300 metres, on marl and limestone soils. Escande's homage to his tutorial genius Jacques Reynaud, the Belle de Nuit ("*Ça fond, ça enrobe – c'est la lune*," he says: "It melts, it coats – it's the moon") is a pure Grenache which its creator claims is grown on flint. Once again, you'll find the Borie de Maurel hallmark of balance, finesse, smooth textures, and perfumed intensity. British readers, finally, might encounter the brilliant Rêve de Carignan, a 14.5% houri of a wine packed with soft, bubbling black fruits yet braced, too, with the taut acid structure of this occasionally magnificent variety. Escande, having studied under a master, is well on the way to becoming one himself.

Borie la Vitarèle
34490 Sainte-Nazaire-de-Laderez, Tel: 04 67 89 50 43, Fax: 04 67 89 50 43

Jean-François Izarn's 10-ha domain contains a number of different terroirs: rich valley-floor soils for Vins de Pays; river-bed pebbles for the perfumed, Syrah-based Les Creisses St-Chinian; limestone for the plummier Coteaux du Languedoc Terres Blanches, mainly Grenache-based; and schist (obviously) for the St-Chinian Les Schistes, a Syrah-Grenache blend. In addition to being a skilled winemaker, Izarn is also a brilliant cook and enthusiastic bonsai grower.

Bousquette
34460 Cessenon, Tel: 04 67 89 65 38, Fax: 04 67 89 57 58

This promising St-Chinian property is, like Foulaquier in Pic-St-Loup and the local Grange des Quatre Sous, Swiss-owned. Eric Perret's vines are organically grown, and the Cuvée Prestige is an ambitious, well-constructed wine packed with the gently licking fire of St-Chinian's remarkable schist terroir.

Cabrol
11600 Aragon, Tel: 04 68 77 19 06, Fax: 04 68 77 54 90

This high-sited (300m), 21-ha domain in Cabardès is run by teacher Claude Cayrol and his brother Michel. The Janus-headed nature of this new-born AOC is celebrated by the two main *cuvées* here: the Syrah-based Vent d'Est, to summarize Languedoc influences, and the Cabernet-based Vent d'Ouest, which glances along the Toulouse corridor towards Aquitaine. No oak is used; the Est

is perfumed and spicy, while the Ouest is denser and richer. Fruit not used for the two main *cuvées* goes into the third Cuvée Réquieu.

Camplazens
11100 Narbonne, Tel: 04 68 45 38 89

Now British-owned, the highlights from this Coteaux du Languedoc La Clape estate, currently being expanded to 40 ha, include a pure Viognier Vin de Pays d'Oc with unusually succulent intensity; the prestige version of the Camplazens Le Château, a wine of sweet, earthy depths; and the ambitious though slightly overweight "garage wine" MO-9. Look for further improvements ahead.

Canet Valette ✪
34460 Cesserons-sur-Orb, Tel: 04 67 89 51 83, Fax: 04 67 89 37 50

Marc Valette's 18-ha domain produces two St-Chinians, outstanding in the great 1998 vintage and subsequently. Une et Mille Nuits (formerly "Tradition") is soft, full, tangy, and sweet-fruited; it's based on all of Valette's grape varieties, but especially on Grenache. Le Vin Maghani (formerly a Fûts de Chêne *cuvée*, based on the estate's best Syrah, Mourvèdre, and Grenache) is bigger and fuller, its seductive depth-charge of moist, spicy, almost fiery fruit wrapped around a sturdy mineral spine. Valette's low yields, crop-sorting, twice daily naked *pigeage* ("you feel great, you smell great"), natural yeasts, and refusal to pump, fine, or filter the harvest give the wines great expressive qualities. Valette, a former cooperative member, also makes a pure Carignan that, if anything, is even more astonishing that that of Jean-Marie Rimbert. It's called Galéjades de Canet Valette (*galéjades* are tall stories). The 1999 vintage was harvested at 18.5% potential alchohol, and fermented (by semi-carbonic maceration) until it would ferment no more, leaving 20 g/l residual sugar: it is an essence of prunes, smoke, and liquorice which powers through to a tantalizingly austere yet sweet-edged finish. It was on the day I tasted this wine that I realised how stupid I had been in dismissing Carignan in the past (September 19th, 2000 as it happened: a millennial Damascus turn). Needless to say, it fits no AOC paradigm and is sold as a Vin de Table.

Capion
34150 Gignac, Tel: 04 67 57 71 37, Fax: 04 67 57 33 94

This is third of the trio of celebrated Aniane Vin de Pays estates, alongside Mas de Daumas Gassac and Granges des Pères. It's now owned by Adrian Buhrer, a Swiss who also owns Saxenburg in South Africa, and whose winemaker Nico van der Merwe thus gets to turn his hand to two vintages a year. The top-of-the-range white Le Sorbier is soft, oaky, exotic, slightly sweet; pleasant enough but a good example of how ill-suited Chardonnay is to the Languedoc – the Marsanne-Roussanne is much more interestingly flavoured. From a big range of reds, most worthwhile is the Syrah-Grenache blend Le Juge.

Casa Blanca
66650 Banyuls-sur-Mer, Tel: 04 68 88 12 85, Fax: 04 68 88 04 08

Alain Soufflet and Laurent Escarpa's Banyuls domain produces a gently mouthfilling Collioure (60% Grenache, 40% Syrah): the 1998 vintage almost seemed to have something of Banyuls' sugary sweetness inside it, with a gently porty finish. The Banyuls itself is made in a lush and tangy Tradition version (based on Grenache Gris), as well as a more succulent, fig-and-raisin "Vintage" version (based on Grenache Noir).

Castelmaure ✪
11360 Eubres et Castelmaure, Tel: 04 68 45 91 83, Fax: 04 68 45 83 56

This small 90-member cooperative cultivates 300 ha in 760 parcels – though the holdings of 12 main members account for 90% of production. "Only 20 years ago," says president Patrick de Marien, "we were considered as good for nothing but table wine." Since 1998, by contrast, thanks to the advice of Michel Tardieu this has been the source of one of the greatest Corbières reds, the Cuvée No 3, a magnificent blend of ripe, low-yielding Syrah, Grenache, and Carignan which combines sweet-fruited, kirsch-like grace and suppleness with some of the mineral fire and fury of the tortured local landscape (half is grown on schist, half on limestone). Another fine Embres et Castelmaure wine is the

Cuvée Pompadour, a clever blend of carbonically macerated Carignan and Syrah with 30% Grenache, aged in older casks for six months. This is warm, ripe, and softly tannic, a classic of the French countryside. The Grande Cuvée, which blends Syrah and Grenache with a little Carignan, is richer, chewier, and more mineral.

Cazeneuve
34270 Lauret, Tel: 04 67 59 07 49, Fax: 04 67 59 06 91

The work of André Leenhardt, president of the Pic-St-Loup growers, shows that this, perhaps the most beautiful sector of the Coteaux du Languedoc, is a promising white wine terroir as well as red. His barrel-fermented blend of Rolle, Grenache Blanc, and Viognier seems to smell of lavender and herbs, and taste both juicy and creamy. Among the red wines, the unwooded Calcaires, too, is full of the perfumes of the *garrigue*. The oak-finished Le Roc des Mates is slightly dryer and less regional in style, while Le Sang du Calcaire is a harvest selection (pure Mourvèdre in 1997, pure Syrah in 1998) of the best fruit given new-oak treatment. The fruit density at this level is more than a match for the oak: these are dark, concentrated, and memorably balanced wines.

La Cazenove
66300 Trouillas, Tel: 04 68 21 66 33, Fax: 04 68 21 77 81

The finest *cuvée* from this Côtes de Roussillon domain is the satisfyingly gutsy yet fresh-fruited Cuvée du Commandant François Joubert.

Cazes
66602 Rivesaltes, Tel: 04 68 64 08 26, Fax: 04 68 64 69 79

This massive 160-ha Roussillon domain produces a wide range of wines of which the best are unquestionably the Vins Doux Naturels, especially the clean, honeyed Muscats and the dark, powerful vintage-dated Grenat Rivesaltes, such as the weighty, densely tannic 1994. Among the non-fortified wines, the tangerine-flavoured pure-Muscat Canon du Maréchal makes a diverting aperitif. Some of the reds are disappointingly light, but the Trilogy Côtes du Roussillon-Villlages is a complex wine of some substance whose gently cooked fruit flavours are marked by the voluptuous warmth of the region. The conversion of this domain to biodynamics over the last half-decade makes it one of France's largest to be following Steiner's and Maria Thun's methods.

Chênes
66600 Vingrau, Tel: 04 68 29 40 21, Fax: 04 68 29 10 91

This 32-ha Roussillon domain is owned and run by one of the Montpellier oenology department's teaching staff, Alain Razungles. All the wines are skilfully vinified, with well-judged barrel fermentation for the whites and ample, well-handled tannins for the reds. The range includes two whites, Les Sorbières (Grenache Blanc and Maccabeu) and Les Magdaliens (Roussanne and Grenache Blanc) as well as the pure Carignan Les Grands' Mères, the Roussillon classic Les Alzines, and a Syrah-Mourvèdre from Tautavel.

Clavel
34160 St-Bauzille de Montimes, Tel: 04 67 86 97 36, Fax: 04 67 86 97 37

Pierre Clavel, son of campaigning regional pioneer Jean Clavel, has 40 ha of vineyard divided between two sites: one in the Méjanelle terroir of the Grès de Montpellier subregion of Coteaux du Languedoc, where the domain's oldest vines are; and one 20 km further north in the hills, where the vines are younger. Best wine in a generally impressive range is the oak-aged Copa Santa, a blend of the oldest Syrah (up to 80%), Grenache, and Mourvèdre grown in La Méjanelle and full of the vigorous, pounding, stony austerities of the region at its truest. The tank-aged Les Garrigues, too, is concentrated and spicy.

Clos Centeilles
34210 Siran, Tel: 04 68 91 52 18, Fax: 04 68 91 65 92

Daniel Domergue is one of the Languedoc's leading ampelographers. Together with his wife Patricia, he has also been one of the pioneers of quality Minervois from this 18-ha domain. "We don't make competition wines," Patricia says; "we make wines to drink at table. *Tout en dentelle* [all in lace]." This graceful and largely unwooded style is certainly a contrast to the direction taken by most of

the avant-garde in Languedoc; you could see it, if you like, as the Belair of its region. The range includes the pure Cinsault Capitelle de Centeilles.

Clos de l'Escandil *see* Aires Hautes

Clos Fantine
34600 Faugères

Olivier Andrieu's 20-ha Faugères domain, run in collaboration with his sisters Corinne and Carole, is assiduously traditional: no wood; lots of Carignan; a championing of "tannic Cinsault"; even a little plea for Aramon. "We don't go in for a lot of fancy techniques. We see our future in the past," says Andrieu, epigrammatically. "Every variety has its value," adds Corinne. The 1998 Clos Fantine was an intense, *garrigue*-scented wine of fine tannic depths; the Cuvée Courtiel is earthier and more challenging.

Clos des Fées ✪
66600 Vingrau, Tel: 04 68 29 40 00, Fax: 04 68 29 03 84

Former sommelier and journalist Hervé Bizeul was attracted to Roussillon by its wonderful patrimony of old vines – which he has turned to brilliant account in a series of finely crafted and beautifully packaged wines. They are preponderantly grown on limy clay soils rather than schist, which may account for their pure-fruited freshness. Les Sorcières du Clos des Fées (Carignan, Grenache, and Mourvèdre) is soft, clean, and sweet-fruited – "for pizzas", Bizeul suggests, half-jokingly. The Vieilles Vignes *cuvée* (which includes Lladoner Pelut as well as Grenache, Syrah, and Carignan, all aged between 50 and 100 years) has more tannic mass and power, while the Clos des Fées itself, vinified in open-ended *demi-muids*, combines the sumptuous fruit of the former with the luxuriously firm grip of the latter. This wine is a blend of 25% of Syrah, Mourvèdre, Grenache, and Carignan, all old vines and brought to maximum maturity. Bizeul's latest purchase is a small 1.16-ha plot of pure Grenache planted in 1952 and known locally as la Petite Siberie due to its cool position in a mountain corridor near to the old iron mines at Calce. The terroir, here, is iron-bearing dark red schist over a limestone bedrock. The first harvest, picked on October 5th, 2001, has produced a wine of comparable dimensions to the others but with a fresher edge and bite to its unctuous, blackberry fruit. All the wines except Les Sorcières are bottled unfiltered.

Clos du Gravillas
34360 St-Jean-de-Minervois, Tel: 04 67 38 17 52

Nicole Bojanowski's domain is one of the leaders in the fine zonal Vin de Pays of Côtes de Brian. The white Cuvée l'Inattendu is only moderately successful, with a slightly clumsy finish, but the red Lo Vièlh is stylish and poised, a real success.

Clos Maginiai
34270 Pic-St-Loup

Promising new organic Pic-St-Loup producer called Zumbaum Tomasi making soft, ripe red wine.

Clos Marie
34270 Lauret, Tel: 04 67 59 06 96, Fax: 04 67 59 08 56

Impressive Pic-St-Loup domain whose top wine is the lushly textured yet well-structured Les Glorieuses. "Simon" is simpler.

Clos des Paulilles
66660 Port-Vendres, Tel: 04 68 38 90 10, Fax: 04 68 38 91 33

Fine, traditional Banyuls and forceful Collioure from this estate owned by the Daure family (*see* Château de Jau). The Banyuls Rimage is deliciously packed with fresh fruit, while the Rimage Mise Tardive is just a little softer. The Cap Béar, by contrast, after a year in the open in demi-johns, is a compost of much tangier, lighter-textured flavours. The syrup-like Rivesaltes of Mas Christine is another VDN from the same team.

Clos Ste-Pauline
34230 Paulham, Tel: 04 67 25 29 42, Fax: 04 67 25 29 42

This recently created Coteaux du Languedoc domain run by Alexandre and

Patricia Pagès produces two *cuvées* of a dense, sweet-fruited low yielding Syrah-Grenache blend, one oaked and one unoaked (though confusingly labelled), plus a third with additional Mourvèdre.

Clos de Truffiers *see* la Négly

Combebelle *see* Comte Cathar

Combe Blanche
Not available

The "Le Dessous de l'Enfer" *cuvée* from this domain in Côtes de Brian is one of the more successful attempts at growing Tempranillo in the Languedoc: it's packed with intense cherry fruit. There is also a well-made white based on equal quantities of Roussanne and Viognier here.

Comberousse
34220 La Liviniere, Tel: 04 68 91 42 63, Fax: 04 68 91 62 15

This 12-ha Coteaux du Languedoc St-Georges d'Orques estate to the west of Montpellier and run by Alain Reder produces a superb white wine based on Rolle, Roussanne, and Grenache Blanc. The 1998 vintage was charged with intense, deep peach-apricot scents and flavours, to the extent that it was hard to believe there was no Viognier in the blend; only the vivid acidity suggested other grape varieties.

Comte Cathare
34220 La Livinière, Tel: 04 68 91 42 63, Fax: 04 68 91 62 15

This single name unites an anthill of activities coordinated with winning enthusiasm and, where possible, a biodynamic vineyard philosophy by Englishman Bertie Eden, the great nephew of Britain's Prime Minister at the time of the Suez crisis. It was founded in 1994 by Eden with financial backing from partners Kevin Parker and Richard Dunn. In domain terms, it includes the 50-ha Château Combebelle in St-Chinian (which includes the former Domaine de la Magnanerie), the 23-ha Domaine de la Bégude in Limoux, the 6-ha Domaine de Montahuc in St-Jean-de-Minervois, and the 60-ha Château Maris in Minervois La Livinière. Comte Cathare is also a négociant, working with the 70-ha Château Ollieux Romanis in Corbières, with the 60-ha Domaine St-Louis de Villeraze in Carbardès, with Domaine du Mal Passé in Faugères, and with Mas Desiré in Roussillon; Combe Aval in Fitou is a cooperative purchase. All of the wines are available to the public at a former tile factory, La Tuilerie, in La Livinière; there is now also a restaurant called Le Relais de Pigasse at Ouveillan on the Canal du Midi. The range is enormous; the wines are competent rather than outstanding. Comte Cathare seems to hesitate between following the path of terroir and AOC or that of varietals and Vins de Pays. The latest venture (and thus probably the best wines from Comte Cathare so far) opts for the latter approach with a range of four lavishly packaged varietals: DGS (Syrah), Umbra (Grenache), La Colline (Cabernet Sauvignon), and 'Oc (Carignan). "It's just simpler paper management for me," says Eden, explaining why they are Vins de Pays rather than AOC. Of the four, the DGS is the best, with its sumptuously creamy fruits and soft, silky tannins: very much a crowd-pleasing varietal rather than a challenging "*vin de terroir*". The style throughout the rest of the range is elegant and urbane; it would be good to see more of the savagery, wildness, and profundity, which the Comte Cathare name evokes, surface in the wines.

Conquêtes
34150 Aniane, Tel: 04 67 57 35 99, Fax: 04 67 57 35 99

Not many growers give up the steady income of vineyards in Champagne for the more uncertain living provided by those in Languedoc, but that's what Sylvie and Philippe Ellner did back in 1994 (though the Champagne vineyards remain in the family). Their 15-ha domain lies at Aniane. In contrast to some of their more celebrated neighbours, both AOC Coteaux du Languedoc (Terrasses de Larzac) wines and Vins de Pays are produced. Conquêtes is the AOC *cuvée*: it's around 70% Syrah with the balance composed of Grenache and Mourvèdre. Intense black fruits with smoky, earthy notes from the Syrah

dominate this forceful wine. The Domaine des Conquêtes, a Vin de Pays based on 60% Cabernet and 40% Merlot, is slightly firmer and more austere, though it shares the burnt-meat character of the AOC wines. There is also an emphatically oaky white Domaine des Conquêtes based on Chardonnay complemented by Viognier and Grenache Blanc.

Cos de la Belle *see* Roc d'Anglade

Coupe-Roses
34210 La Caunette, Tel: 04 68 91 21 95, Fax: 04 68 91 11 73

Promising Minervois domain whose Les Plôts *cuvée* (Syrah, Grenache, and old-vine Carignan) is dark and smoky, with livid meaty fruit.

Courtilles
11590 Cuxac d'Aude, Tel: 04 68 33 57 54

Bernard Schurr is Southcorp's man in the Languedoc (see James Herrick); this 12.5-ha Corbières domain is where he pursues (as the back label has it) his own "dreams". The land lies at Embres in the Durban subzone, and Schurr was amazed to discover what a geological patchwork even a domain this small could furnish. Two reds are produced: the Côte 125 (mostly carbonic maceration, and mostly the domain Carignan plus some purchased fruit) and the Domaine de Courtilles itself (Grenache and Syrah with a little Carignan, about half of the blend barrique-aged). The Côte 125 is a vivid, juicy wine with some of the wildness of the region stamped on it. The 1998 Domaine de Courtilles was a brilliant debut: sweet, chewy, wild, and heady (it included Grenache harvested at nearly 17%). The 1999, by contrast, was a dry and acidulous disappointment (it was a more difficult vintage for Schurr, with rain and grape-worm problems; he also fined and filtered the wine, recognizing later that this was an error). The savoury 2000 marks a return to vigorous, chewy form. "I love chewy wines," says Schurr, promisingly.

des Creisses
34290 Valros

Ambitious new domain owned by Philippe Chessenelong and run with the help of his cousin Louis Mitjavile, the son of François Mitjavile of Tertre Roteboeuf fame. The "basic" Coteaux du Languedoc *cuvée* is already a selection, most of the harvest being sold in bulk: it's pleasant and balanced. More ambitious is the Les Brunes *cuvée*, a Vin de Pays d'Oc blend of Syrah, Mourvèdre, and Cabernet of genuine luxury, voluptuousness, and sumptuousness to go with its lofty price tag.

La Croix Belle
34480 Puissalicon, Tel: 04 67 36 27 23, Fax: 04 67 36 60 45

This is one of the better domains in the promising Côtes de Thongue zonal Vin de Pays. Look for ample fruit in the red Les Calades, a Mourvèdre, Syrah and Merlot blend; the white No. 7 combines even more improbable varieties (Viognier, Chardonnay, Grenache Blanc, and Carignan Blanc with Sauvignon Blanc, Muscat, and Chasan) yet, perhaps surprisingly, it works well, its exotic fruits matched by a little oak.

Embres et Castelmaure *see* Castelmaure

Escourrou
11600 Cabardès

Ambitious new Cabardès domain run by Arnaud Escourrou: the Hommage à Cecile is concentrated and peppery, while the La Régalona is more powerful, tannic and dense.

Estanilles
34480 Cabreolles, Tel: 04 67 90 29 25, Fax: 04 67 90 10 99

Former electrician Michel Louison has been one of the brightest lights in Faugères for many years now, shining from his 34-ha schist-soiled domain at Lenthéric with a range of fine Syrah-based wines. The textured, sweet ripeness, and pure fruit depths of the 1998 Château des Estanilles show the Languedoc in its most irresistable mood.

Félines Jourdan

34140 Mèze, Tel: 04 67 43 69 29, Fax: 04 67 43 69 29

The ways in which Picpoul de Pinet can excite the fastidious gourmet do not appear to be numerous, but Claude Jourdan's are textbook examples: plain, pure lemon. Great oyster wine, which is its rationale, after all.

Ferrer Ribière ✪

64300 Ferrats, Tel: 04 68 53 24 45, Fax: 04 68 53 10 79

Back in 1993, office-worker-turned-winemaker Bruno Rivière met former co-op member Denis Ferrer in the vineyards of Roussillon. The two hit it off ("we had the same ideas and our skills complemented each other") and they formed a joint 40-ha domain together at Terrats, just 40 km from the Spanish frontier. Ferrer looks after the vines; the self-taught Ribière, who seems to have the glum intensity of a *poète maudit*, oversees the wines. "I left the office one day," says Ribière, "the next day I was in the vines. I learned everything by doing and by listening to others. Wine took me like an illness. In truth I don't know how to vinify; I do everything by emotion and by feeling." The result is a fascinating range of wines, some successful, some less so, but all rich in personality. Perhaps appropriately, the vineyards lie in what the French call a "tormented zone": soil types, therefore, include schist, clay-limestone, gravel, marl and pebbles. The whites in general are less memorable than the reds: the Fleur de Lies, for example, a heavily lees-worked blend of Grenache Blanc and Gris with the two Muscats is, says Ribière, a "*vin du passé, un vin culturel*". In present-day sensory terms, it lacks the scented impact of a pure Muscat and the vegetable-garden simplicity of a classic Grenache white. The pure Grenache Blanc Empreinte du Temps, made with low-yielding 76-year-old vines, is barrel-fermented, and the aniseed delicacy of the fruit gets lost in the oak. The old-vine reds, by contrast, are unmissable, particularly the Empreinte du Temps Carignan, made with 123-year-old vines – a wine which contrives to taste as gnarled as the deep-rooted plants that made it. Mémoire du Temps, despite the name, is made mostly from young Syrah vines with a little Grenache and Carignan, and is the sweetest-fruited of the reds, with appetizingly svelte tannins. The 1999 Cana, made from a selection of late-harvested Grenache, Syrah, and Mourvèdre grapes, is one of the most purely mineral wines I have ever tasted, its 14 months in barrique gratifyingly serving to amplify its natural flavours without denaturing them. The extraordinary Selence takes the same approach a stage further: Carignan, Grenache, and Syrah are picked "grape by grape" in November before being macerated for 60 days. "In fact it's jam," Ribière told me. "How do you bottle?" I asked Ribière, meaning to gauge his feelings about fining and filtering. "During an old moon and when the wind's from the southwest," he replied, sorrowfully.

Flaugergues

34000 Montpellier, Tel: 04 99 52 66 37, Fax: 04 99 52 66 44

This fine 34-ha property and its striking château (one of the so-called "follies" of Montpellier) look like becoming the Haut-Brion of the Languedoc if the city continues to expand at its present rate; the vineyards are now bisected by fast roads and occasionally used as car-dumps and television graveyards by witless neighbours. In the face of such slights, Flaugergues is run with great devotion by its owner, Comte Henri de Colbert, a former civil engineer who believes, staunchly, that "a name is not a right but a duty". The terroir – part of the La Méjanelle sector of the Grès de Montpellier – is on the extensive and deep pebble banks of the former Rhône delta; the banks of stones perform every bit as well here as they do in Costières de Nîmes. The best wines of the extensive range are the unoaked Cuvée Sommelière, a digestible yet charracterful blend of 70% Syrah and 30% Grenache, and the Fûts de Chêne *cuvée* which in good years contains Mourvèdre as well as the other two main varieties. Lower yields give this last wine a sweet unction and appealingly soft, chocolatey finish.

Font Caude ✪

34150 Lagamas, Tel: 04 67 57 84 64, Fax: 04 67 57 84 65

Alain Chabanon, whose extensive experience includes spells for Peraldi in Corsica as well as Alain Brumont in Madiran, is a talented winemaker – though

one dedicated to maintaining as low a profile as he can manage. "The world of finance has taken hold of the world of wine," he declares – and he is doing his best to keep the world of finance at arm's length. Having seen "gigantism" chez Brumont, he is also determined to remain small. The fly in this mildly misanthropic ointment is the fact that his wines are so good: demand may exert its own logic. La Merle aux Alouettes (a pun – it's Merlot) is a genuinely great Vin de Pays d'Oc of telling succulence; the Grenache-based Les Boissières, from Montpeyroux, has ethereal cherry scents and cooked fruit flavours; the Esprit de Font Caude, a Syrah-Mourvèdre blend, is both beefier and more glycerous. Chabanon also produces an intensely sweet Chenin Blanc white using raisined grapes called Le Villard.

Força Real

66170 Millas, Tel: 04 68 85 06 07, Fax: 04 68 85 49 00

This 70-ha Côtes du Roussillon-Villages domain (40 ha planted with vines) sited at Millas has its vineyards on schist slopes at between 100 and 300 metres. Mas de la Garrigue is a simple, lively red made from young-vine Grenache with a little Syrah and Carignan. Domaine Força Real, from older vines, has much more of a regional stamp to it, with warm, caramel scents and a high-impact, stony flavour. The top *cuvée* is Les Hauts de Força Real (80% Syrah balanced with Mourvèdre and Grenache given up to 20 months' barrique ageing), a concentrated, stone-and-tobacco scented red lacking only the density and unction of the region's greatest wines.

Foulaquier ✪

34270 Claret, Tel: 04 67 59 96 94, Fax: 04 67 59 96 94

This small, 8-ha domain to the north of the Pic-St-Loup sector of the Coteaux du Languedoc is Swiss-owned (by former architect and winemaker Pierre Jequier) and run with great care and ambition. Initial results (1999 was the first vintage) are little short of dazzling, with a series of three unfiltered wines of great purity and definition: a remarkable achievement for that difficult vintage in the Pic-St-Loup terroir. Grenache and Syrah are used for all three *cuvées*: L'Orphée (70-90% Grenache), Le Rollier (around 50% of each variety) and Les Calades (80% Syrah with some oak ageing in *demi-muids*). The vines, planted in a single parcel at 200 metres, are still young, and quality should rise further as they age. Watch this domain.

Gardiés ✪✪

66600 Vingrau, Tel: 04 68 64 61 16, Fax: 04 68 64 69 36

Jean Gardiés' 30-ha Roussillon estate at Tautavel is one of the swelling band of outstanding domains in this most promising of southern French terroirs, and his achievement with the 2000 vintage is magnificent: no other word will do. The soils are mainly limestone; there is little schist. Les Millères is a wonderful start: floral scents, sweetly spicy flavours. The Vieilles Vignes Tautavel (90% Grenache of 50 years plus) is almost incense-scented, with lyrical, unctuous flavours and a mineral finish; Les Falaises, another old-vine *cuvée* but this time based on Syrah, is pure coffee and meat. Grandest of all is the thunderous La Torre, a Mourvèdre-Carignan blend of extraordinary dimensions, dazzlingly thick cherry fruit, and a grindingly mineral finish. Is this the greatest Mourvèdre outside Bandol? To Languedoc-Roussillon's credit, this is a battle which is beginning to provide much excitement.

Gauby ✪✪

66370 Calce, Tel: 04 68 64 34 19, Fax: 04 68 64 41 77

The burly and exuberant Gérard Gauby's 32-ha biodynamic domain based at Calce is not only one of the best in Roussillon, but also one of the finest domains in southern France. Gauby, like Jean Paux-Rosset at La Négly, ensures very low yields by hard pruning and green harvesting; he also sorts this precious harvest grape by grape. There is a cool, pre-fermentation maceration; wild yeasts are used, and minimum sulphur dioxide. The wines are bottled without fining or filtration. The stamp of terroir, of course, comes storming out of wines produced with such a philosophy, as you can taste in the Les Aleaux Vin de Pays des Coteaux Catalans: it is a pure Mediterranean white, with soft vegetal scents and deep, pure flavours of seeds and fennel bulbs. Astonishingly, this profoundly un-varietal wine is made of Chardonnay. La Jasse is a gratifyingly challenging, almost extractive dry Muscat, while the single vineyard Coume Gineste and La Roque are both stunning whites based on Grenache Blanc and Grenache Gris respectively, fissured with extra mineral depths. The white Vieille Vignes *cuvée* is sumptuous, subtly aromatic, and powerfully though mutely fruited, made from an intriguing blend of Carignan Blanc, Grenache Blanc and Gris, Maccabeu, Malvoisie, and Viognier. There is also a red Vieilles Vignes *cuvée*, made with Grenache of over 50 years and Carignan of over 100 years grown in a variety of sites (limestone, schist, sandstone, and pebbles), plus some older Syrah and Mourvèdre: this is a sappy, stony, full-throttle red of pure-fruited and resonant exuberance. Les Calcinaires is, as the name suggests, grown on limestone alone and is mainly Grenache: explosive, jam-fragrant, and sweet-fruited, this time. Muntada, finally, is preponderantly Syrah: this is the most mineral and earthy of the three wines, with a driving profundity and long, meditative length, produced from yields of 14 hl/ha in the 1999 vintage (unusually fine here in contrast to further east). Like many of the leading producers in the region, Gauby has eased back slightly on the power of his extractions over the last few vintages, providing wines of greater sumptuousness and less brute force.

Gléon Montanié
11360 Durbau, Tel: 04 68 48 46 20, Fax: 04 68 48 46 20
The 1998 Cuvée Gaston Bonnes from Jean-Pierre and Philippe Montanié's property in the Durban sector of Corbières was one of the AOC's successes in that generous vintage. This *cuvée* of 60% Syrah, complemented by Grenache, Carignan, and Mourvèdre, is given a year in barrique.

Gourgazaud
34210 La Livinière, Tel: 04 68 78 10 02, Fax: 04 68 78 10 02
The spicy, warm, friendly wines of this Minervois pioneer owned by the former head of Chantovent, Roger Piquet, has provided many drinkers with their introduction to the AOC. Most ambitious wine is the La Réserve, based on Syrah.

Grand Crès
11200 Ferrals-les-Corbières, Tel: 04 68 43 69 08, Fax: 04 68 43 58 99
The exquisitely perfumed white Vin de Pays d'Oc (based on Roussanne, Viognier, and Muscat) is the best wine of this high-sited 12-ha Corbières domain, situated in the terroir of Lagrasse, though the creamy, strawberry-fruited Corbières Rosé is also very good. The Cuvée Classique red can be a little light, but the Cuvée Majeure (75% Syrah and 25% Grenache) is earthier and richer, without jeopardizing the elegance that is the domain's hallmark. Owner Hervé Leferrer spent six years as *régisseur* at Domaine de la Romanée-Conti, so the finesse comes as no surprise.

Grange des Pères ✪
34150 Aniane, Tel: 04 67 57 70 55, Fax: 04 67 57 32 04
Former physiotherapist Laurent Vaillé's property is sited next to Mas de Daumas Gassac at Aniane, and many feel has eclipsed its neighbour in wine terms, if not in communicative energy, since its founding in 1992. Vaillé trained with, among others, Gérard Chave, Eloi Durrbach and François Coche-Dury, and this background in wine-craftsmanship is evident in every bottle that comes from his cellar. The whites (Roussanne plus Chardonnay) are as polished as the reds (Syrah, Cabernet, Mourvèdre, and Counoise). Oak is used in both with great skill (giving the reds up to two years in wood without disfiguring them makes Vaillé the Guigal of the Languedoc), and the young vines are cropped very low in order to keep concentration levels up. All the wines lack, for me, is a sense of terroir, and in particular that explosively stony, mineral quality that marks the very greatest wines of the region.

Grès St-Paul ✪
34400 Lunel, Tel: 04 67 71 27 90, Fax: 04 67 71 73 76
Dense, exuberant wines from this 26-ha Coteaux du Languedoc domain owned by Jean-Philippe Servière and run with the help of ex-Capion owner Philippe Salasc. The pure-Syrah Antonin and Sirius *cuvées* are especially good: magnificently perfumed and deep in 2000. The property's former river-bed gravels also produce a *cuvée* of honeyed yet elegant Muscat de Lunel called Sevillane. The dry Muscat Libertine is hollow in the middle, while the late-harvest Bohémienne (made from raisined Muscat) is slight.

BRL Hardy *see* La Baume

James Herrick
11104 Narbonne, Tel: 04 68 42 59 90, Fax: 04 68 42 59 99
James Herrick sold the business which bears his name to the Australian company Southcorp in 1999. There are large hectarages (180 ha or more) of Chardonnay planted in three domains (the silt-soiled La Motte, the stonier Garrigue de Truilhas, and the sandy La Boulandière) for the sweet-edged, simple Vin de Pays d'Oc varietal, branded and heavily promoted in the British market. There are also two domain Chardonnays, Domaine de la Boulandière and Domaine la Motte, whose wines have a little extra oaky depth. Good red wines have been produced here in the past, particularly the very first, small-run release of the Cuvée Simone, but at present the range (both Cuvée Simone, now produced in much larger quantities and described as "easy drinking", and the four wines in the "Roman Collection": Atacina, La Provincia, Millia Passum, and Oppidum) is frankly disappointing. Southcorp intends, it says, to make James Herrick "the Lindemans or Penfolds of the South of France." Managing director of Southcorp's operations in France, Bernard Schurr, has proved with the 1998 and 2000 vintages from his own Corbières domain of de Courtilles that he understands what great red wine can be in the Languedoc, so perhaps the ambition is one of substance.

l'Hortus
34270 Valflaunes, Tel: 04 67 55 31 20, Fax: 04 67 55 38 03
This 50-ha domain, named after the slightly lower limestone peak that faces Pic-St-Loup, is one of the leaders of that appellation-to-be. There are two quality levels, Bergerie for "classic" *cuvées* and Hortus for "great" *cuvées*; the reds are Coteaux du Languedoc Pic-St-Loup while the whites are Vin de Pays du Val de Monferrand (for varietal reasons). The style of the reds is restrained yet concentrated, glancing more towards Bordeaux than the southern Rhône; the whites (Hortus is based on Chardonnay and Viognier; Bergerie on Sauvignon, Chardonnay, Viognier, and Roussanne) are more exotic, lush, and glycerous. The 1999 vintage was a particular disappointment here.

l'Hospitalet
11100 Narbonne, Tel: 04 68 45 27 10, Fax: 04 68 45 27 17
This extraordinary domain in Coteaux du Languedoc La Clape is not only a wine estate but also a hotel, workshop, and market for artisans, and a collection of collections (including cars and stones); it was run until recently by the energetic Béatrice Ribourel-Buyck. Just under 30 grape varieties were originally planted on 90 ha in four different sites, rationalized with the help of consultant Michel Rolland into a number of different wines of which the graceful, apricot-fruited white Cuvée Béatrice and vivid, chewy, fleshy, oaky red Cuvée Béatrice are the most impressive. Now owned by Gérard Bertrand.

Jau
66600 Cases-de-Père, Tel: 04 68 38 90 10, Fax: 04 68 38 91 33
This Roussillon estate belonging to former négociant Bernard Dauré and his daughter Estelle doesn't produce the densest or most extracted wines of the appellation, but they are always accessible, balanced, harmonious, and drinkable. Best is the Talon Rouge Côtes de Roussillon-Villages, which turns on the power.

Joliette
66600 Espira-de-L'Agly, Tel: 04 68 64 50 60, Fax: 04 68 64 18 82
This up-and-coming Roussillon domain is a name to watch. The Cuvée André Mercier is simple and straightforward, but the "Villages" Cuvée Romain Mercier is much darker, deeper, and rich-textured, packed with ripe fruit and with increasingly sensitive use of oak.

Joly
34725 St-Saturnin de Lucian, Tel: 04 67 44 52 21

Virgile Joly's small 6.5 ha domain in Coteaux du Languedoc St-Saturnin is one to watch, especially for the spicy, resonant Syrah-Cinsault Virgile.

Jonquières
34725 Jonquières, Tel: 04 67 96 62 58

This 20-ha domain (5 ha of which are Vins de Pays) run by François and Isabelle de Cabissole is another of those in this key sector of the Coteaux du Languedoc (the terroir is St-Saturnin; the region Terrasses de Larzac) that has moved from high yields, machine harvesting, and supplying the local cooperative to much lower yields, hand harvesting, and vinification of the whole harvest on the domain. Nonetheless the style is friendly rather than fierce. "There are tasting wines and there are pleasure wines," says François. "We try to make pleasure wines that aren't too concentrated, too rich, too undrinkable." The light and easygoing Château de Jonquières red fits this bill; the barrel-fermented white and the red La Baronnie are more ambitious: there is added tannic grip and stonier quality of fruit in the latter, without sacrificing the balance and harmony of the house style. The density and succulence of Renaissance, produced from low-yeilding Syrah in 1998, suggests further evolution lies ahead.

Jouclary
11600 Conques-sur-Orbiel, Tel: 04 68 77 10 02, Fax: 04 68 77 00 02

Robert Gianesini and his son Pascal's 30-ha domain in Cabardès produces three cuvées, all of them based on around 50% Merlot balanced by Syrah and Grenache. Best is the sumptuous and silky Guilhaume de Jouclary.

Lambert see Baron'arques.

Lancyre
34270 Valflaunes, Tel: 04 67 55 22 28, Fax: 04 67 55 23 84

The 1998 Vieilles Vignes cuvée of this Coteaux du Languedoc Pic-St-Loup domain sited at Valflaunès had fine, floral qualities and exotic, truffley depths which gave the wine an almost Pomerol-like finish.

Laporte ✪
66000 Perpignan, Tel: 04 68 50 06 53, Fax: 04 68 66 77 52

Raymond and Patricia Laporte's 40-ha, pebble-soiled domain near Perpignan produces three fine reds. Thecle is a Bordeaux-blend Vin de Pays that doesn't taste even remotely Bordeaux-like, but is full of the gruff fire of the south; Ruscino (the Latin name for Roussillon) adds some Syrah and Mourvèdre to the mix to make a still more powerful red with depth-charge tannins. Finally the Côtes du Roussillon Domitia is a sea-scented red with lingeringly mineral flavours of great power and profundity. The Rivesaltes wines are typically sweet and tangy.

Laroche
89800 Chablis, Tel: 04 86 42 89 00, Fax: 04 86 42 89 29

Chablis producer Michel Laroche's 60-ha domain near Béziers (La Chevalière) produces a range of aimiable though unambitious wines peaking with La Croix Chevalière, which could perhaps be good – if the yields resembled those at la Négly, Gauby, or Terre Inconnue. Alas, they are obviously far higher than that at present.

Lastours
11490 Portel-les-Corbières, Tel: 04 68 48 29 17, Fax: 04 68 48 29 14

This inspiring 88-ha Corbières domain, run in part for the benefit of its mentally handicapped workers, has during the 1990s produced some of the AOC's most consistent wines. The basic cuvées (like the Carignan-Grenache Arnaud de Berre) are simple and refreshing; Simone Descamps and La Grande Rompue are deeper, more savoury, more herbal. The top wine is simple called Château de Lastours; after 20 months in new wood, it is relatively light in colour and elegant and composed in flavour, one of the least savage of Corbière's leading wines.

Lhéritier ✪
66600 Rivesaltes, Tel: 04 68 64 41 85

Henri Lhéritier produces two superb, single-parcel Roussillons from his 30-ha domain: the schist-soiled Crest is savage and explosive, "a kick up the backside" in Lhéritier's words; Romani (grown on limestone) is more polished and accessible, more of a stroke on the cheek. There is also a vintage dated Grenat Rivesaltes here, packed with detonating, fruit-saturated sweetness.

Listel see Val d'Orbieu

Lorgeril
11610 Pennautier, Tel: 04 68 72 65 29, Fax: 04 68 72 65 84

Nicolas de Lorgeril is the president of the Cabardès AOC and, with his wife Miren, runs three leading properties there (Châteaux de la Bastide, de Caunettes, and de Pennautier) as well as one in Minervois (Les Hauts de la Borie Blanche). Brainpower does not automatically guarantee viticultural success, but this couple's remarkable achievements (both attended grandes écoles in Paris, and Nicolas is an enarque – a graduate of the Ecole Nationale d'Administration) suggest that Lorgeril should be a name to watch as this new AOC sets about proving itself. He is very much the key player in the appellation: the 350 ha owned or controlled represents almost two-thirds of the entire AOC. In stylistic terms, the most polished and ambitious of all the wines is the Esprit de Pennautier: this 80% Syrah, 20% Merlot blend is dark, very oaky, with lots of smoky-chocolate character. L'Esprit de Bastide (half Malbec, half Syrah) is slightly more accessible, its floral notes and softly savoury flavours striking a more evidently regional note.

Mal Passé see Comte Cathar

Mansenoble
11700 Moux, Tel: 04 68 43 93 39, Fax: 04 68 43 97 21

Under the thought-provoking slogan "Each wine attracts the customer it deserves" former Belgian insurance executive and part-time wine writer Guido Jansegers runs (with Marie-Annick de Witte) this 20-ha Corbières and Vin de Pays domain at Moux, on the northern slopes of the Montagne d'Alaric. The Réserve (a Syrah, Grenache, Mourvèdre, and Carignan blend, half of which is oak-aged) is balanced, fresh, and tasty.

Marcevol ✪
66320 Arboussols, Tel: 04 68 05 74 34

This organic 12-ha Roussillon domain was purchased by the Verhaeghe brothers of Château du Cèdre in Cahors in March 2000; local consulting oenologist Guy Predal is in charge. One 5-ha parcel is at 200 metres on schist soils; the other at 600 metres on acid granites mixed with schist. The basic cuvée is soft, drinkable, and earthy; the Prestige, by contrast, is an outstanding wine (from 2001), thick-textured and sweetly stony, yet (thanks to the altitude) vivid and fresh. Can Felix is a strange, dense, pine and eucalyptus-like white based on Grenache Blanc and Gris with a pinch of Muscat. Expect great things here.

La Marfée
34570 Murviel-lès-Montpellier

Wine-bitten accountant Thierry Hasard has created this small 6-ha domain using vines planted in 15 tiny parcels (or "little gardens" as he calls them) at Murviel-lès-Montpellier; so far the wines have been stored under Hasard's own house in Montpellier (though a purpose-built cellar is on order). "I really believe in stones," he says; he has actually had 20 lorry-loads of stones added to the vineyards to create "macro-porosity", causing outrage to the locals whose forebears had painstakingly removed stones from the very same vineyards. The first vintage was 1997. Two red wines are produced: the Carignan-based Les Vignes qu'on Abat, sweet and flavour-saturated, and Les Champs Murmurés, a perfumed, spicy Syrah-Grenache-Cabernet-Mourvèdre blend. Quality has varied with the vintages, but at best these are dark, dense, smoulderingly smoky reds.

Maris *see* Comte Cathar

Mas Amiel ✪
66460 Maury, Tel: 04 68 29 01 02, Fax: 04 68 29 17 82

This large, historic 150-ha domain, once lost by the Bishop of Perpignan during a game of cards (they don't make bishops like that any more), specializes in Vins Doux Naturels grown on black schist, though three good non-fortified wines are also produced by winemaker Stéphane Gallet (a Normand who trained with Yves Cuilleron in the Rhône) under Vins de Pays legislation. Le Plaisir is a jammy and exuberant pure Grenache. The unfiltered Hautes Terres is a selection of old-vine parcels including Grenache, Carignan, and Cinsault aged in barrique with a much bigger tannic structure and a flavour of hot stones. Carrerade, finally, is a Syrah, Grenache, and Carignan blend packed with explosive fig and plum fruit. Among the stars of a large range of fortified wines is the basic, tank-aged Maury for its clearly delineated berry, prune, and fig fruits backed by fine-grained tannins and the barrique-aged "Vintage" Reserve, all caramel and chocolate. The Grenache-based *oxidatifs* (Mas Amiel has 3,000 glass demi-johns ageing under the hot Roussillon sun) include a 10-year-old Cuvée Spéciale and a 15-year-old Prestige: both flirt with a Madeira-like style of sweet tobacco and raisin scents and tangy flavours in which acidity plumes over the dried fruits. A series of "Millésime" wines are also aged in *bonbonnes* (in contrast to the barrique-aged "Vintage" wines); the 1980, bottled in 1990, once again has a distinctive, Madeira-like scents of cheese, nuts, apples, and figs, with a deep, intense flavour that combines cocoa, tobacco, and minerals. Finally there is a VDN Muscat (80% Muscat à Petits Grains and 20% Muscat d'Alexandrie); schist seems to give a fat, mineralized character which the more floral and citric Muscats grown on limestone (such as St-Jean-de-Minervois) don't have. Plénitude is the name of a pure Muscat d'Alexandie made from partially fermented, raisined grapes and thus produced under Vin de Table legislation: this is an extraordinarily perfumed wine of great complexity and peachy, creamy style. The estate was purchased at the end of 1999 by Olivier Decelle.

Mas Blanc ✪
66650 Banyuls-sur-Mer, Tel: 04 68 88 32 12, Fax: 04 68 88 72 24

This historic, 21-ha Banyuls and Collioure domain belonged to the man who did more than any other to win public recognition for this great schist terroir, Dr André Parcé; it is now run by his son Jean-Michel. In addition to the lush Cuvée Réservée, there are three separate single-vineyard Collioures, though one (Les Junquets which, Côte-Rôtie-like, blends Syrah with Roussanne) is produced in microscopic quantities only. The peppery Cuvée Cosprons Levants is made from the oldest vines, and blends Mourvèdre with Syrah and (the Mas Blanc speciality) Counoise; the dense, dredging Clos du Moulin is Mouvèdre and Counoise only. The range of Banyuls, too, is wide and gratifyingly challenging, from the youngish Rimage and Rimage La Coume, packed with sweet jammy fruits, to the classically older and more oxidative *rancio* Cuvée St-Martin (aged La Coume) and solera-style Hors d'Age.

Mas Cal Demoura
34725 Jonquières, Tel: 04 67 88 61 51, Fax: 04 67 88 61 51

Cal Demoura means "you must stay" in the Occitan dialect, and was the name Olivier Jullien's parents Jean-Pierre and Renée Jullien chose for their house at a time when everyone else seemed determined to leave the Languedoc countryside. Inspired by what his son achieved at Mas Jullien from 1985, Jean-Pierre finally left the local cooperative in 1993 himself, selling most of his vineyards and keeping just 5 ha of the best parcels around Jonquières for his own domain. Infidèle is the top *cuvée*, an honest and straightforward wine based on five varieties (Syrah, Mourvèdre, Cinsault, Carignan, and Grenache) given oak-ageing.

Mas Champart
34360 St-Chinian, Tel: 04 67 38 20 09, Fax: 04 67 38 20 09

As with many St-Chinian producers, the 1998 vintage was outstandingly successful here, especially for the resonantly mineral Causse de Bousquet *cuvée*

(65% Syrah with the balance from Grenache, Mourvèdre, and Carignan), bottled without filtration. The 1999 and 2000 vintages haven't quite matched the quality of the 1998s, but this 10-ha estate, sited on the limestone sector of the AOC, is still one to watch.

Mas des Chimères
34800 Octon, Tel: 04 67 96 22 70, Fax: 04 67 88 07 00

There is a selection of pretty, perfumed reds from this 13-ha Coteaux du Languedoc domain run by Guilhem Dardé.

Mas Crémat
66600 Espira-de-l'Agly, Tel: 04 68 38 92 06, Fax: 04 68 38 92 23

Burgundian dairyman Jean-Marc Jeannin ran this promising Roussillon estate until his recent death; his wife Catherine (a Mongeard-Mugneret) and son Julien are continuing his work. It lies amidst the schists of Espira d'Agly.

Mas Cristine *see* Clos des Paulilles

Mas de Daumas Gassac ✪
34150 Aniane, Tel: 04 67 57 71 28, Fax: 04 67 57 41 03

Aimé Guibert is the Languedoc's most well-known wine producer. First, because his domain has over the last two decades given the region some of the pride and lustre which had eluded it for more than a century. More recently, his fame has been based on having led (ignominiously, some feel) the opposition to Robert Mondavi's project for a winery at Aniane (see page 229). It was Professor Henri Enjalbert who declared, on the basis of geology in the early 1970s, that this 32-ha site in virgin scrubland ought to be a "Grand Cru" of the Languedoc, a testament which Aimé Guibert (formerly a glovemaker to Europe's royal and noble families) publicized with eloquence and unshakeable conviction. The varietal mix and winemaking style were established with the help of fellow Bordelais Professor Emile Peynaud – and the Cabernet-based red which resulted has intermittently led substance to the "Grand Cru" claim with a wine that, although grouchy in youth, holds its substance well through the years. There is little of the aromatic enchantment, however, which Syrah, Grenache, and even old-vine Carignan can provide in the Languedoc, nor the supple tannic mass of these varieties and of Mourvèdre when cultivated with care and low yields. (Oddly, there are small percentages of almost every other French classic red grape variety complementing the 80% Cabernet, including Merlot, Malbec, Cabernet Franc, Tannat, and Pinot Noir, while Nebbiolo, Dolcetto, and Barbera are planted, too.) The white wine, based on Chardonnay, Viognier, and Petit Manseng, is genuinely enchanting in its youth, though its soft exoticism is not necessarily well suited to food, as Tony Blair and Bill Clinton may have discovered when they tackled a bottle together at London's Pont de la Tour restaurant in early 1998.

From 2001, the domain has begun to produce a Cuvée Emile Peynaud – pure Cabernet, from the very first hectare planted on the estate. It is, according to ever-articulate anti-modernist Aimé Guibert, "a gesture of love and gratefulness, a wine that is the symbol of wines of a former time as opposed to modern wines." Aimé Guibert's son Samuel, who trained and worked in New Zealand, is now joining the business, and it will be interesting to see which directions it takes in the years ahead.

Mas Desiré *see* Comte Cathar

Mas de l'Ecriture
34150 Jonquieres

Pascal Fulla, a former lawyer, named his 18-ha Coteaux du Languedoc domain Ecriture ("writing") "because writing is civilization, and wine is civilization too." It's sited amidst the wild fennel of Jonquières (Terraces de Larzac). Declinaisons is his simplest, juiciest *cuvée*; Les Pensées (a philosophical joke: Les Pensées de Pascal) is full of stony purity; the top wine, Ecriture, is a Syrah-Grenache blend of sweet fruit and sweet herbs given lush, spicy oak treatment (Russian and American are used as well as French).

Mas Foulaquier *see* Foulaquier

Mas Jullien ✪
34725 Jonquières, Tel: 04 67 96 60 04, Fax: 04 67 96 60 50

The mercurial, poetic, and intuitive Olivier Jullien is one of the Languedoc's most intriguing wine producers. His Coteaux du Languedoc domain at Jonquières (Terrasses de Larzac) and his wine range has both expanded and shrunk down the years; he now has 15 ha of vines, which he says is ideal, having torn up his underperforming vineyards and planted trees and *sainfoin* "to create a healthy ecosystem" instead. Gone, too, are the old Depierre and Les Cailloutis red *cuvées*, now amalgamated into a single Mas Jullien red; Jullien wasn't happy with his experiment in terroir individuation. Likewise, after much thought, he has finally settled on *demi-muids* for its *élevage*. It is one of the purest, most mineral and in some ways least showy of Languedoc's great reds, but makes a profound bottle after a few years in the cellar. Etats d'Ame ("moods") is Jullien's free-expression, fruitier red, its label sometimes adorned with one of his poems; there is also a typically unusual white based on Carignan Blanc, Grenache Blanc, Chenin Blanc, and Viognier.

Mas de Martin
34160 St- Bauzille-de-Montmel, Tel: 04 67 86 26 33, Fax: 04 67 86 98 82

Former geography and history teacher Christian Mocci has now expanded his biodynamically run Pic-St-Loup domain to 14 ha from its initial 8 ha. The wines of this émigré Corsican are subtle and elegant rather than powerful and thrashing, though they lack neither fat nor density; the use of oak is well-judged. In addition to the AOC wines, there are also some Vins de Pays based on Bordeaux varieties – and Tannat.

Mas de Mortiès
34270 Saint-Jean-de-Cuculles, Tel: 04 67 55 11 12, Fax: 04 67 55 11 12

Rémy Duchemin and Michel Jorcin have 20 ha in their Pic-St-Loup domain. This is another of the many Pic-St-Loup domains where the white wine promises much: rich, viscous, tantalizing, packed with pear and almond. The domain Pic-St-Loup *cuvée* and the Jamais Content *cuvée* are both thyme-flavoured blends of Syrah, Grenache, and Mourvèdre with very old Carignan; the latter is oakier than the former. Que Sera Sera is, as you might have guessed, pure Syrah of majestic purity of fruit preceded by a fanfare of coffee and flower scents, though perhaps more a varietal wine than a *vin de terroir*, at least until the vines age further.

Maurel Fonsalade
34490 Causses-et-Veyran, Tel: 04 67 89 57 90, Fax: 04 67 89 72 04

The range produced at Philippe and Thérèse Maurel's 27-ha domain at Causses et Veyran in St-Chinian includes the voluptuous Cuvée La Fonsalade, made from 50% Syrah plus 30% Grenache and the balance from Mourvèdre.

Monpezat
34120 Pézenas, Tel: 04 67 98 10 84, Fax: 04 67 98 98 78

This Coteaux du Languedoc property run by Christophe Blanc on the stony terraces of Pézenas is one of the few whose best Vin de Pays (the powerfully fruited Cabernet Sauvignon-based Prestige) is as good as its best appellation wine: the dense, complex, and tannic Mourvèdre-dominated La Pharaonne. Neither are filtered.

Mont Tauch
11350 Tuchan, Tel: 04 68 45 29 64, Fax: 04 68 45 45 29

This 300-member cooperative, which merged with the rival Cave Pilote de Villeneuve in 1999, now produces some 45% of all Fitou and 80% of the finer Fitou Montagneux sector. Mont Tauch and its winemaker, Michel Marty, are stout defenders of the AOC's 30% minimum Carignan requirement, which they claim helps give the region's wines their *charactère de cochon*, (literally "boarhood" or cussedness: their wild, savage stamp). There are some 30 major growers among the 300 members, and a selection scheme is underway to classify the best vineyards (paid a 25% premium) and use their wines for the top *cuvées* (paid a 100% premium). Fitou l'Excéption, an oak-aged blend of 40% Syrah with 30% Carignan and Grenache produced in good vintages only, was impressive in 1998 though much lighter in 2000. Terroir de Tuchan, a 40%

Carignan and 60% Syrah blend, is pure and chunky, while Les Douze is a classic Carignan-Syrah-Grenache blend full of game and thyme, drawn and blended from the wines of 12 of the growers working in the selection scheme whose names and photographs appear on the label. Why, I wondered, don't more Fitou producers wish to leave the cooperative and set up on their own? "You have to understand the feeling of isolation that people have here," marketing manager Katie Jones told me. "There are more wild boar than people here. The first fridge didn't arrive until 1960; we only got a cash machine in 1999. We have to change our tyres every 6,000 miles."

Montahuc *see* Comte Cathar

Moulin de Ciffre
34480 Autignac, Tel: 04 67 90 11 45, Fax: 04 67 90 12 05

This 30-ha domain, owned by Jacques Lesineau (formerly at Haut-Gardère in the Graves), occupies a slightly neurotic terroir in that it includes parcels in St-Chinian, Faugères, and Coteaux du Languedoc – and a bit of Vin de Pays des Coteaux de Murviel for luck. Despite this, the range is consistent, steady, and even. Highlights include the oak-aged Cuvée Eole from Faugères; the dark, spicy, and chewy Cabernet-Syrah Vin de Pays Val Taurou; and an excellent, creamy Viognier. Lesineau's Bordeaux background gives him interesting perspectives. "In Bordeaux, Cabernet is phenollically ripe at 12%; here, it still isn't ripe at 13.5% sometimes. You never harvest Cabernet in Bordeaux at 13%, even in the best soils. Here we could do with 14%."

Navarre
34460 Roquebrun, Tel: 04 67 89 53 58, Fax: 04 67 89 70 88

Fine St-Chinian domain at Roquebrun owned by Thierry Navarre. Le Laouzil is herb-flavoured and pure; the barrique-aged Cuvée Olivier is violet-scented, sweet, earthy, and lush, appealing both to hedonists and to those in search of the purer expressions of this remarkable, schistous terroir.

la Négly ✪✪
11560 Fleury-d'Aude, Tel: 04 68 32 36 28, Fax: 04 68 32 10 69

Jean Paux-Rosset's ambitious 50-ha domain uses fruit from his family domain at La Clape, while the Clos des Truffiers also made here takes its fruit from a small parcel at St-Pargoire near Pézenas, part-owned by Bordeaux-based American wine importer Jeffrey Davies. The white wine, Brise Marine, is a salty, weighty, flavour-saturated blend of Bourboulenc with Marsanne and Roussanne; there is also a superb Syrah-Grenache rosé here of true seriousness called Les Embruns. The La Côte (carbonically macerated Carignan blended with conventional Grenache or Grenache and Syrah) is appealingly juicy and zesty, with fresh coffee scents and flavours; La Falaise (hand-sorted Syrah, Mourvèdre, and Grenache) is dense, pure, vivid and peppery, again with the salty finish typical of La Clape. The three most ambitious reds are the dark, gruff, massively concentrated, tapenade-like l'Ancely (overwhelmingly Mourvèdre, stored in *demi-muids*); the Clos des Truffiers itself (sweet, sexy, creamy, floral-smoky Syrah from St-Pargoire) and the formidably intense Porte du Ciel (a fruit-dense Syrah from La Clape, packed with cherry and chocolate liqueur flavours and with a salty-mineral finish). Peter Sisseck of the celebrated Duero estate Pingus gave some initial advice here; the present consultant is Claude Gros.

Nouveau Monde
34350 Vendres, Tel: 04 67 37 33 68, Fax: 04 67 37 58 15

This French-owned branch of the "New World" lies near Béziers on large *galets* (pudding-stones), producing a flower-scented, sweet-textured estate red based on Syrah, Grenache, and Mourvèdre.

Ollieux Romanis *see* Comte Cathar

Oustalet *see* Virginie

Pech Redon
11100 Narbonne, Tel: 04 68 90 41 22, Fax: 04 68 65 11 48

Pleasant, lively tangy wines from this Coteaux du Languedoc La Clape domain run by Christophe Bousquet.

Peyre Rose

34230 Saint-Pargoire, Tel: 04 67 98 75 50, Fax: 04 67 98 71 88

Even in a region as full of individualists as Coteaux du Languedoc, Marlène Soria's domain stands out as spectacularly singular. Pink is the theme colour here, both for the labels and the winery equipment, yet the wines themselves are anything but a simple-minded cliché of "feminine": massively extracted and given long pre-bottle ageing, there is something brutish and primeval about them. There are two *cuvées*, and Syrah dominates each. In the slightly more accessible Cistes, it is complemented with Grenache; in the genuinely leonine Léone, Mourvèdre piles on the power. Can time tame them? Perhaps not; the oldest vintage I have sampled is a 1991 Cistes, still ferocious a decade later. Yet I am glad there is wine like this on the earth to remind us of what might have put hairs on the chests of Odysseus and Achilles. The domain lies near St-Pargoire, making these wines an intriguing comparison with the similarly Syrah-dominated but stylistically dissimilar Clos des Truffiers of Négly.

Piccinini

34210 La Livinière, Tel: 04 68 91 44 32

This 27-ha domain has been one of the pioneers of Minervois and Minervois La Livinière. The wine are simple and pleasant, but light compared to the best of their peers.

Piétri-Géraud

66190 Coullioure, Tel: 04 68 82 07 42, Fax: 04 68 98 02 58

Mother and daughter Maguy and Laetitia Piétri-Géraud make a savoury, light-textured yet persistent red Collioure from their steep, schist terraces: the burgundy of Roussillon. There's also a decadent white Banyuls whose perfumed flavours (violet, lavender, and candied fruit) prove that Grenache Blanc can sometimes rise above it's "white cow" reputation, while the aged red Banyuls Cuvée Joseph Géraud is a vivid prune stew of a wine.

Pithon

66600 Calce, Tel: 04 68 38 50 21

Olivier Pithon, the brother of the Loire Valley's Jo Pithon, has a 9-ha Côtes du Roussillon-Villages domain. Best wines are the choice, fresh-flavoured La Coulée and the lusher, more densely fruited Les Vignes de Saturne.

Pouderoux

66550 Corneilla la Riviere, Tel: 04 68 57 22 02, Fax: 04 68 57 11 63

Robert Pouderoux's 15-ha domain up in the freshness of the Aply Valley benefits from three AOCs: Côtes du Roussillon-Villages, Côtes du Roussillon-Villages Latour de France (for a small parcel), and Maury. Within an exciting range, La Mouriance stands out for its luscious flesh and texture (it is one of France's new-wave barrel-fermented reds).

Préceptorie de Centernach

66650 Banyuls, Tel: 04 68 88 13 45, Fax: 04 68 88 18 55

This project initially began as a joint venture between the Parcé brothers of Domaine de la Rectorie and the Maury cooperative. It didn't work out; so three members (Aurélie Silva Pereira de Abreu, Francis Victor, and Frédéric Trébillac) quit the cooperative to go into full-time partnership with the Parcés for the wines of the Préceptorie, making a total of 38 ha and 40 parcels to draw on, predominantly sited on schist. The results are excellent: look out for the barrique-fermented La Chapelle St-Roch white (Vin de Pays du Val d'Agly), made from Grenache Gris and Maccabeu: fat, vegetal, an odalisque. The red version (from Grenache and Carignan) has plenty of fresh, tangy bite and faintly medicinal fruit. The red and white Coume Marie wines are more elegant, the white musky, the red smoky. Terre Promise, predominantly Grenache grown on clay-limestone rather than schist, is lightly fruited, yet full of falling flaky tannins. There are several Maury wines, too, including the vividly cherryish Cuvée Aurélie Pereira de Abreu and the gutsy, chewy Cuvée TE.

Prieuré de St-Jean de Bébian ✪

34120 Pézenas, Tel: 04 67 98 13 60, Fax: 04 67 98 22 24

Jean-Claude Le Brun and Chantal Lecouty's 30-ha Coteaux du Languedoc domain, purchased from the talented though unpredictable Alain Roux in 1994, has provided some of the New Languedoc's reference bottles. Roux was, like Michel Escande of Borie le Maurel, a follower of Jaques Reynaud of Château Rayas: "Grenache at less than 15% is shit," was typical of the sagely salty advice that Roux passed on to Lecouty. "I wanted," she reflects, "as much concentration as Alain achieved, but with much more elegance"; her pet hate among Languedoc's most ambitious present-day wine is over-extraction. Low yields (25 hl/ha on average) and careful fruit sorting, combined with advice from François Serres (long-time consultant to Rayas), have indeed resulted in a more civilized and drinkable range than the shocking monsters that Roux produced in his early days. The red is a Syrah-Grenache-Mourvèdre blend of tobacco- and leather-scented suavity, smoky fruit, and increasingly soft tannin, bottled unfiltered; Chapelle is the second wine. There is now also a subtly compelling barrel-fermented white based on ripe, low-yielding Roussanne given two days in a cool room before pressing, mixed with four local varieties (Clairette, Grenache Blanc, Bourboulenc, and Terret); the effect is like a decadent southern Pessac-Léognan, with spoonfuls of creamy lemon and apricot fruit.

de la Prose

34570 Pignan, Tel: 04 67 03 08 30, Fax: 04 67 03 48 70

There have been some magnificently stony bottles of Coteaux du Languedoc from this St-Georges d'Orques (Grès de Montpellier) domain, based on low yields of 25 hl/ha at most. The astonishingly herbal Cuvée Prestige (the aftertaste of the 1998 was almost vermouth-like) is a Grenache-Syrah blend, whereas Les Embruns is a pure oaked Syrah that combines some of the cinder-and-smoke characteristics of the variety with further exuberant flavours of *garrigue*.

Puech Chaud

30980 Langlade

Pure Syrah grown in the stony, calcareous soils of Langlade near Nîmes give René Rostaing, now a master of Côte Rôtie, the chance to contrast two very different terroirs – acid in the Rhône and alkaline here. The Rostaing touch is evident in the perfumed fruits and elegant, silky tannins, a stark contrast to Languedoc's more bruising reds (like Peyre Rose). (*See also* Roc d'Anglade.)

Puech-Haut

24160 Saint-Drézéry, Tel: 04 67 86 93 70, Fax: 04 67 86 94 07

Ambitious, 100-ha domain in Coteaux du Languedoc St-Drézery receiving much investment from electrical-transformers mogul Gérard Bru (including advice from Michel Rolland). The wines are pleasant but over-oaky at this stage.

de Ravanès

34490 Thézan-les-Béziers

Impressive Vin de Pays domain working with the zonal denomination of Murviel rather than dull Aude; the varieties, though, are still the Bordeaux classics. The Merlot seems fresher, spicier, and more impressive than the slightly green Cabernet Sauvignon. Les Gravières de Taurou is the top Merlot, while Cuvée Diogène is a Petit Verdot-Cabernet blend.

de la Rectorie ✪

66650 Banyuls, Tel: 04 68 88 13 45, Fax: 04 68 88 18 55

This 25-ha domain is run by brothers Marc and Thierry Parcé and Marc's son-in-law Vincent Legrand with great imagination – and an acute sense of aesthetics, too (Thierry is also a pianist, and brother Pierre a distinguished photographer). Around 30 different wines are made here each year, including two Collioure reds, Le Séris and Coume Pascole, which are relatively pale in colour but have the dry wind of the south blowing through them and a stony finish, too: Séris is preponderantly Grenache whereas Coume Pascole is a Grenache, Syrah, and Carignan blend. A "*vin arride, un vin de pauvre, un vin de* pierre" ("an arid wine, a poor man's wine, a stone wine") is Marc Parce's apt description of Coume Pascole. L'Oriental is an old-vine Banyuls made from Grenache Noir and Gris with some Carignan: pure coffee and aniseed. Best of all are the Cuvée Parcé Frères and Cuvée Léon Parcé sold as a Vin de Liqueur because they haven't had the requisite ageing to qualify as Banyuls: bright, perfumed and exotic red fruits with a lingering, tangy finish. (See also Préceptorie de Centernach.)

Rimbert ✪
34360 Berlou, Tel: 04 67 89 73 98, Fax: 04 67 89 73 98

Jean-Marie Rimbert's 20-ha St-Chinian domain was created in 1997 when he acquired his terraced, schist vineyards after having worked for five years as vineyard manager for Château de Flaugergues. "My pivot is Carignan," says Rimbert – he has 8 ha of the variety, planted over 80 years ago, which he uses for all three of his wines. The exact blend of Les Travers de Marsau, the "cuvée gourmande", changes every year, but it's usually marked by inksquirts of shocking sloe fruit from 50% or more of Carignan; Le Mas au Schiste, the "cuvée prestige", is composed of more of less equal amounts of Carignan, Syrah, Grenache, and Cinsault, one-third of which is barrique aged. Thanks to low yields of 20 hl/ha or so, this is a wine of magnificent intensity, packed with savage scents and flavours of black fruits, hot earth, burnt wood, and burnt meat. The pure Carignan table wine Le Chant de Marjolaine, picked in October at 14.5% or more, is an unforgettable schist liqueur, stony and austere yet fresh with bitter cherry acidity.

Roc d'Anglade
30980 Langlade, Tel: 04 66 81 45 83,

Rémi Pedreno's first vintage at this Coteaux du Languedoc estate (whose land is owned by René Rostaing) was the strikingly Côte Rôtie-like 1999, a Syrah-Grenache blend of coffee and flower scents and pure, mile-long fruit (produced from yields of only 20 hl/ha). Pédreno's is also the hand behind Cos de la Belle, a pure Syrah that constitutes perhaps the greatest Vin de Pays du Gard ever produced. (See also Puech Chaud.)

La Roque
34270 Fontanès, Tel: 04 67 55 34 47, Fax: 04 67 55 10 18

The fortified farm (and former monastery) of Jack Boutin, the pioneering bottler of Pic-St-Loup, constitutes one of the largest properties in the Pic-St-Loup area, with 42 ha of which 35 ha are AOC, including no fewer than 8 ha of Mourvèdre. The unfiltered Cupa Numismae, a Syrah-Mourvèdre blend, is violet-scented but slightly raw in style; there is also a slightly gruff Vieilles Vignes de Mourvèdre cuvée, softened slightly with 10% Grenache.

Roquefort St-Martin
11540 Roquefort les Corbières

Together with the Cuvée No 3 of Embres et Castelmaure, the Grande Réserve of Château Roquefort St-Martin, produced by the cooperative of Roquefort des Corbières in the terroir of Sigean, has been the best of the wines produced in Corbières in cooperation with Michel Tardieu. This limestone-grown blend of Carignan, Grenache, and Mourvèdre has (in the 1998 vintage) splendid truffley depths, a salty edge, and fine, fresh acidity to bring the wine into balance, too. It is made with cool maceration before fermentation, natural yeasts, a 16-month spell in barrique and bottling without filtration: magnificent and cellar-worthy.

St-Louis de Villeraze see Comte Cathar

St-Martin de la Garrigue
34530 Montagnac, Tel: 04 67 24 00 40, Fax: 04 67 24 16 15

This large, well-resourced 62-ha Coteaux du Languedoc estate belongs to ex-supermarketeer Umberto Guida, and is run by the enthusiastic Jean-Claude Zabalia. The standard is consistent: these are carefully made wines, bottled without fining or filtration. Perhaps the best wine for me is an astonishing Picpoul de Pinet, picked very late from low-yielding vines: those who consider this an inarticulate if refreshing choice, the Muscadet of the Midi, should try this

mint-and-verbena-scented, powerfully lemony wine. The earthy, chewy Cuvée St-Martin de la Garrigue is the top red.

Sarda-Malet
66000 Perpignan, Tel: 04 68 56 72 38, Fax: 04 68 56 47 60

This long-established Roussillon domain remains one of the appellation benchmarks, both for the pretty Réserve and for the more ambitious, concentrated and chewier Terroir Mailloles, one of the most harmonious of the AOC's top wines.

des Schistes
66310 Estagel, Tel: 04 68 29 11 25, Fax: 04 68 29 47 17

"Old vines are very important for us," says Jacques Sire, alluding like so many others in Roussillon to the fact that the post-1945 boom in VDN production is now proving a boon for early twenty-first century red wine production. There are 48 ha here, in Tautavel, Maury, and Estagel, including Carignan of more than 80 years and Grenache of over 50. There are three Côtes du Roussillon-Villages wines: the Carignan-rich Cuvée Tradition, full of warmth and vivacious fruit; Les Terraces, a Syrah-rich blend grown on limestone of greater intensity and a smoky, pungent style; and finally the pure-Syrah La Coumille, made from a single parcel in the best years only – elegant, pure and mineral. There is also a fine, tea-scented Maury here and a traditional, tangy Rivesaltes.

Senat
11160 Trausse, Tel: 04 68 78 38 17, Fax: 04 68 78 26 61

Jean-Baptiste Senat's 16-ha Minervois domain (4 ha of which are Vins de Pays) is a good source of ripe, unctuous wines which glance across to the southern Rhône: Senat has no Syrah at all, preferring Grenache, which he balances with old-vine Carignan and Mourvèdre. La Nine is deliciously fruity, while Le Bois des Merveilles is both sweeter and more structured.

Sieur d'Arques
11300 Limoux, Tel: 04 68 74 63 00, Fax: 04 68 74 63 14

This Limoux-based cooperative has shown the way for all those looking for an exit from the impasse of the historic and sometimes superannuated wine styles of the past. Blanquette de Limoux is a pleasant, softly biscuity Mauzac-based sparkling wine of agreeable versatility – the Cava of France, if you like; Crémant versions are not wildly different, since the additional Chardonnay and Chenin merely offers a slightly more international flavour, while those sparkling wines made by the méthode ancestrale here offer a fascinating glimpse of a more rustic, lower-alcohol past. Sieur d'Arques, though, has been instrumental in pioneering still, barrel-fermented Chardonnay here – as well as advocating the division of Limoux up into different terroirs, putting these to the proof via a series of "single-terroir" Limoux wines. Haute Vallée is clearly the best of these with its sappy scents and brisk, cleanly sinewy flavours.

Silène de Payrals see Skalli

Skalli
34202 Sète, Tel: 04 67 46 70 00, Fax: 04 67 46 71 99

Robert Skalli has been the French champion of varietal wines produced within the framework of the Vins de Pays regulations for over a decade. In 1998, however, recognizing the limitations of this approach, Skalli extended the range to include appellation wines. All of the range is packaged and marketed with great skill; quality, however, has often been disappointing, with the varietals being sketchy in character and clumsily acidified, while the first releases of the appellation wines were dry-fruited, slender, and lacking in substance. Recently, however, the varietal Cabernet Sauvignon in the Robert Skalli range has shown a clear improvement with richer tannins and softer balance, while the 2000 launch vintage of Domaine Silène des Payrals in Coteaux du Languedoc (a 30-ha estate sited near the Etang de Thau in Grès de Montpelier) was also dark, dense, and spicily promising, though over-expensive. The Clos Poggiale from Corsica, excluded from that chapter for reasons of space, is coffee-like and concentrated, one of the island's better wines.

Tabatau

34360 Assignan, Tel: 04 67 38 19 60, Fax: 04 67 38 19 54

Promising St-Chinian domain owned by ex-Mas de Daumas vineyard manager Bruno Gracia and his sturdy brother Jean-Paul, a former army captain. Early releases have been pleasant, elegant, tobacco-scented; look for more depth and concentration in the future.

Tardieu ✪✪

84160 Lourmarin, Tel: 04 90 68 80 25, Fax: 04 90 68 22 65

According to the winegrowers of Embres et Castelmaure (qv), Tardieu's techniques in Corbières include a period of cold maceration before fermentation, destalking for all of the Grenache and some of the Carignan, a 10 to 12-day fermentation with the wine being run quickly into barrels after fermentation (thus no long *cuvaisons*), as much contact as possible with the fine lees during 12-months' barrique ageing, and bottling without filtration. (See also Roquefort St-Martin.) Tardieu also makes a scented and creamy Minervois Les Causses from pure Syrah.

Terre Inconnue ✪

34400 St-Series

Tiny garage-style operation run by chemist Robert Creus, his wife Sylvie, and his father Lucien, a former Spanish teacher; all the wines are Vin de Table because Creus can't be bothered with the paperwork involved in AOC legislation. There is no shortage of effort, by contrast, in production, which is modelled on the Tardieu-Laurent approach of tiny yields and fastidious *élevage*. Cuvée Léonie is a pure Carignan, deep and challenging; Los Abuelos is a massively proportioned Grenache (16.5% in 2000); and Sylvie is preponderantly Syrah with low-acid, unctuous, saturated fruit and mineral flavours (yields of 12 hl/ha in 2000). There has been some vintage inconsistency, but expect this to be a star source in the future.

Terre Mégère

34660 Cournonsec, Tel: 04 67 85 42 85, Fax: 04 67 85 25 12

Michel Moreau's Vin de Pays varietal wines are intense but slightly dry and fruitless in style, almost as if the terroir were proving more dominant than the varietal flavours. They include a Merlot and a Cabernet Sauvigon, as well as a Syrah-based Les Dolomies Coteaux du Languedoc, a Viognier, and a Viognier-Grenache Blanc La Galopine Coteaux du Languedoc.

Le Thou

34410 Sauvian, Tel: 04 67 32 16 42, Fax: 04 67 32 16 42

The Comtesse de Ferrier de Montal's Coteaux du Languedoc property is one of those lying on the outskirts of Béziers (Terrasses de Béziers). At present, the wine is wild and herby, though rather light in weight and dry in style; big investments here in 2000 should improve matters.

Toques et Clochers

11303 Limoux Cedex, Tel: 04 68 74 63 00, Fax: 04 68 74 63 12

An annual charity auction in Limoux of Chardonnay barrel samples, the worst of which are over-oaked and under-fruited, but the best of which are varietally true and surprisingly subtle and elegant.

Tour Penedesses

34320 Gabian, Tel: 04 67 24 14 41, Fax: 04 67 24 14 22

This large 40-ha domain straddles both Coteaux du Languedoc and Faugères; there are also some Vins de Pays parcels, too. Alexandre Fouque has no fewer than 15 varieties planted, and the wine range is equally diffuse, with 15 different *cuvées* at present (including a late-harvest Muscat-Terret Blanc). The pure Tempranillo Mas de Couy is only modestly characterful; better are the AOC Montée de Grés, pure and mineral, and the richer Les Volcans.

Tour Vieille

66190 Collioure, Tel: 04 68 82 44 82

A source of two good Collioure wines, the sweet-fruited La Pinède and the more sombre Puig Oriol. Classic Banyuls, too.

Val d'Orbieu

11100 Narbonne, Tel: 04 68 42 75 36

Val d'Orbieu is a large, tentacle-like collection of wine companies and cooperatives based in the Languedoc but whose business interests now stretch to Bordeaux, where it owns Grand-Puy-Ducasse, Meyney, Lamothe-Bergeron, and Rayne Vigneau among other châteaux. It also owns Listel, producer of the technically proficient though organoleptically dull "sand wines" of Aigues Mortes. Val d'Orbieu's most ambitious wines are the Cuvée Mythique, produced since 1990, and more recently a series of "single domain" wines sold under the property name. Cuvée Mythique is a teasing wine about which nothing is ever revealed: no blends, no ageing details, no fruit sources. Since it's produced as a Vin de Pays rather than an AOC, there is considerable freedom for invention; it is beautifully labelled and packaged. All the cooperative will say in reply to questions about it is "*C'est mythique!*" Its success has meant that it is now produced in far larger quantities than the initial 50,000 cases. Since it is a cherry-picking exercise, this means that what was initially one of the best wines in the Languedoc is now merely a good wine of middling concentration which evolves relatively swiftly, acquiring soft, accessible, mellow flavours of spice, soft fruits, and meat.

The top-of-the-line domain wines come from a variety of Languedoc AOCs (Corbières, Fitou, Minervois, St-Chinian), and elevation to their ranks will be decided on tasting alone, by an invited panel of experts. They don't yet have the concentration of flavour that would enable their different terroirs to emerge with the pungent clarity one might hope for: further lowering of yields and bottling without filtration would help. Best is certainly the profound Mourvèdre-based wine of that fastidious viticulturalist and amateur historian Pierre Fil.

Veyran

34490 Causses et Veyran, Tel: 04 67 89 67 89, Fax: 04 67 89 65 77

Gérard Antoine, a former chemist from Paris, is making superb St-Chinian from his domain at Causses et Veyran. The Cuvée Prestige, a 70% Syrah, 30% Grenache blend, is ripe, rich, and beautifully extracted.

Vieux Chêne

66600 Espira-de-l'Agly, Tel: 04 68 38 92 01, Fax: 04 68 38 95 79

Smoky, wild, and savoury characters dominate both the Haut Valoir and the Terres Nègres Altès *cuvées* of this Côtes du Roussillon property.

Virginie

34536 Béziers, Tel: 04 67 49 85 85, Fax: 04 67 49 38 39

Like its rival Skalli, Domaines Virginie (now owned by Castel Frères) has realized that the future of French varietal Vins de Pays is not necessarily an easy or rewarding one, and the company has created the Oustalet brand name for AOC wines. The initial releases (of Coteaux du Languedoc, Corbières, and Minervois) are good though not outstanding; the Syrah-dominated Minervois, with its undulating floral style, is the best.

At a similar quality level are the Référence Chardonnay and Référence Syrah, the latter from a single parcel in Gard grown on rolled pebbles yielding 45 hl/ha and given 18 months in new oak (half French and half American): an appealing wine with blackcurrant, violet, and coffee aromas and a pure, smooth, soaring style with blackcurrants again to the fore. Most intriguing of all, though, is the Paradoxe Blanc, described as a "100% non-interventionist wine" made from Chardonnay vines in exactly the same way as a red wine – in other words with maceration of the skins in the juice, then 14 months' barrique ageing (giving it a greater tannin content than the Viriginie Merlot or Cabernet Sauvignon reds possess). Deep gold in colour, with weighty, vanillin scents and an unctuous, richly textured, chewy peach-skin flavour, tasting this tannic white is akin to catching a glimpse of a dinosaur feeding quietly at the edge of a field.

Corsica

Building Bridges Most wine on Corsica still lacks the definition and density of the best of mainland France. Only when its growers travel and taste what the Languedoc, Rhône, and Southwest have achieved will Corsica's own astonishing terroirs find their voice.

One quarter of a million people live on Corsica, which is fewer than live in the cities of Lyon or Toulouse. All of the island's AOC vineyards add up to under 2,500 ha (6,175 acres) – just a fraction of what is grown in the single AOC of Bordeaux. Corsica is small.

That wasn't, though, what I was thinking as Yves Leccia, the quiet, thoughtful leader of Corsica's wine-growers, drove me from Bastia to Patrimonio. On the map, the journey is nothing. Corsica is capped by a finger that points north, jabbing at France. Bastia lies to one side of the finger's base, and Patrimonio the other. The reality, though, is that you need to drive your car skywards to journey between the two. The road climbs out of Bastia, past the giant rubbish tip that looks down on the city, and keeps climbing. When we eventually reached the saddle of the mountain, Yves suggested we got out to take a look. The view was wide, airy, cartographic; lemon thyme perfumed the air. The Conca d'Oru lay below us, scooped like a length of cork bark. "Corsica," said Yves, "is first and foremost a mountain. There are many places here where the snow never melts. All the true Corsican villages are in the mountains. Corsicans learned to leave the coast for the invaders, who came and went. In spirit, we're a mountain people."

No visitor to Corsica could fail to register that fact. The average height on this, the highest of all Mediterranean islands, is 568 metres (1,863 feet); the peaks rise up to 2,700 metres (8,860 feet). Wine-wise,

there are several implications. The first is that, despite Corsica being France's most southerly vineyard area, it is decidedly not its hottest. Height and wind modify the realities of latitude – as the remarkable freshness of the best of Corsica's white wines, and the almost burgundian grace of some of its reds, proves. The second implication, a reflection of the ways that mountain chains slice up the island, is that the valleys, the towns that dominate their access to the sea, and their vineyard areas are all quite separate from one another. To travel from Patrimonio to adjacent Calvi, for example, is instructive. It involves crossing a desert. Not a sand sea, of course, but a dry, scrubby wilderness of thorn bushes and stones, a long and winding hour of uninterrupted and forbidding inhospitality. Balagne, the region around Calvi, looks very different to hilly, cove-sculpted Patrimonio: it is suddenly flatter and more open. The soil is different, too; the limestone of Patrimonio has given way to granitic sands and clays here. The topography of Corsica, one might almost say, makes each separate AOC an island in its own right, and offers a tantalizing prospect (barely realized as yet) of difference, of distinction, of nuance. We'll explore these briefly in "Adventure of the Land", overleaf.

Where, though, is Corsica today in the wine world? Like many southern French regions, it is at a pivotal point. With one leathery and careworn mask, the island is on the point of extracting itself

definitively from its past of high-volume, low-cost, low-quality production, embraced after the French retreat from Algeria in the early 1960s. No fewer than 20,000 ha (49,400 acres) of vineyards planted with the wrong varieties in the wrong places have been torn up since 1980. With a braver, more youthful mask, it is trying to build on the uniqueness of its soils and grape varieties to create wines of real interest, wines capable of engaging the world's attention along with the best of the Rhône, Provence, or the Languedoc. The wager has not been won yet, as I point out in "Flak", but at least the game is underway. Those grapes are, for red wines, Niellucciu (ie Tuscany's Sangiovese) and the Corsican native Sciaccarellu; and for white wines the Vermentinu (known as Rolle in Provence and Languedoc). In the hands of a grower like Antoine Arena, wines made from these varieties stamp their way into the world, pungent with character, depth, and density, as startling as the discovery of an exotic bird previously thought extinct. Arena is a close friend of André Romero (who has just planted Nielluccio in Rasteau); he is friendly with the Vins de Vienne team of Cuilleron, Villard, and Gaillard. These facts are not coincidental. Arena, through his passion and excitement about great wine, has left insularity behind; he has built bridges which reach to some of southern France's finest cellars. If Corsica is to achieve its winemaking destiny, it needs more Arenas, and it needs more bridges.

Christian Imbert ▲

A few French wine-growers are genuine pioneers; Christian Imbert has been a pioneer three times over. Initially, in his twenties, when he set off on his own to plant fruit trees in the Atlas mountains; later during fifteen nomadic years as a trader in Chad; finally in developing his own forty-two-ha (104-acre) organic wine estate out of the scrub in the underexploited Corsican wine zone of Porto Vecchio. He also founded Uvacorse, an association of growers determined to raise quality standards during the table-wine epoch of the late 1970s. The struggle now is against "the bureaucratic spirit" emanating from Paris and Brussels, and the "Coca-Cola mentality". "La vigne c'est le vin avant l'argent" (the vine is wine before money) is Imbert's motto. "Le Coca-Cola ne passera pas" (Coca-Cola will not prevail).

"I'm crazy, I admit. I do everything I can to produce marginal wines. Exceptional wines, but marginal wines."

ANTOINE ARENA

◀ The crossing from Bastia to Patrimonio takes you over one of this mountainous island's many sky-bare ridges.

The Adventure of the Land

Corsica has one overall appellation – Vin de Corse. Grape growing on most of the island is unthinkable: it is inaccessible mountainside. In practice, then, the Vin de Corse AOC is used chiefly for wines grown along the eastern coastline, between Bastia and Porto-Vecchio, where much of the country's flattest land lies. The least interesting half of Corsica's AOC production begins life here, ninety per cent of it produced by cooperatives. This is also the source of much of Corsica's generally disappointing varietal Vin de Pays (whose volume is almost double the island's AOC volume).

Vin de Corse does, however, have a system of *crus*: Vin de Corse-Porto-Vecchio, Vin de Corse-Figari, Vin de Corse-Sartène, Vin de Corse-Calvi, and finally Vin de Corse-Coteaux du Cap Corse. A little variety and character begins to creep into the equation here. **Vin de Corse-Porto-Vecchio** has steep, spectacular granite slopes overlooking the sea, though there are a mere three producers here. **Vin de Corse-Figari** is also a granite and alluvial vineyard, Corsica's most southerly, and a ferociously windy spot to grow vines. With just five growers and an underused three-grower co-op, it is not much bigger than Porto Vecchio. The small, often chaotic granite slopes of **Vin de Corse-Sartène** constitute Corsica's hottest vine-growing location (its nine private growers plus a co-op make it the biggest of these *crus*). **Vin de Corse-Calvi** is another granite-soiled plains vineyard with wind problems, but its eleven growers include some of the island's more ambitious and skilled, and the result is that wines here compete with the best from Patrimonio and Ajaccio. **Vin de Corse-Coteaux du Cap Corse**, finally, is the oddity among this quintet, in that it is sited on the bony finger that dominates the north of the island, and the soils are schist rather than granite. Because of its incessant high winds, this is another very challenging vineyard area farmed by just four producers, though its historical reputation is the greatest of the five *crus*. Do its wines have *un caractère iodé*, a seaside saltiness? When you taste in the region, perhaps; it does not, though, seem to survive emigration.

The island's two main wine-growing regions have appellations in their own right; there is also a separate appellation for the fortified Muscats of Cap Corse. **Ajaccio** is the more southerly of these two AOCs: it covers 250 ha (618 acres) of widely scattered granite- and sand-soiled slope vineyards set back from Napoleon's home town. The climate is mild and balmy, both less windy and less arid than some of the island's other sectors. Of the two native red varieties, it is the more delicate Sciaccarellu that flourishes in the pink, crystalline

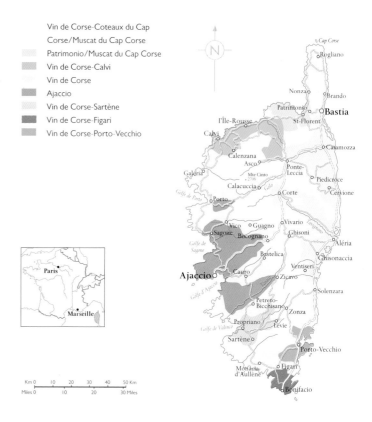

soils here; delicacy, indeed, is a distinguishing characteristic of the light, often understated wines of Ajaccio.

Patrimonio is where most of Corsica's finest wines are to be found. Is this because the vines (especially Niellucciu) enjoy being on its limy clays, such a contrast to the crystalline soils elsewhere? Or that the wind is least problematic here? Or that there are thirty-two wine-growing domains here, and no cooperatives? Probably a combination of all three. The vineyard area itself is relatively small, and many of the vineyards occupy niches in the hills, often some distance from the cellars. The same 450-ha (1,111-acre) area is used for the Vin Doux Naturel AOC of **Muscat du Cap Corse.**

Corsica Flak

The scene is set for Corsica to produce a small range of excellent wines, none of which will have much trouble finding a ready market. Appellation regulations are never perfect, of course, but in general INAO has done a good job of codifying ways in which Corsica's potential can be expressed. It's certainly a shame that dry, unfortified Muscat wines are not permitted in the regulations; and it's also a shame that some of the more experimental wines of growers like Etienne Suzzoni of Culombu and Antoine Arena are forced to go to market as Vin de Table, simply because they don't fit the AOC pigeonholes. But in general, everything is ready.

Now Corsica's wine-growers have to do their bit. As yet, the truth is that most don't. Corsica's political relationship with France is famously difficult; culturally Corsica is more Italian than French. (This is reflected in the island's grape varieties as clearly as in the island's language, the islanders' names, and the number of ferry routes east and south; at sixty km [thirty-seven miles] away, mainland Italy is twice as close as mainland France.) Even the fact that one of the most famous Frenchmen of all time was a Corsican is a matter for ambiguous pride. Perhaps this difficult relationship is one reason why ordinary Corsican wines still seem too insular for their own good.

Corsica: People

Antoine Arena ✪
20253 Patrimonio, Tel: 04 95 37 08 27, Fax: 04 95 37 01 14

Arena is a jovial, middle-aged man who produces an astonishing range of wines from modest and rather jumbled cellars in Patrimonio. He and his wife Marie began their working lives by training to be lawyers, but switched to wine, Arena says, "because it's such a beautiful job." Arena has friends in other winemaking regions of France, but in a way it is Alsace that his wines recall most clearly for me: the late-harvest richness, density, and flavour-saturation of his wines, combined with the fact that at present he uses no oak, gives them a kinship with those created by Zind-Humbrecht. Arena's work completely rewrites the rule book for Vermentinu: made this way, it can happily stand comparison with Pinot Gris or Viognier. His 2000 Carco, for example, billows with scents of bacon and banana; in the mouth it is plump, luscious, and exotic. The 1999, with a year on its fine lees, is a creamier, subtler wine with salty-sweet edges. The 2000 Grotte di Sole Vermentino, which has reached about 16.5% alcohol before giving up fermenting, is honeyed, oozing rich fruit – as is a November-harvested 1999 version packed with apricot and fig (it will have to go to market under Vin de Table legislation). The ever-curious Arena is also working with an old Corsican variety called Bianco Gentile: his 2000 cuvée was picked at 16% potential alcohol, and is a massive and exotic confection of tropical fruits, honey, and melon, with a salty fire at its heart, too. Arena also uses the Carco and Grotte di Sole names for his Niellucciu-based reds. The Carco, a so-called vin de soif (thirst-quencher), is vivid with raspberry fruit; the Grotte di Sole, produced from lower yields, combines something of the bitter-edged sophistication of Tuscany with explosive fruit and mineral flavours. (Few Chiantis, in truth, can compete on an equal footing with this wine.) Arena's Muscat de Cap Corse is as massive as you might expect, almost rivalling the sun-dried Zibibbo Muscats of Pantelleria and, like them, packed with orange citrus sweetness.

de Bernardi
20253 Patrimonio, Tel: 04 95 37 01 09, Fax: 04 95 32 07 66

Jean Laurent de Bernardi's 11-ha Patrimonio domain produces wines that combine perfume and freshness, soft fruit with vivid acid balances. Spice and pepper lurk within his Muscat, too.

Canarelli
20114 Figari, Tel: 04 95 71 07 55

Yves Canarelli's Figari domain has expanded to nearly 23 ha – and is now cultivated organically. The barrel-fermented Vermentino is one of the island's best whites, while the red is increasingly concentrated.

Culombu
20260 Lumio, Tel: 04 95 60 70 68, Fax: 04 95 60 63 46

Those who imagine all Corsicans to be small and dark should travel to Calvi to meet former veterinary student Etienne Suzzoni; he's built like a Maori rugby player. The Domaine Culombu wines are the "ordinary" cuvées, which are pleasant but unexceptional; the best wines are those sold under the Clos Culombu name. These include a richly fruited and perfumed Vermentinu-based white, and a barely less aromatic red in which the toffee-plum fruit of Grenache (40%) meets the herbal refinement of Niellucciu (50%; there is also 10% Syrah). Like Arena, Suzzoni produces some legislation-defying sweet wines including an unfortified sweet Muscat called Dolce Biancu and a cherryish blend of over-ripened but unfortified Aleatico and Sciaccarellu called Dolce Rossu.

Gentile
20217 St-Florent, Tel: 04 95 37 01 54, Fax: 04 95 37 16 69

Some of the wines from this 30-ha Patrimonio domain are inconsistently vinified, but the Sélection Noble red (almost pure Niellucciu given 12 months in foudre) is dark and firmly structured, and the Muscat, too, has fine concentration and buttery depth, with a stony, mineral finish.

Leccia
20232 Poggio-d'Oletta, Tel: 04 95 37 11 35, Fax: 04 95 37 17 03

Yves Leccia's 20-ha Patrimonio domain produces some of the island's most carefully made red and white wines, and a good Muscat, too. The "classic" white has more depth and texture than most, yet with typical island vividness, too; the classic red is carefully crafted and satisfying. The two top cuvées are the salty white E Croce and the warm-fruited red Petra Bianca.

Orenga de Gaffory
20253 Patrimonio, Tel: 04 95 37 45 00, Fax: 04 95 37 14 25

A delicately fruited Blanc de Blancs, a creamy rosé, and a juicily fruited, perfumed, and figgy "classic" red seem more successful from this large 100-ha Patrimonio estate than the "prestige" Gouverneurs, which does not quite have the depth or density to support its oak.

Peraldi
20167 Mezzavia, Tel: 04 95 22 37 30, Fax: 04 95 20 92 91

The memorably named Comte de Poix oversees the leading Ajaccio domain. These are wines of typical delicacy and restraint, clean and elegant. The top red wine, Clos du Cardinale, is made from a single parcel of old vine Sciaccarellu aged in new oak, but it reflects its grape variety, origins, and granite soils more vividly than any winery work. This is a pale, precise, and unshowy wine of elegant curranty fruit, far closer in style to a Santenay or a Jura Poulsard than to a Bandol or a Coteaux du Languedoc.

Pieretti
20228 Luri, Tel: 04 95 35 01 03, Fax: 04 95 35 01 03

Lina Venturi-Pieretti's 9-ha domain is one of only four in the wind-flogged zone of Coteaux du Cap Corse (it was impossible to stand upright in one of her sea-fronted vineyards on the day I visited); her modest winery is sited more or less on a beach of striking blue schist. The Vermentinu-based white is fresher and brisker than many on the island; the red is gentle, downy, and haunting.

Tanella
20114 Figari, Tel: 04 95 70 46 23, Fax: 04 95 70 54 40

The top wines from this Figari domain owned by Jean-Baptiste Peretti della Rocca are called Cuvée Alexandra: the white and rosé are both more allusive and expressive than the Corsican norm, while the red is lusher, softer, and more tannin-clad than most of its peers, with ripe, almost toffeed characters in the 1999 vintage.

Torraccia
20137 Porto-Vecchio, Tel: 04 95 71 43 50, Fax: 04 95 71 50 03

Christian Imbert is one of Corsica's most forceful wine personalities. His 42-ha Porto-Vecchio estate is registered as organic, and he is fiercely anti-wood for vinification and maturation. I find the white and rosé over-neutral; the reds, however, are gentle, tangy, and appealing in an easygoing way. The prestige Oriu (80% Niellucciu) adds a more herb-scented personality, but needs greater depth and density if it is to support the pre-bottle ageing it receives.

Star rating system used on producer spreads   ✪ Very good wine   ✪✪ Excellent wine   ✪✪✪ Great wine

Glossary

abv Alcohol by volume, a percentage measurement of alcohol in a given liquid (such as wine).

acidification The addition of acid to a must or wine: a forceful and sometime violent intervention (q.v.).

assemblage Blending.

autolysis Enzymatic destruction of yeast cells in lees (q.v.), adding flavour and complexity, particularly to sparkling wines following the second, bubble-forming fermentation.

bâtonnage Literally "beating": stirring up of lees in wine, usually in cask.

barrique The *barrique bordelaise* is a 225-litre wooden barrel.

biodynamics See pages 42–43.

botrytis *Botrytis cinerea*, a mould responsible for unwanted and nefarious "grey rot" or "rot" in unripe grapes or grapes destined for red wines, but also responsible for the development of solicited and beneficial "noble rot" in white grapes destined for sweet wines.

brut Sparkling wine or champagne with a *dosage* (q.v.) of up to 15g/l. Extra Brut has 6 g/l or less, and Brut Nature 3 g/l or less.

calcareous Lime-rich.

cap The layer of skins, pips, and sometimes stalks which forms at the top of a vat of fermenting wine.

carbonic maceration Vinification method which involves placing uncrushed berries in a vat under a blanket of carbon dioxide. An intracellular fermentation takes place within the uncrushed grapes in the middle and at the top of the vat, while the weight of the grapes crushes those at the bottom and they undergo a normal fermentation. This method produces fruity, perfumed wines, sometimes with banana or bubblegum scents, and with light tannic structures.

causses Wild, often barren limestone uplands found in a number of French wine regions, like Cahors and Minervois.

cépage Grape variety.

chai Above-ground cellar.

chaptalization The addition of sugar to must to increase a wine's final alcohol content (but not make it sweeter: the sugar is converted to alcohol). Some 17 g of sugar are required for each degree of alcohol. Chaptalization is a major winemaking intervention (q.v.).

château Literally "castle", though the buildings so described are often modest.

clairet Bordeaux term for a very light red wine.

climat Vineyard site or parcel, especially in Burgundy.

clonal selection Selecting and reproducing a single clone of a vine variety for its perceived advantages. This apparent advance often gives rise to monotonous or (if the "advantage" is high yields) poor-quality wines. Contrast massal selection.

clos Enclosed, sometimes walled vineyard.

concentration The removal of water from must (q.v.) or wine by evaporation (q.v.) or reverse osmosis (q.v.), most widely used after a rainy harvest. Cryo-extraction (q.v.), a shortcut in the making of sweet wines, is also a form of concentration.

cooperative Joint-venture entity owned by its wine-growing members, usually to pool winemaking and marketing expenses, meaning that those with tiny holdings do not have to invest in their own winemaking equipment or try to sell their own wines. Over half of France's wine is produced by cooperatives.

corail Term used in the Jura to describe deep rosé or very light red wines.

côte Hillside slope, often propitious for vineyards. The word *coteau*, usually used in its plural form *coteaux*, is also common, and sometimes denotes smaller hills.

coulure Incomplete fruit set, leading to a reduced harvest. Compare *millerandage*.

crémant Originally this term, "creaming", was used to describe sparkling wines bottled at around half normal pressure. The term has now been adopted to describe full-pressure sparkling wines made by the *méthode traditionelle* in parts of France other than Champagne.

cru Literally "growth", usually used to signify a vineyard or larger zone of vineyards of superior quality to the regional norm.

cru classé "Classed growth".

cryo-extraction Freeze-concentration to provide richer musts and therefore sweeter wines.

cuvaison The period during which a fermenting red wine macerates with its skins.

cuve A vat or tank.

cuvée A wine lot.

dégorgement Disgorgement: the removal of sediment after the second fermentation in sparkling winemaking.

délestage Emptying a part-fermented vat then pouring some or all the fermenting wine back over the top of the cap of pips and skins to fill the vat again: a method of extraction (q.v.) and concentration.

demi-muid A medium-sized cask of between 300 and 600 litres.

demi-sec Medium dry.

dosage The amount of sugar syrup added to a sparkling wine at the end of its production cycle.

doux Sweet.

effeuillage Leaf-plucking, to provide better fruit exposure and ventilation.

élevage Literally "raising": everything which is done to a wine between fermentation and bottling.

en primeur Pre-arrival sales.

éraflage Destemming or destalking.

evaporation The removal of water from must (q.v.) by vacuum techniques at low temperature.

extraction The transfer of substances (chiefly tannins, but also including glycerol, sugars, acids, aroma compounds, and mineral traces) from grape solids such as skins during maceration (q.v.).

fermentation The conversion of sugar to alcohol (and carbon dioxide, a by-product) by yeast.

feuillette Little Chablis barrel of between 114 and 132 litres.

filtration The removal of solid particles from a wine by passing it through a filter, an intervention (q.v.) which achieves stability at the cost of lost aroma and flavour.

fining The clarification of a wine by means of adding an agent such as egg white or bentonite, an intervention (q.v.) rarely necessary after unhurried élevage (q.v.).

flor See voile

foudre A large or very large wooden cask, usually old, designed to round and soften a wine via controlled oxidation, but not to give it oaky scents or flavours.

fût See oaked

garage wine See page 169.

grains nobles Grapes affected by noble rot (q.v.).

grand cru "Great growth", though the specific meaning of this term varies widely according to vineyard region.

grand cru classé "Classified great growth".

grand vin "Great wine". In Bordeaux, means the wine which bears the property's name, as opposed to its second wine (q.v.).

green harvesting The removal of bunches of grapes in summer to lower yield.

intervention Wine cannot be made without any human intervention at all, but France's leading wine-growers all now recognize that that the fewer and less heavy-handed the interventions, the better. Great winemakers are not construction engineers, but skilled and observant midwives, skilfully helping a natural process on its way. *See also* non-interventionist.

late harvest Harvesting later than the norm is a risky process, but it is often desirable for rich, amply expressive dry red and white wines, and essential for sweet wines.

lees Yeast residues. Keeping wine in contact with its lees can bring both flavour and textural benefits.

lieu-dit Plot of land; vineyard name; name for an unclassified parcel of land in regions (like Burgundy) where leading parcels have been classified.

liqueur (de tirage) The syrup added to a sparkling wine after disgorgement (q.v.).

liquoreux Sweet.

lutte raisonnée The "reasoned struggle": a term used to describe non-organic viticulture which uses chemicals only when strictly necessary, rather than on a routine, preventative basis. The ideal may be appealing, but the employment of this term is unregulated.

maceration The "soaking" of grape matter in must (q.v.) or wine. Cold maceration (*macération à froid* or *macération préfermentaire*) is carried out before fermentation begins for fruit perfume and flavour. Maceration during fermentation is the means by which extraction (q.v.) is achieved. *See also* carbonic maceration.

malic acid One of the two principal acids in wine. *See also* tartaric acid.

malolactic fermentation Not a true fermentation, but the bacteriological conversion of unstable malic acid to stable lactic acid (plus carbon dioxide), solicited for all red wines and some whites. Its sensorial effect is to soften the acid structure of a wine. Also called secondary fermentation, malo or MLF.

massal selection Selection, usually in a vineyard, of a wide variety of clonal material (by taking cuttings from the healthiest vines) for vine propagation.

méthode ancestrale See *méthode rurale*

méthode champenoise See *méthode traditionelle*

méthode rurale Sparkling wine made by bottling the wine before the first fermentation has finished; such wines will often be relatively low in alcohol, and will contain sediment.

méthode traditionelle The method of making sparkling wine used in Champagne and much copied around France and the world, employing a second fermentation in bottle and disgorgement (q.v.).

micro-oxygenation Alternative to

racking, giving wines the oxygen they need without physically moving them off their lees: *see page 205.*

mildew Common fungal disease affecting vines. Of two types: downy (*mildiou*) and powdery (*oïdium*).

millerandage Abnormal and irregular fruit set, known as "hen and chickens" in English. Compare *coulure*.

mistelle Mixture of grape juice and alcohol.

MLF *See* malolactic fermentation

moelleux Mellow or (literally) "marrowy", meaning sweet though not quite *liquoreux* (q.v.).

monopole A celebrated vineyard site (especially in Burgundy) in single ownership.

mousse The sparkle in a sparkling wine.

mousseux Sparkling.

must Grape juice (*moût*).

mutage Fortification of must or part-fermented wine with spirit to prevent or arrest fermentation.

négociant Term for a wholesale merchant, especially one buying, blending, and bottling wine to be sold under his or her own label. A *négociant-éleveur* also carries out *élevage* (q.v.).

noble rot *See* rot

non-interventionist Term used to describe the approach to winemaking which tries to alter, modify, or "correct" the raw materials delivered by nature to the minimum extent.

non-vintage (NV) Term used chiefly in Champagne to signify a blend of different vintages.

oaked A wine which has received oak treatment. Often labelled *cuvée fûts de chêne* or similar.

oïdium Powdery mildew.

old vines *See vieilles vignes*

oxidation The exposure of wine to air which, if taken to excess, will spoil it. Controlled oxidation, by contrast, can add complexity to wines.

passerillage Grapes which have dried and raisined on the vine, but without the intervention of botrytis (q.v.).

pasteurisation The heating of must or wine to a high temperature to kill micro-organisms. A violent intervention (q.v.).

perlant Term used to describe wines containing a faint prickle of gas.

pétillant A lightly sparkling wine.

petit château A Bordeaux term to describe a wine from an individual property of modest origins.

phenolic maturity A term often used to describe the final or total maturity of a grape (including its skin) as opposed to mere sugar maturity, which indicates no more than the potential achievement of a satisfactory final alcohol level in a wine.

phylloxera Vine pest now called *Dactylasphaera vitifoliae* whose continuing presence in vineyard soils means that most European *Vitis vinifera* vines have to be grafted onto resistant American vine rootstocks.

pièce Traditional 228-litre burgundy cask.

pigeage "Punching down" of the cap (by sticks, paddles or human feet) to aid extraction (q.v.).

plafond limite de classement The percentage extension to an official yield for an AOC.

PLC *See plafond limite de classement*

pourriture grise See botrytis

pourriture noble See botrytis

premier cru "First growth".

premier cru classé "Classified first growth".

press wine In red-wine making, the wine which is pressed from the residue of skins and pips after the liquid part has been drained away.

prise de mousse The acquisition of a sparkle.

pruning Cutting a vine in order to train and trim it.

racking Moving a wine from one container to another.

reduction The opposite of oxidation. Wines in a reduced state (such as barrel samples) are often malodorous; racking or decanting them (i.e. exposing them to oxygen) will freshen them.

remontage Pumping fermenting wine over the cap (q.v.) to aid extraction (q.v.) and prevent reduction (q.v.).

remuage The "riddling" or shaking of bottles of sparkling wine after the second fermentation in order to make their sediment fill the inverted bottle's neck, from where it can easily be removed.

rendement See yield

reserve wines Champagne term for wines stored for several vintages to be used as a blending component. The French word *réserve*, by contrast, has little meaning on wine labels.

reverse osmosis Method of concentration (q.v.).

rootstock The (American or hybrid) part of a grafted vine, which lies underground. Compare scion.

rot *See* botrytis.

saignée Literally "bleeding", meaning the running off of juice in the early stages of red-wine fermentation, either to make rosé wine or to concentrate red wine (or both).

scion The above-ground (vinifera) portion of a grafted vine.

sec "Dry" in the Loire and elsewhere, though treacherously in Champagne this means up to 35 g/l sugar.

second fermentation *See prise de mousse*

second wine Term chiefly used in Bordeaux to denote wine produced from young vines, second-rate parcels or less successful vats, in contrast to the *grand vin* (q.v.) which bears the château name, made from the best components only.

secondary fermentation *See* malolactic fermentation

selected yeast *See* yeast

sélection des grains nobles Selection of individual grapes affected by noble rot.

skin contact Affecting phrase that indicates a period in which the skins of white grapes soak coolly with the juices to extract flavour and perfume (but not, generally, tannin) before fermentation begins.

sorting *See tri*

soutirage See racking

sugar maturity The formation of enough sugar in the grapes to provide adequate alcohol levels – but not necessarily enough to provide rich, complex, satisfying, and fully ripe flavours. Compare phenolic maturity.

sur lie "On lees": a term used in Muscadet (and now elsewhere) to describe wines that have been bottled directly from the fine lees produced at the very end of fermentation and during the early stages of *élevage* (q.v.).

tannin The textural, grippy element of red wines (and to a limited extent of a few experimental white wines: *see page 241*). Tannins vary enormously in style.

tartaric acid The major acid found in wines.

tartrates Crystals of the potassium salt of tartaric acid (potassium acid tartrate) often found in bottles of wine or attached to the base of corks. They are an excellent sign, indicating that the wine has not been over-processed.

terroir "Placeness": *see pages 16-21.*

tri The sorting of harvested fruit to discard damaged grapes, typically on a sorting table (*table de tri*): an essential prerequisite in making great wine.

trie One of a number of passages through a vineyard to pick selected fruit (which might be that affected or unaffected by botrytis, depending on the region and the season).

ullage Word used to describe the head space in a partly filled barrel between the top of the wine and the surface of the cask; a wine stored with such a space rather than fully topped up is said to be "on ullage".

ungrafted *Vitis vinifera* vine planted on its own roots.

varietal Wine made from a single grape variety.

vendange Harvest.

vieilles vignes Old vines: an unregulated term.

vigne French word used to describe both a vine and a vineyard.

vigneron A wine-grower.

vignoble A vineyard or accumulation of vineyards.

vin de garde Wine intended for long storage.

vin de liqueur A *mistelle* (q.v.).

vin de paille "Straw wine": wine made from grapes which have been previously dried on straw mats after harvesting.

vin doux naturel (VDN) Wine fortified part-way through fermentation.

vin gris "Grey wine": pale rosé made by the direct pressing of pale red grapes.

vin jaune "Yellow wine", a Jura speciality: *see page 117.*

vinifera Short form of *Vitis vinifera*, the European grape vine, as opposed to other forms of *Vitis* such as American rootstock material or hybrid vines.

vinification The process of turning grapes into wine.

viticulture The growing of vines.

vintage A wine harvest. The word may also be found on older labels of VDNs (q.v.) to describe wines bottled young; other terms have now superseded the word "vintage" (*see page 225*).

vendange tardive Late harvest.

voile "Veil": the French term for the yeast layer that forms on certain wines left on ullage, akin to the *flor* that occurs in the Jerez region of Spain for fino and manzanilla sherry.

volatile acidity The level of distillable acids (chiefly acetic acid) in a wine. Volatile acidity plus fixed acidity gives the total acidity of a wine.

wild yeast *See* yeast

yeast Fungus responsible for transforming sugar into alcohol (ethanol) and carbon dioxide. Fermentation can be initiated by letting wild or ambient yeasts get to work on the must (q.v.) (a non-interventionist approach) or by using selected yeasts.

yield The amount of fruit cropped for a given area of vines (usually quoted in this book as hectolitres per hectare). Yields vary in France from 10-15 hl/ha (for Sauternes and other sweet wines) to 150 hl/ha or more (in Champagne and for table wines). Vine densities should also be considered, however, since with denser plantings apparently high yields may equate to modest yields per vine; and pressing rates, too, alter the equation (less juice, for example, may be pressed from a given tonnage of grapes in Champagne than in other regions). Yields are limited by law, which is why in some regions (like Champagne) excess yields simply go unpicked.

Vintage Charts

1-3: Weak vintages; consume as soon as possible   **4-7:** Average vintages; hold or drink within ten years   **8-10:** Great vintages; best long-term storage potential

Champagne

1988	9
1989	8
1990	9
1991	4
1992	5
1993	6
1994	4
1995	7
1996	8
1997	6
1998	6
1999	7
2000	7
2001	1
2002	8
2003	6
2004	7

The Loire Valley

	RED	DRY WHITE	SWEET WHITE
1988	6	8	8
1989	9	9	10
1990	9	9	9
1991	5	4	2
1992	2	3	3
1993	4	5	5
1994	4	2	6
1995	9	8	8
1996	8	9	9
1997	7	5	8
1998	5	6	5
1999	5	7	5
2000	6	8	6
2001	5	5	7
2002	8	9	8
2003	10	8	10
2004	6	6	6

Alsace

1988	7
1989	9
1990	10
1991	2
1992	5
1993	6
1994	7
1995	5
1996	7
1997	6
1998	8
1999	6
2000	8
2001	8
2002	8
2003	7
2004	6

Chablis

1988	6
1989	9
1990	9
1991	7
1992	7
1993	4
1994	7
1995	8
1996	6
1997	7
1998	6
1999	8
2000	7
2001	3
2002	9
2003	5
2004	7

The Rhône Valley

	NORTH	SOUTH
1988	8	8
1989	9	10
1990	10	10
1991	8	4
1992	1	3
1993	2	4
1994	6	6
1995	7	8
1996	6	4
1997	8	5
1998	9	10
1999	10	7
2000	8	9
2001	8	9
2002	4	1
2003	10	8
2004	7	8

Provence

1988	7
1989	8
1990	10
1991	5
1992	3
1993	3
1994	4
1995	7
1996	7
1997	5
1998	10
1999	8
2000	8
2001	9
2002	2
2003	9
2004	7

Bordeaux

	DRY WHITE	SWEET WHITE	LEFT BANK	RIGHT BANK
1988	5	10	6	6
1989	5	8	9	10
1990	8	10	10	10
1991	4	3	3	1
1992	5	1	1	3
1993	4	1	4	4
1994	8	3	6	6
1995	7	5	8	8
1996	8	9	9	7
1997	6	9	5	5
1998	9	8	7	10
1999	8	8	7	7
2000	8	3	10	10
2001	9	10	8	7
2002	5	6	5	5
2003	6	9	9	7
2004	5	4	5	5

Burgundy

	WHITE	RED
1988	5	5
1989	9	8
1990	6	9
1991	7	8
1992	5	5
1993	4	7
1994	5	5
1995	8	7
1996	4	4
1997	7	7
1998	5	6
1999	8	9
2000	7	6
2001	5	4
2002	8	8
2003	5	8
2004	6	5

Beaujolais

1988	6
1989	10
1990	7
1991	8
1992	2
1993	3
1994	6
1995	7
1996	4
1997	5
1998	4
1999	9
2000	10
2001	4
2002	8
2003	10
2004	6

The Jura*

1988	9
1989	10
1990	9
1991	6
1992	6
1993	5
1994	5
1995	9
1996	9
1997	4
1998	5
1999	8
2000	9
2001	2
2002	7
2003	5
2004	6

* Ratings are for Vin Jaune
only for 1990 and older
vintages

Savoie

1990	9
1991	4
1992	3
1993	5
1994	5
1995	8
1996	5
1997	5
1998	6
1999	7
2000	7
2001	3
2002	6
2003	8
2004	6

Southwest France

	BERGERAC	MADIRAN	CAHORS	JURANÇON
1988	8	9	8	8
1989	10	9	8	9
1990	9	10	9	8
1991	7	6	4	6
1992	3	5	7	4
1993	5	6	6	10
1994	7	8	7	5
1995	8	10	9	7
1996	9	8	8	10
1997	5	8	7	5
1998	8	10	8	9
1999	7	6	7	5
2000	10	10	10	8
2001	9	9	10	10
2002	6	8	7	7
2003	7	8	6	10
2004	6	7	6	7

Languedoc-Roussillon

1988	8
1989	10
1990	9
1991	3
1992	2
1993	6
1994	6
1995	8
1996	5
1997	4
1998	10
1999	6
2000	8
2001	9
2002	4
2003	6
2004	6

Corsica

1990	10
1991	6
1992	3
1993	7
1994	6
1995	8
1996	6
1997	9
1998	9
1999	8
2000	8
2001	7
2002	5
2003	7
2004	6

Index

Page numbers in **bold** indicate main entries; those in *italics* refer to the illustrations and captions. ***Bold italics*** indicate photo boxes.